CRITICAL SURVEY
OF
POETRY

CRITICAL SURVEY
OF
POETRY

English Language Series

REVISED EDITION

McG-Poe

5

Edited by
FRANK N. MAGILL

SALEM PRESS
Pasadena, California   Englewood Cliffs, New Jersey

REF.
821-009
MAG

Library of Congress Cataloging-in-Publication Data
Critical survey of poetry. English language series/edited
    by Frank N. Magill. — Rev. ed.
        p.   cm.
    Includes bibliographical references and index.
    1. English poetry—Dictionaries. 2. American
poetry—Dictionaries. 3. English poetry—
Bio-bibliography. 4. American poetry—Bio-
bibliography. 5. Poets, English—Biography—
Dictionaries. 6. Poets, American—Biography—
Dictionaries.
    I. Magill, Frank Northen, 1907-   .
PR502.C85   1992   92-3727
821.009'03—dc20   CIP
ISBN 0-89356-834-1 (set)
ISBN 0-89356-839-2 (volume 5)

LIST OF AUTHORS IN VOLUME 5

CRITICAL SURVEY
OF
POETRY

THOMAS McGRATH

Born: Near Sheldon, North Dakota; November 20, 1916
Died: Minneapolis, Minnesota; September 20, 1990

Principal poetry

Longshot O'Leary's Garland of Practical Poesie, 1949; *Letter to an Imaginary Friend: Parts One and Two*, 1970; *The Movie at the End of the World*, 1973; *Passages Toward the Dark*, 1982; *Echoes Inside the Labyrinth*, 1983; *Letter to an Imaginary Friend: Parts Three and Four*, 1985; *Selected Poems*, 1988; *Death Songs*, 1991.

Other literary forms

"Conquering Horse," "Choruses for the City," and "Paradise" (all undated) are three of some fourteen filmscripts completed by Thomas McGrath. These are primarily sociopolitical documentaries, written for such noted directors as Mike Cimino. McGrath was the author of two novels—*The Gates of Ivory, the Gates of Horn* (1987), and *This Coffin Has No Handles* (1988)—and completed a number of interviews and brief biographical and nonfiction prose pieces, as well as short literary essays. He helped to found or served as editor of *Crazy Horse, Masses and Mainstream*, and the *California Quarterly.*

Achievements

Well into his lifetime McGrath began to receive recognition in the upper Midwest. Some readers have complained, however, of critical neglect on a wider scale, which they attribute to literary and political biases. (A few of McGrath's works were initially received more positively outside the United States than within it.) His incredible formal range may have precluded his neat assimilation into any particular literary camp. He produced traditional folk ballads, surrealist free verse, narrative blank verse, and prose poems; he published a collection of very short, haikulike lyrics, as well as a sprawling, two-volume, experimental autobiography in verse, comparable to Walt Whitman's *Leaves of Grass* (1855), William Wordsworth's *The Prelude* (1850), William Carlos Williams' *Paterson* (1963), and Hart Crane's *The Bridge* (1930). He wrote social satire and political invective as well as intimate, personal meditations.

Despite his somewhat ambiguous or incomplete critical acceptance, however, McGrath was awarded—primarily late in his career—a number of distinguished prizes and honors: a Rhodes scholarship, an Amy Lowell Traveling Fellowship in Poetry, two National Endowment for the Arts Fellowships, a Guggenheim Fellowship, and two Bush fellowships. Not long before his death, he was awarded a Senior Fellowship by the Literature Program of the National Endowment for the Arts and was presented the Distinguished Achievement Award by the Society for Western Literature.

Biography

Thomas McGrath was born and reared on a farm near Sheldon, North Dakota, southwest of Fargo. His parents were second-generation Irish homesteaders, and the land they farmed was remote, desolate, and climatically extreme. When roads were impassable and the family's radios inoperable, Tom's father recited poems, sang, and told stories to the family. From an early age, Tom assisted the seasonal crews on their steam threshers and witnessed the lingering Wobbly agitation of that period. In 1939 he was graduated from the University of North Dakota with a Rhodes Scholarship. His financial lot throughout undergraduate school, however, had been poor, reducing him at times to life on the streets. (According to one story, he even stole potatoes one night from the garden of a university president.) Such hardships no doubt played their roles in his lifelong commitment to socialist reform and revolution. In 1940 he attended graduate school in English at Louisiana State University, where he studied with Cleanth Brooks and worked with Alan Swallow in the founding of Swallow Press. Throughout graduate school his interest in the plight of the working class flourished, and, upon graduation with his M.A., and after teaching briefly at a college in Maine, he worked as a labor organizer on the New York waterfront in 1942. He served in the United States Army during World War II and then finally took advantage of his Rhodes Scholarship by attending the University of Oxford.

Back in the United States, McGrath taught at Los Angeles State College from 1951 to 1953. During this time he was called before the House of Representatives Committee on Un-American Activities. His subsequent blacklisting resulted in employment problems for many years, and he was forced to take a variety of temporary odd jobs, including work in a wooden-toy factory. He spent time in Greece, Portugal, Great Britain, and South America, and for ten years he taught at state universities in North Dakota and Minnesota. In 1983 he retired to Minneapolis, Minnesota, where he died in September, 1990.

Analysis

Any glance at Thomas McGrath's oeuvre reveals him to be a poet of formal playfulness. Though his work through the years shows contemporary influences, he never slips into any predictable mode or style and never abandons the concerns he embraced so passionately as a young student in the Depression. His key concerns seem to be human suffering brought about by political and economic oppression, a desire for transformation, and the exile that results from efforts to bring about change. His astounding output—including the two-volume epic *Letter to an Imaginary Friend*—is far too much to examine in a brief overview.

In his earliest work, McGrath's key themes appear mainly in political terms. Indeed, his first several books, selections from which were gathered in *The Movie at the End of the World*, are unarguably Marxist and at times didactic. Each poem has aesthetic integrity, its political concerns being integral rather than extraneous or imposed. Nevertheless, those interests are, in many of these earlier works, particularly overt. An extreme example is "A Little Song About Charity," from *Longshot O'Leary's Garland of Practical Poesie.* In this playful satire with its songlike refrain, the speaker mocks the so-called charity of bourgeois capitalists:

> The boss came around at Christmas—
> Oh smiling like a lamb—
> He made me a pair of gloves
> And then cut off my hands.

This boss comes around again to give the speaker shoes for his birthday, only to cut off the speaker's feet as well. By the end, the readers are told that if they care about their family and about the working class, they must carefully reserve their affections: "Don't waste it on the cockroach boss/ But keep your love at home."

"A Little Song About Charity" is one of the most message-oriented and two-dimensional of McGrath's earliest works. Certainly the whole of *Longshot O'Leary Garland of Practical Poesie* is "practical" or utilitarian, as its title suggests and as the Marxist view of art instructs. Yet a number of the early poems reveal as well the complexities with which McGrath struggled throughout his writing career. "The Dialectics of Love" shows a merging of traditional poetic concerns, private dilemmas, and political ideology. The poem is made up of rhymed couplets, a pattern traditionally suited to poems of wit (such as those of Alexander Pope). Section 1 describes an unfaithful lover's corpse, the earth above him ironically pressing "closer . . . than any lover." The man who in life sought freedom from permanence now experiences the most terrible permanence. In section 2, the perspective widens to include "the human winter,/ And civil war in every sector." Typically for McGrath, personal concerns in and of themselves are not worthy material for poetry (his own marriage was very likely failing at about the time this poem was written). He resists the merely personal, and where it does appear, he connects it nearly always to larger, universal concerns. In "The Dialectics of Love," infidelity in an individual relationship becomes emblematic of an essential human conflict: the desire for security and permanence versus the contrasting desire for freedom. While section 1 derides the changeable lover, section 2 works its way to a realization of the world's inherent mutability. Therefore, "He must seem false who would be true." In other words, the one who is faithful, who is always the same, now seems to this speaker false to life itself.

Characteristically, McGrath next relates this "dialectic" between conflict-ing human needs to the Marxist dialectic, or class struggle. Section 3 sees "Over the public eye and lip/ The seal of personal ownership." The desire to own property is like the wish to keep a relationship constant, or the desire to resist time's havoc. Because such constancy is folly, "personal love/ Changes, if it is pure enough." In the last lines of the poem, the corpse seen earlier, lying in the permanence of death, is now viewed instead as subject to con-stant change, "the transience of the winding year." The idea in section 1 is thus neatly reversed in section 3: in death people are given over entirely to the changes that natural forces inflict.

"The Dialectics of Love," with its metaphysical wit and proper dose of ambiguity, demonstrates the influence of its literary period and of McGrath's graduate study. Its archaic inversions and poeticizing ("When right hand and left divided are/ And the split heart cannot love the more") further shows it to be an immature work. Typically, however, McGrath is more than compe-tent with whatever style he chooses, and "The Dialectics of Love" is no ex-ception.

Other poems of *The Movie at the End of the World* reveal McGrath's themes somewhat more characteristically. The metaphysical permanence-versus-flux dialectic often transmutes into the more earthy conflict of community mem-bership versus exile. The speaker of these poems is solitary, one who watches from a distance, excluded. The sometimes desperately poor young man who left his Irish family's farm for college must indeed have felt a rift: while his education separated him to some extent from his family, his rural roots sepa-rated him from the academic communities at the University of North Dakota and Louisiana State. In the first part of his personal epic, *Letter to an Imag-inary Friend*, he describes this transition from farm life to college and his first encounter with a college dean: "a pithy, pursy bastard" who winds up saying "nothing but *money money.*" The farm boy cannot accept his college scholarship, because the rules require that he live in a dormitory, and he lacks the necessary resources. As a burgeoning Communist in the 1940's and 1950's, McGrath no doubt felt himself alienated more profoundly than ever, and his blacklisting in 1953 both confirmed and enforced this exile.

McGrath was excluded, however, in more ways than one. For most of his career, he was something of a literary outlaw, a status described early in his "Ars Poetica: Or: Who Lives in the Ivory Tower?" Here the speaker suggests some possible roles for the poet: the craftsman and wordsmith, the political caller-to-arms, the documenter of street life and of the real conditions of the working class. Each such suggestion is knocked down, however, by the voices of housewives ("Get out of my technicolor dream with your tragic view and your verses"), editors ("take the red flags out of your poem—we mustn't offend the censor"), hobos on the street ("I respect your profession as much as my own, but it don't pay off when you're hungry"), and even representatives of academia ("Your feet are muddy, you son-of-a-bitch, get out of our ivory tower"). McGrath indeed did not fit neatly into any niche, literary or otherwise, and his exile is evident throughout his work.

This theme of separation typically connects with a companion concern for transformation, particularly in three early poems, "A Long Way Outside Yellowstone," "Love in a Bus," and "Such Simple Love." In each of these pieces the speaker comes upon or is accidentally privy to a couple's lovemaking—an awkward occasion that would doubtless reinforce an already lonely person's separateness. In each of these poems the speaker remarks approvingly of the couple's disregard for convention: in two of the poems the couples are in public places, and in one they are unusually rambunctious, causing the building the speaker also occupies to shake dramatically. In each poem as well the speaker notes that love, however fleeting and inglorious, is the only thing of permanence and worth in the human world, perhaps the only means of transcendence: "their hands touching deny you,/ Becoming, poor blinded beggars, pilgrims on the road to heaven." For McGrath, the only heaven possible is one that happens in material terms. He had perhaps seen too much of tangible human misery—life on the streets, the financial struggles of his family—to accept some dubious, remote, Platonic realm, mystical transcendence, or religious salvation. The material determinism of Marx reflected and reinforced the young poet's inclinations in this regard: the world evolves through material, rather than spiritual, struggle between the classes, and these clashes will necessarily result in some ultimate material change, a revolution and worker's utopia right here on earth.

Despite this ever-present desire for transformation, McGrath never appears naïve. Most of his pieces, even the earliest, engage the theme of incapacity or futility, the ambiguities attendant on any plan for worldly change. In "Such Simple Love," a caustically cynical poem, he says, "But love without direction is a cheap blanket/ And even if it did no one any harm,/ No one is warm." In "A Long Way Outside Yellowstone" there is a similar epigrammatic statement: "Poverty of all but spirit turns up love like aces/ That weren't in the deck at all." In other words, genuine love comes only when material luxuries are stripped away, or when one's material well-being is otherwise nonexistent. This is hardly an optimistic sentiment. In "The Heroes of Childhood," the speaker laments his loss of faith in human gods, including his Marxist heroes. Such poems as "A Letter for Marian" reflect an essential isolation and loss of comradeship, community, and love: "When the telephone rings there's a war on each end./ The message arrives, but there's no one to sign for it."

By the end of section 3 of *The Movie at the End of the World*, McGrath's central concerns and formal virtuosity are more than evident. The fourth and final section, titled "New Poems," continues the development of those concerns. It also heralds, however, a more immediate, spoken voice, a still bolder formal range, and the influence of literary trends of the late 1950's and the 1960's.

This section begins with the playful prose poem "You Can Start the Poetry Now, Or: News from Crazy Horse." The poem gives an account of an actual poetry reading, with the alternating voices of a poet who has stood up to perform and the admonitions of the audience he faces. The poet begins seemingly in midthought, with total disingenuousness: "—I guess all I'm trying to say is I saw Crazy Horse die for/ a split level swimming pool in a tree-house owned by/ a Pawnee-Warner Brothers psychiatrist." The audience interrupts to remind him gently that he can "start the poetry now." The poet, however, continues his previous thoughts, and the audience continually breaks in, increasingly loudly and angrily, to insist that he "START THE POETRY!! START THE POETRY NOW!!" Something of an antipoem, this piece seems to mock conventional notions of the poet's relationship to his public. Certainly this poem itself is formally unconventional.

Yet "You Can Start the Poetry Now" is immediately followed by an end-rhymed poem in six-line stanzas and iambics. McGrath is simply not a predictable poet, and even in many later poems he surprises the reader with dramatic shifts in form and voice. The "New Poems" section reveals the influence of William Carlos Williams ("Legend" appears to be written in variable feet), of Wallace Stevens (the metaphysics and imagism of "from: A Sound of One Hand"), and Whitman ("Return to Marsh Street" with its long cadenced lines). Contemporary influences are also apparent. Through the work of such writers as Robert Bly, many American poets of the 1960's discovered South American and Asian literature, and McGrath was no exception. Such lyrics as "For Alvaro" and "Old Friends" are haikulike in their brevity and lack of abstraction, while "Hoot!" suggests the surreal imagist mode that many writers of the 1960's adopted and that McGrath was to explore further in later books. "Praises" is a tribute to the sensual and metaphorical lushness of vegetables, much along the lines of Pablo Neruda's celebrated odes to socks and salt. Numerous other poems from this section show McGrath's interest in South American writing.

While his later work is somewhat dark, this last section of *The Movie at the End of the World* is for the most part one of relative lightness. He even presents a friendly parody of Bly's poems, the titles of which often begin with a present participle. (McGrath's parody is called "Driving Towards Boston I Run Across One of Robert Bly's Old Poems.") The section ends with an amusing (though serious) rejection of capitalism and the military machine in "Gone Away Blues," as didactic as the much earlier "A Little Song About Charity" but more lighthearted. Some thirty years after his first poems about the plight of the working class, about exile and longing for revolution, McGrath here expresses, with seeming ease, the same concerns.

Probably McGrath's most brilliant output came after *The Movie at the End of the World*. The poems of *Passage Toward the Dark*, for example, have an immediacy, a mature insight, and a dark richness that, arguably, the early and middle-period work simply does not show. Some of his later motifs are more ambitious as well. In the latter part of *Letter to an Imaginary Friend*, McGrath develops a new symbol for revolution: the Blue Star Kachina, a Hopi spirit of radical change, suggesting the transforming power of the imagination and of poetry itself, in all its shapes and modes. Certainly McGrath's poems, which *The Movie at the End of the World* aptly displays, are themselves very like the Kachina. For poetry as versatile and engaging as any in the twentieth century, a reader would do well to explore the work of Thomas McGrath.

Cynthia Nichols

Other major works

LONG FICTION: *The Gates of Ivory, the Gates of Horn*, 1987; *This Coffin Has No Handles*, 1988.

Bibliography

McGrath, Thomas. "Surviving as a Writer: The Politics of Poetry/The Poetry of Politics." Interview by Jim Dochniak. *Sez: A Multi-Racial Journal of Poetry & People's Culture* 2/3 (1981): A-L, special section. This is a twelve-page transcript of an informal interview at the University of Minnesota. McGrath here touches on the childhood sources of his writing, his socialist politics, and his international travels. He distinguishes between tactical and strategic poetry and discusses his struggle to survive financially.

McKenzie, James. "Conversations with Thomas McGrath." *North Dakota Quarterly* 56 (Fall, 1988): 135-150. Compiled here are anecdotes and excerpts from McGrath discussions, interviews, and panel events at the University of North Dakota throughout the years. Topics include McGrath's association with the Beat poets and the autobiographical background to *Letter to an Imaginary Friend*. His former wife Alice McGrath joins in.

North Dakota Quarterly 50 (Fall, 1982). In this special issue, entitled *Dream Champ: A Festschrift for Thomas McGrath*, an assortment of writers, students and friends reflect, sometimes whimsically, on McGrath and his work. Edited by Robert W. Lewis, it includes poems written in honor of McGrath and important essays on his filmscript career and his politics, as well as McGrath's "Statement to the House Committee on Un-American Activities."

Stern, Frederick, ed. *The Revolutionary Poet in the United States*. Columbia: University of Missouri Press, 1988. A two-hundred-page collection of critical essays, retrospectives, and scholarship on McGrath. This book includes work by Diane Wakoski, Hayden Carruth, Studs Terkel, and E. P. Thompson. The volume is a good collection of supplementary material as well, including a chronology of works, biographical sketch, and complete bibliography.

TriQuarterly 70 (Fall, 1987). This issue, edited by Reginald Gibbons and Terrence Des Pres, is devoted entirely to McGrath. The volume, entitled *Thomas McGrath: Life and Poem*, contains some valuable biographical information on McGrath, including a firsthand account of his waterfront years as a labor organizer and agitator. It includes the reminiscences of former students as well.

CLAUDE McKAY

Born: Sunny Ville, Jamaica; September 15, 1889
Died: Chicago, Illinois; May 22, 1948

Principal poetry

Songs of Jamaica, 1912; *Constab Ballads*, 1912; *Spring in New Hampshire and Other Poems*, 1920; *Harlem Shadows*, 1922; *Selected Poems of Claude McKay*, 1953.

Other literary forms

Even though he is probably best known as a poet, Claude McKay's verse makes up a relatively small portion of his literary output. While his novels, *Home to Harlem* (1928), *Banjo* (1929), and *Banana Bottom* (1933), do not place him at the forefront of American novelists, they were remarkable at the time for their frankness and slice-of-life realism. *Home to Harlem* was the first best-selling novel of the Harlem Renaissance, yet it was condemned by the majority of black critics, who felt that the black American art and literature emerging in the 1920's and 1930's should present an uplifting image of the African American. McKay, however, went on in his next two novels to express his admiration for the earthy ways of uneducated lower-class blacks, somewhat at the expense of black intellectuals. The remainder of McKay's published fiction appears in *Gingertown* (1932), a volume of short stories.

McKay also produced a substantial body of literary and social criticism, a revealing selection of which appears, along with a number of his letters and selections from his fiction and poetry, in *The Passion of Claude McKay: Selected Poetry and Prose, 1912-1948* (1973), edited by Wayne F. Cooper. An autobiography, *A Long Way from Home* (1937), and an important social history, *Harlem: Negro Metropolis* (1940), round out the list of his principal works.

Achievements

McKay's contribution to American poetry cannot be measured in awards and citations, nor in visiting professorships and foundation grants. His peculiar pilgrimage took him from Jamaica to Moscow, from Communism to Catholicism, from Harlem to Marseilles. He lived and worked among common laborers most of his life, and developed a respect for them worthy of Walt Whitman. He rejected the critical pronouncements of his black contemporaries and, as Melvin Tolson points out, he "was unaffected by the New Poetry and Criticism." His singular blend of modern political and social radicalism with the timeworn cadences of the sonnet won for him, at best, mixed reviews from many critics, black and white. In any attempt to calculate his poetic achievement, however, one must realize that, with the exception of his early

Jamaican dialect verse (certainly an important contribution in its own right to the little-studied literature of the British West Indies) and some rather disappointing poetry composed late in his life, his poetic career spanned little more than a decade. At the publication in 1922 of *Harlem Shadows*, the furthest extent of his poetic development, he was only thirty-three. McKay should be read as a poet on the way up, who turned his attention almost exclusively to prose after his initial success in verse.

Surely there is no more ludicrous task than to criticize a writer on the basis of his potential, and so one should take McKay as one finds him, and indeed, in those terms, he does not fare badly. His was the first notable voice of anger in modern black American poetry. Writing when he did, he had to struggle against the enormous pressure, not of white censure, but of a racial responsibility that was his, whether he wanted it or not. He could not be merely a poet—he had to be a "black poet," had to speak, to some extent, for countless others; such a position is difficult for any poet. Through it all, however, he strove for individuality, and fought to keep from being bought by any interest, black or white, right- or left-wing.

Largely through the work of McKay, and of such Harlem Renaissance contemporaries as Countée Cullen and Langston Hughes, the task of being a black poet in America was made easier. *Harlem Shadows* marked a decisive beginning toward improving the predicament so concisely recorded by Cullen, who wondered aloud in the sonnet "Yet Do I Marvel" how a well-intentioned God could in his wisdom do "this curious thing:/ To make a poet black and bid him sing."

Biography

Claude McKay was born in 1889 on a small farm in Clarendon Parish, Jamaica. His parents were well-respected members of the community and of the local Baptist church. He received his early education from his older brother, a schoolteacher near Montego Bay. In 1907, he was apprenticed to a wheelwright and cabinetmaker in Brown's Town; this apprenticeship was short-lived, but it was in Brown's Town that McKay entered into a far more fruitful apprenticeship of another sort. Walter Jekyll, an English aristocrat and student of Jamaican culture, came to know young Claude and undertook the boy's literary education. As McKay recalled years later in his autobiography, *A Long Way from Home*, Jekyll opened a whole new world to him:

> I read poetry: *Childe Harold*, *The Duncaid*, *Essay on Man*, *Paradise Lost*, the Elizabethan lyrics, *Leaves of Grass*, the lyrics of Shelley and Keats and of the late Victorian poets, and . . . we read together pieces out of Dante, Leopardi, and Goethe, Villon and Baudelaire.

It was Jekyll who first recognized and nurtured McKay's gift for writing poetry, and who encouraged him to put that gift to work in the service of his own

Jamaican dialect. The result was the publication of *Songs of Jamaica* and *Constab Ballads*. The first is a celebration of peasant life, somewhat after the manner of Robert Burns; *Constab Ballads* is more like Rudyard Kipling, drawing as it does upon McKay's brief stint as a constable in Kingston, Jamaica.

Kingston gave McKay his first taste of city life, and his first real taste of racism. The contempt of the city's white and mulatto upper classes for rural and lower-class blacks was an unpleasant revelation. The most blatant racism that McKay witnessed in Kingston, however, was not Jamaican in origin—it was imported in the form of American tourists. He would come to know this brand of racism much more intimately in the next few years, for, after only eight months in the Kingston constabulary, he resigned his post and left for the United States. In 1912 he enrolled, first at Tuskegee Institute, then at Kansas State College, to study agronomy. His plan was to return to Jamaica to help modernize the island's agriculture. The plan might have succeeded but for a gift of several thousand dollars from an unidentified patron—most likely Walter Jekyll—that paid McKay's way to New York, where he invested his money in a restaurant and married Eulalie Imelda Edwards, an old Jamaican sweetheart. Neither marriage nor restaurant survived long, but McKay found a certain consolation in the bustle and energy of the city. One part of town in particular seemed to reach out to him: Harlem.

In the next five years or so he worked at a variety of jobs—barboy, long-shoreman, fireman, and finally porter, then waiter, on the Pennsylvania Railroad. This was yet another apprenticeship, one in which he further developed the sympathy for the working class that remained with him all his life. Since his youth he had leaned politically toward socialism, and his years among the proletariat solidified his beliefs. His race consciousness developed hand-in-hand with his class consciousness. During this period of apprenticeship and developing awareness, he wrote. In 1918, he began a long association with Max Eastman, editor of the Communist magazine, *The Liberator*. McKay began publishing poems and essays in this revolutionary journal, and eventually became an associate editor. In 1919, in response to that year's bloody postwar race riots, McKay published in *The Liberator* what would become his most famous poem, "If We Must Die." The defiant tone and the open outrage of the poem caught the attention of the black community, and practically overnight McKay was at the forefront of black American poets.

Then came another of the abrupt turns that were so much a part of McKay's life and work. Before his newly won reputation had a chance to flourish, he left for England where he stayed for more than a year, writing and editing for a Communist newspaper, *Workers' Dreadnought*, and, in 1920, publishing his first book of poetry since the Jamaican volumes, *Spring in New Hampshire and Other Poems*. He returned to New York early in 1921 and spent the next two years with *The Liberator*, publishing a good bit of prose and verse and working on his principal book of poems, *Harlem Shadows*. Upon its publication in 1922, observes Wayne Cooper, McKay "was immediately acclaimed the best Negro poet since Paul Laurence Dunbar." Once again, however, he did not linger long over success. He was tired and in need of a change, especially after a chance meeting with his former wife reopened old wounds. Late in 1922, he traveled to Moscow for the Fourth Congress of the Third International. He quickly became a great favorite with Muscovites, and was allowed to address the Congress on the plight of American blacks and on the problem of racism within the Communist Party. As McKay described it, he was greeted "like a black ikon in the flesh." He was, it seemed, on the verge of a promising career as a political activist; but despite his successes in Russia, he still saw himself primarily as a writer. When he left Russia, he was "eager to resume what he considered the modern writer's proper function—namely, to record as best he could the truths of his own experience."

The 1920's were the decade of the Expatriate Artist, but though he spent most of his time in France until settling in Tangiers in 1931, McKay had very little to do with such writers as Ernest Hemingway and F. Scott Fitzgerald; his exile was too different from theirs. During his stay in Europe and North Africa, McKay published all his major fiction, along with a number of magazine articles. His first two novels, *Home to Harlem* and *Banjo*, were financially successful, in spite of the outraged reaction they drew from most black American critics. *Gingertown*, a collection of short stories, was not nearly so successful, and McKay's third novel, *Banana Bottom*, was a critical and financial disaster. Financially ruined, McKay was forced to end his expatriate existence.

With the help of some American friends, McKay returned to New York in 1934. He hoped to be of service to the black community, but upon his return, observes Wayne Cooper, "he found a wrecked economy, almost universal black poverty, and little sense of unity among those black writers and intellectuals he had hoped to work with in years ahead." As for his literary ambitions, the Harlem Renaissance was finished; black writers were no longer in vogue. Not only could he not find a publisher, he was unable to find any sort of a job, and wound up in Camp Greycourt, a government welfare camp outside New York City. Fortunately, Max Eastman was able to rescue him from the camp and help him to get a job with the Federal Writers' Project. In 1937 he was able to publish his autobiography, *A Long Way from Home*. Once again, he was publishing articles in magazines, but his views isolated him from the mainstream black leaders; he felt, again in Cooper's words, that "their single-minded opposition to racial segregation was detrimental to any effective black community organization and to the development of a positive group spirit among blacks." McKay's thought at this time also shows a drift away from Communism, and a growing disillusionment with the fate of the "Grand Experiment" at the hands of the Soviets.

A Long Way from Home was neither a critical nor a financial success. Neither was his next and last book, *Harlem: Negro Metropolis*, a historical study published in 1940. By then, in spite of the steady work provided him by the Federal Writers' Project, his literary reputation was declining steadily. Despite his final acceptance of American citizenship in 1940, he could still not bring himself to regard America as home. His exile from both the black leadership and the left-wing establishment was becoming more and more total; worse still, his health began to deteriorate rapidly. Once again, like Walter Jekyll and Max Eastman in earlier years, a friend offered a hand. Ellen Terry, a Catholic writer, rescued McKay from a Harlem rooming house, and McKay's life took one last unexpected turn. As a young man he had rejected the fundamentalist Christianity of his father, and during his varied career had had little use for religion. Through his friendship with Terry, and later with the progressive Chicago bishop, Bernard Scheil, McKay experienced a change of mind and heart. In the spring of 1944 he moved to Chicago, and by fall of that year he was baptized into the Roman Catholic church.

At last he seemed to have found a refuge, though his letters reveal a lingering bitterness over his lot. With his newfound faith, however, came a satisfying involvement in Chicago's Catholic Youth Organization and the opportunity to go on writing. His health continued to decline, and on May 22, 1948, McKay died of heart failure. He had recently finished preparing his *Selected Poems of Claude McKay* for publication. It is probably just as well that the volume appeared posthumously, as it took five years to find a publisher; at the time of his death, all of his works were out of print.

After a requiem mass in Chicago, McKay was brought back to Harlem for a memorial service. He was buried in Queens, "a long way from home."

Analysis

At the conclusion of his essay "The Renaissance Re-Examined," which appears as the final chapter of Arna Bontemps' 1972 book, *The Harlem Renaissance Remembered*, Warrington Hudlin insists that any true appreciation of the Harlem Renaissance hinges on the realization that this celebrated literary phenomenon "'opened the door' for the black writing of today. The Renaissance will always be remembered for this reason. It will be valued for its merits. It will come again to importance because of its idea." The poetry of Claude McKay must be read in much the same light. Though it is easy enough to find fault with much of his verse, he did help to "open the door" for those who would follow; as such, he deserves to be valued for his merits, judged by his strengths.

Though progressive enough in thought, McKay never felt compelled to experiment much with the form of his poetry. In content he is a black man of the twentieth century; in form he is more an English lyricist of the nineteenth, with, here and there, Miltonic echoes. The effect is, at times, a little peculiar, as in "Invocation," a sonnet in which the poet beseeches his muse to

> Let fall the light upon my sable face
> That once gleamed upon the Ethiopian's art;
> Lift me to thee out of this alien place
> So I may be, thine exiled counterpart,
> The worthy singer of my world and race.

Archaic trappings aside, there is a kind of majesty here, not bad work for a young man in his twenties. The Miltonic ring is probably no accident; McKay, it must be remembered, received something of an English gentleman's education. As the work of a black man pursuing what had been to that time primarily a white man's vocation, McKay's "Invocation" bears comparison with John Milton's "Hail native Language." One of the young Milton's ambitions was to vindicate English as poetic language, deserving of the same respect as Homer's Greek, Vergil's Latin, or Dante's Italian. McKay found himself in the position of vindicating a black man's experience of a white culture as a worthy subject for poetry.

Not all of McKay's verse concerns itself specifically with the theme of interracial tension. Among his poems are love lyrics, idyllic songs of country life, and harsher poems of the city, where "the old milk carts go rumbling by,/ Under the same old stars," where "Out of the tenements, cold as stone,/ Dark figures start for work." A recurring theme in McKay's work is the yearning for the lost world of childhood, which for him meant memories of Jamaica. This sense of loss is the occasion for one of his finest poems, "The Tropics in New York":

> Bananas ripe and green, and ginger-root,
> Cocoa in pods and alligator pears,
> And tangerines and mangoes and grape fruit,
> Fit for the highest prize at parish fairs.

The diction here is simple; one can almost hear Hemingway in the loving list of fruits. The speaker's memory stirs at the sight of a shop window. In the midst of the city his thoughts turn to images of "fruit-trees laden by low-singing rills,/ And dewy dawns, and mystical blue skies/ In benediction over nun-like hills." Here, in three straightforward quatrains, is the mechanism of nostalgia. From a physical reality placed by chance before him, the observer turns his eyes inward, visualizing a happy scene of which he is no longer a part. In the final stanza his eyes are still involved in the experience, only now they have grown dim, "and I could no more gaze;/ A wave of longing through my body swept." All of the narrator's senses tune themselves to grief as the quickening of smell and taste turns to a poignant hunger for "the old, familiar ways." Finally, the poem closes on a line as classically simple and tersely musical as anything in the poems of A. E. Housman: "I turned aside and bowed my head and wept."

Indeed, the poem is reminiscent of "Poem XL" in A. E. Housman's *A Shropshire Lad* (1896):

> Into my heart an air that kills
> From yon far country blows:
> What are those blue remembered hills,
> What spires, what farms are those?

It is a long way, to be sure, from Shropshire to Clarendon Parish, Jamaica, but the issue here is the long road back to lost experience, to that "land of lost content" that shines so plain, "The happy highways where I went/ And cannot come again." Any fair assessment of McKay's verse must affirm that he knew that land, those highways, all too well.

That same fair assessment, however, must give a prominent place to those poems upon which McKay's reputation was made—his poems of protest. McKay, in the estimation of Arna Bontemps, was black poetry's "strongest voice since [Paul Laurence] Dunbar." Dunbar's "racial" verse is a good indication of the point to which black American poetry had progressed by World War I. His plantation-style dialect verse tries, with a certain ironic cheerfulness, to make the best of a bad situation. At their best, these poems exhibit a stinging wit. At their worst, they are about as dignified as a minstrel show. In his poems in literary English, Dunbar is more assertive of his racial pride, but with an emphasis on suffering and forbearance, as in "We Wear the Mask." This poem, which could be read in retrospect as an answer to those critics and poets who would later disown Dunbar for not being "black" enough, speaks of the great cost at which pain and anger are contained:

> We smile, but O great Christ, our cries
> To Thee from tortured souls arise.
> We sing, but oh, the clay is vile
> Beneath our feet, and long the mile;
> But let the world dream otherwise,
> We wear the mask.

The anguish is plain enough, yet the poem, couched in a prayer, seems to view this "wearing of the mask" as an ennobling act, as a virtuous sacrifice. McKay was not inclined to view things in quite that way.

From the spring through the fall of 1919, numerous American cities were wracked by bloody race conflicts, the worst of which was a July riot in Chicago that left dozens dead and hundreds injured or homeless. While he was never the object of such violence, McKay and his fellow railroad waiters and porters walked to and from their trains with loaded revolvers in their pockets. Not unexpectedly, his reaction to the riots was far from mild; his concern was not with turning the other cheek, but with returning the offending slap. When the sonnet "If We Must Die" appeared in *The Liberator* it marked the emergence of a new rage in black American poetry:

> If we must die, let it not be like hogs,
> Hunted and penned in an inglorious spot,
> While round us bark the mad and hungry dogs,
> Making their mock at our accursed lot.

Again, the form is of another century, the language dated, even by late nineteenth century standards—"O kinsmen! We must meet the common foe! . . . What though before us lies the open grave?" The message, however, is ageless, avoiding as the poem does any direct reference to race.

On the heels of much-publicized violence against black neighborhoods, the implications were clear enough, but the universality of the poem became more obvious with time. A Jewish friend of McKay's wrote him in 1939, "proclaiming that . . . ["If We Must Die"] must have been written about the European Jews persecuted by Hitler." In a more celebrated instance, Winston Churchill read the poem before the House of Commons, as if, in the words of black poet and critic, Melvin Tolson, "it were the talismanic uniform of His Majesty's field marshal." The message reaches back to Thermopylae and Masada, and forward to Warsaw, Bastogne, and beyond. In its coverage of the bloodbath at the New York State Prison at Attica, *Time* (September 27, 1971) quoted the first four lines of McKay's sonnet as the "would-be heroic" effort of an anonymous, rebellious inmate. McKay might not have minded; he stated in his autobiography that "If We Must Die" was "the only poem I ever read to the members of my [railroad] crew." A poem that touches prisoners, railroad workers, and prime ministers alike must be termed a considerable success, despite any technical flaws it may exhibit.

Even so, one must not altogether avoid the question of just how successful McKay's poems are as poems. James Giles, in his 1976 study, *Claude McKay*, remarks on the disparity "between McKay's passionate resentment of racist oppression and his Victorianism in form and diction," finding in this conflict "a unique kind of tension in many of his poems, which weakens their ultimate success." Giles is probably correct to a point. In many cases McKay's art might have found fuller expression had he experimented more, let content more often shape form; he had shown abilities in this direction in his early Jamaican poems, and he was certainly open to experimentation in his later prose. The simple fact, however, is that he consistently chose to use traditional forms, and it would be unfair to say that it was a wholly unsuccessful strategy.

Indeed, the very civility of his favorite form, the sonnet, sometimes adds an ironic tension that heightens, rather than diminishes, the effect of the poem. For example, one could imagine any number of grisly, graphic effects to be achieved in a *vers libre*, expressionistic poem about a lynching. In

McKay's "The Lynching," though, one cannot help feeling the pull of an understated horror at seeing the act translated to quatrains and couplets: "and little lads, lynchers that were to be,/ Danced round the dreadful thing in fiendish glee." No further description of the "dreadful thing" is necessary. When McKay uses his poems to focus on real or imagined experience—a lynching, a cornered fight to the death, an unexpected remembrance of things past—his formal restraint probably works most often in his favor.

In poems that set out to convey a self-conscious message, however, he tends to be less successful, not so much because the form does not fit the content as because poetry and causes are dangerous bedfellows. Some of McKay's other angry sonnets—"The White House," "To the White Fiends," "Baptism"—may leave readers disappointed because they preach too much. McKay's specifically sociological, political, and, later, religious views receive better expression elsewhere, in his prose. Perhaps that is why he did not devote so much of his time to poetry after the publication of *Harlem Shadows*. In any case, his position in black American poetry is secure. Perhaps he should be judged more by that which was new in his poems, and that which inspired other black writers to carry on the task, as later generations have judged the Harlem Renaissance—as a bold and determined beginning, a rolling up of the sleeves for the hard work ahead.

Richard A. Eichwald

Other major works
LONG FICTION: *Home to Harlem*, 1928; *Banjo*, 1929; *Banana Bottom*, 1933.
SHORT FICTION: *Gingertown*, 1932.
NONFICTION: *A Long Way from Home*, 1937 (autobiography); *Harlem: Negro Metropolis*, 1940.
MISCELLANEOUS: *The Passion of Claude McKay: Selected Poetry and Prose, 1912-1948*, 1973 (Wayne F. Cooper, editor; contains social and literary criticism, letters, prose, fiction, and poetry).

Bibliography
Bronz, Stephen H. "Claude McKay." In *Roots of Negro Racial Consciousness: The 1920's, Three Harlem Renaissance Authors.* New York: Libra Publishers, 1964. This earnest but somewhat dated study is a very accessible introduction to McKay as representative of the Harlem Renaissance. Bronz finds McKay's poetry powerful and dramatic and the novels and stories weak but interesting.
Cooper, Wayne F. *Claude McKay: Rebel Sojourner in the Harlem Renaissance.* Baton Rouge: Louisiana State University Press, 1987. This first full-length biography of McKay is a fascinating and very readable book. Special attention is paid to McKay's early life in Jamaica and the complex

influences of his family. Includes nine photographs and a useful index.

Gayle, Addison, Jr. *Claude McKay: The Black Poet at War.* Detroit: Broadside Press, 1972. This brief study looks closely at four poems—"Flame-Heart," *Harlem Shadows*, "To the White Fiends" and "If We Must Die"—as they demonstrate McKay's growing skill and militancy throughout his career. Gayle argues that McKay was an important revolutionary poet.

Giles, James R. *Claude McKay.* Boston: Twayne, 1976. This study examines McKay's work as it was influenced by his homeland of Jamaica, the Harlem Renaissance, the Communist Party, and the Roman Catholic church. Giles asserts that McKay's fiction represents his major achievement. The book includes a chronology and a briefly annotated bibliography.

LeSeur, Geta. "Claude McKay's Marxism." In *The Harlem Renaissance: Revaluations*, edited by Amritjit Singh, William S. Shiver, and Stanley Brodwin. New York: Garland, 1989. This article examines McKay's struggle to find in Marxism the solution to the "Negro question" and looks at his trip to Russia to assess Marxism in action firsthand in 1922 and 1923.

ARCHIBALD MacLEISH

Born: Glencoe, Illinois; May 7, 1892
Died: Conway, Massachusetts; April 20, 1982

Principal poetry

Songs for a Summer's Day, 1915; *Tower of Ivory*, 1917; *The Happy Marriage*, 1924; *The Pot of Earth*, 1925; *Streets in the Moon*, 1926; *The Hamlet of A. MacLeish*, 1928; *Einstein*, 1929; *New Found Land: Fourteen Poems*, 1930; *Conquistador*, 1932; *Poems 1924-1933*, 1933; *Frescoes for Mr. Rockefeller's City*, 1933; *Public Speech*, 1936; *Land of the Free*, 1938; *America Was Promises*, 1939; *Brave New World*, 1948; *Actfive and Other Poems*, 1948; *Collected Poems 1917-1952*, 1952; *New Poems 1951-1952*, 1952; *Songs for Eve*, 1954; *The Collected Poems of Archibald MacLeish*, 1962; *The Wild Old Wicked Man and Other Poems*, 1968; *The Human Season: Selected Poems 1926-1972*, 1972; *New and Collected Poems, 1917-1976*, 1976; *On the Beaches of the Moon*, 1978; *Collected Poems, 1917-1982*, 1985.

Other literary forms

In addition to some twenty volumes of poems, Archibald MacLeish presented innumerable lectures, to college students, librarians, and the general public. Some of these are recorded in the volumes of prose essays he published, many on the public role of the poet as guardian of his own society. Several others concern social issues of the 1930's through the 1960's. The essays analyzing poems and commenting on the responsibility of the poet, such as *Poetry and Opinion: The "Pisan Cantos" of Ezra Pound* (1950) and *Poetry and Experience* (1961), illuminate MacLeish's own work as well as distinguish him from such contemporaries as Ezra Pound and T. S. Eliot.

The other major literary genre in which MacLeish worked was verse drama. One of his earlier works, *Nobodaddy: A Play* (1926), whose title is derived from William Blake's name for the Old Testament God of vengeance and restrictions, presents an interpretation of the stories of Adam and Eve and Cain and Abel. A closet play, it dramatizes the relationship between self-conscious humanity and indifferent, alien nature. In 1934 he collaborated with Nicholas Nabokoff on a ballet, *Union Pacific*, but much of his creative energy in the 1930's was devoted to writing hortatory verse plays for radio, such as *The Fall of the City* (1937), *Air Raid* (1938), and *The American Story: Ten Broadcasts* (1944). These works approach propaganda in their enthusiasm for the freedom of democracy and their attempts to warn Americans against the dangers of Fascism.

Of the later plays, *The Trojan Horse* (1952) presents implicit criticism of the McCarthy era while *This Music Crept By Me upon the Waters* (1953) dramatizes the individual's quest for happiness and the transitory, paradoxical nature of that happiness. *J. B.* (1958), MacLeish's most popular and widely-read play, is an adaptation of the story of Job to modern American life; it ran successfully on Broadway for ten months.

Achievements

MacLeish's reputation has remained undeservedly small in the light of his contributions to both literature and public life. His name is known for a handful of lyrics that are widely anthologized. Academic scholars have paid relatively little attention to his work, considering its scope and quality. Nevertheless, his works have received many awards, including three Pulitzer Prizes: in 1932 for *Conquistador*, in 1953 for *Collected Poems 1917-1952*, and in 1959 for his drama *J. B.* Among many other literary awards, he was given the prestigious Bollingen Prize in 1953. In addition to his achievements as a writer, MacLeish was highly successful in government and academic posts.

MacLeish is probably most noteworthy for his refusal to "escape" into his art, for his effort to be a whole human being: husband, father, teacher, soldier, public servant, as well as poet. Unlike Eliot and Pound, who longed nostalgically for the lost order of past European culture, MacLeish committed himself to the New World—to both the present and the future. He sought, through experiments with traditional verse forms and metrics, to adapt the techniques of poetry and drama to the American idiom and contemporary life. He wrote not for posterity but for his contemporaries. As Hyatt Howe Waggoner points out in *The Heel of Elohim* (1950), MacLeish was the only poet of the early twentieth century who understood and wrote about the modern revolution in physics, the space-time continuum, and the four-dimensional universe. This pervasive awareness of profoundly shocking scientific discoveries may turn out to be one of MacLeish's major contributions to modern literature, but most significant is MacLeish's attempt to fulfill the ancient but neglected tradition of the poet as prophet—in Percy Bysshe Shelley's words, the poet as "unacknowledged legislator of mankind."

The present critical consensus is that MacLeish has written some magnificent lyric poems, that the longer works, such as *Conquistador*, are flawed, and that some of them, such as *The Hamlet of A. MacLeish*, tend to be derivative. Given the size of MacLeish's corpus, its variety, and the topical political content of some works, it is probable that decades must pass before he can be judiciously ranked as a writer. As a whole man, speaking to other men of his time, he must be admired. He not only reflected upon the timeless paradoxes of being human but also acted as a Socratic gadfly, pricking the consciences of his fellow citizens of a threatened republic.

Biography

Archibald MacLeish was born in Glencoe, Illinois, on May 7, 1892. Some aspects of his early life seem to have influenced his mature concept of the poet. His father was a Scots immigrant, that circumstance perhaps explaining MacLeish's preoccupation with westward migration and his emphasis on America as a melting pot. More important, both his parents fostered a strong sense of moral responsibility in the young MacLeish. After attending the Hotchkiss School, MacLeish was graduated from Yale with a B.A. degree in 1915, showing his propensity for being a well-rounded man by distinguishing himself in sports, academics, and the writing of poetry. He went on to Harvard Law School, marrying Ada Hitchcock in 1916; but his education was interrupted by his enlisting in the Army in 1917. MacLeish served in France, attaining the rank of captain. He returned to Harvard and received his law degree in 1919 and then taught for a year before joining a Boston law firm. After practicing law and trying to write poetry for three years, MacLeish quit his job and moved his wife and two children to Paris to devote his full efforts to poetry. During the five years of his expatriation, MacLeish associated with other American writers such as Pound, John Dos Passos, F. Scott Fitzgerald, and Ernest Hemingway, the latter becoming a close friend. MacLeish's poems of this period show the influence of the poetics of Pound and Eliot and also of the spare style of Hemingway. His poems of this period tend also to reflect the introspective influence of the decadent poets.

Unlike many other American expatriates of the 1920's, MacLeish never intended to abandon his homeland. Having achieved recognition as a poet, in 1928 he returned to the United States, to a farm at Conway, Massachusetts. From that point on, his writings express a strong patriotic commitment. In the next year MacLeish traveled on foot and mule through Mexico, tracing the path of Hernando Cortes and preparing to write his epic, *Conquistador*. In the meantime he published *New Found Land* which, as the title suggests, heralded a renewed affirmation of America. Thus MacLeish turned away from the preoccupation with European tradition and the past that characterized Eliot and Pound, and embraced the promise and the problems of his native land.

MacLeish became increasingly vocal about the problems of America in the Great Depression, acting out his belief that a poet must speak to his own time about real issues, rather than to an elite group of aesthetes. He joined the editorial board of the new *Fortune* magazine and wrote articles of distinction on contemporary social issues. During the 1930's, he spoke out for the preservation of democracy not only through his poems but also through exhortative verse radio plays and a poetic commentary on photographs illustrating rural poverty. The last work in particular led in 1939 to MacLeish's controversial appointment by President Roosevelt to the post of Librarian of Congress. In the early 1940's, MacLeish also served as director of the Office of Facts and Figures, assistant director of the Office of War Information, Assistant Secretary of State, and after the war, as head of the United States delegation to the founding of UNESCO. During the political debates of the 1930's and 1940's, he remained both anti-Marxist and anti-Fascist, a staunch supporter of American democracy, and a severe critic of the big capitalists who, he felt, were exploiting the land.

In 1949, MacLeish returned to private life and to teaching. He was Boylston Professor of Rhetoric and Oratory at Harvard until 1962. From 1963 to 1967, he was Simpson Lecturer at Amherst College. During this later phase of his career MacLeish turned in his plays and poems to the fundamental and universal issues of human life. After the death of Robert Frost in 1962, MacLeish succeeded him as the unofficial poet laureate of the United States, publishing, for example, a poem on the 1969 moon landing in *The New York Times*. This poem typifies MacLeish's concept of the role of the poet. While it describes a specific political and scientific feat, the poem concludes with an ironic twist that broadens the context of this historical event into a reflection on man's universal preoccupation with the mysteries of existence. The moon landing shows technology capturing man's oldest symbol for time, change, and imagination; once on the moon, however, man discovers its essence as a symbol of reflection: he sees an impossible sight, his own home, the earth, rising like the moon before his eyes. By following his seemingly impossible aspirations, man finds knowledge of himself and his illusions.

Analysis

Public and private man, humanist, social critic, poet, Archibald MacLeish presents a rare wholeness of vision throughout his long career as a writer. This is not to say that his poetry remains static, that for over fifty years he wrote the same poem over and over again. Indeed, his focus and style shift at two major points, dividing his corpus roughly into three stages: the 1920's, the 1930's, and the postwar period. As Hyatt Howe Waggoner points out, MacLeish was the first among a very few twentieth century poets who have recognized, grasped, and used in their work the discoveries of post-Newtonian physics. He refused to polarize poetry and science because to do so would be escapism. It is the poet's role to express the mysteries of existence and experience. To oppose poetry to the contemporary understanding of nature and the universe, of origins and time and space, is to rob the poet of his subject and his mission. Throughout his works, MacLeish reiterates the value of the real, the concrete experience of the senses and feelings. Philosophically, he resembles the British empiricists of the eighteenth century, though without being reductive about experience. He distrusts abstractions, in the political arena no less than in the aesthetic. MacLeish is always in agreement with William Wordsworth's concept of the poet, "a man speaking to men." Unlike Eliot and Pound, he did not write for posterity nor for an elite group of preservers of western culture. He sought a metaphor for contemporary man, particularly American man. Like the eighteenth century English Augustans, he wrote social criticism with a public voice, with a sense of civic responsibility. Unlike neoclassicists of all periods, however, from Alexander Pope to Eliot, MacLeish refused the temptation to look back with nostalgia to a golden past. Rather, he sought to remind his readers of the true American dream. In *A Continuing Journey* (1968), he defines this dream as a reverence for the dignity of man, his self-determination, and his possibilities for unbounded knowledge.

If MacLeish were only a public poet, only addressing contemporary social issues, he would soon lose his audience. His genius inheres in his synthesis of the "public-private world in which we live." He is always a poet, a superb craftsman meditating on the exigencies of human experience. The main fact of human experience for MacLeish is man's finiteness, the inevitability of death. In fact, the three stages of his poetic development can be understood according to their attitude toward death. Early in his career, MacLeish lost his brother in World War I; he also suffered the death of a child. In the first period, there is an outcry against meaningless death. Man's transient existence in the vast universe of twentieth century physics offers a temptation to deep bitterness, but MacLeish refuses to yield to it. In later prose essays and poems, he criticizes the existentialists, who reduce man's lot to absurdity. The poetry of the second stage, written in the 1930's, turns away from the search for the relationship between man and the universe, focusing instead on death in its more political and historical context: death from war, oppression, and hunger. In the final period, MacLeish returns to death as a topic, but now as a concrete, highly personal event. He writes elegies for his friends, for other writers. He dwells on growing old, on his own inevitable death. These later poems invite comparison with the last poems of William Butler Yeats. They are affirmative, yet also ironic and sometimes tragic. In terms of the paradox presented in John Keats's "Ode on a Grecian Urn," these poems choose the death that results from living rather than the immortality of stasis.

In *New and Collected Poems, 1917-1976*, MacLeish included the poems he published in the 1920's, together with three earlier poems published in 1917 in *Tower of Ivory*. The poetry of this early period reflects to some degree the influences MacLeish encountered during his five years in France. These poems had elicited critical comments that tended to denigrate them by stressing their derivative nature, though, in general, such evaluations are unfair. It is true that influences tend to be obvious, but the poems also embody MacLeish's personal synthesis of technique and vision. These works develop a core of personal symbols, using the techniques of the French symbolists as well as the Poundian juxtaposition of concrete images and the fusion of ancient myth and modern life used so successfully by Eliot in *The Waste Land* (1922). The early poems show an almost Metaphysical wit in their use of paradox and irony, also revealing traces of William Shakespeare, William Blake, Keats, and Yeats, to name a few. Hemingway, his close friend during the expatriate period, seems, surprisingly, to have influenced MacLeish's style in a very lasting way. Throughout his career he tends to use short concrete words grouped into coordinate clauses, with relatively little subordination. He seems to want to state the "bare facts," not to embellish them. Yet the poems of the 1920's reveal highly successful experiments with music and sound. Critics agree that MacLeish was a technical master of the musical aspect of lyric poetry.

The Happy Marriage is a sequence of sonnets about love, paradoxical in the manner of John Donne, using plain language yet with striking musical effects. The poems are not allusive; they dwell on real life as opposed to books, on great moments of sense perception as opposed to ideas and abstractions. Not "love" or the "lover," but particular, concrete visual and tactile moments of sensation compose man's reality. In *The Dialogues of Archibald MacLeish and Mark Van Doren* (1964), MacLeish states that Algernon Charles Swinburne was his initial source, and intense sensibility is evident in these poems, as in the earlier *Tower of Ivory*, though they are never decadent.

The Pot of Earth is a long narrative poem using a ritual taken from Sir James G. Frazer's *The Golden Bough* (1890-1915) as an epigraph; it works through allusion as an ordering structural and thematic principle in the story of a contemporary girl's reproductive cycle. The fertility ritual, part of the cult of Adonis, describes women cultivating plants in pots of earth. The plants grow rapidly under the sunlight, but wither for lack of roots. After eight days the plants, along with images of the dead Adonis, are thrown into the sea or springs. This use of Frazer invites comparison with *The Waste Land*; the two works utilize the lore from Frazer in a parallel manner. The resulting poems, however, are very different in subject matter, mode, and tone. Whereas Eliot reflects on the sterility of Western culture after World War I, associating it with abortive fertility rites and degraded or impotent lovers, MacLeish expresses the age-old rhythms of the female life cycle, its inescapable connection with nature and death. While the species lives on, the individual, who rebels against her unwilled participation in the cycle, dies. *The Pot of Earth* itself is "pregnant" with the techniques and symbols that MacLeish developed in succeeding works. Images of the moon, sun, sea, and leafy trees shadowed against the moon or sun recur throughout MacLeish's works, sometimes as opaque images or details and sometimes as symbols fraught with almost allegorical significance. The themes born here are meditation on death, man's (here woman's) relationships to time, nature, and the revolving planets, and the flesh as intractable reality, somehow mysteriously connected with "self."

In this poem, sensuous, concrete images of nature work together with the narrative structure to communicate the tension between the individual heroine (or victim) of the poem and the inexorable rhythms of nature in which she participates by maturing, making love, conceiving, bearing a child, and dying as a result. The epigraph of the poem, from Hamlet's "mad" talk with Polonius about Ophelia, establishes the sun as a symbol of the male fertilizing principle.

Hamlet's "let her not walk i' the sun" puns on the word "sun," meaning that his (the son's) love for her is threatening. In the same way, MacLeish uses the sun as both a death-bearing fertilizing principle and beckoning romantic love. The moon is a relatively clear symbol, in its influence on the tides, of the inevitable cyclical processes of nature: birth, maturity, death, and rebirth. The individual, however, is not reborn; the species is. The tragedy of the individual thus inheres in a conflict with nature's preservation of the species. MacLeish plays with point of view in the poem to bring out this conflict. Part I, "The Sowing of the Dead Corn," begins with an objective third-person description of nature's "death," winter, shifting to a limited third-person with insight into the young girl's fear of menstruation. This is carried further into a first-person interior monologue, jumping from the thirteen-year-old to the seventeen-year-old girl. The loss of virginity on Easter Sunday is told in the third person through juxtaposed natural images of sowing, together with brief explanatory statements.

Part II, "The Shallow Grass," begins with the marriage of the young woman, juxtaposing her behavior with the sensuously depicted newly plowed fields which function typically as an objective correlative for the body of the bride. The poem moves back and forth from nature, in the context of the Adonis ritual, to the particular woman, now pregnant, just beginning to try to separate her identity from her uncontrollable body. Part III, "Carrion Spring," reveals her as a "reaped meadow," dead. In Parts II and III, the poet turns to the reader and comments cryptically on the mystery of the process. In tone, *The Pot of Earth* is not optimistic; its insistence on the absolute presence of flesh and bone, on their mysterious inviolability, is present in *The Happy Marriage* and ties in with the conclusion to *Einstein*, another long poem of the 1920's.

MacLeish's technique of structuring in *The Pot of Earth*—allusion to the Adonis ritual—is similar to his use of marginal glosses in both *Einstein* and *The Hamlet of A. MacLeish*. Both long poems rely on marginal glosses to provide order and context for their verses; the latter is similar in tone to *The Waste Land*, and similar in conception to the "Hamlet" of Jules LaForgue. The speaker is a poet beating his breast in the void, bewailing the inadequacies of words and knowledge. The ghost of Shakespeare's *Hamlet, Prince of Denmark* (c. 1600-1601) represents the mystery of meaning that man assumes to be at the center of experience. There is a sense of the moon as the boundary of the human corner of the vast indifferent universe. The poet-speaker bemoans the pain of mortal existence, without any illusion of a responsive chord in the universe. *The Hamlet of A. MacLeish* typifies his more personal poems in that it is both autobiographical and universal. He mentions the loss of his brother and child, while always remaining a representative figure, the poet-man facing the exigencies of life in a universe without meaning. Along with *Einstein*, this poem is among MacLeish's most pessimistic, and he rejected its self-pitying aspects during the following decade.

Streets in the Moon, like *Einstein*, grapples with the image-defeating concepts of modern physics such as the time-space continuum and the fourth dimension. Whereas *Einstein* suggests a laboratory notebook, being a factual description of man's felt disjunction with a vast, yet closed and indifferent universe, *Streets in the Moon* is a series of more "poetic" lyrics. These poems on various topics, such as death, technological man, and poetics, range from the playful to the nostalgic. Their language tends to be plainer, more abstract and conversational than that of earlier poems. They are united, however, by their uses of the moon as a symbol and the Einsteinian universe as setting. Many of the poems are ironic in the disparity between their titles and their contents. The moon, always haunting MacLeish's poems, seems to be a Janus-faced symbol, with contradictory meanings. It is a traditional beacon of imagination, of the dream world of myth and symbol, but it is also a satellite in the indifferent universe, representing a time-space continuum that mutely destroys man's aspirations toward meaning. Even MacLeish's most famous lyric, taken from *Streets in the Moon*, "Ars Poetica," is permeated by the symbolic moon.

"Ars Poetica," a twenty-four line poem with a Horatian title implying high seriousness, has been taken both too seriously and not seriously enough by some critics. The title suggests a disquisition on the true nature of poetry. Companion poems such as "Some Aspects of Immortality," "Man!," and "Hearts' and Flowers'," however, reveal a technique of ironically deceptive titles. The titles do relate to the subject at hand, but not in the imposing or sentimental way the reader expects. For example, "Hearts' and Flowers'" sounds like a sentimental valentine, but it is a musical compilation of scientific descriptions of sea anemones. The further irony results from the erotic rhythms and connotations of the scientific words. Thus the reader comes full circle from romantic expectations, through surprise at the scientific terminology, and back to erotic and romantic response on an intuitive level. "Ars Poetica" operates analogously. At first reading it appears to be, not a treatise on poetics, but a paradoxical, anti-intellectual riddle. It has been rejected by some readers (and with some justification) as the epitome of art for art's sake. In the 1920's, MacLeish's poetry was much more attuned to aestheticism than it was later. The first section of "Ars Poetica" states that a poem should be a concrete object, using four similes to suggest the desired qualities of muteness and palpability: a "globed fruit," "old medallions," stone casement ledges, and the "flight of birds." In other words, a poem should be felt and experienced, not rationally analyzed. It should be a "real" and immediate experience, like the inviolate life of the flesh referred to in earlier poems. Certainly it is paradoxical to ask that a poem, a collection of words, be silent and wordless.

The second eight lines of "Ars Poetica" begin and end with the same two lines comparing the poem's motionlessness in time to the moon's climbing.

The first uses a kind of philosophical synaesthesia to communicate the time-space continuum that informs *Einstein* and *Streets in the Moon*. The moon, of course, does not climb; only from the perspective of an earthly observer, man, does it appear to do so. The earth turns (and man with it) and the moon circles the earth, but all he sees is an apparently static moon that yet moves higher and higher. Thus the poem seems to have deceptive qualities. The poem, like the moon rising behind the branches of a tree which serve as a standard to gauge its movement, passes through the memories and experiences of the mind. Whether these mental events are the poet's or the reader's is not clear. Possibly MacLeish refers to the creative process, the relationship between the poet's personal experiences and the impersonal work he forges from them. Most often quoted are the final eight lines which argue that a poem should not be read as a statement of some idea or external meaning. Rather, a poem is a created object, a whole self-contained experience. Here there is a suggestion of Eliot's objective correlative, which MacLeish had also frequently used in the poems of the 1920's. An image is offered for the reader to experience directly, to feel the emotion that the poet wants to express. Metonymy rather than metaphor is the appropriate figure of speech. The image or poem is an instance of the emotional complex rather than an analogue of it. The obvious trap in "Ars Poetica" is to extort "meaning" in the sense of a general theory of poetics from a poem that warns against interpreting poems as vehicles of meaning. Thus it sets the reader up to expect a theory of poetry, thwarts that expectation by its content, yet does fulfill the title's promise in a negative way.

The final volume of MacLeish's initial stage, *New Found Land*, is a transitional work. Like his other collections, it offers a variety of lyrics on death, time and space, travel and migration, and it uses various experimental styles in combination with the recurrent symbols of sun, moon, sea, and leafy branches. Many of MacLeish's best-known lyrics are to be found here; but they are nostalgic, looking back to the Old World and the preoccupations of MacLeish's expatriate years. Only with "American Letter," at the end of the volume, is the promise of the collection's title fulfilled. "American Letter" shows the poet reluctantly turning from the sirens of Old World culture, the tempting foreign olive and palm trees. This poem is often described as an affirmation of America, but it is a difficult, painful affirmation. America is strange because it is neither a land nor a race. It is only a promise of a New World. MacLeish is in a sense a "reborn" American, avowing his kinship with the land and the mixed blood of America.

MacLeish's return to the United States in 1928 and his tramp through Mexico following the path of Cortes marked a rather dramatic change in the purpose and preoccupations of his poems. His research for *Fortune* magazine plunged the poet into awareness of social problems caused by the Great Depression. His poetry became oriented toward the New World, the present time, and the immediate future; he criticized society, but with an affirmative faith in the possibilities for freedom's triumph. The first poem of this period, *Conquistador*, builds on the narrative techniques used in his earlier works but with a new kind of subject matter. *Conquistador* is closer to a true American epic than most other attempts, such as William Carlos Williams' *Paterson* (1946-1958) or Hart Crane's *The Bridge* (1930). It explores the historical, cultural, and ideological origins of the New World, and what it finds is violence and the rape of the land, a theme shared by the subsequent volume, *Frescoes for Mr. Rockefeller's City*.

Conquistador makes no explicit value judgments; it merely presents the story of Cortes' discovery and violent capture of Mexico. The facts are presented, however, in the context of Dante's *Inferno*. The Dedication is from the deepest pit of hell, from Ulysses' speech to his sailors as he leads them out of the world of men toward their death. Ulysses' sin is his driven, unprincipled search for new realms to explore and conquer; he is severely punished for venturing out of his appropriate realm, using deception to inspire his followers. A persistent motif of MacLeish's poetry is man's insistent drive to push westward, to explore, but mostly to discover the "land's end." This drive is neither praiseworthy nor evil in itself, but it has often led to trouble. In addition to the framing quotation from Dante, *Conquistador* uses a kind of modified terza rima, based not on rhyme but on other techniques of sound repetition, predominantly assonance and consonance. A further echo of the *Inferno* is the Prologue, which is reminiscent of Book VI of Vergil's *Aeneid* (c. 29-19 B.C.), the descent to the underworld, and the context for *The Divine Comedy* (c. 1320). The speaker of the poem descends to find the dead followers of Cortes to obtain the story of Bernál Díaz, one of the soldiers whose actual record of the journey MacLeish had read. It is Díaz's somewhat disjointed memories, difficult to recover, that form the substance of the poem. Because it is made up of somewhat harshly juxtaposed concrete images, *Conquistador* resembles Pound's *Cantos* (1925-1972), yet it is unified by a single plot, the conquest of Tenochtitlan, and a single narrative consciousness, that of Bernál Díaz.

Conquistador picks up one of MacLeish's earliest themes, applying it to the writing of history. In *The Happy Marriage* and even in "Baccalaureate," one of his very first poems, MacLeish contrasts book-learning and abstract ideas with felt concrete experience. In the Preface to *Conquistador*, Díaz protests against the "official" historical accounts of the conquest of Mexico, especially the one written by a priest named Gómara. Such records falsify reality by labeling it with dates and neat words. For Díaz and the other soldiers, the conquest was a matter of blood and terror and guilt and finally death. It was a collection of acutely felt sense impressions and emotions. The style of the poem, written in fifteen books, embodies the confusion of Díaz's ghost as he summons his long-submerged memories. They are hazy and missing links, but acute when they surface. Clauses are repeatedly strung together with "and," as a child would speak.

Critics have read *Conquistador* as a poem more about the consciousness of the narrator than about the conquest of Tenochtitlan. MacLeish, however, seems to aim at objectivity by finding the most real, most accurate account available, the story of a participant in the action. The unglorious, unheroic attitude of the soldier lends realism to a story that might be idealized by a more distanced third-person narrative. MacLeish is essentially an empiricist; thus the sense impressions of one subject are the only accurate matter of knowledge. As always with a first-person point of view, the reader is left to evaluate the narrator and his reliability, to weigh the facts for himself. The ironic distance between author and narrator becomes greatest in the final book, in which Díaz describes the "beautiful victory," meaning the utter destruction of a highly developed culture which would never again live. Díaz calls it a "Christian siege," words which are oxymoronic in themselves. The ethnocentric attitudes of the Spaniards follow MacLeish's interesting attempt in Book II to represent the alien yet beautiful culture of the Aztecs through the speech of Montezuma on death. It is almost impossible to make rational sense out of the words because they seek to transcend Greek-Judeo-Christian categories of thought.

Frescoes for Mr. Rockefeller's City, published a year after *Conquistador*, weaves its implicit criticisms of the rape of the land and its natives into a more explicitly North American tapestry. These lyrical poems are a series of written paintings metaphorically intended to adorn New York City. Many of them attack the major capitalists, such as Andrew Mellon, J. P. Morgan, and Cornelius Vanderbilt, who built the railroads and controlled the stock market. MacLeish seems to blame them not only for massacring the Indians and alienating the earth with technology, but also, more immediately, for causing the Depression. In "Oil Painting of the Artist as Artist," MacLeish clearly criticizes the expatriate artists with whom he lived and learned during the 1920's. While his criticism of exploitative capitalists might suggest that MacLeish became a Communist during the 1930's, his poem "Background with Revolutionaries," a sarcastic critique of Lenin, actually earned him the venomous wrath of his Communist contemporaries. From 1928 on, MacLeish had a clear conception of Jeffersonian democracy as a standard for American government. He did not fall into the political extremes of Communism in the 1930's or of McCarthyism in the 1950's. Two other volumes of the 1930's, *Public Speech* and *America Was Promises*, while also criticizing the abusers of democracy, are both powerfully affirmative in their overall impressions. *Public Speech* sets forth brotherly love as the means for healing. *America Was Promises* juxtaposes the ideals of the Founding Fathers with the exploitations of capitalists, but it ends on the idea that America's promise is still intact for those who wish to seize it by preserving freedom.

The long final stage of MacLeish's career synthesized the poles of the two earlier, formative stages. In the 1920's he studied poetic techniques, both traditional and modern, dwelling in the realm of art for art's sake, expressing fine shades of sensibility and railing against the fact that man must live and die in a vast mathematical universe without inherent meaning. In the 1930's, on the other hand, MacLeish faced his homeland squarely, shouldering his heavy social responsibilities as a poet in a suffering and disillusioned republic. The 1940's were another transitional phase, in which MacLeish was still dwelling on public issues, but returning as well to earlier preoccupations, such as the Einsteinian universe and man's place in it.

"Actfive" is a successful synthesis of many of MacLeish's earlier techniques and themes, a poem in which he asks what the nature of the world will be after the attempted genocide and atomic bombs of World War II. The context is Shakespeare's metaphor that "All the world's a stage." The poem is essentially an allegory, a technique that MacLeish uses often in the short, Blakean lyrics of his later period. God has departed, the King is unthroned, and man is murdered. "Actfive" seeks a hero, surveying the ineffectual types proposed in the modern era: the scientist, the magnate of industry, the revolutionary, the Nietzschean great man, the victim, the State, the narcissistic ego, and the masses. The poem is as negative as a realistic understanding of World War II requires, yet it ends on a note shared by *Einstein* and by William Faulkner's speech accepting the Nobel Prize. The "something inviolate" of *Einstein*, the mysterious, concrete life force inherent in flesh and bone will survive. Faulkner's belief that man will not merely endure but will prevail is anticipated in MacLeish's hope that man will dare to endure and love. The poems of *Actfive and Other Poems* are lyrics that look back to the "Metaphysical" wit of the 1920's and forward to the more Yeatsian poems of the later years. They are paradoxical and meditative, seeking a new reconciliation of private and public voice.

The lyrics of the 1950's through the 1970's are studded with gems. Nature is no longer the vast universe of contemporary physics, but the age-old habitat of man. MacLeish's style becomes markedly plain, the syntax often blunt. Many of the poems deal with death as a very concrete event, adopting the accepting attitude of Keats's "To Autumn." The majority of the lyrics use a technique new for MacLeish. They hinge, sometimes ironically, on a single correspondence between a natural image and a human idea or feeling. The correspondences range from emblems to metaphor to allegory. The natural images tend not to be static but rather brief processes or structures of experience, such as the sudden flight of birds from a tree. There may be a strong Japanese influence in MacLeish's new technique and simplicity. Related to the use of analogy is a strong thematic concern with the ordering of experience, as captured in Wallace Stevens' poem "Anecdote of a Jar." Thus, MacLeish becomes simultaneously more intellectual and more concrete. He becomes far more personal in his subject matter and voice, while at the same time appealing to a wider audience. Not everyone shares his concern over the abuses of capitalism, but most readers do share a concern about death's imminence. Many of the later poems are topical, but in a more personal way than the poems of the 1930's. They are elegies for MacLeish's friends and comments on the sickness of the McCarthy era. "National Security" presents the political sickness of the 1970's by dealing with Cambodia, Laos, and Vietnam as three names locked in a classified file. Two juxtaposed metaphors produce the bitter irony of the lyric: the names as classified files and the names as bodies whose blood oozes from the file drawer, through the Capital, and into the continent.

The lyric "Old Man's Journey," published in 1968, is typical of the later poems. It is a sixteen-line poem, in rhyme scheme identical to a Shakespearean sonnet except for the extra couplet at the end. To accentuate the pattern, the poem is spaced as three quatrains followed by two couplets. Unlike traditional sonnets, the poem is not iambic pentameter. It is predominantly tetrameter, although the rhythms and lengths of the lines vary to suit the sense of the poem, as in free verse. Thus technically the poem typifies MacLeish's synthesis of constrictive, traditional poetic forms with contemporary innovations, especially in free verse. Using musical sound repetitions, thirteen of the poem's lines describe the salmon's relentless return upstream to its birthplace to die. Only the title, line four, and the appended couplet reveal the analogical nature of the natural description. The salmon is somewhat anthropomorphized with the goal of eternity and the idea of memory. Line four explains that return to the nostalgic past is a human compulsion, a fault. As in most of his later lyrics, MacLeish does not expound upon the human significance of the poem. The emblem or analogy, the image drawn from nature, receives the emphasis, the reader being forced to draw his own conclusions. The poems speak by implication. The salmon becomes infected with restlessness at the memory of its birth place, so it halts its journey and swims upstream to die. In human terms this suggests the way old people's minds often dwell on their earliest experiences, but it could also imply a return to a geographical place or to earlier values. The final couplet broadens the context of the poem through literary allusion even as the earlier long poems use marginal glosses and epigraphs from *The Golden Bough*, *Hamlet*, and the *Inferno*. Here, as in *Conquistador*, the reference is to Dante's version of Ulysses as a wanderer compelled to explore ever farther from home. "Old Man's Journey" thus implies that just as a salmon's nature drives it to return at last to the stream where it was spawned, so man's nature drives him to remembrance or literal return to his earliest experiences on the way to death.

Such lyrics as these, however, are best read for their concrete images of nature, allowing their human implications to unfold on an intuitive level. While MacLeish clearly rejected any hint of art for art's sake by 1930, his best poems live up to the injunctions of "Ars Poetica" that a poem is not an abstract exposition but rather a self-contained object.

Eve Walsh Stoddard

Other major works

PLAYS: *Nobodaddy: A Play*, 1926; *Union Pacific—A Ballet*, 1934 (with Nicolas Nabokoff); *Panic: A Play in Verse*, 1935; *The Fall of the City: A Verse Play for Radio*, 1937; *Air Raid: A Verse Play for Radio*, 1938; *The States Talking*, 1941; *The American Story: Ten Broadcasts*, 1944; *The Trojan Horse: A Play*, 1952; *This Music Crept By Me upon the Waters*, 1953; *J. B.: A Play in Verse*, 1958; *Three Short Plays: The Secret of Freedom, Air Raid, The Fall of the City*, 1961; *Herakles: A Play in Verse*, 1967; *Scratch*, 1971; *Six Plays*, 1980.

NONFICTION: *Housing America*, 1932; *Jews in America*, 1936; *Background of War*, 1937; *The Irresponsibles: A Declaration*, 1940; *The American Cause*, 1941; *A Time to Speak: The Selected Prose of Archibald MacLeish*, 1941; *American Opinion and the War*, 1942; *A Time to Act: Selected Addresses*, 1943; *Poetry and Opinion: The "Pisan Cantos" of Ezra Pound*, 1950; *Freedom Is the Right to Choose: An Inquiry into the Battle for the American Future*, 1951; *Poetry and Experience*, 1961; *The Dialogues of Archibald MacLeish and Mark Van Doren*, 1964; *The Eleanor Roosevelt Story*, 1965; *A Continuing Journey*, 1968; *The Great American Frustration*, 1968; *Champion of a Cause: Essays and Addresses on Librarianship*, 1971; *Riders on the Earth: Essays and Reminiscences*, 1978; *Letters of Archibald MacLeish: 1907-1982*, 1983 (R. H. Winnick, editor).

Bibliography

Cohn, Ruby. *Dialogues in American Drama*. Bloomington: Indiana University Press, 1971. Although this volume does not contain much analysis of MacLeish's earlier plays since the author believes they are merely unsuccessful adaptations of his poetry to dramatic form, Cohn's incisive reading of *J. B.: A Play in Verse* makes this volume worth consulting.

Drabeck, Bernard A., and Helen E. Ellis, eds. *Archibald MacLeish: Reflections*. Amherst: University of Massachusetts Press, 1986. This oral autobiography, drawn from recorded conversations the editors pursued with MacLeish from 1976 to 1981, is a valuable, unique compendium of MacLeish's commentary on his own poetry and prose and that of his peers. The preface by Richard Wilbur is especially helpful in placing MacLeish's achievements in centennial perspective.

Falk, Signi. *Archibald MacLeish*. New York: Twayne, 1966. The best extant source of exposition and biographical information on MacLeish, even though it is basically a handbook or primer on him rather than a full-fledged bio-critical study. Falk methodically examines each work in MacLeish's oeuvre and offers a sound critical judgment of its merits.

Kirkpatrick, D. C., ed. *American Writers Since 1900.* New York: St. James Press, 1983. This standard reference tool contains a chronology of Mac-Leish's life and a comprehensive bibliography of his work. The short, evaluative article by Robert K. Johnson is a worthy overview of MacLeish's achievements in poetry and drama.

Leary, Lewis G., Carolyn Bartholet, and Catharine Roth. *Articles on American Literature, 1950-1967.* Durham, N.C.: Duke University Press, 1970. And Leary, Lewis G., and John Archard. *Articles on American Literature, 1968-1975.* Durham, N.C.: Duke University Press, 1979. These reference volumes contain comprehensive bibliographies of periodical articles related to Mac-Leish's criticism.

MacLeish, Archibald. *The Letters of Archibald MacLeish, 1907-1982,* edited by R. H. Winnick. Boston: Houghton Mifflin, 1983. Published posthumously, these letters represent the most important source of autobiographical information on MacLeish's life and the sources, influences, and personal memories of his most famous poems and plays. Contains a helpful index.

Smith, Grover. *Archibald MacLeish.* Minneapolis: University of Minnesota Press, 1971. This pamphlet in the well-known University of Minnesota series offers a concentrated analysis of MacLeish's poetry with some attention to the poetic drama, *J. B.: A Play in Verse.* The short biography and bibliography is a useful starting place for research.

LOUIS MacNEICE

Born: Belfast, Ireland; September 12, 1907
Died: London, England; September 4, 1963

Principal poetry
Blind Fireworks, 1929; *Poems*, 1935; *Poems*, 1937; *The Earth Compels*, 1938; *Autumn Journal*, 1939; *Selected Poems*, 1940; *The Last Ditch*, 1940; *Poems 1925-1940*, 1940; *Plant and Phantom*, 1941; *Springboard: Poems 1941-1944*, 1944; *Holes in the Sky: Poems 1944-1947*, 1948; *Collected Poems 1925-1948*, 1949; *Ten Burnt Offerings*, 1952; *The Other Wing*, 1954; *Autumn Sequel: A Rhetorical Poem in XXVI Cantos*, 1954; *Visitations*, 1957; *Eighty-Five Poems*, 1959; *Solstices*, 1961; *The Burning Perch*, 1963; *The Collected Poems of Louis MacNeice*, 1966 (E. R. Dodds, editor).

Other literary forms
Although he was a poet first and foremost, Louis MacNeice published a number of important works in other genres. His only novel *Roundabout Way* (1932), not very successful, was published under the pseudonym Louis Malone. MacNeice's only other venture into fiction was a children's book, *The Penny That Rolled Away* (1954), published in England as *The Sixpence That Rolled Away*.

An area in which he was no more prolific, but much more successful, was translation. The combination of his education in classics with his gifts as a poet led him to do a successful translation of Aeschylus' *Agamemnon* (1936). E. R. Dodds, an eminent classics professor at Oxford and literary executor of MacNeice's estate, calls the translation "splendid" (*Time Was Away,* 1974, Terence Brown and Alec Reid, editors). W. B. Stanford agrees that in spite of the almost insurmountable difficulties of Aeschylus' text, MacNeice succeeded in producing an eminently actable version, genuinely poetic, and generally faithful to the original. MacNeice's translation of Johann Wolfgang von Goethe's *Faust* (1951) for radio presented very different problems—in particular, his not knowing German. The radio medium itself also produced problems in terms of what the audience could follow. MacNeice collaborated with E. L. Stahl on the project, and on the whole it was successful. According to Stahl, MacNeice succeeded in rendering the work's unusual combination of the dramatic with the lyric, producing excellent versions of the various lyrical passages.

MacNeice wrote several plays for the theater and nearly one hundred radio scripts for the BBC. Except for *The Agamemnon of Aeschylus,* his theatrical works are not notable, although *Station Bell* was performed by the Birmingham University Dramatic Society in 1935 or 1936, and a similar play, *Out of the Picture,* was performed in 1937 by the Group Theatre in London, which had also done *Agamemnon*. The verse play was accounted a failure, while having its moments of very good poetry and wit. It was similar to the plays that W. H. Auden and Christopher Isherwood were producing for the Group Theatre in the 1930's: cartoonlike parodies in the service of leftist political views. MacNeice's play does, however, show a serious concern with love. Much later, in 1958, MacNeice wrote *One for the Grave* (published in 1968), patterned on the medieval morality play. It exemplifies his growing interest in allegory, described in *Varieties of Parable* (1965). During World War II, MacNeice wrote documentary dramas for radio, contributing much that was original, though not of lasting literary value, to the genre. His later radio dramas, such as *Out of the Picture,* and his late poems tend toward allegory and quest motifs. *The Dark Tower* (1947) is the most successful of these dramas in its equilibrium between realism and allegory.

MacNeice also wrote an unfinished prose autobiography, published posthumously as *The Strings Are False* (1965); several works of mixed poetry and prose, most notably *Letters from Iceland* (1937) with Auden; and several volumes of literary criticism. These works illuminate MacNeice's poetry, offering insight into the self-conscious relationship of one poet to his predecessors and his craft. *Modern Poetry: A Personal Essay* (1938) is significant as a manifesto of one of the new poets of the 1930's, who believed that poetry should speak directly to social and political issues. *The Poetry of W. B. Yeats* (1941), written before the major scholarly commentaries on William Butler Yeats, offers lucid insights into particular poems, as well as illuminating MacNeice's own goals as a poet. *Varieties of Parable*, a posthumous printing of MacNeice's Clark Lectures of 1963, elucidates his concern with writing poetry that operates on two levels simultaneously, the realistic and the symbolic, moral, or allegorical.

Achievements

MacNeice is most notable as an exemplar of Socrates' maxim that the unexamined life is not worth living. The major question surrounding his reputation is whether he ranks as a minor or a major poet, whether his poems show a progression of thought and technique or an essential similarity over the years. No one would deny that his craft, his mastery of prosody and verse forms, is of the highest order. Most critics agree that in his last three volumes of poems MacNeice took a new point of departure. Auden asserts in his memorial address for MacNeice (*Time Was Away*) that posterity will endorse his opinion that the later poems do advance, showing ever greater craftsmanship and intensity of feeling. Auden claims that of all his contemporaries, MacNeice was least guilty of "clever forgeries," or dishonest poems. This honesty, combined with an ingrained temperamental skepticism, is at the root of both his major contributions to poetry and what some people see as his flaws. MacNeice is a philosophical poet, Auden says, without a specific body of beliefs, except for a fundamental sense of *humanitas* as a goal and standard of behavior. He is a harsh critic of general systems because he is always faithful to the complexity of reality.

MacNeice's achievements as a poet are paradoxical: he combines an appeal to large audiences with highly learned allusions and he focuses on everyday events and political issues while also exploring ultimate metaphysical questions. Most interesting is his transition from the 1930's view that the poet is chiefly a *communicator*, almost a journalist, to the belief that poetry should operate on two levels, the real and the allegorical. It is these contradictory qualities, along with the literary-historical value of recording a thoughtful person's ethical responses to the trials of modern life, that will ensure Mac-Neice's poetry a lasting reputation.

Biography

Louis MacNeice was born on September 12, 1907, in Belfast, the son of a well-respected Church of Ireland Rector. Because his early childhood experiences inform the imagery and ideas of almost all his work, the details of MacNeice's early life are important. His father, John Frederick MacNeice, and his mother, Elizabeth Margaret, were both natives of Connemara in the west of Ireland, a bastion of wild tales and imagination. Both parents communicated to their children their strong attachment to the Ireland of their youth as opposed to the stern, dour, Puritanical atmosphere of Ulster. MacNeice's father was extraordinary among Protestant Irishmen in his outspoken support for Home Rule and a united Irish republic. Thus the young poet started life with a feeling of displacement and a nostalgia for a culture and landscape he had never seen. Life in the Rectory was, of course, pervaded by religion and a sense of duty and social responsibility. MacNeice had a sister, Elizabeth, five years his elder, and a brother, William, in between, who had Down's Syndrome and therefore did not figure heavily in the other children's play. The children were fairly isolated and developed many imaginative games. Louis showed a tendency toward Gothic preoccupations in his fear of partially hidden statues in the church and in the graveyard that adjoined his garden. Of special significance is his mother's removal to a nursing home and subsequent death when Louis was seven. She had provided comfort and gaiety in the otherwise secluded and stern life of the Rectory. Louis, the youngest, had been particularly close to her and his poetry reflects the rupture in his world occasioned by her loss. Without their mother and intimidated by the misery of their father, the MacNeice children became particularly subject to the influences of servants. On the one hand, the cook, Annie, was a warm Catholic peasant who spoke of fairies and leprechauns. On the other hand, Miss MacCready, who was hired to take care of the children when their mother became ill, was the antithesis of both Mrs. MacNeice and Annie, a puritanical Calvinist, extremely dour and severe, lecturing constantly about hell and damnation.

In 1917, MacNeice's father remarried. Though she was very kind and devoted, the new Mrs. MacNeice had a Victorian, puritanical outlook on life which led to further restrictions on the children's behavior. Soon after the marriage, MacNeice was sent to Marlborough College, an English public school, further confusing his cultural identity. From this point on, England became his adopted home, but the English always regarded him as Irish. The Irish, of course, considered him an Anglo-Irishman, while he himself always felt his roots to be in the west of Ireland. Both at Marlborough and later at Merton College, Oxford, MacNeice was in his milieu. At Marlborough he was a friend of Anthony Blunt and John Betjeman, among others. He flourished in the atmosphere of aestheticism and learning. At Oxford he encountered Stephen Spender and the other poets with whom he came to be associated in the 1930's. MacNeice studied the classics and philosophy at Oxford and these interests are second only to the autobiographical in their influence on his poetry. He was graduated from Oxford with a double first in Honour Moderations and "Greats."

Having rebelled against his upbringing by drinking heavily and rejecting his faith at Oxford, MacNeice in a sense completed the break by marrying a Jewish girl, Mariette Ezra. Together they moved to Birmingham, where he was appointed lecturer in Classics at the University. In Birmingham, MacNeice encountered the working class and taught their aspiring children at the University. He had always been protected from the lower classes of Belfast and in English schools had lived among the upper classes. The new contact with working people led to a healthy respect for the ordinary man and a broadening of MacNeice's social awareness. At the same time, he was becoming recognized as a member of the "poets of the thirties," with Auden, Isherwood, Spender, and C. Day Lewis, whose sense of social responsibility led them to espouse Marxism. MacNeice never became a Communist, but he did write about social issues and questioned the comfortable assumptions of traditional English liberalism. While at Birmingham, MacNeice became friendly with E. R. Dodds, who was later to become his literary executor. In 1934 he and his wife had a son, Dan, and in 1936, she left them both abruptly for an American graduate student at Oxford, Charles Katzman. This abandonment, parallel to the death of his mother, haunted MacNeice for many years and is reflected in his poetry. In the later 1930's, MacNeice traveled twice to Spain, reporting on the Spanish Civil War, and twice to Iceland, the second time with Auden. In 1936 he became lecturer in Greek at Bedford College for women at the University of London. In 1939 and 1940, he lectured at colleges in the United States, returning to what he felt to be his civic responsibility to England following the outbreak of World War II.

From 1941, MacNeice worked for the British Broadcasting Corporation as a scriptwriter and producer, except for the year and a half in 1950-1951 that he served as Director of the British Institute in Athens, Greece. In 1942 he married a singer, Hedli Anderson; they had a daughter, Corinna, the following year. In the 1940's and 1950's MacNeice traveled extensively, to India, Greece, Wales, America, Africa, Asia, France, and Ireland. His premature death in 1963 was the sort of paradoxical experience he might have used in a poem on the irony of life. He was going far beyond the call of duty for the BBC by descending a chilly manhole to check the sound transmission for a feature he was producing. He suffered from exposure, contracted pneumonia, and died. Such a death appears to represent the antithesis of the poetic, yet for MacNeice, poetry spoke about the ordinary as well as the metaphysical and it was intended to speak to the ordinary man. His death resulted from the performance of his ordinary human responsibility, his job.

Analysis

Louis MacNeice was an extremely self-conscious poet. He wrote several books of literary criticism, gave lectures on the subject, and often reflected upon the role of the poet in his poems. In an early essay, written in 1936, he reveals his allegiance to the group of poets represented by W. H. Auden, who believed their chief responsibility to be social rather than purely artistic. MacNeice divided art into two types: parable and escape. William Butler Yeats and T. S. Eliot, while unquestionably great, represent the latter, the less valid route. MacNeice always retained his belief in "parable-art," that is, poems that appear naturalistic while also suggesting latent moral or metaphysical content—although he came to realize in later years that journalistic or overly realistic art has its defects while "escape-art" often addresses fundamental problems. MacNeice's lasting conception of the poet's task is remarkably close to William Wordsworth's in the Preface to the *Lyrical Ballads* (1800): the poet should be a spokesman for and to ordinary men. In order to communicate with a large audience, the poet must be representative, involved in current events, interested in the news, sports, and so on. He must always place the subject matter and the purpose of his art above a pure interest in form. In *Modern Poetry: A Personal Essay*, he echoes Wordsworth's dictum that the poet must keep his eye on the object. A glance at the titles of MacNeice's poems reveals the wide range of his subjects; geographical locations, artists, seasons, classical and mythical figures, types of people, technological objects, and types of songs are a few representatives of the plurality embraced by his poems. Furthermore, like Wordsworth, MacNeice studies external objects, places, and events closely, though his poems often end up really being about human consciousness and morality, through analogy or reflection on the experience.

Thus, MacNeice's fundamental approach to poetry also resembles Wordsworth's. Many of his poems are a modernized, sometimes journalistic version of the locodescriptive genre of the eighteenth century, arising from the description of a place, object, or event, followed usually by a philosophical, moral, or psychological reflection on that event. Although MacNeice attempts to use a plain, simple style, his training in the Classics and English literature tends to produce a rich profusion of allusive reverberations. The relationship between the topical focus of the poem and the meditation it produces varies from association to analogy to multiple parallels. In technique, MacNeice differs from the imagistic, symbolist thrust of T. S. Eliot, Ezra Pound, and the modern American poets influenced by them. The framework of Mac-Neice's poems is primarily expository; he tells rather than trying to show through objective correlatives.

As Terence Brown argues in *Louis MacNeice: Sceptical Vision* (1975), MacNeice is most notable as a poet of ideas. In his study of Yeats he emphasizes the importance of belief in giving substance to a poet's work. Many critics have mistakenly criticized MacNeice's poetry on this basis, finding it superficial and devoid of philosophical system. Brown argues cogently that MacNeice is deceptively philosophical because he remains a skeptic. Thus the few positive beliefs underlying his poetry appear negative. Many of his poems question epistemological and metaphysical assumptions; depending on one's interpretation, MacNeice's "final" position may seem positive or negative. Many of his poems represent what might loosely be called an Existentialist position. Although he never stops evaluating the validity of religion, MacNeice ceased to believe in God in his late teens, after being brought up in the home of a future Anglican bishop. The loss of God and Christianity left a huge gap in the metaphysical structure of MacNeice's thought, and he resisted replacing it with another absolute system such as Marxism. He retained a strong sense of moral and social duty, but he found no objective sanctions for value and order. In his poems he explores the conflicting and paradoxical facts of experience. For example, he believes that a new social order will benefit the masses, but he is honest enough to admit his fondness for the privileges of the elite: good education, clothes, food, art. He remains obsessed with the Heraclitean theory of flux, that we can never step into the same river twice. Yet when we face the absence of certainty, belief, and absolute value, we can celebrate plurality and assert ourselves against time and death. Brown distinguishes the modernity of MacNeice in "a sceptical faith, which believes that no transcendent reality, but rather non-being, gives being value."

The most striking technical features of MacNeice's poems evince his sometimes conflicting concerns with reaching a large audience of ordinary people and with reflecting philosophically on experience. In line with the former, he attempts to use colloquial, or at least plain, language, and often to base his rhythm and style on popular musical forms, from the folk ballad, nursery rhyme, and lullaby to modern jazz. His concern with contemporary issues, coupled with his classical training, makes irony and satire inevitable. Like the

English Augustans (with whom he did not want to be identified), MacNeice cannot help contrasting reality with the ideals of past literature, politics, and belief systems. His satire of contemporary society tends to be of the urbane, gentle, Horatian type, only infrequently becoming harsh and bitter. Other stylistic features mark his concern with metaphysical issues. He uses analogy and paradox, accreting many resonances through classical and biblical allusions, usually simultaneously. Many poems pose unresolved questions and problems, circling back on their beginnings at the end. The endings that repeat initial statements or questions would seem to offer closure, or at least a definite structure, to the poems, but paradoxically they do not. Rather, they emphasize the impossibility of answering or closing the issue. Another stylistic feature that recurs throughout MacNeice's work is the list, similar to the epic catalogs of Homer. Rather than suggesting greatness or richness as they usually do in epics, MacNeice's catalogs represent the irreducible plurality of experience.

In addition to the question of his belief system or lack thereof, critics have disagreed over whether MacNeice's work develops over time or remains essentially the same. The answer to this question is sometimes viewed as a determinant of MacNeice's rank as a poet. An argument can be made for both positions, but the answer must be a synthesis. While MacNeice's appreciation of the complexity of life, its latent suggestions, grows as his poetry develops, certain interrelated clusters of themes and recurring images inform his work from beginning to end. For example, the places and events of his childhood shape his problematic identity and world view, including his obsessions with dreams and with Ireland as a symbol of the more Gothic, mysterious, and mystical sides of experience. Connected with his upbringing in the home of an Anglican rector is a preoccupation, mentioned above, with disbelief in God and religion, and faith in liberal humanism. The disappearance of God results in complex epistemological and moral questions which also pervade many poems. Another related thematic cluster is a concern with time, death, and Heraclitean flux. Closely related to this cluster is an increasing interest in cycles, in repetition versus renewal, reflected in many poems about spring and fall.

Although these themes, along with recurring images of train journeys, Ireland, stone, dazzling surfaces, and time represented as space, among others, continue to absorb MacNeice's attention, the types of poems and emphases evolve over time, particularly in response to changes in the political temper of the times. His juvenilia, written between 1925 and 1927, reflects the aesthetic focus of his student years, playing with sound and rhetorical devices, musing on sensation, death, God, and self-consciousness. MacNeice did not really emerge as a poet until the 1930's, when his teaching, marriage, and life among the workers of Birmingham opened his eyes to the world of social injustice and political reality. At that point he was influenced by Auden,

Stephen Spender, and C. Day Lewis, and came to see the poet's role as more journalistic than purely aesthetic.

The poems of the 1930's reflect his preoccupation with the disheartening political events in Spain and Germany and his belief that the existing social order was doomed. The poetry of this period is more leftist than at any other stage in MacNeice's career, but he never espouses the dogmas of Marxism. During World War II, his poetry becomes more humanistic, more positive in its treatment of man. MacNeice's faith in human nature was fanned by the courage and generosity he witnessed in his job as a fire watcher in London during the war. After the war his poems become at first more philosophical, reflecting a revaluation of the role of art and a desire for belief of any kind, not necessarily in God. At this point the poems express an existential recognition of the void, and a disgust with the depersonalization of England after the war; they also play with looking at subjects from different perspectives. His last three volumes of poems, published in 1957, 1961, and posthumously in 1963, represent what most critics consider to be the apotheosis of MacNeice's career. The lyrics of his latest poems are austere and short, often using tetrameter rather than pentameter or hexameter lines. Many of these poems are "parable-poems" in the sense that MacNeice described in his Clark Lectures of 1963, published as *Varieties of Parable* (1965); that is, they use images to structure a poem that is in effect a miniature allegory. The poems appear to be topical or occasional, but they hold a double or deeper meaning.

Because MacNeice was essentially a reflective, philosophical poet, his poetry records an ongoing dialectic between the shaping forces of his consciousness and the events and character of the external world. Thus certain techniques, goals, and preoccupations tend to recur, though they are different in response to historical and personal developments in MacNeice's life. Since he was a skeptic, he tends to ask questions rather than give answers, but the more positive values that he holds become clearer by the last years of his life. In particular, the idea of a kingdom of individuals, who lay claim to their freedom and create their lives, is implicit in many of the later poems, after being introduced in "The Kingdom," written around 1943. The members of this kingdom counteract flux and fear by their genuineness, their honest seeing and feeling, their incorruptibility. The Greek notion of *arête*, sometimes translated as virtue or excellence, but without the narrowly moral meaning usually attached to "virtue," comes to mind when one reads the descriptions of exemplary individuals in "The Kingdom." This kingdom is analogous to the Kingdom of Christ, the ideal Republic of Plato, and the Kingdom of Ends in Immanuel Kant's moral system. Yet it does not depend on absolutes and thus it is not an unattainable ideal but a mode of life that some people manage to realize in the ordinary course of life. Moreover, the members of this kingdom belong by virtue of their differentness, not because they share divine souls or absolute Ideas of Reason.

MacNeice sees himself in terms of stages of development in such poems as "Blasphemies," written in the late 1950's, where he describes his changing attitude toward God and belief. The poem is a third-person narrative about his own feelings toward religion since his childhood. In the first stanza he is seven years old, lying in bed pondering the nature of the unforgivable sin against the Holy Ghost. In the second stanza he is seventeen, striking the pose of a blasphemer, parodying prayers. The middle-aged writer of the autobiographical poem mocks his earlier stance, seeing the hollowness of rebellion against a nonexistent deity. The third stanza describes how, at thirty, the poet realized the futility of protest against an absence, and turned to a new religion of humanism and realism, facing facts. The mature MacNeice undercuts these simple new faiths by ending the stanza with a question about the nature of facts for a thirty-year-old. Stanza four finds the poet at forty attempting to appropriate the myths of Christianity for purely symbolic use, and realizing that their lack of absolute meaning makes them useless to him. At the age of forty he has reached a crisis of sorts, unable to speak for himself or for mankind. The final stanza sums up MacNeice's ultimate philosophical position: that there are no ultimate beliefs or postures. He finally throws off the entire issue of Christianity, finding divinity neither above nor within man.

The irreducible reality is that he is not Tom, Dick, or Harry, some archetypal representative of ordinary man. He is himself, merely fifty, a question. The final two lines of the poem, however, in typical MacNeice fashion, reintroduce the problem of metaphysics that he has just dismissed. He asserts that although he is a question, that question is as worthwhile as any other, which is not saying too much. He then, however, uses the word "quest" in apposition to the word "question," reintroducing the entire issue of a search for ultimate meaning. To complete the confusion, he ends with a completed repetition of the broken-off question which opens the poem: What is the sin against the Holy Ghost? The repeated but augmented line is an instance of the type of incremental repetition used in folk ballads such as "Lord Randall," and it suggests the kind of dark riddle often presented in such songs. The final question might be just idle intellectual curiosity or it might imply that ultimate questions of belief simply cannot be escaped by rationality.

MacNeice's dedicatory poem, "To Hedli," which prefaces the 1949 *Collected Poems 1925-1948*, serves as a good introduction to his technique and themes. The poem is clearly occasional and autobiographical, using the first-person point of view that he often eschews in later poems. While employing fairly plain diction, the poem is a sestina, a highly restrictive verse form made up of six stanzas, each having six lines ending with the same six words throughout the poem. In addition, the final word of each stanza is repeated as the last word of the first line in the succeeding stanza. MacNeice takes a few liberties, adding a tercet, or half-stanza, at the end, and substituting the word "returning" for "turning" in stanza four. The poem is typically self-reflective, calling into question the poetic efforts represented in the collected poems, regretting the unanswered questions present in the volume. The content of the poem thus radiates out from a highly specific event, the collecting of MacNeice's poems from 1925-1948, and their dedication to the listener of the poem, his second wife Hedli. From this focus the poem reaches back to the poet's past practices and beliefs and outward to suggest a broad metaphysical stance. The poem is therefore typically occasional, personal, and philosophical. Although the poem does not make explicit reference to World War II, its recent horror is implicit in the anger of those who believed they knew all the answers and the "grim past" which has silenced so many poets.

Two recurrent themes that pervade this poem are the need for belief and the motif of repetitive cycles, with the question of renewal. The sestina form, so highly repetitive, mirrors the concern with cycles. Stanza one calls the poetic moments in the collection "April Answers." In MacNeice's works, spring and fall always signal, on one level, the cycles of time and life. In "Day of Renewal," he says he has measured all his experience in terms of returning autumns. The answers that come in April are the positive side of cycles; they herald renewal if not rebirth. The poems, or answers, implicitly compared to perennial plants, seem to have "withered" off from their bulbs or roots, their questions. The questions, or sources of the poems, are akin to the frozen barrenness of winter, perhaps representing despair. Stanza three picks up the metaphor implicit in the word "withered" by comparing the "Word" to a bulb underground. MacNeice is writing this poem during the period when he began attempting to deal with religious matters symbolically, so it is clear that "Word" has no literal Christian significance. It is rather the source of true poetry, informed by some body of belief. The cycles of renewal in MacNeice's past work are contrasted with a larger cycle in which this word is awaiting a new generation of poets who will produce "full leaf" and "bloom" of meaning and image.

The alternating stanzas, two and four, criticize more clearly what MacNeice sees as his own weaknesses as a poet. He has lived too much in the present, in a no-man's-land of belief, between unknown gods to come and the rejected gods of his ancestors. This position parallels, though without the defined system of belief, Yeats's prophecy in "A Second Coming." There is a milder sense than Yeats's of the crumbling of the old order in the outpouring of angry sound from those who knew the answers, perhaps enthusiasts for Communism. Stanza four explains MacNeice's past contentment with "dazzle," the poetic mirroring of intense moments in the flux of life, and with chance gifts washed up by the sea of life. These gifts were fragments from older castaways who could never return. This statement suggests that while nature repeats its cycles endlessly, men die. The final half stanza suggests that the poet is growing older and has nothing but half answers; his end is in sight.

Stanza five begins with the word "But," clearly contrasting the poet's past contentment with his present goals. He refers to the autumn in which he is writing this dedicatory poem (November, 1948) and parallels the leaves' turning brown with the gilt's flaking off his poetic images. The poem ends with a definite desire for some fundamental answers to metaphysical questions. Unlike later poems, "To Hedli" at least implies that such answers may exist.

Among the earlier poems in the 1949 collection, "An Eclogue for Christmas" (December, 1933) marks an early point of departure, a turning toward serious poems of social commentary. In his fragmentary prose autobiography, *The Strings Are False* (1965), MacNeice describes his absorption in his home life during the early 1930's. His sister, in "Trees Were Green" (*Time Was Away*), comments on the special pleasure Christmas always represented for her brother. MacNeice explains that when he had finished writing this poem he was taken aback by the depth of his despair over Western culture's decay. Like many of the poems of this period, "An Eclogue for Christmas" combines colloquial language with a classical form, the eclogue, which is a dialogue between shepherds, often on love or poetry, or the contrast between city and country life. The two speakers of MacNeice's poem, *A.* and *B.*, represent the city and the country, the country in this case being the world of the landed gentry in England. There is no disagreement between the two speakers; they mirror each other's prophecies of doom in terms of the societies they represent. Neither city nor country escapes the horrors of the times. *B.*, the representative of country life, tells *A.* not to look for sanctuary in the country. Both places are equally bad. The poem describes a time like that in Yeats's "A Second Coming," but in a more dominant way than "To Hedli." It seems that MacNeice could clearly see the coming of World War II. The poem satirizes contemporary upper-class British society as mechanistic, slick, and superficial. The rhythms of jazz pervade the hectic and chaotic life of the city, and people like *A.* become automatons. Rather than being individuals like those in MacNeice's later "The Kingdom," people are grotesque in their efforts to be unique.

The motif of cyclical return is what motivates the poem, the reflection on Christ's birth as represented by "old tinsel and frills." This is a hollow repetition, not a renewal or rebirth. The elaboration of technological "improvements" has alienated people from the genuine reality of life. The cyclicity of history is suggested in the metaphor of the Goths returning to silence the pneumatic drill. Yet MacNeice is such a skeptic that he is unable to make a wholesale condemnation of modern industrial society. He admits that a narcotic beauty can be perceived in the lights and bustle of the city, which he here calls an "organism" rather than a machine. *B.* attacks the country gentry in Marxist terms, as a breed whose time is about to end. He alludes to the destruction of the "manor wall" by the "State" with a capital "S," and also to private property as something which is turning to "poison and pus." Much of this part of the dialogue is carried on in questions, so it is difficult to assign a positive attitude to either speaker, let alone the author. *A.*, who seems closer to MacNeice, counters the Marxist-inspired questions of *B.* with questions about the results of violent revolution. *A.* is clearly the skeptic who sees the problems inherent in capitalist society but cannot accept the Marxist solution. *A.* interrupts *B.*, telling him not to "gloat" over his own demise, suggesting the irony of an upper-class Communism. The poem ends with self-mocking assertions on the part of both speakers; they have no choice but to cling to the few good, real things they have in life.

Like so many of MacNeice's poems, this one circles back to its opening occasion, the significance of Christmas. The ending holds out a somewhat flippant hope for renewal, but it is extremely "ephemeral," like the few positive ideas in the last part of the poem. Thus, "An Eclogue for Christmas" shows MacNeice facing an "evil time," the discord and injustices of modern industrial society, but unwilling and unable to accept the premises of a new regime founded on violence and the subordination of the individual to the State. This skepticism sets him apart from the group of poet-friends surrounding Auden.

Six years later, in the fall of 1938, MacNeice wrote *Autumn Journal*, a long poem in twenty-four cantos, commenting specifically on the depressing political events of the time: the Munich Pact and the Spanish Civil War. In a prefatory note he categorizes the poem as half lyric and half didactic, hoping that it presents some "criticism of life" with some standards beyond the "merely personal." The poem, however, is a journal (as the title states) and its record of events is tinged by fleeting personal response. It is a huge, complex version of his shorter poems in its intertwining threads of autobiography, travel, politics, philosophy, morality, and poetics. The personal-ethical response to political events is the strongest of these threads, coloring the entire poem. Because it takes its impetus from the private and public events of the days and months of late 1938, from late August until New Year's Eve, it does not have an overall architectonic structure; each individual canto rounds itself out as a separate unity which is enhanced by its relationship to the whole.

The poem as a whole is given closure by the parallels between the dying summer at the beginning, the dying year at the end, and the threatened death of European civilization from the impending world war throughout. The narrative is basically chronological, following the poet's first day of the fall term, through trips to Oxford and finally to Spain. The narrative technique resembles stream of consciousness, the thoughts and memories of the poet creating the subject matter. The poem is more fluently lyrical than many of MacNeice's poems, which have been criticized as being "flat." It uses an alternating rhyme scheme like that of ballad stanzas (abcbdefe . . .), but the effect resembles terza rima.

As in most of MacNeice's works, the meditations are rooted in specific observations of actual times, places, and events. Canto I begins with a catalog of concrete images of summer's end in Hampshire, ordinary people leading ordinary lives, insulated within their families. The poet-narrator is in a train, as in so many of his poems. The train ride comes to symbolize the journey of life, the time line of each individual. In an ambiguous tone, MacNeice mentions his dog lying on the floor of the train, a symbol of lost order. This is picked up both more seriously and more ironically in Canto VII when the dog is lost while political treaties are dying and trees are being cut down on Primrose Hill in order to make an antiaircraft station. The loss of the dog is the close of the "old regime." In MacNeice's personal life, the "old regime" represents his marriage to Mariette, but in larger terms it is the demise of traditional Western capitalist society. At the end of this canto, the speaker tries to work up enthusiasm for a war which he cannot romanticize. He realizes exactly what it is, yet he also realizes that he may have to become uncritical like the enemy, like Hitler propagandizing on the radio.

Canto VIII builds, through satirical popular song rhythms, to a climax of fear about the outbreak of war. At the end of the canto the poet learns that the crisis is averted through the sacrifice of Czechoslovakia. He does not explain his response directly except to say that he has saved his own skin as an Englishman in a way that damns his conscience. The poet-narrator feels a terrible conflict between a natural desire to avert war and a sense of duty, which might in earlier times have been called honor, to face up to the threat of Hitler and defeat him. This conflict is implicit until Canto XII, in which he describes people, himself included, lacking the heart to become involved in ethics or "public calls." In his private debate with his conscience, MacNeice recalls the soldiers training across the road from his home when he was a child during World War I. Having described the beginning of classes in Canto IX, cynically and mockingly stating that *we* are safe (although the Czechs are lost), the poet is reading Plato in preparation for teaching his philosophy course. The ethical differences between Plato and Aristotle form an important context for the progress of MacNeice's feelings and thoughts in the poem. In Canto XII, he rejects Plato's ideal forms as a world of capital initials, preferring instead the Heraclitean world of flux, of sensation. He admits at the end of Canto XII that his desire is to be "human," in the fullest sense, to live in a civilized community where both mind and body are given their due. He undercuts this desire by satirizing the professors of humanities who become "spiritually bankrupt" snobs, yet conceding his own willingness to take the comforts that such a profession provides. Though the connection is not explicitly made here, the reader must keep in mind the overwhelming threat to civilization that forms the background of these reflections. *Autumn Journal* traces MacNeice's emotional and moral journey from reluctant self-interest to reluctant determination to do his share to protect humanity in the impending war.

Canto XIII is a mocking, slightly bitter rejection of the elitist education, particularly in philosophy, that MacNeice has received. The bitterness arises from the disjunction between the promise and world of thought and the real world he must inhabit. He must be happy to live in the world of appearances and plurality, life in the particular rather than the eternal and ideal realm. The poet's synthesis between skepticism and moral and civic responsibility is revealed in the next canto where he describes a trip to Oxford to help drive voters to the polls. While he cannot commit himself to political ideologies, he does mobilize himself to act for a "half-believed-in principle." Imperfect though it is, the parliamentary system is England's only hope for political progress. Here MacNeice comes to the important realization that to shun politics for private endeavor is to risk the conditions that support or allow that private endeavor. As he drives back to London at the end of Canto XIV, MacNeice has a new understanding of the need for all Englishmen to unite against the threat of Fascism. This new resolution allows the cheerful final image of the sun caressing the plurality of nature, wheelbarrows full of oranges and apples. This serenity is undercut in the following canto by a nightmarish effort to escape through drink the horrors that threaten, horrors associated in MacNeice's mind with his childhood fears and bad dreams.

In Canto XVII, at nine o'clock on a November morning, the poet savors a moment of almost Keatsian escape in a bath, allowing responsibility to die. Metaphorically he speaks of the ego merging into the bath, thus leading himself into a meditation on the need of man to merge, or at least interact, with those outside himself. Significantly, MacNeice affirms Aristotle's ethical notion that man's essence is to act, as opposed to Socrates' idea that man's crowning glory is to think. The canto ends with his refusal to "drug" himself with the sensations of the moment. This climactic decision to act is followed by cantos satirizing industrialized England, implying, as William Blake does in *Songs of Innocence* (1789) and *Songs of Experience* (1794), that church and state conspire to allow social injustice. While MacNeice is not a Communist, he fairly consistently condemns *laissez-faire* economics as an instrument of evil. While Canto XVIII is very bitter about England's social and political failure to act, it ends with the affirmative statement that the seeds of energy and choice are still alive. Canto XX, trying to sound bitter, relaxes into a nostalgic longing for Christmas, a week away, a "coral island in time." This beautiful image is typical of MacNeice's conflation of space and time. Any poem about consciousness exists in the stream of time, but to be comprehensible the passing of time must be anchored to spatial reference points. MacNeice frequently concretizes this space/time relationship by metaphorically imaging time as a geographical space. Christmas here is an ideal moment, described through an allusion to the lotus eaters of the *Odyssey* (c. 800 B.C.). The remainder of the canto speaks respectfully of Christ but ends on a satirical note about people exploiting the season to beg for money. This carries additional overtones, however, because if one remembers the spirit of Christmas rather than the selfish pleasures it brings, nothing is more appropriate than to celebrate Christ's birthday by giving money to beggars.

Canto XXI returns to the notion of Canto XVII, that one must live a life beyond the self, in spite of the wish to quit. The poem, like the year, ends with MacNeice's train journey through France to Spain. Significantly, the poem skips Christmas, implying that neither the hollow religion of Christianity nor the personal pleasures of the holiday have a meaningful place in the ethical and political events at hand. MacNeice goes to face the New Year in Spain, a place where metaphorically all of Europe may soon stand in time. He goes to confront his duty as a man of action and a citizen of a free country. His New Year's resolutions, detailed in the penultimate canto, reveal his self-criticisms and determination to seek the roots of "will and conscience," to participate. The final canto is a sleep song, gentle in tone, allowing some peace after the hard-won resolutions of Canto XXIII. MacNeice addresses himself, his parents, his ex-wife, and all people, to dream of a "possible land" where the individual can pursue his natural abilities in freedom and understanding. He tells of his hope to awaken soon, but of his doubts to sleep forever.

Most critics agree that MacNeice's final three books of poems, *Visitations*, *Solstices*, and the posthumous *The Burning Perch*, achieve new heights of technical precision and depth of meaning. The themes of flux and renewal become even more prominent than in the past. According to his own statements in literary criticism, MacNeice was attempting to write more "parable-poems." The use of the train journey and of Christmas Day in *Autumn Journal* exemplifies the multiple layers of meaning he could achieve in describing an actual event, object, or place. In these later poems there is more respect for the mysterious, the dark side of experience. The focus on life as a paradox is playfully yet darkly expounded in poems resembling folk ballad riddles, poems such as "A Hand of Snap-shots," "The Riddle," and parts of "Notes for a Biography." In particular, the poems of *The Burning Perch* give brief nightmare sketches of the Gothic side of experience. Connected to the motifs of riddles and paradoxes is a new concern with perspective or various ways of knowing, as in Part I of "Jigsaws," "The Wiper," "The Grey Ones," and perhaps "Budgie."

"The Wiper," from *Solstices*, is a perfect example of the kind of "parable-poem" MacNeice sought to write in his later years. On the literal level it starts with a concrete description of the driver's and passengers' perspective of the road from inside the car on a dark, rainy night. The first stanza portrays the glimpses of the shiny asphalt when the windshield wipers clear the window, only to blur it when they move back the other way. The focus shifts to the nature of the road and then to an outside view of the wet cars on the road.

The fourth stanza turns to the memory of the car's passengers, to the relationship between past and present, while the final stanza looks not very invitingly to the "black future," literally the dark night ahead on the road. Only through subtle double meanings does MacNeice suggest the allegorical or symbolic nature of the poem. The words "mystery" and "always" in stanza two and "black future" in stanza five are the only obvious indicators of a level of meaning beyond the literal.

The poem symbolizes life as a journey with the potential of being a quest, a potential limited by the restrictions of partial blindness. The riders in the car can see only brief snatches of a black road, a mysterious road with unknown dimensions. The darkness of night, the meaningless void of existence, is broken intermittently by the lights of other people insulated and partially blinded in their own "moving boxes." Significantly, while each driver is able to see very little through the dark and rain, his or her car gives off light that illuminates the way for other drivers, if only transiently. The dials in the cars measure speed and distance covered. In Aristotle's terms, these are indicators of efficient causes, but the final cause, the destination and the daylight, is not indicated. The final line of the poem is highly characteristic of MacNeice in its qualified, pessimistically positive assertion. In spite of ignorance and clouded perceptions, living in a world of night and rain, the drivers manage to stay on the road.

MacNeice is a poet of contradictions, a learned classicist who sought to write in a colloquial idiom and appeal to a broad audience, a man who sought belief but was unable to accede to the dishonesty of systematizing. His poems are above all honest. They study life in the fullness of its antinomies and paradoxes.

Eve Walsh Stoddard

Other major works

LONG FICTION: *Roundabout Way* (published under the pseudonym Louis Malone), 1932.

PLAYS: *The Agamemnon of Aeschylus,* 1936 (translation); *Out of the Picture,* 1937; *Christopher Columbus,* 1944 (radio play); *The Dark Tower and Other Radio Scripts by Louis MacNeice,* 1947 (radio plays); Goethe's *Faust, Parts I and II,* 1951 (radio play, translation with E. L. Stahl); *The Mad Islands and The Administrator,* 1964 (radio plays); *One for the Grave,* 1968; *Persons from Porlock and Other Plays for Radio,* 1969 (radio plays).

NONFICTION: *Letters from Iceland,* 1937 (with W. H. Auden); *I Crossed the Minch,* 1938; *Modern Poetry: A Personal Essay,* 1938; *Zoo,* 1938; *The Poetry of W. B. Yeats,* 1941; *Astrology,* 1964; *The Strings Are False,* 1965; *Varieties of Parable,* 1965.

CHILDREN'S LITERATURE: *The Penny That Rolled Away,* 1954.

Bibliography

Brown, Terence. *Louis MacNeice: Sceptical Vision.* New York: Barnes & Noble Books, 1975. This book is concerned with the themes in MacNeice's poetry. The author presents the argument that the poet's real contribution is as a proponent of creative skepticism. The result is a dependable, authoritative study. Contains a good bibliography and notes.

Brown, Terence, and Alec Reid, eds. *Time Was Away: The World of Louis MacNeice.* Dublin: Dolmen Press, 1974. These essays, a grab-bag collection including personal tributes, reminiscences, and evaluations of MacNeice's work, are of uneven quality. Several pieces are of interest—including one by MacNeice's sister which contains personal biographical information. Other selections look at MacNeice's Irishness, his poetry, and his reaction to his mother's death. Includes W. H. Auden's "Louis MacNeice: A Memorial Address" to introduce the collection.

Longley, Edna. *Louis MacNeice: A Study.* London: Faber & Faber, 1988. The first complete study after MacNeice's death. Explores the dramatic nature of MacNeice's poetry, stresses the importance of his Irish background, and credits William Butler Yeats's influence hitherto downplayed. This piece of historical criticism moves chronologically linking MacNeice's life and times. Special attention is given to his English, war, and postwar poems. An appreciation of MacNeice's poetry, it contains a select bibliography and is an excellent guide to the poet's work.

McKinnon, William T. *Apollo's Blended Dream: A Study of the Poetry of Louis MacNeice.* New York: Oxford University Press, 1971. After a skeletal biography the author suggests that MacNeice has been underestimated and proposes to reevaluate his work in a new perspective. He characterizes him as a poet-philosopher and then goes into a detailed analysis of his linguistic techniques. Although rather dry in approach, this is a valid study with interesting perceptions of the poet.

Marsack, Robyn. *The Cave of Making: The Poetry of Louis MacNeice.* New York: Oxford University Press, 1982. This book looks at MacNeice as a poet of the 1930's and focuses on despair and disillusionment in his work. Contains commentary on the poet's craft and process based on papers, drafts, and notes made available to the author. Extensive notes and an excellent bibliography make this a helpful companion to reading MacNeice.

Moore, Donald B. *The Poetry of Louis MacNeice.* Leicester: Leicester University Press, 1972. This descriptive study traces the poet's development chronologically, starting with early influences and following him through the war years and to his death. Tracks thematic lines such as self, society, and philosophy through MacNeice's work. The final chapter gives a retrospective and general critical overview. Includes a select bibliography with citations of related works.

Smith, Elton Edward. *Louis MacNeice.* New York: Twayne, 1970. This study concerns the significance of MacNeice's poetry more than its relationship to his life, even though it surveys his work in chronological order. Traces MacNeice's move to a new style and tone of expression. The final chapter succinctly presents the pattern of the poet's development that has emerged from the study. Contains good notes and bibliography.

SANDRA McPHERSON

Born: San Jose, California; August 2, 1943

Principal poetry

Elegies for the Hot Season, 1970; *Radiation*, 1973; *The Year of Our Birth*, 1978; *Patron Happiness*, 1983; *Streamers*, 1988.

Other literary forms

Sandra McPherson has published a number of essays about contemporary poetry, among them "You Can Say That Again" (*Iowa Review*, Summer, 1972), "The Working Line" (*Field*, April, 1973), "Saying No: A Brief Compendium and Sometimes a Workbook with Blank Spaces" (*Iowa Review*, Summer, 1973), "Secrets: Beginning to Write Them Out" (*Field*, Spring, 1986), and "The Two-Tone Line, Blues Ideology, and the Scrap Quilt" (*Field*, Spring, 1991).

Achievements

Since the mid-1960's, Sandra McPherson has been one of the United States' most important poets. Well received by critics and readers for poems noted for their empathy and unusual syntactical arrangements, McPherson has earned numerous high-profile literary grants and awards, including two Ingram Merrill grants (1972 and 1984), three National Endowment for the Arts grants, the Helen Bullis Prize from *Poetry Northwest*, the Bess Hokin Prize from *Poetry*, the Emily Dickinson Prize from the Poetry Society of America, and the Blumenthal-Leviton-Blonder Award from *Poetry*. Her first book, *Elegies for the Hot Season*, was a selection of the National Council on the Arts university press program. Her second book, *Radiation*, received the Pacific Northwest Booksellers Prize. *The Year of Our Birth* was nominated for a National Book Award, and *Streamers* was nominated for both the *Los Angeles Times* Book Award and the Bay Area Book Reviewers Association Award.

Biography

The unusual facts of Sandra McPherson's biography come to figure both directly and indirectly in many of her poems. Born in San Jose, California, she was given up for adoption at birth. Her adoptive parents lived in San Jose; McPherson grew up there and went to San Jose State University. Not only has McPherson's adoption helped to form her worldview, but her adult reunion with her birthparents in 1981 has also provided the poet with a heightened sense of both the random and orderly forces at work in the universe. Now that she is intimate with two sets of living parents, many of McPherson's poems, especially those in *Patron Happiness*, have come to focus on the similarities between her own ways of perceiving and those of her blood relatives. They also take up attendant questions concerning identity formation and the way a person's life inevitably progresses along unforseeable paths. (See "Earthstars, Birthparents' House," "Wings and Seeds," "Helen Todd: My Birthname," and "Last Week of Winter" in *Patron Happiness* and "The Pantheist to His Child" and "Big Flowers" in *Streamers*.)

After continuing her education at the University of Washington, where she studied with the celebrated poets David Wagoner and Elizabeth Bishop, McPherson worked for a short time as a technical writer for Honeywell, a defense contractor. Poems that reflect this experience are "Preparation" and "Resigning from a Job in the Defense Industry" in *Elegies for the Hot Season*. After marrying poet Henry Carlile (whom she later divorced) in 1966, she gave birth the following year to a' daughter, Phoebe. She has taught at the University of Iowa's writing workshop, Portland State University, the University of California at Berkeley, and the University of California at Davis. Since 1987 her interests have included the aesthetics of blues music and African-American quilts.

Analysis

In her poems, Sandra McPherson repeatedly takes up the issue of survival. She is especially concerned with the tenuous life of objects and beings at the mercy of forces outside their control. In "World of Different Sizes," from her first book, *Elegies for the Hot Season*, she admits a desire to help small objects or beings survive. Her subjects range from slugs and flowers to cats and dogs to human beings and the natural world at large. The lives of children and women as well as adult love relationships are also favorite topics. Usually written in the voice of a narrator who is empathic with whatever or whoever is threatened, her poems express a deep admiration for the idiosyncrasies of the world's fragile inhabitants. McPherson sees relationships between the inability of a being to protect itself and special traits of that being. The poet believes that those traits are highly deserving of care and admiration, because they cannot be found in any other being and therefore will disappear when that being dies. For McPherson, the beauty of a thing is closely related to its degree of helplessness. As she intimates in "Worlds of Different Sizes," she believes that all things—no matter what their size— have an invisible and endangered spirit that is laboring for life.

McPherson's belief in the delicate and essential inward energy of plants and animals (and sometimes even inanimate objects) produces a poetry that continuously examines that aspect of things which gives them their distinctive identity. In her poem "The Plant," she recognizes a houseplant's distinctive life, suggesting that its blossoms emerge from a special place in the plant, a kind of botanical soul. As in many of McPherson's poems, however, this soul is finite and cannot always weather the menacing forces of its environment.

McPherson's work is not important merely because of her ability to prize those beings threatened by uncontrollable forces. Her genius lies in her talent for wedding this extraordinary empathic faculty with her own idiosyncratic syntactical mode. Her idiom is clearly her own—and it virtually resists mimicry. Few other poets write like Sandra McPherson. Her poetic language does not soar like that of Dylan Thomas or Theodore Roethke in passionate lyric bursts. She is one of the most significant poets of her era because she renders her concern for the unique qualities of vulnerable beings in a poetic diction that is often contrapuntal, involuted, highly detailed, and, in her best poems, mysterious and surprising. The linguistic structure she creates is often as unusual as the subjects she is describing. The great aesthetic strength of McPherson's poetry is that in key ways her verse is like many of her subjects: exclusive, irreproducible, one-of-a-kind. Her poems can be difficult; they frequently require close reading in the way many of Marianne Moore's poems do. People, animals, and things are depicted not only with a care for detail but also with an eye for aspects of the subject that have heretofore gone undescribed.

McPherson's poems are often marked by a shimmering, highly refined voice, one that speaks out of an uncanny identification with the inner life of fellow creatures. While McPherson's growing canon will probably leave a lasting mark, her voice also seems somehow fearful of its own mortality, of its human fragility. Beginning with Wallace Stevens, most of the major poets of the twentieth century lament the fact of human mortality. Yet few poets use tone and imagery to render convincingly the nervous fear that not only is one capable of dying but indeed that one may die at any moment. One of McPherson's earlier poems, "Lions," uses lions as images of incompletely socialized, unpredictable, and dangerous human instincts. This simultaneous and self-conscious awareness of one's own power to kill and ability to die is echoed in McPherson's language and serves to amplify her assertion that all beings—especially those that survive at the pleasure of others—must be the focus of wonder and care.

To examine McPherson's five books in order of their appearance is to witness in midcareer the evolution of a style of poetic language that simultaneously describes and mirrors the tenuous and idiosyncratic nature of its subjects. Her first book provides a small preview of the complex syntactical and imagistic poetics she has come to employ more and more. The title poem is the best in a remarkably sophisticated first volume. In the two-part "Elegies for the Hot Season," snails and caterpillars are the foci of her empathy as well as metaphors for the finite lives of humans. In the first section, called "The Killing of the Snails," the narrator remembers how her father would circle the house on humid moonless nights during the summer, hunting for snails to destroy. She could hear him on the other side of the walls as he crunched them with his feet. The next day she would search for them. The signature characteristics by which one can recognize the poems of McPherson's fifth book are prefigured here in her attention to detail and imaginative phrasing. Like her later poetry, this first section does not end with an obvious thematic turn. There is surprise in the section's closure; the poet does not dwell on what might be a young girl's horrific fascination. Rather, she notes the perseverance and perhaps the retribution of the surviving snails.

The second section, "The Killing of the Caterpillars," does not, however, end the poem by focusing on the persevering traits of caterpillars. In this sequence the narrator has watched her neighbor torch nests of tent caterpillars in the branches of his cherry tree. The neighbor is a musical "conductor," but the music is the sound of immolation, the burning caterpillars. The exploding larvae begin their strange, hallucinatory fall through the branches. McPherson finds the exact metaphor to describe the scene and renders it here in exotic imagery and exquisite free verse sound. The fiery caterpillars have been part of a terrible and oddly beautiful show. After they burn out into black crisps, the narrator's fixation with burning appears in her attention to light, specifically that of her father's flashlight illuminating the dead caterpillars. The poem ends with a hopelessness that had been temporarily suppressed by the closing retribution of the first section. In many ways "Elegies for the Hot Season" establishes a paradigm for the kinds of poems that McPherson has written since it first appeared. With an imaginative care for specific visual details, the poem focuses on the fragile existence of small, nonhuman creatures and demonstrates a sympathy for their circumstance. Furthermore, "Elegies for the Hot Season" considers the deadly human power of the environment those creatures inhabit.

At least two other poems from *Elegies for the Hot Season* are representative of McPherson's range. "Resigning from a Job in the Defense Industry" is not an overcharged political manifesto; rather, it considers the manner in which people in the narrator's workplace would cope with their life of building weapons of mass destruction. Typically, McPherson's narrator found herself fascinated with names. Her coworkers attempted to minimize the nearly unimaginable gravity of their work by distracting themselves. Some decorated their holiday plants and trees. Others made art for the company talent show. Like the poet's artistic impulse, the creative process of the coworkers was a gesture against the mechanics of death. In "His Body," which expresses a woman's view of her lover's body, the narrator is fascinated by the unusual aspects of a being's physical self. In this case, these aspects correspond to the invisible characteristics that distinguish one human being from all others. While the language is syntactically straightforward, the poem manifests McPherson's penchant for clever observation. While "His Body" closes on a loving note, it also affirms the poet's belief that being alive dictates the condition of isolation.

McPherson continues her inquiry into identity in her second book, *Radiation*. Employing a quote from French poet Paul Valéry as an epigraph, she establishes a severe context for the poems that follow. Is it true that good people are fundamentally evil? That evil people have good hearts? Valéry understands that his hypothesis is unprovable, and McPherson, too, recognizes that the notion that each individual may actually be a character opposite, like a film negative, is probably too simple. Yet the epigraph provides her with a tool for understanding human nature: People may not be duplicitous character opposites, but they are certainly not entirely how they project themselves. Human beings are, rather, complex entities who can be both savage and caring. The kind may at times be cruel, and the cruel may at times be kind. In McPherson's view, such irony must be accepted if one is to appreciate one's dual position as destroyer and caregiver. One's survival and the survival of others may depend on one's recognizing one's own animality.

McPherson believes that human beings are animals in the best and worst sense of the word. People are born feral, and several poems in *Radiation* concern the instinctively self-directed nature of humankind. In "Peter Rabbit" McPherson retells the children's story of Peter, the small rabbit that disobeys his mother and wanders far from home, barely escaping from Mr. McGregor's garden and losing his pretty blue jacket in the process. The poem is narrated by a bright child to whom the story is being read. The child knows that mothers, too, can be unkind, even Mother Rabbit. Though the child sympathizes with Peter, the child also knows that Peter is not always good, that he is a thief. At the same time, the child understands that being bad may be part of being alive. In the next lines the child recognizes an affinity with Peter—almost a complete identification. McPherson creates an endearing children's diction to dramatize the innate good-bad split in human beings. Such a language emphasizes the child's innocence, but innocence here does not mean moral purity. The child needs protection, despite the fact that the child can be "naughty" and knows it. The child is needy and desirous of all good things, including Peter's safe deliverance from Mr. McGregor. The child also knows how the story will end. Endlessly yearning for pleasures, the child wants to put off the inevitable displeasure of that cessation.

Like many of the poems in *Radiation*, "Peter Rabbit" is a more penetrating investigation of the issues McPherson began to explore in *Elegies for the Hot Season*. The poems of the second book take greater associative leaps, each image leading quickly to another. When she was writing these poems, she was clearly influenced by the work many of her peers were doing with "deep imagery," a style of writing characterized by leaping, often surreal images intended to stir buried emotions in the reader. Such images were usually referred to as archetypes, especially by proponents of Jungian poet

Robert Bly's theories regarding poetry and the operations of the unconscious mind. This kind of archetypal imagery is effective in McPherson's "Cinderella," a poem that retells the old story by placing an aging Cinderella at a window out of which, at the end of the poem, she stares, full of longing. Soon, however, Cinderella finds a gold leaf, and she is again temporarily satisfied. The poem first leaves the reader with a sensation of deliverance. Just as Peter Rabbit escaped the foot of Mr. McGregor, and just as the child narrator hopes for a provider of infinite pleasures, Cinderella is once more saved from her life of drudgery—or so it may seem, for this Cinderella is perhaps too much like the child in Peter Rabbit. She has not learned what all adults must learn: to find redemption in the self.

In *The Year of Our Birth* themes involving the painful realities of children, women, parents, and the natural world are rendered in a complex style often marked by great associative leaps, deep imagery, ellipses, and uncommon syntax. The poems of *The Year of Our Birth* are among McPherson's most ambitious, difficult, and rewarding. One critic found her rhythms awkward, but he may have misunderstood McPherson's deliberately contrapuntal accents, which are intended to reflect the peculiarities of both the thing perceived and the process of perception.

Such a surprising syntactical arrangement begins "Children," a poem about the complex symbiotic relation between mother and daughter. The poet establishes a strange and affecting density in the first line by mixing the pronoun "you" into the sentence four times. The effect of this and other techniques is a certain indeterminacy. The reader is temporarily adrift, trying to establish meaning and order. McPherson intends to disrupt the conventional, linear style of expression, because she wants the poem's language to mirror the relationship between the mother and daughter—that is, a state out of equilibrium, always in dynamic flux, indeterminate.

McPherson uses similar diction as well as a more radical, leaping imagery in "A Coconut for Katerina," an extraordinary poem about a friend's miscarriage. The poem never explicitly states that its subject is a miscarriage. The reader's immediate dislocation is like Katerina's flustered consciousness. One must suspend typically linear thought in order to follow the poem's movement. As with many of the poems in *The Year of Our Birth*, reading "A Coconut for Katerina"—perhaps the poet's best poem—requires an intuitive approach. Filled with poetic surprises, the entire first stanza works against structural order, and the sentence of the second stanza is actually a fragment. The third sentence suggests that Katerina is holding up a coconut as if for display. Many of the poem's lines shift direction in meaning, until understanding is obscured by the shifts.

Such shifting, indeterminate writing can be disarming when first encountered, but, when a reader learns to release the desire for instantaneous conventional interpretation, the poem takes on a salient life. In this poem, the reader can eventually come to sense that Katerina is despondent over a mis-carriage, despondent to the point of a near psychotic experience. Many of McPherson's poems require an unusual way of reading; not only must the reader float from strange image to image in the associative drift of a dis-tressed consciousness, but that reader also must allow those images first to pique emotional responses and, second, to come to the surface of the reader's own consciousness. The reader experiences the situations and resulting feel-ings McPherson is uncovering. Reading in this way provides a free-floating sensation.

Immediately following the strange images of milk at the end of the first stanza, the reader finds rope imagery. The atransitional movement from milk to rope is an example of McPherson's rapid leaps. The poem is elliptical in that it provides few linking terms. McPherson eschews transitions and re-quires her readers to shift rapidly. The sudden introduction of the first-person narrator is another quick shift. Who is she or he? Later in the poem, the narrator is transformed into the first-person plural "we." Perhaps the narra-tor is a friend, then a group of friends. The narrator apparently empathizes intimately with Katerina, experiencing the anxiety she feels. Yet the narrator is simultaneously conscious of something more. Katerina—like the children, Peter Rabbit, the snails, the caterpillars, and all the other objects of McPher-son's concern—is representative of the vulnerable being who must suffer ran-dom fates.

McPherson is of great literary importance because in taking such risks with language she is advancing one of the collective projects of twentieth century American poetry: to render thought processes and emotional life via poetic language. A poem such as "A Coconut for Katerina" is not simply decoded; rather, it is experienced, felt. The sequence of archetypal moments in the poem provides a surprisingly fast series of imaginative episodes that correspond to those of Katerina and her friends. The reader knows a central facet of their lives. To empathize with them is, in McPherson's view, a good thing. The poem ends with a series of sea and water images, which generate an awareness of future possibilities.

The poet's care for all things vulnerable is an explicit concern of many other poems in *The Year of Our Birth*. "In a Garden" offers a proposition in less dense language than either "Children" or "A Coconut for Katerina." In "Centerfold Reflected in a Jet Window," McPherson is frightened for all women, especially her daughter, who are too often exploited by certain kinds of men. The narrator is sitting in an airplane behind a man who is staring at a naked woman in a magazine. First she imagines the woman exposed and freezing outside the plane. Quickly the woman is transformed into the narra-tor's freezing daughter. Eventually the poem employs another surreal and deep image—that of a disappointed old woman who is riding inside the earth, alone, wanting love after giving it all her life.

McPherson's fourth major book, *Patron Happiness*, is also deeply concerned with women who aspire to succeed in a tragically unloving world. One of its most affecting poems is "The Steps," subtitled "Mother Once in the '40's." The poem is about a mature woman who faints every other year or so and who seems to desire some kind of lighter, otherworldly existence. A kind of mystic feminist fantasia, the poem asserts a woman's desire to transcend her mundane and empty existence after her children are grown. The poem intimates that her survival depends on her periodic dream states, in which she can know a less binding, more rapturous state of being. The trance becomes a method of adapting to a world that conspires against her fulfillment.

If the poems of McPherson's first three books primarily depict a world of vulnerable beings menaced by dark forces, *Patron Happiness* exhibits a romantic option by which those who are endangered may find some solace. Just as "A Coconut for Katerina" closes on a note of regenerative possibility, poems such as "The Steps," "Helen Todd: My Birthname," and "Urban Ode" seem to favor a life of speculative wonder. In these poems the imagination can serve as comfort or relief. For example, in "Helen Todd: My Birthname" McPherson imagines the identity she would have had if her birthparents had kept her. The poem is one of McPherson's most popular, because its subject is striking and its execution poignant. The poet's imagination allows her to know two lives in the one being. Astonished to learn her birthname, Helen Todd, she converts this astonishment to an empowering realization that she may actually have doubled her life.

"Urban Ode," the last poem in the book, has a theme of openness to the enabling possibilities of the imagination. It begins in a diner from which an angry boy has been quietly ejected after flinging a chair that just misses the narrator. The boy's behavior leads the narrator to ponder his probable painful loneliness—a loneliness that she, too, has felt. Now, after hours of therapy and piano playing, however, she may be past the debilitating effect of that loneliness. The poem ends with images of children running around a bush. One of the children asks her friend Ava to come see a jay, but Ava says no because she has already seen a jay. She knows what it is, what it looks like. While Ava disregards something she has already seen, her friend has learned to see wonder in the bird—and, by extension, in all common things. Because McPherson is uncertain that such potential can exist in herself, the poem is not a sure affirmation of imaginative potential. McPherson herself wonders whether this state of surprise that can negate a paralyzing loneliness is truly possible for adults.

Like *Patron Happiness*, McPherson's *Streamers* chronicles her development from great worry and doubt to a modest hope. With a naturalist's eye for details, the book often focuses on marine and plant life while carrying on her inquiries into the renascent methods of the vulnerable. The book also demonstrates McPherson's new interest in poems that are longer than her usual one- or two-page length. The best poem in the volume is the title piece, which draws a comparison between the lives of persevering women and the cyanea, a stinging jellyfish that can attain a diameter of seven feet. Written in forty-one irregular stanzas, the poem is set initially at the sea, where the narrator and a friend are propped on elbows, looking down from a dock at a large jellyfish. Unlike other women, this woman friend has not left for other parts of the world; she owns five houses but lives alone. The poem, about women finding independent means to happiness, shifts from the friend's reminiscences and observations to those of the narrator, with an intervening quotation from Sherlock Holmes about the great distracting vision of beautiful women. The key to the poem lies in the elasticity of the jellyfish, its "streamers," which never seem to harden. Unlike the friends who have left their husbands (and perhaps unlike men who too often survive by armoring themselves emotionally), the two women come to see that achieving vitality and an adaptable flexibility is the key to retaining their own identity as independent women while surviving. "Streamers" moves toward this conclusion in a long, undulant wave of comparisons. Unlike many of McPherson's earlier poems, its syntax is relatively natural, as close to conversational as she ever writes.

The volume ends with "Kindness," a poem of twenty-three regular four-line stanzas, comparing flowers to the tensionless hands of the narrator's lover. The narrator understands that she has come to love this man because he chooses "not to threaten" and she can therefore live a less anxious life. Like "Streamers," "Kindness" moves with an easy, uncomplicated pace. Like "Streamers"—and many of McPherson's other poems—it draws its surprising conclusions from intriguing likenesses. The lover is as gentle as a plantain, and both he and the narrator are like naturalists, in love with the things of the natural world as well as with each other. Where some people might callously destroy the undefended, mysterious beings of the world, this man kindly accepts their enigmatic or unknowable selves.

"Streamers" and "Kindness" are representative of McPherson's ongoing poetic and thematic growth. Over more than twenty years, she has demonstrated an extraordinary talent for perceiving the unique attributes of common things and rendering her insights in a language that is as distinctive as the things themselves. Her evolution from *Elegies for the Hot Season*, published in 1970, to *Streamers*, published in 1988, is marked principally by an increased confidence in the redemptive powers of the imagination and the regenerative powers of sentient beings. As she becomes somewhat less anxious about the dangers of an unfeeling environment and a bit more comforted by the enduring possibilities of imagination, her poetry demonstrates a less apprehensive voice while retaining its diligence, complexity, and insight.

Kevin Clark

Bibliography

Boruch, Marianne. "No Perimeters." *American Poetry Review* 18 (March/April, 1989): 41-43. In this review of *Streamers*, Boruch applauds McPherson's sense of discovery and surprise. Boruch discusses "Fringecups" and "The Feather," analyzing McPherson's deliberate manner of coming to realizations. The review finishes with a declaration that, like those of William Carlos Williams, McPherson's poems are rare because they do not compromise.

Jackson, Richard. Review of *Patron Happiness*. *Prairie Schooner* 59 (Winter, 1985): 109-116. Jackson's review is a positive evaluation of *Patron Happiness*, which he sees as recording a romantic journey toward personal identity.

McPherson, Sandra. "Dialogue with Sandra McPherson." Interview by Cecilia Hagen. *Northwest Review* 20, nos. 2/3 (1982): 29-55. In this lengthy and wide-ranging interview, McPherson discusses her intuitive closeness to nature, her writing styles, contemporary poets, world and national history (including the Vietnam War), politics, feminism, liberalism, her travels, and her first three books of poems. Of particular interest are her comments about American literary politics, especially as applied to Western poets, and her references to Elizabeth Bishop.

Stitt, Peter. Review of *The Year of Our Birth*. *The Georgia Review* 33 (Summer, 1979): 463-470. The most critical of all pieces written about McPherson's work, this review of five books by different poets devotes only two adjectival paragraphs to *The Year of Our Birth*. Stitt dislikes the opening poem, and he finds the rhythms of others awkward. He does cite "Centerfold Reflected in a Jet Window" and "Senility" as good poems.

Young, David. "Overview." *The Longman Anthology of Contemporary American Poetry*. 2d ed. London: Longman, 1989. One of the best, most insightful pieces written about McPherson, Young's brief introduction presents a highly laudatory description of her work. He commends the intricacies of her poems as well as her imaginative and specific manner of observation. Young discusses "Gnawing the Breast," "Games," "The Museum of the Second Creation," "Resigning from a Job in the Defense Industry," and "A Coconut for Katerina."

HAKI R. MADHUBUTI
Don L. Lee

Born: Little Rock, Arkansas; February 23, 1942

Principal poetry

Think Black, 1967, 1968, 1969; *Black Pride*, 1968; *Don't Cry, Scream*, 1969; *We Walk the Way of the New World*, 1970; *Directionscore: Selected and New Poems*, 1971; *Book of Life*, 1973; *Earthquakes and Sunrise Missions: Poetry and Essays of Black Renewal, 1973-1983*, 1984; *Killing Memory, Seeking Ancestors*, 1987; *Say That the River Turns: The Impact of Gwendolyn Brooks*, 1987.

Other literary forms

Although Haki R. Madhubuti began his writing career as a poet and continues to write poems, he soon asserted that poetry was not only an aesthetic process, but also a sociopolitical act. Two themes permeating his work, then, are also political goals: black unity and black power (through that unity). Because his efforts as a poet and writer demand total dedication to his political concerns—whether in his personal life-style or in his publishing ventures—Madhubuti has essentially chosen the role of poet-as-prophet. As he puts it, "*black* for the blackpoet is a way of life." It should come as no surprise, then, that less than half of his published writing has been poetry (despite its having been his initially favored genre), for Madhubuti does not intend to elevate his status in the black community by his writing so much as he seeks to transform the community through the writing act itself. To that end, he has become one of the foremost social essayists in the Black Nationalist movement, along with Imamu Amiri Baraka (LeRoi Jones), Maulana Ron Karenga, and Julius K. Nyerere.

From the early pamphlet *For Black People (And Negroes Too)* in 1968 to the book *Enemies: The Clash of Races* in 1978, Madhubuti has consistently used the social essay to espouse and develop the ideals, difficulties, and goals of what has come to be called "cultural nationalism." His book *From Plan to Planet, Life Studies: The Need for Afrikan Minds and Institutions* (1973) perhaps best expresses the emphasis on "social content" in Madhubuti's use of the essay and "Blackpoetry," which, as he says in the preface to *Don't Cry, Scream*, is to "tell what's *to be* & how to *be* it," as vehicles for black liberation. The book, a collection of thirty brief essays organized into four distinct sections, is unified by the underlying premise that black survival, meaning the survival of all peoples of African descent anywhere in the world, including Africans, is threatened both by the political power of European and American governments and by the racism—latent and manifest—in those two Aryan-derived cultures.

In the attempt to unify the diaspora of African culture, Madhubuti begins by examining the individual's situation in an oppressive culture and asserts the necessity to *"create* or *re-create* an Afrikan (or black) mind in a *predominantly* European-American setting." (*Afrikan* here and throughout Madhubuti's writing is so spelled in order to indicate a harder *c* sound indigenous to African languages before the "contamination" of sound and spelling—implying sociopolitical domination—by European colonialism: the change in the "standard" spelling is seen as a "revolutionary" act.) This first section, appropriately untitled in recognition of the difficulty involved in establishing a cultural perspective with which to begin a plan of unity, might be called "To See with Afrikan Eyes." The second section, "Life Studies," moves from the concern for the black individual to the problems inherent in the local black community. Here Madhubuti shifts from the necessity of self-esteem, or "positive identity," to the necessity for a black value system, *Nguzo Saba*, that subordinates individual success to the best interests of the black community as a whole. The code of *Nguzo Saba* nurtures self-reliance through cooperative education, business, and industry (urban or rural). To this end, he asserts that widely diverse and geographically scattered communities can form a "psychological unity" that will result in a Black Nation. Madhubuti's synthesis here achieves less theoretical complexity but more pragmatic clarity than similar ideas from his sources: Nyerere's *ujamaa*, African-based socialism; and Karenga's *kawaida*, African tradition and reason.

From this plan for cultural unity despite geographical disparity, Madhubuti focuses on the responsibility of the artist in "The Black Arts." Black artists, in these recommendations, bear the role of "culture stabilizers" who affirm racial identity, maintain political purpose, and define cultural direction in accordance with the principles of the previous section. They are, by implication, prophets who create and fulfill the prophecy of a Black Nation. Through cooperative publishing, teaching, and distribution, the artists help create new wealth, thus new power, for blacks in America—but only insofar as the black community gains unity, not merely in any sense of individual achievement. In the fourth section, "Worldview," Madhubuti extends the prior concerns for individual, community, and artist to blacks throughout the world. Loosely based on Nyerere's concepts and drawing upon ideas in Frantz Fanon's *The Wretched of the Earth* (1965), as well as many other sources, he analyzes the rise of European colonialism from a cultural nationalist viewpoint and reasserts the necessity for the values defined in section two on a global as well as a national scale. While Nyerere bases his doctrine on a philosophy of issues that reaches toward love to nurture the culture, Madhubuti, revising those ideas, asserts that the "nationbuilding" of love within the community must focus on people—black people—not on issues. (*Love* is defined by him as "familyhood," "mutual involvement in one another," and "the brotherhood of man.")

The implicit contradiction throughout the essays, however, is that whites are not only perceived as the enemy of blacks in America, but as "the world's enemy." No such contradiction in "a brotherhood of man" exists as long as Madhubuti speaks of blacks. In fact, it is worth noting that, aside from his condemnation of European and American colonialism (in its various forms), he argues from a pro-black rather than an antiwhite position. His antagonism to negative positions is explicitly stated: "Our struggle should not be based upon the *hate* of anything." In addition to this central contradiction, there are a number of flaws, particularly in unidentified sources and poor documentation, that weaken the polemic of this volume. It remains, however, an important tool in understanding the poetry of Madhubuti; in fact, considered with *Enemies: The Clash of Races*, the work may be said to overshadow the poetry itself,for Madhubuti has moved increasingly to this literary form as his primary means of expressing his sociopolitical (which is to say artistic) vision.

One further major literary concern for Madhubuti has been literary criticism, especially the definition of "new Blackpoetry" in the light of the concepts of *ujamaa* and *kawaida*. His collection of critical essays, *Dynamite Voices: Black Poets of the 1960's* (1971), is significant in two respects: it established a responsibility for the black critic to evaluate seriously the merits of the emerging "cultural nationalist school" of black poets, and it provided a model for doing so (if sometimes uneven and superficial in its judgments). Here, too, Madhubuti shows a tendency for his social criticism to overrun his literary evaluation, but the book will remain an important contribution to the development of aesthetic standards for black literature. (Some of Madhubuti's insights have already been explored and expanded much more carefully and thoroughly than in his own book by Stephen Henderson and Addison Gayle, Jr.) In this context, it is also necessary to note that Madhubuti regularly contributes a column, "Worldview," and book reviews to his journal *Black Books Bulletin*. Other reviews, short essays, polemical statements, and introductions are widespread in anthologies and journals such as *The Negro Digest* (now *Black World*), *Third World*, and *The Black Scholar*. In addition to his writings, recordings of Madhubuti are also available that add a great deal to the printed poem on the page. Like the work of Dylan Thomas, much of the delight in hearing Madhubuti's poetry—based as it is on the improvisations and unpredictable qualities of jazz and urban black speech patterns—is lost when his voice is absent. More so than for a great many poets, his work becomes more powerful when heard.

Achievements

Perhaps Madhubuti's single most impressive accomplishment has been not his success with new forms of poetry, his articulation of new social criticism, his formulation of new aesthetic principles, or his success as a publisher and editor, but his ability to accomplish all of these goals, for which, he asserts, a black poet must struggle. Madhubuti *is* the black poet of his proposed "total dedication" to black liberation and "nationbuilding." In his embodiment of his principles and commitment, Madhubuti has reached into corners of the black community that have been heretofore untouched by black literature or liberation politics. Within four years of the publication of his first book, he had "sold more books of poetry (some 250,000 copies) than probably all of the black poets who came before him combined" (*The Black Collegian*, February-March, 1971). One would be hard-pressed to name *any* American poet who could boast such a large figure in such short time—twenty-five thousand copies, ten percent of Madhubuti's sales, might be considered a phenomenal success. Clearly, Madhubuti's popularity does not rest on library or classroom purchases; it is based on the very "market" he seeks to speak to: the black community. Having defined his audience as exclusively the blacks of America in his social criticism, he has found a quite remarkable response from that desired audience even though he is frequently blunt in his sarcastic ridicule of blacks who aspire to imitate whites. In taking the black community seriously as an audience, Madhubuti has discovered that the audience accepts him seriously. This interaction, then, seems to be the epitome of the "mutual involvement" between artists and community of which he writes in his social criticism.

Madhubuti's popular reception, however, has not diminished his success in a more narrowly defined black literary community. His influence on young black poets and writers of the 1970's is pervasive; one sees imitations of him and dedications to him in many black literary journals. His extensions of Baraka's theoretical positions in cultural nationalism have forced older black critics to reexamine and reevaluate their criteria for black aesthetic standards. His publishing and editing efforts have enabled many young black writers to reach print, as attested by his numerous introductions and reviews of their work. Most important, however, Madhubuti has succeeded continuously in educating (he would say *reeducating*) ever-increasing numbers of individuals within the black community to participate in that dialogue and to perpetuate it within the community. He has been, and remains, an essential leader in working toward black pride, unity, and power, or as he puts it, in giving "identity, purpose and direction" to black "nationbuilding."

Biography

Haki R. Madhubuti (Don L. Lee), born in Little Rock, Arkansas, moved to Chicago with his parents Jimmy and Maxine Lee midway through his childhood. After graduating from high school, Madhubuti continued his education at Wilson Junior College, Roosevelt University, and the University of Illinois at Chicago Circle. His formal education has been tempered, however, by a wide range of jobs which have increased his rapport with varied classes and individuals within the black community. After serving in the United States Army from 1960 to 1963, Madhubuti returned to Chicago to begin an apprenticeship as curator of the DuSable Museum of African History, which he continued until 1967. Meanwhile, he worked as a stock department clerk for Montgomery Ward (1963 to 1964), a post office clerk (1964 to 1965), and a junior executive for Spiegel's (1965 to 1966). By the end of 1967, Madhubuti's reputation as a poet and as a spokesman for the new black poetry of the 1960's had grown sufficiently to enable him to support himself through publishing and teaching alone.

In 1968-1969, Madhubuti was writer-in-residence at Cornell University. Similar positions followed at Northeastern Illinois State College (1969-1970) and the University of Illinois at Chicago Circle (1969-1971), where he combined poet-in-residencies with teaching black literature. From 1970 to 1975, Madhubuti taught at Howard University, except for a year at Morgan State College where he was writer-in-residence for 1972-1973. The extensive popular reception of his poetry and the increasing frequency of his social essays made him a favorite if controversial reader and lecturer with black college students across the country. His influence and popularity also enabled him to found, in Chicago, the Institute of Positive Education in 1971, which publishes *Black Books Bulletin* edited by Madhubuti; he is also the publisher and editor of Third World Press. In conjunction with his writing concerns, which are virtually synonymous with his political commitments, Madhubuti has held important executive positions with a number of Pan-African organizations such as the Congress of African People. Madhubuti's publishing, editing, teaching, and writing continue to maintain his stature within the Black Nationalist movement.

Analysis

Much of Haki R. Madhubuti's poetry was initially greeted by outright condemnation on the part of white critics whose standards of aesthetic judgment were antagonistic, to say the least, toward the nationalist assumptions inherent in much of the new black poetry of the 1960's. Jascha Kessler, for example, in a review in *Poetry* (February, 1973), said that in "Lee all is converted to rant/ . . ./ [he] is outside poetry somewhere, exhorting, hectoring, cursing, making a lot of noise/ . . . you don't have to be black for that/ . . ./ it's hardly an excuse." Madhubuti's sociopolitical concerns, in short, were viewed as unfit for poetic rendering, and his urban, rap-style jazz rhythms and phrases in his poems were dismissed as simply disgruntled, militant ravings. Ironically, that sort of reception—and inability to move beyond the parameters of the New Criticism—supported exactly what the new black poets were claiming: white critical standards forced blacks to write as if they were white themselves and thereby denied them their own cultural heritage and suppressed their experience of oppression. Indeed, this is the dilemma in which the young Lee found himself; if he were to "succeed," he would need (even as a poet) to obliterate his own identity as a black man.

The writings of Amiri Baraka, probably more than any other poet's, as well as his independent studies in African culture (probably begun at the DuSable Museum), violently ruptured the assumption that accommodation to the dominant culture was the sole means by which blacks could survive in America. With the break from accommodationist thought, as Marlene Mosher suggests in *New Directions from Don L. Lee* (1975), Madhubuti began his struggle to create identity, unity, and power in a neo-African context that would preserve his heritage and experience while creating a possibility for the black community as a whole to free itself from the oppressive constraints of mainstream American culture. Madhubuti progressed from the accommodationist period through a reactive phase, then through a revolutionary program, to a prophetic vision. These four aspects of his poetry are distinct not only in the ideological content of his work, but also in the structure of the poems themselves. Once the prophetic vision had been embraced, it was necessary to begin a pragmatic clarification of that vision; the necessity to describe specifically the new Black Nation led, ironically, to an increasing devotion to prose, and thus Madhubuti's poetry seemed nearly to disappear—at least in publication—after his book of poems, *Book of Life*. That the vision of his poetry should result in the suspension of his poetry writing in favor of concrete description was, for those who laud his poetry, a great loss. It is not, however, incomprehensible, for Madhubuti, in urging the embodiment of his poetic vision and in describing *how* to build that vision in realistic terms, is actually carrying out what he first proposed as the goal of his work: to construct an African mind and to create a Black Nation. One assumes, then, that his activities left little time for him to pursue his poetry. Fortunately, he began again to publish books of poems in 1984.

The period of accommodation in Madhubuti's work is available only through autobiographical references found in the early poems of the reactive phase. This early "pre-poetic" time is, appropriately, marked by a lack of articulation. Without his own voice, there are no poems, no prose, no statements of any kind. To speak as oneself for one's community was to react to that accommodation. Madhubuti's "confession" of that period, therefore, is marked by bitterness, hatred, and condemnation of almost everything he associated with white America, including himself. Several poems in his first book, *Think Black*, are testimonial as well as vengeful; it is clear in these poems that Madhubuti had been "liberating" himself for several years, and only then was testifying to that personal struggle through accommodation. He was to say later, in "Black Sketches" (*Don't Cry, Scream*), that he "became black" in 1963 and "everyone thought it unusual;/ even me."

Both the accommodationist period and the reactive phase are seen in *Think Black*, but the point of view is nearly always that of a reaction against accommodation. In "Understanding But Not Forgetting," Madhubuti speaks of his family life and his "early escape/ period, trying to be white." Among his images are those of an intellectual accommodationist who "still ain't hip," an uneducated grandmother "with wisdom that most philosophers would/ envy," misery-filled weekends with "no family/ but money," a twenty-two-year-old sister with "five children," a mother involved in prostitution but "providing for her family," and a cheating white newspaper distributor who kept "telling/ me what a good boy I was." Reexamining his childhood and adolescence in this poem, Madhubuti concludes: "About positive images as a child—NONE," and further that "About negative images as a child—all black." In his attempt to understand his social conditioning and view it in the larger context of American culture, he is forced to conclude that education, democracy, religion, and even the "BLACK MIDDLE CLASS" (to which he has aspired) have failed him because of "the American System." It is, in fact, those very outcasts of the black community itself—the grandmother and the prostitute-mother, who "read Richard Wright and Chester Himes/ . . ./ [the] bad books," that offer examples of survival against overwhelming oppression.

Madhubuti had not, however, accomplished much more at that time than rejection of the value system which had created his anger and despair: the awareness of *how* to "think black" is vague. The last poem in the book, "Awareness," is a chant of only three words: "BLACK PEOPLE THINK." In the variations of syntactical arrangement of these words, however, one is left with the unmistakable impression that he will struggle to learn from those outcasts of mainstream society just what it does mean to "THINK BLACK." These lessons are the heart of his second book, *Black Pride*, which is still reactive but nevertheless substantial in its discovery of identity. While many of these poems remain confessional, there is an increase in the clarity of Madhubuti's sociopolitical development. In the brief lead poem, "The New Integrationist," he announces his intention to join "negroes/ with/ black/ people." The one-word lines of the poem force the reader to contemplate not only the irony in his use of "integration," but also the implications inherent in the labels "negro" and "black." It is an appropriate keynote for the fulfillment of that vague awareness with which his first book ended.

Perhaps the growth in self-identity that characterizes *Black Pride* begins, paradoxically, most clearly in "The Self-Hatred of Don L. Lee." The confessional stance of the poet first acknowledges a love of "my color" because it allowed him to move upward in the accommodationist period; it "opened sMall [sic]/ doors of/ tokenism." After "struggling" through a reading list of the forerunners of cultural nationalism, Madhubuti then describes a breakthrough from "my blindness" to "pitchblack/ . . ./ awareness." His "all/ black/ . . ./ inner/ self" is now his strength, the basis for his self-identity, and he rejects with "vehement/ hatred" his "light/ brown/ outer" self, that appearance which he had previously exploited by accepting the benefits of tokenism. While Madhubuti had escaped accommodation by this time, he had not yet ceased to react to it; instead of having skin too dark, he had skin too light. He was, as black oral tradition puts it, "color-struck." He had, however, moved much deeper into the problem of establishing an identity based on dignity rather than denigration.

The growth of identity and black pride still remains, then, a function of what is not blackness instead of what is, or will become, Madhubuti's new Black Nation. In several poems such as "The Primitive," Madhubuti describes the loss of black values under American slavery and the subsequent efforts of blacks to imitate their oppressors who "raped our minds" with mainstream images from "Tv/ . . ./ Reader's Digest/ . . ./ tarzan & jungle jim," who offered "used cars & used homes/ reefers & napalm/ european history & promises" and who fostered "alien concepts/ of Whi-teness." His message here is blunt: "this weapon called/ civilization/ . . ./ [acts] to drive us mad/ (like them)." For all of his vindictive bitterness, however, Madhubuti addresses himself to the black community more than he does to white America—self-reliance for self-preservation emerges as the crucial issue. As he suggests in the final poem "No More Marching Now," nonviolent protest and civil rights legislation have been undermined by white values; thus, "public/ housing" has become a euphemism for "concentration camps." His charge is typically blunt: "you better wake up/ . . ./ before it's too late."

Although the first two volumes of Madhubuti's poems exist in the tension between accommodation and reaction, they do show growth in the use of language as well as in identity and pride. His work, at times, suffers from clichéd rhetoric and easy catch-phrases common to exhortation, but it also possesses a genuine delight in the playfulness of language even while it struggles forward in the midst of serious sociopolitical polemic. In his division of "white," for example, where the one-syllable word is frequently cut into the two-syllable "whi-te" or the second syllable is dropped completely to the next line, Madhubuti demonstrates more than typographical scoring for the sound of his poem, for he displays the fragmentation between ideals and the implementation of those ideals in American culture. In contrast, "Black man" appears frequently as one word, "blackman," sometimes capitalized and sometimes not—to emphasize the gradual dissolution of the individual's ego, to suggest the necessity for unity in the community for which he strives. Capitalization, in a similar way, sometimes connotes pride in his use of "BLACK." At other times, he uses derogatory puns, such as when "U.S." becomes "u ass." His models are street language, urban speech patterns, jazz improvisation, the narrative form of the toast, and the general inventiveness of an oral tradition that belongs wholly to black culture.

These early poems continue to develop both thematically and technically in Madhubuti's next two books, *Don't Cry, Scream* and *We Walk the Way of the New World*, in which he began to outline his revolutionary program. Mosher suggests that these works are consciously much less antiwhite and much more problack in their sociopolitical commitment. Madhubuti's artistic commitment fused completely with his politics; as he says in the preface to *Don't Cry, Scream*, "there is *no* neutral blackart." Black poetry is seen as "culture building" rather than as a tool to criticize either white society or blacks who seek assimilation. In this programmatic work, the hate, bitterness, and invective of the earlier two books give way to music, humor, and a gentler insistence on change. The poems are more consciously crafted than previously, but they do not compromise their essentially urgent political fervor.

In perhaps the most widely anthologized poem by Madhubuti, "But He Was Cool or: he even stopped for green lights," he humorously undermines the stance of black radicals who are far more concerned with the appearance of being a revolutionary than with a real commitment to working for change in the black community. His satire here is more implicit than explicit, for the reader views the "supercool/ ultrablack" radical in "a double-natural" hairstyle and "dashikis [that] were tailor made." His imported beads are "triple-hip," and he introduces himself "in swahili" while saying "good-by in yoruba." Madhubuti then becomes more explicit in his satire by dividing and modifying "intelligent" to read "ill tel li gent," but he quickly moves back to implication by a rapidly delivered "bop" hyperbole that describes the radical as "cool cool ultracool/ . . ./ cool so cool cold cool/ . . . him was air conditioned cool" and concludes that he was "so cool him nicknamed refrigerator." The dissonance of the last word with the "ice box cool" earlier in the delivery clashes not only in sound, but also in economic and political connotation. This radical is so busy acting the role of a revolutionary that he has been seduced by the very goals of Western culture that Madhubuti is rejecting: money, power, and sex. By his superficial use of gestures, the "radical" has taken himself even farther away from an awareness of the real needs in the black community. In the aftermath of riots in "detroit, newark, [and] chicago," the would-be revolutionary must still be informed that "to be black/ is/ to be/ very-hot." Despite the humor, music, and wordplay in one of Madhubuti's most consciously and carefully "aesthetic" poems, the message is still primarily political. Although the poem does react to the shallowness of the radical, it is worth noting that the poem is no longer essentially reactive in its tone; by the very act of informing the radical of his ignorance in the closure of the poem, the implication is established that even this caricature has the possibility of redemption in Madhubuti's version of Black Nationalism.

Throughout *Don't Cry, Scream*, Madhubuti begins to embrace a wider range of sensibilities in the black community while continuing to denounce those who would betray the needs of black people. In "Black Sketches," he describes Republican Senator Ed Brooke from Massachusetts (then a self-proclaimed liberal advocate of civil rights) as "slashing/ his wrist/ because somebody/ called him/ black," and portrays the conservative (relative to Madhubuti) Roy Wilkins as the token figure on the television show, "the mod squad." He is relentless in his attack on black leaders who work within mainstream politics. In another poem, however, "Blackrunners/ blackmen or run into blackness," Madhubuti celebrates the Olympic medal winners Tommie Smith and John Carlos for their Black Power salutes in 1968 during the awards ceremony. One could hardly describe their gesture as revolutionary, but Madhubuti accepts and praises their symbolic act as a sign of solidarity with his own sense of revolutionary change. In other poems, he is equally open to the role of black women, intellectuals, and Vietnam veterans. By the final poem of the volume, he is even willing to concede that the "negroes" whom he has denounced in earlier work may also be receptive to his political message. In "A Message All Blackpeople Can Dig (& a few negroes too)," Madhubuti announces that "the realpeople" must "move together/ hands on weapons & families" in order to bring new meanings "to/ . . ./ the blackness,/ to US." While not exactly greeting antagonists with open arms (the parenthetical shift to the lower case in the title is quite intentional), his emphasis has changed from the coarse invective found in *Think Black* to a moral, political force that proceeds in "a righteous direction." Not even whites are specifically attacked here; the enemy is now perceived as "the whi-timind," attitudes and actions from "unpeople" who perpetuate racism and oppression. The message, in short, is now much closer to black humanism than it ever has been before: "blackpeople/ are moving, moving to return this earth into the hands of/ human beings."

The seeds for a revolutionary humanism planted at the close of *Don't Cry, Scream* blossom in *We Walk the Way of the New World*. The flowers are armed to be sure, but in signaling this change, the author's introduction, "Louder but Softer," proclaims that the "cultural nihilism" of the 1960's must give way to the "New World of black consciousness" in which education and self-definition (in the context of the community) will create not noisy, pseudorevolutionaries but self-confident leaders who pursue "real" skills—"doctors, lawyers, teachers, historians, writers"—for ensuring the survival and development of African-American culture. Madhubuti's scope and purpose in this book is no less committed than it has been before, but it is far more embracing, compassionate, and visionary. His concern is the establishment of "an ongoing process aimed at an ultimate definition of our being." The tone of urgency ("We're talking about our children, a survival of a people") remains constant and clear, but its directions have moved completely "from negative to positive." While the ideas are not new in *We Walk the Way of the New World*, they do form Madhubuti's most consciously articulated and poetically designed program: of the three sections that shape the

book, "Black Woman Poems," "African Poems," and "New World Poems,"
he says, "Each part is a part of the other: Blackwoman is African and Africa is Blackwoman and they both represent the *New World.*" What is new in
the fourth volume, then, is the degree of structural unity and, to a certain
extent, a greater clarity in describing the specific meaning of *Nguzo Saba*, a
black value system: "design yr own neighborhoods/ . . . teach yr own chil-
dren/ . . . but/ build yr own loop/ . . ./ feed yr own people/ . . ./ [and]
protect yr own communities."

The unifying metaphor for the book is the pilgrimage into the New World.
Arming the heroic, everyman figure "blackman" (unnamed because he is
potentially any black man in the service of community rather than in pursuit
of individual, egotistical goals) with a knowledge of the contrasts between
black women who are positive role-models (with their love tied inextricably
to black consciousness) and black women who aspire to imitate white
middle-class, suburban women, Madhubuti then distinguishes the values of
precolonial Africa from those which have become "contaminated" by Western industrialization. Here his emphasis is on rural communalism, loving
family life, and conserving natural resources. By the final section, "blackman" has ceased to function as a depersonalized hero and is embodied in
the individuality (having derived such from the community) of real black
men, women, and children. This section largely recapitulates the themes and
messages of earlier work, but it does so in an affirmative tone of self-
asserted action within *kawaida*, African reason and tradition. In the long
apocalyptic poem "For Black People," Madhubuti dramatically represents a
movement of the entire race from a capitalistic state of self-defeating in-
activity to a socialistic economy where mutual love and respect result in an
ecologically sound, peacefully shared world of all races (although the "few
whi-te communities/ . . . were closely watched"). The movement of the
poem, symphonic in its structure, is, in fact, the culmination of Madhubuti's
sociopolitical growth and artistic vision to this point.

With *Book of Life*, Madhubuti introduces little new thought, but his ideas
are expressed in a much more reserved political tone and poetic structure.
His role is that of the visionary prophet, the wise sage offering advice to the
young children who must inevitably carry on the struggle to build the New
World which he has described. Indeed, the book's cover shows a photograph
of his own son in the center of a star, and the volume is dedicated to him
"and his sons, and their sons." Throughout the book, photographs of
Madhubuti sitting or fishing with his son testify to his affirmation of the future. His introduction still affirms "black world unity" and looks to *kawaida*
as the source of this new African frame of reference, but only six new
poems speak explicitly to the political dimensions of his vision. The second
section, captioned after the title of the book, is composed of ninety-two
meditations that echo Lao-tzu's *Tao-te Ching* (c. third century B.C.). The

language is simple but profound; the tone is quiet but urgent; the intended audience seems to be his son, but the community overhears him; the poetics are nearly devoid of device from any cultural context, but the force of the didacticism is sincere and genuine. Madhubuti, thinking of black poets who talk "about going to the Bahamas to write the next book," denounces those "poets [who] have become the traitors." It may well be that his sense of betrayal by black artists whom he had expected to assist him in his struggle for the New World and his own growing quietism combined to bring an end to his poetry—at least since the 1973 publication of this work. He seems to have followed his own proverb in *Book of Life:* "best teachers/ seldom teach/ they be and do."

Madhubuti demonstrated an astonishingly rapid growth in his poetry and thought—in only six years. With that sort of energy and commitment, it is not surprising that he should do what he has asked of others, shunning the success of the "traitors": to be and do whatever is necessary for the building of the New World. For Madhubuti, that necessity has meant a turning away from publishing poetry and a turning toward the education of the future generation. One might quite easily dismiss Madhubuti as a dreamer or a madman, but then one would need to recall such visionaries as William Blake, who was dismissed too much too soon.

Michael Loudon

Other major works

NONFICTION: *Dynamite Voices: Black Poets of the 1960's,* 1971; *From Plan to Planet, Life Studies: The Need for Afrikan Minds and Institutions,* 1973; *Enemies: The Clash of Races,* 1978. *Earthquakes and Sunrise Missions: Poetry and Essays of Black Renewal, 1973-1983,* 1984; *Say That the River Turns: The Impact of Gwendolyn Brooks,* 1987; *Black Men: Obsolete, Single, Dangerous?,* 1990.

Bibliography
Basel, Marilyn K. "Haki R. Madhubuti." In *Contemporary Authors,* edited by Deborah A. Straub. Vol. 24. Detroit: Gale Research, 1988. This essay is an excellent lengthy analysis of Madhubuti's life and works. Basel emphasizes Madhubuti's importance to African-American literature, saying that he has come to symbolize the best in African-American art and experience. Supplemented by a primary and secondary bibliography.

Hurst, Catherine Daniels. "Haki R. Madhubuti." In *Afro-American Poets Since 1955,* edited by Trudier Harris and Thadious M. Davis. Vol. 41 in *Dictionary of Literary Biography.* Detroit: Gale Research, 1985. This article in a reference book is very important as it provides a primary bibliography of the poet's work, a concise biography, and an analysis of his work. An excellent introduction for all students.

McAninch, Jerry B. "Haki R. Madhubuti." In *American Poets Since World War II*, edited by Donald J. Greiner. Vol. 5 in *Dictionary of Literary Biography*. Detroit: Gale Research, 1980. Like Catherine Daniels Hurst's article, McAninch provides essential background information on the life and work of Madhubuti. He especially describes Madhubuti's commitment to civil rights for African Americans, pointing out that the poet changed his name from Don L. Lee to one in Swahili in 1973.

Madhubuti, Haki R. "Hard Words and Clear Songs: The Writing of Black Poetry." In *Tapping Potential: English Language Arts for the Black Learner*, edited by Charlotte K. Brooks, et al. Urbana, Ill.: Black Caucus of the National Council of Teachers of English, 1985. In this article, Madhubuti outlines some of his poetic philosophy. He explains why he writes, as a poet, and as an African American. Helpful to understanding Madhubuti's outlook.

Mosher, Marlene. *New Directions from Don L. Lee*. Hicksville, N.Y.: Exposition Press, 1975. This volume is the only available book-length study on Madhubuti, so it is extremely valuable to any student of his work. Mosher provides criticism and interpretation of Madhubuti's important writing up to the mid-1970's. Includes a bibliography and an index.

CHRISTOPHER MARLOWE

Born: Canterbury, England; February 6, 1564
Died: Deptford, England; May 30, 1593

Principal poetry
Hero and Leander, 1598 (completed by George Chapman); "The Passionate Shepherd to His Love," 1599.

Other literary forms
Christopher Marlowe's literary reputation rests primarily on four plays: *Tamburlaine the Great, Parts I* and *II* (1587, first octavo edition, 1590); *The Famous Tragedy of the Rich Jew of Malta* (1589, first quarto edition, 1633); *The Troublesome Raigne and Lamentable Death of Edward the Second* (1592, first quarto edition, 1594); *The Tragicall History of D. Faustus* (1588, first quarto edition, 1604). Two unfinished plays, *The Tragedy of Dido, Queene of Carthage* (1586-1587, with Thomas Nashe) and the fragmentary *The Massacre at Paris* (1593), round out his dramatic canon. He produced two important translations: *Elegies* (1595-1600), which treats three books of Ovid's *Amores* (before A.D. 8), and Lucan's first book of *Pharsalia* (A.D. 62), first entered in the Stationers' Register as *Lucan's First Book of the Famous Civil War Betwixt Pompey and Caesar* (1593, the earliest extant edition is dated 1600).

Achievements
His plays established Marlowe as the foremost of the University Wits, a loosely-knit group of young men, by reputation generally wild and rakish, that included Thomas Lodge, Thomas Nashe, George Peele, and the older, perhaps less unruly, John Lyly. Their work largely established the nature of the English drama which would reach its apogee in the work of William Shakespeare. Marlowe shares with Thomas Kyd the honor of developing the English conception of tragedy. Marlowe also developed the rather clumsy blank verse of the day into the flexible vehicle of his "mighty line," using it to flesh out his tragic characters as they fell from greatness. He shares the honor of reshaping the dramatically crude chronicle play into the mature and subtle history play. His *The Troublesome Raigne and Lamentable Death of Edward the Second* bears comparison with William Shakespeare's *Richard III* (1592-1593) and anticipates Shakespeare's "Henriad."

Marlowe's nondramatic poetry has attracted an impressive, even a disproportionate, amount of critical attention, considering that it consists simply of one lyric poem, known in several versions, and one narrative poem, generally considered to be an 817-line fragment of a longer projected work. Had Marlowe's dramatic work been only middling, it is unlikely that his poetry, excellent as it is, would have been so widely noticed and esteemed. C. F. Tucker Brooke observes in his *The Works of Christopher Marlowe* (1964) that

Hero and Leander, Marlowe's narrative fragment, was enormously popular with the Elizabethans and that the literature of the period is rich in allusions to the poem. His lyric poem "The Passionate Shepherd to His Love" also enjoyed an early and continuing popularity from its first appearance in *The Passionate Pilgrim* (1599) and *England's Helicon* (1600), two widely circulated collections of English verse. A version of the poem is included in Isaac Walton's *The Compleat Angler, or the Contemplative Man's Recreation* (1653).

While Marlowe attracted much casual comment among his contemporaries, serious criticism of his work was rare until the nineteenth century. After the Puritan diatribe of T. Beard in *The Theatre of Gods* [sic] *Judgements* (1597) and W. Vaughn's consideration in *The Golden Grove* (1600), no serious criticism appeared until J. Broughton's article, "Of the Dramatic Writers Who Preceded Shakespeare" (1830). From 1883 onward with Herford and Wagner's article, "The Sources of Tamburlaine," Marlovian criticism grew at an increasing rate. Two critics initiated the very extensive body of modern scholarship which began in the first decade of the twentieth century: Frederick S. Boas with his edition and commentary of the works (1901), and Brooke with an article, "On the Date of the First Edition of Marlowe's *Edward II,*" in *Modern Language Notes* (1909). Boas' contribution culminated in the monumental *Marlowe: A Biographical and Critical Study* (1940). While both writers concentrated on Marlowe's drama, they also began a serious examination of his poetry. From 1910 onward, the volume of criticism has been almost overwhelming. *The New Cambridge Bibliography of English Literature* (1974) cites literally hundreds of books and articles. The annually published *MLA International Bibliography* shows no slackening in scholarly interest.

While most of the criticism bears on concerns other than the poetry, criticism dealing with *Hero and Leander* and, to a lesser degree, with "The Passionate Shepherd to His Love," is more than respectable in quantity. Interest covers many aspects of the poems: the rhetorical and prosodic forms, with their implications for aesthetics and comedic intent; bibliographic matters dealing with publication history, textual variations, and their implications for questions about authorship; mythological bases and sources; possible autobiographical elements; and moral and ethical values, often centering on sexuality and implied homosexuality. The foregoing list is not exhaustive, and any given study is likely to include several of the aspects while using one of them to illuminate one or more of the others. Marlovian criticism boasts the names of many outstanding modern scholars; a sampling would include J. A. Symonds, T. S. Eliot, U. M. Ellis-Fermor, F. S. Tannenbaum, Mario Praz, J. Q. Adams, M. C. Bradbrook, J. Bakeless, L. Kirschbaum, W. W. Greg, Helen Gardner, F. P. Wilson, C. S. Lewis, and Louis L. Martz.

Biography

Biographical interest in Christopher Marlowe has been keen and perhaps too often controversial. Public records are relatively numerous, considering that he was a sixteenth century Englishman who died before he was thirty years old. His baptism, progress through school and university to the M.A. degree, and the details of his death are documented. Contemporary references to Marlowe and his works are likewise plentiful. The variety of interpretation placed upon this evidence, however, is truly astonishing. What is quite clear is that Marlowe was born into a relatively affluent family of tradesmen in Canterbury. His father was in the shoe trade, possibly as a shoemaker, possibly as an employer of shoemakers. In any case, in January, 1579, Marlowe entered King's School, an institution operating just beyond Canterbury Cathedral. In December, 1580, he enrolled in Corpus Christi College, Cambridge, on a scholarship. In 1584, Marlowe was graduated with the B.A. degree but continued his studies, still on scholarship. Marlowe's attendance was, at least occasionally, irregular, and he was engaged from time to time upon some sort of secret work for the government, the nature of which remains unclear despite much speculation. It involved travel on the Continent; it may have involved spying at home or abroad. When, in 1587, the university determined to withhold the M.A. degree from Marlowe, the Privy Council intervened in the name of the Queen and insisted that Marlowe's services to the crown were sufficient grounds for granting the degree.

Upon leaving Cambridge, Marlowe immediately immersed himself in the political and intellectual life of London, on the one hand, in the aristocratic circles of Sir Walter Raleigh and Sir Thomas Walsingham, and on the other, in the bohemianism of the London actors and playwrights. Both groups apparently contributed to the underworld contacts that tavern life and secret government service would suggest. As early as 1588, Robert Greene attacked Marlowe indirectly as an atheist, a charge which reappeared from time to time. In 1589, Marlowe was involved in a brawl with a certain William Bradley which ended with Bradley's death at the hands of one Thomas Watson. Both Marlowe and Watson were jailed temporarily because of the affair, which was finally adjudged to have been a case of self-defense.

By 1592, both *Tamburlaine the Great, Parts I* and *II*, and *The Tragicall History of D. Faustus* had been produced and published. Meanwhile, Marlowe's reputation as a dangerous fellow had grown. In that year, he had been bound over to keep the peace by a brace of frightened constables, and he appears to have been one of the atheist playwrights attacked in Robert Greene's *Groatsworth of Wit Bought with a Million of Repentance* (1592). On May 12, 1593, Marlowe's fellow University Wit, friend, and former roommate, Thomas Kyd, during or shortly after torture, wrote a letter to the Lord Keeper, Sir John Puckering, accusing Marlowe of ownership of papers, found in Kyd's room, which denied the divinity of Christ.

Whether or not Kyd's confession influenced them, the Privy Council issued a warrant for Marlowe's arrest and ordered him to report to them daily. On

May 30, Marlowe spent the day at the Bull Inn in Deptford in the disreputable company of the double-agent Robert Poley, and two other possible spies, Nicholas Skeres and Ingram Frizer. The coroner's report indicates that they had walked in the garden during the day and then had eaten supper together. Following a quarrel about the bill, Marlowe is said to have taken Frizer's dagger from his belt and beaten him about the head with it. Frizer managed to grasp Marlowe's arm, reverse the blade, and force it into Marlowe's head. The jury found that the stab wound was the cause of death and declared the death to be instant and accidental.

On the whole, the jury was composed of competent men, the sequence of events plausible, and the jury's conclusion sound. Short, then, of the discovery of more telling evidence, all theories of a plot of premeditated murder against Marlowe must be taken as only more or less interesting conjectures. Perhaps it was inevitable that the facts about a famous man whose life was both colorful and secretive would excite equally colorful speculation about the facts which lie beyond the official records and public accusations.

Analysis

Christopher Marlowe's lyric poem "The Passionate Shepherd to His Love" is known in several versions of varying length. C. F. Tucker Brooke's 1962 reprint of his 1910 edition of Marlowe's works cites the six-stanza version of *England's Helicon*, with variant readings provided in the notes. Frederick S. Boas, in *Christopher Marlowe: A Biographical and Critical Study*, puts the case for holding that only the first four stanzas are certainly Marlowe's. Fredson Bowers, in the second volume of his monumental *The Complete Works of Christopher Marlowe* (1973), offers a "reconstructed" four-stanza version of the original poem printed alongside the six-stanza version of *England's Helicon*. All versions provide a delightful and innocuous exercise in the pastoral tradition of happy innocent shepherds sporting in a bucolic setting. Simply put, a lover outlines for his sweetheart the beauties and pleasures she can expect if she will live with him and be his love. Nature and the rejoicing shepherds will provide the pair with entertainment, clothing, shelter, and all things fitting to an amorous paradise.

The stanza is a simple quatrain rhyming in couplets. While it is a fine example of Elizabethan taste for decoration and is very pleasing to the ear, it presents nothing especially clever in its prosody. A few of the couplets are fresh enough in their rhymes, such as "falls/ madrigalls," "kirtle/ Mirtle," and "buds/ studs," but the rest are common enough. The alliteration falls short of being heavy-handed, and it achieves neither clearness nor subtlety. The poem's appeal, then, seems to lie mostly in its evocation of young love playing against an idealized background, its simple language and prosody forming part of its overt innocence.

Sir Walter Raleigh's famous response, "The Nymph's Reply to the Shepherd," also published in *England's Helicon*, sets all of the cynicism associated with the *carpe diem* poetry of a John Donne or an Andrew Marvell against Marlowe's pose of innocence. Raleigh's shepherdess argues that the world and love are too old to allow her to be seduced by "pretty pleasures." She speaks of aging, of the cold of winter, of the sweet appearance which hides bitterness and approaching death. She scorns his offers of beauty, shelter, and love as things which decay and rot. Were youth, love, and joy eternal, and old age well provided for, then she might love. Both poems are set-pieces and imply nothing except that both poets were makers working within established traditions. The innocence of Marlowe's poem argues nothing about his own personality and much about his ability to project himself imaginatively into a character and a situation. In doing this, he produced a gem, and that is enough.

In contrast to the simple, single-leveled "The Passionate Shepherd to His Love," *Hero and Leander* is a more complex, more sophisticated poem. Whatever ultimate plans Marlowe may have had for the completed poem, the two completed sestiads are in the comic mode as they portray the fumbling yearnings and actions of two adolescents faced with passions with which they are totally unprepared to deal. The story of young love, then, is constantly undercut with one sort of comedy or another.

Perhaps the easiest clues to Marlowe's comic intention lie in his choice of epic style and heroic couplets, both of which lend themselves to witty parody because they are traditionally used seriously. The epic tradition allows Marlowe to pay his lovers elaborate, and obviously exaggerated, compliments through the use of epic similes and through comparison with the classical tales of gods and heroes. The heroic couplet allows him to emphasize the fun with variations of the meter and with comic rhymes, generally feminine ones.

The retelling of the famous tale of two ill-fated lovers—whose trysts require Leander to swim across the Hellespont to visit Hero in her tower—begins soberly enough, as a mock-epic should. By the ninth line, however, Marlowe begins a description of Hero's garments which is wildly ornate and exaggerated in style. Her dress, for example, is lined with purple and studded with golden stars; the sleeves are green and are embroidered with a scene of Venus, naked, viewing the slain and bloody Adonis; her veil reaches to the ground and is so realistically decorated with artificial vegetation that men mistake her breath for the odor of flowers and bees search it for honey. The picture, thus far, could pass as an example of Elizabethan taste for the gaudy, and becomes clearly comic only in retrospect.

The twenty-fifth line, however, presents a figure which sets the anticlimactic tone informing the whole piece. Hero's necklace is described as a chain of ordinary pebbles which the beauty of her neck makes shine as diamonds. Later on, her naked beauty causes an artificial dawn in her bedchamber, to Leander's delight. The improbabilities are piled on thickly: her hands are not subject to burning because sun and wind alike delight in them as playthings; sparrows perch in her shell buskins; Cupid could not help mistaking her for his mother, Venus; and Nature itself resented having been plundered of its rightful beauty by this slip of a girl. Marlowe points up the comedy of the Cupid passage with a feminine rhyme: "But this is true, so like was one the other,/ As he imagined Hero was his mother." He signs the comic intent of the Nature passage with an outrageous conceit and compliment: "Therefore in sign of her treasure suffered wrack,/ Since Hero's time, hath half the world been black." Throughout the two sestiads, similar tactics are employed, including much additional use of comic feminine rhyme (Morpheus/ visit us, cunning/ running, furious/ Prometheus, kist him/ mist him, and yv'ry skin/ lively in) and mocking versions of the epic simile.

The compelling argument for Marlowe's comedic intent, however, lies in this treatment of situation, theme, and character. Boas reflects a view commonly held by critics at the turn of the twentieth century when he argues that Marlowe's purpose was to tell the stories of the lovers, working in as much mythology as possible. He does not see the comedy as anything but incidental, and congratulates Marlowe on rescuing the grossness of Ovidian comedy with "delicate humor." Brooke, also an early twentieth century Marlovian, regards *Hero and Leander* as an essentially original work to be judged independently of George Chapman's continuation of the poem. Brooke treats the poem as an extended example of masterful heroic verse with no hint that such verse could be used here as an adjunct of comedy.

The French critic Michel Poirier comes nearer to Marlowe's comedic intent in his biography, *Christopher Marlowe* (1951, 1968), in which he describes the poem as belonging to the genre of Renaissance hedonism. He sees the poem as a "hymn to sensuality, tastefully done." He too sees the poem as erotic, but argues that it avoids equally ancient crudeness and the rough humor of the medieval fabliaux. Philip Henderson's essay "Christopher Marlowe" (1966) points up the by-then-dominant view by observing that *Hero and Leander* is not only a parody but also a very mischievous one, written by a poet who is so disengaged from his poem that he is able to treat it wittily and with a certain cynicism. John Ingram in *Christopher Marlowe and His Associates* (1970) harks back to an earlier view in claiming that no other Elizabethan poem equals it for purity and beauty. He notes nothing of the ironist at work.

A. L. Rowse, an ingenious if not always convincing literary historian and critic, sees *Hero and Leander,* in *Christopher Marlowe: His Life and Work* (1964), as a sort of rival piece to Shakespeare's *Venus and Adonis.* He goes so far as to suggest that Marlowe and Shakespeare read their poems to each other in a sort of combat of wit. However that may be, Rowse is probably right in seeing the poem as being carefully controlled, in contrast to the view, well-represented by Boas, that the poem is structurally a mere jumble.

Rowse sees the poem as organically unified by the careful playing off of this mode and that technique against a variety of others.

In his essay "Marlowe's Humor," included in his most useful book *Marlowe: A Collection of Critical Essays* (1964), Clifford Leech rejects earlier criticism holding that the comic passages were the work of other writers and pits C. S. Lewis' denial, in his *English Literature in the Sixteenth Century* (1954), that *Hero and Leander* contains any humor at all against T. S. Eliot's assertion in *Selected Essays* (1950-1972) that Marlowe was at his best when writing "savage comic humor." Leech's position is that the poem is dominated by a humor at once gentle and delighting, not to say sly. He supports his position with a shrewd analysis of the subtle effects of tone and verse form. Louis L. Martz, in *Hero and Leander: A Fascimile of the First Edition, London, 1598* (1972), also sees Marlowe's tone as comic and as conveyed through the couplet, and he characterizes the poem as being carefully structured as a triptych, with the Mercury fable, usually viewed as a digression, as the central picture, flanked by tales depicting mortal love. He sees Marlowe's digression as intentional and Ovidian. Martz, as a whole, comes down firmly on the side of those who see the poem as a thoroughgoing comedy.

Philip Henderson keeps to the comedic interpretation but also brings boldly to the fore a factor in the story long recognized but generally treated as minor, incidental, and otherwise unaccountable—that of homosexuality as a theme. In *Christopher Marlowe* (second edition, 1974), he argues that the passage describing Leander's body is "rapturous," but that the element is reduced to farce by Leander's encounter with Neptune as he swims the Hellespont. At the same time, Henderson firmly denies that Rowse's description of Marlowe as a known homosexual has any basis in fact. On balance, Henderson concludes that the critics' urge to find irony and sensational undertones obscures recognition of the beauty properly belonging to *Hero and Leander,* and he notes further that the insistence upon seeing comedy throughout Marlowe's work is a modern one. William Keach, tracing Marlowe's intentions in "Marlowe's Hero as 'Venus' Nun" (*English Literary Renaissance,* Winter, 1972), argues that Marlowe is largely indebted for the "subtleties and complexities" of his poem to hints from his fifth century Greek source, Musaeus. Keach sees both poets as ironists and argues that Hero's activities as a priestess of love who is puritanically virginal are essentially silly.

John Mills, in his study "The Courtship Ritual of Hero and Leander" (*English Literary Renaissance,* Winter, 1972), sees Hero at the opening as a compound of innocence and sexuality, with all the confusions that such a compound can make, both in her own mind and in those of men who observe her. Mills's interest lies, however, not so much in this condition itself as in the web of classical elements and allusions in which it is contained. He argues, in effect, that the poem depends upon an overblown, stereotypical, and mannered attitude toward romantic sex which he compares to Vladimir

Nabokov's theory of "poshlust." Mills concludes that Marlowe's "poshlustian comedy" arises out of the actions being played out in a physical and material world of sexuality in such terms that Hero and Leander, and innocent readers, are persuaded that their activities are really spiritual. In another essay, "Sexual Discovery and Renaissance Morality in Marlowe's 'Hero and Leander'" (*Studies in English Literature, 1500-1900*, XII, 1972), published immediately after that of Mills, William P. Walsh argues that Marlowe is ironic in basing the story on love at first sight and making his characters slaves of their irrational passion. His notion is that the lovers themselves, not sexuality, are the objects of humorous comment with which they are not entirely out of sympathy. His development of the theme is detailed and astute, and he points out, in discussing the invented myth of the Destinies' love affair with Mercury, the generally overlooked argument that Marlowe makes for reproduction as the true object of sex, as against pleasure for its own sake. Walsh suggests that the inability of Hero and Leander to see beyond their dream of a sexual paradise at once positions them for the eventual tragic ending traditional to their story, yet keeps them reduced to comic stature in Marlowe's portion of the poem.

In writing *Hero and Leander*, then, Marlowe displayed ingenuity and erudition by telling an ironically comic tale of the mutual wooing and seduction of a pair of inexperienced but lusty young lovers. The telling is intricately and objectively organized and describes a rite of passage which is neither sentimentalized nor especially brutalized. The result is a highly skilled *tour de force* in the tradition of the Elizabethan maker, cynical enough, perhaps, but confessional or autobiographical only tangentially, if at all. Coupled with "The Passionate Shepherd to His Love," *Hero and Leander* establishes Marlowe's claim to a high place in the select company of those British poets who have produced a slender but superior body of lyric poetry.

B. G. Knepper

Other major works

PLAYS: *The Tragedy of Dido, Queene of Carthage*, 1586-1587 (with Thomas Nashe); *Tamburlaine the Great, Parts I and II*, 1587 (commonly known as *Tamburlaine*); *The Tragicall History of D. Faustus*, 1588; *The Famous Tragedy of the Rich Jew of Malta*, 1589; *The Troublesome Raigne and Lamentable Death of Edward the Second*, 1592; *The Massacre at Paris*, 1593.

TRANSLATIONS: *Elegies*, 1595-1600 (of Ovid's *Amores*); *Pharsalia*, 1600 (of Lucan's *Pharsalia*).

MISCELLANEOUS: *The Works of Christopher Marlowe*, 1910, 1962 (C. F. Tucker Brooke, editor); *The Works and Life of Christopher Marlowe*, 1930-1933, 1966 (R. H. Case, editor); *The Complete Works of Christopher Marlowe*, 1973 (Fredson Bowers, editor).

Bibliography

Bakeless, John. *The Tragicall History of Christopher Marlowe*. 2 vols. Cambridge, Mass.: Harvard University Press, 1942. In this massive study, Bakeless incorporates the efforts of such earlier important Marlowe biographers as Leslie Hotson (1925), C. F. Tucker Brooke (1930), and Mark Eccles (1934). The work remains valuable because of its thoroughness, and Bakeless' interpretations have been only slightly superseded by discoveries of later scholars.

Bloom, Harold, ed. *Christopher Marlowe: Modern Critical Views*. New York: Chelsea House, 1986. This volume consists of thirteen selections, mainly excerpts of previously published books that are landmarks in Marlowe criticism. Analyses of six plays and *Hero and Leander* are uniformly authoritative. Of special interest is Lawrence Danson's essay on Marlovian skepticism, which provides an excellent perspective on the playwright-poet's career as a whole. The bibliography at the end of the volume includes most of the major critical studies of Marlowe.

Leech, Clifford. *Christopher Marlowe: Poet for the Stage*. Edited by Anne Lancashire. New York: AMS Press, 1986. Consisting partly of revisions of previously published articles, this posthumous book is especially important for its lucid analyses of *The Tragicall History of D. Faustus* and *The Troublesome Raigne and Lamentable Death of Edward the Second*. Leech sees Marlowe's tragic heroes as ultimately solitary victims. His treatment of *Hero and Leander* is an admiring response to the poet's comic skills.

Levin, Harry. *The Overreacher: A Study of Christopher Marlowe*. Cambridge, Mass.: Harvard University Press, 1952. A critical as well as a biographical study, this landmark book is excellent on both the nondramatic works and the plays. Levin develops the thesis that central to Marlowe's work is the confrontation between the ideals of human beings and their realization that they have inherent limitations, which Levin sees as the essence of Marlovian tragedy.

Pincuss, Gerald. *Christopher Marlowe*. New York: Frederick Ungar, 1975. This brief illustrated book is a good introduction to Marlowe and the theater for which he wrote. Begins with a chronology of the playwright's life and concludes with a representative bibliography adequate for all but the most advanced scholar.

Steane, J. B. *Marlowe: A Critical Study*. Cambridge, England: Cambridge University Press, 1964. After reviewing the facts and theories of Marlowe's life, Steane devotes individual chapters to the plays and poems (the latter including not only *Hero and Leander* but also Marlowe's translations of Lucan and Ovid). The sections on the plays are noteworthy primarily because of the analyses of Marlowe's poetic style and Steane's thesis that the changing style reveals how Marlowe became increasingly pessimistic and unstable during his brief life and career.

ANDREW MARVELL

Born: Winestead-in-Holderness, England; March 31, 1621
Died: London, England; August 18, 1678

Principal poetry
The First Anniversary of the Government Under His Highness the Lord Protector, 1655; *Miscellaneous Poems*, 1681; *Complete Poetry*, 1968.

Other literary forms
In 1672, with the publication of *The Rehearsal Transpros'd*, Andrew Marvell became a pamphleteer. In this animadversion on the works of Samuel Parker, Marvell vigorously supported King Charles II's stand in favor of religious toleration. No other work by Marvell was so widely received in his lifetime as this urbane, witty, slashing satire. According to Marvell's contemporary Gilbert Burnet, "From the King down to the tradesman, his books were read with great pleasure." Parker's counterattack quickly engendered Marvell's second pamphlet, *The Rehearsal Transpros'd: The Second Part* (1673). *Mr. Smirke: Or, The Divine in Mode* (1676), was Marvell's defense of Herbert Croft, the Bishop of Hereford, against Dr. Francis Turner's pamphlet attack. His next pamphlet, *An Account of the Growth of Popery and Arbitrary Government in England* (1677), resulted in the government's offering a reward for the identity of the author. *Remarks upon a Late Disingenuous Discourse* was published posthumously in 1678. Some three hundred letters are also extant and available in Margoliouth's edition, as well as in those of Captain Edward Thompson and Alexander B. Grosart.

Achievements
In his own century and for some time afterward, Marvell's reputation rested much more on his prose pamphlets, a few political poems, and his political activities, than on his achievement as a lyric poet. Most of his poems, including all of the lyrics, remained unprinted until the posthumous edition of 1681. By then the Metaphysical mode was no longer in fashion, and the book of Marvell's poems seems to have been desired more for its excellent engraved portrait of the politician and pamphleteer than for anything else. Appreciation of Marvell's poetry was increased by Charles Lamb's essay of 1818, but it remained sporadic until after the publication of T. S. Eliot's essay on the occasion of the tercentenary of Marvell's birth in 1921. Except for a quantity of imitations of his verse satires, some of which were attributed to him, his influence on other poets was slight. By far his widest poetic audience is in the present day. He has had a modest influence on some twentieth century writers, such as Marianne Moore.

Today Marvell is recognized as a lyric poet of the first rank, although how uniformly excellent his poems are, individually or collectively, remains a subject of debate. Certainly the quality is somewhat irregular. Nevertheless, with a rather small corpus he has been awarded at least three apt distinctions. That three-quarters of his work is in eight-syllable form and much of it is brilliant has earned him the title "master of the octosyllabic." A few fine poems on a difficult subject have caused him to be called "Cromwell's poet." Finally, while his work includes civic, pastoral, and georgic material, he is, more than any other poet in English, the "garden poet."

Biography

Andrew Marvell was born on March 31, 1621, at Winestead-in-Holderness, Yorkshire. He was the fourth child and only surviving son of Andrew Marvell, Senior, a clergyman. In late 1624, the Reverend Marvell became lecturer at Holy Trinity Church in Hull, to which the family moved. The poet grew up there and was for the rest of his life associated with Hull, representing the city in Parliament for the last eighteen years of his life. On December 14, 1633, the young Marvell entered Trinity College, Cambridge. In 1637 Marvell was converted by Jesuits and ran away to London, whence his father retrieved him and returned him to Cambridge. Sometime in 1641 Marvell left Cambridge, having received the B.A. degree but without completing the requirements for the M.A.

Marvell may then have spent some time working in the commercial house of his brother-in-law, Edmund Popple, in Hull. His activities during the turbulent 1640's are not well recorded, but it is known that during that period he spent four years abroad, learning Dutch, French, Italian, and Spanish. He studied the gentlemanly art of fencing in Spain, and in Rome he paid a visit to the impoverished English Catholic priest, Flecknoe, whom he made the butt of a satiric poem. Engaged in this Grand Tour, Marvell seems to have avoided any direct part in the English Civil War. Marvell returned to England in the late 1640's, publishing a congratulatory poem (probably written in 1647) for a volume of Richard Lovelace's verse in 1649, and contributing one poem to a volume lamenting the death of the young Lord Hastings in June, 1649. From 1650 to 1652 Marvell was tutor to Mary Fairfax, daughter of the parliamentary general, Lord Fairfax, whose resignation in June, 1650, left Cromwell dominant. That same month, Marvell must have composed "An Horatian Ode upon Cromwell's Return from Ireland," in which he applauds Cromwell's activities up to that point and anticipates his success in the coming campaign against the Scots. Because the poem also shows great sympathy and regard for the late King Charles in the brief passage dealing with his execution, a good deal of critical attention has been paid to the question of whether Marvell's praise of Cromwell is genuine, ironic, or intended to create an image toward which it might be hoped that the real Cromwell would gravitate. Marvell is elsewhere so prone to see more than one side of a question that it does not really seem remarkable that he may have recognized good qualities in both King Charles and Cromwell. "Upon Appleton House" and "Upon the Hill and Grove at Bill-borow," which describe two Fairfax estates, must be presumed to date from Marvell's days with the Fairfaxes; it is likely that a number of the lyrics, including "The Garden" and the Mower poems, also date from that period. In 1653 Marvell left the Fairfax employ and sought, through John Milton, a position with the Commonwealth government. When his association with Milton began is uncertain, but it is known that they became and remained very close friends. In September, 1657, Marvell received a government post, becoming Latin Secretary, sharing (with Milton) responsibility for correspondence with foreign governments. He retained this post until the dissolution of the Commonwealth government. During the Cromwell years, Marvell wrote a number of poems in praise of Cromwell. These include "An Horatian Ode upon Cromwell's Return from Ireland," *The First Anniversary of the Government Under His Highness the Lord Protector*, 1655, and "A Poem upon the Death of His Late Highness the Lord Protector." Although Cromwell and his son, and perhaps close associates, presumably saw these poems, they seem not to have been widely circulated. Only *The First Anniversary of the Government Under His Highness the Lord Protector* was printed, and that anonymously.

In 1659 the Corporation of Hull chose Marvell to represent them in Parliament. He remained a member for the rest of his life, being twice reelected. He seems to have made the transition to the Restoration of Charles II with relative ease, and from his position in Parliament joined other friends of Milton in protecting that poet from serious harm under the new regime. During this period Marvell's satiric talents blossomed. His satiric verse included three "advice to a painter" poems parodying a poem by Edmund Waller and lampooning various influential persons and their policies. More important by far were his prose pamphlets, especially the first, *The Rehearsal Transpros'd*. This was an attack on the pamphlets of Samuel Parker, a rising Church of England divine, who strongly supported conformity and had tangled in print with the nonconformists, especially John Owen. The question of toleration versus conformity was a very important one in the politics of 1672, with Charles II, for his own reasons, trying to put through a policy of toleration. Marvell's powerful and witty book quickly went through multiple editions. Parker strongly counterattacked with a new pamphlet, causing Marvell (despite an anonymous threat to cut his throat) to reply with *The Rehearsal Transpros'd: The Second Part*. Parker did not reply further. Marvell's last three pamphlets are of considerably less importance. *Mr. Smirke: Or, The Divine in Mode* used with less success and for a less crucial cause the techniques of the two parts of *The Rehearsal Transpros'd*. Next, *An Account of the Growth of Popery and Arbitrary Government in England* evoked the government offer of a reward for the name of the author, who died before action was taken on an informer's report. The title of this work precisely indicates the concerns that Marvell voiced in it, suggesting that leading government figures were involved in a plot to make England Catholic again. By 1674, Marvell himself was involved in clandestine activities as a member of a pro-Dutch "fifth column," apparently operating under the name of "Mr. Thomas" and making secret trips to Holland. Marvell's death, on August 18, 1678, was the result of his physician's treatment of a fever and not, as was suspected by some, a political murder. His last pamphlet, *Remarks upon a Late Disingenuous Discourse* is his least readable work and is of little importance.

Analysis

Andrew Marvell is firmly established today in the ranks of the Metaphysical poets, and there is no question that much of his work clearly displays the qualities appropriate to such a position. He reveals a kinship with the Metaphysical poets through his ingenious use of extended logic, even when dealing with emotions; his yoking of very dissimilar things, of the mundane (even profane) with the sublime, of large with small and far with near; and his analytic quality. His use of puns, often woven into intricate groups, may be added to the list. Like John Donne and the other Metaphysical poets, Marvell shapes his rhythm with careful attention to his meaning. Marvell's admiration for Donne shows not only in having written some strongly Donne-like poetry ("On a Drop of Dew," "Young Love," and parts of "Upon Appleton House," for example), but in his gratuitously full use of one of Donne's poems in a pamphlet written late in Marvell's life. It might be added that Marvell's prose works, especially his most successful, show the same Metaphysical qualities.

Where Donne's best-known poetry (as well as Marvell's most Donne-like work) resembles puzzles from which attentive reading gradually extracts greater clarity, a similar approach to Marvell's best and most "Marvellian" passages (for example, "a green thought in a green Shade") causes them not to become more clear so much as more dazzling. Marvell has been called "many-sided," "ambiguous," "amphibian," "elusive," and "inconclusive." He is. He has been said to have a vision that is "complex," "double," or "ironic." He does.

Marvell's work often shows a remarkable ability to make opposites interdependent, to create a *concordia discors*. Such is the relationship of Cromwell and King Charles in "An Horatian Ode upon Cromwell's Return from Ireland," and of retirement and action in "Upon Appleton House" and "The Garden." Sometimes, no less remarkably, he achieves moments of what can only be called "fusion," as in the "annihilation of all that's made" in "The Garden," or in the last few lines of "To His Coy Mistress." He will at times surprisingly mix levity and gravity, as in "To His Coy Mistress" and parts of "Upon Appleton House." His use of qualifiers is unusual ("none, *I think*," or "*If* these the times").

Marvell employed decasyllabics for his last two Cromwell poems, inventing a stanza combining lines of eight and six syllables for the first. Three fourths of his work was in octosyllabics, however, and he has been rightly called the "master of the octosyllabic."

Certainly the most widely anthologized and best known of Marvell's poems is "To His Coy Mistress." It is not only a seduction poem, but also a *deduction* poem, in which the theme of *carpe diem* is presented as a syllogism: (1) If there were world enough and time, the lady's coyness would not be a crime; (2) There is not world enough and time; (3) therefore, this coyness may or may not be a crime. Marvell must have been aware that his poem depended upon flawed logic; he may have meant it to be ironically typical of the desperate reasoning employed by would-be seducers.

In the first section of the poem, the speaker describes the vast amounts of time ("An age at least to every part") and space (from the Ganges to the Humber) he would devote to his love if he could. This apparently gracious statement of patience is then juxtaposed with the striking image of "Time's wingéd chariot hurrying near" and the resultant "Deserts of vast eternity." "Deserts," meaning "unpeopled places," is emphasized by the shift of the stress to the first syllable of the line. There follows the arresting depiction of the drawbacks of postmortem chastity, with worms "trying" the lady's "long-preserved virginity," as her "quaint honor" turns to dust. Imagery of corruption was not unusual in *carpe diem* poems, and it also occurs (the *momento mori* theme) in visual arts of the period; Marvell's lines are, however, remarkably explicit and must have been devised to shock and disgust. The passage represents, as Rosalie Colie notes in *"My Ecchoing Song"* (1970), "sound psychology" in frightening the lady into the comfort of her lover's arms, an event that the next two lines suggest may indeed have occurred at this point, as the speaker rescues himself from the danger of excessive morbidity with the urbanely ironic comment, "The grave's a fine and private place,/ But none, I think, do there embrace." This makes the transition to the last section of the poem, wherein the speaker, having shown that however limitless time and space may intrinsically be, they are to mortals very limited, offers his solution. The answer is to take energetic action. The formerly coy mistress, now described (either in hope or in fact) as having a "willing soul" with "instant fires," is invited to join the speaker in "one ball" of strength and sweetness, which will tear "thorough the iron gates of life." This third section of the poem is an addition not typical of *carpe diem* poems, which usually suggest rather than delineate the consummation. The amorous couple, the speaker indicates, should enthusiastically embrace the inevitable and each other. Like the elder Fairfaxes in "Upon Appleton House," they should "make Destiny their choice" and devour Time rather than waiting for Time to consume them. In its three sections, "To His Coy Mistress" presents first a cheerful and generous offering of limitless time and space, then a chilling reminder that human life is very limited, and finally a frenzied but extraordinarily powerful invitation to break through and transcend all limits.

If "To His Coy Mistress" makes the case for action versus hesitation, "The Garden," the best-known hortensial work of the "garden poet," considers the question of action versus contemplation. Like much of Marvell's work, it employs a rich texture of wordplay and classical and Christian allusions. It is a retirement poem, in which the speaker begins by celebrating his withdrawal from the busy world of human endeavor. This theme is one rich in tradition, and would have been attractive during the uncertain and dangerous times in which Marvell lived. In this poem, however, the speaker retires not merely from the world of men, but, in a moment of ultimate retirement, from the world of material things. As the poet contemplates the garden, his mind and his soul momentarily transcend the material plane.

In the first stanza, the speaker comments on the folly of seeking human glory. Men "vainly" ("from vanity," and also "in vain") "amaze" themselves (surprise themselves/trap themselves in a maze) in their efforts to achieve honors (represented by the palm, oak, and bay leaves used in classical victors' wreaths). Even the best such victory represents success in only one area of endeavor, for which the victor receives the decoration of a wreath woven from a single species, a wreath which in its singleness "upbraids" (braids up/ rebukes) his "toyles" (coils of hair/efforts). In contrast, repose is rewarded by "all flowers and all trees." Addressing Quiet and Innocence personified, the speaker uses a typically Marvellian qualifier when he says that their sacred plants "if here below,/ Only among the plants will grow," suggesting that quiet and innocence may be really unobtainable on Earth. The solitude experienced by the lone visitor among the plants of the garden is nevertheless worth seeking, for, in comparison, "Society is all but rude"—society is nearly "coarse," or (an inversion and a pun) society is almost "rustic." The next three stanzas describe the physical, sensual values that the garden offers in contrast to those of the world. As the "society" of the garden is superior to that of men, so the sensuality of the garden is more intense than that of men: "No white or red was ever seen/ So amorous as this lovely green" (the colors of fleshly passion are less "amorous" than the green of the garden), and the beauties of the trees exceed those of any woman. The gods Apollo and Pan knew this, the speaker says, since they pursued the nymphs Daphne and Syrinx, not for their womanly charms, but in order to obtain their more desirable dendritic forms.

In the fifth stanza the speaker reaches a height of sensual ecstasy as the various garden fruits literally thrust themselves upon him, in what Rosalie Colie rightly calls a "climactic experience." It is powerfully sexual, yet the speaker is alone and in the garden, as Adam once was in Eden. And then the speaker, "stumbling" and "Insnared," falls, reminding the reader of the Fall in Eden. Marvell's speaker, however, is still alone and still—indeed, more than ever—in the garden. The next two stanzas describe what is occurring "Meanwhile" on the mental and spiritual planes. The mind withdraws from the lesser pleasures of the body to seek its own kind of happiness. Within the mind, an interior paradise, are the images of all things in the physical world, just as the sea was thought to contain creatures corresponding to all terrestrial species. Yet the mind, unlike the sea, can create, imaginatively, "Far other worlds and other seas," transcending the mundane, and "Annihilating all that's made/ To a green thought in a green shade," an image that R. I. V. Hodge in *Foreshortened Time* (1978) calls "arguably the most intriguing image in Marvell's poetry or in the whole of the seventeenth century." Many explications have been offered for this couplet; the central notion seems to be that through the action of the mind in creating the far other worlds and seas, the physical world ("all that's made") is compacted, or by contrast appears to be compacted, into a single thought. It is, however, a "green" thought—a living, fertile thought which is the source, through the action of the mind, of the transcendent worlds and seas. Indeed, perhaps the thinker himself has almost been annihilated; "in a green shade" could indicate not only that the thinker is shaded by the trees, but also that he *is* (for the moment) a shade, an insubstantial shadow of his physical self. The green thought is, perhaps, the Platonic pure *idea* of garden from which all gardens derive. It could be suggested that this is the true garden of the poem.

In stanza seven, the soul leaves the body in a flight indicative of its later, final flight to heaven. In the next stanza the garden is compared explicitly to Eden—not merely Eden before the Fall, but Eden before Eve. Three times, in successive couplets, the speaker states that Paradise enjoyed alone is preferable to Paradise shared. Such praise of solitude can hardly be exceeded, even in the considerable Christian literature on the subject, and perhaps Marvell, relying on his readers' knowledge that Adam had after all requested Eve's company, expected his readers to identify this stanza as a momentary effusion, not shared by the poet himself, on the part of the poem's persona. The reader is reminded, at least, that mortals in the fallen world can only approximate paradisical ecstasy, not achieve it, until they leave this world for a better one. The speaker, now quite recalled from his ecstasy, observes "this dial new." The term may indicate a literal floral sundial, in which small plots of different plants marked the hours around a circle; it clearly and more importantly indicates the entire renewed postlapsarian world, under the mercy of God the "skillful gardener," who provides the "milder sun" (the Son, Christ, God's mercy). The bee, who is industrious rather than contemplative, "computes its time [thyme] as well as we!" This is a typically Marvellian paradox. The bee's industry is reminiscent of the negatively viewed "incessant labors" of the men in the first stanza; the bee, however, is performing wholesome activity in the garden, reckoned with flowers. The situation is analogous to that of the speaker in stanza five who fell, but did not Fall, remaining in the garden.

The poem's persona at first rejected the world of action for the garden's solitude and the contemplative exercise thereby made possible. Contemplation has led to physical, then to mental, then to spiritual ecstasy, but the ecstatic moment is limited because the speaker, dwelling in a world that remains thoroughly fallen, is not yet "prepared for longer flight." Refreshed by his experience and noting that the "dial" is *new*, the speaker can accept the action of the bee and recognize action, as well as contemplation, as an appropriate part of human existence.

Another poem dealing with the question of withdrawal versus action is "Upon Appleton House," which clearly raises the issue of involvement in the English Civil War and subsequent disturbances. The poem falls into two halves, each depicting both action and retirement, and builds toward a resolution in the form of Lord Fairfax's daughter Mary, who was under Marvell's tutelage. A genre of the time was the "country house" poem, in which a country estate was described, and its inhabitants and their way of life thereby praised. "Upon Appleton House" begins in this manner, with the first nine stanzas devoted to the house itself. Employing a variety of conceits, Marvell finds the modest size and decoration of the structure preferable to the overblown grandeur of other houses. It is on a human scale, with "short but admirable Lines" that "In ev'ry Figure equal Man." Nevertheless, it is less modest than its owner, Lord Fairfax. When he arrives, the house sweats, and from its square hall sprouts a "Spherical" cupola, outdoing the proverbially impossible task of squaring the circle.

A source of building material for the house was the ancient nunnery whose ruins were still evident, wherein had dwelt the nuns whose order had in former times owned the estate. By recounting a historical episode connected with the nunnery, Marvell shows how it is also a source of the estate's present occupants. An ancestral Fairfax had wooed the "blooming Virgin" Isabel Thwaites, "Fair beyond measure" and an heiress. She was induced to enter the nunnery at Appleton, from which she could ultimately be extracted only by a Fairfacian raid. This tale, told in stanzas eleven to thirty-five, falls into two distinct parts. The first (stanzas eleven to twenty-eight) is essentially a nun's eloquent invitation to Isabel to withdraw to the secluded life of the cloister. The joys of this "holy leisure," behind walls that "restrain the World without," are attractively and enthusiastically described, though Marvell would not wish to portray otherwise so Catholic an institution. The passage wherein Isabel is compared to the Virgin Mary, and the later picture of the nuns "in bed,/ As pearls together billeted,/ All night embracing arm in arm," may be meant to raise doubts in the reader's mind that would be confirmed when he is told that "The nuns smooth tongue has suckt her in." After debating what to do, the betrothed Fairfax decides to remove her from the nunnery by force. In a rather burlesque episode, the nuns, whose "loud'st cannon were their lungs," are dispossessed of their prize and, in the next stanza, which flashes forward to the Dissolution, of their nunnery.

Action in this case has been far superior to withdrawal. It leads ultimately, however, to another withdrawal, that of Sir Thomas Fairfax, son of the celebrated couple. After a heroic military career he retired to Appleton House, but the flower beds there, which he shaped like the bastions of a fort, show that he was incapable of retiring fully. Stanzas thirty-six to forty describe the flower-fort, wherein flower-cannons discharge salutes of scent and the bee stands sentinel. There follows (stanzas forty-one to forty-five) a lamentation by the poet over the present unhappy state of England, "The garden of the world ere while," and praise of Fairfax, "Who, had it pleasèd him and God," could have prevented it. In this first half of the poem, then, Marvell has first described the house as an illustration of the greatness of its owner, then shown the virtue of action over withdrawal, then indicated that a man of great action can never fully retire. Finally, he has shown regretful acceptance of Fairfax's retirement, with the clear statement that England suffers without ameliorative action on someone's part. In the second half of the poem the same ideas will be reiterated and enhanced, except in the last part the focus will be not on Fairfax but on his daughter Mary ("Maria"), whose embodiment of the values of retirement and action will effect a resolution.

From the flower fort, the speaker can look down over the meadow (stanzas forty-six to sixty) onto the public world of action. It is a world capable of topsy-turvy, this "Abyss" of a meadow, from which it is a wonder that men rise alive. Men (seen from the hill) look like grasshoppers, but grasshoppers (perched on the tall grass) "are Gyants there." Cows look like beauty spots or fleas, and when the land is flooded, "Boats can over bridges sail" and "Fishes do the stables scale." It is a dangerous world, where the Mowers "massacre the grass," which is very tall, and the rail (humbly close to the ground) is accidentally killed: "Lowness is unsafe as hight,/ And chance o'retakes what scapeth spight." The earlier lamentation over England's condition in stanzas forty-one to forty-three invites the reader, if invitation were needed, to read this section as an allegory of England, although it may be carrying the allegory too far to see the hapless rail as Charles I, as has been suggested. The mowers who cause the carnage, leaving the field like a battlefield "quilted ore" with piles of hay that look like bodies, are not evil. As they dance in triumph, their smell is fragrant and their kisses are as sweet as the hay. Marvell compares the meadow at the outset with stage scenery, constantly changing. Describing a series of scenes as the hay is harvested and piled and the cattle set loose in the field to crop the last few inches of grass, he ends with a flood. The flood is caused by the opening of sluices up-river, but the reader is meant to think of the biblical Flood.

Taking refuge from the drowned world, the speaker "imbarks" (embarks/ encloses in bark) himself in the "green, yet growing ark" of an adjacent wood. The trees are as tightly woven together as are the families of Fairfax and Vere

(Fairfax's wife's family). From without, the wood seems absolutely solid, but inside it is "passable" and "loose." The nightingale, a bird of solitude, sings here, and "highest oakes stoop down to hear,/ And listning elders prick the ear." The nightingale may represent Mary Fairfax, twelve years old when Marvell became her tutor, in which case the "Elders" would be her parents. At any rate, while the song of solitude is attractive, the "Sadder" sound of the stockdoves, whose necks bear "Nuptial Rings," is more pleasing. This indication, even within the wood, that private withdrawal may not be desirable, prepares for the later part of the poem, when Mary herself appears. In a lengthy section very reminiscent of "The Garden," the speaker revels in the delights and the security of the wood, a place "where the world no certain shot/ Can make, or me it toucheth not." He wishes never to leave the wood, and requests, in a passage that reminds many readers of Christ's crucifixion, that the vines and brambles fetter him and the "courteous Briars nail [him] through."

Noticing that the flood has subsided, he finds the meadow equally attractive. It is "newly washt," with "no serpent new." The "wanton harmless folds" of the river attract the speaker, who abandons himself to the pleasures of angling, achieving in stanza eighty-one such harmony with the landscape that it is difficult to distinguish between him and it. The sedge surrounds his temples, his side is a riverbank, and his "sliding foot" may remind the reader of the "Fountains sliding foot" in "The Garden." The sudden arrival of Maria, however, extracts him from this reverie by means of an odd inversion wherein she, the pupil, reminds the presumably adult speaker of his responsibility. Calling himself a "trifling Youth," he hastily hides his fishing gear.

Essentially the rest of the poem is devoted to praise of Maria, a creature neither of withdrawal nor of action, but a fusion of both. Among the imagery giving her awesome power are echoes of the Last Judgment: she has "judicious" eyes, she "already is the Law," and by her the world is "wholly vitrifi'd." Nature collects itself in silence, and the sun blushingly conceals himself. As the halcyon, flying "betwixt the day and night," paralyzes nature and turns it blue, so Maria gives her surroundings the stillness of glass and imbues them with her (their) qualities: "'Tis She that to these Gardens gave/ That wondrous beauty which they have," and so also with the woods, meadow, and river. Intelligent (learning languages in order to gain wisdom, which is "Heavens Dialect"), without vanity, and raised in the "Domestick Heaven" of Appleton House, she is not the new branch that a male heir would be on the "Farfacian oak." Instead, she is a sprig of mistletoe that will one day be severed "for some universal good." Presumably this will be her marriage, which will be of considerable political importance. The product of the seclusion of Appleton House, she is thus the ideal person to take action to affect the world at large; in her the apparent opposites of withdrawal and action are harmoniously fused. The final stanza of the poem features a pattern of conceits reminiscent of the first stanza, and compares the fishermen carrying their boats to tortoises, echoing the tortoise in stanza two. The fishermen are "rational amphibii," amphibians who can think; but they are also thinkers who can operate in two mediums: human beings need both contemplation and action.

This concord of opposites, which is more powerful than compromise and is presented with reason and wit, represents those characteristics central to Marvell's work.

C. Herbert Gilliland

Other major works

NONFICTION: *The Rehearsal Transpros'd*, 1672; *The Rehearsal Transpros'd: The Second Part*, 1673 (for modern editions of the two preceding entries, see *The Rehearsal Transpros'd and The Rehearsal Transpros'd: The Second Part*, 1971; D. I. B. Smith, editor); *Mr. Smirke: Or, The Divine in Mode*, 1676; *An Account of the Growth of Popery and Arbitrary Government in England*, 1677; *Remarks upon a Late Disingenuous Discourse*, 1678.

MISCELLANEOUS: *The Poems and Letters of Andrew Marvell*, 1927, 1952, 1971 (H. Margoliouth, editor).

Bibliography

Chernaik, Warren L. *The Poet's Time: Politics and Religion in the Work of Andrew Marvell*. Cambridge, England: Cambridge University Press, 1983. For Chernaik, Marvell is a poet-prophet whose political ideas are consistent, militant, and rooted in his religion. His readings of "Upon Appleton House" and "An Horatian Ode upon Cromwell's Return from Ireland" are extensive and perceptive. He also discusses Marvell's later (post-1666) satiric poetry and his political polemics.

Hunt, John Dixon. *Andrew Marvell: His Life and Writings*. Ithaca, N.Y.: Cornell University Press, 1978. Hunt's intent is to provide a context against which some of Marvell's major poems ("Upon Appleton House," "An Horatian Ode Upon Cromwell's Return from Ireland," and "Last Instructions to a Painter") can be read. Since Hunt's focus is artistic, the book is profusely illustrated. Includes a one-page chronology of Marvell's life and sixty-six engravings and emblems.

Klause, John. *The Unfortunate Fall: Theodicy and the Moral Imagination of Andrew Marvell*. Hamden, Conn.: Archon Books, 1983. Klause finds "lingering preoccupations" rather than consistent viewpoints in Marvell's writing. In his extensive analyses of the Cromwell poems, "The Garden," and "Upon Appleton House," Klause finds Marvell "adapting" to political realities. Complemented by an extensive bibliography of primary and secondary sources.

Patterson, Annabel M. *Marvell and the Civic Crown*. Princeton, N.J.: Princeton University Press, 1978. Patterson focuses her attention on "Marvell the Writer," who corrected and modified other ideas rather than formulate his own. Trying to "fill the gaps" in Marvell's criticism, she omits analyses of many popular poems and instead focuses on the relatively neglected polemical writings and the "painter" and "statue" poems, though she does discuss in detail the Cromwell and Fairfax poems.

Rees, Christine. *The Judgment of Marvell.* London: Pinter, 1989. Rees argues that Marvell's poetry concerns choice or the impossibility of choosing, and his choices involve the life of pleasure, as well as those of action and contemplation. Using this three-fold division, she offers extensive commentary on approximately twenty-five well-known poems.

Stocker, Margarita. *Apocalyptic Marvell: The Second Coming in Seventeenth Century Poetry.* Athens: Ohio University Press, 1986. Stocker's book offers a corrective view of Marvell, a poet committed to an apocalyptic ideology that informs all of his poems. Contains lengthy analyses of Marvell's major poems such as "An Horation Ode Upon Cromwell's Return from Ireland," "Upon Appleton House," and "To His Coy Mistress," as well as the often overlooked "The Unfortunate Lover." Supplemented by an extensive bibliography.

Wallace, John M. *Destiny His Choice: The Loyalism of Andrew Marvell.* Cambridge, England: Cambridge University Press, 1968. Because he believes Marvell played a more significant role in the politics of his period than he did in its literature, Wallace reads Marvell's political poems in their historical context. After a discussion of the Civil War debates, Wallace devotes chapter-long explications to the two Cromwell poems, "Upon Appleton House," and "Last Instructions to a Painter."

JOHN MASEFIELD

Born: Ledbury, Herefordshire, England; June 1, 1878
Died: Boar's Hill, England; May 12, 1967

Principal poetry

Salt-Water Ballads, 1902; *Ballads*, 1903; *The Everlasting Mercy*, 1911; *The Widow in the Bye Street*, 1912; *The Story of a Round-House and Other Poems*, 1912; *Dauber: A Poem*, 1913; *The Daffodil Fields*, 1913; *Philip the King and Other Poems*, 1914; *Good Friday and Other Poems*, 1916; *Sonnets and Poems*, 1916; *Lollington Downs and Other Poems*, 1917; *The Cold Cotswolds*, 1917; *Rosas*, 1918; *A Poem and Two Plays*, 1919; *Reynard the Fox: Or, The Ghost Heath Run*, 1919; *Enslaved and Other Poems*, 1920; *Right Royal*, 1920; *King Cole*, 1921; *The Dream*, 1922; *Sonnets of Good Cheer to the Lena Ashwell Players*, 1926; *Midsummer Night and Other Tales in Verse*, 1928; *South and East*, 1929; *The Wanderer of Liverpool*, 1930 (poems and essay); *Minnie Maylow's Story and Other Tales and Scenes*, 1931; *A Tale of Troy*, 1932; *A Letter from Pontus and Other Verse*, 1936; *Ode to Harvard*, 1937; *Some Verses to Some Germans*, 1939; *Guatama the Enlightened and Other Verse*, 1941; *Natalie Masie and Pavilastukay: Two Tales in Verse*, 1942; *Wonderings (Between One and Six Years)*, 1943; *I Want! I Want!*, 1944; *On the Hill*, 1949; *Poems*, 1953; *The Bluebells and Other Verse*, 1961; *Old Raiger and Other Verse*, 1961; *In Glad Thanksgiving*, 1967.

Other literary forms

John Masefield wrote books of poems and verse plays, prose plays, novels, and other prose works, including histories.

Achievements

Masefield's poetry appealed to a very wide audience. His first book of verse, *Salt-Water Ballads*, sold out in six months, and his narrative poems were very popular. *The Everlasting Mercy* was a sensation in his day. Some of his lyric poems, including "Sea Fever," have become standards of English poetry. He received many honorary degrees, including those from Oxford and Cambridge. In 1930, he was elected to membership in the American Academy of Arts and Letters, and he was president of the Society of Authors in 1937. In 1961, he was made a Companion of Literature by the Royal Society of Literature, and also in that year he won the William Foyle Poetry Prize. In 1964, the National Book League gave him a prize for writers older than sixty-five.

Biography

John Masefield was born June 1, 1878, in Ledbury, Herefordshire. His very early years were happy ones, although the children in the family spent their time with their nurse and saw little of their parents; they saw their mother only between teatime and bedtime at six o'clock. She died a few weeks after giving birth to a sixth child when John was six-and-a-half years old. Their grandparents died a year after their mother, and the family, in reduced circumstances, moved into the grandparents' home. John occasionally visited his godmother, wrote his first poems when he was about ten, and went to boarding school. His father died at age forty-nine after suffering from mental disorders. Taking over as guardians, his aunt and uncle suggested that John be trained to go to sea in the merchant marine. Although he wanted to write or paint, he decided to pursue seafaring because the son of a governess whom he had liked enjoyed being a cadet on the school ship H.M.S. *Conway*.

Masefield joined that ship when he was thirteen and left it when he was sixteen, having learned a good deal of mathematics and navigation. He became an apprentice on a four-masted cargo barque sailing for Chile, which did not touch land for three months. During the voyage, he had some trouble with seasickness and experienced the fury of Cape Horn storms. He was released from service after he became seriously ill with sunstroke and a possible nervous breakdown. After a hospital stay in Valparaiso, he went home. His aunt nagged him into going to sea again; but he deserted ship in New York, causing his uncle to cut him off financially.

The seventeen-year-old Masefield could not find work in that depression year; thus, he and an acquaintance became vagrants, getting occasional work on farms and sleeping out, an experience that gave him great empathy for the down-and-out. After some months, he returned to New York City, living in Greenwich Village, almost starving but writing poetry. He finally obtained work with long hours at a bar and then moved to Yonkers to work in a carpet factory, reading the English poets in his spare time. At nineteen, he was suffering from tuberculosis and malaria. He returned to England (earning his way back on a ship) hoping to be a writer there. Poor and sick, he obtained a clerk's position in a London bank, which he held for three years. He regained his health, became reconciled with his aunt and uncle, and was especially close to his sisters. He managed to meet William Butler Yeats and to become part of the Yeats circle. In 1901, he became exhibition secretary for an art show in Wolverhampton. His poems were being published regularly in magazines, and his first book of verse, *Salt-Water Ballads*, was very popular.

When he met Constance de la Cherois Crommelin, she was thirty-five and he was twenty-three, but despite the difference in their ages, they were married in 1903, after Masefield had obtained an editorial position. They took a house in Greenwich; then John left Constance and his baby daughter Judith for a nighttime editorial position in Manchester. He wrote articles and reviews and worked seven days a week for the publisher; yet, he still managed to write plays, one of which, written in 1907, was produced. (Curiously, also, one of his stories was pirated for the stage.)

About the time that his son Lewis was born, Masefield became infatuated briefly with Elizabeth Robins, an American actress and author who became a veritable goddess to him. He called her "mother" and wrote to her, sometimes many times a day. After she withdrew from his life, he had a burst of creativity that produced *The Everlasting Mercy*, a long narrative poem that caused a great stir.

After settling into a country house in Lollington, he became a Red Cross worker in a French hospital during World War I. In 1915, he visited Gallipoli for the Red Cross, and, in 1916, he traveled to the United States on a lecture tour, but also with the intention of enlisting Americans' sympathy with Britain in the war: he had been in touch with British intelligence. He also organized theatricals and verse reciting contests in his area.

When Masefield's wife Constance was recovering from an operation for a brain tumor, the family moved to the Cotswolds; later they lived in a village near Dorchester, called Clifton Hampden, in the upper valley of the Thames. Masefield died in 1967, after refusing to have his leg amputated when he developed gangrene from an infected toenail. He was cremated, as he had wished, and his ashes were deposited in the Poets' Corner in Westminster Abbey.

Analysis

John Masefield's difficulties in life, his early poverty, ill health, and arduous labors, caused him to develop a reflective attitude toward the world. While he is often thought of as a writer of rollicking sea and narrative poems, his poetry is usually concerned in some way with the tragedy of human life; it is seldom simply humorous. He seemed to value most highly his more formal philosophical poems, although his lighter pieces have been the most popular. Many of these poems seem simple because he chose to speak in the vernacular about common experiences. His own experiences, however, gave him great empathy with the down trodden, and he deliberately chose to treat such matters, as he points out in "Consecration." He will not speak of the great, he says, but of the lowly and scorned; and he ends the poem with a heartfelt "Amen."

Masefield's poems about the life of the common sailor are firmly rooted in the ballad tradition. He makes use of a dramatic speaker as he skillfully interweaves narrative and lyrical material. A number of such poems deal with death at sea; some treat the subject lightly, in a manner of a sea chantey, but the harsh realities underlie the touches of humor. In "The Turn of the Tide" and "Cape-Horn Gospel I," the soul or ghost wants to continue working on the ship after death. Masefield's most famous work, "Sea Fever," is about these two realities, the harshness and the appeal of life at sea. The title suggests a disease; the sea can be a kind of addiction. Masefield's refrain repeatedly emphasized that the speaker "must go down to the seas again," while alliteration effectively evokes the rhythms of wheel and wind and sail. The speaker responds to a call; he has no choice in the matter. The life is like that of the vagrant gypsy, or, not so explicitly, like the gull's and the whale's. The life of the sea fascinates, but it is also lonely, gray, and painful. The middle stanza of the three, however, contains none of these negative images, suggesting that the very heart of the matter is the delight in the movement of the ship. In the last stanza, the wind no longer pleasantly makes the white clouds fly; it is as sharp as a "whetted knife." From this life the speaker, in the last two lines, desires two things: "quiet sleep and a sweet dream when the long trick's over." The sea journey is suddenly the journey of life, with a final sleep at the end. According to the glossary that Masefield supplied for the *Salt-Water Ballads*, a trick is "the ordinary two-hour spell at the wheel or on the lookout," but the "long trick" suddenly suggests the trip itself and life itself, for Masefield has transformed the realistic situation into a symbolic one with a single word.

"Cargoes" is a different type of sea poem, without a speaker or story line. Three ships are described briefly, each in one short stanza. Masefield here is an imagist presenting only the pictures, with no explicit connections between them and no commentary on them. The inclusion of the last freighter, the British coaster, seems ironic, since it is less attractive than the ships of the past; it is actually dirty and sails in less attractive seas. Including it may also seem ironic because of its cargo: such humble items as coal and tin trays. It can scarcely be compared with the quinquereme from Nineveh with its glamorous apes and ivory, or with the Spanish galleon with its jewels and gold; yet it is the modern representative of a tradition that goes back to the ancients. A third irony is that it actually exists, whereas the others are gone, though, of course, it too will become a thing of the past. Here, Masefield makes skillful use of meter and stanza form, the unusual number of spondees imparting a feeling of strength, reinforced by the periodic use of two short lines rather than a single long one. Masefield made light of objections that a ship from Nineveh was not plausible because Nineveh was two hundred miles inland. As Constance Babington Smith notes in *John Masefield: A Life* (1978), he responded to a question of an Eton boy: "I can only suggest that a Ninevean syndicate must have chartered the ship; even so it was odd." The first line of the poem is musical in its repetition of sounds, including the *n*, short *i*, and *v*. It is not improbable that the poet chose Nineveh for its alliterative and evocative qualities.

As the modern freighter in "Cargoes" is less distinguished than its antecedents, the modern city in "London Town" is less pleasant than the country and the small town. Masefield is speaking in his own voice here, for in the last line he speaks of the land in which he was bred, and the countryside described is his homeland. The poet alternates stanzas in praise of London with stanzas in praise of the country, but all those in praise of London end with a defect or a deficiency, with a varied refrain in favor of leaving the place. In two of these stanzas, the deficiency is given in only a half line of contrast, as in the statement that the world is busy there, while the mind grows "crafty." The alternate stanzas praise the countryside without reservation and are prefaced with a joyous song like "Then hey" or "So hey." The poem is joyous in the delight of the poet in returning to the world of nature, but the criticism of the city is sobering. In the last stanza about London, it hardly matters that the tunes, books, and plays are excellent if "wretchedly fare the most there and merrily fare the few." The city is a tragic place, for beneath its artifice there is misery and poverty. The irony is somewhat like that of Masefield's long narrative poem *Reynard the Fox: Or, The Ghost Heath Run*, in which the hunters seek an exciting diversion, while the fox is only trying desperately to survive.

Masefield's homeland, described in the country scenes in "London Town" and other poems, includes the Malvern Hills mentioned at the beginning of the fourteenth century poem *The Vision of William, Concerning Piers the Plowman*, and the influence of that work is apparent in Masefield's long narrative poem *The Everlasting Mercy*. Masefield had resolved to write about the lowly, and some of the lowly are anything but perfect. Saul Kane bit through his father's hand and went to jail nineteen times, but he tells the reader in a monologue that is part soliloquy and part public attestation that he regrets breaking his mother's heart. He says, "Now, friends, observe and look upon me" to see evidence of the Lord's pity; it is an address to the reader that is reminiscent of the medieval religious lyrics in which Christ tells the reader to look at how his side bleeds or in which the Blessed Virgin invites the reader to weep with her. The effect is that the figure, whether it be Christ or Saul Kane, becomes a static moral picture. It is short-lived here, however, as Saul plunges into his story of a poaching-rights argument, boxing, and celebration.

The otherworldly passages in the poem are instrumental in Saul's religious conversion to a different way of life, the first of them being Saul's remembrance on his way to the celebration of how the bell ringer had seen spirits dancing around the church at Christmas. The whole eerie scene becomes vivid to him, and he prays when he thinks of Judgment Day. After the party, he leans out the window and is tempted by the devil to throw himself down, even as Christ was tempted. He decides not to kill himself and feels exalted; he wants to excoriate the righteous, who would secretly like to be whores and sots and who "make hell for all the odd/ All the lonely ones of God." After this realization, he runs through the town and rings the fire bell. After he speaks out to the squire's parson for his actions toward the poor, he is upbraided by the mother of a lost child whom he had befriended; when she summons the mystical imagery of the Book of Revelation, he shrinks away.

After he insults a Quaker woman who visits the bar and she leaves, exhorting him, he suddenly feels, in a mystical passage about tide, sun, moon, and bells ringing for someone coming home, that he has been converted. Feeling that he was born to "brother" everyone, he sees everything symbolically, from mole to plowman, and says that Christ will plow at the "bitter roots" of his heart.

First Christ and then Saul become plowmen, a transformation reminiscent of *Piers Plowman*. At the end of the work, where the meter changes from iambic tetrameter to a more lyrical trimeter, he seems to have awakened to the beauty of nature. The poem is enhanced by its many ironies, such as that Saul should experience the world of the spirit while he is drunk, and that Saul, of all people, could become a patient plowman and a Christlike figure. Some of the names in the story are symbolic: certainly Saul and Miss Bourne, the Quaker, and possibly Saul's last name, Kane (Cain). Although Saul is not exactly Everyman, his life in its aimlessness, belligerence, and unhappiness embodies a tragic pattern of human existence that is not uncommon. Masefield was not religious in the traditional sense, but he seems to have believed in reincarnation and to have been fascinated by religion, a number of his works being on religious themes. This poem was a sensation in its time; it was considered shocking for its direct language and crudity. J. M. Barrie, however, described it in the *Daily Chronicle* of November 29, 1912, as "incomparably the best literature of the year."

Because his story-poems, sea-poems, and songs are so vivid, Masefield's more subdued philosophical poems have been generally neglected. "CLM," a tragic work about women and motherhood, was written during his wife's second pregnancy, when he was romantically involved with Elizabeth Robins, whom he called "mother." The letters of the poem's title stand for the name of Masefield's actual mother. Speaking of his prenatal life, the poet sees the fetus as common earth and as a leech. Pregnancy is "months of birth," and birth itself is hell. His present life involves the death of "some of her," some cells he received from her; thus, the subject of death is first raised in connection with his own life. Not until the second stanza does the reader become aware that the speaker's mother is dead. Both the womb and the grave are dark. There is a cluster of images associated with his desire to see her again, together with the uncertain nature of such an encounter: gates of the grave, knocking, "dusty" doors, her "dusty" beauty, and passersby in the street. He feels that he has not repaid his debt of life to her and to other women, and he uses the images of men triumphing over women, trampling on their rights and lusting after them, to convey men's selfishness and their subjugation of women. At the end of the poem, in an ironic and tragic reversal of his desire to see his mother again, he tells the grave to stay shut so that he will not be shamed. The shut grave image stands in strong contrast to the image of its opening earlier in the poem.

Much of Masefield's more philosophical poetry was concerned with beauty.

Some of his ideas on this theme were embodied in the narrative poem *Dauber*, in which a young artist becomes a sailor because he wants to paint ships and sea life as they have never been painted before. His insensitive shipmates, however, destroy his paintings. When he dies in a fall from the yardarm during a storm, his last words are, "It will go on." Ironically, he is mourned not as an artist but as a fine sailor-to-be.

The worship of beauty and the linking of beauty and tragedy in human life were recurrent themes in Masefield's sonnets. Beauty exists in nature and within the individual, despite the reality of death, and beauty exists in a life to come. Beauty and death are related, for, as he says in one sonnet, the life that was is "Pasture to living beauty." The beautiful may die, but Beauty will go on. The personified Beauty of many of his sonnets seems to be an amalgam of the goddess Nature, the world soul of Platonic philosophy, God, the Beatrice of Dante, and the women in the poet's life. "On Growing Old" asks Beauty to be with him as he sits amidst the imagery of age and death: an old dog, his own coldness by the fire, the yellow leaves of a book, the embers. The word "her" indicates that Beauty possesses the seas and cornland where he is no longer able to go. Comparing himself to a beggar in the Strand, he asks Beauty for gifts—ironically, not youth, but wisdom and passion, which he compares to bread and to rain in a dry summer. They are necessities in the closing darkness of old age and death, for with them "Even the night will blossom as the rose."

Masefield, then, was a more philosophical poet than is generally realized. Beauty was a kind of goddess in his work, and a kind of quest as well; he was fascinated by the interrelationship of beauty with tragedy and death. It was also no accident that he chose to retell in his verse the tragic tales of Troy, of Arthur, and of Tristan and Isolt, for he dealt in many of his poems with the tragedies and ironies of human life.

Rosemary Ascherl

Other major works

LONG FICTION: *Captain Margaret*, 1908; *Multitude and Solitude*, 1909; *Last Endeavour*, 1910; *The Taking of Helen*, 1923; *Sard Harker*, 1924; *Odtaa*, 1926; *The Hawbucks*, 1929; *The Bird of Dawning*, 1933; *Basilissa*, 1940.

SHORT FICTION: *A Mainsail Haul*, 1905; *A Tarpaulin Muster*, 1907.

PLAYS: *The Tragedy of Nan and Other Plays*, 1909; *The Tragedy of Pompey the Great*, 1910; *The Faithful*, 1915; *The Coming of Christ*, 1928; *End and Beginning*, 1933; *The Play of Saint George*, 1948.

NONFICTION: *Sea Life in Nelson's Time*, 1905; *On the Spanish Main*, 1906; *Shakespeare*, 1911; *Gallipoli*, 1916; *Chaucer*, 1931; *The Nine Days' Wonder*, 1941; *So Long to Learn*, 1952; *Grace Before Ploughing*, 1966.

MISCELLANEOUS: *A Book of Both Sorts: Selections from the Verse and Prose*, 1947.

Bibliography

Drew, Fraser. *John Masefield's England*. Cranbury, N.J.: Associated University Presses, 1973. This volume is a thematic study of Masefield's portrayal of English life and customs. Drew maintains that this is the key to Masefield's work. His celebration of England was the continuation, not the reversal, of his early stress on the common man. His interest in English life included seamanship and fox-hunting. Useful comparisons with Rudyard Kipling, Joseph Conrad, and others are included.

Dwyer, June. *John Masefield*. New York: Frederick Ungar, 1987. A very simply written, short but comprehensive introductory study. Discussions of the novels and plays, as well as the poems are included. Dwyer maintains that Masefield in part abandoned his rough, common style for a more refined voice as he gained popularity. She attempts a psychological analysis of the verses, endeavoring to show Masefield's loneliness beneath his public persona of national triumph.

Hamilton, W. H. *John Masefield: A Critical Study*. New York: Macmillan, 1922. An influential study, this work celebrates Masefield for his narrative poems, especially *Reynard the Fox*. Hamilton contends that the novels are much less successful. In almost all of his work, Masefield stresses the value of England. He was deeply patriotic, although he abhorred war. The author criticizes Masefield's overemphasis on productivity: this often led him to write inferior work. An amusing chapter collects parodies of Masefield's work.

Knight, G. Wilson. "Masefield and Spiritualism." In *Mansions of the Spirit: Essays in Literature and Religion*, edited by G. A. Panichas. New York: Hawthorne Books, 1967. Knight, one of the greatest twentieth century Shakespearean critics, applies his thematic style of criticism to Masefield. The sea should not be taken only literally in the poems and plays but also as a symbol of the spiritual. Knight maintains that Masefield's poems often express the conviction that man can become acquainted with spiritual powers of various sorts. Knight stresses the recurring use of words and phrases which illustrate this stance. He rates Masefield as one of the great poets of the twentieth century.

Lamont, Corliss. *Remembering John Masefield*. Cranbury, N.J.: Associated University Presses, 1971. Lamont, an American philosopher, was a friend of Masefield for more than forty years. He includes valuable selections from Masefield's letters, expressing Masefield's distaste for modern poetry. The true and noble, in Masefield's view, is the proper object of poetry. World Wars I and II have diverted poets from the proper path. Lamont maintains that Masefield's poems express a coherent philosophy, a suggestion Masefield rejects. The work includes a tribute to Masefield by Robert Graves and a memoir by the poet's daughter.

Sternlicht, Sanford. *John Masefield*. Boston: Twayne, 1977. This excellent survey stresses the long narrative poems. The author contends that *The Ever-lasting Mercy* is Masefield's greatest achievement. Through his rough, vital style, Masefield paved the way for other twentieth century poets to write in a realistic way about the seamier side of life. Masefield himself strongly defended traditional morality. Sternlicht attributes the decline in Masefield's critical reputation to his "old-fashioned" views and his aversion to experiment in verse.

EDGAR LEE MASTERS

Born: Garnett, Kansas; August 23, 1868
Died: Melrose Park, Pennsylvania; March 5, 1950

Principal poetry

A Book of Verses, 1898; The Blood of the Prophets, 1905; Songs and Sonnets, 1910; Songs and Sonnets, Second Series, 1912; Spoon River Anthology, 1915; Songs and Satires, 1916; The Great Valley, 1916; Toward the Gulf, 1918; Starved Rock, 1919; Domesday Book, 1920; The Open Sea, 1921; The New Spoon River, 1924; Selected Poems, 1925; The Fate of the Jury: An Epilogue to Domesday Book, 1929; Lichee Nuts, 1930; The Serpent in the Wilderness, 1933; Invisible Landscapes, 1935; The Golden Fleece of California, 1936; Poems of People, 1936; The New World, 1937; More People, 1939; Illinois Poem, 1941; Along the Illinois, 1942; The Harmony of Deeper Music: Posthumous Poems, 1976.

Other literary forms

Edgar Lee Masters' prolific output included seven early unproduced plays (all published before Spoon River Anthology), four verse dramas, two later volumes of plays, and many volumes of prose.

Achievements

Masters' long and varied career was distinguished by prolific productivity and a versatile display of poetic talent; he tried almost every poetic form, from classical imitation to verse drama to epic, and he handled them all with seeming ease and technical finesse. The sheer bulk of his writing—well over fifty books in his long lifetime—necessarily resulted in repetitiveness, unevenness, and frequent superficiality; and at his worst his poetry is mere magazine verse. Yet, his undeniable talent had early support from such noted critics and writers as Amy Lowell, John Cowper Powys, Ezra Pound, William Marion Reedy, Harriet Monroe, Harry Hansen, Louis Untermeyer, and Percy H. Boynton; and, at his best, his work surmounts changing fashions in poetic taste and even his own occasional lapses in style, technique, and taste.

Masters was long considered a one-book author. That book, Spoon River Anthology, was immensely popular in his lifetime—it went through some seven editions before he died—and even today it is the sole title by Masters known to many students of American literature, in part because of the popularity of stage and television adaptation of parts of the book. Given the immense praise, almost amounting to adulation, accorded the book upon its publication, it was small wonder that his reputation thereafter began its long, slow decline; none of his subsequent books had either the popular or the critical appeal that it did.

Much of Masters' importance as a poet, no doubt, derives from his ability to appeal to both the ordinary reader and the scholar, the same trait found in such contemporaries of Masters as Robert Frost, Edwin Arlington Robinson, and Robinson Jeffers and in later poets such as James Wright. This diverse readership has led to Masters' being accorded a certain place in studies of American poetry and the "Chicago Renaissance," but rarely have these studies amounted to anything like genuine analysis. Even though he failed to maintain his popular acclaim after *Spoon River Anthology*, selections from that book continue to be included in virtually every anthology of American literature and to be taught to succeeding generations of students.

Biography

Although he was born in Kansas, Edgar Lee Masters is the quintessential Illinois poet, having moved there as an infant and remained there, first in small Sangamon valley towns and later in Chicago, until he was fifty-five years old. Masters' mother was interested in literature, music, and the church, and his father was a successful attorney and politician, twin emphases that also served to dominate Masters throughout his life. Largely self-taught, he spent one year at Knox College, where he studied German, Greek, and law. In 1892, the year after he was admitted to the Illinois bar, he moved to Chicago, working first as a bill-collector for the electric company, while attempting to get established in law, and writing verse pseudonymously for several Chicago newspapers. He spent the following twenty-five years as a successful attorney in Chicago, eight of those years in partnership with Clarence Darrow. The first of his many books appeared pseudonymously in 1898; by 1915, when *Spoon River Anthology* was published, he had published several other collections of poetry and unproduced plays and had come to the attention of the British critic John Cowper Powys, who cited Masters as one of three significant new American poets.

For several years, Masters had been contributing verse to the St. Louis *Mirror*, a weekly edited and published by William Marion Reedy. In 1913, Reedy had introduced Masters to J. W. MacKail's translations published as *Select Epigrams from the Greek Anthology* (1928), and Masters' subsequent first-person free-verse epitaphs of ordinary small-town characters became the work known as *Spoon River Anthology*. The success of the book led Masters to relinquish his law practice in 1923 and move to New York City, where he spent most of the rest of his life. His life in New York was marked on the one hand by ready access to the publishing world and, on the other, by numerous affairs; married twice, Masters also had many love affairs, at least fifteen of which are indexed in his autobiography. From 1931 to 1944, he lived in the Hotel Chelsea in New York, a traditional residence for writers, and then in various convalescent homes until shortly before his death in such a home in a Philadelphia suburb.

Analysis

Edgar Lee Masters had written hundreds of undistinguished, even mediocre, poems before *Spoon River Anthology*; most of these were typical of the time, derivative and rigidly imitative of European models and metrical forms; not surprisingly, these early poems, even when published in book form (as his first four collections were), were generally ignored. Masters' discovery of *Select Epigrams from the Greek Anthology* and its great influence on his own subsequent work in *Spoon River Anthology* even led him to an ironic touch of self-criticism, as when his character Petit the Poet, speaking from the grave as do the other inhabitants of Spoon River's cemetery, expresses the remorse at his placing so much emphasis on "little iambics" while remaining oblivious to all the important events in the world around him. Masters' accomplishment in this collection was so profound in its originality and its willingness to venture into new patterns that he could scarcely help offering such a reflective comment on his earlier work.

What Masters accomplished in the book for which he is best known was little short of a revolution, although in retrospect a revolution of which he was merely one of the principals. Masters had befriended the young Carl Sandburg and helped him get his *Chicago Poems* published in 1916, and Masters, influenced by William Marion Reedy, gradually realized and expressed in various early critical statements that American poetry had to try to offer a distinctively American perspective, not merely to lie buried under layers of technically precise but moribund verse. Both Sandburg and Masters, along with their fellow Midwesterner Vachel Lindsay, were part of this concerted move to free native verse from the constraints of more formal poetry, even though the preponderance of educated and critical opinion opposed and belittled their efforts.

Hence, Masters' accomplishment in *Spoon River Anthology*, based as it was on "realism"—simplicity of language and form, taking ordinary persons for subjects, a commonsensical attitude toward experience, and much of Walt Whitman's celebration of America—resulted in an original work that was immensely popular. Masters' happy ability to combine realistic, plain subject matter with a mystical celebration of both the natural world and the small Midwestern town was unique and, ironically, at the same time a poetic dead end. Masters once observed that World War I meant the end of the world he depicted in *Spoon River Anthology*, partly because the innocence and simplicity he described was no longer possible, and partly because even more revolutionary poetic influences, such as that of T. S. Eliot, were at work. While popular audiences continued to purchase *Spoon River Anthology* and Masters' later books, it was obvious that the world out of which that book came had virtually ceased to exist.

Spoon River Anthology is a collection of 244 dramatic monologues—mostly in free verse—by a host of people of all social and occupational levels speaking from their graves in the Spoon River cemetery. Masters faithfully describes their sense of frustration with the dreary, limited, and consistently unfulfilled lives they had lived. Though the book seemed, to some of its initial readers, unnecessarily defeatist and even obscene, especially as the "genteel tradition" attempted to fight what was already a lost cause for literary propriety, Masters was able to develop what he had attempted, an awakening of "the American vision [and] love of liberty." The sheer honesty of his portrayals thus necessarily shocked some sensitive souls. The speakers, unhindered by the propriety forced upon them in life, speak freely of their frustrations with small-town life, sentiments similar in quality to those subsequently expressed by Sherwood Anderson in *Winesburg, Ohio* (1919) and by Sinclair Lewis in *Main Street* (1920). Critics evaluating *Spoon River Anthology*, ironically, spent far more time disputing whether the first-person portraits were "poetry" than in considering the extent to which the criticisms were valid. Masters' indebtedness to Walt Whitman (and to Ralph Waldo Emerson) was recognized, especially in his rejection of rigid verse forms, but there seemed to be little understanding of Masters' intent or ironic perspective.

The 244 first-person portraits—and the 321 portraits in the less successful sequel, *The New Spoon River*—represent virtually all the professions and classes of people in a "typical" small American town, especially a Middle-Western small town. A mere catalog would indicate that these speakers were teachers, druggists, bankers, housewives, soldiers, laborers, dentists, carpenters, prostitutes, lawyers, and so on. While some of these assorted personages aspired to ambitions and careers clearly out of reach for their time, talent, and place, almost all of them felt frustrated; very few seem to possess the innate "greatness" that would enable them to sense a larger vision in their lives that would someday take them far from and above their humble origins. For the most part, their limited abilities, petty perspectives, and stilted ambitions suggest that neither in life nor in death could they have completely escaped the village.

Yet Masters did not depict these people as consistently evil, idle, imbecilic, corrupt, or depraved; rather, his objectivity and honesty did not allow him to take sides in presenting their stories; he impersonally depicts both good and evil, even in the same person. Without some passing of judgment, the collection was certain to offend the established genteel view of the day that required moral certitude to be praised and evil to be punished. In no sense are Masters' "bad" characters dealt with more harshly than his "good" ones. Indeed, the sheer objectivity with which he views his characters enables them to offer their own comments on their lives, thus reflecting evil or virtue in their own words, not through authorial intrusion. Hence, as satire, the volume is excellent, although it is far from an incessantly pessimistic assemblage of worthless defectives. Even Amy Lowell, one of Masters' first sympathetic readers, found the book depressing—a "long chronical of rapes, seductions, liaisons, and perversions"—thus suggesting that the sophisticated reader too could miss Masters' intention to "awaken the American vision" and "love of liberty."

In reality, Masters' plan in *Spoon River Anthology* is deliberately and carefully structured; as Masters said, he put "the fools, the drunkards, and the failures . . . first, the people of one-birth minds [in] second place, and the heroes and enlightened spirits . . . last, a sort of *Divine Comedy*. . . ." Though many of the speakers do tell the truth about themselves without self-consciousness, some are completely hypocritical, and others are unaware of the implications of what they say about themselves. "A. D. Blood," for example, is a town official noted for both his pomposity and his hypocrisy; Masters offers his own unspoken commentary on Blood's puritanic life by telling of a "worthless" young couple's lovemaking each night on Blood's tombstone. "Editor Whedon," who in life "pervert[ed] truth" for "cunning ends," lies in death "where the sewage flows from the village,/ And the empty cans and garbage are dumped,/ And abortions are hidden." Some of the unfortunates were victims of well-meaning but unrealistic patriotism, as in the cases of "Harry Wilmans" and "Knolwt Hoheimer"; the latter asks of the words on his tombstone, "Pro Patria," "What do they mean, anyway?" "Margaret Fuller Slack" is, as her first two names suggest, a frontier feminist who had to decide "Should it be celibacy, matrimony or unchastity?" and who, after rearing eight children, found too little time to write and to become as "great as George Eliot": she died from lockjaw after washing her baby's clothes and says, at the end of her speech, "Sex is the curse of life!"

The favorable portraits, although fewer in number, are generally effective and touching. "Anne Rutledge," Lincoln's first love, who died before they could marry, tells poignantly of how Lincoln was changed and marked by the loss. "Lucinda Matlock," one of the most effective of the poems, tells how she was able to find fulfillment in the small town and in marriage; she asks,

> What is this I hear of sorrow and weariness,
> Anger, discontent and drooping hopes?
> Degenerate sons and daughters,
> Life is too strong for you—
> It takes life to love life.

The kind of life that destroyed weaker souls was one in which she exulted and gloried.

Tennessee Chaflin Shope, who had been "the laughing-stock of the village," especially ridiculed by the "people of good sense" such as a clergyman, reacted to the ridicule by asserting the "sovereignty of [his] soul"; before Mary Baker Eddy had even begun "what she called science," he had "mastered the 'Bhagavad Gita,'/ And cured [his] soul." Jonathan Swift Somers, Spoon River's poet laureate, says in his monologue that after a person has done all that he can to control his life and destiny, his soul might catch fire, enabling him to see the evil of the world clearly; at such a time, that person should be thankful that "Life does not fiddle," that is, meddle with or cheat him. What makes Somers' epitaph especially noteworthy is the fact that Masters appended a portion of Somer's unfinished epic, "The Spooniad," in which the poet ostensibly offers a dramatic portrayal of the conflict between the liberals and the old guard in Spoon River; in "The Spooniad," Masters perfectly imitates the rhythms and diction of a classical epic, but with the point of showing how the town's early history culminated in A. D. Blood's murder. Even though much of *Spoon River Anthology* can be said to reflect Masters' cynicism, his favorable portraits, even more than the unfavorable ones, illustrate the extent to which a few select speakers can see above the mundane pettiness in small-town life and sense the extent to which their lives have great intrinsic value.

The excesses of naïve idealism, of course, can easily be seen in those monologues spoken by unsophisticated villagers; yet this is also the case with those who have some awareness of the larger world. Archibald Higbie, in the monologue bearing his name, admits that he "loathed" and "was ashamed" of Spoon River and that he had escaped its influence as he traveled through Europe, pursuing his gifts as an artist. Since Spoon River had "no culture," its residual influence could only bring Higbie shame. Yet his work, ostensibly of Apollo, still contained the visage of Lincoln, and all he could do, "weighted down with western soil," was to pray for "another/ Birth," one "with all of Spoon River/ Rooted out of [his] soul." A similar inordinate emphasis on the "ideal" that existed far from the village, especially in the form of European art from a "simpler" day, can be found in "Caroline Branson": the speaker, after lamenting the loss of another's love, says, not unlike Emily Dickinson, that "only heaven" knows the secret of the "nuptial chamber under the soil"; she too asks for "another trial" and concludes by beseeching, "Save me, Shelley!"

These miniature autobiographies or "autoepitaphs," then, offer candid reflections by ordinary folk who tell frankly what kinds of persons they were and how they lived. Though the majority have lived "lives of quiet desperation," bitter, thwarted existences in a drab little village, Masters does suggest by his careful linking of narrative to narrative and general movement from despair to hope that such an existence does not necessarily lead to self-pity and posthumous despondency, but can—in the words of "Fiddler Jones"—lead to "a thousand memories,/ And not a single regret."

None of Masters' later volumes had either the popular or the critical acclaim of *Spoon River Anthology*, and few today hold readers' interests. Among the more memorable later volumes are *Domesday Book* and its sequal, *The*

Fate of the Jury. Domesday Book has often been compared to Robert Browning's *The Ring and the Book* (1868-1869) in that both long poems present a variety of witnesses to a murder as a means of leading the reader to a recognition of the multiplicity of truth; it has also been compared with Theodore Dreiser's *An American Tragedy* (1925). The story, a simple one, is of Barrett Bays, a rabbit hunter, who finds the corpse of a woman on the Illinois River shore near Starved Rock; he sees that the victim is Elenor Murray, his onetime lover. The subsequent coroner's inquest clears Bays of any guilt in the matter, but the coroner, William Merival, is not satisfied. The reader gradually learns that the victim, a "free spirit" who had worked as a nurse in France during the war and whose relationships have led to the breakup of at least one marriage, was a far more complicated person than anyone in the town realized. Merival assembles a coroner's jury and subpoenas various witnesses. Most of *Domesday Book* comprises statements by these witnesses, including the victim's parents, a teacher, a priest, a piano teacher, a physician, and even the sheriff and the governor. Since each one has only a partial glimpse of the young woman, the resultant composite amounts to a skillful picture of a small town as well as of the deceased. Granted, Masters did extend the verse narrative to too great a length, and granted, too, he was repetitious—inevitable when such partial sources of information are cited. The free verse of *Spoon River Anthology* was replaced by blank verse that seemed to many readers and reviewers a monotonous, infelicitous choice. *Domesday Book* remains better in its parts than in the whole, and Masters' attempt to go beyond anything he had attempted previously can today be praised more for the effort and the vision than for the sheer poetic pleasure and drama he was able to create.

The *Fate of the Jury*, by contrast, is less than half as long as *Domesday Book*, and it picks up where the earlier book ended. In the later book, Masters allows the jurors and the coroner himself to speak about the case: one juror is a suicide; another (an editor) speaks while on his deathbed; a clergyman disappears after talking with the coroner; and the coroner himself, whose story is the frame for the book, eventually marries a young widow as relief from the pathos and pressure of the prolonged case; unfortunately, there is mental illness in the widow's family, and shortly after the two are married she goes insane and dies. Thus, the "fate" of the jury—as well as of the coroner and the original victim—is a pathetic, possibly even tragic, decline into even further despair.

Domesday Book and *The Fate of the Jury* suffer from prolixity, stylistic roughness, and pretentious, empty rhetoric. Still, Masters' admitted gift for characterization and for a dramatic, realistic rendering of small-town life in all its squalor and inconsistency is well served by the two books, even though they suffer when compared to better examples of the genre such as Stephen Vincent Benét's *John Brown's Body* (1928) and Edwin Arlington Robinson's

Cavender's House (1929). Masters wrote some half-dozen later dramatic poems, but none of them achieved even the limited fame and success of *Domesday Book* and its sequal. The use of a narrative framework composed of courtroom testimony was natural enough for Masters, who so effectively combined the law with poetry, but the richness of the characterization, as in *Spoon River Anthology*, remains his greatest accomplishment, as well as constituting the single most important parallel with Browning, whose name is so often invoked in relation to Masters. This skillful use of characterization, again in common with courtroom practice, was especially effective when contrasting testimony offered tangential perspective on the truth, with no single speaker or witness having more than a small part of the whole truth. Each speaker in *Domesday Book* and its sequel clearly felt that he or she had the "truth" about the events under investigation; but the primary truth that is revealed is less about the victim than about the speaker.

Though Masters the poet sometimes falters, Masters the psychologist remains a superlative student of character motivation; nevertheless, his achievement is just now beginning to be appreciated. As craftsmanlike and formally successful as many of his lyrics may be, it is likely that his ultimate reputation will rest primarily on his free-verse dramatic monologues and two longer blank-verse dramatic narratives. While he tried virtually every poetic form and technique and wrote on a vast array of topics, all of which resulted in repetitiveness, unevenness, and superficiality, his best work transcends mere changes in literary taste and fashion; it is probable that his ultimate rank will be considerably higher than that which he enjoyed during the first half of the twentieth century.

Paul Schlueter

Other major works

LONG FICTION: *Mitch Miller*, 1920; *Children of the Market Place*, 1922; *The Nuptial Flight*, 1923; *Skeeters Kirby*, 1923; *Mirage*, 1924; *Kit O'Brien*, 1927; *The Tide of Time*, 1937.

PLAYS: *Althea*, 1907; *The Trifler*, 1908; *The Leaves of the Tree*, 1909; *Eileen*, 1910; *The Locket*, 1910; *The Bread of Idleness*, 1911; *Lee: A Dramatic Poem*, 1926; *Jack Kelso*, 1928; *Gettysburg, Manila, Acoma*, 1930; *Godbey*, 1931; *Dramatic Duologues*, 1934; *Richmond*, 1934.

NONFICTION: *Levy Mayer and the New Industrial Era*, 1927; *Lincoln, the Man*, 1931; *The Tale of Chicago*, 1933; *Vachel Lindsay: A Poet in America*, 1935; *Across Spoon River*, 1936; *Walt Whitman*, 1937; *Mark Twain, A Portrait*, 1938; *The Sangamon*, 1942.

Bibliography

Flanagan, John. *Edgar Lee Masters: The Spoon River Poet and His Critics.*

Metuchen, N.J., Scarecrow Press, 1974. Flanagan describes the reception of Masters' work by American and European critics and stresses the importance of relatively neglected works by Masters, including his *Domesday Book* and his biography of Abraham Lincoln.

Hallwas, John E., and Dennis J. Reader, eds. *The Vision of This Land: Studies of Vachel Lindsay, Edgar Lee Masters, and Carl Sandburg.* Macomb: Western Illinois University Press, 1976. This volume of essays explores the works of three major poets from Illinois. Edgar Lee Masters practiced law for forty years. Charles Burgess' essay examines legal arguments in his poetry, and Herb Russell discusses his literary career in the years immediately after the publication of his *Spoon River Anthology* in 1915.

Masters, Hardin Wallace. *Edgar Lee Masters: A Biographical Sketchbook About a Famous American Author.* Rutherford, N.J.: Fairleigh Dickinson University Press, 1978. This book contains numerous reflections on Edgar Lee Masters by his son. Hardin Masters presents a sympathetic view of his father's poetry, but he does indicate that Edgar Lee Masters was a vain and often insensitive father and husband. Includes a thorough list of the more than fifty books written by Masters.

Primeau, Ronald. *Beyond Spoon River: The Legacy of Edgar Lee Masters.* Austin: University of Texas Press, 1981. Primeau makes extensive use of Masters' 1936 autobiography *Across Spoon River* in order to demonstrate the extensive influence of major writers such as Ralph Waldo Emerson, Johann Wolfgang von Goethe, and Percy Bysshe Shelley on Masters. Primeau argues persuasively that Masters' poetry written after his *Spoon River Anthology* does not merit the relative oblivion into which it has fallen.

Vatron, Michael. *America's Literary Revolt.* Freeport, N.Y.: Books for Libraries Press, 1969. Vatron proposes that we read the poetry of Vachel Lindsay, Edgar Lee Masters, and Carl Sandburg as expressions of "political Populism." Although this interpretation is somewhat forced, it does remind us of the historical and political context in which their poetry was written.

WILLIAM MATTHEWS

Born: Cincinnati, Ohio; November 11, 1942

Principal poetry

Broken Syllables, 1969; *Ruining the New Road*, 1970; *The Cloud*, 1971; *The Waste Carpet*, 1972; *Sleek for the Long Flight*, 1972; *An Oar in the Old Water*, 1973; *Sticks and Stones*, 1975; *Rising and Falling*, 1979; *Flood*, 1982; *A Happy Childhood*, 1984; *Foreseeable Futures*, 1987; *Blues If You Want*, 1989.

Other literary forms

Curiosities (1989) is a collection of nineteen essays, ranging from personal reflections on William Matthews' travels in Italy to critical commentaries and reviews of the works of various fellow poets. With Mary Feeney he has translated poems from the French by Jean Follain.

Achievements

A prolific poet and a master of the "deep" or surreal image, in the mode of James Wright and Robert Bly, William Matthews has attracted consistent critical acclaim from fellow poets, from the publication of his first full-length collection, *Ruining the New Road*, in 1970, but as of 1990 his work had not yet been mentioned with any regularity in scholarly studies of contemporary American poetry. He received a fellowship from the National Endowment for the Arts in 1974, following publication of his second book of poems, and a Guggenheim Fellowship after his fourth book appeared, in 1979. In 1988 he spent a month at the Villa Serbonelli on a grant from the Rockefeller Foundation. Noted for his often-aphoristic wit and for his ability to bridge the "inner" and "outer" dimensions of the human condition, Matthews ranges easily among Brahms, basketball, blues, and his own backyard.

Biography

"I used to have a morning paper route, played baseball and basketball, had a dog named Spot. Troy, Ohio." So William Matthews writes in his autobiographical essay "Moving Around" (1976). Troy is a town of around twenty thousand located about seventy miles north of Cincinnati, where he was born in 1942. When Matthews' father left his job with the Soil Conservation Service for a position with a student exchange program, the family moved back to Cincinnati. This move altered Matthews' small-town view of the world at a crucial age of his life (about age twelve). He visited Europe with his family and has remained an avid traveler.

Sent to a boarding school in the Berkshire Hills of Massachusetts, he began writing poems, though he was not to become a serious poet until after his undergraduate days at Yale University, where he received his B.A. in 1965.

Having married while at Yale, he moved to the University of North Carolina in Chapel Hill, where the couple's two sons (William and Sebastian) were born and where he did graduate work, receiving his master's degree in 1966. Also at North Carolina he started the literary magazine *Lillabulero*, which ran between 1966 and 1974, and was codirector of Lillabulero Press.

After a year as instructor in the English department at Wells College (1968-1969), Matthews taught at Cornell University, where his first full-length collection, *Ruining the New Road*, was published in 1970, to be followed two years later by *Sleek for the Long Flight*. Following his divorce in 1974, Matthews moved to the University of Colorado, where he taught for a year. Between 1976 and 1980 he served as a member of the panel on literature for the National Endowment for the Arts, on the board of directors of the Associated Writing Programs, and as an advising editor for L'Épervier Press.

Between 1978 and 1983 Matthews taught as full professor and director of creative writing at the University of Washington. After that he became an editor for the Atlantic Monthly Press. Remarried, he settled in New York City.

Analysis

In his poems and essays, William Matthews refers frequently to poets as diverse as Horace and Richard Hugo, Wallace Stevens and W. H. Auden, Elizabeth Bishop and Galway Kinnell. Yet the allusions are not limited to other poets. Novelists such as Vladimir Nabokov and Russell Banks are part of that world, and European writers of various periods populate it: Victor Hugo, Gustave Flaubert, Gabriele D'Annunzio, Vergil. Still, such a strictly literary "Who's Who" would give a reader a false impression of Matthews' range. The list would have to include Ted Williams, Jack Nicklaus, and Archie Moore, and it would encompass musicians as various as Wolfgang Amadeus Mozart and Bob Marley, though the emphasis would definitely be on jazz and blues (Janis Joplin, Bessie Smith, Dexter Gordon, Stan Getz). Sigmund Freud also makes frequent appearances in Matthews' work. Perhaps it is indicative of his world that in a poem entitled "Self-Knowledge" one encounters him reading Horace while listening to a Bud Powell tape.

What is elusive in Matthews' poems is more difficult to account for than the range of his reference or allusion. In the prefatory poem to his first full-length collection, *Ruining the New Road*, Matthews teases his audience with the suggestion that "the search party" does not involve an actual lost child, but that poet and reader are "deep in symbolic woods": "The search is that of art." No sooner does he offer that premise, however, than he insists, "There was a real lost child./ I don't want to swaddle it/ in metaphor." Even as he proclaims what he does not want to do, he does it; not only is the infinitive "to swaddle" metaphoric but it is also "loaded" for any reader of the King James Version of the New Testament. His definition of his stance as a writer is as applicable to his later poems as it was to his earlier efforts: "I'm just a journalist/ who can't believe in objectivity." To make such a statement in the poem is to "digress," as he admits, from the poem's supposed subject, so he concludes by informing the reader, "The child was still/ alive. Admit you're glad."

Especially in the first three collections, Matthews seems to be at some pains to contrive a surreal metaphoric base, as in "Cuckold": "You can hear the silverware/ catching its eager breath/ inside the sleeping drawer." Early, too, he established himself as a virtuoso of the simile—both simple, "We twist away like a released balloon" ("Moving"), and complex, "In sleep we issue from the earth/ like prayers the nuns have swallowed/ but can't keep down" ("Der Doppelgänger"). The poems of his first book are often quite spare, and the lines tend to be rather short.

In *Sleek for the Long Flight* and *Sticks and Stones*, Matthews was to carry this minimalist impulse to nearly the ultimate point, producing three one-line poems, while at the same time exploring the prose poem. His unusual blending of the inner, dreamlike world of the surreal and the outer, quotidian world of the domestic is evident in various ways throughout the long, narrow-lined "The Cat," which begins with "a hail of claws" as the cat lands "in your lap." Matthews greets the cat with playful, Homeric epithets: "Fish-breath, Wind-/ minion." What is most striking, however, is how Matthews moves from a domestic simile, "One night you lay your book/ down like the clothes/ your mother wanted/ you to wear tomorrow," to a surreal metaphor, "The cat exhales the moon." One moment the speaker can be quite direct: "This is the only cat/ I have ever loved." In the next lines, however, he moves to the whimsical, "This cat has written/ in tongue-ink/ the poem you are reading now," and then angles toward the profound: "the poem scratching/ at the gate of silence."

One remarkable poem from *Sleek for the Long Flight* is "Stone," dedicated to fellow poet Charles Simic, which begins with wordplay: "The creek has made its bed/ and wants to lie in it." Matthews delights in moments such as these, in which language seems to deconstruct itself. His best poems are always densely textured; that is, they are not only thoughtful or provocative or profound but also metaphorically rich and musical.

Sticks and Stones, published in a limited edition of six hundred copies by a small press, is a transitional collection. Its most ambitious effort is "The Waste Carpet," a four-page satire on the ecological "apocalypse" which gets quite playful: "Three Edsels forage in the southeast corner,/ a trio of ironical bishops."

In his next three collections, however, Matthews was back to major key: *Rising and Falling*, *Flood*, and *A Happy Childhood*. "Memory," Matthews writes in "Moving Again," the second poem of *Rising and Falling*, "is our root system." The poem opens with one of his patentable similes: "At night the mountains look like huge/ dim hens." Now divorced, he sees his sons infrequently: "If I lived with my sons/ all year I'd be less sentimental/ about them." This mingling of the surreal metaphoric element with the mundane statement typifies Matthews' most effective poems. From the top of the mesa, the speaker imagines, he and his sons look down on their new home. Matthews weaves an assonantal long *i* through the lines:

> The thin air
> warps in the melting light
> like the aura before a migraine.
> The boys are tired. A tiny magpie
> fluffs into a pine far below
> and farther down in the valley
> of child support and lights
> people are opening drawers.

An imagined resident opens a drawer and finds a forgotten telephone number. The elusive quality of this ending is not really clarified by comments Matthews offers about two names in the poem (Nicky and Verna) in his essay "Moving Around."

The image of rising and falling permeates the collection of that title, involving activities from climbing a hill to music, basketball, snorkeling, and the sexual act. The poems of *Rising and Falling*, which remains among the strongest of Matthews' collections, also revolve around death, and the juxtaposition of the highly erotic "Isla Mujeres" (isle of women) and "Living Among the Dead" is surely no coincidence. "It was when I learned to read," Matthews writes, "that I began always/ to live among the dead." It is easy to love the dead, he argues, because they are perfected, complete, but "to love a child is to turn/ away from the patient dead." One of his most startling similes comes from this poem: "My sons and I are like some wine/ the dead have already bottled."

The confrontation of death is more immediate in "Bystanders," a narrative poem from *Flood*, in which a fatal accident on a snowy hill draws onlookers together, helpless in the face of inevitability. What is most remarkable about this poem is the extreme understatement, its flat narration: "A woman wiped blood from his crushed/ face with a Tampax, though he was dead,/ and we stood in the field and stuttered." Matthews simply presents the event, drawing only the subtlest of conclusions: "So we began to ravel from the stunned/ calm thing we had become/ by not dying." Against this quiet metaphor he places the noise of the cleanup; the "staunch/ clank" of the snowplow's chains.

Because he understands language and because he loves words well, Matthews dares trust neither language nor words. This attitude toward language, which is now associated with deconstruction, is especially evident in such poems from *A Happy Childhood* as "Good," a series of eight ten-line poems which opens the collection. The poems are an exercise in form, for no two of them possess the same stanzaic arrangement. The opening poem, for example, which reflects on a friend who was an only child, is arranged in tercets with the seventh line set up alone. The next one, a love poem of sorts, in which the speaker mentions the loss of his "stolen good," is also set up in tercets, but with the last line apart from the others. The third poem in the series (and they do not seem really to constitute a "sequence") opens with the single, "floating" line and involves a change in point of view from first to third person: "Romantic, you could call him." Yet, the poem's subject resembles Matthews himself: "He walks the balance beam/ of his obsession like a triumphant/ drunk passing a police test." In the second tercet he likens the persona to a man in love with "a woman fools would find plain" (presumably "the muse").

In the fourth poem of the series he alternates couplets and tercets in commenting on the "good lie" of art. In the next poem, which is divided into two five-line stanzas, he tortures the word "good" through the satiric comments of the eighteenth century founder of Methodism, John Wesley, who argued that "'my good man' means 'good for his debts,'/ and not for nothing." Returning to the first person in the sixth poem of the series, Matthews probes himself "to the very bone," for which he digs "like a dog, good dog." The body of that poem yields rather playfully to the spirit in the next, which is written in the third person: "The body's dirty/ windows are flung open, and the spirit squints// out frankly." (This enjambment of the line across a stanza break is fairly common in Matthews' poems, and it creates an odd tension: the free flow of line against the imposition of stanza.) The concluding poem of the series, arranged in couplets, reintroduces the first-person speaker, who expresses his gratitude to those who have influenced his poems and freed them so that "they go their own strange ways."

This series, then, becomes a sort of *ars poetica*, touching on most of Matthews' poetic concerns, either directly or indirectly. The counterpoint series, "Bad," appears several pages later in the book, and Matthews also pairs up such poems as "Manic" and "Depressive," "Fat" and "On a Diet," "Right" and "Wrong." He also arranges strings of adjectival titles—for example, "Charming," "Restless," "Masterful." In fact, although the lengthy title poem of the book concludes, "Who knows if he's happy or not?" *A Happy Childhood* is Matthews' most playful collection, reminding the reader that the letter *J* in his "Poet's Alphabet" stands not only for "jazz" but also for "jokes" and "for how much jokes are about language." Among Matthews' jokes is his decision to end the book with the poem "Wrong."

Foreseeable Futures and *Blues If You Want* frequently turn on the subjects of music and poetry, though any comment on "subjects" in Matthews' work should take account of his essay "Dull Subjects," in which he observes that the subject matter of a poem is often only its point of departure, the raw material that is to be transformed. Thirty of the thirty-six poems in *Foresee-*

able Futures are composed in fifteen lines set up as five tercets, strongly enjambed so that form and line seem constantly to be testing each other. In "By Heart," which opens with an observation on Sidney Bechet's clarinet solo in "High Society" in 1937, Matthews poses a familiar question: "Which came first, style or content?" The rather scholarly historical stance, the history of jazz in this case, combined with the inclination to offer up just such a question, reveals much about Matthews' poetic voice. Throughout his work he assumes the distance not only of the journalist but also of the intellectual, and the wit that follows the question above is part of that stance: "To this trick/ question Drs. Xtl and Yrf and Professor Zyzgg/ have given honorable gray hours." Even as he teases the academics here, Matthews can not resist joining them, even though his definition of style, which follows, is "poetic" (metaphorical): "Style is that rind// of the soul we can persuade to die with us."

Yet the world of Matthews' poems has not become "academic" in the often-pejorative sense of the term. It remains typical of his books that one can move from reference to the philosopher and poet George Santayana in one poem to the strikingly dramatic "Caddies Day, the Country Club, a Small Town in Ohio" in the next. Perhaps Matthews' best poems are those such as "It Don't Mean a Thing If It Ain't Got That Swing," from *Blues If You Want.* This five-page poem moves from the following sort of passage:

> A grackle unrolls like a carpet of sandpaper
> its brash lament. A car with an ulcerated
> muffler stutters past. Inside, the girl has on
> those panties, the pale color of key lime pie . . .

to the following:

> and thus what we lazily call "form"
> in poetry,
> let's say, is Language's desperate
>
> attempt to wrench from print
> the voluble body it gave away
> in order to be read.

These two passages manifest everything from Matthews' often-startling similes and metaphors and his erotic touch to his indulgence of the cerebral. As Matthews says in "Poet's Alphabet": "Human consciousness is so composed that we can't have experience without a commentary on it. This makes us both silly and interesting. . . . It makes us want to make poems."

Ron McFarland

Other major works

NONFICTION: *Curiosities*, 1989.

TRANSLATION: *Remaining at a Loss: Thirty Prose Poems by Jean Follain*, 1972 (with Mary Feeney).

Bibliography

McCullogh, Ken. "William Matthews." In *American Poets Since World War II*, pt. 2, *L-Z* edited by Donald Greiner. Vol. 5 of *Dictionary of Literary Biography*. Detroit: Gale Research, 1980. The most thorough account of Matthews' life and work, with some critical attention to the latter; however, several of his books, including many of his most important poems, have appeared since this entry was written.

Marowski, Daniel G., ed. "William Matthews." In *Contemporary Literary Criticism*, vol. 40. Detroit: Gale Research, 1986: 318-325. This selection of reviews from literary journals and newspapers provides useful secondary material on Matthews' work.

Matthews, William. "A Conversation with William Matthews." *Black Warrior Review* 1 (Spring, 1975): 57-77. A useful but dated discussion with the poet.

_____. "Talking About Poetry with William Matthews." *Ohio Review* 13 (Spring, 1972): 32-51. Of interest for information on Matthews' first two collections, *Ruining the New Road* and *Sleek for the Long Flight*.

HERMAN MELVILLE

Born: New York, New York; August 1, 1819
Died: New York, New York; September 28, 1891

Principal poetry
Battle-Pieces and Aspects of the War, 1866; *Clarel: A Poem and Pilgrimage in the Holy Land*, 1876; *John Marr and Other Sailors*, 1888; *Timoleon*, 1891; *The Works of Herman Melville*, 1922-1924 (volumes 15 and 16).

Other literary forms
Herman Melville is best known for his novels, which include *Moby Dick* (1851), *The Confidence Man* (1857), and *Billy Budd, Foretopman* (1924). During his lifetime he also published a collection of short stories and sketches entitled *The Piazza Tales* (1856), as well as ten other short stories in various popular magazines. In addition to his novels and short stories, Melville contributed numerous essays, poems, and reviews to literary journals; the most famous of these is surely his review of Nathaniel Hawthorne's *Mosses from an Old Manse* (1846), published as "Hawthorne and His Mosses." In this review Melville indicates that his reading of Hawthorne altered the course of his literary growth. Since his death, four of Melville's journals, kept during such journeys as those to England and Israel, have appeared in print, as has *The Letters of Herman Melville* (1960, Merrill R. Davis and William H. Gilman, editors).

Achievements
During his lifetime, Melville's public literary achievements were lamentably few. It is only in the last several decades of the twentieth century that his work has received just recognition as the product, in the words of Howard P. Vincent (the principal editor of Melville's poems), of America's "most powerful literary genius." Substantial testimony to Melville's contemporary significance in American and world letters is indicated by the increase in the number of doctoral dissertations written about his work, from one in 1933 to twenty-two in 1980. Only two of the 1980 dissertations, however, deal exclusively with his poetry.

Even so, two book-length studies of his poetry have appeared in the 1970's, and the number of scholarly articles which treat it continue to increase steadily. In his 1947 edition of the poetry, Vincent observes that few readers of Melville's novels are aware that he is also a poet of no little talent. Vincent's efforts went largely unnoticed, however, until the 1970's or so. In the 1970's, several of Melville's poems have been regularly anthologized, along with the usual selected prose works. In modern times critics generally acknowledge Melville and Walt Whitman as the two best poets of the Civil War. Besides his 1866 *Battle-Pieces and Aspects of the War*, however, Melville, like Whitman, wrote many other poems. In his edition of Melville's poems, Robert Penn Warren states that he agrees with Randall Jarrell's judgment that Melville, Emily Dickinson, and Whitman are the best poets of nineteenth century America. Increased interest in Melville's poetry seem to confirm this judgment.

Biography

Herman Melville was born in New York City on August 1, 1819, into a family of some affluence. His father, Allan Melville, was a prosperous importer, and his mother, Maria Gansevoort, was of the wealthy and distinguished Albany Gansevoorts. When Herman was eleven, however, his father's business failed and the family entered a period of irreversible decline; Allan Melville died two years later, hopelessly mad. Several of Melville's biographers maintain that the younger Melville carried the stigma of his father's predicament with him the rest of his life, always fearing that either failure or inherited madness would overtake him. Certainly he failed many times to appeal as a writer to a popular audience, and his wife at one time contemplated leaving him because of his alleged insanity. Now, long after his death, Melville has achieved an appreciative audience, and his "insanity" may well be judged the by-product of restive genius.

Following his father's death, Melville worked at numerous odd jobs, such as bank clerk, teacher, and, of course, ordinary seaman. His first tenure at sea occurred in 1839 when he shipped aboard the *St. Lawrence*, a merchant ship sailing between New York and Liverpool. Two years later he embarked upon his South Sea island adventures, joining the crew of the *Acushnet*, a whaling vessel bound for the South Seas out of the harbor of New Bedford, Massachusetts. He returned home in 1844 and began writing about these adventures, producing the immensely successful *Typee*, his first novel, in 1846. Shortly thereafter he married Elizabeth Shaw, published his second, slightly less successful novel, *Omoo* (1847), which also draws on his South Sea escapades, and settled down in New York into a life of relatively pleasant domesticity.

Following these early successes, Melville soon discovered that both his reputation and his financial rewards as an author were falling rapidly. Critics found *Mardi* (1849) inscrutable, *Redburn* (1849) and *White-Jacket* (1850) promising improvements, but *Moby Dick* and *Pierre* (1852) immoral books. Nevertheless, along with Richard Henry Dana's *Two Years Before the Mast* (1840), *White-Jacket* did much to influence making American maritime laws more humane; the cruel practice of flogging, for example, became outlawed by an act of Congress. With the failures of *Moby Dick* and *Pierre*, Melville began to consider poetry. He had tried his hand at writing verse at least as early as *Mardi*, which contains twenty-two poems, and again in *Moby Dick* with two more. After trying three more works of prose, *Israel Potter* (1855),

The Piazza Tales (which enjoyed a measure of success), and *The Confidence Man* (a dismal failure), Melville seems to have turned all his literary talent to the writing of poetry.

For the remainder of his career, from 1857 until about 1886, when he appears to have begun work on *Billy Budd, Foretopman*, his last novel, Melville wrote only poetry. According to Sidney Kaplan, one of the contemporary editors of *Battle-Pieces and Aspects of the War*, Melville began to chronicle systematically the events of the War in poetry, to become *the* poet of the Civil War. For this purpose he made a deliberate study of prosody and poetic theory. Like his last several novels, *Battle-Pieces and Aspects of the War* was a failure at the bookstores. Melville, who had by this time received an appointment as a district inspector of customs for the New York harbor, remained undaunted (though not uninjured) by an unappreciative public, and began work, probably in 1867, on his longest poetic work, *Clarel: A Poem and Pilgrimage in the Holy Land*. This poem, running to more than eighteen thousand lines and largely based on Melville's own pilgrimage to Israel in 1856-1857, was printed privately with the financial assistance of his uncle, Peter Gansevoort. The other two volumes of his poetry, *John Marr and Other Sailors* and *Timoleon*, were also privately printed in limited editions of twenty-five copies, which were probably distributed only to interested family and friends. The novel *Billy Budd, Foretopman* remained in manuscript at Melville's death in 1891 and did not appear in print until 1924.

The notices of Melville's death were condescending at best and some were unabashedly disrespectful, expressing surprise and consternation at learning that he had not already died some years before. It was not until the appearance of Raymond Weaver's biography, *Herman Melville: Mariner and Mystic* (1921), that Melville was rediscovered. Since that time, his reputation has consistently and deservedly improved, and today he is recognized by all serious readers of literature as one of America's greatest prose writers and one of her great poets.

Analysis

As he does in his novels, Herman Melville, in his poems, pursues his personal struggle to discover some degree of certainty in a world in which such a task was becoming increasingly difficult. For the Deists of the eighteenth century, God had receded to the role of watchmaker who, after the machine-like world was constructed, left it to run its course. In the nineteenth century, with the impact of historical criticism of the Bible and of Charles Darwin's theory of evolution, God seemed to have disappeared altogether. Such awareness, however, was confined to the most perceptive thinkers; the masses of people put off such challenges for a later day. Melville was one of those thinkers who refused to put off an intellectual or spiritual challenge which came his way. He was for his time a seer, a prophet. It is probably for this reason that Melville, while speaking with an ever clearer voice today, found himself misunderstood and finally unheard in his own time. Melville's personal struggle has become that of our time.

Melville sought to reconcile the antinomies of existence. Since the advent of the Christian era, the most serious of these contraries, life and death, could easily be reconciled by the promise of eternal happiness—for the faithful, that is, although one of eternal torture and hellfire for unbelievers. By Melville's time, the promise of an afterlife had become less certain, and, to some, improbable and even naïve. This is the kind of conflict which preoccupied Melville, and which he confronted with courage and commitment.

Melville's first book of poems, *Battle-Pieces and Aspects of the War*, was harshly criticized for its unconventional metrics. One reviewer, writing for *The Round Table* on September 15, 1866, asserted that the poet displayed a "disregard of the laws of verse" and that he "ha[d] but little sense of melody, and almost no sense of proportion." Educated readers of the mid-nineteenth century still expected both to see and to hear regular patterns of rhyme and rhythm—not the irregular, experimental patterns of Whitman, Dickinson, and Melville. As in the better poetry of Whitman and Dickinson, however, irregularities of rhythm and rhyme, when they occur in Melville's better poems, do indeed "seem an echo to the sense" (from Alexander Pope's *An Essay on Criticism*, 1711). Perhaps what is true of Melville's ideas is true of his sound patterns; just as twentieth century minds are required to grasp Melville's penetrating analysis of human estrangement from time-honored but time-worn ideas of God, so twentieth century ears are necessary to connect sound with sense in his poetry.

The second poem of *Battle-Pieces and Aspects of the War*, "Misgivings," embodies most of Melville's major themes, as well as displays his formal innovations. The poem, fourteen lines long, suggests the sonnet form; but it exhibits several radical departures from traditional sonnet structure. Instead of fourteen lines of fairly regular iambic pentameter, Melville has two seven-line stanzas. The first five lines of the first stanza are in iambic tetrameter with only one anapest to vary the pattern; line six adopts the familiar iambic pentameter of the sonnet. The final line of the first stanza, however, contains two anapests and two amphimacers, so six lines of the first stanza retain a four-stress rhythm. The second stanza is another matter. Only the first three lines are iambic tetrameter, with a trochee, two spondees, and an anapest for variation. The fourth line is composed in iambic trimeter with a spondee, but the next two lines expand swiftly, by use of monosyllabic and disyllabic words, into perfectly regular iambic pentameters, leading to the slower concluding alexandrine (iambic hexameter), which contains three anapests. The rhyme scheme is ababacc for each stanza, except for the fifth line of stanza two, which does not rhyme with any other line in the poem.

Although Melville's formal innovations struck many of his readers as disagreeable, unpoetic, even clumsy, they are strictly functional. The sound pattern in "Misgivings" complements, with consummate artistry, the poem's meaning. The poem opens as "ocean-clouds" are observed sweeping over "inland hills" during "late autumn brown"; these clouds of huge expanse bring with them destructive storms which fill "the sodden valley" with "horror." The pathetic fallacy developed in the first three lines, that an inanimate valley may be filled with terror, prepares the reader for the fourth line's arresting observation, as well as for its abstract significance. The destructive storm, which comes in dreary autumn, is to be followed by the frozen, paralyzing (even deadly) winter, striking terror in the hearts of the valley's inhabitants, even causing "the spire" to fall "crashing in the town."

That very concrete image, a crashing spire, may first suggest the destruction of a church or of religion. The spire crashes in a town, however, suggesting a further association of the spire with societal order. The poet seems to suggest, then, that the very fabric of his country's civilization is vulnerable to the destructiveness of this storm. The splitting of the Union in 1860 seemed to promise just such destruction. The poet next laments that such promised devastation may be explained metaphorically as "The tempest bursting from the waste of Time/On the world's fairest hope linked with man's foulest crime."

This couplet echoes Melville's reading of at least two of William Shakespeare's plays, *Macbeth* (1606) and *The Tempest* (1611). The action of *The Tempest* comes bursting on the stage as the play opens with a storm of its own, the result of a waste of Time. Prospero, denied his rightful dukedom of Milan for twelve years, has eked out a meager existence on a remote Mediterranean island far from Milan; seizing the opportunity that fate has suddenly provided him, he manages to reassemble the offending parties by having his servant Ariel create the illusion of a storm; he finally attains the justice denied him during these twelve years, this great waste of time. The second line of the couplet recalls the "fair is foul and foul is fair" motif in *Macbeth*. That which seems fair, Macbeth's hospitality toward King Duncan, is in fact most foul, for Macbeth plots and carries out Duncan's murder. In Melville's poem, "the world's fairest hope," the United States, the modern world's first experiment in democracy, has actively legitimized, from its birth, "man's foulest crime," slavery. For the eighty-four years since Independence, Americans have squandered Time by committing a crime they have declared, in principle at least, to be barbarous and unspeakably cruel. The land of the free has enforced and even legislated slavery, freedom's exact opposite.

The metrical architecture of this crucial "Time-crime" couplet is astonishing. The first five lines establish the mood and set the scene for disaster. Religion, civilization, and even nature herself, as in *Macbeth* and *The Tempest*, all seem to herald the speed of doom. The swift pace of these five lines is slowed, however, first by the increase of an extra foot in the "Time" line and then by a much more complicated process in the final line of the stanza. Such a slowing is indeed appropriate, for the poet has commented that this scene moves him to "muse upon my country's ills." Although the sixth line contains five feet and the seventh only four, the last line is lengthened by two anapests which introduce two amphimacers, in each of which the first and last syllables receive primary stress: "fairest hope" and "foulest crime." So the four-foot line actually contains six primary stresses, creating an effect of gravity. Indeed, the poems' subject is most grave. Finally, the precision of "Time-crime" need only be stated, for surely slavery has been time's crime.

The poem's suggestion that Nature herself also participates in this crime is now stated in the first line of the next stanza: "Nature's dark side is heeded now." Recognizing Melville's dependence on Calvinism's claim that all men are innately depraved ("In Adam's fall/ We sinned all"), one is led to conclude that the "Nature" that Melville names here is that of man's essential depravity, although Melville did not restrict himself to metaphors drawn from Christianity. He drew on other religious traditions as well, particularly on Zoroastrianism, a Near Eastern faith which posits the existence of a good god of light, Ahura Mazda, and one of evil darkness, Ahriman (Angra Mainyu), who struggle for the souls of men. Melville introduced Zoroastrianism into his works when in *Moby Dick* he made Ahab's mysterious servant Fedallah a Parsee, a modern term for an adherent of Zoroastrianism. The line "Nature's dark side is heeded now" may just as likely suggest the cosmic struggle between the gods of light and darkness in which the god of darkness now has the upper hand. Certainly the participation of nature in the storm indicates that the struggle here is one of cosmic or exterior proportions and not merely one of interior conscience.

In the following line Melville observes parenthetically "(Ah! optimist— cheer disheartened flown)." In *The Mystery of Iniquity: Melville as Poet, 1857-1891* (1972), William H. Shurr calls this line "an unequivocal statement of Melville's . . . antitranscendentalist polemic." Certainly in a world which heeds "Nature's dark side," there can be little room for transcendental optimism, and the spondee which opens the line would seem to place emphasis on that optimism. The line concludes, however, with the phrase "disheartened flown." The next two lines, made up of monosyllabics and disyllabics, now move swiftly toward the conclusion. The first of these two lines maintains the tetrameter rhythm of the stanza's initial two lines; the next, or fourth, line, however, has four primary stresses but only three feet.

This tetrameter line followed by a trimeter seems to mock first the adults in the town and then those of the country for not having foreseen the inevitable doom of death and destruction: "A child may read the moody brow/ Of yon black mountain lone." The image of a "black mountain" could refer, as some have suggested, to the black race preparing both to liberate themselves and to be liberated. Considering Melville's use of Zoroastrianism, however, the phrase seems to duplicate the terrible evil suggested in the first line of the stanza by the spondaic phrase, "dark side." Something else a bit more subtle is happening here, however, and this subtlety shows Melville at his best as a sound-technician.

The diphthong in "mountain" and the voiced vowel in "lone" set up a pattern which carries over into the following, regularly pentameter line: "With shouts the torrents down the gorges go." While the diphthong of "mountain" appears again in "shouts" and "down," the voiced vowel of "lone" recurs in "torrents," "gorges," and finally in the nonrhyming verb "go." This line is the only one of the poem which does not rhyme; it is lengthened by a foot; and it assonates with the preceding line. All these factors bring emphasis to bear on this line. The next line gives a clue why: "And storms are formed behind the storm we feel." Note the continued assonance of the voiced vowel in "lone" now appearing in "storms," "formed," and "storm." Melville also skillfully retains the liquid "r" in five of these "lone" assonating syllables: "torrents," "gorges," "storms," "formed," and "storm."

Recalling the sweeping storm which opens the poem, the emphasis called for here is very artfully accomplished and should now become apparent. The "storm" is not merely a metaphor from Nature which "we feel"; it has now become an actual storm stirred by men. The storm's metaphorical torrents are, in fact, the shouts of real men, and the poem moves to this apocalyptic conclusion: "The hemlock shakes in the rafter, the oak in the driving keel."

Now since the poison of the hemlock has finally done its work on the rafters of the human soul, the very oak or strength of the steering body, the ship of state, trembles at the horror of the storm. As was suggested in the image of the town's crashing spire, the very fabric of civilization shakes at the discovery of its own evil. This sonnet, then, draws a picture which is perfectly consistent with Melville's worldview in his novels and in many other poems. Melville feels the responsibility to admonish the world of its threatened doom. When our world of "seem" is the exact opposite of the way we perceive it, then our continued existence is indeed imperiled.

"Shiloh, a Requiem" relates some of the results of the country's disgorging. The poem is a lament for the shocking loss of life (and "the waste of Time") which one of the bloodiest conflicts of the Civil War has brought on the country. The poem opens on a cloudy day following the battle of April 6 and 7, 1862. The bursts of cannon and tortured shouts are completely absent now as "Skimming lightly, wheeling still,/ The swallows fly low/ Over the field." As in "Misgivings," Melville is here an artist of sound; for the light skimming and wheeling of the birds echo the passage of bullets through the unresisting air. "Skimming lightly, wheeling *still*," Melville says; the echoes of the bullets remain even today to haunt the visitor to this battlefield which has now become a national monument. Ironically the poet notes that the men who died here were "Foemen at morn, but friends at eve," and he continues with this succinct observation: "What like a bullet can undeceive!" Such a warning speaks to any culture of any time.

Clarel, his long narrative of a spiritual journey, has no images as immediate as those of *Battle-Pieces and Aspects of the War*'s sweeping storms and dying foemen; rather, in the ten years separating the two works Melville has become more philosophical and contemplative. This tone certainly prevails in *Clarel*'s "Epilogue," as the poem's opening lines indicate. The poet asks in a brief question of sweeping scope: "If Luther's day expand to Darwin's year,/ Shall that exclude the hope—foreclose the fear?" Expressing some measure of impatience with the debate suggested by such a question, the poet asserts: "The running battle of the star and clod/ Shall run forever—if there be no God." Finally he advises Clarel to "keep thy heart yet but ill resigned/ . . . thy heart, the issues there but mind."

In the final analysis, Melville seems to be saying, the heart offers the greatest certainty in an uncertain world; indeed, even "Science the feud can only aggravate." If one relies on the heart, however, "Emerge thou mayst from the last whelming sea,/ And prove that death but routs life into victory." These are noble lines. Robert Penn Warren labels them an affirmation. One must note carefully, however, that the statement is conditional: "Emerge thou *mayst*." Melville is still unwilling to subscribe to any dogma, whether religious or scientific (whether of Luther or of Darwin), but he can find solace in his knowledge of the human heart and in the power of human feeling. As for the certainty for which Clarel has made his pilgrimage, the poet's position appears to be finally that of an optimistic agnostic. In other words, Melville seems not to have excluded the hope (to paraphrase from the opening couplet) for some sort of benevolent release from pain and realization of a glorious after-life, but, at the same time, neither has he embraced such a hope as an absolute certainty.

A later poem from *John Marr and Other Sailors* recaptures some of the skepticism of *Clarel*, as well as the pessimism of *Battle-Pieces and Aspects of the War*. "The Aeolian Harp" relates how the haunting tones of a wind harp cause the poet to conjure up "A picture stamped in memory's mint" of a dismasted, waterlogged wreck which floats aimlessly about but which consequently drifts "Torpid in dumb ambuscade" as a constant threat to the destruction of another unwarned and unprepared vessel. What is of particular interest here is not the symbolism of Melville's indifferent and unfeeling demon of disaster (another Moby Dick?) but the poet's allusion once again to Shakespeare's *The Tempest*. He compares the vision evoked by the wind harp's "wailing" with the sort of illusions Ariel creates in the play. The wind harp's illusion is ". . . less a strain ideal/ Than Ariel's rendering of the Real." This reference to Ariel is particularly apropos in this poem, for the storm that Shakespeare's Ariel brews forces Ferdinand, Alonso, Gonzalo, Antonio, and others to Prospero's island domain and is replete with terrifying corposants, thunderclaps, and trembling waves. So convincing is Ariel's play that these

Neapolitans abandon ship and swim to Prospero's island for safety. The illusion recalled in Melville's poem promises no safety for the hapless victims of this ship, which crashes heedlessly into any unfortunate enough to cross its treacherous course.

Finally, the poet concludes: "Well the harp of Ariel wails/ Thoughts that tongue can tell no word of!" So horrible is this "picture stamped in memory's mint" that the relating of it requires the impetus of the haunting wind harp, now become wholly Ariel's harp. Thus Melville reveals the power of the poet's imagination. Perhaps because his century viewed man's relationship to God and the world in harsher terms, he demanded a poetic world more austere and even more forbidding than the world of Shakespeare's *The Tempest*.

Melville is not, however, always so severe. The later poems of *Battle-Pieces and Aspects of the War*, for example, are enthusiastically patriotic and finally positive. The poem "Malvern Hill," celebrating the victory of Union forces at Malvern Hill in Virginia on July 1, 1862, concludes with these hopeful lines: "Wag the world how it will,/ Leaves must be green in Spring." His poem, "Falstaff's Lament over Prince Hal Become Henry V," is a delightfully humorous portrait of Shakespeare's rejected father-figure, Sir John Falstaff. The discarded old man drowns his sorrow in sack or wine: "Come drawer [tapster], more sack here!" The comic old gentleman shrewdly observes, however, that "now intuitions/ Shall wither to codes." Prince Hal, now become King Henry V, tosses aside the virtues of spontaneity for the rules and responsibilities of a crown. Melville's predicament as a poet is something like that of the English prince; having come to be a full-fledged poet in his middle age, surely he came to the genre carrying few illusions about the vicissitudes of a world where Darwinism and critical analysis of traditional Christianity challenged established faith. Melville's poetry is inevitably sobering and grave, yet his quest for some degree of certainty, to reconcile a world of opposites, led him to write poetry which is vibrant, sensitive, and sonorous. In one of his last poems, "Art," Melville emphatically declares that, in the poet's poem, opposites "must mate,/ And fuse with Jacob's mystic heart/ To wrestle with the angel—Art."

John C. Shields

Other major works

LONG FICTION: *Typee*, 1846; *Omoo*, 1847; *Mardi*, 1849; *Redburn*, 1849; *White-Jacket*, 1850; *Moby Dick*, 1851; *Pierre*, 1852; *Israel Potter*, 1855; *The Confidence Man*, 1857; *Billy Budd, Foretopman*, 1924.

SHORT FICTION: *The Piazza Tales*, 1856; *The Apple-Tree Table and Other Sketches*, 1922.

NONFICTION; *Journal Up the Straits*, 1935; *Journal of a Visit to London and the Continent*, 1948; *The Letters of Herman Melville* (1960, Merrill R. Davis and William H. Gilman, editors).

Bibliography

Bloom, Harold, ed. *Herman Melville: Modern Critical Interpretations.* New York: Chelsea House, 1986. In his helpful introduction, Bloom discusses the importance of the thirteen articles presented. Major critics interpret Melville's themes, forms, symbolism, and comedy in *Moby Dick*, the tales, *Billy Budd, Foretopman*, and other works. Includes a useful chronology, a bibliography, and an index.

Branch, Watson G., ed. *Melville: The Critical Heritage.* London: Routledge & Kegan Paul, 1974. Brings together the records of the nineteenth century's critical reception of Melville in reviews, essays, and other documents, all of which help readers understand the uneven reception of Melville's genius: Until 1938, he was not considered appropriate for university studies, yet now, he is recognized as a great American writer. An index accompanies the text.

Chase, Richard, ed. *Melville: A Collection of Critical Essays.* Englewood Cliffs, N.J.: Prentice-Hall, 1962. Major twentieth century critics included here are D. H. Lawrence, Alfred Kazin, Robert Penn Warren and F. O. Matthiessen. Eleven articles illuminate Melville's novels, stories, and writing style. The critics cover the relation of novelistic, romantic, and epic elements in his work. His poetic development is traced and his place in the American literary tradition is debated.

Dimock, Wai-chee. *Empire for Liberty: Melville and the Poetics of Individualism.* Princeton, N.J.: Princeton University Press, 1989. Dimock's literary analysis uses metaphors of space, dominance, and fate to show Melville's vision of the human soul. The isolated self builds "thick walls" and "interior spaciousness" (Moby Dick himself) to pursue freedom and to resist the downward pull of doom. Indian-hating in the American "empire" takes on metaphysical dimensions in this difficult but rewarding study. Includes notes and an index.

Miller, Edwin Haviland. *Melville.* New York: George Braziller, 1975. Melville is a difficult subject for biographers because he did not reveal himself intimately in letters, diaries, or journals. Therefore his books, and accounts of him by others are where the inner man is found. Using these sources, Miller writes a fascinating and illuminating account. Two plates and fifteen half-plates, a select bibliography, and an index assist the reader.

Mumford, Lewis. *Herman Melville.* New York: Literary Guild, 1929. Using letters, notebooks, and memoirs, Mumford writes candidly about Melville's life and thoughts. He interprets the great white whale, Moby Dick, as a symbol of the universe in which we live: indifferent to human life which lives in illusions. Contains an important biography that brings Melville into our times. Supplemented by an index.

SAMUEL MENASHE

Born: New York, New York; September 16, 1925

Principal poetry
The Many Named Beloved (1961); *No Jerusalem But This* (1971); *Fringe of Fire*, (1973); *To Open* (1974), *Collected Poems* (1986).

Other literary forms
Samuel Menashe is known primarily for his poetry.

Achievements
Samuel Menashe has won critical recognition for being one of the most individual and daring poets of his time. Eschewing all the poetic fashions of the late twentieth century, Menashe writes a tightly chiseled verse that nevertheless is full of visionary experience and intensity. Poets and critics as diverse as Hugh Kenner, Donald Davie, and Kathleen Raine have called attention to Menashe as a demanding and exemplary poet. Menashe has achieved more popularity in Great Britain than in America, perhaps because his sense of a personal sacredness is more in tune with the English poetic tradition than with the more public celebration associated with poets such as Walt Whitman. To an unusual degree, Menashe has created a demanding, radically personal body of poetry that speaks to essential issues of human experience and belief.

Biography
Samuel Menashe was born in New York City, the child of Jewish immigrants. His early exposure to Yiddish and Spanish were crucial in bestowing upon him the sensitivity to linguistic nuance evident in the care he lavishes upon every word in his poems. Menashe especially attributes his verbal gifts to the influence of his mother, who was multilingual. He served in the United States Army during and after World War II and studied at the Sorbonne in Paris, writing a doctoral thesis on poetic experience and gaining an advanced degree.

Menashe has traveled widely in Europe and the Near East and despite the local settings of his poetry, is quite cosmopolitan as a writer, possessing an awareness of many literatures and cultures. He is an impressive and eloquent reciter of verse who captivates audiences when he reads aloud from his own work and that of his favorite poets. Menashe lives in an apartment in downtown New York City and frequently gives public readings of his poetry, both in New York and elsewhere.

Analysis

The poetry of Samuel Menashe is very distinctive. His poems are all quite short and seem as if they are trying to grasp the essence of their subject in the most simple and fundamental way. Although the length of his poems entitles him to be styled a minimalist, their concerns are not at all minimal; rather, they are all-embracing, almost transcendent in their scope. Menashe's poems are easy to comprehend on their surface. Puzzling out the intended meaning of the poems is not particularly challenging for the reader. The richness of Menashe's poems lies in the way their embroidery and orchestration of language illuminates the tenderness and wisdom of his thought.

Menashe has been influenced by many different poets. In the bareness and austerity of his language he recalls twentieth century poets in the modernist tradition, particularly those of the "Objectivist" school such as George Oppen, Louis Zukofsky, and Charles Reznikoff—most of whom, like Menashe, were of Jewish descent. Unlike these poets, however, Menashe is less interested in the object in itself than in the highly subjective range of human emotions and spirituality. Thus Menashe also has a completely different set of ancestors. His very personal sense of beauty and glory recalls the Bible as well as such maverick religious poets as William Blake, Emily Dickinson, and Gerard Manley Hopkins, who all, like Menashe, excelled in imbuing very short forms with mystery and spirituality.

This latter tradition is most overt in the poems in Menashe's first volume, *The Many Named Beloved.* These poems are the longest and most ornate in Menashe's canon, although still brief and compact compared to the works of most other poets. Some of the most successful poems in the collection are small narratives or parables. A good example is "Promised Land." In this poem, the speaker stands "at the edge/ of a world/ beyond my eyes/ beautiful." Like the biblical Moses, the speaker never manages to enter the promised land he contemplates. Unlike his scriptural predecessor, however, he does not truly yearn to enter this paradise. He realizes that beauty is most vivid when it cannot quite be attained.

Alluding to a Jewish tradition that knows exile and estrangement far more vividly than it knows fulfillment and consummation, the poem concludes, "The river/ We cannot cross/ Flows forever." To cross the river would be to end the exile, to find a definite salvation. The "cannot" in the above clause implies that humankind by nature is forbidden to cross this river, which in some ways is the border between mortality and immortality. Yet there are more subtle reverberations to the "cannot." These become clear when the whole line is read. "Flows forever" gives an impression of permanence and continuity, not loss or despair. The poem implies that the river is kept flowing by the very way in which its existence allows exile to be maintained. The river's activity is ultimately positive rather than negative, in keeping alive human aspirations and never letting them become resolved into a settled, final state. This is why exile is, in Menashe's phrase, "green with hope" and not green with envy.

In this poem and in others, Menashe uses religious terms and images. Yet he is not a believer in formal religion; unlike some modern poets such as T. S. Eliot, he is not interested in religion as dogma, doctrine, or ritual. Rather, he is excited by the hope and by the poetic magic that religion at times expresses.

The poems in *No Jerusalem But This* mark a new phase in Menashe's career. There is far less "high" language in these poems. Menashe is less reliant on visionary rhetoric and more content to let his poems speak on their own terms. From this point onward, no comparisons with other poets are relevant; Menashe's career becomes a solitary journey. This solitary emphasis can be seen in the poem that includes the collection's title line. This is probably Menashe's most important and memorable poem. "The Shrine Whose Shape I Am" is a kind of hymn, but it is not the sort that could be included in any religious ceremony. This shrine is not a conventional object of worship or reverence, but rather the speaker's body itself.

Menashe, though, is very canny in that he is not proposing any pagan cult of the body. Instead, he focuses on how the body marks the boundaries of the self and its world. The body for Menashe signifies not earth or blood but the spirit of life itself. This spirit is symbolized in the early lines of the poem by fire. "Flames skirt my skin," the speaker says, as he describes his form as having a "fringe of fire."

The poem goes on to state, "There is no Jerusalem but this." There is no reason to look for Jerusalem, the holy city, in Heaven, where religious thinkers have often placed it. Nor is any Jerusalem on earth—whether the actual Jerusalem which, when the poem was written, had only recently been made part of the new state of Israel or any other site said to be a sacred abode—sufficient in the view of the poem to express human spirituality fully. If there is no Jerusalem in either Heaven or earth, then Jerusalem must be within the self or body. Yet Menashe is not saying that Jerusalem definitely does exist within the self or body, only that if there is a Jerusalem at all this is where one would find it. This limitation of Jerusalem to the human form is not at all a reduction. This Jerusalem is as wondrous and evocative as any heavenly or earthly city. It is "breathed in flesh by shameless love." The speaker's belief is as vivid as that of any biblical figure: "Like David I bless myself/ with all my might." There is no sense that the speaker's spiritual condition is impoverished when compared to the past.

Still, all is not bliss. The tragedies as well as the triumphs associated with other Jerusalems are also present in this one. The speaker finds that he cannot share the certainty that he attributes to previous ages. "I know that many hills were holy once," he states. "But now in the level lands to live/ Zion ground down must become marrow." In the absence of any larger belief, the physical husk of human skin and bones must sustain any hopes for transcendence. Yet these hopes are, by nature, ephemeral. Menashe is sensitive to the frailty of bone as well as the pulse and color of flesh. The human body is inevitably subject to time and decay. Thus the speaker, in living Jerusalem within his own body, in a way is bound to reenact, or more truly act in his own way, the suffering of Jesus. "And through death's domain I go/ Making my own procession." Each human life holds the pathos and the dignity to be found in larger shapes within traditional religion. Menashe lovingly conveys the connections between human hopes for a higher world and the way these hopes are played out in, and by, the course of an individual life.

Poems of this sort, filled with rich, interior reflection, are not the only type to be found in this volume. There are some excellent poems with a natural setting. These poems may seem surprising from a poet of Menashe's visionary intensity, but they are like his other verse in that his eye is never on the setting as such. Instead, he focuses on the metaphorical potential of that setting. In "Sheep Meadow" Menashe conveys a delicate but very accurate sense of this famous green stretch of New York's Central Park, here glimpsed in winter, when it is usually least noticed. Menashe is so much a poet of his beloved New York City that this park scene is as close to pure "nature" as he tends to get. Yet the poem magnificently captures a personal sense of the atmosphere of the place.

He opens by comparing speaking French on the Sheep Meadow to "a very rich hour/ of the Duke of Berry," the allusion being to the well-known medieval illustrations. By making this comparison, Menashe instantly transforms what would otherwise have been a nondescript, perhaps even banal, scene into one rife with imaginative possibility. He does this, moreover, without ruining the spontaneity of the scene by a heavy-handed reference to high culture. The medieval reference is made offhandedly and naturally, not with an air of pomposity or pretension. From this imaginative base the poem glides strategically into its actual setting. Menashe depicts the snowy meadow "hedged by trees/ on the south side/ where the towers/ of the city rise." The Sheep Meadow is a locus of stillness and peace within the fantastically complex and aggravated edifices of a great metropolis. Its calm and quietness stand out even more within such surroundings than they would if the field lay in the open country. The calm of the Sheep Meadow is not a careless calm but a deliberate and meditative one. It can serve as a resting place for "one of those hours/ in early afternoon/ where nothing happens/ but time makes room." The off-rhyme between "noon" and "room" is emblematic of the close and comfortable but never completely static or placid relationship between nature and the human mind that the poem portrays. Even though nothing dramatic or striking occurs during this sojourn of reverie in the meadow, the serene near-stillness is worthy of notice, because it does not answer to the usual mandate of time. The awareness that time is passing typically leads one to believe that unless something dramatic happens an hour is unimportant. The poem suggests, however, that this equation should be altered. By saying that "time makes room" for this sort of reflective thought, the poem leads the reader to consider whether the spaces in which thought lingers outside the strict limits of time may ultimately evade the logic of day-by-day necessity that reigns outside the park. The poem starts out with an image, goes into the description of a place, and concludes with a finely honed evocation of a mood.

In Menashe's *To Open*, as well as the poems that were uncollected until the appearance of *Collected Poems* in 1986, the poet maintains the general type and tone of his verse. Yet in these poems his technique becomes even more refined and masterful. Just as in the shift from the first to the second volume an emphasis on emotional depth and idiosyncratic reverence replaced one on rhetorical grandeur, so does the course of Menashe's poetry after the second volume exhibit less of a stress on subject matter and more of a focus on linguistic concreteness and complexity. The poems become still shorter. Yet even in those of only two or three lines there is as much intricacy as most poets would put into far longer forms. A fine example is "Tears." This poem is so brief that its entire length could be conveyed in one sentence. "Without tears/ The eyes die/ Of dryness—/ You must cry/ To water/ The eye." This miniature container holds enormous conceptual and linguistic depth and skill.

Tears are traditionally far more often the by-product of poetry than its subject. Even when poems take tears as their subject, as in Alfred, Lord Tennyson's "Tears, Idle Tears," they are at least ostensibly supposed to be lamented, not celebrated. Menashe's poem implies, however, that tears are ultimately beneficial. Without tears, the eye would die of dryness. This is to say, without the emotional release of crying the eye would be imprisoned in a cold self-sufficiency, incapable of knowing or feeling any experience outside it. Tears, although apparently an expression of pain, in fact serve to demonstrate a sentimental attachment on the part of the human eye (and mind) to phenomena that are not inherently part of it. As usual, Menashe's content is a wise aphorism strategically designed to counter conventional wisdom.

Yet content is not the only factor here. The very words in which the content is expressed redouble the force of their meaning. Menashe's language is not only meant to sound striking and beautiful but also actually to affect the meaning that is conveyed through it. In fact, it can even be said that the language assists in constructing this meaning. The dominant rhyme in the poem is, in terms of sound, a long *i*, usually expressed visually by the letter *y*. The repetition of this rhyme binds the words together in one phonetic unit of meaning. Yet by more often than not standing at the end of a line (for example, "die," "cry," "eye"), the *y* sound protrudes out of each line just as tears protrude out of the eye. Like the tears, the *y* sound is crucial in communicating feeling and meaning from one isolated unit (whether a mind or a poetic line) to another. Menashe here masterfully combines a large philosophical and emotional sweep with a meticulous concern for the smallest and most closely wrought hint of verbal meaning. He holds in balance the big and the little, the macrocosmic and the microscopic, in order to create an inimitable, superbly controlled piece of poetry.

A similar triumph of closely wrought language is "Waves." In the first stanza, the waves are described: "Waves crest, waver, fall." The monosyllabic, consonant-filled phrases give the impression of hardness and exactitude. Yet they also convey the air of objects that are full of unrest, not at repose with one another. This tension is resolved in the following and final stanza, "Masts sway/ at anchor/ over the bay." The inclusion of the two-syllable word "anchor" conveys a sense of expansive firmness that truly does anchor the language, while the rhyme between "sway" and "bay" mimics the anchor's limitation of the motion represented by swaying as the masts rest in alert peace on the bay. Once again, the language and the scene that it depicts go hand in hand. As with all Menashe's poems, the amount of rewarding labor expended on the part of both reader and writer goes far deeper than the mere appearance of a few words on the page.

Nicholas Birns

Bibliography

Birkerts, Sven. Review of *Collected Poems. Partisan Review* 54 (Fall, 1987): 649-650. Birkerts, one of the leading practical critics of poetry, describes Menashe as a "poet of subtle breath stops and fine detail" who produces "calibrated minims" in which rhyme and construction are paramount.

Davie, Donald. "The Poetry of Samuel Menashe." In *The Poet in the Imaginary Museum.* New York: Persea Books, 1977. One of the longest and most in-depth discussions of Menashe's work. Davie, a distinguished poet and one of Menashe's main critical champions, gives an invaluable survey of both Menashe's work and his temperament, providing a representative sample of his most important poems. Davie is especially valuable on the linguistic and religious aspects of Menashe's poetry.

Heller, Michael. Review of *Collected Poems. The New York Times*, March 8, 1987, p. 32. In the most prominent review of Menashe's *Collected Poems*. Heller, himself a noted poet whose verse possesses qualities similar to Menashe's, sees Menashe's poetry as the work of a "lapidarian" and discusses the formal techniques of his rhymes. Heller aptly observes how even Menashe's most "disarmingly simple" poems possess "uncanny force."

Menashe, Samuel. Interview by Fred Bornhauser. In *Contemporary Authors*, edited by Hal May, vol. 115. Detroit: Gale Research, 1985. In one of the most wide-ranging and revealing interviews ever given by Menashe, the poet discusses both his life and his poems, placing special emphasis on the interrelationship between language and emotion. Menashe also comments, at times rather pointedly, on the critical response to his poems.

WILLIAM MEREDITH

Born: New York, New York; January 9, 1919

Principal poetry

Love Letter from an Impossible Land, 1944; *Ships and Other Figures*, 1948; *The Open Sea and Other Poems*, 1958; *The Wreck of the Thresher and Other Poems*, 1964; *Earth Walk: New and Selected Poems*, 1970; *Hazard, the Painter*, 1975; *The Cheer*, 1980; *Partial Accounts: New and Selected Poems*, 1987.

Other literary forms

William Meredith worked as the opera critic for *Hudson Review* from 1955 to 1956. He wrote the libretto, based on a Robert Louis Stevenson story, for Peter Whiton's opera *The Bottle Imp*, which was produced in 1958. Meredith edited and introduced a selected edition of Percy Bysshe Shelley's poetry (1962); in 1968, along with Mackie L. Jarrell, he edited and introduced *Eighteenth Century English Minor Poets*. He translated Guillaume Apollinaire's poetry in a work that appeared in 1964 as *Alcools: Poems 1898-1913*. In 1986 a volume of Bulgarian poetry, edited and introduced by Meredith, was published. In addition, he has written a variety of reviews and essays.

Achievements

Meredith's place in the New England literary tradition and twentieth century American poetry is secure. Early in his career his poetry was highly imitative and academic. He eschewed experimentation, and he maintained a reticence and control that constricted his development and caused some to dismiss his understated, formal style as not engaging. Starting with the appearance of his *Ships and Other Figures* in 1948, however, Meredith moved consistently toward a less academic style and a more immediate voice. Since then, his importance to American poetry has steadily increased.

Meredith's superlative accomplishments have been widely praised by his peers. He is the recipient of several honors, including the Yale Younger Poets Award, three annual prizes awarded by *Poetry*, the Loines Prize, the Van Wyck Brooks Award, two Rockefeller Foundation grants, a National Endowment for the Arts grant, the International VAPTSAROV Prize for Literature, the Pulitzer Prize for Poetry, and an American Academy of Poets Award. Meredith has been a Guggenheim Fellow, a Ford Foundation Fellow, and a Woodrow Wilson Fellow at Princeton University. He is a member of the American Academy and National Institute of Arts and Letters (for which he has served as secretary) and Chancellor of the Academy of American Poets. In addition, Meredith has served as consultant in poetry to the Library of Congress.

Biography

William Morris Meredith was born on January 9, 1919, in New York City and spent his childhood in Darien, Connecticut. He attended the Lenox School in Massachusetts and then Princeton University, where he received a B.A. and was graduated *magna cum laude* in 1940. Until 1941 he worked as a copy boy, then reporter, for *The New York Times.* During World War II, Meredith was first a private in the United States Army Air Corps, then a Navy pilot. In 1944, *Love Letter from an Impossible Land* was published while Meredith was a lieutenant. After the war, he became a Woodrow Wilson Fellow, then an instructor in English and a Resident Fellow in creative writing at Princeton University. *Ships and Other Figures,* published by Princeton University in 1948, is largely a product of his time at this university. During the Korean War he served as a carrier pilot, was promoted to lieutenant commander, and received two Air Medals.

Meredith's association with Connecticut College began in 1955 and has continued, with a few interruptions, throughout his teaching career. With the publication by Alfred A. Knopf of *The Open Sea and Other Poems* in 1958 and several other volumes of poetry, Meredith has composed a significant body of creative work. Moreover, he has written in other genres, has been afforded many honors, and has taught at a variety of institutions, including the University of Hawaii, Middlebury College, Bread Loaf, and Carnegie-Mellon University. He has served as a member of the Connecticut Commission of the Arts and as director of the Humanities Upward Bound Project for Connecticut College.

Analysis

William Meredith's interest in exploring ways to order human existence in the face of chaos has remained his principal thematic concern. Although the complexity of this thematic focus has deepened, the subtle shift in Meredith's thematic vision, according to Guy Rotella, has to do with "the degree of confidence he feels in any of the methods and results," along with his understanding of "the threats to its successful completion and to the maintenance of its gains." Meredith's disciplined and at time austere approach to this dilemma can be deceptively straightforward. He is a sophisticated poet who with his precise and elegant voice finds, frequently within small and otherwise unnoticed domestic and natural events, the sublime. His moral quest for personal, public, and artistic order, even while acknowledging humankind's tendency toward disorder, is a steadfast source of amazement and poetic inspiration.

Published in 1944 as part of the Yale Series of Younger Poets, *Love Letter from an Impossible Land* is one of Meredith's apprentice works, a collection of poems (a few written while Meredith was still an undergraduate) that is highly imitative. This work displays a willing commitment to traditional form, meter, and rhyme. Meredith's academic style mirrors the work of many poets, including Matthew Arnold, William Butler Yeats, and W. H. Auden, as well as the Metaphysical poets of the seventeenth century. Although these poems are products of war, they do not impugn its moral validity. Meredith views the many negative results of war—chaos, despair, and death—with a discriminating eye as he attempts to ascertain meaning and purpose in a world that appears to be self-destructing. Several poems here are predictable studies in form, the ultimate purpose appearing to be maintaining the form in question rather than permitting any organic expansion of theme. Others show a willingness to debate spiritual issues, a directness of thought (Meredith's restraint and impersonal tone hinder this), and a use of colloquial diction.

Although many poems in this volume, especially those that adhere to a prescribed form, are not as successful as those that transcend traditional boundaries, this is not to say that all the poems that fall into the imitative category fail. Employing the form of a sonnet and an impersonal voice, "In Memoriam of Stratton Christensen" subtly inquires about the meaning of Stratton Christensen's death. The speaker states, "Your death is a puzzler that will tease them on," refusing to admit that the young airman's loss of life can be totally understood.

By far the most successful poems in this collection are those that stray from academic formalism, employing a more immediate voice and striking imagery. "Love Letter from an Impossible Land," "June: Dutch Harbor," and "Notes for an Elegy" are poems that could have been written by an experienced hand. In these poems, Meredith allows a more mature voice to emerge. In "Notes for an Elegy," the comforting tones usually supplied by an elegy vanish as the speaker attempts to comprehend another airman's death, a death not met during battle. The speaker claims that death is "a fair price" for the power of flight, which he equates with freedom. After discussing the aviator's death and the hope that God will "lift [him] gently," the speaker concludes, "The morning came up foolish with pink clouds/ To say that God counts ours a cunning time,/ Our losses part of an old secret, somehow not loss." Ambiguity persists (for example, in the words "cunning" and "secret"), as death retains an inscrutable aura. The airman's death may not be as significant or easily explained as the speaker desires, yet he searches for signs that will counteract what appears to be a random and tragic event.

Written while Meredith was a Woodrow Wilson Fellow at Princeton University, his second volume, *Ships and Other Figures*, is another uneven collection of mostly benign, imitative poetry. The urgency displayed by several war poems in *Love Letter from an Impossible Land* has disappeared. The immediacy of death, which Meredith vividly confronts in his first collection, is muted in this book. Henry Taylor suggests that "one feels the absence of peril in these poems, the safety of academe." Meredith's fascination with fixed forms, order, and how order can reflect and contain what is created, dominates these poems, hindering their immediacy and thematic development. Frequently the speaker's voice is lost in the poet's unflagging determination to perform within the confines of a particular form or in a cultivated flatness of voice that at times is bereft of passion or sincerity.

"Carrier," one of Meredith's war poems, succeeds in capturing some of the introspective urgency found in his earlier war poems. The carrier is personified as "huge and peacock vain," a mother who watches "her sprung creatures" as they fly away and "disappear." The airmen who fly from her deck must view her, upon return from a mission, as a safe haven where they can recoup their energies for other missions. Nevertheless, the danger of battle is distant in the poem. The speaker states that there is "far-off dying" with which the personified ship and the crew must contend, but the poem ends without bringing the deadly uncertainty of battle to the reader.

One of the more engrossing poems in this collection (which is revised and retitled in *Partial Accounts: New and Selected Poems*) is "Homeric Simile." The pitch of an air battle is likened to the developmental section of a composition for string quartet. The poem begins with a bomber on a night mission. The threat of "the hostile terrain" below the aircraft is real; the people manning the bomber sense the possibility of death as the navigator leads them to the target. What seems to be a logically staged event becomes chaotic, and the artificial order shatters. Fire and smoke appear below; tracers and searchlights rise to meet the aircraft; friends in other airplanes are killed. Yet the momentary confusion of battle gives way to a musical performance in which "the calm intelligent strings do their duty." The battle is compared to a group of instruments working toward a clear, unified end. The dissonance the instruments have encountered during developmental sections of the composition ultimately concludes in triadic harmony "after uncertain passage." Order eventually returns to the airmen's and the musicians' worlds. Meredith's urge to find order and meaning, even in the face of chaos and death, supersedes, and in some way legitimizes, the horrors of a war.

Ten years passed before Meredith's third volume of poetry was published. In many respects *The Open Sea and Other Poems* can be viewed as his first mature collection. Meredith's penchant for order survives, yet he adds another dimension by questioning the conditions of order and meaning. The poems here are intellectually superior to and more sophisticated than his previous work. The volume contains poems that still adhere to fixed forms and display technical and artistic skill; however, Meredith also displays a willingness to experiment with these forms. Richard Howard writes, "This third book insists on the autonomy of art, and with it of form." "The Open Sea" (a sestina), "Sonnet on Rare Animals," and "The Illiterate" (a Petrarchan sonnet) display Meredith's graceful concern with form but do not overshadow or stifle his artistic desire to express thoughts about possession and loss. "The Chinese Banyan," set in iambic trimeter, evinces a newfound willingness to go beyond mere acceptance of a prescribed order. His tone is at times playful and deceptively commonplace, as in "Bachelor" and "Thoughts on One's Head (IN PLASTER, WITH A BRONZE WASH)." When he demonstrates the most control over his lines, as in "Rus in Urbe," the preciseness of the language impinges on the subject matter of the poem. The carefully pruned garden can produce fruit, which implies that well-measured lines might offer meaning rather than contrived artifice. Occasionally Meredith falters, as in "In Memory of Donald A. Stauffer," and his poems begin to sound like work found in his second volume. Even a poem such as "To a Western Bard Still a Whoop and a Holler Away from English Poetry," which is a sincere yet misguided attempt in quatrains to express Meredith's dissatisfaction with the experimentation of Allen Ginsberg and the Beats, falls flat.

The beautiful sestina "Notre Dame de Chartres" is an excellent example of how a more mature Meredith limns humankind's attempt to order chaos through art and find a hint of salvation and meaning within that order. Meredith's tone is relaxed as he explores the urge to order. When the faithful find the "Sancta Camisa" (holy shirt) after fire has destroyed the first church and town, they raise a far greater church, "the vast basilica," which will house the shirt in royal fashion. Yet it is "faith that burned / Bright and erroneous" that creates the architectural marvel. The inclusion of the word "erroneous" suggests that the manifestation of order, in this case the cathedral, arises from a loving faith that somehow is tainted and perhaps even false. Yet the final stanza suggests that despite the speaker's obvious reservations, he finds some validity in the order created by "the blessed shirt," which "spoke to the stone that slept in the groin of France."

The publication of *The Wreck of the Thresher and Other Poems* in 1964 marked Meredith's entry into the ranks of important contemporary poets. Gone is the occasionally overbearing concern with fixed form and the infringement of institutional authority. The poems found here are more personal (although never confessional) and less academic, using a voice that is sometimes reminiscent of the better poems in *Love Letter from an Impossible Land*. Meredith's friendships with both Robert Frost and John Berryman, which developed between the publication of *The Open Sea and Other Poems* and this volume, are evident in his use of colloquial language, his narrative technique, and his wry humor. Frost's influence is perhaps best illustrated in "Roots," in which Mrs. Lemmington reflects on her past, her mortality, and her ultimate return to the earth. Her fascination with roots as inversions of branches and leaves is a metaphorical and biological fusion of the historical past and future with the present. As with Frost, the tree (as well as the sea in Meredith's case) becomes a contemplative symbol.

Again, Meredith is concerned with order in a world that is fraught with disorder and chaos. Death is the arbitrary destroyer of any ordering done by humankind, whether on a grand scale or in the quiet confines of one's home. In "On Falling Asleep to Birdsong" the speaker, who is near sleep, hears the lone call of a whippoorwill. Rather than finding solace in the call, which must be very familiar, the speaker thinks about his parents and his own mortality. Convinced that "this is a question of will," he dreams of nightingales, and this thought leads him to Ovid's story of the rape of Philomela. Unable to break free of his own mortality, the speaker hears the whippoorwill's call again and understands its implication of courage in the face of disorder and mortality.

The poem "The Wreck of the *Thresher*" represents Meredith at his most eloquent. This poem is a probing, if somewhat dramatic elegy inspired by the *Thresher* disaster of 1963 in which the nuclear submarine's crew perished. The limits of technology, which is an extension of the human urge to order, are addressed, as are the mystery of human existence and nature's capacity to assimilate human grief. The speaker concedes that all attempts to create order are regularly threatened, that safety, especially the safety of technology, is mostly imagined, and that destruction haunts all human activity. He admits that "the bottom here is too far down for our sounding;/ The ocean was salt before we crawled to tears." The mysteries of the sea and death remain unfathomable. Although the speaker acknowledges the fragility of any attempt to order, especially where the sea is involved, he also leaves the reader with a sense that without the perpetual and valorous urge to invent and reinvent order, only disorder, chaos, and death are left.

Earth Walk: New and Selected Poems contains fifty-three poems, fourteen of which are new works. Meredith's selection of his previous work is heavily weighted toward *The Open Sea and Other Poems* and *The Wreck of the Thresher and Other Poems.* His introduction reveals an awareness that the poems in his two latter volumes are more accomplished and that those selected "engage mysteries I still pluck at the hems of." Meredith's choices also emphasize his near obsession with human ordering; these poems tend to examine and approve humankind's attempt to stave off despair by creating order. The new poems in this volume are straightforward, utilizing an assortment of points of view and a cultivated innocence that at times startles and deceives. Meredith does not abandon the fixed form, but his formal poems tend to be less hampered than many of his earlier attempts. His tone is both conversational and immediate. Many poems are open and narrative in nature without heavy use of rhyme, as in "In Memory of Robert Frost." The numerous gains made in earlier volumes are reaffirmed and strengthened here. The poem "Earth Walk" is a fine example of the new flexibility in Meredith's style. The poem's freedom with point of view, the irregular rhyme, the brief, almost playful allusions to space technology and mortality, and the wry, casual humor illustrate his ability to move beyond his original confines and to explore earth's riddles freely.

In "Winter Verse for His Sister" Meredith utilizes a contemplative tone as the speaker, a thinly disguised Meredith, practices for death by going "to that other house/ Where our parents did most of their dying,/ Embracing and not embracing their conditions." The natural world appears to be indifferent, above the questions being asked or at least "noncommittal," as the speaker fruitlessly tries to discover some meaning in life and death—something Mer- . edith grudgingly must leave unresolved.

Another poem that tackles nature's mysteries is "Walter Jenks' Bath," in which a young African American contemplates the meaning of atoms and how they compose matter. The boy's conclusion is best illustrated by the last few lines of the poem: "Even if I died the parts would go on spinning,/ Alone, like far stars, not knowing it." Meredith's spirit is present in this young man's realization that there is a viable connection between the particles that compose his body and those of the universe. Within this connection, however extemporaneous, the boy imagines an inclusive, orderly system.

Meredith's sixth collection of poetry, *Hazard, the Painter,* is a slim volume containing only sixteen poems, all of which are somewhat autobiographical. In his opening note to the reader, Meredith states, "Resemblances between the life and character of Hazard and those of the author are not disclaimed but are fewer than the author would like." The poems focus on the life of a less-than-important middle-aged American painter who is a witness to his own slow decay as well as a country "in late imperial decline." Meredith does not attempt to present Hazard as a complete individual; the poems are an incomplete portrait of his tenuous and at times disordered life. Most events examined in this volume are small domestic occurrences, rituals that make up everyday life; there are also satirical meditations on existence and hesitant reflections on death. The colloquial spontaneity of these poems, an influence of Berryman more than Frost, can be ingratiating. Beneath the surface of Hazard's daily perambulations and interior monologues, Meredith is at work, taking a hard look at the United States in the 1970's. The disintegration Hazard discovers is a direct threat to his concept of order and meaning.

In "Hazard Faces a Sunday in the Decline," the painter yearns for a vanished civility as he presides over his family's dinner table. He is comfortable in the material sense and cautiously optimistic, yet he recognizes his culture's deterioration as well as his family's failings. He accepts the challenge before him (although he can never succeed in imposing his personal order upon the world) and reflects, "Someone has fed us and blessed us," but adds, "with the manners of bohemia. Among barbarians,/ a lot is expected of us, ceremony-wise./ We rise to that expectation." In "Hazard's Optimism" he grapples with his own shortcomings as well as "morale in a morbid time." He has been working on one painting for two years. Much of his time is spent daydreaming, not at his canvas. His lack of success with his painting is emblematic of humankind's ultimate failure to give a lasting order to existence. Yet his attempt to bring temporary order to life through his art, in the face of decay and death, is all-important. The struggle permits Hazard, and others who challenge disorder, a small portion of dignity.

Hazard's concerns about America are most evident in "Nixon's the One." As Hazard tries to remove McGovern-Shriver stickers from his cars after the Democratic Party's loss in the 1972 presidential race, he muses, "Who were all those cheering on the gray glass/ screen last night, loving their violent darling,/ America, whom they had married to money?" His poignant, rather estranged acknowledgment "that his nation has bitterly misspoken itself" is disheartening. In Hazard's mind, the country has become a vast desert of consumerism, greedily oblivious to a senseless war as long as profits continue to materialize.

Hazard senses that life and death are controlled by random forces. Nature cannot be permanently ordered by humankind. In "Squire Hazard Walks" he casually ruminates on death and how "the cat will be disassembled/ in his own time by underground technicians." Yet any attempt to draw a personal analogy is stymied by Hazard as his "thought turns chicken." The life-sustaining order that he so desperately needs comes in the last poem, "Winter: He Shapes Up." Meredith returns symbolically to the quatrain and to slant rhymes. Hazard is painting again, "gnawed by a vision of rightness." He reasons that life, whether it be public or private, can be measured only by "a few things made by men,/ a galaxy made well." This is all that is afforded humankind. Hazard realizes that in the face of chaos, he must paint, attempt to nurture order, and endure, even though he sees the incongruous realities before him.

The Cheer contains thirty-five poems that are highly reflective of Meredith's primary thematic interest. Some of the poems are formal, but much of the work found in this volume is informal, and some leans towards experimentation, as in "Give and Take." Meredith's thematic interests are well seasoned by his acceptance, or at least recognition, of the painful limits and possibilities of human existence, as shown in "Examples of Created Systems." There is never a suggestion, however, that the individual should acquiesce and accept decay and disorder. Again, Meredith finds value in the heroic posture of resistance. He says in the opening piece, "The Cheer," that "words addressing evil won't turn evil back/ but they can give heart./ The cheer is hidden in the right words." Despair is not the answer: "Against evil, between evils, lovely words are right." The poet brings cheer, and not a small amount of hope, to a world that sits perilously close to despair, chaos, and death.

As an icebreaker works to clear a path through the ice on the river at midnight in "Winter on the River," the temporary relief and order the vessel brings symbolize the prescribed formula against the harsh realities of this world. Humankind's dependence on nature, which constantly intrudes on the human will to create and order, is evident as the icebreaker moves past the speaker and the ice-making cold reclaims the river. Antithetical states are constantly observed and analyzed in Meredith's poetry. To defeat or at least to delay the inevitable negative state is a formidable task.

"Two Masks Unearthed in Bulgaria" and "Homage to Paul Mellon, I. M. Pei, Their Gallery, and Washington City" show how creativity (not only in the artistic sense) can defy mortality by producing meaningful constructs that act as bridges between generations and centuries. Even though a specific creation is made within a certain time frame, it can transcend temporality because it employs materials that connect it to the past and the future. Such a realization permits the creative mind to continue in the face of chaos, because it implies continuity, a way to bring thoughts of order and meaning to bear on ever-present decay.

Several poems in this volume view mortality with a discerning eye. In "Trelawny's Dream," Edward John Trelawny struggles with his part in his friend Percy Bysshe Shelley's death. Speaking from middle age, Trelawny has spent most of his life attempting to understand the meaning of the tragedy and assuage his feelings of guilt. Trelawny's attempt to find meaning in the deadly tragedy, the loss of a great poet and his companions, is his way of bringing order to an event that defies explanation. The inexplicable randomness of death is what Trelawny is facing; he states, "Though I am still a strong swimmer/ I can feel this channel widen as I swim." Although Trelawny must ultimately fail, his heroic attempt to find meaning gives his troubled life dignity and purpose.

Meredith's eighth volume, *Partial Accounts*, is a retrospective collection of nearly fifty years of writing. Of the 104 poems included in the volume, only eleven are new. The recent material is very much in tune with his mature work and his thematic concerns. Meredith refuses to yield to confessionalism and other poetic trends; this collection is modest and illustrates his lifelong desire, which is documented in "What I Remember the Writers Telling Me When I Was Young," to use a polished reticence to tackle the sublime. The title of the book suggests that something positive has been accomplished, yet there is still much to do. Meredith's understanding of existence and the ramifications of life's tendency toward chaos would never permit him to make a greater claim. Philosophical closure, even if attractive, is not permitted in a world that resists order and defies explanation with its randomness. The poet remains quite optimistic in the face of the bleak reality confronting everyday life. Again, Meredith sees the poet's role as one that brings good cheer, a little comfort, hope, and a temporary refutation of disorder. "The Jain Bird Hospital in Delhi" focuses on the Jains' small acts of compassion to injured birds as evidence of humanity's potential for caring and an undeniable connection between humankind and nature.

Another poem that represents what Meredith has worked so many years to say is "Among Ourselves," which looks at the way people seem to court stories of suffering and disaster but never relish their personal tales of happiness and success. After the guests have departed, the speaker asks, "Why do we never recount that,/ friends? And our lives,/ what about them? Our sweet, deliberate lives?" Meredith's determination to spread good cheer rather than supporting the bleaker, mortal side of existence is understandable, yet he has been criticized for his imperturbability.

One of the more important new poems in this collection is "The American Living-Room: A Tract." The quiet, personal, and self-critical voice Meredith employs in this poem quickly brings the reader into the speaker's confidence. The speaker states, "Ideally, you should be in your own/ when you read this." After a diatribe on individualism and on how fortunate Americans are to have enough rooms to label one the living room when many people have nothing, he comments that the living room is used for living but is also a repository of absurdity and clutter. The occupant can be identified by the room's contents: "To others/ this room is what your scent is to a dog./ You can't know it or help it." The final stanza moves away from the nature of living rooms to the nature of poetry: "With us in America, a person who has a printed poem/ is likely to have a living room." Poetry "has somehow gone along/ with the privileges of the nation/ it intends to change, to dispossess of material demons." Meredith's outcry against American materialism—which, in a way, fuels the reader's ability to purchase his book—is only temporary, for he has a modest request. His poem (and indeed all of his poetry) "would like nothing better/ than to be added to the dear clutter here." Again, Meredith calls his readers to look beyond the difficulties of life and be thankful, and he hopes they will accept his poetry into the clutter of their lives, where it might, if only for a brief time, offer a renewal of spirit and a modicum of order.

Robert Bateman

Other major works

TRANSLATION: *Alcools: Poems 1898-1913*, 1964.

EDITED TEXTS: *Shelley*, 1962; *Eighteenth Century English Minor Poets*, 1968 (with Mackie L. Jarrell); *Poets of Bulgaria*, 1986 (translated by John Balaban).

MISCELLANEOUS: *The Bottle Imp*, 1958.

Bibliography
Howard, Richard. "William Meredith: 'All of a Piece and Clever and at Some Level, True.'" In *Alone With America: Essays on the Art of Poetry in the United States Since 1950*. New York: Atheneum, 1980. An enlightening (al-

though short) study of Meredith's work through *Hazard, the Painter.* Howard's concern with Meredith's quest for "order and delight," using a style that "is partly evasive and sly, party loving and solicitous," is informed and scholarly.

Ludwig, Richard M. "The Muted Lyrics of William Meredith." *Princeton University Library Chronicle* 25 (Autumn 1963): 73-85. An early and essential critical study of Meredith's first three volumes of poetry. The article includes other writers' comments about Meredith, a biographical sketch, and a comprehensive list of early Meredith publications.

Meredith, William. "The Frost Tradition: A Conversation with William Meredith." Interview by Gregory Fitz Gerald and Paul Ferguson. *Southwest Review* 57 (Spring, 1972): 108-117. This interview, originally produced for television, provides a brief look at Meredith's thoughts and influences. The questions cover a wide range of topics, including his World War II poetry, much of his work up to *Earth Walk*, the importance of Frost and others, the translating of Apollinaire's poetry, and Meredith's fascination with form.

Rotella, Guy. *Three Contemporary Poets of New England: William Meredith, Philip Booth, and Peter Davison.* Boston: Twayne, 1983. Among the most thorough and important analyses of Meredith's poetry available. The text includes biographical notes and a detailed bibliography. Rotella places Meredith firmly in the New England tradition, concluding that he is an important twentieth century poet who is not strictly "an unreconstructed academic formalist," as some critics claim, but a poet who "still seeks hopefully for an ordered life and art, for meaning and value, to affirm and to praise."

Taylor, Henry. " 'In Charge of Morale in a Morbid Time': The Poetry of William Meredith." *Hollins Critic* 16 (February, 1979): 1-15. One of the more probing investigations of Meredith's poetry through *Hazard, the Painter.* Taylor sees Meredith's voice, beginning with *The Wreck of the Thresher and Other Poems*, as civilized and "engaged in encounters of inexhaustible interest." Taylor views his frequent use of form as "method, not a barrier."

JAMES MERRILL

Born: New York, New York; March 3, 1926

Principal poetry

First Poems, 1951; *The Country of a Thousand Years of Peace and Other Poems*, 1959, 1970; *Water Street*, 1962; *Nights and Days*, 1966; *The Fire Screen*, 1969; *Braving the Elements*, 1972; *Divine Comedies*, 1976; *Mirabell: Books of Number*, 1978; *Scripts for the Pageant*, 1980; *The Changing Light at Sandover*, 1982; *From the First Nine: Poems 1946-1976*, 1982; *Late Settings*, 1985; *The Inner Room*, 1988.

Other literary forms

The Seraglio (1957, 1987) and *The (Diblos) Notebook* (1965) are both novels. *Recitative* (1986) collects a number of James Merrill's essays. He has also written plays: *The Immortal Husband* (first produced in 1955 and published in *Playbook* the following year) and *The Bait*, published in *Artists' Theatre* in 1960.

Achievements

James Merrill has been a major voice in American poetry ever since 1967, when he won his first National Book Award for *Nights and Days*. *Braving the Elements* won the Bollingen Prize in Poetry, and *Divine Comedies* won the Pulitzer Prize. He was awarded another National Book Award for *Mirabell: Books of Number*. *The Changing Light at Sandover*, which combines *Divine Comedies*, *Mirabell*, and *Scripts for the Pageant* with a coda, won the National Book Critics Circle Award. Known as a lyric poet and recognized as a master of traditional poetic forms, Merrill stands among the first rank of poets in the United States.

Biography

James Ingram Merrill was born in New York City to Charles Merrill, an extremely powerful and successful stockbroker and founder of the firm that is now Merrill Lynch. His mother, Hellen Ingram Merrill, was Charles Merrill's second wife. When James Merrill was twelve years old, his parents were divorced. His father married a third time, and that marriage also ended in divorce.

Merrill was graduated in 1947 from Amherst College, where he wrote a senior thesis on Marcel Proust. He served in the U.S. Army from 1944 to 1945. For fifteen years, beginning in 1959, he spent part of each year at his home in Greece. He has traveled widely in other countries, but makes his primary home in Stonington, Connecticut.

Analysis

James Merrill's poetry is lyrical, and most of it is written in traditional forms. He is, indeed, a master of the lyric; his ingenious rhymes and subtle utilization of the envelope quatrain (one of his favorite forms), the sonnet, and other forms are almost overwhelming. Helen Vendler, one of the country's best-known critics, has called his lyrical gift "ravishing." The poems in his first six books were mostly short ones, but with the publication of *Divine Comedies* he began writing a series of long narrative poems that he brought together in *The Changing Light at Sandover.* Since then a considerable amount of critical attention has been given to this novel in verse. Merrill's concerns include the family, love, change and metamorphosis, the appeal of opposites, and the differences and similarities of imagination and reality. In many poems these concerns are almost inextricably intertwined. Themes from one book appear again in subsequent volumes, as do characters, sometimes commenting on the former work. His methods include humor, especially the humor of irony and of puns, the quoting or paraphrasing of the work of other writers, various narrative techniques, and one technique that might be called philosophical—the construction of a new order for the universe. Informing both his themes and his methods is his immense sense of play.

Merrill's *First Poems* includes "Transfigured Bird," four variations on a theme from childhood. Critics have assumed that the child in the poem is Merrill himself. This poem indicates a number of things about the child: his sense of isolation, his loneliness, and, most important, his discovery that things are often not what they seem at first glance. This book and the one that followed it eight years later, *The Country of a Thousand Years of Peace,* both include poems about love, but the poet's carefully controlled forms and reticent language seem to evade the expression of feelings. For this reason, many critics found Merrill's early work cold and viewed his poetic technique as a mask that seemed to hide his emotions. As W. H. Auden had done, Merrill addressed his love poems to an anonymous "you," thus disguising his homosexuality. This reticence seemed to be particularly handicapping because Merrill chose not to explore the world of current events or the world of ideas, where emotion would not be essential. His personal subject matter seemed to cry out for feeling. This second volume includes Merrill's first poem about the world of the Ouija board—a world that would assume major significance in the later work, but which he dismisses at this point.

Water Street represents a major change. In this volume the narrator's voice becomes identifiable as that of Merrill himself. For the first time poems that are clearly confessional are included; yet they are confessional only in that they begin to utilize material that is perhaps neurotic, distressing, or humiliating and anguish-filled. Merrill is not one of the confessional poets who spill their lives and feelings wantonly. Having always valued good manners, he does not violate them here; he writes with restraint, but with power and feeling. In fact, the last stanza in the book is a kind of introduction to the new way he will treat his material. "If I am host at last," he writes, "it is of little more than my own past./ May others be at home in it." Thus he begins to push aside the mask.

Memories of childhood and loneliness are still evident, as in "A Vision of a Garden," in which Merrill shows the reader the picture of a solitary little boy who draws a face with his finger on a winter-frosted window. This poem, while beginning with the child, ends with the adult who has found a lover "whose words whose looks alone undo/ such frosts." There are poems about the family, too, and in this volume Merrill plunges deeper into both family and romantic relationships.

In his third book, *Nights and Days*, which won the National Book Award, he includes a series of seven sonnets, exploring his feelings about his parents. Although violence and anger are masked, powerful emotion is communicated when he writes that in his father's blue gaze he can see "the soul eclipsed by twin black pupils, sex/ and business; time was money in those days." Although the chief character of the book's final poem is a woman (who in one scene wears makeup that turns her face into a clown's mask), the poem's title, "Days of 1964," alludes to the titles used by C. P. Cavafy for poems about homosexual liaisons. In this volume Merrill moves closer to expressing his true feelings.

Judith Moffett writes of Merrill's next book, *The Fire Screen*, that it does not seem to advance the work. On the other hand, Stephen Yenser finds that in it the narrative impulse predominates, and that in use of anecdote and character "Kostas Tympakianakis" points toward Merrill's later long narratives. In almost every collection Merrill includes at least one poem that concerns family; in this volume, it is "Mornings in a New House," which includes the lines that give the volume its title. He shows a cold man in a new house in front of its fireplace. He thinks about the fire screen stitched in crewel by his mother when she was a child. The screen, depicting giant birds and flowery trees, is a kind of embroidery made from lustrous threads, but threads that have been crossed, recrossed, and knotted—not unlike, perhaps, the relationships between mother and child. Love is a theme of several of these poems, but it is artfully veiled. In the volume's first poem, "Lorelei," the narrator speaks of an unnamed loved one, saying that each stepping-stone has stranded "you." Next Merrill's typical opposites appear, and he changes, saying, "Does not. Not yet. Not here./ Is it a crossing? Is there no way back?"

Merrill's next book, *Braving the Elements*, is significant in several ways. First, it is replete with puns and numerous other wordplays, as his previous books were, but they are even more evident and delightful here. He uses these methods in "The Emerald," another poem about both family and love. In this poem his mother gives him an emerald ring that his father had given her when when his son was born. It is for his future wife, she says. Although the poem says that he does not tell his mother, he is telling the reader that he is homosexual, that he will not marry and father children.

> I do not tell her, it would sound theatrical,
> *Indeed this green room's mine, my very life.*
> *We are each other's; there will be no wife*;
> *The little feet that patter here are metrical.*

In the final poem in the book, the last four words, arranged in a cross pattern, illustrate Merrill's persisting love for antithesis. The words, to be read first down and then across, are "Nought/ Sought/ Waste   Erased." They cancel one another out in one sense, but in another sense, if nothing is looked for, then the time one might have spent looking is not erased at all, but is available for other purposes. Still, it may be wasted because nothing worthwhile was tried. Merrill would have it both ways.

Although Merrill has frequently used narrative elements in his poems, and has in fact written two novels, in this volume he presents his most significant narrative so far. "Days of 1935" combines his concern with family, his childhood loneliness, and his narrative imagination. The little rich boy who has appeared in many previous poems knows about the Lindberg kidnapping and in his fancy constructs his own kidnappers, Floyd and Jean, who seem extremely interesting, however sinister. In the end, however, although they have snatched him out of his ordinary life and transported him into their illicit one, they let his parents take him back. He is abandoned to his mother's "Grade/ A controls" and his father's provisions, the latter implying that the father was more likely to give gifts than time or love. This pattern of rescue and return is one that will repeat itself in his grown-up love affairs—the excitement of the early interest and then the desertion. Merrill draws this parallel clearly in another poem in this volume, "Days of 1971," in which he defines love:

> Proust's Law (are you listening?) is twofold:
> (a) What least thing our self-love longs for most
> Others instinctively withhold;
>
> (b) Only when time has slain desire
> Is his wish granted to a smiling ghost
> Neither harmed nor warmed, now, by the fire.

One of Merrill's most significant books, *Divine Comedies* was published in 1976; it contains "The Book of Ephraim," a long narrative poem that was to become part 1 of the trilogy *The Changing Light at Sandover.* Judith Moffett says of it, "This suspension bridge joining the body of Merrill's earlier poetry to his *Sandover* trilogy may well be ultimately adjudged his finest single piece of writing." This long poem, essentially the beginning of a journey of discovery about the nature of God, grew out of the experience Merrill and his friend and lover, David Jackson, had over a period of years with a Ouija board. The two had shared houses since 1955 in Stonington, Connecticut; Athens, Greece; and Key West, Florida. Soon after they had moved into their Stonington house, the two were whiling away an evening at the Ouija board when something extraordinary began to happen. The cup that they were using for a pointer began to spin furiously and spelled out letter after letter, which Merrill began copying down as rapidly as possible. They were being visited by a familiar from the spirit world, one Ephraim, who explained that he was a homosexual Greek Jew who became a servant of the Roman Emperor Tiberius. The first story line in the book has to do with the relationship between JM (Merrill) and DJ (Jackson) and their relationship to the garrulous, humorous, but not altogether reliable Ephraim. One of Ephraim's major teachings is that God is imagination. Ephraim serves as an instructor to the two younger men about the science of the soul after death. The second line in the plot involves characters from a novel that Merrill was writing and whose manuscript he lost in a taxi in Georgia. These characters are Eros, a person who seems to resemble Ephraim; Sergei Markovich, who may incorporate characteristics of Merrill; a Mrs. Rosamund Smith; Leon Cade, a Vietnam veteran who has suffered some horrifying experiences in the war; and others. The third line has to do with the writing of the poem. Both JM and DJ comment on what Ephraim tells them, express doubts, and have reservations. Later, other characters appear, including Hans Lodeizen, a young Dutch poet who died of leukemia in 1950; Maya Deren, an avant-garde dancer and filmmaker who was a friend of both JM and DJ; and the poet W. H. Auden, who had recently died.

Besides opening up the exploration of the question of the nature of God, this poem continues Merrill's interest in the nature of love. In fact, as Merrill approaches middle age, he finds that "we've wanted/ Consuming passions; these refine instead . . . Yield such regret and wit as MERRILY/ GLOW ON when limbs licked blazing past recall/ Are banked where interest is minimal." This poem is full of typical Merrill wordplays and, though focused on an otherworldly chronicle, still evidences Merrill's concern with family. Details about JM and DJ's everyday life and worries are included with the more esoteric and metaphysical work. The poem describes David Jackson's aged parents living in the West, still "at each other's gnarled,/ Loveless mercy." It speaks as well of Merrill's father, who

> in his last illness complained
> Of the effect of medication on
> His real self—today Bluebeard, tomorrow
> Babbitt. Young chameleon, I used to
> Ask how on earth one got sufficiently
> imbued with otherness. And now I see.

This passage again illustrates Merrill's opposites, and his fascination with illusion and reality.

Mirabell, which becomes Part 2 of the Sandover trilogy, is unlike "The Book of Ephraim" in several ways. In "The Book of Ephraim," Merrill wrote the story; in this second part, and again in part 3, the spirits dictate the material. After Ephraim's book was finished, one day in 1976 Merrill and Jackson were engaged in what they considered would be a friendly chat with the spirits. Instead, some strange, dreadful powers intruded and ordered Merrill to write "poems of science," because, they insisted, the work was not finished yet. After accepting their dictates, Merrill and Jackson found themselves giving hours every day to the Ouija board. Merrill spent additional hours transcribing and trying to make sense of the voluminous messages, and eventually gave them both a poetic shape and a narrative structure. What resulted is a mythology to account for the new science that has discovered black holes and other astronomical anomalies, as well as the mysteries of the cell and physical chemistry. This is an intriguing reversal of the world's other genesis mythologies in that all of those were prescientific whereas this mythology provides stories to explain the scientifically known. In the beginning Merrill was uneasy because he did not have control of the material and resented that "it's all by someone else." Moreover, both Merrill and Jackson were uncomfortable with some of the things the spiritual messengers told them, especially their insistence on determinism and elitism. Nevertheless, Merrill eventually came to look forward to the enormous work of each day; he told Helen Vendler in an interview published in 1979, "I woke up day after day beaming with anticipation."

The spirits provide the myths to explain God Biology, who is referred to thereafter as God B. These spirits who begin *Mirabell* are bats. They have numbers for names and are metaphorically the rebellious angels; they are also antimatter itself, as well as the negative electrical charge within the atom. Other characters arrive also—many of them, fortunately, more benevolent. Auden has a large role, as does JM and DJ's old friend Maria Mitsotaki. These two act, in a certain sense, as surrogate parents for JM and DJ, Auden addressing them as "MY BOYS" and Maria calling them "MES ENFANTS." These two characters have several other functions as well. Auden suggests poetic techniques to JM when the poet is struggling for an adequate form. Furthermore, he is at first the most skeptical of all the students. This works very well, because Auden had a skeptical, inquiring nature, yet his eventual adoption of the traditional Anglican faith is well known. His voice can thus lend authenticity to the bizarre proceedings. Maria, unlike Auden, was not a public figure; she was a Greek friend of JM and DJ. She serves as both a mother figure and an example of life's strange unknowns: They discover that her death was not natural but instead a suicide. Later they also learn that her brilliant mind is really that of one of the Five Immortals.

In part 3 other friends, four angels, the Nine Muses, two numbered familiars, and other characters also appear. *Mirabell* is the most dense of the three parts and includes a great many explanations that have a certain tedium. The last two books continue the exploration of the nature of God but concentrate much more on humankind's relationship with nature. The spiritual teachers are appalled at overpopulation and at massive destruction of nature's riches. All of this is lightened by Merrill's puns, spoonerisms, and other kinds of wordplay, and by comments from JM and DJ on what they are being told.

Scripts for the Pageant became part 3 of the trilogy, and in it JM and DJ discover that the *Mirabell* spirits were not completely informed and hence told them some things that were wrong. It also introduces God B's twin, Psyche/Chaos/Mother Nature. It contains further disturbing revelations. The two learned in "The Book of Ephraim" that the first law is SURVIVE and the second is NO ACCIDENTS; now they are instructed about "V Work," the only work that really counts. Further, the spirit guides insist that humans sinned when they discovered how to split the atom and that a kind of apocalypse is coming. The four major characters, drawn together by their strange lessons, puzzle over the happenings. The final stanza of "Samos," the canzone that introduces the last part of *Scripts for the Pageant*, addresses their mutual confusion.

> Samos. We keep trying to make sense
> Of what we can. Not souls of the first water—
> Although we've put on airs, and taken fire—
> We shall be dust of quite another land
> Before the seeds here planted come to light.

This passage is full of puns and wordplay, but it also illustrates the familial feeling of the four students, JM, DJ, Auden, and Maria.

In fact, when it is time for Maria to take her leave to be born again in Bombay, her last speech is of friendship and love. She says that her old life had too few attachments, and then, anticipating her new life, says, "YET IF LOVING'S 88/ PERCENT IS CHEMICAL I ANTICIPATE/ FORMING SOME STRONG NEW BONDS." There is more than a comment on love here; there is also a punning reference to the fact that Maria is to be reborn as a biochemist. Numerous changes have also occurred in this volume, but one of the most startling has to do with Maria. In the "NO" section the readers learn that she is really Plato.

When *The Changing Light at Sandover* appeared, Merrill added a coda both to give a sense of closure to the entire work and to keep the process going. At the end of *Scripts for the Pageant* the poem insists on swirling up, to hear God B one last time. The coda involves returns and also the possibility of new beginnings. Many of the pronouncements in *Mirabell* were as grim as Old Testament prophecy. Perhaps a case could be made for *Scripts for the Pageant*'s making subtle correspondences with the first four books of the New Testament. The coda then may correspond to the New Testament's Book of Acts. The correspondence between the visions of Saint John in Revelation and some of the revelations in this account must not be discounted either.

The Changing Light at Sandover is Merrill's most notable achievement. It will surely be read and studied for years, and it places him among that elite group of poets who have also dared to write their metaphysical visions: William Butler Yeats, William Blake, John Milton, and Dante. It is not surprising that a poet who is a master of poetic forms would turn his hand (or his psyche) to a system. While the systems of Blake, Milton, and Dante were concerned primarily with humanity's relation to God, and Yeats's work was partially concerned with this connection, Merrill's work is more concerned with humans' relationship to the earth on which they live. That this relationship has far-reaching and even theological implications should be no surprise.

It must be noted, however, that although the critic could study the system for its theology, the entire premise—in fact, the machinery that brings the "revelations"—is based on play. One plays with a Ouija board; it is a kind of game. This spirit of play permeates the entire work and is evident especially in the varieties of humor. Some of this is the humor of irony; some of it comes from puns, to which Merrill is addicted; some of it comes from other kinds of wordplay. The entire work merits study for its wordplay alone. One of Merrill's most effective techniques is using a word and meaning more than one of its meanings—frequently several of them at once. This is a technique that was used by Marianne Moore, who introduced some of her best ideas into her work this way. A study of the roots of the words Merrill has carefully chosen yields further clues to the depth of his humor (and his thinking as well).

Throughout Merrill's work, family relations, the nature of love, changes, and the differences between appearance and reality have occupied his attention. He began by writing poems that were relatively short, but branched out into the long narrative poem, which gave him the room to let his imagination range across the whole universe and throughout history (and even prehistory) and to launch sorties into the world of ideas. There is no doubt that the writing of *The Changing Light at Sandover* changed and enlarged his work remarkably.

The year in which *The Changing Light at Sandover* appeared also saw the publication of *From the First Nine*, a selection from Merrill's first nine books of poetry. *Late Settings*, published in 1985, includes some fragments that had been cut from the final *The Changing Light at Sandover*. "From the Cutting-Room Floor" includes bits starring William Carlos Williams, Marianne Moore, and Gertrude Stein, who appears as hostess of *Meet the Press in*

Heaven, interviewing Elvis Presley. The understated humor of these pieces is delightful. The two most important poems in this volume, however, are "Clearing the Title," which has to do with new beginnings, and "Santorini: Stopping the Leak." The latter makes a number of references to persons and places seen in *The Changing Light at Sandover.* The narrator finds himself in the night kicking off his bedclothes, and the sheets flap "like bats in negative"—surely akin to the bats in *Mirabell.* He also passes a chapel to Saint Michael, who was one of the important characters in *Scripts for the Pageant.* Also, the narrator has had X rays to remove a plantar wart on his foot, but as readers know from *The Changing Light at Sandover,* too many X rays can burn up the soul. Now he finds that he has a small ghost-leak in the "foot-sole."

The Inner Room reveals a new twist in Merrill's poetic technique. He had seldom used prose poems, but this volume contains a series of them in a section entitled "Prose of Departure." Because these poems describe a trip to Japan, they include a number of haiku. The Japanese influence is further evident in that the poems echo Bashō Matsuo's travel journals. The most significant part of this book, however, is the brief play *The Image Maker.* The chief character in this play is a *santero,* a carver and repairer of saint statues in a Caribbean village. He is obviously a maker in the Aristotelian sense. He and his society practice Santeria, a Latin American religion that combines Christian concepts with Yoruba lore from West African religions. In Santeria the saints have double characters, their beneficent Christian side and an opposite side that belongs to a pagan deity, Chango, who is violent and chaotic. Merrill's work has always been concerned with doubleness, and this situation provides him with an opportunity to explore it. Although the *santero* has the skill to shape the saints' figures and dress, their inner lives belong equally to good and evil. Thus the maker can provide a symbol but has no control over the actions resulting from his creations. When the *santero* is called away from his combined home and workplace by the voice of the damaged Saint Barbara, who imitates the voice of his sickly and whining mother, the *santos* come to life and their wild and evil selves prevail. Francisco kills the pet dove, and Barbara sets fire to a wall calendar, thus destroying all the holy days. When the *santero* returns, he cleans up the mess, then appeases Chango with cigar smoke and a ceremony, and returns to his work of repairing Barbara.

Merrill here continues some of the concepts from *The Changing Light at Sandover.* Just as the familiars from another world had insisted, the creative artist of any kind does not have control over the effects of creation. God B and Mother Nature lament this fact in *The Changing Light at Sandover.* Although not knowing how a created work will turn out has negative aspects, it can have positive aspects as well. The discovery in the work not only may affect the work but also can have profound effects on the maker. Merrill says, "Writing his or her poems changes a poet, over the years, in ways that perhaps time or society by themselves couldn't."

Moreover, the artist does not know when he or she begins how the product will turn out. The artist is often surprised, because the materials for the work discover their possibilities as the process proceeds. This play affirms the "V Work" and provides, as well, a miniature of one of the major concepts of *The Changing Light at Sandover*—the multifaceted nature of beings. In a simple yet profound way, it demonstrates that cleaning up is one of the virtues and explores once again the complex relationship between reality and illusion.

There is no doubt that the Sandover trilogy has affected Merrill's work. This does not mean that the subsequent poems are lesser. It may mean that as his work continues to take new turns the later work may be glossed by *The Changing Light at Sandover* rather than the reverse. Merrill's work is of major importance for its poetic technique, for his brilliant use of language, and for the quality of the imagination he displays. Moreover, his exploration of metaphysical concerns that are universal and timeless puts it among works of important thought.

Ann Struthers

Other major works

LONG FICTION: *The Seraglio*, 1957, 1987; *The (Diblos) Notebook*, 1965.

PLAYS: *The Immortal Husband*, 1955; *The Bait*, 1960.

NONFICTION: *Recitative*, 1986.

Bibliography

Bloom, Harold, ed. *James Merrill.* Modern Critical Views Series. New York: Chelsea House, 1986. Harold Bloom's introduction to this collection of essays is especially valuable. There is a chronology and an index.

Labrie, Ross. *James Merrill.* Boston: Twayne, 1982. This volume in the Twayne's United States Authors series is the first full-length study of Merrill's poems, fiction, and plays. Contains separate chapters on Merrill's life and art, his plays, his fiction, and his poems of the 1940's and 1950's, and a chapter that analyzes the *Divine Comedies.* Includes an interesting section on Merrill's view of art. Supplemented by a two-page chronology of the poet's life, notes and references, a select bibliography, and an index. Suitable for all students.

Lehman, David, and Charles Berger, eds. *James Merrill: Essays in Criticism.* Ithaca, N.Y.: Cornell University Press, 1982. This volume collects a number of essays on Merrill's work. Especially useful are David Lehman's "Elemental Bravery: The Unity of James Merrill's Poetry," Willard Spiegelman's "Breaking the Mirror: Interruption in Merrill's Trilogy," and David

Jackson's "Lending a Hand." This volume has an index, notes, and a bibliography.

Moffett, Judith. *James Merrill: An Introduction to the Poetry.* New York: Columbia University Press, 1984. Moffett traces Merrill's themes of childhood, family, love, and masking, and the influences on his work of Proust and opera. She uses a chronological method, beginning with his first book, privately published by his father when Merrill was only sixteen. She admires Merrill's work but is critical of passages that she finds too obscure. This volume is an easy-to-read entry into Merrill's work. The text is supplemented by notes, a good selected bibliography, and an index.

Vendler, Helen. "James Merrill." In *Part of Nature, Part of Us: Modern American Poets.* Cambridge, Mass.: Harvard University Press, 1980. The section on Merrill provides informative commentary on *Braving the Elements, Divine Comedies,* and *Mirabell: Books of Number.* Vendler says that in *Braving the Elements* Merrill finally found a use for all of his many talents, including his fondness for narrative and his gift for euphony. Includes a foreword by Vendler and a bibliography of books discussed.

Von Hallberg, Robert. "James Merrill: Revealing by Obscuring." In *American Poetry and Culture, 1945-1980.* Cambridge, Mass.: Harvard University Press, 1985. Von Hallberg asserts that much of Merrill's style—his elegance, good manners, and literary language—comes from his position as part of the American upper class. He addresses Merrill's subversion of his own texts and briefly argues that *The Changing Light at Sandover* was written at least partly out of consideration for David Jackson, his companion.

Yenser, Stephen. *The Consuming Myth: The Work of James Merrill.* Cambridge, Mass.: Harvard University Press, 1987. This study emphasizes Merrill's proclivity for seeing duality while still being aware of the interconnectedness of things. This book is more detailed and complex than Moffett's and addresses in greater depth Merrill's literary references. The text is supplemented by an index, extensive notes, a useful list of Merrill's works, and photographs.

THOMAS MERTON

Born: Prades, France; January 31, 1915
Died: Bangkok, Thailand; December 10, 1968

Principal poetry

Thirty Poems, 1944; *A Man in the Divided Sea*, 1946; *Figures for an Apocalypse*, 1947; *The Tears of the Blind Lions*, 1949; *The Strange Islands*, 1957; *Selected Poems*, 1959, 1967; *Original Child Bomb*, 1962; *Emblems of a Season of Fury*, 1963; *Cables to the Ace*, 1968; *The Geography of Lograire*, 1969; *The Collected Poems*, 1977.

Other literary forms

Better known for his nonfiction prose than his poetry, Thomas Merton has written an autobiography, *The Seven Storey Mountain* (1948); four journals, *The Secular Journal* (1959), *The Signs of Jonas* (1953), *Conjectures of a Guilty Bystander* (1966), and *The Asian Journal of Thomas Merton* (1973); and numerous books of theology and devotion, including *Seasons of Celebration* (1950), *No Man Is an Island* (1955), and *Contemplative Prayer* (1969). His other works include an early novel, published posthumously, *My Argument with the Gestapo* (1969); translations of Church Fathers, including *Clement of Alexandria* (1962) and *The Wisdom of the Desert* (1960); and several works about Eastern religion: *The Way of Chuang Tzu* (1965), *Mystics and Zen Masters* (1967), and *Zen and the Birds of Appetite* (1968). Merton published numerous articles on a similar range of topics in periodicals such as *Commonweal*, *The Catholic Worker*, *The American Benedictine Review*, *Jubilee*, and *The Sewanee Review*. A selection of his photographs and calligraphy has been published by John Howard Griffin in *A Hidden Wholeness*, 1970. His literary essays, introductions, and related materials are collected in *The Literary Essays of Thomas Merton* (1981).

Achievements

A teacher of English literature turned Cistercian monk, Merton bridges two worlds, bringing his considerable skill as a prose stylist to his religious works and turning Catholic dogma into poetry. He has been acclaimed by many critics, with some justification, as the most important religious writer of the mid-twentieth century—a superlative that is, of course, impossible to establish. One thing, however, is certain: neither as influential or skillful a poet as T. S. Eliot or W. H. Auden, nor as important a theologian as Karl Barth or Dietrich Bonhoeffer, Merton is impressive in both areas; among his contemporaries, only C. S. Lewis can rival him. Beyond this there is Merton's importance as an antiparadigm for modern society. His life and writings reveal a mind unwilling to rest in any of the easy philosophies of twentieth century Western culture.

Biography

Thomas Merton was born near Prades, France, in the Pyrenees, on January 31, 1915. His father, Owen Merton, a post-Impressionist painter of some note, was a New Zealander who met his American wife, Ruth, while both were art students in Paris. Because of the dangers of World War I, Merton's family soon moved across the Atlantic to Douglastown, Long Island, to be near his maternal grandparents. There his brother John Paul was born in 1918 and shortly afterward, in 1921, his mother died of stomach cancer. While the younger brother remained in America with his grandparents, young Merton's father took him to Bermuda, France, and England in order to find fit subjects to paint. The stay in France was one of the formative influences on Merton's life, for there he was deeply moved by the "medieval" aspects of French village life, including the Catholic churches that he saw but never entered.

After his removal to England, Merton began his serious education by matriculating at Oakham School in Rutland in 1929. Almost immediately after this, his father contracted brain cancer and died in 1930 after a period of invalidism. This death left the fifteen-year-old Merton orphaned, yet, because of a settlement from his grandfather, financially secure. Only minimally supervised by his grandparents across the Atlantic and a guardian in London, Merton spent his adolescence and early twenties in increasing commitment to two things—literature and dissipation.

He started off on a disastrous walking tour of Germany during one of the academic holidays at Oakham and came back with an infection that developed into a near-fatal case of blood poisoning. In 1936 he matriculated at Clare College, Cambridge, where he began a year of dissipation unusual even for college freshmen, one of the few sober moments of which, it seems, was the winter holiday which he spent touring Rome and visiting the many impressive churches there. On the recommendation of his guardian, he left Cambridge at the end of the school year, realizing that he was wasting his time there. He left England and took up residence with his grandparents on Long Island and matriculated at Columbia University.

At Columbia he was accepted into a circle of literary-minded undergraduates including several who were later successful as writers and editors—Edward Rice, Robert Lax, and Robert Giroux. This relationship led him to channel some of his restless energy into several of Columbia's student publications—forming a habit of regular and prolific writing that never left him. With his friends, he discovered the teaching of Mark Van Doren—a circumstance that convinced Merton to major in English and write a master's thesis under Van Doren, entitled "Nature and Art in William Blake" (1939). His conversion to Catholicism was a process of which the external causes are more difficult to identify than those of his conversion to writing. Among the discernible influences, however, were his enrollment in a course in scholastic philosophy under visiting Professor (later Father) Daniel Walsh, his discovery of the theological writings of Jacques Maritain, his study of the "mysticism" of Blake, and his reading of the journals of Gerard Manley Hopkins. On November 16, 1938, he was baptized a Catholic.

Soon after Merton's conversion two important things happened. First, he began to write poetry, and, second, he began to entertain ideas of devoting himself totally to God by entering one of the religious orders, deciding finally on the Franciscans. He was conditionally accepted, but just days before entering the novitiate, he compulsively confessed doubts about his former way of life to the Franciscan priest who was arranging his vocation. He was consequently turned down as unstable.

Disconsolate, he accepted a position teaching English at the Franciscan St. Bonaventure's University in Olean, New York, as a means of living as close to the monastic life as he could manage as a layman—reciting the Breviary daily and writing religious verse. During this time, dissatisfaction still plagued him; he had gradually given up his dissipations, but life at a Franciscan school in upstate New York seemed too easy—not the total dedication to God that he desired. Two alternate vocations presented themselves to him: joining, in voluntary poverty, the Friendship House in Harlem, a Catholic social agency run by Catherine de Hueck Doherty, or entering the Gethsemani Monastery near Louisville, Kentucky, the Cistercian Abbey he visited for a retreat during Holy Week of 1941. The decision was a difficult one, but the attraction of a contemplative life won out, and he entered Gethsemani on December 10, 1941, only three days after America's entry into World War II.

For a period of time in the late 1940's, Merton considered leaving the Cistercians for the eremitical life of the Order of the Carthusians. He finally perceived this as a temptation, and by the time he progressed through the novitiate, vows, minor clerical orders, and finally the priesthood in 1949, the desire had left him. As soon as he entered Gethsemani, his superiors recognized his abilities as a writer, commissioning him to write books on various monastic topics and especially encouraging his poetry. His four volumes of poetry published in the 1940's attest both to his talent and the initial encouragement of his superiors.

Merton, however, saw his vocation as a writer totally opposed to that as a monk, preferring the humble anonymity of silence to the clatter of the typewriter. In short, he wrote under obedience to his Abbot. The irony of this situation should not escape anyone who reads the poet whose influence over Merton's personal and poetic life is greater than any other—Hopkins. Hopkins, like Merton, an undergraduate convert to Catholicism given to journal writing and poetry, was denied permission to compose verse by his superiors in the Jesuit order. Merton solved his dilemma with a compromise, finding that writing books on theology was actually helping rather than hindering his contemplative tendencies but receiving permission to stop writing poetry. Consequently, he published no volumes of poetry between 1949 and 1957—the period that was his most prolific for prose.

The last period of Merton's life, the decade before his death in 1968, is in many ways the most complex. It is characterized by his sudden and prolific rededication to poetry, his increasing reinvolvement in the world through his social criticism and interest in the civil rights movement, his commitment to the ecumenism and monastic renewal mandated by Vatican II, his increasing interest in Asian religions, and, finally, his retreat in 1965 to a secluded hermitage on the grounds of Gethsemani Abbey where he could devote himself to a life of total prayer and contemplation which incorporated practices both Catholic and Zen. At this stage, he also took up calligraphy and photography as Zen disciplines. This growing love of Oriental religions and ideas led him to leave Gethsemani in the fall of 1968 for an Asian trip to speak at several religious conferences and, more important, to learn at first hand of Hinduism, Sufism, and Buddhism. He visited the Dalai Lama and other religious leaders in India, Sri Lanka, and Thailand, kept a journal, and wrote several poems about his experiences. On December 10, 1968, twenty-seven years to the day after his entry into the monastic life, he delivered a paper in Bangkok, Thailand, to a religious conference; he retired to his room that afternoon and, because of faulty wiring in a large electric fan, died accidentally of electric shock. He left in manuscript a considerable body of work, both poetry and prose—much of which has been published posthumously.

Analysis

As a prose writer who published more than forty volumes of autobiography and theology, Thomas Merton is surprisingly homogenous, dealing with the same themes and subjects, presenting the same insights from slightly different perspectives. Even his books on Asian religions develop Oriental refinements on insights he had already developed from a Western point of view—inner peace and how to achieve it. His poetry, however, is amazingly diverse. In *The Collected Poems*, a volume of more than a thousand pages, echoes can be heard of a widely diverse group of literary figures who attracted his interest: John Donne, T. S. Eliot, James Joyce, Richard Crashaw, Gerard Manley Hopkins, William Blake, George Herbert, Andrew Marvell, Hart Crane, Ezra Pound, William Carlos Williams, and the Provençal troubadours.

This list, however, is not an indication that Merton was a slavishly derivative poet; its diversity alone indicates that part of his creativity was his ability to assimilate so much material. Yet he does more than assimilate; the vast difference between his first volume of verse, *Thirty Poems*, and his last, *The Geography of Lograire*, bespeaks a mind both open to new experiences and able to re-create itself poetically. Unlike many other poets, Merton has more than one thing to say, and much of the aesthetic enjoyment of reading his work is hearing him discover a voice suitable to his subjects.

Thirty Poems contains poems that Merton wrote during his secular years after his conversion to Catholicism and during his first years as a novice at Gethsemani. The thirty short poems are composed in a lyric mode, mainly on religious themes. Some of them are travel poems ("Song for Our Lady of Cobre," "Night Train," "Aubade: Lake Erie"), while most reflect cessation of motion in the dual stability of place ("The Trappist Abbey: Matins") and liturgy ("The Communion," "The Holy Sacrament of the Altar"). The thirty poems chart a journey away from a dangerous world toward a monastic retreat—Merton's physical and mental journey recorded in *The Seven Storey Mountain*—"The Flight Into Egypt," to borrow the title of one of them. Merton's rejection of the world is evident in such poems as "Dirge for the Proud World," "Lent in a Year of War," and the poignant lament, "For my Brother: Reported Missing in Action, 1943."

In *Thirty Poems*, as in much of Merton's early poetry, Hopkins is a strong influence. Merton had even begun a doctoral thesis at Columbia on Hopkins—a project terminated by his monastic vocation. Not only does Merton owe much of his general religious imagery to Hopkins in *Thirty Poems*, he also owes the title and subject matter of "The Blessed Virgin Compared to a Window" to Hopkins' "The Blessed Virgin Mary Compared to the Air We Breathe."

A Man in the Divided Sea, Merton's second volume of poetry, written simultaneously with his first and dedicated to Mary, Queen of poets, is a longer continuation of *Thirty Poems*. The themes of travel ("Tropics," "Calypso's Island," "The Ohio River—Louisville"), rest ("A Letter to My Friends on Entering the Monastery," "After the Night Office—Gethsemani Abbey," "The Trappist Cemetery—Gethsemani"), and retreat from the world ("Poem: 1939," "Dirge for a Town in France," "Ode to the Present Century") function in the same way. This longer, richer volume contains themes missing in the earlier one, notably the sacramental view of nature, in which the woods, fields, and hills around Merton's Abbey become a mystical path running parallel to the liturgical one. Poems such as "April," "Advent" (a poem about winter nights), and "Trappists, Working" (a poem about laboring in the fields) take their place in *A Man in the Divided Sea* beside poems such as "The Candlemas Procession" and "Song for the Blessed Sacrament."

The depth of Merton's reading also becomes evident in this volume, for there are poems on subjects from Greek myths, poetic treatments of several saints, and aubades in imitation of the Provençal troubadours. Merton, like many of his poetic generation, imitates T. S. Eliot: "April" and "Ash Wednesday" owe titles, imagery, and prosody to the Eliot of *The Waste Land* (1922). More important than these influences is that of the seventeenth century Metaphysical poets. Merton admits in his autobiography that Andrew Marvell's rhymed octosyllabic couplets shaped, to a large extent, his early poetry, and one can still hear echoes of Marvell in *A Man in the Divided Sea*, even if

Merton chose not to publish many of his rhymed poems. "An Invocation to St. Lucy" has its forerunner in a poem of Marvell's greater predecessor, John Donne ("A Nocturnal upon St. Lucy's Day"), and some of the sensual Catholic imagery found in Richard Crashaw emerges in "The Biography." "Transformation: For the Sacred Heart" owes its subject and some oddities of phrasing to George Herbert, while an occasional psalm paraphrase in Merton has its equivalent in Herbert and other seventeenth century poets.

"Figures for an Apocalypse," the title poem of Merton's third volume, is his first published attempt at a long poem—a type to which he became increasingly committed. It is a poem in eight sections roughly paralleling the biblical book of the Apocalypse but modernizing it drastically. The seriousness of subject matter is tempered by some passages of exuberant satire, especially Section III, subtitled "Advice to my Friends Robert Lax and Edward Rice, to get away while they still can." Section VI, "In the Ruins of New York," is notable for its view of that city blooming into flowers and grasses after the apocalypse cleanses it.

The rest of *Figures for an Apocalypse* consists of short, lyric poems in the mode of Merton's two earlier volumes dealing with the same themes. "Canticle for the Blessed Virgin" and "Duns Scotus" are Hopkinsian, as are the frequent nature poems—"Landscape: Wheatfields," "Evening: Zero Weather," "Winter Afternoon," and "Spring: Monastery Farm." "Natural History" is, perhaps, Merton's most derivative poem, for in it he even adopts some of Hopkins' syntactical oddities, including the ungrammatical omission of relative pronouns. This exuberant imitation of poets he liked could have led Merton into slavishness, except for an equally exuberant tendency to mix the seemingly unmixable. "Spring: Monastery Farm," for example, combines Hopkins' nature with complex astronomical imagery drawn from Donne's "Good Friday, 1613." "Duns Scotus," similarly, is derived from Hopkins' "Duns Scotus's Oxford," but its syntax and some of its imagery echo not Hopkins but the William Blake of "The Tyger." As one might expect, Blake, the subject of Merton's master's thesis and a poet whose mysticism opened a spiritual door to Merton, also leaves his mark on Merton's poetry. The surprising fact, however, is that Blake's influence is not discernible until *Figures for an Apocalypse.* Blake's influence grows, while that of Hopkins diminishes in Merton's later poetry.

Two small volumes, *The Tears of the Blind Lions* and *The Strange Islands*, are transitional, indicating the direction of Merton's later poetry while retaining some of the influences and themes of his earlier work. Dedicated to Jacques Maritain, the French lay theologian and philosopher whose books helped lead Merton to conversion and who later became his personal friend, *The Tears of the Blind Lions* is the last volume of poems that Merton published before his eight-year cessation of poetic composition in the 1950's. It no longer includes poems of travel and of retreat from the world; even the liturgical poems are mostly gone; the volume is sustained by poems about saints and some fine nature poems such as "On a Day in August" and "In the Rain and the Sun." Hopkins' hold on Merton is apparent in these two poems and also in "Song" and "Hymn for the Feast of Duns Scotus." The abandonment of his favorite early themes, however, is significant, for in the 1950's Merton gradually repudiated the idea that a monk is someone who retreats from the world in favor of its opposite—that a monk is an ordinary man of the world who cannot escape his responsibilities to it. Merton's interest in civil rights and disarmament began about that time, but he had not yet found a poetic voice for it.

Dedicated to his teacher and friend Mark Van Doren and Van Doren's wife, Dorothy, *The Strange Islands* is the transitional volume on the other side of Merton's poetic hiatus. It represents the initial stage of Merton's shift from the short, lyrical poems of his early years to his long, complex, satirical last poems. The volume is divided into three parts: the first, which consists of short poems mixed with several of medium length; the second, which is a long drama in both verse and prose entitled "The Tower of Babel"; and the third, which is composed of short lyrics. One can still hear Hopkins in "The Annunciation" and some notable nature poems such as "Spring Storm," but the predominant mood is satiric, not only in "The Tower of Babel" but also in poems such as "Sports Without Blood—a Letter to Dylan Thomas." Merton's habit of including prose passages in his poems, beginning with "The Tower of Babel" and continuing in his later volumes, is evidence of the increasing influence of modernism on his verse, although it is also reminiscent of Blake's *The Marriage of Heaven and Hell* (1790).

Original Child Bomb, Emblems of a Season of Fury, and *Cables to the Ace* in different ways represent Merton's new style. *Original Child Bomb* consists of a single long prose poem, satiric in tone, which arranges the details surrounding the explosion of the first atomic bomb. The first poetic treatment of Merton's social and political concerns, it is an eloquent statement.

Emblems of a Season of Fury is primarily a volume of poems about people. Saints such as Macarius the Elder, Macarius the Younger, and Fulbert, and philosophers such as Averoës and Lee Ying are juxtaposed with Ernest Hemingway and James Thurber. There is a strongly satirical mood not only in such juxtaposition but also in many of the individual poems, such as "An Elegy for Five Old Ladies." Some reflect Merton's social and political concerns ("And the Children of Birmingham," "Chant to Be Used in Processions Around a Site with Furnaces"), and many, such as *Original Child Bomb*, are prose poems.

Dedicated to Robert Lax, *Cables to the Ace* is a long poem in eighty-eight sections, with prologue and epilogue, and alternates verse with prose poetry. Its tone is satiric: quotations from Shakespeare, William Wordsworth, and Meister Eckhardt and allusions to *Finnegans Wake* are juxtaposed with references to the Vietnam War and Zen.

Merton was still working on *The Geography of Lograire* when he died, leaving the longest of his poems unfinished. Epic in scope and modern in mode, its antecedents were Hart Crane's *The Bridge* (1930), William Carlos Williams' *Paterson* (1946-1958), and especially Ezra Pound's *Cantos* (1925-1972). Its development is paratactic: autobiographical allusions, references to anthropological studies, and obscure historical matters interweave to develop Merton's twin themes of the blindness of Western culture and the despera-tion of the cultures it has oppressed. Divided into four sections, "South," "North," "East," and "West," the poem juxtaposes the words of oppressed groups such as the Mayas, English Ranters, Kanakas, and Sioux with the words of their oppressors. The wide but specialized knowledge that the poem requires, together with its broken syntax, makes this Merton's most difficult poem. In the opinion of many critics, however, it is his most rewarding.

In addition to his separately published volumes of poetry, Merton's *The Collected Poems* includes unpublished early poetry, humorous verse, concrete poems, fragments, French poems, and, most important, his translations from French, Spanish, Latin, Portuguese, Chinese, Greek, and Persian. Merton's interest in concrete poetry can be traced to Herbert as well as to modern practitioners of that genre; a particularly interesting one is a rectangle con-structed out of the Latin *Natura abhoret vacuum* ("Nature abhors a vac-uum") in which the *u*'s in the last word expand in various ways to fill out several lines. Notable among the translations are the numerous poems of Chuang Tzu, the early Taoist (especially "Cutting up an Ox"), and the seven poems of Raissa Maritain, including her moving "Chagall."

Robert E. Boenig

Other major works

LONG FICTION: *My Argument with the Gestapo,* 1969.

NONFICTION: *Cistercian Contemplatives,* 1948; *The Seven Storey Mountain,* 1948; *What is Contemplation?,* 1948; *Exile Ends in Glory,* 1948; *The Waters of Siloe,* 1949; *Seeds of Contemplation,* 1949; *What Are These Wounds?,* 1950; *Seasons of Celebration,* 1950; *The Ascent to Truth,* 1951; *A Balanced Life of Prayer,* 1951; *The Sign of Jonas,* 1953; *No Man Is an Island,* 1955; *The Living Bread,* 1956; *The Silent Life,* 1957; *Silence in Heaven,* 1957; *Thoughts in Soli-tude,* 1958; *The Secular Journal,* 1959; *The Wisdom of the Desert,* 1960 (trans-lation); *Disputed Questions,* 1960; *New Seeds of Contemplation,* 1961; *The Behavior of Titans,* 1961; *The New Man,* 1962; *Clement of Alexandria,* 1962 (translation); *The Merton Reader,* 1962; *Life and Holiness,* 1963; *Raids on the Unspeakable,* 1964; *The Way of Chuang Tzu,* 1965; *Conjectures of a Guilty Bystander,* 1966; *Mystics and Zen Masters,* 1967; *Zen and the Birds of Ap-petite,* 1968; *Faith and Violence,* 1968; *Contemplative Prayer,* 1969; *The Cli-*

mate of Monastic Prayer, 1969; *Opening the Bible*, 1970; *Contemplation in a World of Action*, 1971; *The Asian Journal of Thomas Merton*, 1973; *The Literary Essays of Thomas Merton*, 1981.

MISCELLANEOUS: *A Hidden Wholeness*, 1970 (photographs and calligraphy).

Bibliography

Cooper, David A. *Thomas Merton's Art of Denial: The Evolution of a Radical Humanist.* Athens: University of Georgia Press, 1989. This work is an excellent study of the congruence of contemplative thought and social criticism in the writings of Merton. Cooper stresses both the unity and the evolution in Merton's reflections on his commitment to spiritual values and his role as a social critic.

Hart, Patrick, ed. *Thomas Merton, Monk: A Monastic Tribute.* New York: Sheed & Ward, 1974. This study is a very thoughtful assessment of Merton's significance as a writer by fellow monks who knew him well. The essays by Jean Le Clerc, Thérèse Lentfoehr, and James Fox stress the originality of his writings on monasticism and spiritual renewal.

Kramer, Victor A. *Thomas Merton: Monk and Artist.* Kalamazoo, Mich.: Cistercian, 1984. The eighth chapter in this book is entitled "Experimental Poetry." Kramer analyzes the links between poetry and contemplative thought in Merton's last two books of poetry *Cables to the Ace* and *The Geography of Lograire.* Contains an annotated bibliography of studies on Merton.

Labrie, Ross. *The Art of Thomas Merton.* Fort Worth: Texas Christian University Press, 1979. This thoughtful book examines Merton's stylistic creativity and analyzes well the impressive blend of prose and verse poems in *Cables to the Ace.* Labrie argues persuasively that Merton was a major lyric poet.

Merton, Thomas. *Collected Poems.* New York: New Directions, 1977. This posthumously published book is the most complete collection of Merton's poetry from the poems written in the early 1940's until *The Geography of Lograire,* completed only six months before his death in December, 1968. This book enables readers to appreciate the evolution of Merton's skill as a poet.

Mott, Michael. *The Seven Mountains of Thomas Merton.* Boston: Houghton Mifflin, 1984. This is an authorized and very well-researched biography of Merton from his birth in France in 1915 until his death in Thailand in 1968. Mott interviewed several people who knew Merton personally. This volume is an essential introduction to the life and works of Merton. Contains a very thorough list of primary and secondary sources, as well as an index.

W. S. MERWIN

Born: New York, New York; September 30, 1927

Principal poetry

A Mask for Janus, 1952; *The Dancing Bears*, 1954; *Green with Beasts*, 1956; *The Drunk in the Furnace*, 1960; *The Moving Target*, 1963; *The Lice*, 1967; *Animae*, 1969; *The Carrier of Ladders*, 1970; *Writings to an Unfinished Accompaniment*, 1973; *The First Four Books of Poems*, 1975; *The Compass Flower*, 1977; *Feathers from the Hill*, 1978; *Finding the Islands*, 1982; *Opening the Hand*, 1983; *The Rain in the Trees*, 1988; *Selected Poems*, 1988.

Other literary forms

A talented translator, W. S. Merwin has translated numerous works including *The Poem of the Cid* (1959), Persius' *Satires* (1961), *The Song of Roland* (1963), *Voices*, by Antonio Porchia (1969, 1988), *Transparence of the World: Poems*, by Jean Follain (1969), and poetry by Pablo Neruda and Osip Mandelstam. He has also written plays: *Rumpelstiltskin*, produced by the British Broadcasting Corporation (BBC) in 1951; *Pageant of Cain*, produced by BBC Third Programme in 1952; *Huckleberry Finn*, produced by BBC television, 1953. *Darkling Child* was produced in London by Arts Theatre in 1956, *Favor Island* was produced by Poet's Theatre in Cambridge, Massachusetts, in 1957, and *The Gilded West* was produced in 1961 in Coventry, England, by the Belgrade Theatre. Merwin's prose work includes *The Miner's Pale Children* (1970), *Houses and Travellers* (1977), a memoir of childhood entitled *Unframed Originals* (1982), and *Regions of Memory: Uncollected Prose, 1949-1982* (1987), edited by Cary Nelson.

Achievements

The achievement of W. S. Merwin is both impressive and distinctive. His body of work encompasses a wide range of literary genres and includes poetry, plays, translations, and prose. His development as a poet has spanned great literary distances, from the early formalism of *A Mask for Janus* to the spare, simple language and openness of the verse form he refined in *The Lice*. His later poetry has often displayed a prosaic, almost conversational quality, as in "Questions to Tourists Stopped by a Pineapple Field," from *Opening the Hand*.

Although Merwin himself has carefully avoided making in-depth comments or pronouncements about his poetry and has not engaged in the often-fussy critical debate that has shadowed his career, his work continues to show evidence that the exploration of the power and enigmatic nature of language is one of his great concerns. His many remarkable translations have perhaps been a stimulating influence on his own innovations of poetic form. In moving away from the rather mannered style of his early verse with its reliance on myth, rhyme, and punctuation to a poetry of silence and absence, Merwin, according to Sandra McPherson, began "researching the erasures of the universe."

Merwin received early recognition for his poetry with the selection of *A Mask for Janus* as the 1952 Yale Series of Younger Poets Award winner. He has been the recipient of many other grants, fellowships, and awards over the years since then. He received a *Kenyon Review* fellowship in 1954; the American Academy Grant, 1957; an Arts Council of Great Britain bursary, 1957; a Rabinowitz Research Fellowship, 1961; the Bess Hokin Prize, 1962; a Ford Foundation Grant, 1964; the Chapelbrook Award, 1966; the Harriet Monroe Memorial Prize (*Poetry*, Chicago), 1967; a P.E.N. Translation Prize for *Selected Translations, 1948-1968*, 1969; a Rockefeller grant, 1969; a Pulitzer Prize for *The Carrier of Ladders*, 1971; the Academy of American Poets Fellowship, 1973; the Shelley Memorial Award, 1974; a National Endowment for the Arts Grant, 1978; and a Bollingen Prize, 1979. In 1987 Merwin received the Governor's Award for Literature of the State of Hawaii. He is a member of the American Academy.

Biography

William Stanley Merwin was born in New York City on September 30, 1927, and grew up in Union City, New Jersey (where his father was a Presbyterian minister), and in Scranton, Pennsylvania. From his own accounts his parents were strict and rather cheerless. His earliest poems, written as a child, were austere hymns for his father. He received his bachelor's degree in English from Princeton University, New Jersey, in 1947. While at Princeton, he was befriended by the critic R. P. Blackmur and became very interested in the work of Ezra Pound. Like Pound, he was a student of romance languages and began to value translation as a means of remaking poetry in English. As a student he even grew a beard in imitation of Pound's and eventually went to visit Pound at St. Elizabeths Hospital. In 1949 he followed Pound's example and left the United States to become an expatriate. His sojourn was to last some seven years. From 1949 to 1951 he worked as a tutor in France and Portugal. In 1950 he lived in Mallorca, where he was tutor to Robert Graves's son, William. After that he made his living for several years by translating from French, Spanish, Latin, and Portuguese. From 1951 through 1953 he worked as translator for the BBC's Third Programme. In 1954 he was married to Diana Whalley. During 1956 and 1957 Merwin was playwright-in-residence for the Poets' Theatre in Cambridge, Massachusetts, and in 1962 he served as poetry editor for *The Nation*. He was an associate at the Theatre de la Cité in Lyons, France, during 1964-1965. In 1971 he won the

Pulitzer Prize for his collection *The Carrier of Ladders.* Since 1978 Merwin has made his home in Hawaii, where he lives with his wife, Paula.

Analysis

Beginning with his first book of poetry, *A Mask for Janus*, W. S. Merwin has explored how language structures and creates experience. He has also been devoted to myth, or mythmaking, as a way of making sense of experience. While experimenting with language and myth, he has examined the possibilities of developing poetic forms suited to expressing what language can reveal about the mind and existence. In his search, Merwin has had rich resources to draw from, such as the other languages of his many translations and his firm grounding in earlier poetic traditions. His background led him first to master orthodox forms and later to move beyond them.

Published in 1952, *A Mask for Janus* used myth and traditional prosodic forms to explore such themes as the birth-death cycle and the isolated self. In "Meng Tzu's Song," the speaker meditates on concerns of identity and solitude:

> How can I know, now forty
> Years have shuffled my shoulders,
> Whether my mind is steady
> Or quakes as the wind stirs?

At first reading, this poem has the flavor of a translation. Ed Folsom, writing in *W. S. Merwin: Essays on the Poetry* (1987), notes that while the verse in *A Mask for Janus* was seen by some critics as an example of traditional craftsmanship, it was also stiff at times, wordy, and overwrought. In recalling and using the structures and tonalities of a more formal poetry, however, Merwin was able to develop his mastery of those elements and earn his release from them.

Merwin continued his use of myth and the narrative form in *The Dancing Bears* and *Green with Beasts*. In "East of the Sun and West of the Moon" (*The Dancing Bears*), Merwin uses the myth of Psyche and Cupid to explore the problem of identity. Through language that is often elegant and precisely shaped into neat thirteen-line stanzas, he offers clues to the enigma of inner and outer reality. In what may be read as a clarifying statement, Merwin reveals his belief that "all metaphor . . . is magic," and "all magic is but metaphor." Here, he employs his magic to explore the hidden realms of being.

The preoccupation with myth and a formal, poetic style followed in his next two works, *Green with Beasts*, and *The Drunk in the Furnace*. Yet there is also a strange new energy working as Merwin begins moving away from Greco-Roman myths and toward the creation of his own. In "The *Portland* Going Out" (*The Drunk in the Furnace*), the apparent randomness of the disaster that strikes a passing ship recalls to the poet the mystery of life and death and thus of existence itself.

The *Portland* had passed close by the poet's ship on its way out of the harbor to an ill-fated rendezvous with a storm, where it put "all of disaster between us: a gulf/ Beyond reckoning." This glimpse into the abyss works ironically as a reaffirmation of life.

There are several other poems in this collection that revolve around images of the sea. Alice N. Benston, writing in *Poets in Progress* (1962), calls the sea the "perfect symbol for Merwin." The duality inherent in the sea as both life-giver and symbol of nature's indifference to humanity provides Merwin with a metaphor for the unknown.

The poems in *The Drunk in the Furnace* take some other new and significant directions. For example, several examine the poet's youth and the family members who helped shape his early experiences. These poems are not reverential but sober, almost bitter reflections on his memories of "faded rooms," his grandfather left alone to die in a nursing home, and his grandmother's failure to see her worst sins as she reminisces about her life. The sarcastic tone of "Grandfather in the Old Men's Home" seems directed at the society in which Merwin was brought up—a society that he would later reject.

The family poems in *The Drunk in the Furnace* and others such as "Home for Thanksgiving" and "A Letter from Gussie" in *The Moving Target* allow Merwin to explore his past further before turning away to begin a new journey. It is as if these poems generate and voice his realization and declaration that he will no longer be bound by the expectations of the culture into which he was born. Nor will he recognize any longer the restraints of the poetic forms that served as his early models.

The new style toward which Merwin was moving in *The Moving Target* emerges more fully realized in *The Lice*. Here he abandons narrative, adopts open forms, and eliminates punctuation:

> The nights disappear like bruises but nothing is healed
> The dead go away like bruises
> The blood vanishes into the poisoned farmlands
> Pain the horizon
> Remains

With *The Lice*, in effect, Merwin leaves the shore, lifts off the launching pad, and enters a new realm where the poem becomes the vessel for voyages toward "nameless stars." While numerous critics have pointed to the overall negativism and pessimism of *The Lice*, hope is undeniably evident in the very act of poetic discovery, as Merwin sheds his skin and emerges as something born not only "to survive," but indeed "to live."

In *The Lice* lie keys to an understanding of the work that will follow. The stark, even dumbfounding silences in a poem such as "December Among the Vanished"—in which "the old snow gets up and moves taking its/ Birds with it"—attract Merwin away from a world that seems to be in the process of self-destruction and toward a new, strange sensibility. A new spareness, a new simplicity and immediacy inform these poems. Gone are the earlier elaborate, formal structures. According to Ed Folsom and Cary Nelson in their introduction to *W. S. Merwin: Essays on the Poetry*, Merwin had begun to lose, at this stage, his faith in language and for a time was not even sure he could write words to articulate experience. In an interview with Edward Hirsch in 1987, Merwin explained how he came to distrust language, believing that experience cannot be articulated.

The Lice also reveals a new, more serious concern with the deadly corrosiveness of politics and the wanton destruction of the environment by greedy corporations. Behind the poet's initial anger and numbing frustration over mass environmental destruction, however, is a recognition of the potential for other responses to the earth's tragedy. He listens carefully, trying to hear the hidden voices in nature. These voices, and the voices emanating from his inner self, offer the possibility of discovering new consciousness—new poems—as long as as he does not allow his anger to deafen him or the state of the world to distract him.

In listening for these other voices, the poet remains open to the discovery not only of the world but also of himself. In "For a Coming Extinction," he asks the reader to join voices with "the sea cows the Great Auks the gorillas" and, using the speech of innocents, to testify to the inherent significance of all life.

A new tone emerges in Merwin's poetry in *The Carrier of Ladders*, which was awarded the Pulitzer Prize in 1971. The tone is one of rebirth and reaffirmation. Thus far he has stared into the dark night of his disillusionment with a world corrupted by human beings, and has seen only his own reflection. However much he regrets the alienation that such a vision brought forth, he realizes at this stage that to live and create he must seek the renewal of his own spirit.

To do so, the poet will have to step into the darkness, the unknown, and accept both what is there and what is not there. In "Words from a Totem Animal" (*The Carrier of Ladders*), Merwin writes,

> My eyes are waiting for me
> in the dusk
> they are still closed
> they have been waiting a long time
> and I am feeling my way toward them

The language and form of *The Carrier of Ladders* are perfectly suited to the poet's task of trying to see things with new eyes. This poetry is less judgmental and more open to the experiences of being alive. The simplicity of the diction, and the clear, fresh immediacy of tone draw the reader into the poems. There the poet waits, "standing in dry air" and "for no reason"— praying simply that his words may be clear.

During the 1970's, Merwin continued his search for oneness with nature and the knowledge of self such a quest promises. The childlike innocence achieved in the poems of *The Carrier of Ladders* continues to characterize much of the poetry in *Writings to an Unfinished Accompaniment*, *The Compass Flower*, and *Finding the Islands*. Scattered throughout these books are references to the sea, fish, owls, dogs, cows, stones, mountains, clouds, the moon, and the stars.

In "Gift" (*Writings to an Unfinished Accompaniment*), Merwin comes to realize that the revelation he seeks must be found through trust in what is given to him. An almost mystical stillness resides in these poems, as if one could hear the "sound of inner stone."

With *Opening the Hand*, Merwin looks outward toward more familiar landscapes and situations and fixes his hermetic gaze upon them. In a poem about the death of his father, told as through a dream, the poet hallucinates images that seem to haunt him like ominous premonitions. His concern with ecology is also evident in this collection. In "Shaving Without a Mirror," he seems to be waking up from a night outdoors, listening for forest voices. The awe he feels, and his urge to surrender to the experience of being alone in the wilderness, confirms his sense of the interrelatedness of all things, a sense that first emerged in *The Lice*.

"What Is Modern" (*Opening the Hand*) is a poem charged with irony. Merwin comments on the American culture's ridiculous preoccupation with defining modernity. An undeniable sense of humor and a refreshing looseness characterizes the poem: "is the first/ tree that comes/ to mind modern/ does it have modern leaves." While grounded in the particular, the recognizable and commonplace, the poetry of *Opening the Hand* still achieves the same obsidian polish of earlier poems whose spare diction and muteness gave an ethereal rather than concrete quality to things.

The Rain in the Trees combines many of the qualities in the work of the 1960's and 1970's, while continuing his experiments in style and form. The subjects include his family, nature, travel, John Keats, language, the Statue of Liberty, Hawaii, and love. In such diversity of subjects come surprise and freshness. The poems mirror his wanderings and his restlessness in pursuit of the ineffable.

In "Empty Water," Merwin uses incantatory speech to invoke the spirit of a toad whose eyes were "fashioned of the most/ precious of metals." He chants for the toad's return:

> come back
> believer in shade
> believer in silence and elegance
> believer in ferns

believer in patience
believer in the rain

A joy in the primal unity and the inherent beauty of all life is evident throughout *The Rain in the Trees*. In "Waking to the Rain," the poet wakes from a dream "of harmony" to find rain falling on the house, creating the one sound that reveals the silence that surrounds him.

Since the early 1980's, Merwin has made Hawaii the base from which he makes journeys to the great cities of the mainland United States to lecture and give readings. His devotion to poetry and his life as a wandering poet have given him a folk hero's aura. The question of where Merwin's work will fit into the body of contemporary American poetry continues to be asked by critics and readers alike. The publication, in 1988, of his *Selected Poems* is a testament to the achievement of one of the most impressive and elusive American poets writing today.

Being of the generation that began writing in the 1940's and 1950's, he had his poetic roots in more classically influenced, technically controlled verse forms. His disaffection with the formal poetic styles of his predecessors was shared by other poets of his generation such as James Wright and Robert Bly. What he had to say required new ways of communicating, new vessels that would journey toward new realms of perception. By immersing himself in the literature of other cultures, both as a student of languages and as a translator, Merwin has been able to bring a sense of the archetypal source of all poetic expression to his work. His ability to look at a tree and describe the space between its leaves may be unique among contemporary poets. Merwin has referred to his poems as houses that he makes out of virtually anything and everything he can find. These houses made of words are places where the reader can enter and experience "the echo of everything that has ever/ been spoken."

Francis Poole

Other major works

PLAYS: *Rumpelstiltskin*, 1951 (radio play); *Pageant of Cain*, 1952 (radio play); *Huckleberry Finn*, 1953 (teleplay); *Darkling Child*, 1956; *Favor Island*, 1957; *The Gilded Nest*, 1961.

NONFICTION: *The Miner's Pale Children*, 1970; *Houses and Travellers*, 1977; *Unframed Originals*, 1982; *Regions of Memory: Uncollected Prose, 1949-1982*, 1987 (edited by Cary Nelson).

TRANSLATIONS: *The Poem of the Cid*, 1959; *Satires*, by Persius, 1961; *Spanish Ballads*, 1961; *The Song of Roland*, 1963; *Selected Translations, 1948-1968*, 1968; *Twenty Love Poems and a Song of Despair*, by Pablo Neruda, 1969; *Products of the Perfected Civilization: Selected Writings of Chamfort*, 1969; *Voices*, by Antonio Porchia, 1969, 1988; *Transparence of the*

World: Poems, by Jean Follain, 1969; *Asian Figures*, 1973; *Selected Poems*, by Osip Mandelstam, 1973, 1989 (with Clarence Brown); *Iphigenia at Aulis*, 1978 (with George E. Dimock, Jr.); *Selected Translations, 1968-1978*, 1979; *Four French Plays*, 1985; *From the Spanish Morning*, 1985; *Vertical Poetry*, 1988.

Bibliography

Benston, Alice N. "Myth in the Poetry of W. S. Merwin." In *Poets in Progress*, edited by Edward Hungerford. Evanston, Ill.: Northwestern University Press, 1962. Originally from *Triquarterly*, this essay discusses Merwin's first four volumes of poetry. Benston explores Merwin's concept of the poet as mythmaker, proposing that this concept is what drives his poetry making. He goes beyond retelling fables, she insists, and has actually taken myth as a creed.

Byers, Thomas B. *What I Cannot Say: Self, Word, and the World in Whitman, Stevens, and Merwin*. Urbana: University of Illinois Press, 1989. Byers' chapter on Merwin, "W. S. Merwin: A Description of Darkness," focuses primarily on *The Lice* and attempts to define Merwin's place in the American poetic tradition descended from Ralph Waldo Emerson and Walt Whitman. He believes that Merwin is busy refuting and revising Whitman's poetic concept of the self as connected to all living things. According to Byers, Merwin sees, as Stevens did, the self as inevitably isolated, even though his poetics recognize the need to see oneself as related to other people and other things in order to become more ecologically aware. Includes notes, a bibliography, and an index.

Christhilf, Mark. *W. S. Merwin the Mythmaker*. Columbia: University of Missouri Press, 1986. Christhilf discusses Merwin's contributions to the postmodernist movement (with *The Moving Target*) and his assumed role of mythmaker, noting that the poet became ambivalent toward this role in the 1980's. In a useful discussion, Christhilf traces the mythmaking concern in American poetry across four decades. His comments on Merwin's memoir *Unframed Originals* are also useful in understanding the poet's growing uncertainty about the place of personal experience in poetry—a concern shared with his contemporaries Robert Bly and James Wright.

Davis, Cheri. *W. S. Merwin*. Boston: Twayne, 1981. This study makes the poetry and prose of Merwin accessible to the reader new to his work. While well aware of the variety in Merwin's writing, Davis attempts to reveal what gives it unity. She examines his attitudes toward language and silence, his concern for animals and ecology, and his beliefs about poetry and nothingness. Chapters 1-5 look at his books of poetry from *A Mask for Janus* through *The Compass Flower*. Chapter 6 discusses the prose poetry of *The Miner's Pale Children* and *Houses and Travellers*.

Merwin, W. S. "The Art of Poetry: XXXVII." Interview by Edward Hirsch.

Paris Review 101 (1987): 57-81. Merwin recollects his childhood fascination with Indians and his nightmares that the whole world had become cities. The entire interview reflects his strong environmental concerns. He also talks about literary influences: John Berryman; R. P. Blackmur, his teacher; and Ezra Pound on medieval poetry and the importance of the ear in poetry. He discusses his political activities and involvement in the anti-nuclear movement. Finally, he explains how with *The Moving Target* he came to distrust language, believing that experience transcends articulation.

Nelson, Cary, and Ed Folsom, eds. *W. S. Merwin: Essays on the Poetry.* Urbana: University of Illinois Press, 1987. The editors provide a good introductory essay, comparing Merwin to Pound (both students of romance languages), William Carlos Williams, and Wallace Stevens. William H. Rueckert's notes are a help to readers of *The Lice*, and Ed Folsom discusses Merwin's change in style beginning with *The Compass Flower.* Includes several other essays whose authors often explore the poet's work in manuscript, as well as comprehensive bibliographies, full notes, and a thorough index.

CHRISTOPHER MIDDLETON

Born: Truro, England; June 10, 1926

Principal poetry

Poems, 1944; *Nocturne in Eden: Poems*, 1945; *Torse 3: Poems 1949-1961*, 1962; *Nonsequences/Selfpoems*, 1965; *Our Flowers & Nice Bones*, 1969; *The Lonely Suppers of W. V. Balloon*, 1975; *Pataxanadu and Other Prose*, 1977; *Carminalenia*, 1980; *Woden Dog*, 1981; *111 Poems*, 1983; *Serpentine*, 1985; *Two Horse Wagon Going By*, 1987; *Selected Writings*, 1989.

Other literary forms

In addition to collections of poetry and short prose, Christopher Middleton has also published an impressive number of translations, edited volumes, and critical essays.

His translations from German cover a wide variety of genres, including poems by Johann Wolfgang von Goethe, Friedrich Hölderlin, Eduard Mörike, Hugo von Hofmannsthal, Georg Trakl, Paul Celan, Günter Grass, and others. He has also translated Friedrich Nietzsche's letters and such major works of modern German prose as Robert Walser's *The Walk and Other Stories* (1957) and *Jakob von Gunten* (1969), Christa Wolf's autobiographical narrative *The Quest for Christa T.* (1970), and Elias Canetti's critical study of Kafka's letters to his fiancée, *Kafka's Other Trial: Or, Letters to Felice* (1974). Middleton has also edited or coedited several anthologies of verse and prose in translation: *No Hatred and No Flag, 20th Century War Poems* (1958), which was published a year later in German as *Ohne Hass und Fahne*; *Modern German Poetry, 1910-1960: An Anthology with Verse Translations* (1962, with Michael Hamburger); and *German Writing Today* (1967). He has also published German translations of his own works, including two pieces from *Pataxanadu and Other Prose*, "The Pocket Elephants" (1969, *Der Taschenelefant*), and "Getting Grandmother to Market" (1970, *Wie wir Grossmutter zum Markt bringen*). He is also the author of a libretto for a comic opera, *The Metropolitans* (1964, music by Hans Vogt).

Middleton's critical essays have appeared in numerous journals, and many have been collected in *Bolshevism in Art and Other Expository Writings* (1978) and *The Pursuit of the Kingfisher* (1983).

Achievements

Middleton's main achievement is that of a mediator among the disparate worlds of poetry, translation, and academic scholarship. He frequently includes translations in his volumes of poetry, and regards the act of translation as a preeminently poetic endeavor, while his critical works appear as the natural by-products of his familiarity with the history and the direct practice of literature.

Middleton has gained wide recognition as a translator, which is to say that he is recognized for his absence, for not being obtrusively present in the works he reproduces in English. Good translators are always difficult to recognize: on the one hand, they are denied the glory of the first creator of the text (after all, the translator's words are not "his own"), while on the other hand, those bilingual readers best able to appreciate the merits of a translation are precisely the same readers who have no need of one, since they can always read the work in the original. Middleton's many translations, together with his essays on translation, stand as major contributions to a difficult, challenging, and often underestimated art.

Middleton's poetry has also attracted much attention. He was awarded the Sir Geoffrey Faber Memorial Prize for Poetry in 1963, and a selection of his works was anthologized that same year in *Penguin Modern Poets 4*. Reviewers have usually been quick to mention Middleton's open allegiance to the traditions of European modernism, and they have often praised his accuracy of detail, together with his "fine sense of the absurd." They have also frequently noticed a certain obliquity—not to say obscurity—in Middleton's approach; one reviewer observed that Middleton "handles his insights with great finesse, but always from a distance as though with tweezers." In a similar vein, others have regretted in his works "the quick change from style to style," "the absence of any unifying personal pressure," and "something constrictingly intellectual." These problems are often regarded as endemic to a self-conscious postmodernism; but in fact, these same poetic peccadilloes of flexibility and distance would be praised as virtues in a translator, while "intellectual" references to what one critic called "the *disjecta membra* of a scholar's workshop" can be seen simply as the natural expression of a *modus vivendi* operating between the creative and the professional life. In short, Middleton views poetry as a form of translation, translation as a form of creation, and both as legitimate and important subjects and objects for academic study. In a world plagued with divided loyalties and petty territorial rivalries, this example is indeed a major achievement.

Biography

Christopher Middleton was born on June 10, 1926, in Truro, Cornwall, where his father was organist at the cathedral. The family soon moved to Ely, and in 1930 they moved on to Cambridge, where his father later became Senior Lecturer in Music. Middleton's early childhood atmosphere of cathedrals and music was followed by a series of boarding schools in idyllic pastoral settings, where he took up classical studies. He began to write poems at the age of sixteen. Although he later rebelled against the security of his childhood, he acknowledges that it was "a source for ideas of order." "Ideas of order" became very important for the young Royal Air Force aircraftsmaninterpreter (later sergeant-interpreter) arriving among the ruins of Germany just at the end of World War II. Middleton remained in the R.A.F. until 1948, then returned by way of southern France to Oxford, where he read German and French and received his B.A. in 1951. He was lecturer in English at the University of Zurich, Switzerland, from 1952 to 1955, during which time he completed his Oxford Ph.D. thesis on the works of Hermann Hesse. In 1953 he married Mary Freer. From 1955 to 1965 he was Senior Lecturer at King's College, the University of London, except for one year, 1961-1962, when he was Visiting Professor at the University of Texas at Austin. This brief introduction to the American Southwest marked a crucial turning point in Middleton's career, and Texas joined London and the South of France as a recurring geographical locus for his poems. In 1966 he returned to the University of Texas, where he continues to serve as Professor of German Literature.

Analysis

Christopher Middleton's poems may be understood as poetic tributes to the recurrent possibilities of order. Typically, he subjects an emblem of a conventional and preexistent order (a classical or political theme, a work of art, a still-life on a breakfast table) to linguistic changes which disorder and reorder the given elements in such a way that what emerges is a new and provisional order that contains and signals its own explosive instability. In other words, the poet does not claim to uncover the "real" significance of anything; and the uniqueness of Middleton's poetry-of-process lies at least partly in the fact that the changes that take place in his poems always seem somehow slightly accidental, not fully under control, perhaps not even fully the responsibility of the poet. To lay claim to such control and responsibility would be to defeat the very point of the procedure by undermining the surprising freedom that comes with the startling rediscovery of things long thought familiar. This helps to explain Middleton's evident lack of interest in "inspiration," or the creation of order *ex nihilo*; he chooses rather to subject the available material of an imperfectly ordered world to sensational transformations, performing a trick that, as one critic put it, "makes the things hover in the air like a mirage." For Middleton, creation is recreational re-creation, and his poems have much in common both with translations and with collages. By merging classical elements (images of order) with modernist techniques (procedures of disorder), Middleton is able to avoid both the chill stasis of a sterile classicism and the self-defeating absurdity of an all-too-radical modernism; in his sensitive hands, old forms of order become as disquieting as the marble torsos of Giorgio Chirico or René Magritte, or as radiant as Paul Cézanne's weighty apples.

Middleton's modernized classicism is evident even in the titles of most of his volumes of poetry, titles which he always takes care to explain. *Non-*

sequences/Selfpoems is chosen for its echoes of nonsenses and consequences, and because "the poems are always consequent-nonsequent."/(Such self-negating hyphenated compounds are posted in Middleton's explanations like warning signs; he mentions elsewhere the "lucky-unlucky" publication of his first two volumes of poetry, or his preference for a "stark-ambiguous" style.) The title of *Pataxanadu and Other Prose* blends Samuel Taylor Coleridge's exotic dream-poem with Alfred Jarry's "pataphysics," the "science of imaginary solutions." *Carminalenia* merges two words from a line of Propertius to convey both a literal Latin sense of "Softsongs" but also, as Middleton notes, a latent suggestion of something "criminal."

The title *Torse 3* refers to one of the meanings of the word "torse," a certain kind of geometrical surface; its etymological cousins include "torsion," "tortuous," and "torture." The final twist in this collection is a poem about order, the fifth and last of "Five Psalms for Common Man," which may be taken as Middleton's most direct statement about the subject. Here the first definitive assertion—"Order imagined against fear is not order"—breaks the logical rule of identity, as "order" quickly becomes plural, a dialectic of order and disorder: "Out of a rumbling of hollows an order is born/ to negate another existing order of fear." A few lines later, the Psalmist sings that "Another order of fear is chaos," while throughout the poem, things either happen or they do not happen: fear "only negates or does not negate existing order," while "images of chaos . . . accord or do not accord." Out of this logical-sounding but ambiguous tangle emerges the final statement: "The orders revolve as improvisations against fear,/ changed images of chaos. Without fear, nothing." Thus the circle of transformation is complete: order against fear cannot be order, but without "orders of fear" (or chaos—which has no plural) there can be no order at all. Other writers have described this dilemma in terms of the creator's struggle against entropy; but Middleton seems to suggest that order is only the obverse of entropy, undifferentiation momentarily disguised.

Nonsequences/Selfpoems introduces the "Texan theme" into Middleton's work, where it immediately takes up permanent residence. Images of politics—of social order—also occupy more territory here than in *Torse 3*, as Middleton develops methods for integrating political material into his vision of the poet's dangerous game. In "Difficulties of a Revisionist," a political extension is added to the notion of the poet as translator or maker of kaleidoscopic collages: "All day fighting for a poem. Fighting against what?/ And for what? What? being its own danger, wants/ to get rescued, but from its rescuer?" Which side is the poet to be on in the struggle for a new revisionary vision, if the poem—"its own danger"—is struggling to be saved from its poet? Danger lurks also in the poem entitled "Dangers of Waking," in which the "reports and messages" brought by children to the recumbent narrator are progressively magnified into the nightmare news of barbed wire, prison cells, and "the killing of this or that/ man, thousand, or million." This poem appears rather late in the volume, and serves as a counterbalance to an earlier description of "Navajo Children" accepting lollipops from tourists in Canyon de Chelly, Arizona.

Repressions past and future stalk the pages of *Nonsequences/Selfpoems* which shows Middleton at his bleakest. Even the more pastoral and private images of order appear as if at the mercy of angry mobs just over the distant horizon. The natural-unnatural world harbors savages and phantoms: cats crunch the headbones of mice, the Cyclops' broken eye clings like a slug on a carrot, houses are haunted by shaggy monsters and street-crossings by "this unknown thing." All the poet's combinatory gifts are helpless to rectify or mitigate the horrors of the past; "January 1919" begins with one of Middleton's bitterest lines—"What if I know, Liebknecht, who shot you dead"—and ends with an appeal to "Look upon our children, they are mutilated." In the final poem, "An Englishman in Texas," the poet presents himself as a kind of sky-struck survivor eager to shed the shreds of past identity in order to exist fully in the present; this last nonsequence voices his wish to "drop character,/ its greed for old presences, its dirt" in order to "move once,/ free, of himself, into some few things."

Our Flowers & Nice Bones, Middleton's next volume of poetry, takes its title from a letter by Kurt Schwitters, and represents Middleton's most sustained Dadaistic sortie into such experimental forms as concrete poetry, "found" poems, and works in which sound is invited to take precedence over sense. The poet's quest for order seeks its method either in the visual effect of letters on the page ("Birth of Venus," "Milk Sonnet") or in the shock of finding an unintentional poem ready-made, or a poetic possibility in the merging of two or more such "finds" (such as "Found Poem with Grafts," a true poetic collage). He also organizes poems in terms of sound, either by inventing a mock language of suggestive nonsense (like the Teutonic Latin Finneganese of "Lausdeo Teutonicus" or the Mexican yodeling of "Armadillo Cello Solo") or by taking existing words through transformations based on their sounds (as in the jazzy bass be-bop of "Ballade in B").

One of the most interesting applications of this technique occurs in "Computer's Karl Marx," since the substitution of sound for sense also serves as a means of parodying the monotonous jargon of Marxist orthodoxy. The poem's epigraph is a quotation from Nikolai Bukharin about "the reorganization of production relations." Taking the words "production relations" as a source of raw sound-material for the manufacture of other words of Latin origin, Middleton reorganizes vowels and consonant clusters to produce such transmogrified tonal echoes as "conscript prostitutes/ rusticate prelates." Another poem in this collection, "Pavlovic Variations," offers additional insight into Middleton's attitude toward translation. As one learns from a postscript, the title of the poem comes not from Pavlov—as readers trained to respond to allusions will immediately have assumed—but from a Yugoslavian poet named Miodrag Pavlovic. The opening section of the poem is Middleton's English rendering of a German translation of one of Pavlovic's works, whose classical landscapes and political themes are then explored and developed in five subsequent variations. Middleton's poetic techniques have been compared with those of visual artists and with the Impressionists in particular; but in *Our Flowers & Nice Bones* he borrows systems of order—whether at the level of individual letters, syllables, words, or themes—at least equally from the world of music.

The Lonely Suppers of W. V. Balloon is the most accomplished of Middleton's books of verse, beginning even with the unidentified hovering balloon depicted on the dust jacket, an elaborately equipped bubble of a globe with a suspended Spanish galleon for a gondola, complete with cannon and banners, and dangling ballast of birdcage and winecask. In this collection Middleton is at his best, displaying a rare and sensitive mixture of whimsy and provocation, game and threat, entirely accurate as if by accident. One of the most beautiful poems in the volume, "A Cart with Apples," shows Middleton's poetry-of-process at its most masterful. The poem paints a simple still life of an apple cart standing in a field of roses; but through the transforming play of attributes, of fullness and roundness, shadows and primary colors (blue, rose, and yellow), every object—cart, apples, field, and all their interwoven shadows—comes to share in the full, round, colorful reality of every other object until the image achieves a vivid shimmering density worthy of Cézanne. This is Cubist poetry, enriching its objects with layers of perspective while preserving the essence of their unity. Unlike paintings, poems accumulate their being in linear time; but here the quality of the light shifting from stanza to stanza is a poetic reflection of Claude Monet's attempt to capture the shifting colors absorbed and reflected by the façade of the Rouen Cathedral. "A Cart with Apples" offers a vision so much a part of the idea of southern France that one recognizes it without having seen it, just as one knows that the setting is southern France although it is never actually mentioned. Something of the quality of Mediterranean light is captured here with simple words and a lucid technique that clearly reflects Middleton's ideas about the transformational nature of order.

The title poem in this volume, "The Lonely Suppers of W. V. Balloon," is another magical still life: a Texas evening, a bottle of wine on the table ("seadark wine," for an inveterate inverter of tropes) and a thunderstorm raging outside. It is a poem about, among other things, gratitude: "Thank the thunderstorm," the poet says, because "Here we sit, love . . . and believe/ What floated past the window was Balloon's lasso,/ His anchor was the lightning." Thus, through the intercessionary charm of a word as weird as "balloon," the Englishman conjures up a moment of deep peace with the desert phantoms, so that what passes in the dark is not a noose, but a lasso, and even the flash of lightning can be an image of steadfastness. Yet Balloon's world is not without its dangers, as is suggested by "Briefcase History," a case history of the poet's briefcase done in the style of Guillaume Apollinaire. The briefcase, made from scavenged war materials, is celebrated as a trusted veteran and friend. Nevertheless, the poem ends with an ominous twist— game or threat?—as the poet suddenly tells the travel-worn container of so many mementoes: "you have never contained an explosive device/ never have you contained an explosive device/ yet."

While both *Our Flowers & Nice Bones* and *The Lonely Suppers of W. V. Balloon* contain examples of prose poetry, Middleton's next collection, *Pataxanadu and Other Prose*, consists entirely of short prose parables, enigmas, and fragments in the tradition of Franz Kafka and Jorge Luis Borges. These prose sketches frequently echo themes from earlier poems, though here newly subjected to the quasilogical rules of prose and to its mimetic possibilities. Most of the narrators of these prose sketches see themselves as isolated historians writing with a sense of duty and urgency about political or familial situations. The assumptions underlying their specific attitudes are revealed only between the lines, as the dreamlike merges with the matter-of-fact, and classical motifs mix with visions of a totalitarian future. The confessional order imposed by eyewitness testimony is here locked in soft-spoken but deadly combat with the disorder of randomness or the false order of political oppression. Unlike most of the pieces, the five title sketches in *Pataxanadu and Other Prose* are generated through a system of lexical substitutions originally developed by Raymond Queneau, which Middleton applies to passages from Sir Thomas Malory, Sir Thomas Urquhart's translation of François Rabelais, Jonathan Swift, Herman Melville, and Charles Doughty. In a sense, these are prose equivalents of the "found" poems in *Our Flowers & Nice Bones*; but here their "finding" involves the deliberate systematic distortion of the original text—a method answering Arthur Rimbaud's call for the "systematic disruption of all the senses"—and the results are remarkably droll (Melville's mates, Starbuck, Stubb, and Flask are "translated" into Stealbudget, Stuff, and Flaunt). *Pataxanadu and Other Prose* also comes with its own key in the form of a review by Middleton's anagrammatical avatar, Doctor Philden Smither, of an imaginary monograph by a certain Professor Erwin Ignaz Steintrommler on the historical significance of short prose. Prof. Steintrommler's Germanic pedantry is gently spoofed: he argues, for example, that since all users of language necessarily lie, "the shorter the prose is, the less will be the likelihood of falsification"—a position that leads logically to silence as the supreme form of truth. But Steintrommler's examples are all "real," ranging from Aesop's fables to Daniil Kharms and Kenneth Patchen, and they offer a valuable reminder of the richness of the tradition of short prose, one which has yet to be fully recognized as a distinct and important genre.

Carminalenia is more sparse and spare than his previous volumes. Familiar themes recur, and there is also a translation of Apollinaire's "The Palace of Thunder," but the obliquity of many of the poems, the privacy of their references and the mystery of their connections, makes this easily the least accessible of all Middleton's works. This privacy extends to the appended notes, where Middleton compares a poem to the experience of diving through a shoal of fish. Middleton's homage to the privacy of his illuminations recalls the style of Wallace Stevens, which finds an obvious echo in the poem entitled "A Very Small Hotel Room in the Key of T." Middleton continues to raise questions about the limits of generic frontiers when he entitles one blank verse piece "The Prose of Walking Back to China." In a prose poem entitled "Or Else," the poet uses the title phrase as a refrain to retract every statement as soon as it is uttered in favor of an alternative version, itself immediately supplanted by yet another version, and so on. This is another classic example of Middleton's method of composition based on the principle that order is always self-destructing, that it exists only as a perpetual urge to order; once frozen and taken for granted, it becomes a lie, a target.

The world of Middleton's poems is steeped in a kind of all-pervasive "or-elseness," and his most rewarding works are those in which this quality is directly enlisted in the service of the poem's patterned destruction-and-transfiguration. The latent "or-elseness" of a given work is also opened up by translation, which uncovers new possibilities of order in the mediating language. Middleton has described the task of the poet and translator as a matter of "astonishing speech into incandescence," but it is this same incandescence of unstable matter that also astonishes the poet into speech.

Gene M. Moore

Other major works
LONG FICTION: *Jakob von Gunten*, 1969 (translation).
SHORT FICTION: *The Walk and Other Stories*, 1957 (translation).
PLAY: *The Metropolitans*, 1964 (opera libretto).
NONFICTION: *The Quest for Christa T.*, 1970 (translation); *Kafka's Other Trial: Or, The Letters to Felice*, 1974 (translation); *Bolshevism in Art and Other Expository Writings*, 1978; *The Pursuit of the Kingfisher*, 1983.
ANTHOLOGIES: *No Hatred and No Flag, 20th Century War Poems*, 1958 (published in 1959 in German as *Ohne Hass und Fahne*); *Modern German Poetry, 1910-1960: An Anthology with Verse Translations*, 1962 (edited with Michael Hamburger); *German Writing Today*, 1967.

Bibliography
Bête Noire, (Spring, 1991). A special issue of this British literary magazine, focusing on Christopher Middleton.
Bryfonski, Dedria, ed. "Christopher Middleton." In *Contemporary Literary*

Criticism. Vol. 13. Detroit: Gale Research, 1980. Excerpts from critical responses to Middleton's work through *Pataxanadu.* Several of the critics represented are themselves poets, including Thom Gunn, Douglas Dunn, Jay Parini, and Ian Hamilton (better known as a biographer); also represented is the critic John Simon.

May, Hal, and James G. Lesniak, eds. "Christopher Middleton." In *Contemporary Authors New Revision Series.* Vol. 29. Detroit: Gale Research, 1990. A biographical sketch with a chronological overview of Middleton's work. Includes a primary bibliography and references to secondary sources.

Smith, Stan. "Christopher Middleton." In *Contemporary Poets,* edited by James Vinson and D. L. Kirkpatrick. 4th ed. New York: St. Martin's Press, 1985. Rather than a chronological overview, Smith provides a concise analysis of the defining characteristics of Middleton's work, with an emphasis on his reaction against the "parochialism" of contemporary English culture and his affinity with the dislocating vision of European modernism. "Many of Middleton's poems," Smith notes, "turn Hitler's and Stalin's death camps into universal symbols of 20th-century history." Includes a primary bibliography.

Young, Alan. "Christopher Middleton." In *Poets of Great Britain and Since 1960,* edited by Vincent B. Sherry, Jr. Vol. 40 in *Dictionary of Literary Biography.* Detroit: Gale Research, 1985. A thorough and sympathetic account by one of Middleton's best critics. As in Stan Smith's shorter piece (see above), Young stresses Middleton's challenge to the reigning assumptions of contemporary British poetry; Young sees Romantic as well as high modernist elements in Middleton's work. Includes a primary bibliography and references to secondary sources.

JOSEPHINE MILES

Born: Chicago, Illinois; June 11, 1911
Died: Berkeley, California; May 12, 1985

Principal poetry

Lines at Intersection, 1939; Poems on Several Occasions, 1941; Local Measures, 1946; Prefabrications, 1955; Poems, 1930-1960, 1960; Civil Poems, 1966; Kinds of Affection, 1967; Saving the Bay, 1967; Fields of Learning, 1968; To All Appearances: Poems New and Selected, 1974; Coming to Terms: Poems, 1979; Collected Poems, 1930-1983, 1983.

Other literary forms

In addition to her many volumes of poetry, Josephine Miles wrote more than a dozen books developing her theories of poetry and applying these theories to particular poets and eras. Among the most widely read of these works are Eras and Modes in English Poetry (1957, revised 1964) and Style and Proportion: The Language of Prose and Poetry (1967, revised 1984). These books are detailed structural analyses of English poetry and prose; all of Miles's criticism expounds her theory that the structure of language changes to reflect the time spirit that the language expresses. Her one play, House and Home, was first performed in 1960 and was published in First Stage in 1965.

Achievements

Miles's contribution to American poetry is valuable and unusual. She combined poetry of political commitment with sound scholarship and theory to produce a body of work that is at the same time of the tower and of the streets. Her work is a challenge both to the poet/propagandist and to the "art for art's sake" poet.

Miles's many awards and honors include a Guggenheim Award in 1948, the Oscar Blumenthal Prize in 1959, an American Council of Learned Societies Fellowship in 1965, a National Endowment for the Arts grant in 1967, and an American Academy of Poets Fellowship in 1978. Although her critical works have been to some extent superseded, Miles's poetry has guaranteed for her a lasting place in twentieth century American literature.

Biography

Josephine Louise Miles was born on June 11, 1911, to Reginald and Josephine Miles, a Chicago couple. When she was still an infant, Miles was diagnosed as having rheumatoid arthritis, a disease which plagued her all of her life. When she was five, her father, who was in the insurance business, moved the family to Southern California, hoping that the climate there would be beneficial to his daughter's condition. The family moved back to Evanston, Illinois, for a time, but Miles had identified California as her spiritual home. The family eventually settled down in Los Angeles, and Miles, after finishing at Los Angeles High School, attended the University of California, Los Angeles. After receiving her B.A. in 1932, she enrolled in graduate school at the University of California at Berkeley. She completed her M.A. in 1934 and her Ph.D. in 1938.

Although she had written poems since childhood, it was during her graduate school years that she first began to publish seriously and to gain recognition. Her first poems were published in an anthology, *Trial Balances* (1935), and this work earned for her two awards. Her first book, *Lines at Intersection*, appeared in 1939 and contains the best poems of her graduate school period.

In 1940, Miles began teaching at Berkeley as an instructor, and she remained there for the rest of her life. In 1947, she was the first woman to be tenured by Berkeley's English department, and in 1952 she was made a full professor. Miles never married, devoting her life to teaching, research, and poetry; during her years at Berkeley, she published more than two dozen books, in addition to numerous articles and reviews. She retired in 1978 and was given the status of Distinguished Professor Emerita. She died in Berkeley of pneumonia on May 12, 1985.

Analysis

Josephine Miles's poetry reflects both her political involvement in liberal causes and her intense concern with the sounds and structures of English. Over the decades of her writing, the poems became less formal and closed as their political content increased. Her topics shifted from minute observations of daily activities to analysis of the poet's role in the chaotic contemporary world. Nevertheless, even her most strident political poems show careful craftsmanship and attention to sound.

Miles's first published poems are tightly structured and intellectually dense. Her often-anthologized "On Inhabiting an Orange," published in the anthology *Trial Balances* in 1935, precedes her first collection. "All our roads go nowhere," the poem begins. "Maps are curled/ To keep the pavement definitely/ On the world." Because of these conditions, people's plans for "metric advance" must "lapse into arcs in deference/ to circumstance." The poem develops its single metaphor with clarity and sureness, using common metaphysical geometric images to provide the pleasure afforded by this kind of poetry. It is not surprising that her first work received two awards, the Shelley Memorial Award (1936) and the Phelan Memorial Award (1937).

Her first collection, *Lines at Intersection*, is a series of poems of everyday events arranged by time of day—morning poems, noon poems, evening poems. The individual works are mostly formal in structure, but they are more impressionistic than the early poems, and their music is more subtle. These poems incorporate such devices as internal rhymes, unusual metrical patterns, Dickinsonian slant rhymes, and incremental repetition. The poems are personal but not intimate, providing new perspective on such familiar things as the morning paper, the door-to-door salesman, baseball games, and theater performances. A few of the poems still show her preoccupation with mathematics and geometry, while others foretell one of her future concerns: the world of business, which was to become a major metaphor for the contemporary world. *Lines at Intersection* was well received, with favorable reviews in *Poetry* and elsewhere.

Miles's second collection, *Poems on Several Occasions*, shows a marked divergence from her earlier work in content. These poems, too, are arranged by time of day, and they also represent the life cycle from birth to death; moreover, these poems use the same stylistic devices as those of her earlier collection. This group, however, begins to define Miles's social commitments. By this time, Miles was becoming more aware of the inequalities, injustices, and false promises of contemporary America. Her titles show her new perspective: "Market Report on Cotton Gray Goods," "Committee Report on Smoke Abatement in Residential Area," "Committee Decision on Pecans for Asylum." The America in these poems is as unattractive as that of Allen Ginsberg in the 1950's and 1960's, and often for the same reasons. Business transactions take the place of personal contact, and there is a vast gap between what society would provide and what people want and need. Yet the poems are by and large wistful and do not actively suggest interference with the processes of oppression.

Local Measures marks a change in style: These poems are more conversational and irregular than Miles's earlier works. Their subjects include daily observations, social topics, and the relation of art to life. More of these poems are free verse or highly individualized forms. Dancing and motion pictures are analogues to poetry; the collection, written while Miles was working on her analysis of poetic forms in different periods of history, reflects her own search for a form appropriate to herself and her time. The mutual reflection of art and life is a theme approached again and again, as in "Redemption." Films, dances, even the jewelry that appears in these poems show Miles's attempts to define and thus master the process of creation.

Prefabrications combines her concerns for art and the social world. This rich and varied collection of sixty poems demonstrates the sense of community and continuity she was developing in the poetic theory on which she was working at the same time. Some of these poems, such as "The Plastic Glass," express the belief that the essentially human transcends the shabbiness and emptiness of life's surfaces. Others, such as "The Student," seek a source or definition of that humaneness, often using metaphors and images that are accessible to all but particularly compelling to academics. Indeed, in this and other poems in the collection, the academic life itself becomes a metaphor of the teaching-learning dialogue with the world. Some of the poems are about art. "Two Kinds of Trouble," a long poem, compares the social structures that made it hard for Michelangelo to communicate his vision with the problems of contemporary artists—a different kind of trouble.

Miles's *Poems, 1930-1960* included selections from all of her earlier books and a new group of poems, "Neighbors and Constellations," for the most part negative assessments of the possibility of meaningful intercourse among members of the human community. These poems, however, marked a turning point in her attitude, and the next collections showed a more active involvement in causes combined with a belief in the possibility of success.

Civil Poems and *Kinds of Affection* show that Miles was in and of Berkeley in the 1960's. These two collections center on pollution, poverty, destruction of beauty for purposes of greed, experimentation with animals, gun control, the war, the bomb, technology. An index to these poems would please nostalgia buffs, but the poems are less calls to action than expressions of the notion that social involvements are in fact ways of loving, or "kinds of affection." Among references to Dag Hammarskjöld, Molotov cocktails, and other hallmarks of the time, Miles returns again and again to the subject of commonality, the sharing underneath that survives all divisions. *Fields of Learning* does not diverge greatly from the previous two collections, but includes more science and slightly less politics. The world of these poems is filled with deoxyribonucleic acid, AMPAC, free neutrons, and gravitational electromagnetic fields. Yet despite their heavy freight of theoretical physics and technology, these poems are not inaccessible. They communicate a sense of human potential that exists not because of, but in spite of, technological advancement.

To All Appearances, while still political, is in many respects a return to earlier themes. Many of these are quiet poems of family and friendship. Their form is (usually) free verse, but in content the work is often reminiscent of *Local Measures.* One of the most memorable of the group is "Conception," which begins:

> Death did not come to my mother
> Like an old friend.
> She was a mother, and she must
> Conceive him.

The poem elaborates on its controlling metaphor, as do some of Miles's earliest poems, but here the appeal is as much emotional as it is intellectual. In general, these poems seem more direct than her earlier work. She uses "I" often in poems of reflection on her experiences inside and outside the university community.

Miles's last major collection (exclusive of her *Collected Poems, 1930-1983*) was *Coming to Terms* in 1979. This powerful collection gathers together the many strands of her lifelong preoccupations and weaves them into a single fabric. These are poems of social and aesthetic interest, asking the broadest questions and providing penetrating answers. The critics received the work with highest praise; Miles's last years were filled with honors and awards. More than one reviewer found the long poem "Center" to be Miles's strongest work. The poem poses the question "What are we here for?"—"we" being poets, creators, and humane visionaries. Her answer, not unlike that of the God in Johann Wolfgang von Goethe's *Faust*, is that we are here to make the best mistakes:

> Give us to err
> Grandly as possible in this complete
> Complex of structure, risk a soul
> Nobly in north light, in cello tone . . .

The result of such risk and error is a re-vision, a new perspective from which to view the possible. Human creativity in all of its forms becomes a medium "To take, as a building, as a fiction, takes us,/ Into another frame of space/ Where we can ponder, celebrate, and reshape." Miles's late view of poetry as process, or becoming, is similar to Wallace Stevens' final aesthetic. In this poem, Miles shows her own adjustment of vision, from the downward glance at the fatal curve of Earth in "On Inhabiting an Orange" to the upward and outward vistas of the possible from "the center."

    Collected Poems, 1930-1983 gives an overall view of Miles's development and includes her last poems, for the most part scenes of Berkeley and of the university. (She lived only about a year after the appearance of this volume, which was popular as well as critically acclaimed, and she was awarded *The Nation's* Leonore Marshall Poetry Prize in 1983.) Her careful craftsmanship and metrical felicity can be appreciated in this final publication, a well-edited work which illustrates the range of her poetic gift. Her "search for a common language" antedated Adrienne Rich's better-known one and combined some of the same ingredients. This collection shows how her hopes for community within human society paralleled her search for what she called "commonality" in language. Her intellectually and emotionally persuasive metaphors, her subtle music, and the potency and optimism of her later work make Miles a significant contributor to twentieth century American poetry.

Janet McCann

Other major works

    PLAY: *House and Home*, 1960.

    NONFICTION: *Wordsworth and the Vocabulary of Emotion*, 1942; *Pathetic Fallacy in the Nineteenth Century: A Study of a Changing Relationship Be-*

tween Object and Emotion, 1942; *Major Adjectives in English Poetry from Wyatt to Auden*, 1946; *The Primary Language of Poetry in the 1640's*, 1948; *The Primary Language of Poetry in the 1740's and 1840's*, 1950; *The Primary Language of Poetry in the 1940's*, 1951; *The Continuity of Poetic Language: Studies in English Poetry from the 1540's to the 1940's*, 1951 (includes preceding three volumes); *Eras and Modes in English Poetry*, 1957, revised 1964; *Renaissance, Eighteenth-Century, and Modern Language in English Poetry: A Tabular View*, 1960; *Ralph Waldo Emerson*, 1964; *Style and Proportion: The Language of Prose and Poetry*, 1967, revised 1984; *Poetry and Change: Donne, Milton, Wordsworth, and the Equilibrium of the Present*, 1974; *Working Out Ideas: Predication and Other Uses of Language*, 1979.

Bibliography

Beloof, Robert. "Distances and Surfaces." *Prairie Schooner* 32 (Winter, 1958-1959): 276-284. This fine, readable article examines Miles's poetry in terms of poetic strategies. Beloof's analysis is detailed, thematic, and logical.

Chase, Karen. Review of *Collected Poems, 1930-1983*, by Josephine Miles. *World Literature Today* 58 (Summer, 1984): 423. A very favorable review of Miles's career. Excerpts from selected poems are briefly discussed to reveal Miles's versatility.

Guillory, Daniel L. Review of *Collected Poems, 1930-1983*, by Josephine Miles. *Choice* 24 (March, 1984): 978. Guillory suggests a favorable comparison could be made between the poetry of Miles and the poetry of William Carlos Williams. Important themes in Miles's poetry are listed, as well as a thematic and chronological progression.

Smith, Lawrence R. "Josephine Miles: Metaphysician of the Irrational." *Pebble* 18-19-20 (1979): 22-35. A very interesting and insightful article examining some of the major symbols and themes in Miles's poetry. Careful attention is given to many of Miles's poems.

EDNA ST. VINCENT MILLAY

Born: Rockland Maine; February 22, 1892
Died: Austerlizt, New York; October 19, 1950

Principal poetry

Renascence and Other Poems, 1917; *A Few Figs from Thistles*, 1920; *Second April*, 1921; *The Harp-Weaver and Other Poems*, 1923; *The Buck in the Snow and Other Poems*, 1928; *Edna St. Vincent Millay's Poems Selected for Young People*, 1929; *Fatal Interview*, 1931; *Wine from These Grapes*, 1934; *The Flowers of Evil*, 1936 (*Les Fleurs du Mal*, translation; with George Dillon); *Conversation at Midnight*, 1937; *Huntsman, What Quarry?*, 1939; *Make Bright the Arrows*, 1940; *There are No Islands Any More*, 1940; *Invocation to the Muses*, 1941; *Collected Sonnets*, 1941; *The Murder of Lidice*, 1942; *Collected Lyrics*, 1943; *Poem and Prayer for an Invading Army*, 1944; *Mine the Harvest*, 1954; *Collected Poems*, 1956.

Other literary forms

Edna St. Vincent Millay was known during her early career for her verse plays, the most successful being the first, *Aria da Capo*, first produced in 1919 and published in 1921, followed by *The Lamp and the Bell* and *Two Slatterns and a King*, also published in 1921, and *The Princess Marries the Page* (written during her student years at Vassar), published in 1932. Her reputation as a writer of verse for the stage was such that she was invited to write the libretto for a Deems Taylor opera commissioned by the Metropolitan Opera Company of New York. The result of her collaboration with Taylor was a successful presentation of *The King's Henchman* (1927), a variation of the Tristan story. Millay tried to rework the material of the opera libretto into a drama but finally condemned the result as hopelessly contaminated; she was never able to rid it of the influence of the libretto.

Conversation at Midnight and *The Murder of Lidice* are sometimes classified as plays, the former receiving performance after Millay's death and the latter being written for wartime radio broadcast after the Nazis destroyed the Czechoslovakian town of Lidice and slaughtered its male inhabitants. *The Murder of Lidice* cannot be considered as more than hastily written propaganda at best, and *Conversation at Midnight* suffers if one looks for the conflict and engagement of drama in it. Millay conceded after its completion that it was not really a play but a series of poems with a fixed setting.

In addition to working with dramatic forms, Millay, in the beginning years of her career, wrote topical commentaries for the New York weekly, *Vanity Fair*, under the pseudonym Nancy Boyd; they were collected in a 1924 volume as *Distressing Dialogues*, the title used by the magazine as the pieces appeared. Although these early essays helped to support the young poet, Millay was never willing to have them published under her name. She was, however, proud of her collaboration on *Flowers of Evil* (1936), the translation of Charles Baudelaire's *Les Fleurs du mal* (1857), although scholars find more of Millay in the translations than the original may warrant. Millay's letters have been collected and published and a recording she made of selected poems is still available.

Achievements

Millay's meteoric rise as a popular poet seems to have been, in part, a product of her times and the independent style of life that she represented. This fact may account for the later critical dismissal of her work. Millay's poetry is, in many ways, conventional in its formal aspects, often showing strict attention to rhyme and traditional metrical patterns. Her nineteenth century literary forebears were Alfred, Lord Tennyson and A. E. Housman. She showed no interest in the experimental work being done by T. S. Eliot, Ezra Pound, and others of her generation. In her strong allegiance to the lyric, to traditional verse forms, and to conventional diction, she guaranteed that she would not take her place in the mainstream of influential twentieth century poets, although she was very much aware of contemporary currents. Once her initial popularity waned, Millay's work was judged to be something of a sport in a century in which the breaking of forms was thought to be the best representation of the breaking of traditional views of the world.

Ironically, much of Millay's early popularity came from her image as a rebel and nonconformist—a representative of emancipated Greenwich Village culture, a perfect example of the liberated woman of the 1920's. This reputation was primarily promoted by the publication of *A Few Figs from Thistles*, a collection of flippant and audacious poems which seemed a manifesto for the new woman and her independent, nontraditional attitude toward modern life. The image of the short-lived candle burning at both ends and giving its lovely light forged an identity for Millay that her serious poems could never alter, and the proverbial candle seems in retrospect almost an ironic paradigm for Millay's own poetic career.

In spite of Millay's waning popularity in the last decades of her life and the harsh judgment of critics who were suspicious of her early widespread popularity, Millay's poetic accomplishment is considerable, and she deserves a more sensitive reading than she has been accorded in the years since her death. She is very much an American poet in her eclecticism. As a champion of the individual and of freedom from tyranny of any kind, she deserves a place in the American tradition beside poets as widely divergent as Walt Whitman and Archibald MacLeish. As a poet willing to insist on the validity and strength of real emotion and thought in women and on their individuality in relationships, Millay replaced hitherto largely convention-bound material with fresh insights. In her frank introspection and exploration of psychological states, she opened the way for the modern confessional poets who followed her.

Biography

Although Edna St. Vincent Millay is not usually thought of as a New England poet, she was born in Maine and spent the first twenty years of her life there, most of them in Camden, where her mother moved with her three young girls after a divorce in 1900. Millay and her sisters were encouraged to develop their musical and poetic talents and to read widely in the classics and in English and American literature. Millay's mother supported the family by working as a nurse, and from her example, Millay learned early the independence and self-reliance which were to influence her poetry. She learned to value and trust her personal voice, leading many of her readers to search her poems for the details of her personal life that they were thought to reveal.

With the aid of a patron, Millay was able to attend Vassar College the year after the publication of "Renascence," the beginning of her public career as a poet. After graduation from Vassar, Millay moved to New York and, living in poverty, began her association with Greenwich Village and the Provincetown Players. This period of five or six years before her marriage provides the backdrop against which Millay is remembered and with which she is identified, although it represents a very small portion of her life. It was during this period that her famous friendships and love affairs with Floyd Dell, Arthur Fricke, and Edmund Wilson, among others, began, and during which the Provincetown Players produced *Aria da Capo*. She won fame and national popularity with the publication of *A Few Figs from Thistles* in 1920. After several years in Europe, marked by the beginning of the bad health that was to plague her for the rest of her life, Millay returned to the United States and in 1923 became the first woman to win a Pulitzer Prize for poetry. In the same year, she married a Dutch importer who gave up his business to provide a stable environment for her—on a farm at Austerlitz, New York, and in an island home off the coast of Maine.

Taking an active part in the general outcry of American intellectuals and artists against the death sentencing of Nicola Sacco and Bartolomeo Vanzetti, Millay called on the governor of Massachusetts and wrote public statements and several poems, including "Justice Denied in Massachusetts." She was arrested along with others keeping vigil at the time of the execution. In this, as in everything she did, Millay acted with total conviction and unflinching courage—qualities which give strength to her poems, although these same unabashed qualities set her apart in an age that increasingly demanded ironic distance as a prerequisite for serious verse.

Millay received several honorary doctorates and was elected to both the National Institute of Arts and Letters and the American Academy of Arts and Letters. By the end of the 1930's, however, after publication of *Conver-*

sation at Midnight, her reputation had suffered a serious decline, a decline accelerated by the work that she published too hurriedly in the service of wartime propaganda: *Make Bright the Arrows* and *The Murder of Lidice* represent the lowest ebb in her reputation as a serious poet. In the summer of 1944, she suffered a severe nervous breakdown accompanied by serious "writer's block" that lasted for more than two years. Just as she was beginning to take up her work again in 1949, her husband died suddenly. The shock resulted in hospitalization again. She returned later that year alone to her farm in Steepletop, New York, where she died of heart failure a little more than a year after her husband's death. A volume of new poems, *Mine the Harvest,* was published in 1954 and her *Collected Poems* in 1956.

Analysis

The theme of individual liberty and the frank acknowledgment of emotion are everpresent in Edna St. Vincent Millay's poems. She speaks as clearly for a democracy of persons, in whatever relationship, as Walt Whitman does and with no hint of snobbery or elitism. She values the simple and common in nature; the reader never finds her straining after exotic effects. Millay is a realist in her expectations, and she refuses conventional romantic attitudes— a refusal which often results in the ironic tone of some of her love poems. It is not surprising that she acknowledged her fondness for Andrew Marvell, the poet of "The Passionate Shepherd to His Love" and "The Nymph's Reply."

Millay's volumes of poetry contain no "major" poems which have entered the canon of literature in the way in which those of Robert Frost, T. S. Eliot, or William Butler Yeats have. Her early volume, *Renascence,* with its title poem written before she entered Vassar, may hold little interest for contemporary readers, although it was highly praised by Harriet Monroe, the editor of *Poetry* magazine. Much of the strength of the other volumes lies in the sustained effect of sonnet sequences and collections of lyrics. There is evidence of growth, however uneven, in Millay's development as a poet, as her work moves from the devil-may-care irony and unabashed emotion of the early poems to a more considered and mature production.

The one form in which Millay excelled is the sonnet, both Shakespearean and Petrarchan. She has been described as a transitional poet, and this is nowhere better born out than in her control of a conventional and circumscribed form in which she was equally comfortable with traditional or modern subject matter and attitudes.

"Euclid Alone Has Looked on Beauty Bare," published in *The Harp-Weaver and Other Poems,* is an accomplished classical Petrarchan sonnet written early in Millay's career. It takes as its subject the holy, dazzling beauty of pure form or idea available only to the Greek mathematician, Euclid, who perceived a pure beauty which has not been matched by the prattling of subsequent generations seeking imitations of beauty clothed in human form. The octave ends with a command to let the geese gabble and hiss (an allusion both to the use of geese as watchdogs in ancient times and to those who mistakenly cry out that they have sighted Beauty). The sestet presents a vivid description of the blinding and terrible light that Euclid bore when he "looked on Beauty bare," suggesting that lesser men are fortunate that they have not seen Beauty whole, as it would be too much for them to bear. (In the sestet, the word "bare" has become an adjective of personification as well as one carrying its original meaning of "pure," "unadorned.") Lesser men are lucky if they have even once heard Beauty's sandal on a distant rock; those seekers after Beauty who are not Euclids are doubly fortunate to have heard only a distant echo of Beauty's step, for they could not have borne the blinding intensity of Euclid's vision.

This sonnet is seemingly simple and straightforward. It is more complex than it first appears, however, for by the poet's own personification of Beauty (now clothed—in sandals, at least), she acknowledges herself to be one of those lesser mortals who followed Euclid. She ironically accepts her own conventional restrictions. Euclid's vision is of "light anatomized," not of Beauty in the traditional, personified female form.

Fatal Interview, the chronicling of a love affair from inception through intense passion to sad conclusion, represents Millay's longest sustained sonnet sequence. The book's title comes from John Donne's sixteenth elegy in a series about a tragic affair, beginning, "By one first strange and fatal interview." Although the sonnets do not evince the full range of intense emotion that one might expect, Millay manages to treat her subject with the objectivity, control, and irony that mark her love poems as the products of the modern woman, freed from the stereotype of woman as the passive, overwhelmed love object. The passions of love and sexual ecstasy find their way into these poems, but always present too is an awareness of the fleeting nature of even the most passionate relationships and a refusal to accept a bondage that involves the loss of individual integrity. She knows that love can be "stung to death by gnats."

"Well, I have lost you; and I lost you fairly" is the initial line of sonnet forty-seven, and there is a pride expressed in losing well on the speaker's own terms. Nights of weeping she will not deny, but day finds her dry-eyed and fully operative in the world that goes on after love is lost. A more slyly played relationship or one of lesser intensity might have preserved the relationship through another summer, but at too high a cost for lovers who have experienced so much intensity and honesty. The price in "words I value highly" is one that Millay as poet and woman will not, cannot, pay. "Well, I have lost you" is simple and straightforward; a sign of control over pain and grief. Sonnet thirty and others preceding it have made it clear that Millay's realism, her defense against the grief of loss, is a reaction inherent in her philosophical stance in the world; this fact, however, does not lessen the real poignancy of the sonnet. These are the statements of a highly intelligent and sensitive woman who suffers because of the awareness that never leaves her. In "Love is not all: it is not meat nor drink" (sonnet thirty) the speaker is conscious that men have died for lack of love even though it is not technically one of the physical necessities of life such as food, drink, and shelter. The sonnet accepts love as a dear necessity for life, but there is in the concluding lines the nagging realization that if it were necessary, she might sell this love for peace, or these passionate memories for food. Although at this moment she is inclined to think she would not, the acknowledgment of the possibility clearly marks the distance between Millay's poem and Elizabeth Barrett Browning's "How do I love thee?" In a more flippant early lyric entitled "Thursday," the gulf between Millay and the more conventional Browning is absolute and unbridgeable.

Among Millay's poems for her mother, "The Ballad of the Harp-Weaver" and "In the Grave No Flower" are two which display careful simplicity and controlled depth of feeling. "The Ballad of the Harp-Weaver" was criticized by Edmund Wilson for being slight, superficial, and sentimental. He characterized it as a poem for a woman's magazine. The poem is more effective than Wilson suggested and wholly appropriate to its subject: the rich gifts of the spirit given to a child by a mother who, in her poverty, cannot provide the material food and clothing that her child needs. The ballad form controls the simple narrative of the parable, and if the reader accepts the perfect union of form and subject that Millay achieves, the poem is more than a modest success.

"In the Grave No Flower" names with loving specificity common weeds that, by their rank fecundity and stubborn resistance to the plow, inherit the earth, in contrast to the barren grave where there is and can be no flower. This lyric demonstrates Millay's control of intense grief, heightened by her ability to express it with devastating simplicity. The reader has only to compare "In the Grave No Flower" to the early "Elegy Before Death," written on the death of a close friend, to see the distance that Millay has come in her growth as a poet.

Millay's best poems may be love sonnets or lyrics of passion or elegy (even "The Buck in the Snow" is an elegy of sorts), but as a poet she is willing to risk the most ordinary of subjects. A poem called simply "Menses," although not one of her best, is an interesting example of the risk-taking that marked Millay both in her personal and in her poetic life. This poem celebrates the settled relationship, the accommodations made between two people out of the love and understanding which comes with adjustments to the most unglamorous cycles of life. The occasion of the poem is a surface duel between a man and a woman who is undergoing the emotional upheaval associated with her monthly menstrual cycle. The poem is, for the most part, an interior dramatic monologue spoken by the man ("to himself, being aware how it is with her"), who turns aside an incipient quarrel, having "learned/ More things than one in our few years together." Millay's risk-taking in this poem is found with her decision to give to the man the voice in this special situation, and with the woman, driven by physical forces, half-awaiting the relief his understanding will bring her. A simple rendering of the symbiotic daily relationship of two people, this poem is deeply meaningful and, in its own way, as spectacular and surprising as a moment of passion might be in one of Millay's love sonnets.

Millay's poetic subjects range more widely than her reputation suggests, for the complexity of her poetry has been obscured by the personal image created during the early years of her career. She is not only the poet whose candle consumes itself and the night and "gives a lovely light!"; she is an accomplished poet of a wide range of complex emotions, themes, and forms.

Donna Gerstenberger

Other major works

PLAYS: *Aria da Capo*, 1919; *The Lamp and the Bell*, 1921; *Two Slatterns and a King*, 1921; *The King's Henchman*, 1927 (opera libretto); *The Princess Marries the Page*, 1932.

NONFICTION: *Distressing Dialogues*, 1924 (published under the pseudonym Nancy Boyd).

Bibliography

Brittin, Norman A. *Edna St. Vincent Millay*. 1967. Rev. ed. Boston: Twayne, 1982. Brittin has rewritten his 1967 biography of Millay (he uses the name "Vincent" as her friends and family called her, in the earlier edition), providing more discussion of her prose works and less space to the biography. He brings out her feminist ideas and her relation to the poetic movement of High Modernism. The chronology and useful annotated bibliography have a few new items, but not many. An essential reference.

Cheney, Anne. *Millay in Greenwich Village*. University: University of Alabama Press, 1975. A map of the Greenwich Village section of Manhattan accompanies the introduction to this study of Millay's village years, from 1918 to 1925. The men in her life at that time, Floyd Dell, Edmund Wilson, Arthur Fricke, and the man she married, Eugen Boissevain, are discussed in a chapter devoted to each, with an analysis of the poems dated in the period of each romance. Ten pages of photographs of Millay and New York document this important period in American literary history. Includes notes, a bibliography, and an index.

Drake, William. *The First Wave: Women Poets in America, 1915-1945*. New York: Collier Books, 1987. Drake captures the essential meaning to women poets in the period between the two world wars of the rising movement for female independence, the Freudian backlash to that movement, and the effect of a wave of anticommunism on the critical reception of women poets. Millay's place in this story is well documented and argued, including her avoidance of the psychoanalytical trap and her need for nurturing but not stifling care. A full page photo shows Millay and Lola Ridge being arrested for protesting the Sacco-Vanzetti case. Contains excellent notes, a bibliography, and an index.

Gould, Jean. *The Poet and Her Book.* New York: Dodd, Mead, 1969. In seventeen chapters, Gould retells Millay's life from sources oral and written. Many fascinating anecdotes reveal Millay's personality in her childhood, her adolescent and college years, her travels, and her marriage. Readers learn about her friends, her illnesses, and her publishing history. This book is useful for a nonpolitical understanding of her strengths and weaknesses. Sixteen pages of photographs accompany the text.

Sheean, Vincent. *The Indigo Bunting: A Memoir of Edna St. Vincent Millay.* New York: Harper, 1951. The title refers to a small North American bird that sings when other birds are still. So Sheean characterized Millay, his friend for many years. This intimate close-up shows the extent of Millay's culture, her knowledge of Latin literary classics, and music and art history. Her personal fascination shines through these pages of recollections.

Stanbrough, Jane. "Edna St. Vincent Millay and the Language of Vulnerability." In *Shakespeare's Sisters: Feminist Essays on Women Poets*, edited by Sandra Gilbert and Susan Gubar. Bloomington: Indiana University Press, 1978. From her Vassar days onward, Millay's public image was as a rebellious, liberated, self-assured woman. But Stanbrough argues from evidence in her poetry that inwardly, Millay felt anguish at women's victimization in a world they could not control. She used a child narrator, wrote about "ancient secrets," and protested against war and totalitarian regimes, all from her sense of extreme vulnerability.

VASSAR MILLER

Born: Houston, Texas; July 19, 1924

Principal poetry
Adam's Footprint, 1956; *Wage War on Silence*, 1960; *My Bones Being Wiser*, 1963; *Onions and Roses*, 1968; *If I Could Sleep Deeply Enough*, 1974; *Small Change*, 1976; *Approaching Nada*, 1977; *Selected and New Poems: 1950-1980*, 1982; *Struggling to Swim on Concrete*, 1984; *If I Had Wheels or Love: Collected Poems of Vassar Miller*, 1991.

Other literary forms
Despite This Flesh (1985), poems and stories on the nature of physical handicap and its sufferings by various writers, was edited by Vassar Miller.

Achievements
Considered by many to be the best poet to have emerged from Texas, Miller was widely hailed at the publication of her second book of poems, *Wage War on Silence*, which was nominated for the Pulitzer Prize in 1961. Three of her other books have won awards from the Texas Institute of Letters. In 1982, she shared with the poet William Barney the poet laureateship of Texas. Her poetry is noted for its formal craftsmanship, its distinct precision of language and rhyme in traditional form, and its account of a life of loneliness and suffering from cerebral palsy and of a strong faith in Christianity expressed with erotic passion.

Biography
Vassar Miller was born and reared in Houston, Texas, the daughter of a successful real estate developer whose family house, on Vassar Street, where she still resides, is the scene of many of her poems on childhood and on the anguish of coping with chronic illness and debilitation. Her father had early encouraged her by giving her a typewriter and coaching her first efforts at poetry; some of her poems give harrowing glimpses into the despair of a child whose mother physically rejected her. Miller attended the University of Houston for her B.S. and M.A. degrees; she wrote her master's thesis on mysticism in the poetry of Edgar Arlington Robinson. For a time, she taught in a private school in Houston and was a participant in such literary conferences as the Breadloaf Writers' Conference in Vermont in 1968 and the Southwest Writers' conferences of 1973 and 1983, held at the University of Houston. Illness discouraged her from teaching, but for years she was a familiar figure in her neighborhood streets, propelling her three-wheeled bicycle, until a local ordinance restricted its use. Miller is revered in Texas as a

voice of resilient faith whose work eschews the major trends of modern poetry but is rich in the values of Anglo-American tradition, both in candor
and in tempered self-reliance.

Analysis

Vassar Miller's earliest poetry springs from her close study of the New
England poet Edgar Arlington Robinson, an exacting formalist whose elegant
short poems recounted the bitter lives and emotional corruption of villagers
in his imaginary Maine town of Tilbury. Miller's graduate thesis on Robinson worries out the thread of faith and hope running through Robinson's
poetry, which he composed at a time when New England had ceased to be
an important economic region of the United States and its citizens had resigned themselves to lives of failure and cynical resentment. Her study zeroed
in on his portrayals of trapped individuals and how they dealt with their
plight, either by suicide or drunkenness or by tapping some inner resource of
faith.

Adam's Footprint, which collects her earliest poetry, explores her world of
pain, physical and emotional, in compact stanzas of eight lines with neat envelope or alternating rhyme schemes. One may detect in them the echo of
hymns, based loosely on ballad measure but here straightened out into full
eight- and ten-syllable lines. In an interview published in *Heart's Invention:
On the Poetry of Vassar Miller* (1988, edited by Stephen Ford-Brown), Miller
described her childhood notebooks as "filled with miserable imitations of
equally miserable hymns." Later, she would turn to Emily Dickinson and
master a variable, minimalist lyric of excruciating pointedness. Nevertheless,
the hymn would remain a base measure of her rhythmic imagination, as it
did for Dickinson herself. Both writers are to be credited with having composed secular literary hymns in which sensuous, erotic longings have their
place in religious meditation.

Adam's Footprint develops carefully a series of metaphors of the body
through feet and coordinated motions, as Miller describes her experiences as
a handicapped child. In the title poem, she compares her infirmity to being
outcast, an exile like Adam, whose footprint marks the path others of misfortune must follow. Even here, however, Miller carefully avoids self-pity;
the poem's scrupulous artistry is the adequate sublimation of her pains. The
real ballet of elegant motions occurs in the mind, in the artist's skillful execution of her words even as she cries out against her freakish disability.
Another poem, "Spastic Child," laments another child's inability to speak,
in a poem lushly confident to express his pain for him. The artist of these
poems is the alter ego of the crippled infant, a second, idealized self technically projected out of the subject's own suffering intellect.

The sonnet, one of Miller's favorite forms, is a perfect vehicle for the ar-
gumentative lyric she writes in *Adam's Footprint*, with its eight-line assertion

or question and its six-line rebuttal. In "The Magnitude of Zero," Adam is the first child, here called the "first citizen," to "whom earth splays huge upon my nothing's rack." Verbs such as "trudge," "quail," and "splays" underscore the labored movements of the subject. "The Final Hunger" begins, "Hurl down the nerve-gnarled body," as the reader follows her to painful sleep in another very forceful sonnet. Miller is equally adept at the Petrarchan and the Shakespearean sonnet forms. "Beside a Deathbed," in the Shakespearean mode, closes on a feminine, two-syllabled rhyme, "lying,"/"dying," a small flourish of her technical mastery.

Miller's poetry took a new direction in Texas writing; the tradition of verse in the Southwest is dominated by female poets whose subjects included inspirational thoughts, moral homilies, studies of the landscape, and overall expressions of Christian faith and calm endurance. Miller's probing lyrics delve deep into a world of error and torment, failure and unrequited erotic longings. Though other women had hinted of their dissatisfactions with life on the ranch and in the small prairie towns, Miller's poetry is overtly stark, even brutal in its portrayal of a life of toil and loneliness.

It was perhaps coincidence that she should come of age just as the confessional poets were publishing their own first works on similar themes, although with far more intensity. Her second book, *Wage War on Silence*, bore some resemblance to the poems of Robert Lowell, Sylvia Plath, and Anne Sexton, who make up the core of the confessional movement of the 1960's, and whose poems dissect their own witheringly painful lives in the public arena of literature. Miller became associated with the women writers of the movement and doubtless benefited by the connection. Her favorite among them was Sexton, to whom she later dedicated one of her poems. In fact, Miller's literary associations all take her back to New England, from Dickinson to Robinson and contemporary writers, among whom she has found a parallel preoccupation with the inner life, a subject often avoided by other Texas poets until recently.

"Without Ceremony," a Shakespearean sonnet with the "turn" or riposte saved for the final closing couplet, is an impassioned prayer for mercy addressed to Father Pain, the Word "in whom our wordiness dissolves/ When we have not a prayer except ourselves." Piety on the one hand rejects artfulness in prayer but, on the other, is proffered with immaculately textured artifice. Unresolved in Miller's poetry is this double standard, this conflict between a pure, unrehearsed experience of her faith and the demands of art. The poems insist upon the reality of their emotions and settings but frame them within the ordered, compact structure of verses. Part of the power of such writing lies in its tension between conflicting attitudes: a singeing, violent emotion and the limpid formality of its expression. Like the poet Denise Levertov, who admires Miller's writing, Miller insists on the most exacting measures for poetry that describes the chaos of modern life. Both poets reject out of hand the mode of spontaneous composition as unfit for true poetry.

Songs abound in *Wage War on Silence*; some, such as "Love Song for the Future," are in the racing rhythms of trochaic meter, where the beat falls on the first syllable of the foot and pushes the language along in a quick, dancing motion, as in John Donne's line "Go and catch a falling star." Miller's opening lines are "To our ruined vineyards come,/ Little foxes, for your share." The rhyme scheme is *ababcdcd*, a lacing pattern that enhances the quickness and neatness of the language. The theme of the poem is the dying wilderness, the animal kingdom Saint Francis of Assisi loved, which is doomed by a "world of steel," the town and city. Innocence of all kinds perishes as the landscape is urbanized and the adult world of commerce and greed takes over.

Though not a regional poet in the conventional sense of local-color anecdotes and reminiscences of the land, Miller is subtly regional in her metaphorical landscapes; the wilderness is her own emotional life, but it stands equally for the disappearance of ranch land and wild meadow in urban Texas, for the sprawl of cities such as those her own father helped to develop into megalopolises. Concrete and steel are her images for alienation and loss; childhood is the moist grass and the garden where she recalls a few fond memories of her father and of her still pliant body. The city is the stiffening ground of painful adulthood, and by that indirect means she copies the changes of her region.

"So you are what we name,/ And what we name we love," she writes in the first stanza of "For a Christening," in a six-syllable line that is soothing, melodious, and songlike, crafting a hymn to innocence as a child is baptized. "Each man's sorrow is an absolute" is the noble opening of "The Common Core," which gives grim solace to those who suffer, in a patterned verse like the "songs of experience" William Blake wrote for children. There is much injured innocence in Miller's world, where she often takes on the persona of a child confiding its pains to adult readers.

In another striking lyric, "Defense Rests," she tells the reader cunningly that "Love/ is too much for the heart to bear/ alone." The poem weaves together eros and faith, sexual longing and religious commitment, and ends by appealing to Christ for comfort of her earthly needs, since he alone in her religion has both suffered and known the love of others, including Mary Magdalene and John the Baptist. Such open confessions of need coupled with powerful religious devotion recall seventeenth century religious verse, the sometimes torrid poetry of John Donne, Henry Vaughan, Richard Crashaw, and Thomas Traherne, among whom passionate prayer mixed with erotic imagery is, if not the norm, the common thread that prompted T. S. Eliot to praise their "undissociated sensibility." Miller restores some of that wholeness of passion when she combines soul and self in the same passage.

My Bones Being Wiser, published in 1963, shows increasing maturity in the writing. The forms are not so rigidly enforced, and the language has become more fluid and open, while at the same time sparer in its music. "The leaves blow speaking/ green, lithe words/ in no man's language," begins the poem "Precision," with its deft touch, its suggestive language bordering on dream imagery. The naïve voice perceives talking trees and animate nature, as imagination goes beyond mere selfhood and encompasses the immediate surroundings of her world. This is the "wisdom" of the title, the surer grasp of meaning in her experience. Even the sonnets are more delicate and reflective, as in "Reverent Impiety," with its caustic premise, "I will not fast, for I have fasted longer/ Than forty days" in a life of agonizing debility. The dominant influence of these poems is the taciturn energy of Dickinson, whom Miller closely approximates with stunning lines of her own, though not with Dickinson's reckless daring. "Though you elude my leash of love," she chides her longed-for lover in "Complaint," her rapture is boundless "like the damned."

When one combs such books by Miller, it is not plot one notices but the separate poems on each page. Plot may exist in the slow shift of subject from early life and first passion to these smoother, more mature reflections on unfulfilled longing. Miller's publishers are often asked to sort through the manuscripts she sends and to make books out of them, rather than to depend on her for final arrangement of the work. Fortunately for Miller, her books have found conscientious editors who have discovered a usable thread of narrative running through her poems. Yet one would be mistaken to make too much of how the poems unwind a tale or yield some hidden premise in their relations to one another. Her books record the slow passing of days and years, slight shifts in faith and perspective on the world. The poem, however, is the real focus of experience, as it records a sudden fascination with a word or vowel, a delicate experiment in a new rhythm, a use of slang or even a curse word, or a new metaphor to be worked into a villanelle or sonnet.

Noticeable in *Onions and Roses* (1968) and *If I Could Sleep Deeply Enough* (1974) is the theme of middle age taking hold throughout the poetry. The poet is writing from her mid-forties to the age of fifty, and the reader can detect how elegy and lament are increasingly foregrounded in these books. Sleep is no longer a restful escape from the day's pain, but deepens its meaning as a figure of death. The formalism has relaxed; sonnets and regular stanzaic lyrics flank free verse compositions, a form in which to posit misgivings and doubts in her faith, wrestlings with the Lord, and her acerbic wit or crankiness. The open lyric allows her to experiment with even tighter concision, in brief poems of eight or nine lines, as in "In a Land of Indistinct Seasons," with its spare image of a "crystal pane" where someone has "let the summer out/ and the autumn in." Even here, Miller eschews that other dictate of modern poetry, thought as process or ambiguity. Her language is honed, refined, reduced to a compactness of result, finished and enclosed in its precise certainty of expression.

Approaching Nada, a brief sequence of lyric meditations, written over a three-day period in March, 1977, while the poet was on a trip to Phoenix, Arizona, tests the limits of her imagination and faith in what many consider her greatest poem. Written in irregular, eight-syllable lines of mainly trochaic meter, a muscular rhythm for driving home one's thoughts, *Aproaching Nada* allows the reader to feel the willfulness of her argument as she confronts her lifelong belief in God. The *nada* of the poem is Spanish for "nothing," and the surrounding desert of Phoenix confirms the absence of things rather than supporting her vision. "Many words do not compose the Word," she admits, but "Somewhere between silence and ceremony springs the Word." Here as nowhere before Miller expands her sense of faith and religion to include a world of vision across all faiths, a sense of God running through Native American, Quaker, Catholic, Protestant, and beyond. God here is the collective longing for spiritual comfort. God is the Nothing, the spirit beyond imagination or words, present in everything but without substance or human conception. The recognition of the spirit's Nothingness raises her religious views to the mystical insight that no religion or spiritual way can take possession of God; spirit resides in the human condition in spite of one's individual ways.

> These poets of the Nada
> obeyed Him. So poets, mystics of
> the bruising thing
> climb up bloody concretes
> to leave nailed high
> white pieces of themselves.

The poet is, as Abbé Bremond wrote, "un mystique manque," a failed visionary who

> like the mouse will scuttle
> clean to the border
> of the ineffable,
> then scurry back
> with tidbits of the Vision.

To approach Nada or the nothing is to release the illusions of godliness one has cherished, and to accept with finality the ineffability of spirit, its transparent presence in the void.

Trying to Swim on Concrete opens with an impassioned sonnet, "Admission," addressed to her father, whom she loved best of all men. "You were my absolute, if such there lives/ Within the prison of the relatives." This and her new work collected in *If I Had Wheels or Love* mark a slow shift back to closed form as the dominant mode of her verse, with the sonnet and tercet stanza the dominant forms. A few poems, such as "Whitewash of Houston," a longish tirade against the squalid life of Houston, are prosy and open, but mainly the poet is back to song, to iambic pentameter lines of delicate music such as the opening of "Assertion," "I am no scholar in the ways of love," and "I have been out of the weather of love," in "Seasonal Change." In "Affinity," Miller pays homage to another influence on her life and thought, the great religious short-story writer Flannery O'Connor, who also suffered a lifelong debilitating illness while she wrote. "Had disease and early death not shut/ your door, you might have left the family pew,/ thumbing your nose at every holy 'Tut!' "

The "uncollected poems" that close *If I Had Wheels or Love* are her starkest examinations of the meaning of death, her own and others. In several of these poems, she bids farewell to deceased friends and tries to foresee her own end, while in others she continues her flirtations with potential lovers as the other extreme of her resilient spirit. "You, smiling friend," she writes in "Love Song," a Petrarchan sonnet, "say only that you like me,/ And that, at least for now, is quite enough." She returns to Adam's exile, her metaphor for the loneliness of her own invalid childhood, in "Fiat," which opens, "Eden is closed forever, if it was/ Opened to us at anytime." In one of her loveliest lyrics, "Rivers," she turns to her region directly to write "Rio de Brazos de Dios" on the long, winding river that drops down into the Gulf of Mexico at Freeport: "river of rest and rescues,/ bear me with lullabies,/ safe to the arms of Jesus."

Though Miller is a poet whose range of techniques is limited, the forms within which she works are brought to mastery and high finish. These forms frame her tale of suffering love and of spirit tested by a life of pain and profound introspection.

Paul Christensen

Other major works
ANTHOLOGY: *Despite This Flesh*, 1985.

Bibliography
Davy, Taylor Claudia Mestelman. "Benediction of Bone: The Poetry of Vassar Miller, a Psychological Study of the Evolution of Poetic Voice and Self." *Dissertation Abstracts International* 51 (September, 1990): 846A. This brief abstract, which summarizes the content of a Ph.D. dissertation at Indiana University of Pennsylvania, takes an approach that is based on the theories of humanistic psychologist Abraham Maslow. Davy presents her own "evolutionary writing pyramid" as a device for "correlating the poetic process with psychological development" and applies it to Miller's poetry. An order number is provided for those who wish to examine the full dissertation.
Ford-Brown, Steven, ed. *Heart's Invention: On the Poetry of Vassar Miller*,

Houston: Ford-Brown, 1988. The first collection of essays on the poetry and life of Vassar Miller, *Heart's Invention* contains eight essays by other poets and literary critics, and an interview by Karla Hammond. "Allowing for Such Talk," a critical essay by Paul Christensen, explores the regional aspects of Miller's poetry and the role of religion in her work. Thomas Whitbread, in "Vassar Miller and Her Peers: A Causerie," traces the stylistic influences of contemporary poets on Miller's work. In "Passionate Scriptures of the Body," the poet Robert Bonazzi, who edited and published Miller's *Selected and New Poems: 1950-1980*, analyzes the intricate metrical structures of her poems as the metaphor of physical perfection by a severely handicapped writer. Bernetta Quinn's "Vassar Miller's Anatomy of Silence" compares some of the shorter forms of Miller's work to religious meditations.

Kaplan, Susan. "Vassar Miller." In *Contemporary Poets*, edited by James Vinson and D. L. Kirkpatrick. 4th ed. New York: St. Martin's Press, 1985. Kaplan calls attention to the humorous sense of incongruity in Miller's poems, a "glib spirit" that gives energy to her best work. Though her poems are generally focused inwardly, Kaplan says, Miller is so "unabashedly honest" that her collections seem to have a multiplicity of voices.

JOHN MILTON

Born: London, England; December 9, 1608
Died: London, England; November 8, 1674

Principal poetry

Poems of Mr. John Milton, 1645; *Paradise Lost*, 1667, 1674; *Paradise Regained*, 1671; *Samson Agonistes*, 1671; *The Poetical Works*, 1952-1955.

Other literary forms

Although John Milton's poetry represents only about one-fifth of his total literary production, the prose works are more obscure, largely because he wrote in genres that no longer appeal to a large audience. Milton's prose is usually read today for what it reveals about his biography and his thought. His most prominent theme was liberty—religious, domestic, and civil. The following examples are notable: five antiprelatical tracts (1641-1642); four tracts justifying divorce (1643-1645); and five pamphlets defending the English Puritan cause against the monarchists (1649-1654). The tract *Of Education* (1644) and the classical oration upholding freedom of the press, *Areopagitica* (1644), are the most familiar titles among the prose works. The remaining titles consist largely of academic exercises, letters, additional pamphlets, works of history, and treatises. Milton left in manuscript at his death a Latin treatise on religion, *De doctrina Christiana libri duo Posthumi* (1825), a work which provides valuable clarification of his religious beliefs.

Achievements

By common agreement, literary historians have ranked Milton second among English poets. He wrote during the English Renaissance, when authors were attempting to develop a national literature in the vernacular. In this endeavor they had exceedingly rich sources to draw upon: the classics, many recently translated, which provided both genres and themes; the Judeo-Christian tradition, an area of broad interest and intensive study following the Reformation; and national sources—historical, folk, mythical; and literature from the Continent, particularly Italy and France. By the time Milton began writing, William Shakespeare and his contemporaries had created a national drama that surpassed that of other nations, and Ben Jonson had adapted such classical lyric genres as the ode and the epigram to English verse. As yet no poet had succeeded in creating an epic poem based upon a classical model, a task which the age considered the highest achievement of the creative mind.

It remained for Milton to undertake this formidable task, one for which he was well prepared. Among English poets of the first rank he was the most deeply and broadly learned—in classical languages and literature and in works of the Judeo-Christian tradition. From early life, he considered poetry to be a true vocation, and his development as a poet suggests that he emulated Vergil and Edmund Spenser, beginning with lyric genres and progressing by degrees to the epic. Milton's strongest inclination as a poet was to produce a synthesis of classical and Christian elements, a blend which critics have labeled his Christian humanism.

Milton contributed poems of lasting value and interest to English literature in both major and minor genres. He stressed the importance of the individual will by making his most common theme that of the soul in ethical conflict— the wayfaring, warfaring Christian. He developed a style peculiarly "Miltonic." In the verses which Milton would have seen as fitting his ideal of "simple, sensuous, passionate," Matthew Arnold discovered "touchstones," or examples of the sublime in poetry. Finally, he adopted the blank verse of English drama as a vehicle for the long poem on a serious theme.

Biography

John Milton was born into an upper-middle-class family in London, his father being a scrivener with real estate interests, sufficiently affluent to assure Milton that he did not have to follow a profession in order to live. John Milton the elder, who achieved recognition in his own right as a composer and musician, encouraged his son in his studies and enrolled him in St. Paul's School, then a quality day school in London. When he entered Christ's College, Cambridge, at sixteen, Milton had an excellent grounding in Latin and Greek.

Even though he was once suspended from Cambridge, he was a serious and successful student, taking two degrees (B.A., 1629; M.A., 1632). While at Christ's College, he wrote a significant amount of lyric poetry, and he altered his original intention of being ordained. Leaving Cambridge in 1632, he returned to his father's estates at Horton and, later, Hammersmith, remaining there until 1638. Although he continued to write poetry, his essential purpose appears to have been further systematic study of classical and Renaissance literature, history, and philosophy.

Approaching thirty, he set out in 1638 to tour France, Switzerland, and Italy, a journey which lasted fifteen months and enabled him to glean impressions of European nature, art, and architecture that later enriched his poetry. During the tour he also visited such learned men as Hugo Grotius and Giovanni Diodati and attended the meetings of learned societies.

Returning to England upon the outbreak of civil war in 1639, he became engaged in the pamphlet war against the bishops. For a period of about fifteen years, Milton turned his primary attention to the writing of polemic prose, which he regarded as promoting the cause of liberty. His poetic output was small, consisting of a few sonnets and lyrics and translations from the Psalms. For a brief time he became a schoolmaster, though his school enrolled only a handful of students, two of whom were Milton's nephews. His marriage to Mary Powell in 1642 lasted until her death following childbirth in 1652; a second marriage ended with the poignant death of Katharine Woodcock in 1658. His work as a controversialist brought his merit to the attention of the government of Oliver Cromwell, and he was appointed Secretary of Foreign Tongues to the Council of State in 1649. He was totally blind by 1652 and had to dictate his correspondence and creative work.

By the late 1650's, he began composing *Paradise Lost*; his three major poetic works occupied the remaining years of his life. As the Restoration approached, he tried in vain to stem the tide by writing more antimonarchial and anticlerical pamphlets. During the years following the Restoration, he lived quietly in London with his third wife, Elizabeth Minshull, receiving friends and composing and revising his poems. He was much troubled by gout and died of its complications in 1674.

Analysis

The greater part of John Milton's lyric poetry was written during his residences at Cambridge (1625-1632) and at Horton-Hammersmith (1632-1638). The work of the Cambridge period includes numerous occasional poems in English and conventionally allusive Latin epigrams and elegies. These early lyrics may owe something to Milton's "Prolusions," which are academic exercises on a set theme with predictable lines of argument, ornamented with numerous classical allusions. Such prose assignments may well have contributed to Milton's rich style and his firm sense of genre.

The poems cover a wide variety of topics: the death of bishops, of an infant, of the university carrier; the anniversary of the Gunpowder Plot; and religious topics. In "At a Vacation Exercise," written before he was twenty, Milton intimates that he will use his native language for "Some graver subject" than the one which the hundred-line lyric develops. His lyric "On Shakespeare," included with the commendatory poems in the second folio (1632), had a theme of special interest to the young Milton, the fame that comes to a poet. In this lyric, as in others, the style and diction indicate a debt to Edmund Spenser.

Among the poems written during the Cambridge period, the ode "On the Morning of Christ's Nativity" (1629) remains the most significant, perhaps the best nativity hymn in English poetry. The verses depict Christ as a triumphant redeemer—sovereign over nature, baneful to demons, and warmly human. In a rhyme-royal proem (four stanzas), Milton establishes the occasion and setting, and then celebrates the Nativity in thirty-seven stanzas, each being of eight verses, varying in length and rhyming aabccbdd. The hymn has three structural divisions: stanzas I-VII portray the peace of nature and the civilized world at the time of Christ's birth; stanzas VIII-XV celebrate the promise of Christ for the future, with images of music and harmony; stanzas XVI-

XXXVII foretell the results of Christ's birth for the near future, the cessation of oracles and the collapse of pagan religions. Milton associates Christ with Pan and Hercules, freely drawing upon classical mythology and reading it as Christian allegory; at the same time, he follows a different Christian tradition by equating the pagan gods with devils. The ode is remarkable for its exuberant metrical movement and its rich imagery of light and harmony.

Two of Milton's best-known lyrics, "L'Allegro" and "Il Penseroso," cannot be dated with certainty, though they are usually assigned to the period 1629-1632. "L'Allegro" celebrates the pleasures of the mirthful man, while "Il Penseroso" celebrates those of the contemplative man, whose joyous mood may be tinged with melancholy. These companion poems, both written in iambic tetrameter, employ a similar structure. "L'Allegro" begins in early morning and concludes in the evening; its companion begins in the evening and ends with morning. The speaker in each poem moves through a series of settings, and both poems express the delight and pleasure to be derived from nature and art, their chief appeal being to the senses of sight and sound.

The poems of the Horton-Hammersmith period demonstrate the growth of Milton's poetic power and give promise of further development, *A Maske Presented at Ludlow Castle* (1637) and "Lycidas" (1637) being the most notable. The masque is a brief dramatic entertainment, characterized by a simple plot and conflict, usually presented by amateurs and employing elaborate costumes, fanciful situations, song, dance, and highly poetic passages. The poem represents Milton's first important use of blank verse and his first significant work on the theme of temptation. The mythical Comus, whose name has replaced Milton's original title for the masque, inhabits a wood and entices travelers there to taste his liquor, which transforms them into monstrous shapes and makes them his followers. Milton's heroine, the Lady, becomes separated from her brothers in this wood and is tempted by Comus but refuses. Although he can force her to sit immobile in a chair, he can attain no power over her mind or will. The brothers, assisted by the guardian spirit Thyrsis, arrive on the scene, drive Comus away, and secure her release through the aid of the water nymph Sabrina. Thereupon the two brothers and the Lady are presented to their parents. The theme of temptation enables Milton to celebrate the power of the human will to resist evil, a central theme of his major poems. In *Comus* (1634) the temptation occurs in a natural setting, almost a pastoral milieu; in later works the setting and character are altered to present the theme in greater complexity.

The occasion of Milton's pastoral elegy "Lycidas" was the death of Milton's fellow student at Cambridge, Edward King, who drowned in the Irish Sea in 1637. At the time of his death he had a career as a clergyman open before him. Milton follows the conventions of the pastoral elegy, King being treated as a shepherd whose songs have ended, and for whom all nature mourns. The invocation of the muse, rhetorical questions, the fixing of blame, the procession of mourners, the catalog of flowers—all of these conventional elements find a place. The traditional elegiac pattern of statement of loss, reconciliation, and looking toward the future is also followed in "Lycidas." Milton uses the convention of allegory in pastoral poetry to meditate on fame and to attack abuses within the Church. The elegy employs a complex rhythm and rhyme pattern which is indebted to the Italian *canzone*.

Over a period of approximately thirty years, Milton wrote twenty-three sonnets, among them some of the most memorable lyrics in English. As with other genres, he made contributions to the form, in this instance both thematic and stylistic. Although the first six sonnets, five of them in Italian, are conventional in style, the English sonnets that follow mark new directions that influenced the history of the sonnet form. The first sonnets were love poems, and most early English sonnets were written in the tradition of Francis Petrarch's sequence to Laura. William Shakespeare and John Donne had left influential poems on the themes of friendship and religion. To Milton the sonnet became a poem written not in sequence but on an occasion of personal or public significance—on his twenty-third birthday, on his blindness, on the death of his wife, on the massacre in Piedmont, on the public reception of his divorce tracts. While many of the sonnets reflect Milton's strong religious and moral convictions, they are not, strictly speaking, religious poems.

From the standpoint of style, he broke the traditional quatrain division and introduced an inverted Latinate syntax which allowed freedom in the placement of modifiers. The result was numerous enjambments and an alteration of the pauses within the lines of the sonnet. As in his longer poems, Milton juxtaposes Latinate diction and syntax with simple English diction and meter, creating a powerful tension. These stylistic innovations and the rich allusive texture that Milton brings to the sonnet combine to make the sonnets seem more restricted and concentrated than those of the Elizabethan period. When, a century after Milton, the pre-Romantics revived the sonnet as a lyric form, the predecessor whose work they emulated was Milton.

Although he had been planning to write an epic poem for nearly forty years before *Paradise Lost* was published in 1667, Milton did not seriously begin the composition before the period 1655-1657, when he was approaching fifty years of age. He had thought of an epic based upon either British history or a biblical theme; when the time came, he chose the biblical theme and developed it on the grandest scale possible. From a Christian perspective, he set out to narrate all important events in man's temporal and spiritual history, to answer all important questions, to tell what one poet called "the story of all things." Not content to narrate the fall of man from grace, Milton included in his statement of the theme, as announced in the Prologue to Book I, man's restoration and his ability to gain immortality. The theology of *Paradise Lost* is essentially orthodox Protestant, although a few unusual theological views were discovered after students of Milton closely examined the epic in the light of his treatise on theology, *De doctrina Christiana libri duo Posthumi.*

Milton adheres to numerous epic conventions established by Homer and Vergil, his classical predecessors in the form: action set in various realms, divine and human characters, a stated theme, invocation of the muse, epic games, epic similes, warfare, speeches, dreams, catalogs, roll calls, elevated style, and twelve books (or multiples of twelve). A remarkable departure from the practice of earlier epic poets, as T. J. B. Spencer has pointed out, is that numerous minor epic conventions, particularly those concerning warfare and conflict, are more often associated with the demonic than with the human or the divine. Milton specifically rejects warfare as a subject unworthy of the epic, preferring to celebrate the suffering hero who endures adversity for the sake of conscience and right. In a mythical perspective, Christ represents the hero of Milton's epic, for he is the character who acts, who creates and restores. Yet, Adam receives more attention in the poem and undergoes a change of fortune; for mankind, Milton's readers, he becomes the hero.

As Northrop Frye pointed out, it is instructive to examine *Paradise Lost* as a myth, even though Milton believed that he was narrating events that actually took place—some poetic license and elaboration being permitted. The mythical structure of the epic is cyclic, involving actions primarily of the Deity (constructive) and Satan (destructive). The earliest point in the narrative is the occasion for Satan's revolt, the recognition of Christ as Son of God before the assembled angels in Heaven. Following a three-day war in Heaven, Satan and millions of followers are cast out; and God creates the universe and the human order to restore spiritual beings to vacant places in Heaven. This purpose is challenged by Satan, who journeys to earth to tempt man and bring about his fall. Although Satan achieves his objective, God repairs the loss by giving man the law and redeeming him, enabling man to regain the opportunity of entering Heaven after Judgment Day.

Since Milton follows the epic convention of beginning *in medias res*, the narrative is not presented chronologically. Instead, after stating the theme, Milton begins the first book with Satan and his followers in the depths of hell. Although the poetic structure of *Paradise Lost* may be approached in various ways, the most common is to divide the epic into three major parts or movements, with four related books in each: I-IV; V-VIII; IX-XII. Books I-IV introduce the theme, settings, lines of narrative development, characters (divine, demonic, human), and motivation. In Book I Satan and Beëlzebub are found suffering in hell, a place which Milton describes as holding a multitude of torments. They resolve never to submit but to continue their vain attempt against God through guile. Rousing his followers, Satan has them build an enormous palace, Pandemonium, as the site of a council of war (Book II). After Moloch, Mammon, Belial, and Beëlzebub have proposed plans of action to the council, the plan of Satan, as presented by Beëlzebub, is accepted—that they attempt to thwart God's plan by subverting another world and its beings, a mission which Satan volunteers to perform. He sets out to travel through chaos to earth, while his followers divert themselves with epic games.

In Book III the setting is changed to Heaven where another council takes place. God the Father, presiding over the assembled angels, informs them of Satan's mission, predicts its success, explains the necessity for a redeemer, and accepts Christ's voluntary sacrifice to save mankind. The council in Heaven (III, vv. 80-415) provides the essential theological basis for the poem, clarifying the redemptive theology of Christianity as Milton understood it. This done, Milton returns to Satan, who deceives the angels stationed by God for man's protection and travels to the peak of Mount Niphates overlooking the Garden of Eden. The fourth book introduces the human characters, Adam and Eve, whom Milton describes as ideal human types, living in an idyllic setting. Even Satan finds the creation of God beautiful, though the beauty does not deter him from his destructive plan. Instead, he approaches Eve in the form of a toad and creates in her mind a troubling dream, until the angels appointed to watch over the Garden discover him and drive him out.

Books V-VIII, the middle books of *Paradise Lost*, contribute to the narrative in at least three important ways: they enable Milton to show God's concern for man by sending Raphael to instruct Adam of the danger represented by Satan, the function which George Williamson has described as "the education of Adam." They permit him to provide exposition through an account of the war in Heaven and of the creation. Finally, they enable him to prepare the reader to accept as credible the fall of perfect beings whose only duty was to obey a plain and direct command of God. Book V opens with Eve narrating her dream to Adam, the dream created by Satan, in which an angel tempts her to disobey God's command and eat of the forbidden tree. The dream follows closely the actual temptation sequence in Book IX and so foreshadows the more complex temptation that follows. Adam reassures her that dreams imply no guilt, and the angel Raphael arrives to begin his explanation of the revolt of Satan. In Book VI the angel narrates the three-day war in Heaven. James H. Hanford has shown that in the narrative Milton describes the types of combat then known—single warriors battling for victory, classic battle formations, artillery, and, finally, an elemental kind of strife like that of the Titans, in which the angels rend up hills to hurl them at their opposition. On the third day Christ appears to drive Satan and his host out of Heaven.

The seventh book provides an account of the creation of the universe and all living things by Christ, who forms the whole from chaos, bringing order and harmony. To Milton the creation is consciously and intentionally harmonious and hierarchical. In Book VIII, Adam explains what he can recall about his own creation and asks Raphael questions about astronomy. When he acknowledges to the angel that he sometimes inclines to Eve's view because her wisdom seems superior, Raphael warns him not to abandon his responsibility as her guide, emphasizing the importance of hierarchy.

The final group of books includes an account of man's fall (IX), its immediate aftermath (X), and the long-term consequences (XI-XII), the final two books representing the education of fallen Adam. In Book IX, Satan returns to the Garden under cover of darkness and enters the body of the serpent. The serpent approaches Eve, who has persuaded Adam to let her work apart, and tempts her to disobey God through promises of greater power. When she returns to Adam, he understands what has happened, and at her invitation eats the forbidden fruit, not because he has been deceived but because he wishes to share Eve's fate. The immediate results include inordinate and ungovernable passions in both and disorder in nature. In Book X, Christ appears in the Garden to pass sentence on man, but his words hold out hope of triumph over Satan. As he is returning to hell, Satan meets the allegorical figures Sin and Death, who are paving a broad way to link hell and the earth. His triumph before his followers in hell is eclipsed when they are transformed into serpents which greedily approach apple trees growing outside the great hall, only to discover the fruit to be bitter ashes. Meanwhile, Adam and Eve have understood that God's will must prevail and have begun to take some hope in the promise given them by the Savior.

In Book XI, the archangel Michael is sent by God to explain to Adam the effects of sin upon his descendants, so that Adam can understand and accept God's plan for mankind. Adam sees the effects of sin, understanding the cause of disease, death, and erroneous choices among men. He witnesses the flood that destroys the world and acknowledges it as just. In Book XII, Michael narrates the bringing of the law through Moses, the birth of Christ, the establishment of the Church, and the history of Christianity until Judgment Day. Having understood the entire scope of human history, Adam gratefully accepts God's plan for the restoration of humanity, and he and Eve depart from the Garden, having lost the original paradise but having gained the ability to attain a "paradise within."

For the exalted theme of *Paradise Lost*, Milton achieves an appropriately elevated style which appeals primarily to the ear, creating the "organ tones" for which it is celebrated. He chose blank verse because he believed it to be the closest equivalent in English meter to the epic verse of the classics; yet the stylistic unit is not the line but rather the sentence, and, at times, the verse paragraph. The more prominent stylistic qualities include the following: Latinate diction and syntax ("the vast profundity obscure"), frequent inversions, words either archaic or used in unfamiliar senses, collocations of proper names, epic similes, compound epithets, compression, and, most prominently, the schemes of repetition—the most frequent being polyptoton, antimetabole, and chiasmus.

The style reveals a weaving of related images and a richly allusive texture that can be grasped only after repeated readings. Christopher Ricks has shown, for example, that references to the "hands" of Adam and Eve recur in poignantly significant contexts, creating a cumulative effect with one image. When Milton uses a biblical name, as Ricks notes, he often "transliterates"; that is, provides the literal equivalent in English. Thus, when Satan is named, "adversary" may appear immediately thereafter; "pleasant" occurs in passages that mention Eden—as if to remind the reader that names embody meanings of which he is unaware. Further, reading mythology as allegory, Milton freely associates mythical characters with biblical counterparts—Proserpine with Eve, Deucalion with Noah, Ceres with Christ. Finally, the reader learns to interpret biblical characters typologically, as Milton did, where characters in the Old Testament anticipate the New—Adam, Noah, and Moses, for example, all being types of Christ. Through these poetic techniques, Milton achieves a style so complex that its interest and appeal can never be exhausted.

Milton's brief epic *Paradise Regained*, written in blank verse and published with *Samson Agonistes* in 1671, represents a sequel to *Paradise Lost*, its hero Christ being a second Adam who overcomes temptation that is much more extensive than that experienced by Adam. Milton makes several assumptions about the temptation of Christ in his source, Luke 4:1-14, an account of events which occurred before the beginning of Christ's ministry: first, Christ does not fully understand either his mission or the role of the Messiah; second, he can be genuinely tempted; third, his withstanding temptation assures his success in the role of redeemer. To Milton, the Book of Job represented the ideal model for the brief epic; it appears that no other poem in English or in the classics influenced the form significantly.

The temptations of Christ, narrated in the four books of the poem, offer easy access to those things which Satan supposes a hero of his kind would want. At the beginning of the narrative, Christ has been fasting in the desert for forty days following his baptism, an event which had attracted Satan's interest. Satan had heard God's recognition of Christ following the ceremony and had supposed that Christ might be the offspring of Adam destined to bruise his head. Resolving to subject Christ to temptations, Satan approaches him in disguise and invites him to turn stones into bread in order to allay his hunger. After Christ's refusal, Satan next offers a banquet, also refused because Christ recognizes the giver as evil. When Satan realizes that Christ cannot be tempted by ordinary means, he concludes that he is indeed someone extraordinary and appeals to Christ's supposed ambition by offering first wealth, then the Parthian kingdom, then Rome, and, later, all kingdoms of the world in return to fealty to Satan. In rejecting these offers, Christ reveals that his kingdom is not of the world. Undeterred, Satan offers all the learning—philosophy, poetry, history—of Athens, declined by Christ as unnecessary to him and inferior to that of the Hebrews.

Satan raises a storm in the desert in the hope of terrifying Christ and transports him through the air to the pinnacle of the Temple, where he urges Christ to cast himself down and be rescued from death by God. When Christ replies, "Tempt not the Lord thy God," Satan recognizes his divine nature and falls himself, leaving Christ in the protection of angels who minister to him.

Barbara Lewalski has pointed out that the temptations in *Paradise Regained* are designed to reveal Christ's roles as priest, prophet, and king. The prophet in the wilderness denies himself, the king acknowledges no kingdom of this world, and the priest rejects the false and unnecessary learning for the true.

For his only tragedy, *Samson Agonistes*, Milton adapts a Greek model of the genre to a biblical episode, the story of Samson, as found in Judges XIII-XVI. The title signifies Samson the wrestler or athlete; Milton's hero represents a type of Christ from the Old Testament, though Samson, unlike Christ, falls from favor and undergoes a series of temptations before being restored. Since Milton wrote the tragedy in verse (1,758 lines in blank verse) and since he clearly states that he did not intend the work for the stage, it is usually studied as a dramatic poem.

Samson Agonistes, said to be the English tragedy which most closely follows the Greek model, employs numerous Greek conventions. It takes place on the final day of the hero's life and follows the unities of time, place, and action. Milton divides the major episodes of the play not by acts but by the choral odes, as in Greek drama. The chorus performs its usual functions— providing exposition, advising the hero, announcing arrivals, and interpreting for the audience.

The tragedy opens with a despairing Samson, blind and enslaved to work in a Philistine mill, being visited on a holiday by a group of his countrymen, who form the chorus. Samson blames himself for the loss of God's favor because he revealed the secret of his strength to his wife Dalila, who betrayed him to the Philistines. The men of Dan announce the arrival of Samson's father Manoa, who is negotiating with the Philistines for his son's release, a prospect which brings Samson little comfort, since he believes that idleness will only increase his sense of guilt. Manoa's effort, however, invites Samson to choose a life of ease and rest much unlike the life he has known, and this he rejects. Dalila arrives and informs Samson that she now wishes that he would return to her and renew their marriage. Her suggestion only arouses his anger, and she leaves, satisfied that she will enjoy fame among her own people. The next visitor is the Philistine champion Harapha, a giant who has come to challenge Samson to prove his strength once again through physical combat; but Harapha discreetly leaves after Samson defies him. This meeting renews Samson's understanding that his strength derives from God, yet it suggests to him that single combat is no longer his role.

A Philistine officer arrives to command Samson to attend the celebration in Dagon's temple in order to divert the audience with feats of strength. At first Samson scornfully refuses the command as impious and idolatrous, but, after an inward prompting, changes his mind and accompanies the officer to the temple. As the Chorus and Manoa await Samson's return, they hear a fearful noise, and a messenger arrives to announce that Samson has destroyed the temple and has perished in the destruction, along with thousands of Philistines. The chorus recognizes that Samson has been restored to God's favor and has acted in accordance with divine will.

As in his other major works, Milton in *Samson Agonistes* expands and modifies his source while remaining faithful to its original meaning and spirit. The effort of Manoa to obtain Samson's release, the appearance of Dalila during his imprisonment, and the character of Harapha are all Milton's additions. They enable him to interpret the character of Samson as more complex than the biblical character and to show him undergoing a series of temptations. Although the poetic voice is less intrusive in *Samson Agonistes* than in the epics, Milton, as Hanford has pointed out, identifies rather closely with the blind hero of the tragedy.

There can be little doubt that religion, as Milton understood it, stands as the major theme of his poetry. The protagonists of his four greatest poetic works—the Lady in *Comus*, Adam in *Paradise Lost*, Christ in *Paradise Regained*, and Samson in *Samson Agonistes*—undergo an elaborate temptation (or a series of temptations) and either triumph or come to terms with failure. Critics recognize that Milton does not excel in characterization, one reason being that his characters are subordinate to his narrative and thematic purposes. Nor does Milton possess a gift for humor or comedy; his infrequent efforts in those directions usually appear heavy-handed.

His religious perspective is Protestant, with greater emphasis upon the will than was common for his time. Milton's view of salvation would have been called "Arminian" during the seventeenth century—that is, Christ provided for the salvation of all who willingly accepted him. To Milton this assumption takes on classical overtones derived perhaps from Aristotle and Ovid, among others. In kind of Aristotelian teleology, he assumes that one right choice makes a second easier, and thus man through the proper exercise of his will moves toward the perfection of human nature. Conversely, a wrong choice makes subsequent right choices more difficult and may lead to the degradation of human nature. In his poetry Milton seeks to celebrate right choices and to guide readers in their own choices. His poetry of the will and of ethical conflict is expressed in literary genres of lasting interest and in a style so sublime and so rich in poetic meaning that one discovers new beauties with each successive reading.

Stanley Archer

Other major works

PLAY: *Comus*, 1634 (masque, printed in 1637 under the title of *A Maske Pre-*

sented at Ludlow Castle).

NONFICTION: *Of Reformation Touching Church Discipline in England*, 1641; *Of Prelatical Episcopacy*, 1641; *Animadversions upon the Remonstrant's Defence Against Smectymnuus*, 1641; *The Reason of Church-Government Urg'd Against Prelaty*, 1642; *An Apology Against a Pamphlet . . .* , 1642; *The Doctrine and Discipline of Divorce*, 1643; *Of Education*, 1644; *The Judgement of Martin Bucer Concerning Divorce*, 1644; *Aeropagitica*, 1644; *Tetrachordon*, 1645; *Colasterion*, 1645; *The Tenure of Kings and Magistrates*, 1649; *Eikonoklastes*, 1649; *Pro Populo Anglicano Defensio*, 1651; *Pro Populo Anglicano Defensio Secunda*, 1654; *Pro Se Defensio*, 1655; *A Treatise of Civil Power in Ecclesiastical Causes*, 1659; *Considerations Touching the Likeliest Means to Remove Hirelings Out of the Church*, 1659; *The Readie and Easie Way to Establish a Free Commonwealth*, 1660; *The History of Britain*, 1670; *Of True Religion, Heresy, Schism, and Toleration*, 1673; *De doctrina Christiana libri duo Posthumi*, 1825; *Complete Prose Works of John Milton*, 1953-1982 (8 volumes). MISCELLANEOUS: *Works*, 1931-1938 (18 volumes).

Bibliography

Bloom, Harold, ed. *John Milton.* New York: Chelsea House, 1986. One of the Modern Critical Views series, it contains a selection of some of the best Milton criticism from the last thirty years. Includes a bibliography and an index.

Broadbent, John Barclay, ed. *John Milton: Introductions.* Cambridge, England: Cambridge University Press, 1973. Still the best general introduction to the work of Milton available. Twelve chapters cover his life and times, his poetic formation, his science, his theology, and his art and music. Suggestions for resources and further reading are offered in each chapter. Contains an index.

Danielson, Dennis R. *Milton's Good God: A Study in Literary Theodicy.* New York: Cambridge University Press, 1982. To some extent this is a reexamination of William Empson's thesis in his *Milton's God*, but mainly it is an analysis of Milton's theology and how it is related poetically to the task he set himself in *Paradise Lost.* Supplemented by a select bibliography and an index.

Hunter, G. K. *Paradise Lost.* Boston: Allen & Unwin, 1980. The great advantage of this short study is its ability to make the poem enjoyable. It suggests ways of reading the text that still take full account of Milton's art, complexities, and contradictions. Contains a bibliography and an index.

Martz, Louis L. *Poet of Exile: A Study of Milton's Poetry.* New Haven, Conn.: Yale University Press, 1980. Sixteen chapters center on *Paradise Lost* as a poem of exile. Two separate sections cover the rest of the poetry, and a fourth section looks closely at the interaction with Ovid in *Paradise Lost* in terms of heroic and pastoral love. Contains appendices and an index.

Milner, Andrew. *John Milton and the English Revolution: A Study in the Sociology of Literature.* Totowa, N.J.: Barnes & Noble Books, 1981. Written from a Marxist perspective, it sets Milton's major poems in the world of the defeat of a rationalist world vision as expressed in Independency and the subsequent need to reorder that vision after the Restoration. It takes particular issue with Christopher Hill and is part of a wider historicist debate. Contains notes, a bibliography, and an index.

Ricks, Christopher. *Milton's Grand Style.* Oxford, England: Clarendon Press, 1963. Ricks examines Milton's epic style in *Paradise Lost*, well aware of the controversy surrounding it. In a scholarly manner, he shows that many of the criticisms are unfounded and that Milton's verse possesses both sublimity and flexibility. Includes indexes.

N. SCOTT MOMADAY

Born: Lawton, Oklahoma; February 27, 1934

Principal poetry
Angle of Geese and Other Poems, 1974; *The Gourd Dancer*, 1976.

Other literary forms
Although he prefers to call himself a poet, N. Scott Momaday is best known for his novel, *House Made of Dawn*, which won the Pulitzer Prize for fiction the year following its publication in 1968; a second novel, *The Ancient Child*, appeared in 1989. Other important prose works are autobiographical. *The Journey of Tai-me*, privately published in 1967, became part of *The Way to Rainy Mountain*, an exploration of personal and cultural history, which came out in 1969. A second autobiographical book, *The Names: A Memoir*, appeared in 1976. Momaday's weekly column for *Viva*, the Sunday magazine of the Santa Fe *New Mexican*, should also be included among autobiographical forms. The text that Momaday wrote to accompany David Muench's photographs in *Colorado* (1973) reasserts his persistent sense of affinity for particular landscapes. An early essay, "The Morality of Indian Hating" (*Ramparts*, 1964), reflects an interest that Momaday has continued to explore in essays, prefaces, and speeches: an examination of the Native American people in their relationship to themselves and to the invading European culture. Momaday's vision of nature owes much to his study of American Romantic literature.

Achievements
Momaday's most impressive achievement has been to demonstrate the possibility, viability, and value of Native American literature. When *House Made of Dawn* won the Pulitzer Prize in 1969, at least one critic presumed that its author was the first Native American to write a novel. Although that critic discovered that many novels had been published by Native Americans, their works remain neglected. Writers such as Oliver La Farge had adapted Amerindian themes, and from time to time collections of tales and of poems in translation made by ethnologists had appeared. It has been Momaday, however, who has brought impeccable academic as well as tribal credentials to the writer's task and produced a body of work that has merited critical praise and scholarly attention. Although his work is not popular with either the general public or the academic critics, both groups acknowledge its importance. The achievement is twofold. A specifically Native American tradition in American literature, exemplified by authors such as Gerald Vizenor, Leslie Silko, Louise Erdrich, and James Welch, is now recognized. Second, tra-

ditional native literary forms, as Momaday and other authors incorporate them into their writings, have greatly enriched the whole of American literature.

Biography

Six months after his birth in February, 1934, Navarre Scott Momaday was solemnly given the Kiowa name *Tsoai-talee* (Rock-Tree Boy) by Pohd-lohk, his step-grandfather. A year later, the Momadays moved from Oklahoma to New Mexico, and from 1936 to 1943 they lived in various places on the Navajo reservation: Shiprock, New Mexico, and Tuba City and Chinle, Arizona. Although there were stays in Oklahoma, Kentucky, and Louisiana, the reservation was home. After three years near the Army Air Base at Hobbs, New Mexico, the family moved in 1946 to the pueblo of Jemez, New Mexico, where Momaday's parents taught in the day school. Momaday lived at Jemez until his last year of high school, when he attended Augusta Military School in Virginia, from which he was graduated in 1952.

Studies occupied the next eleven years. After attending the University of New Mexico and Virginia Law School, Momaday was graduated from the University of New Mexico in 1958. Following a year of teaching at Dulce, on the Apache reservation, he entered Stanford University as a creative writing fellow. He received his Ph.D. degree in 1963, and in the following years taught at the University of California in Santa Barbara and in Berkeley, at Stanford, at New Mexico State University, and at the University of Arizona. It was in 1965, after the death of his grandmother, that Momaday made the journey north from Oklahoma to South Dakota that was to inspire *The Way to Rainy Mountain*. Shortly afterward, a Guggenheim award enabled him to spend a year at Amherst, Massachusetts, where he studied the work of Emily Dickinson. In 1969, the Gourd Dance Society of the Kiowas, to which his father had belonged, initiated Momaday as a member. Interrupting his years of teaching at American universities, Momaday spent several months in Moscow in 1975 as the first Fulbright lecturer in American literature in the U.S.S.R. Momaday became a teacher of literature and creative writing at the University of Arizona, living in Tucson with his wife and daughters.

Analysis

Two themes predominate in all of N. Scott Momaday's work, both poetry and prose. First, he celebrates material, sensory existence. The writer lovingly examines nature and the artifacts of human life, from the smallest creature to the most vast panorama. Whether describing a ghost town in Colorado or the coming of rain to a Southwestern desert, he is concerned to express the perceptual and emotional experience of physical life with eloquence and precision. The prose is often lush; the poetry can be spare, but exceedingly resonant.

A second preoccupation is with imagination, that power of mind that transforms and illumines the perceptible world and endows it with meaning. Momaday sees language as the primary vehicle for this transformation and affirms again and again the elemental importance of words. Collective imagination working upon natural existence creates culture, and in his examination of the contrasts and interweavings of the cultures of his experience, Momaday explores them as products of the human imagination. In an early essay, he speaks of two Kiowa legends, which he then shows to be emblematic of Kiowa thought and history and of the Kiowas' response to their history. In the same essay, he points to the metaphorical language of a non-Indian historian whose imagery betrays his fundamental bias and underlies a whole theory of civilization versus savagery.

Momaday's prose works—his essays, autobiographies, and fiction—treat the dynamic of the two elements—sensory life and the power of imagination—discursively and sometimes analytically. His poetry, on the other hand, focuses most often on the fundamental meeting of nature and imagination in the act of perception itself. This is a consummately introspective procedure, and the poetry collected in *The Gourd Dancer* demonstrates a loving attentiveness to the natural world as it impinges on the mind.

The number of Momaday's published poems is small—*The Gourd Dancer* contains fewer than fifty—and he has spoken of the slowness of writing. Nevertheless, the poems derive from a wide variety of traditions, from the eighteenth century epigram to Whitmanian self-celebration to Native American ceremonial lyrics. They consist of free verse, metrical verse, prose-poems, and syllabic verse. Throughout Momaday's poems, in those reflecting his time in the Soviet Union, astronauts' lunar explorations, a vision of planetary holocaust, reflections on landscape—and in his prose works as well—there is woven this theme of the relationship between material reality and the signifying imagination.

The subtlest and most complex of Momaday's poems is probably that entitled "Before an Old Painting of the Crucifixion." The poem is a meditation on being and nothingness. The painted scene evokes in the speaker an imaginative reconstruction of the death of Jesus as a historical event, and he muses on the despair that comes with his recognition of nonbeing. The painting also calls to mind the sea, and memory evokes a recent vision of nature. Nature, however, holds ultimate emptiness for the speaker, whose consciousness of death permits him to see the void beyond death and alienates him from the merely natural process of dying. No inherent significance resides in natural life, and mere imagination remains the only (largely unavailing) defense against the inconsequent passage of time.

It is a profoundly pessimistic poem, and one with a specifically European, post-Cartesian formulation. Momaday has a great admiration for Emily Dickinson, and he has quoted her poem beginning "Farther in summer than the birds" as a realization of this alienation from nature, along with the anguish that such knowledge brings. This perception of man and nature, he believes, is also contrary to the vision of nature in Native American thought. Traditional Indian philosophy regards man as part of nature, indivisible from its processes and kin to all its creatures.

The poem entitled "Angle of Geese" draws implicitly on this cultural tradition. This poem had its genesis in a particular event, the death of a friend's child, and it also alludes to a geese-hunting trip Momaday went on as a young adolescent. The goose in the poem is not mere meaningless nature, however, but ancestral, and the poem implies a usable wisdom in nature and affirms human continuity with all forms of life.

The development of Momaday's use of traditional materials can be traced through the poems that appear in his novel, *House Made of Dawn*, and in the two autobiographical works, *The Way to Rainy Mountain* and *The Names*. In general, he moves from using traditional texts, to inclusion of material learned at first hand, to personal and family traditions and incorporation of general elements of form and content.

The Kiowas' sacred mountain (Devil's Tower in South Dakota) is named *tsoai*, "Rock-Tree," and *talee*, added to it, makes "Rock-Tree Boy," Momaday's Kiowa name. In *The Names*, Momaday extends the process of personal mythologizing begun in *The Way to Rainy Mountain* by inventing an episode in which his great-grandmother's husband, Pohd-lohk, presents him to the family, relates to him the history of the people, and finally gives him the name Tsoai-talee.

In "The Delight Song of Tsoai-talee," appearing in his first collection, *Angle of Geese and Other Poems*, Momaday draws on Indian traditions and on the nineteenth century American Romanticism that he has admired particularly in Tuckerman and Dickinson. The first-person emphasis, as well as the catalog of items in the natural world, call to mind the second song that Benally sings in *House Made of Dawn*. Unlike the Navajo song, however, in which each item has a specific meaning in a highly complex religious symbology, Momaday's poem reflects more than anything else Walt Whitman's expansive identification of his own persona with emotionally felt nature. *The Names* carries other echoes of this Whitmanian exuberance, notably in the Epilogue with its imaginary journey across the land.

The one poem that does appear in *The Names*, however, is written in pentameter couplets and echoes Wallace Stevens in its image and themes. This poem is printed in *The Gourd Dancer* as the first in a set of four poems on the imaginary "Plainview." Taken together, the four Plainview poems reflect the scope of Momaday's fascination with differing cultural perspectives and traditions. The punning title introduces the multiple themes of place and perception. Plainview is a location on the Midwestern landscape of which Momaday has written frequently with both familiarity and reverence. The vastness of space implies infinity at the same time that it emphasizes the particularity of objects perceived. Plainview also refers to sight, for whatever is in "plain view" should be visible, whole and unambiguous. In this sense the title is ironic, since in fact four Plainviews are given, each from a different perspective.

"Plainview: 1" is an explicit study in the act of perception. The speaker places himself in relation to the object of vision—the eleven magpies—and records the metamorphoses of shape and light he observes as wind and clouds pass over the grass. The same sense of underlying emptiness prevails here as in the earlier poem, "Before an Old Painting of the Crucifixion," and finally the speaker decides that the birds themselves are an illusion. The poem suggests a theme elaborated in the other three: that landscape itself is the product of imagination.

"Plainview: 2" makes use of specifically Native American themes and forms. The speaker's vision of the old Indian, drunk and pathetic, stands in contrast to the old man's nostalgic vision of his horse. The incantatory repetition and the celebration of the horse reflect native tradition. This version of what is in "plain view" stresses the irony of that title in the disparity between the visibly vulgar and the invisible beauty that lives in imagination and recollection.

"Plainview: 3" is simply a triple set of metaphors comparing the rising sun with a string of glass beads, a drift of pollen, and a prairie fire. Once again the reader is asked to examine the process of perception, this time in the comparison of visual images. The brief poem recalls Imagist works.

Finally, "Plainview: 4" mixes modes, oral and written, prose and poetry. History comes to life in the landscape as the speaker muses on the woman he often dreamed of, a white woman who had been a Kiowa captive. The haunting excerpts from traditional frontier ballads, heard only in the mind's ear as the speaker contemplates the abandoned house, bear out Momaday's comments on the importance of oral tradition to cultural continuity. The poem invokes history and tragedy, but finally both are as evanescent as the magpies in the first poem of the set. Only the wind whistles through the empty house.

The Way to Rainy Mountain is more complex than *The Names*, more highly wrought, less conventionally autobiographical. In structure and theme it fuses most successfully the introspective European viewpoint and the communal vision of the oral tradition. Momaday's recollections and anecdotes begin to take their place in legend and lore, and history metamorphoses to myth. He frames his prose narratives with two poems, "Headwaters" and "Rainy Mountain Cemetery," which begin and end the book.

The two poems use conventional meter and rhyme, yet echo the traditional Kiowa materials as Momaday interprets them in the text. In "Headwaters" the speaker stands at noon on the plains, meditating on the hidden vitality and even violence immanent in the silent landscape. Only the moss on the hollow log suggests the marshland that is there and the waters swelling out of the land. The waters themselves point to a deeper, archaic source of primitive life forces, as the author's exploration in the chapters that follow takes him to the sources of his family, his people, and his definition of human life. The poem's title refers to one of the geographical objects of Momaday's journey—the ancestral home of the Kiowas at the headwaters of the Yellowstone River. The image of the insect at the mouth of the log recalls the Kiowa creation myth of the people's emergence through a hollow log; this image of a figure within a circle reappears at the end of the introduction in Momaday's recollection of the sight of a cricket outlined against the moon "like a fossil" and immediately following the drawing by Momaday's father, Al Momaday. The image is a talisman for the centripetal nature of the journey as one that reaches within for self-knowledge.

"Rainy Mountain Cemetery" the poem that closes the book, refers to both the starting point and the goal of Momaday's journey. The pilgrimage began with Momaday's visit to his grandmother's grave, where he was inspired to visit the places that she had seen more perfectly in the mind's eye, as she recollected the historical migration of the Kiowa people. The poem is the speaker's graveside meditation on her, although, in keeping with Kiowa tradition, her name remains unspoken. The speaker reflects on the silence and, implicitly, on the nothingness which is all that remains after death. The name on the stone, he says, is no more than the stone's name, and the word "stone" ends both the first and last lines of the poem, setting an off-rhyme against the first and third lines of the second stanza. The only unrhymed line ends in the word "name." The poem reiterates Momaday's preoccupation with the power of language, stated most explicitly in the often-quoted passage from section VIII in which he asserts the creative power of language and links it to Kiowa traditions of naming. In "Rainy Mountain Cemetery," then, silence is nonexistence, and the name on the tombstone nothing but a shadow—the absence of light. The poem concludes the metamorphosis that the book has both documented and achieved: the physical has been transformed into myth. The physical world, vibrant on every page, is transformed to words and lives beyond itself in the imagination. The same is true for the life of the people and that of the individual. This, Momaday says, is the human miracle: the creation of self through imagination by means of words.

Between the publication of *The Names* in 1976 and the appearance of his second novel, *The Ancient Child*, in 1989, Momaday was in much demand as a lecturer and interview subject. During the period he published several important essays, including an introduction to Native American literature for a new literary history of the United States. Although he continued to write poetry, no new collections were published.

At this time, Momaday worked more intensively on another interest, graphic arts, exhibiting prints, drawings, and paintings in several shows. Momaday's work in visual arts intersects with his sense of language and poetry, as the title of one essay, "Landscape with Words in the Foreground," suggests. A series of drawings of shields embodies the connection. The shield motif recalls the cover design that Al Momaday, the poet's father, made for *The Way to Rainy Mountain.* Momaday's drawings include words, usually texts from his prose poems or retellings of traditional stories, as elements in the graphic presentation. Two of these shield pictures are reproduced in Charles Woodard's book of conversations with Momaday, *Ancestral Voice* (1989). The move toward mixing and integrating visual and verbal modes began in Momaday's publications with his drawings for *The Gourd Dancer*; the shield series emphasizes the modernist tendency in Momaday's work that was implicit earlier in the collage structure and mixed media of *The Way to Rainy Mountain.* The shield drawings combining picture and text as a graphic element suggest the work of modernists such as Pablo Picasso and the Italian futurists, whose work, like Momaday's, also grew out of the symbolist and post-symbolist tradition of nineteenth century romanticism.

Fourteen years in the making, Momaday's second novel, *The Ancient Child*, reflects his preoccupation with his dual creative identity as poet and painter. The novel's protagonist, Locke Setman, is an accomplished, successful painter, a cosmopolitan man of the world at home in the great cities of Europe and America. But he is dissatisfied, suffering from a malaise of the spirit. His spiritual guide and mentor is Grey, a young Navajo woman who resembles Emily Dickinson (she wears white in her dreams and spends much time putting together books of her poems). Both Grey and Locke Setman are alter egos for Momaday, with clear parallels in his own life and intellectual development: the poems Grey writes are Momaday's poems from *The Gourd Dancer.* The ending of this uneven novel is extremely ambiguous: the protagonist, like his counterpart, the bear-boy of the ancient legend, leaves the articulate, language-centered life of human beings. His eventual return is uncertain. What this ending suggests about the direction of the poet's own work is also uncertain.

Helen Jaskoski

Other major works

LONG FICTION: *House Made of Dawn*, 1968; *The Ancient Child*, 1989.

NONFICTION: "The Morality of Indian Hating," 1964; *The Way to Rainy Mountain*, 1969; "The Man Made of Words," 1970; *Colorado*, 1973 (with David Muench); *The Names: A Memoir*, 1976.

MISCELLANEOUS: *The Complete Poems of Frederick Goddard Tuckerman*, 1965 (editor).

Bibliography

Mason, Kenneth C. "Beautyway: The Poetry of N. Scott Momaday." *South Dakota Review* 18, no. 2 (1980): 61-83. Mason treats *The Gourd Dancer* as a unified work; he traces thematic progression through the three parts and offers close readings of poems in each section.

Roemer, Kenneth J. *Approaches to Teaching "The Way to Rainy Mountain."* New York: Modern Language Association, 1990. The brief first part introduces a bibliography/filmography on Momaday of special use to teachers. The second, major portion collects seventeen essays dealing with background contexts, forms and themes, and teaching the book in writing and in literature courses. An interview with a Kiowa elder closes the discussions.

Scarberry-Garcia, Susan. *Landmarks of Healing: A Study of "House Made of Dawn."* Albuquerque: University of New Mexico Press, 1990. This first monograph on *House Made of Dawn* examines analogues and sources in published translations and studies of Navajo chantways and myths.

Schubnell, Matthias. *N. Scott Momaday: The Cultural and Literary Background.* Norman: University of Oklahoma Press, 1985. A comprehensive account of Momaday's life and work to 1985, this study focuses particularly on Momaday's intellectual debt to European traditions including Romanticism and symbolism. The book includes an extensive bibliography and a long chapter on the poetry.

Trimble, Martha Scott. *N. Scott Momaday.* Boise, Idaho: Boise State College, 1973. The first monograph on Momaday and his work, this pamphlet introduces major themes through publication of *The Way to Rainy Mountain* and *Angle of Geese and Other Poems.*

Velie, Alan R. *Four American Indian Literary Masters.* Norman: University of Oklahoma Press, 1982. The chapter on Momaday's poetry contains detailed explication of "Angle of Geese," "The Bear," "Buteo Regalis," as well as discussion of "Before an Old Painting of the Crucifixion" and "The Fear of Bo-Talee." Velie concentrates on post-symbolist theory and the influence of Yvor Winters and Frederick Goddard Tuckerman.

Woodard, Charles L. *Ancestral Voice: Conversations with N. Scott Momaday.* Lincoln: University of Nebraska Press, 1989. The longest published interview with Momaday, the book transcribes hours of conversation in 1986-1987. Topics range from Momaday's sense of "bear power" and a "blood knowledge" of prehistoric migrations to his appreciation for Shakespeare and Dickinson to his sojourns in the U.S.S.R. Included are reproductions of twenty-three of Momaday's prints and drawings.

JOHN MONTAGUE

Born: Brooklyn, New York; February 28, 1929

Principal poetry

Forms of Exile, 1958; *Poisoned Lands and Other Poems*, 1961; *A Chosen Light*, 1967; *Tides*, 1970; *The Rough Field*, 1972; *A Slow Dance*, 1975; *The Great Cloak*, 1978; *Selected Poems*, 1982; *The Dead Kingdom*, 1984; *Mount Eagle*, 1988.

Other literary forms

John Montague has published his short stories, a novella, a collection of his essays, two volumes of poems translated into English (one from Irish, the other—in collaboration with his second wife—from French), and several anthologies of Irish literature.

Achievements

Montague is one of the preeminent poets writing in English in the second half of the twentieth century, perhaps best known for his poems about "the Troubles" (past and present) in Ireland. Among his many awards and prizes are the Butler and O'Shaughnessy awards, from the Irish American Cultural Institute; the Bartlett Award from the Poetry Society of Great Britain; a Guggenheim Fellowship; the Hughes Award; honorary degrees from the State University of New York and University College, Cork; and a festschrift, *Hill Field*, in honor of his sixtieth birthday.

Biography

John Montague was born in Brooklyn of Irish parents in 1929. His father, James Montague, had gone there for employment in 1925, joining a brother who ran a speakeasy. James's wife, Mary (Molly) Carney, and their two sons joined him in 1928; John, the third son, was produced by this reunion. In 1933 the three brothers were sent to County Tyrone in Northern Ireland, the older two moving in with Carney relatives in Fintona, the youngest staying with two unmarried Montague aunts in Garvaghey. John's mother returned to Ireland in 1936, settling in Fintona (his father did not return until 1952).

Montague was reared apart from his mother and brothers, though he spent some holidays with them. He excelled at local schools, developed a stammer that has persisted through his life, and won a scholarship to a boarding school in Armagh. He spent summer holidays during World War II with cousins in the South of Ireland. Having enrolled at University College, Dublin, he received a B.A. in history and English in 1949. He traveled in Austria, Italy, and France; in 1952 he received his M.A. in Anglo-Irish literature.

Montague traveled to the United States in 1953, spending a year at Yale University, a summer at Indiana University, and a year in the University of Iowa Writers Workshop, where he received an M.F.A. in 1955. There he met Madeleine de Brauer, his future wife. He traveled in Mexico, spent a year at the University of California at Berkeley, and was married in his wife's native France before returning to Dublin in 1956.

He worked for the Irish tourist board for three years, became associated with Liam Miller's Dolmen Press, helped found Claddagh Records, and published his first book of poems before moving to Paris in 1961, where for two years he was correspondent for the *Irish Times*. He lived in Paris during most of the 1960's, but also in the United States and Ireland. His first marriage ended in divorce; in 1972 he was married to Evelyn Robson, who, like his first wife, is French.

They settled in Cork, where they have maintained a home since 1972. Montague taught at University College, Cork, from 1972 to 1988. His daughters were born in 1973 and 1979. He continues to travel widely, generally dividing most of the year among Ireland, the United States, and France. He holds the position of distinguished professor in the New York State Writers Institute at Albany.

Analysis

The main subjects of John Montague's poetry are Ireland, his family, and love. He writes about people and places he knew growing up in County Tyrone, about sectarian strife in Ulster and its historical sources, and about relatives, especially his parents, seeking to understand them and his relationships with them. He has examined love from all angles: from outside and within, as desired and feared, found and lost, remembered in joy and pain.

If Ireland, family, and love are Montague's main subjects, his main theme is loss, a theme clearly seen in his poems about exile, a topic he has explored thoroughly. The title of his first book of poems, *Forms of Exile*, points to this preoccupation. "Emigrants," the shortest of its poems, confronts a major fact of Irish life since the 1840's: economic exile. Its "sad faced" subjects could be Montague's own parents, bound for Brooklyn.

"Soliloquy on a Southern Strand" looks at another sort of exile. After many years in Australia, an Irish priest reflects disconsolately on what has become of his life. He feels cut off from Ireland, alienated from the young people around him on the beach, discouraged about his vocation. In "A Footnote on Monasticism: Dingle Peninsula," Montague thinks about "the hermits, lonely dispossessed ones," who once lived on the peninsula. He feels a degree of kinship with these "people hurt into solitude/ By loss of love." Dispossession, another form of exile, and "loss of love" appear in this early poem to be equivalent.

More than half the poems in *Forms of Exile* allude to religious belief and practice, a subject seldom mentioned in Montague's later books. Clearly, despite his sympathy for the Irish priest in Australian exile and his qualified empathy with the Dingle hermits, Montague is distancing himself from the more parochial aspects of Irish Catholicism. "Rome, Anno Santo" looks unsympathetically at "the ignorant Irish on pilgrimage." "Incantation in Time of Peace" expresses doubt whether prayer can prevent the coming of "a yet more ominous day" in Ireland.

"Cultural Center" (later retitled "Musée Imaginaire") contemplates artworks from different cultures in a museum, each representing a civilization's values. Among them, commanding the speaker's attention and that of a nun in the museum, is a "minatory" Catalan crucifix. The "rigid figure" on the cross, its "sharp body twisted all awry," bespeaks a religion harsh but undeniably real. At the nun's waist swings a miniature modern crucifix: "a minute harmless god of silver plate," as "inoffensive . . . and mild" as the nun herself. Given these "conflicting modes" of imaging Catholic Christianity, clearly Montague prefers the strength and authenticity of the "lean, accusing Catalan crucifix"; yet his misgivings about the values it represents are obvious.

Although love would develop into one of Montague's chief subjects, there is more fear than love in *Forms of Exile*. When love does appear, it is merely observed, not actually experienced: in "Irish Street Scene, with Lovers," for example, and "Song of the Lonely Bachelor."

"The Sean Bhean Vocht" introduces an old woman who, symbolically, is Ireland personified, a repository of "local history" and "racial memory." "As a child I was frightened by her," Montague says, but it is not entirely clear what has replaced fear: fascination, respect, perhaps a hint of affection. Montague's ambiguity in this regard suggests that he has only begun to work through his feelings toward Ireland.

Poisoned Lands and Other Poems overlaps with *Forms of Exile*: 40 percent of its poems appeared in the earlier book. In its new poems, Montague continues to write about Ireland, reflecting on his relation to it and its relation to the world. Several of these poems attempt to shape and understand childhood memories. "The Water Carrier" describes the chore of fetching water with precisely rendered details, then stops short. "Recovering the scene," Montague says, "I had hoped to stylize it,/ Like the portrait of an Egyptian water-carrier:/ Yet halt, entranced by slight but memoried life." Realizing that he cannot be that detached from memory, he concludes,

> I sometimes come to take the water there,
> Not as return or refuge, but some pure thing,
> Some living source, half-imagined and half-real
>
> Pulses in the fictive water that I feel.

Memory itself is that "fictive water," a resource on which to draw. "Like Dolmens Round my Childhood, the Old People" evokes the lives of country neighbors. As megalithic structures dot the Irish countryside, mysterious and yet matter-of-factly present, so these figures populate the landscape of the poet's memory. "For years they trespassed on my dreams," he says, "until once, in a standing circle of stones,/ I felt their shadow pass// Into that dark permanence of ancient forms." He has commemorated the old people without sentimentality and made peace with their memories.

The outside world began to impinge on his local world when he was a schoolboy, as he recalls in "Auschwitz, Mon Amour" (later retitled "A Welcoming Party"). Newsreel images of concentration-camp survivors brought home to him the irrelevance of Ireland's "parochial brand of innocence." Having learned something about evil in the wider world, he has yet to comprehend what he has seen. For now, there is nothing to do but return to school and toss a football. The "Irish dimension" of his childhood, he says, came from being "always at the periphery of incident."

In poems such as "Auschwitz, Mon Amour" and the sarcastic "Regionalism, or Portrait of the Artist as a Model Farmer," Montague's disaffection with Irish provincialism gives him an exile's sensibility, in the tradition of one of his masters, James Joyce. "Prodigal Son" reflects on his annual visits to Ulster: It is a nice place to visit, but he would not want to live there. (Montague is well aware that the self-selected exile of the artist has little in common with exile imposed by economic circumstance, such as he alludes to in the opening poem of *Poisoned Lands and Other Poems*, "Murphy in Manchester.")

Within the new poems in this collection, the subject of religion all but disappears. Love is alluded to occasionally, mostly in passing; yet the volume does include Montague's first full-fledged love poem, "Pastorals." It is a dialogue between two lovers, a cynic who sees love as but the "movement of unlawful limbs/ In a marriage of two whims" and an idealist who views it as a sanctuary where "hearts long bruised . . . can trace/ Redeeming patterns of experience."

The first section of *A Chosen Light* is a gathering of love poems. "Country Matters" and "Virgo Hibernica" recall love unspoken; the inhibiting shyness of adolescence. The latter acknowledges "the gravitational pull/ of love," but the former concludes that "the word of love is/ Hardest to say."

"All Legendary Obstacles" memoralizes the reunion of separated lovers. A number of subsequent poems in the section draw upon less ecstatic (less "legendary") experiences, including the strains within a marriage. "Loving Reflections," for example, moves in its three parts from tenderness to an angry argument to grim determination to hold on to the relationship.

Montague begins to explore family connections seriously in *A Chosen Light*, particularly in "The Country Fiddler" and "The Cage." His uncle and godfather John Montague, for whom he was named, had been a country fiddler, but his "rural art [was] silenced in the discord of Brooklyn," and he died in American exile. His nephew, born there, became his uncle's "unexpected successor" when sent to Ireland at age four to live. Montague also sees his craft, poetry, as "succession" to his uncle's "rural craft" of music.

In "The Cage" Montague calls his father "the least happy/ man I have known," who drank himself to "brute oblivion." When he finally returned to Ireland in 1952, after twenty-seven years in Brooklyn, he and his son were briefly reunited; by then, however, the son was but an occasional visitor to Tyrone and would soon head for the United States himself. Mingled in the poem are Montague's conflicting feelings toward his father: pity, revulsion, respect, affection.

"The Road's End" grew out of one of Montague's visits home. He retraces childhood steps, noting changes: overgrown thorns, a disused well, abandoned homes. "Like shards/ Of a lost culture," he says, "the slopes/ Are strewn with cabins, emptied/ In my lifetime." His sense of loss is strong.

In *Tides*, only two poems allude to Montague's blood kin, "Last Journey" and "Omagh Hospital," and both move from their specific subjects to the larger world of Northern Ireland. The former is subtitled "i.m. James Montague," but salutes Ulster's, as well as his father's, memory, citing the "place-names that sigh/ like a pressed melodeon/ across this forgotten/ Northern landscape." In "Omagh Hospital," Montague's dying Aunt Brigid pleads to be taken home, but he pictures her house, "shaken by traffic/ until a fault runs/ from roof to base." The house that has become uninhabitable is not only the family home but the whole province, rent by a grievous "fault."

Tides has an increased proportion, and a stunning variety, of love poems. The first two of the book's five sections concentrate on the darker side of love. "Premonition" and "The Pale Light" provide horrific, nightmare images. "Summer Storm" scales down to the more prosaic hell of a couple arguing, Montague returning here to his theme of love gone sour. "Special Delivery," in which "the worm of delight/ . . . turns to/ feed upon itself," reinforces this theme. The two poems in these sections that actually celebrate love are those that, at first glance, might seem least capable of doing so: "The Wild Dog Rose" and "The Hag of Beare." "The Wild Dog Rose" focuses on a haglike woman who has lived a solitary life of few expectations and fewer pleasures. Her one encounter with a man was a terrifying attempted rape. Yet love is not absent from this apparently loveless life: The poem ends with a glimpse of transcendent, absolutely selfless love. The poem elicits not pity for the old woman but admiration for her great heart. In "The Hag of Beare," another crone comes to a higher love, at the end of a life utterly different from that briefly sketched in "The Wild Dog Rose." Having known all fleshly pleasures, now denied by age and infirmity, the Hag of Beare expresses her willingness to welcome "the Son of Mary," like so many men before, "under my roof-tree."

The middle section of *Tides* introduces a frankly erotic note into Montague's love poetry. "A Dream of July" celebrates "Ceres, corn goddess," whose "abundant body is/ Compounded of honey/ & gold," and similar imagery of honey and gold can be found in "The Same Gesture" and "Love, a Greeting" (as earlier it was found in "Virgo Hibernica"). Love here is primarily physical, exuberant, largely unassociated with responsibilities, and—as in the title poem, "Tracks"—without commitment.

Poems in Montague's first two books of poems are not randomly arranged, but a greater degree of order obtains in books three and four, which group poems into thematically related sections. Moreover, in *Tides*, the fourth book, sea imagery, often metaphorical, helps unify the volume as a whole. Montague's fifth book, *The Rough Field*, is more highly organized still. Though it contains a number of individual poems capable of standing on their own (eight appeared in previous Montague books), in fact it is one long poem composed of many parts.

Montague began work on *The Rough Field* in the early 1960's, concluding it a decade later, after a new outbreak of sectarian violence struck Ulster. Montague says that he began with "a kind of vision . . . of my home area, the unhappiness of its historical destiny." Violent confrontations in Belfast and Derry gave added point to the project and contributed materials that Montague incorporated into the completed work: "the emerging order/ of the poem invaded," as he says in part 9, "by cries, protestations/ a people's pain."

"Rough Field" translates the name of the townland, Garvaghey, where Montague grew up: "Rough Field in the Gaelic and rightly named/ . . . Harsh landscape that haunts me." He weaves together family stories, incidents from his childhood, and episodes from Irish history since the sixteenth century. The book is populated by members of his family, people from Tyrone whom he knew growing up, and historical figures from Hugh O'Neill (1545-1616) to Bernadette Devlin (b. 1947). It evokes the landscape and dwells on the place-names of Tyrone, and of Ulster in general, sites of ancient or recent historical significance. Interspersed among Montague's poems, often with ironic effect, are a variety of "found" texts: excerpts from historical documents, memoirs, letters, newspapers, and the like. The "conversation" among the various voices in *The Rough Field* (Montague's several voices and these "found" voices) contributes to the book's multilayered complexity.

Its complexity notwithstanding, the book is unified by its steady focus on one place (and the continuity of its problems) as well as by recurring images— the rough field, houses, swans—and recurring concerns: home, inheritance, exile; memory; dreams; loneliness; things lost; things broken, shaken, scattered, shattered, including buildings, families, lives, dreams, tradition, a culture, a province. *The Rough Field* is further unified by successfully linking the personal, the familial, the regional, the national, the global, Montague's Garvaghey becoming a microcosm of "the rough field/ of the universe." Finally, it is unified by successfully linking past and present: generation joined to generation ("This bitterness/ I inherit from my father"), century to century (contemporary exile in the United States and the seventeenth century "Flight of the Earls"). *The Rough Field*, treating a serious theme with artistry and authority, is widely considered Montague's greatest work.

A Slow Dance is a rich mixture, its five sections linked by recurring images: warmth and cold and, especially, dance. The slow dance, Montague has said, is the "dance of death and life," and this volume reveals a heightened sense of both mortality and vitality.

Section 1 takes the reader "back to our origins"—individually to the womb, collectively to primordial cave—and there the dance of life and death begins. "The humid pull/ of the earth" is immediate; the dance begins "in . . . isolation" but ends in complete identification with the natural world, human "breath mingling with the exhalations of the earth." The section collapses time and dissolves distinctions between civilizations, so that legendary poet-king Sweeny coexists with Saint Patrick, and (in "For the Hillmother") the Christian Litany of the Blessed Virgin provides the form for a pagan invocation to nature as the source of life. The section is about life, with death only hinted at.

Section 2 opens with a birth, but in "Courtyard in Winter," the poet meditates on the suicide of a friend. Montague grieves that he could not "ease the single hurt/ That edged her towards her death," but he does not give in to guilt or despair. Rather, "I still affirm/ That nothing dies, that even from/ Such bitter failure memory grows." Much of the rest of the section consists of lyrical evocations of nature, of which "Windharp" is perhaps the best known.

The opening section collapses time and telescopes civilizations in the service of life; the third does the same in the service of death, "The Cave of Night" substituting for the womb/cave. Ancient Celtic blood sacrifice is juxtaposed to armed struggle in Belfast. Killing with sword and rifle, the slaughtering of a pig in a farmyard and of soldiers on a battlefield, are essentially the same in this hellish section, ruled over by the "Black Widow goddess." The section ends, fittingly, with a poem called "Coldness."

The reader turns with relief in the fourth section to the warmer world of family. Problems here—parents unable to live together, a child denied "the warm circle" of its mother's company—are problems that can be comprehended, sometimes even dealt with. Loneliness is here (it is never far in Montague's poetry), but "human warmth" is, too.

The final section of *A Slow Dance* is Montague's tribute to his friend the composer Séan Ó Riada. The "slowly failing fire" dies out, and the book ends with a cry of anguish:

a lament so total
it mourns no one
but the globe itself
turning in the endless halls

of space.

The book, which begins by celebrating "The whole world/ turning in wet/ and silence," thus ends lamenting the same turning world. The "globe itself/ turning" enacts the "slow dance" of life and death.

The Great Cloak focuses on love—no poems here about growing up, family, or Ireland. Montague examines the breakup of one marriage, the beginning of another, and the interval between. The poems are short (averaging about half the length of those in *A Slow Dance*), uncomplicated, accessible. Their imagery is predominantly visual (attentive to the play of light and shadow) and tactile (hands touching, caressing).

In the first section, sexual encounters are brief respites from loneliness. Loneliness and worse—nothingness, the void—seem implicit in the ominous image that closes the section: "profound night/ like a black swan/ goes pluming past."

The second section, less self-absorbed, sadly sifts through the fragments of a broken marriage. It is an inventory of losses. "Darkness" finds Montague trying to understand his estranged wife's feelings, and in four other poems he goes so far as to speak with her voice: "I sing your pain/ as best I can," he says, in his own voice. The longest and best poem in the book, "Herbert Street Revisited," returns to the Dublin street where, newly wed, Montague and his wife made their first home. It is a generous-spirited celebration of the love they shared.

"Anchor," title of the last section, expresses a wish; the new relationship Montague explores here seems less fixed, less certain, than the title suggests. "Walking Late," for example, ends with the couple circling "uncertainly/ towards a home." Only in "Protest," which records the birth of their child, and the handful of poems that follow it does the tone of voice become confident enough to warrant the section's title.

Montague's *Selected Poems* draws from all of his previous books of poems and includes a few that would appear later in *The Dead Kingdom* or *Mount Eagle*. Some poems, particularly early ones, show substantive revisions, and the order in which they appear is not always that of the earlier books.

Like *The Rough Field*, *The Dead Kingdom* is a single long poem—an arrangement of shorter poems, ten of which appeared in previous books. Unlike *The Rough Field*, *The Dead Kingdom* has a narrative line. It begins when news arrives in Cork that Montague's mother has died. "The 'thread' or plot," Montague has written, "is the long drive North" to attend her funeral.

The drive north takes Montague through the Midlands, calling up bittersweet memories of summers in County Longford. Over half the poems in the book's first two (of five) sections connect with "this neutral realm." "Abbeylara" affectionately recalls summers with Carney relatives, but now they are dead, their house abandoned, their carefully tended garden gone wild. The small piece of land to which they gave order is "reverting to first chaos/ as if they had never been."

Two poems in section 1 meditate on transience itself. In "Process," "time's gullet devouring" all that people value becomes an abyss of "fuming oblivion," across which one can but cast "swaying ropeladders" such as "love or friendship,/ an absorbing discipline." "Gone" recalls things great and small that have been "hustled into oblivion" and stoically salutes "the goddess Mutability,/ dark Lady of Process,/ our devouring Queen." Terms such as "chaos," "oblivion," and "the void" spatter the first half of the book, and the metaphor of "time's gullet" and the "devouring Queen" is reinforced by multiple references to appetite, feeding, and digestive organs.

In section 3, the border of Northern Ireland revives thoughts of violent conflicts there. Weather and mood alike turn cold and dark as he returns to the "bloody ground" where he was raised. More despairing than in *The Rough Field*, Montague can but "sing a song for the broken/ towns of old Tyrone" and "for the people,/ so grimly holding on." He calls his wish for "an end to sectarianism" a "forlorn hope."

As in *A Slow Dance*, the almost unrelieved gloom of section 3 gives way to the warmer—even when painful—images of family in section 4. In a series of flashbacks Montague reviews his parents' lives, together and apart (a photograph of the young couple introduces the section).

Music has woven its way through all Montague's books, but none of them is as filled with music as *The Dead Kingdom*, which invokes everything from popular songs ("Kathleen Mavourneen," "Paddy Reilly") to Mary Mulvey's music box and "the sound/ of bells in monastic/ sites." Montague himself calls for song in several poems (for example, "sing a song for/ things that are gone"). The principal singer, however, is his father, teaching his son the words to "Ragtime Cowboy Joe"; singing "Molly Bawn" to his own Molly, after his long-delayed return to Ireland; lending his "broken tenor" to Christmas carols in Midnight Mass. Montague understands that, back in Brooklyn, his "father's songs/ couldn't sweeten the lack of money" that had contributed to the family's fragmentation. Yet Montague recognizes that "the healing harmony/ of music" had been his father's rope ladder across oblivion, and he regrets that his mother's funeral is "without music or song" to "ease the living" and "sweeten our burden."

Montague continues to examine the subject of exile in its various forms, under its various names: "emigration," "transportation," "diaspora," "dispossession." At last, his mother dead, he brings himself to mention the form of exile he himself has experienced most painfully: being rejected by his mother in childhood. "You gave me away," he says to her posthumously ("The Locket"), "to be fostered/ in Garvaghey" ("A Muddy Cup"), "to be fostered/ wherever charity could afford." This, he says, was the "primal hurt," to be "an unwanted child": "All roads wind backwards to it" ("A Flowering Absence").

"It is hard to work so close to the bone," Montague has said of these poems about his mother. After a lifetime of excavating the strata of his life, Montague has finally reached emotional bedrock. To have been "fostered" is to have been exiled most radically. Yet "The Locket," "a last song/ for the lady who has gone," ends with a "mysterious blessing": The poet learns, after his mother's death, that the locket she had always worn contained an old photograph of "a child in Brooklyn."

His responsibilities in Tyrone finished, Montague turns his attention to the living woman in his life—

> I place my hopes
> beside yours, Evelyn,
> frail rope-ladders
> across fuming oblivion

—and heads "back across the/ length of Ireland, home."

Mount Eagle is neither arranged as a coherent whole, like *The Rough Field* and *The Dead Kingdom*, nor organized into distinct sections, like *A Chosen Light, Tides, A Slow Dance*, and *The Great Cloak*. Rather, like Montague's first two books, *Forms of Exile* and *Poisoned Lands and Other Poems*, it is something of a miscellany, though its poems are generally arranged by subject. The volume includes a quartet of poems related to "the Troubles" in Northern Ireland, each rendering a sharply etched vignette. There is a late harvest of childhood memories, usually recalled, not for their own sake, but for a connection Montague wishes to draw with something in later life. "The Leap," for example, draws an analogy between daring jumps years before across the Garvaghey River and, referring to his second marriage, a new "taking off . . . into the uncertain dark." Four poems are culled from a father's affectionate observation of his young daughter's investigations of their world. Only one poem alludes to Montague's father, and then in passing; none mentions his mother.

Perhaps a third of the poems could be classified under the general heading of "love." "Fair Head" recalls an early, unconsummated love; several other poems, more characteristically, commemorate consummations. "The Well-Beloved" muses on the process by which smitten lovers, each idealizing the other, descend into married life, and wonders what it takes to "redeem the ordinary." The startling "Sheela na Gig," inspired by the grotesquely sexual female figures carved on medieval Irish churches, synopsizes male human behavior in terms of "banishment" from "the first home" at birth and then a lifetime of trying "to return to that [anatomical] first darkness." Birth, too, is banishment: the first experience of exile.

The most interesting new development in *Mount Eagle* is its attention to nature. "Springs" expresses the ecologically correct wish to "erase/ from this cluttered earth/ our foul disgrace." "Peninsula" is a much more appealing celebration of "Dame Nature's self-/ delighting richness." Several poems draw upon Native American nature myths, including the title poem, wherein an eagle trades its freedom to disappear into, and become "the spirit of," a mountain. The poem may encode Montague's own intent to dedicate himself to a new sort of poetry: less subject to the buffeting of life's winds, perhaps less confessional, more abstract. (Montague has acknowledged that "Mount Eagle" is a homonym for his own name.) The last seven poems in *Mount Eagle*, which include "Luggala" and "The Hill of Silence," could be indicative of this new direction in his work.

Richard Bizot

Other major works
LONG FICTION: *The Lost Notebook*, 1987.
SHORT FICTION: *Death of a Chieftain and Other Stories*, 1964.
NONFICTION: *The Figure in the Cave and Other Essays*, 1989; *Born in Brooklyn*, 1991.
TRANSLATIONS: *A Fair House: Versions of Irish Poetry*, 1973; *November*, by André Frénaud, 1977 (with Evelyn Robson).
ANTHOLOGIES: *The Dolmen Miscellany of Irish Writing*, 1962; *The Faber Book of Irish Verse*, 1974; *Bitter Harvest: An Anthology of Contemporary Irish Verse*, 1989.

Bibliography
Irish University Review: A Journal of Irish Studies 19 (Spring, 1989). This "John Montague Issue," edited by Christopher Murray, includes an interview with Montague, seven articles on his work, an autobiographical essay by Montague ("The Figure in the Cave"), and Thomas Dillon Redshaw's checklist of Montague's books (see below).
Kersnowski, Frank. *John Montague*. Lewisburg, Pa.: Bucknell University Press, 1975. The first book-length study of Montague's work (actually a slim monograph), this work surveys his career through *The Rough Field*. Its chief value may be its readings of individual poems and stories. Does not include an index.
Mariani, Paul. "John Montague." In *Poets of Great Britain and Ireland Since 1960*, pt. 2, *M-Z*, edited by Vincent B. Sherry, Jr. Vol. 40 of *Dictionary of Literary Biography*. Detroit: Gale Research, 1985. A well-informed overview of Montague's life and work, through *The Dead Kingdom*, with a

good selected bibliography of work by and about Montague.

Montague, John. *The Figure in the Cave and Other Essays.* Edited by Antoinette Quinn. Syracuse, N.Y.: Syracuse University Press, 1989. This is the essential source for information about Montague's life, especially in the first four (very autobiographical) essays and in the detailed chronology of his life at the end.

Redshaw, Thomas Dillon, ed. *Hill Field: Poems and Memoirs for John Montague on His Sixtieth Birthday, 28 February 1989.* Minneapolis: Coffee House Press, 1989. Ten brief memoirs offer glimpses into various phases of Montague's life. Its most useful feature is the editor's "The Books of John Montague, 1958-1988: A Descriptive Checklist."

MARIANNE MOORE

Born: Kirkwood, Missouri; November 15, 1887
Died: New York, New York; February 5, 1972

Principal poetry
Poems, 1921; *Observations*, 1924; *Selected Poems*, 1935; *The Pangolin and Other Verse*, 1936; *What Are Years*, 1941; *Nevertheless*, 1944; *Collected Poems*, 1951; *Selected Fables of La Fontaine*, 1955 (translation); *Like a Bulwark*, 1956; *O to Be a Dragon*, 1959; *Tell Me, Tell Me*, 1966; *The Complete Poems of Marianne Moore*, 1967, 1981.

Other literary forms
Marianne Moore left a voluminous correspondence with literary figures in America and England, work that when published will demonstrate that she was as original-minded in personal and critical prose as she was in verse. She wrote occasional reviews and lectured on campuses and at poetry centers. This work, too, shows her imaginative daring, the "idiosyncrasy and technique" that she valued. A sampling of her prose as well as of her verse was published as *A Marianne Moore Reader* (1961). A selection of essays, *Predilections*, appeared in 1955.

The words "collected" and "complete" in a title may promise more than the book delivers; in Moore's case, the contents are only those examples of her work that she wished to keep in circulation. Because she frequently revised extensively, a genuinely complete edition must be variorum. The best available selection is *The Complete Poems of Marianne Moore*. Most of Moore's manuscripts and correspondence, as well as a collection of her furnishings and personal items, are housed in the museum of the Philip H. and A. S. W. Rosenbach Foundation, Philadelphia. *The Complete Prose of Marianne Moore* (1986) includes all of Moore's published prose work, from her early stories to her mature essays and reviews; as editor of *The Dial* from 1921 to 1929, and later, as her poetic reputation grew, she had the opportunity to write on a broad range of twentieth century poets and fiction writers.

Achievements
If she had lived longer she would have sympathized with the aims, if not with the more fervid rhetoric, of the revived feminist movement; but in her day Moore sought recognition without regard to gender. Her daring paid off, since her work impresses most critics, male or female, as that of a major figure among poets of modernism; she is considered to be an artist on a par with Wallace Stevens, William Carlos Williams, and Ezra Pound.

Praised by Eliot as "one of those few who have done the language some service," Moore quickly made a reputation among other poets. She won the Dial Award in 1924, and in 1925 was the object of discussion in five consecutive issues of *The Dial*. Her work, however, long remained little known to the public. The "beauty" that she sought was the product of an individualistic decorum, a discipline of self and art that yielded the quality she admired in the poem "The Monkey Puzzle" (*Selected Poems*, 1935) as "porcupine-quilled, complicated starkness." The quilled and stark imagery is slow to attract admirers other than the *cognoscenti*, but by the 1950's her work was receiving wide recognition.

She had, indeed, a year of wonder in 1952, receiving the National Book Award, the Bollingen Prize, and the Pulitzer Prize. Since that time, some of her poems have appeared in every reasonably comprehensive anthology of modern verse. Either the 1935 or the 1967 version of "Poetry" is almost always included. Other choices vary: "The Pangolin," "What Are Years?," "Virginia Britannia," and "A Grave" are among those poems most frequently anthologized.

Biography

The relaxation in Marianne Moore's later verse and the rise of public acclaim demonstrate that late in her life the poetic self that had begun in a reticence that approached diffidence, that had armored itself as much against temptation from within as against threat from without, had burst through its early encasements to take on the role of moralist and even of sociopolitical adviser. A degree of tolerance for the self and the world perhaps made her choices easier, although it did not always benefit her art.

Moore seems to have had an inborn disdain for the self-indulgent. After a girlhood in Missouri and Pennsylvania and an education at Bryn Mawr College, she taught commercial subjects at the United States Indian School in Carlisle, Pennsylvania, for three and a half years while perfecting her art as a poet. Her verse began to appear in *The Egoist* (London), *Poetry*, and other journals of the new poetry. By 1918, she had settled in Manhattan and become a member of the literary circle that included William Carlos Williams, Wallace Stevens, and Alfred Kreymborg. Her first volume, *Poems* (1921), was brought out in London. The period of the Dial Award was followed by her appointment in 1925 as an editor—soon to be editor-in-chief—of *The Dial*. She guided the journal through its heyday as the premier American periodical of literature and the arts. The work excited her, demonstrated her firm taste, and made her acquainted with most of the prominent writers of the time. After *The Dial* was discontinued in 1928, Moore never again worked at a salaried job. Although she earned occasional small checks for verse and reviews, her career as a writer, according to Driver, was subsidized by the former backers of *The Dial*. In the same year that the publication ended,

Moore and her mother—a close adviser until her death in 1947—moved to Brooklyn, where the poet's brother John, a Navy chaplain, was stationed.

Useful though it was, the period with *The Dial* was an interruption. Moore had published *Observations* (1924) before going to work on the journal; her next book, *Selected Poems*, did not appear until 1935. This volume reprinted several pieces from earlier books and also some more recent work from magazines. The slim *The Pangolin and Other Verse* appeared in 1936. Moore lived quietly for the next two decades, publishing additional thin volumes. In the 1950's, the growing acceptance of modernism and the approval indicated by her numerous awards helped bring public attention; she became, indeed, something of a celebrity. Doubtless interest was furthered by her darting and witty conversation with interviewers, as well as her shrewd adoption of a three-cornered hat as a badge of eccentricity. It became routine to see a photo story in *Life* magazine on Moore's trip to the zoo, to read of her as unofficial hostess for the mayor of New York, and to find *The New Yorker* printing the hilarious exchange of letters that resulted from the request in 1955 that she think up names for a new model from Ford. (The final choice—not one of her suggestions—was "Edsel.") When in 1965 she left her Brooklyn apartment for one in Manhattan, the move was recorded on the front page of *The New York Times*.

Yet Moore could never be accused of self-importance. She enjoyed attention, but was wary—"I am often taken advantage of," she said—and continued to work at essays, reviews, and poetry. In some of her late verse she is sententious or playful. In other pieces she continues to focus on an object, a "thing" that provides her with observable fact that she can carpenter into an aesthetic stairway, a means of rising to discovery. Readers will frequently find in the work of her early and middle decades, and sometimes even in her late poems, the delight, the quilled beauty that is her legacy.

Analysis

In Marianne Moore's best work the imagined and the perceived are interdependent; she merges the two to create her usefully idiosyncratic reality. Often she finds in her universe suggestions of ethical principle. When she integrates statement of principle with sufficient circumstance, she makes the presentation seem not merely a lesson but also a fundamental component of the aesthetic structure of her world.

That "we"—speakers of English, one supposes—have not successfully integrated the world of imagination with that of the senses is part of the closing observation in her best-known poem, the 1935 version of "Poetry." This piece unfortunately has been the victim of ill-advised revision. Its argument was clear in the 1921 printing; after publishing a much-altered version in her 1924 book, Moore in 1935 returned to the 1921 version. The 1935 printing, however, introduced an ambiguity that illustrates how much may depend on so supposedly trivial a device as a punctuation mark.

The 1935 version, the one that became well-known, opens with a first line that seems to dismiss poetry as "all this fiddle." This is best taken as a bit of rueful humor about Moore's own dedication, since she clearly was in no way contemptuous of her art. The poetry she likes is that which contains the "genuine," a quality that she shows by example and then by assertion to be equivalent to "useful." In what is perhaps a caution against the dangers of her own frequent practice of working from pictures or written descriptions rather than from first-hand experience, she remarks that the too "derivative" may become "unintelligible," and adds that people do not admire "what they cannot understand." In the 1921 version, a period followed "understand," making it clear that the next several examples that the poem gives are included in the "phenomena" mentioned in line 18. But after "understand" in the 1935 version, Moore puts a colon, seeming to indicate that the content of the following lines is to be taken as examples of objects that, because they are unintelligible, are not admired. This material, however, consists of several notations of the sort of exact reality that Moore likes to use—a "tireless" wolf, a "twitching critic"—and lines 16 to 18 accept the usefulness of such detail by declaring that, together with other matter, all such "phenomena" are important. The reader not deterred by the apparent contradiction will next find a warning that mere specification of "phenomena" does not make art, followed by the observation that real poetry is not yet with "us," that it will arise only when poets become "literalists of the imagination" who produce "imaginary gardens with real toads in them." This much-discussed phrase is a careful statement of her own intention: to disclose the universe ("imaginary gardens") suggested by the objects perceived by the senses (such as "real toads"). The ending remark is that "in the meantime" the reader will have to be satisfied with one or the other of the two components of true art: raw material in "all its rawness" and "the genuine." The real poet, it appears, will be the one who merges these elements.

"Poetry" is uncharacteristically broad in its interests. Moore's usual stance in her early work is that of one on guard against threat, controlling and armoring the self. She sees mankind as living in danger, as though over an abyss, an emptiness largely composed of people's ignorance of purpose or significances, together with a suggestion that the universe, insofar as it may heed mankind at all, is indifferent or hostile. One must be rock-hard, alert, wary. In "The Fish" (*Poems*) she portrays the dark colorations, the lack of hiding places, the "iron edge" of the forces that impel life forms into seemingly chaotic motion. Yet these life forms represent the intelligence, the consciousness of an enduring cliff of reality and of spirit that withstands all "abuse" and "accident." The view is ultimately optimistic; but the optimism is sparse, the opponent determined, grim, almost victorious. The sense of threat, of a necessary caution in attempts to profit from or even to understand the oceanic indifference that surrounds man, is emphasized in "A Grave" (*Observations*). Here the "sea," the abyss of, perhaps, the universe, society, or self-indulgence, offers the incautious nothing but a grave; it subdues the rapacious with its own superior rapacity; it lies under all activity of man and bird and shell, and, though men may at times create a harmony that seems to deny its power, in the end it extinguishes all that is "dropped," that thoughtlessly stumbles into it.

One protection is decorum, a discipline that keeps focus on the essential, that avoids all gluttony and greed. Moore frequently celebrates objects, creatures, and places that exemplify this spare rectitude. Thus, she presents as an appropriate home for man the town that has an abundance of delights but no excess, the town of "The Steeple-Jack" (*Selected Poems*). The excess that Moore criticizes is that of the artifice that is too clever, too luxuriant in ornament and ingenuity. In "The Jerboa" (*Selected Poems*), stanzas headed "Too Much" condemn the wealth of Egyptian courtiers who accumulated luxuries while poverty and drought afflicted the common people; stanzas headed "Abundance" celebrate the true wealth of the jerboa, the self-sufficient rodent that, unlike the pharaoh's over-indulged mongoose, knows a natural "rest" in its desert home. In such early poems, Moore finds in the relatively uncomplicated lives of animals, usually exotic ones that have no traditional symbolism in the English-speaking world, and occasionally in examples from the worlds of flora and of human craftsmanship, the delight that arises from the primary values she recommends. These are the values that make for survival in a world of hard requirements: honesty in function and behavior, modest simplicity in bearing, and courage.

The combination of discipline and excitement, of decorum and ardor, is supported by Moore's style. Instead of using the accentual-syllabic measure that determines the length of lines in most poetry in English—a repetitive arrangement of stressed syllables which gives verse a sound quite different from prose—Moore counts syllables. This gives her the freedom to use the syntax normal to prose. Her syntax is at times exotic, but this results from her fondness for ellipses and abrupt juxtapositions that require of the reader some of the dexterity of her own perception. The syllabic measure enables her to use feminine rhyme, which puts the stress on syllables other than those that rhyme. She commonly parallels line lengths from stanza to stanza. In "The Jerboa," for example, the first and second lines of each stanza have five syllables, the third lines each have six, the fourth lines have eleven, and similar parallelism is maintained throughout. She also indents to put together those lines which rhyme. Internal correspondences of sound are frequent. Despite this workmanship, however, the effects are almost entirely visual: read aloud, a Moore poem sounds like thoughtful prose. Yet the suggestion of verse is there; and it is strengthened by Moore's obvious delight in accumulating specific, colorful detail. Fastidious, seemingly reticent, avoiding the glaring and the grotesque, gaining impact by conveying the sense of tightly controlled, unsentimental emotion, the style suggests possibilities for a verse that English has not yet fully exploited.

The theme of most of Moore's early work is summed up in "An Octopus" (*Selected Poems*) as "relentless accuracy." Although in the poetry that she published in mid-career she continues to emphasize need for discipline and heroic behavior, she begins to relent a bit, to add to her exposition an emphasis on love and spiritual grace. She always gives particulars, grounding cautionary generalization firmly in sensory reality. She no longer limits her typical poem to one "thing," one animal or object, however, and she more often considers directly the human behavior that is the underlying subject. The broadening of range shows in the great poem "The Pangolin" (*The Pangolin and Other Verse*), an admiration of the interrelationships of grace as that quality is seen in the observed features of the animal, the architecture and stone ornamentation of a cathedral, and the behavior of men when "kindly" toward one another. In such "splendour" Moore finds a suggestion of the spiritual. The poem is a marvelous interweaving of delighted observations of the animal, appreciative examination of the cathedral, recognition of man's "vileness" but also of his "excellence," and intimation, by question and by assertion of renewal, of the existence of a grace beyond the mundane.

Other poems from *The Pangolin and Other Verse* show similar acceptance of a world beyond the self. Intricate and skillful interweaving of detail and unobtrusive comment makes "Virginia Britannia" a celebration of the possibilities of the American continent, leading to the question: "How could man ignore and destroy?" In "Smooth Gnarled Crape Myrtle"—the title hints at paradox—the poet ends with a rueful "Alas!" for mankind, the creatures who in artifice honor the peace, plenty, and wisdom, the friendship and love, that they do not in fact allow to direct their behavior. In "Spenser's Ireland" (*What Are Years*), a gentler humor accepts certain peculiarities as native to the Irish (among whom the poet lists herself), even while the poem renews Moore's frequent assertion that one is never really free until or unless one is "captive" to a "supreme belief."

The poem "What Are Years?" is Moore's most direct presentation of her values. Perhaps too direct for some tastes, it appeals to others by its accessibility. After noting that people cannot understand the nature of their guilt or innocence, but that all are "naked" to the dangers of existence, the speaker moves on to define courage as "resolute doubt," the strength of spirit to remain strong even when defeated. The chief exponent of such strength is the one who "accedes to mortality," who accepts the fact of death and yet struggles to live, keeps returning to the struggle even though imprisoned in a world of mortality. An ambiguous "So" begins the last stanza: one who feels strongly, who is intensely aware of mortality, "behaves," keeps the ego disciplined. The pattern is that of the caged bird who, though captive, continues to sing. Despite his lack of "satisfaction," presumably of desire for flight and freedom, he knows "joy," the spiritual strength to go on living and to triumph over circumstance. This joyous discipline, it appears, "is" mortality, is knowledge of death, yet also "is" eternity, awareness of something beyond the mortal.

Survival calls, above all, for fortitude, the quality honored in "Nevertheless" (*Nevertheless*). Here the speaker's admiring delight in the way plant life manages to survive, not by withdrawing but by reaching out, by extending its growth, leads to the observation that to achieve "victory" one cannot be merely passive; one must "go/ to it." Two of Moore's most delightful poems are "A Carriage from Sweden," applauding the "unannoying/ romance" of the decorative yet functional cart that the speaker has seen in a museum; and "The Mind Is an Enchanting Thing," celebrating the play of the human mind that is both "trued" by belief and complex enough to experience "conscientious inconsistency."

"In Distrust of Merits" praises the sacrifices of Allied soldiers in World War II; the speaker contrasts hate and love, declares that the worst of enemies is the self, and, vowing never to hate people of other skin-colors or religions, decries the error of hate and egocentrism. The speaker then backs up: presumably those who love are "not competent" to make such vows until they have replaced with "life" the scene of death that has resulted from their neglect of others. The guilt is shared by everyone, for wars are "inward." The speaker must learn to live for the beauty that arises from patient (that is, thoughtful and loving) action, not as the "dust," the human being who lives in arrogance.

Moore wrote no long poems. Although in her work of the 1950's she appears to have moved away from reticence, she still often prefers to attribute declarative or striking statements to someone else: few poets have been as given to the indirect, sometimes oblique, view of experience afforded by use of quotations, photographs, and other products of someone else's observation. Moore likes to approach at second-hand, so to speak, to comment on and to expand the significance that she finds suggested or confirmed by others. Most such material she takes from her reading, but in some cases one may suspect that she puts quotation marks around a phrase of her own that she wants to hold up for inspection without seeming to impose herself on the reader. This fondness for operating at one remove from the subject suggests that she would find work as a translator congenial. It is not surprising to note that in 1945, after W. H. Auden proposed to a publisher that she translate the *Fables choisies, mises en vers* (1668-1694) of the French poet Jean de La Fontaine, she began what became an eight-year labor of translation, amounting to two and a half times as much verse as she printed in the *Collected Poems* (1951).

Moore's approach is not the literal translation often demanded by the language teacher, but it remains closer to the original than do most of the translations of, for example, Ezra Pound or Robert Lowell. She was attracted to the task because of La Fontaine's craftsmanship and, one may assume, because his skeptical, world-weary examples of competitive behavior in a sophisticated world of affairs provided vicarious experience of a world with which Moore had little direct contact. Thorough critical assessment of Moore's translation is yet to come. Hugh Kenner praises her for discovering "a badly needed idiom, urbane without slickness and brisk without imprecision"; and Donald Hall finds that her versions have a "fire of visual imagery" that is lacking in the originals. Laurence Stapleton observes that, good as they are, *Selected Fables of La Fontaine* took her on "a detour from her own best work." The translations, however, await extended study by someone who knows both French and English well enough to be aware of nuances and who has a firm conception of what a translation should be.

Whatever her hopes that *Selected Fables of La Fontaine* might expand her scope, Moore's last three volumes continue to explore her familiar themes: resistance to threat and intrusion, admiration for the disciplined and delightful. She adds, however, much of what used to be called "occasional" verse, prompted by some event of the moment. The poems of *Like a Bulwark* show these late tendencies. The title poem admires one "firmed" by the assault of fate, leaned and strengthened by his sturdy resistance. Delight in a certain complexity in existence appears in "Then the Ermine": in a quotation that Moore may have devised, she describes the ermine's color as "ebony violet." In "The Sycamore," this pleasure in the parti-colored expands to glorification of "anything in motley." Too often overlooked is "Apparition of Splendor," wherein works of art, the forests of the earth, and traditional fairy tales all contribute to celebrate the courage of the porcupine, which defends itself without aggression. Observation of particulars in skating, tennis, dancing, music, canoeing, pomology, and painting lead in "Style" to an exclamation of joy as the speaker rapturously contemplates artistry wherever it occurs.

Several poems make direct use of Christian tradition, although their intention is not to argue specific doctrine but to use this tradition as a vehicle for values. In "Rosemary," Moore represents beauty and love as enwreathed to form "a kind of Christmas-tree," a celebration of Christ's birth. "Blessed Is the Man" may be viewed as a version of the beatitudes, Moore's metrical objections to the intemperate and her praise of the "unaccommodating" man who has faith in the unseen.

In some poems of *Tell Me, Tell Me*, Moore's last book made up primarily of new poems, ardor is as warm as ever. "Arthur Mitchell," a brief admiration of a dancer, shapes its stanzas to imitate the twirl of the performer. The closing imagery of "Sun" (a poem first published in 1916) implies comparison of the power of the sun—standing, one deduces, for courage of spirit—to a work of spiritual art, a gorgeously wrought hour-glass. The poem is almost a prayer: the speaker appeals to "Sun" to eradicate the "hostility" found in "this meeting-place of surging enmity," this world, or, even, one's own soul.

The reprinting of "Sun" implies a continuity of thought and feeling. Moore seems, however, to have been conscious of a lessening of her powers. "The Mind, Intractable Thing" is, despite its seemingly playful title, a saddening poem when compared with the sprightly dance of feeling in the earlier "The Mind Is an Enchanting Thing." In the late poem, the speaker still exclaims over her subject, but the details are autumnal, the delight colored by near despair as she complains that the "mind" does not help her, that she does not know how to "deal with" terror and wordcraft. One need not take the poem too literally for, as the several good poems in the volume show, Moore retained great abilities to the end of her life.

Following the discovery in the 1960's that Moore's work is not after all impenetrable, book-length studies are accumulating, and the school anthologies that give most Americans the only experience they have with good poetry regularly print some of her poems. The proselike surface of her art is now understood to be supported by a skill with diction and metrics that, as she put it, is "galvanized against inertia." Most poet-critics have continued to be admiring. Randall Jarrell declared that Moore has discovered "a new sort of subject" and "a new sort of connection and structure for it," and John Ashbery speculated that she would eventually be ranked as the best American modernist poet.

Moore has had detractors, of course. In her early years such traditionalists as Louis Untermeyer and Margaret Anderson denigrated her work because it does not have the marked rhythm and heightened language that their Romantic taste demanded. Somewhat later, such middle-of-the-road critics as Oscar Cargill and Babette Deutsch gave her writing only carefully qualified praise. Feminists have struggled to accommodate Moore in their systems. Emily Stipes Watts declares that her reputation is "evaporating" because she follows what are in Watts's view masculine standards. Helen Vendler and Bonnie Costello admire her greatly and are rather possessive about her as a fellow member of what they see as their beleaguered gender; but they are bothered by male critics' applause, suspicious that such praise is only another tactic for putting a woman on a pedestal. Moore's work will survive the obtuse and the silly. Quilled beauty may put off the timid, but it will nevertheless prevail, because by its rigor, grace, and artistry, it achieves aesthetic triumph.

Bernard F. Engel

Other major works

PLAY: *The Absentee*, 1962.

NONFICTION: *Predilections*, 1955.

MISCELLANEOUS: *A Marianne Moore Reader*, 1961; *The Complete Prose of Marianne Moore*, 1986.

Bibliography

Costello, Bonnie. *Marianne Moore: Imaginary Possessions.* Cambridge, Mass.: Harvard University Press, 1981. Having studied the notebooks, clippings, pamphlets, and books from which Moore's many quotations are derived, Costello provides a guide to understanding Moore's poetry. Each chapter discusses a poetic element: symbols, images, poems on poetry, and three of Moore's critical essays and forms. Two poems, "Pangolin" and "Plumet Basilisk," receive a lengthy analysis. Notes and an index accompany the text.

Hadas, Pamela White. *Marianne Moore: Poet of Affection.* Syracuse, N.Y.: Syracuse University Press, 1977. Hadas brings out the human qualities in the objects and animals that are often the subjects of Moore's poems. She shows how Moore bridges the scientific knowledge of animals and the human fields of music, art, and language. Five chapters deal with the biography, poetic style, fascination with animals, self-defensiveness, and vision of heroism in the poet's life and art. This useful book helps to make difficult poems more understandable and ends with notes, a bibliography, and an index.

Molesworth, Charles. *Marianne Moore: A Literary Life.* New York: Atheneum, 1990. Access to Moore's letters to her mother and brother provided Molesworth with valuable biographical material. The book is organized by the places where Moore lived: first Missouri, then Pennsylvania, and finally Brooklyn and Manhattan in New York City. The story of Moore's life revealed here shows how carefully she made decisions about each step she took. She lived a long life as both a major poet and a beloved American personality. Sixteen pages of photographs, notes, and an index complete the work.

Stapleton, Laurence. *Marianne Moore: The Poet's Advance.* Princeton, N.J.: Princeton University Press, 1978. Stapleton chronicles the continuity of Moore's "courageous act of self-exploration" in a detailed examination of her poems, essays, and translations. A chapter devoted to her translation of Jean de La Fontaine's animal fables indicates the sure understanding of French seventeenth century salon life that allowed Moore to bring the poems to life in English. Includes notes and an index.

Tomlinson, Charles. *Marianne Moore: A Collection of Critical Essays.* Englewood Cliffs, N.J.: Prentice-Hall, 1969. Twenty-one articles by leading critics and poets are grouped in five sections: an interview with Moore; early comments by Ezra Pound, T. S. Eliot and others; later comments by Wallace Stevens, William Carlos Williams, Randall Jarrell, and Kenneth Burke; the Jean de La Fontaine translations; and articles from the 1960's. Such a collection of analysis and comment will never be out of date.

Vendler, Helen. "On Marianne Moore." *The New Yorker* 54 (October 16, 1978): 168-194. Drawing on the Tomlinson and Stapleton books, Vendler offers her provocative insights into Moore's character and poems. "Marriage" is talked about, and the assessment of Moore's male critics who have tended to belittle her achievement helps to form a more accurate view of her work.

WILLIAM MORRIS

Born: Walthamstow, England; March 24, 1834
Died: London, England; October 3, 1896

Principal poetry

The Defence of Guenevere and Other Poems, 1858; *The Life and Death of Jason*, 1867; *The Earthly Paradise*, 1868-1870; *Love Is Enough: Or, The Freeing of Pharamond*, 1872; *The Aeneids of Virgil*, 1875 (translation); *The Story of Sigurd the Volsung and the Fall of the Nibelungs*, 1876; *Chants for Socialists*, 1884, 1885; *The Pilgrims of Hope*, 1885-1886; *The Odyssey of Homer*, 1887 (translation); *Poems by the Way*, 1891; *The Tale of Beowulf*, 1895 (translation).

Other literary forms

William Morris' first publication was a series of short prose romances and a review of Robert Browning's *Men and Women* (1855) in *The Oxford and Cambridge Magazine* (1856). Except for his translations of several Icelandic sagas and his journal of two expeditions to Iceland (1871, 1873), Morris wrote no significant prose until 1877, when he began his career as a public lecturer. Some of his lectures were published as pamphlets; those he considered the more important were collected in *Hopes and Fears for Art* (1882) and *Signs of Change* (1888). Other lectures appear in *The Collected Works of William Morris* (1910-1915, May Morris, editor); *William Morris: Artist, Writer, Socialist* (1936, May Morris, editor); and *The Unpublished Lectures of William Morris* (1969, Eugene D. LeMire, editor). During this period he also contributed to the Socialist journal *Commonweal*, which he edited from 1885 until 1890 and in which he published two utopian dream-visions—*A Dream of John Ball* (1888) and *News from Nowhere* (1891). *Icelandic Journals* are an important supplement to the Norse stories in *The Earthly Paradise* and *The Story of Sigurd the Volsung and the Fall of the Nibelungs* and, less directly, to *Love Is Enough*, written the year after his first visit to Iceland. His Socialist prose, both fiction and nonfiction, provides a necessary context for the *Chants for Socialists* and *The Pilgrims of Hope*, and should be of interest to anyone concerned with the relationship between the aesthetic earthly paradise of his poetry and the political earthly paradise of his socialism.

Morris' Utopian fiction is closely related to the series of prose romances he wrote during the last dozen years of his life: *A Tale of the House of the Wolfings* (1888), *The Roots of the Mountains* (1890), *The Story of the Glittering Plain* (1891), *The Wood Beyond the World* (1894), *The Well at the World's End* (1896), *The Water of the Wondrous Isles* (1897), and *The Sundering Flood* (1897). It is in these works that the thematic concerns of his earlier poetry reach their final development.

A selection of Morris' letters appears in *The Letters of William Morris to*

His Family and Friends (1950, Philip Henderson, editor). The first volume of a complete edition of his letters, edited by Norman Kelvin, has been published under the title *The Collected Letters of William Morris* (1984).

Achievements

With the publication of *The Earthly Paradise* in 1868 and 1870, Morris was acknowledged a major poet and, two decades later, considered the logical successor to Alfred, Lord Tennyson as poet laureate. His strength as a poet lies in his grasp of human psychology and his inventiveness with narrative forms. The dramatic monologues of *The Defence of Guenevere and Other Poems* are remarkable for their daring psychosexual realism, and, both for this reason and because they are short enough to anthologize, they have come to be the poetry for which Morris is most widely known. The longer narrative poems that followed, *The Life and Death of Jason* and *The Earthly Paradise*, experiment with techniques of distancing and so forgo the dramatic immediacy of his earliest work; however, they continue Morris' exploration of sexuality and broaden it into a profound analysis of the relationship between erotic desire and the creative impulse. The complexly structured *Love Is Enough* and the epic *The Story of Sigurd the Volsung and the Fall of the Nibelungs*, which Morris considered his poetic masterpiece, furthered his experiments with narration. Along with his prose fiction, his longer poems constitute a major exploration of narrative technique. In the twentieth century, his poetry has been partially overshadowed by his essays and prose fiction and by his accomplishments as a designer, typographer, and political activist. Instead of displacing Morris' achievement as a poet, however, his other work should be judged with it as part of a total effort to transform the thought and life-style of Victorian England. Precisely because his interests extended beyond poetry, Morris exemplifies the bond between poetry and other forms of artistic and political expression.

Biography

William Morris was born on March 24, 1834, in the village of Walthamstow, a few miles northeast of London. His father was a well-to-do broker who maintained a household characterized by old-fashioned self-sufficiency. Morris' early life was centered in his family, who encouraged his tastes for literature and medievalism. At the University of Oxford, which he entered in 1853, he developed close ties with Edward Burne-Jones, and a group of friends ("the Brotherhood") who shared these interests. The year after Morris left Oxford, the Brotherhood undertook the publication of *The Oxford and Cambridge Magazine*, which Morris financed and, for a while, edited, and to which he was a regular contributor. In the same year, he articled himself to the architect G. E. Street, but, following the example of Burne-Jones, who had determined to become an artist, he gave up architecture after a few months in Street's office and became a disciple of the Pre-Raphaelite painter Dante Gabriel Rossetti.

Under the spell of Rossetti, Morris joined in the artist's project to paint scenes from Sir Thomas Malory's *Le Morte d'Arthur* (c. 1469, 1485) on the interior walls of the Oxford Union. Lingering in the congenial atmosphere of the university, he wrote most of the poems he later published in *The Defence of Guenevere and Other Poems*, and paid court to Jane Burden, a hauntingly beautiful woman whom Rossetti had persuaded to sit for him as a model. Morris and Jane Burden were married in 1859 and established themselves at Red House, near Upton, ten miles south of London. The house, of considerable architectural interest, had been designed for them by Morris' friend Philip Webb. Morris himself took an active role in planning the interiors of Red House, and this concern led to the establishment of a firm—Morris, Marshall, Faulkner and Company (later, Morris and Company)—dedicated to the improvement of British interior design. The firm produced stained glass, wood carving, metalwork, furniture, wallpaper, fabrics, and carpets, and in time exercised a significant role in modifying Victorian tastes.

The period at Red House, during which his daughters Jane (Jenny) and Mary (May) were born, was the happiest in Morris' married life. In response to the growing business of the firm, however, he moved back to London in 1865, and with this move began Jane Morris' gradual estrangement from her husband and her involvement with Rossetti—a relationship about which little is certain but much has been said. Morris' disappointment with his marriage is reflected in *The Earthly Paradise*, which he had begun at Red House but completed in the years after his return to London.

Search for a weekend and vacation home led Morris to Kelmscott Manor in a distant corner of Oxfordshire, a house he leased in 1871 and with which he was soon strongly identified. In the same year, he took the first of his two expeditions to Iceland—an outgrowth of the study of Icelandic language and literature which he had begun in 1868 and which was to exert a formative influence on his subsequent writing.

Although the 1870's saw the publication of *The Story of Sigurd the Volsung and the Fall of the Nibelungs* and a major reorganization of the firm, the decade is more strongly marked as the beginning of Morris' political activism. His original concerns were foreign policy and the destruction of historical buildings in the name of "restoration." Soon, though, he had also begun lecturing on the theory of design and manufacture. These efforts to influence public policy confronted Morris with the intransigence of the political and economic establishments, and this experience, along with the influence of John Ruskin, whose writings Morris had admired since his days as an Oxford undergraduate, led him to socialism. In the 1880's Morris became one of the central figures in the British Socialist movement. He edited the journal *Commonweal*; he traveled and lectured up and down the country; he fought, risking his own imprisonment, for the Socialists' freedom of speech; he set forth his notion of an ideal society in the Marxist romances that remain his most widely read books—*A Dream of John Ball* and *News from Nowhere.*

Ultimately, dissension within the Socialist League and his own general fatigue led to a partial withdrawal from political activities in the 1890's. It was during these last years of his life that Morris established the Kelmscott Press and published a number of books, for which he designed the type, layout, and binding. It was also during this period that he returned to the themes of his earlier writing in a series of prose romances that have in recent years found a popular audience. Morris died on October 3, 1896, and was buried in Kelmscott churchyard.

Analysis

Like other Victorian poets, William Morris is best understood in relationship to the Romantic poets whose work preceded his. Like Alfred, Lord Tennyson and Robert Browning, he sought an alternative to the Romantic preoccupation with self by writing in literary forms from which the self of the poet was distanced or removed. Unlike Tennyson and Browning, but in part through their example, he had discovered such forms by the time of his first collection of verse. Excluding himself from his poetry, however, was not enough; Morris went on to find and test ways of replacing the self with a collective consciousness. It is this effort that gives shape and purpose to his literary career.

Tennyson and Browning had found congenial settings for many of their important poems in classical Greece or Rome, Arthurian England, or the Italian Renaissance. Morris set his earliest poems in the Middle Ages, and this setting freed him—at least partially—from the restraints of his times and allowed him to express emotional and intellectual states for which there were no Victorian equivalents. The violence and sexuality of *The Defence of Guenevere and Other Poems* would have been difficult or impossible to treat in poems dealing with contemporary England. Moreover, the poems are spoken either by dramatized personae or by the anonymous voice of the traditional song or ballad. Thus, the contemporary poet is excluded from the text and thereby relieved of the need to moralize or interpret its subject by Victorian standards.

The contents of *The Defence of Guenevere and Other Poems* fall into three categories: poems based on Arthurian materials, poems based on Jean Froissart's *Chronicles* (1373-1410) of the Anglo-French wars of the fourteenth century, and poems linked not by their common source but by their strong, often hallucinatory symbolism.

The title poem exemplifies the first group. In it, Guenevere uses an extended autobiographical apology to forestall the knights who are about to execute her as an adulteress. Because it is a dramatic monologue, the central ambiguity of the poem remains unresolved: Is Guenevere really a repentant victim of circumstances, or is her speech simply a ploy to gain time? It is, of course, both. If she is a victim—if she allowed herself to be led into marriage with a man she did not love—then her victimization signals the same weakness, the same passive sensuality, that precipitated her infidelity. Yet her confession of weakness is itself a seduction of her accusers. In a world determined by sexual desire, her passivity becomes a form of strength. By absenting himself from the poem, Morris allows these contradictory interpretations to interact and thus, in effect, to complicate its meaning. The Guinevere of *Idylls of the King* (1859-1885) is an expression of Tennyson's need to confirm Victorian sexual morality. Morris' Guenevere, in contrast, calls the relevance of moral order itself into question. Ultimately, Lancelot will come to her rescue, and that, in the end, is all that matters.

The Froissartian poems dramatize characters with a real, although usually minor, place in history. They give the lie to the accusation that Morris sentimentalized the Middle Ages. In poems such as "The Haystack in the Floods," "Sir Peter Harpdon's End," and "Concerning Geoffrey Teste Noire," the slow English defeat in the last years of the Hundred Years' War is portrayed with grim realism. In the first and shortest of the three poems, the lovers Jehane and Robert have been taken in ambush and Jehane offered the choice of becoming the lover of an enemy and so saving Robert's life—or at least postponing his death—or refusing and thus bringing about Robert's immediate murder and her own trial by water as a witch. Instead of brooding over her dilemma, she falls asleep, leaning against the wet haystack beside which they had been ambushed. After an hour, she awakens, speaks a quiet "I will not," and sees her lover decapitated and his head beaten to pieces. Again, the power of the poem lies in the absence of authorial comment. Nothing stands between the reader and Jehane's purely instinctual response. Overwhelmed by circumstances, her consciousness is reduced to a sequence of images, culminating in "the long bright blade without a flaw" with which Robert is executed; and the poem is all the more intense for this refusal to verbalize her emotional state.

In the third group of poems, Morris' concentration on imagery results in a poetry comparable to that of the French symbolists. (Like the symbolists, Morris at this point in his career was strongly influenced by Edgar Allan Poe.) Poems such as "The Wind" and "The Blue Closet" are richly evocative but elude precise decipherment. The first depicts a speaker who is psychotic; the second, based on a painting by Dante Gabriel Rossetti, uses deliberate inconclusiveness to suggest a deteriorating consciousness. The longest of the fantasy poems, "Rapunzel," offers a more positive account of the psychosexual development of its protagonist Prince from youth to maturity and seems to foreshadow Morris' later concern for the relationship between art and the erotic drives; any interpretation of the poem, however, is bound to be tenuous.

The success of these early poems in confronting the reader with states of passionate intensity has made it difficult for some critics to understand Morris' decision to write in a very different style in the narrative poetry of the 1860's. If the immediacy of *The Defence of Guenevere and Other Poems* is missing in *The Life and Death of Jason* and *The Earthly Paradise*, though, the shift in style is in no sense a falling off. The manner of the earlier poems would not have worked in a longer narrative. Intensity can be sustained only so long; in time, it becomes unbearable or ludicrous. Moreover, the dramatic monologues and dialogues of *The Defence of Guenevere and Other Poems*, rich in psychological complexity, limit the role of the reader to that of an observer. The poems that followed reflect Morris' growing concern with the full nature of the experience of art; hence, the storyteller, since his role is now a matter of consequence, must be restored to a position of importance.

The storytellers of *The Life and Death of Jason* and *The Earthly Paradise* are not, however, merely extensions of William Morris. Storytelling in *The Earthly Paradise* is complex; the basic assumption of the two works is clear in the simpler narrative of *The Life and Death of Jason*. Morris' subject is classical; his models, however, are not the primary Homeric epic but the imitative secondary epic of Apollonius of Rhodes, his chief source for the materials of the poem, and, explicitly in the invocation to Book XVII, the medieval poet Geoffrey Chaucer. Thus, *The Life and Death of Jason* is not a direct imitation of a classical narrative, but the imitation of an imitation. The chief result of this device is to distance the storyteller from his story. It is no longer *his* story. Rather, it belongs to tradition. It is his task in the present to retell the tale, not to use it as a mode of self-expression; and, given the emphasized distance from the original narrative, the possibility of self-expression is limited. It is the story itself that dictates narrative structure and determines closure—not the narrator's sense that he has had his say. "Another story now my tongue must tell," the poet announces as, having completed his narrative of "the Winning of the Golden Fleece," he undertakes his account of the events that occurred to Jason ten years after his return to Argos. Similarly, when this final episode is completed and capped with the death of Jason, the poem concludes with the assurance that "now is all that ancient story told."

In its original form, *The Life and Death of Jason* was to have been a much shorter poem, "The Deeds of Jason," within the narrative frame of *The Earthly Paradise*. Despite its independent publication, the poem is best understood in that context. *The Earthly Paradise* is an enormous work—more than four times the length of *Idylls of the King* and almost twice as long as Browning's *The Ring and the Book* (1868-1869). The poem consists of a Prologue ("The Wanderers") and a related series of narrative interludes framing twenty-four stories drawn from classical and Germanic sources and arranged according to the cycle of the year, from March to February, with two stories for each month. In addition to this narrative frame, the poem begins with an apology and ends with an epilogue, and prefaces each month's storytelling with a twenty-one-line lyric appropriate to the season, all in a first-person voice that may be identified with Morris. If the poet is present in these occasional verses, it is only as an accretion; and this deliberately adventitious role emphasizes his dissociation from the narratives themselves.

The Wanderers are fourteenth century Vikings who flee a plague-stricken Norway in search of a fabled Earthly Paradise—a land of immortal life and happiness—across the Atlantic. After a lifetime of disappointed expectations, they reach an island "midmost the beating of the steely sea," to which long ago Grecian colonists had been sent and where, cut off from the outside world, classical civilization has flourished long into the Christian era. The Wanderers, now old men, decide to remain here and, along with the Greek elders, agree to pass the time telling stories drawn from their two traditions. The obvious lesson of this narrative frame is that the quest for a geographical earthly paradise is vain, and that timelessness and beauty, if they exist at all, are to be found in art. Yet the art available to the storytellers, like that of *The Life and Death of Jason*, is carefully limited in its effects. It is not directly self-expressive. It is, at best, a temporary illusion. For the space of the storytelling, its auditors may forget their cares, but the sequence of stories itself— from spring to winter—reminds the reader that they are only a respite, never a real escape from the relentless movement of time and decay. Thus, *The Earthly Paradise* is less a celebration of the power of art than a study of the limits of artistic experience. Its most telling literary analogues are not the medieval frame narratives from which it takes its general structure, but John Keats's "Ode to a Nightingale" and "Ode on a Grecian Urn"—Romantic poems in which the nature of art is probed and tested.

The Wanderers' quest suggests a model of the artist's career. Like the protagonist of another Romantic poem about art, Percy Bysshe Shelley's *Alastor* (1816), they seek a real equivalent to the figments of their imagination—and, since their quest is in part motivated by artistic accounts of an earthly paradise, by the imaginative vision embodied in traditional art and oral storytelling, the failure of this quest teaches them the fundamental irreconcilability of the imagination and the natural world. It is therefore a necessary discipline that prepares them to accept the more limited notion of art that enables them to tell the tales of *The Earthly Paradise*. As such, their geographical quest corresponds to the stage of early Romanticism characteristic of many Victorian writers. (The story of their adventures is, fittingly, Romantic autobiography: the only first-person narrative available to them is the account of their own failure.)

In contrast, the Argonauts of *The Life and Death of Jason*, the classical tale originally to have followed immediately after the Wanderers' Prologue, are motivated by two realizable aims—seizing the Golden Fleece and returning safely with it to Argos. The classical counterparts of the Wanderers exemplify, in other words, a classical reasonableness in setting goals for themselves. Yet Jason, having accomplished all this, ends his life dissatisfied. His heroic deeds brought to pass, he is left sitting aimlessly on the sand by the rotting hulk of his ship, at length to be crushed in sleep by its falling stem. The Wanderers are able to transform their failure into successful art and so give form and meaning to their lives. Jason, without art, is trapped in memories he is powerless to reshape to the purposes of old age.

This notion of art as strictly limited yet necessary is present in the opening lines of the Apology. Morris, referring to himself as "the idle singer of an empty day," compares his work first to the Christmastide illusion of a wizard who made the spring, summmer, and fall appear through windows on three sides of a room, "While still, unheard, but in its wonted way,/ Piped the drear wind of that December day"; then, to "a shadowy isle of bliss" like that which the Wanderers come upon "Midmost the beating of the steely sea." These images argue that the full power of art is realized only when its limitations are perceived. The wizard's spell is powerful because his audience never loses awareness of the winter it temporarily displaces; the island is blissful precisely because it holds its own against the sea. The Camelot of Tennyson's *Idylls of the King* is, like the Wanderers' storytelling, a city "built to music." Its relationship to the real world is always ambiguous, however, and it is this ambiguity that spawns the doubt that destroys Arthur's kingdom. For ambiguity, Morris substitutes a tension between the recognized claims of the actual and those of the imaginary, through which each heightens, by contrast, the experience of the other. Art, by giving up its claims to replace actuality, thus subtly pervades and enhances the real world—just as the "lesser arts" of Morris and Company were able to exert an influence over day-to-day life unavailable to the "fine arts" of Victorian England.

In keeping with the project, the twenty-four narratives of *The Earthly Paradise* are generally familiar in subject and simple in narrative style. Certain of the stories, however—in particular, those in the second half of the collection—violate this rule, perhaps reflecting the strains of Morris' personal life, perhaps his impatience with simplicity itself. Both in length and tone, "The Lovers of Gudrun" (November), which Morris based on the Icelandic Laxdaela Saga, seems to break out of its narrative frame. Two overlapping groups of stories, those dealing with erotic quests and those dealing with artists, appear to have particularly caught Morris' imagination: "The Story of Cupid and Psyche" (May), "Pygmalion and the Image" (August), "The Land East of the Sun and West of the Moon" (September), "The Man Who Never Laughed Again" (October), and "The Hill of Venus" (February). Eros, for Morris, may be sublimated in art or idealized love, but its basic nature as irrational drive is never forgotten. Each of these stories recapitulates, in its own way, the journey and disillusionment of the Wanderers. The protagonists of the first three eventually find fulfillment of their desires, but only after a nadir of despair in which all hope for the recovery of imaginative life is lost. Put to the test, the man who never laughs again is unable to resist the claims of the imagination and is destroyed by the strength of his own desire. In Morris' version of the Tannhäuser legend, Walter's acceptance of the limits of art—here, the erotic fantasy world of the Venusberg—leaves him in a nightmare limbo of "hopeless" joys and "horrors passing hell." Significantly, in this, the final story in the collection, the tension between the imaginary and the actual has itself become a source of frustration. Just as his empathic re-creation of the figures on the Grecian Urn leads Keats to "A burning forehead, and a parching tongue," Morris' storytelling returns full circle to the painful self-consciousness he had originally sought to banish. The earthly paradise afforded by narrative art can, it turns out, provide just the opposite of an escape from the pains of desire.

This discovery lies behind *Love Is Enough*, the most complex and in some ways most personally revealing of Morris' longer poems. Written after his 1871 journey to Iceland, it is the first of his literary works to reflect his firsthand experience of the scenery and ambience of the North. The core plot is a version of the erotic quests of *The Earthly Paradise*, but carried to an unexpected conclusion. Pharamond deserts his kingdom in search of Azalais, a maiden in a Northern valley about whom he has dreamed obsessively. Years and much hardship later, he finds her and they are united. He then leaves her, however, to return to his old kingdom, now under a new ruler. The poem ends with Pharamond contemplating the changes that have taken place and deciding to return to—yet still apart from—Azalais. This fable is presented as a masque celebrating the wedding of an Emperor and Empress who, along with the peasant couple Giles and Joan, and the mayor, who functions as a master of ceremonies, comment on the story. Within the masque, Love acts as a commentator on, and at times agent in, the fable; a series of lyric poems ("The Music") add yet another interpretative dimension to Pharamond's quest.

While these framing devices invite comparison with *The Earthly Paradise*, they are not merely a more complicated attempt to distance Morris—and the reader—from his central romantic narrative. Instead, they signal Morris' new concern for the role of the audience. *The Earthly Paradise* deflects attention from the story to the act of storytelling; *Love Is Enough* deflects it from the story to the act of story-receiving. The audience witnessing the masque is carefully chosen to represent the nobility, the bourgeoisie, and the working class. Each group's response is different; each uses art for its own purposes; each perceives the story of Pharamond in a somewhat different context. Together, they make up a composite cultural response. Further, it is important to note that this response includes an awareness of the performance of the work. The actor and actress who play the parts of Pharamond and Azalais are the subject of audience discussion. The point, however, is not that the audience is conscious of theatrical artifice—in the way that the listeners to the tales in *The Earthly Paradise* are conscious that what they are hearing is literary artifice—rather, awareness of the human participants in the masque gives art a grounding in actuality: the story of Pharamond is more "real" because "real" human beings perform it. The truth of art, Morris suggests, lies not in its imitation of life but in its integration with human experience.

It follows from this view that the artist who seeks this integration must concern himself with the lives of his audience and with the kind of life in which art is most vital. Although the Emperor and Empress are developed as romantic figures, it is Giles and Joan who are granted the fullest experience of the masque. Their range of response is unhindered by a sense of public role; at the end of the performance, they propose to invite the actor and actress home with them to "crown the joyance of to-day," thus completing the integration of art and life; and, significantly, they have the last word in the poem. It would seem that the peasant couple represent the consciousness toward which Pharamond himself grows in the course of his life. The subtitle of the poem, "The Freeing of Pharamond," refers to his freedom first from the role of king and, finally, from the role of romantic quester. He must forgo the need for dominance either as a ruler or as a heroic lover if he is to find happiness with Azalais. For this reason *Love Is Enough* represents an important stage in Morris' development as a social revolutionary. Yet it is revolutionary in theme only, not in tone. The dominant feeling of the poem is pain, and the figure of Love who controls the action of the masque is markedly sadistic. Here, more than anywhere else in the longer poems, Morris' own erotic frustration seems to determine the ambience of the narrative.

The link between a revolutionary consciousness and eros marks *Love Is Enough* as a turning point in Morris' literary career. It follows from the poem that Morris was beginning to recognize a conflict between his intentions as an artist and the limitations of his bourgeois audience. This conflict is pronounced in *The Story of Sigurd the Volsung and the Fall of the Nibelungs*, for Morris' epic is a poem written for a sensibility markedly different from that of the late Victorian reading public.

As early as 1870, Morris had been fascinated by the *Volsunga Saga*, a prose translation of which he had published in that year. What struck him about the Icelandic poem was its artless understatement—"All tenderness is shown without the use of a tender word, all misery and despair without a word of raving, complete beauty without ornament." It is, as a result, "something which is above all art." If the powerful effects that Morris admires in the saga do not have verbal equivalents in the text, then they must be outside it, in the reader's supplying what has gone unsaid. Appropriately, the poet of such work is anonymous—"some twelfth century Icelander, living the hardest and rudest of lives," whose work is more a collection of material than an original composition. Thus, the reader not only is forced to supply the emotional force of the poem but also is given no identifiable narrator on whom to rely. Further, because Victorian conventions represent an inappropriate supplement to his work, Morris wrote the poem in language that discourages a response based on contemporary assumptions of behavior and morality. He relies heavily on an often archaic Anglo-Saxon vocabulary that forces the reader to perceive the text as embodying an alien mode of expression. The poem makes little effort to engage the modern reader, and for that reason it may seem difficult to read. Only when one has adapted oneself to its style does the poem's power become apparent.

Even its narrative form is un-Victorian. If the structure of a novel organized according to the developmental pattern of human life defines what his contemporaries expected from the plot of an extended narrative, then Morris chose a story that ignores this expectation. His central figure, Sigurd, does not appear until the second of the poem's four books and is killed before the end of the third. In the course of the poem various characters—Sigurd, Regin, Brynhild, Gudrun—come into prominence and then pass away. Morris uses imagery and symbolism to suggest organic wholeness, but these devices do not obscure the lack of novelistic unity fundamental to *The Story of Sigurd the Volsung and the Fall of the Nibelungs*. Instead of a narrative organized around the development of individual character, it traces the collective fate of a people. The reader, to respond to this subject, must be able to identify structure with a collectivity rather than with an individual life; and it is for this reason that the poem is closely related to Morris' later Marxist writings.

Although *The Story of Sigurd the Volsung and the Fall of the Nibelungs* effectively ended the major phase of Morris' poetic career, it was not a dead end. After 1876, his chief energies shifted from writing poetry to changing society so that poems like the above work could be read; and when he returned to imaginative literature, it was with the recognition that the audience he was seeking could be reached best by prose. The archaic language and collective consciousness of *The Story of Sigurd the Volsung and the Fall of the Nibelungs*, however, reappear in *A Tale of the House of the Wolfings* and the romances that followed.

Except for his translations of *The Odyssey of Homer* and *The Tale of Beowulf* and for a few of the short pieces collected in *Poems by the Way*, the only verse that Morris published in the last twenty years of his life was directly related to his efforts to popularize socialism. The subject of his *Chants for Socialists*, which appeared in Socialist journals and pamphlets during the mid-1880's, is clear from titles such as "The Voice of Toil," "No Master," "All for the Cause," and "The March of the Workers." The power of such poetry may have passed with its historical occasion; however, that Morris could write verse that caught the imagination of the common man was no mean accomplishment.

The Pilgrims of Hope is a fictional narrative, the concluding sections of which are based on the 1871 Paris Commune. As Karl Marx did, Morris saw the events in France as a stage in the overthrow of bourgeois culture, and for this reason his portrait of the Communards is biased and perhaps sentimentalized. Moreover, the poem, which appeared serially in *Commonweal*, was hastily written, and it was only after Morris was well into it that he seems to have hit upon the theme that would bring it to a conclusion. Despite its lapses, however, *The Pilgrims of Hope* is successful in its realistic portrait of working-class London and urban socialism. It also suggests some of Morris' own problems in justifying his status as a businessman with his socioeconomic beliefs. Yet, just as *Love Is Enough* links eros and revolution, the later poem connects Marxism with a love triangle made up of the protagonist, his wife, and a socialist comrade. Indeed, their decision to go together to Paris and fight for the Commune is less strongly felt as a commitment to socialism than as an—explicitly suicidal—resolution of the tensions in their relationship. Not only does the medium of the poem return Morris to the erotic concerns of his earlier poetry; that return itself argues that, beneath his commitment to social action, those concerns remained unresolved—a view confirmed by the prose romances of the 1890's, in which he returned to the theme of the erotic quest, now envisioned not simply as an act of the individual protagonist, but as a component of the social history of a people.

Seen in isolation, Morris' career as a poet is inconclusive; seen in terms of his work as a whole, its pattern of development becomes clear. If, like Tennyson and Browning, Morris sought to free his poetry of Romantic self-consciousness, his alternative was more radical than theirs. Typically, the Romantic poem confronts the reader with the self of the poet—in William Wordsworth's terms, "a man speaking to men"—whose presence demands a personal response. Tennyson, Browning, and the Morris of *The Defence of Guenevere and Other Poems* replace the self of the poet with a collection of other selves. These alternative figures may no longer speak with the authority of the poet, but the relationship between reader and poem is basically the same: one responds to the poem as one responds to a fellow human being, either directly, in the dramatic monologues, or at second hand, in narrative verse. In the poetry he wrote after *The Defence of Guenevere and Other Poems*, Morris rejects this model. *The Earthly Paradise* removes even the art of storytelling from the world of the reader. The complicated structure of *Love Is Enough* "frees" not only Pharamond but also the reader from identification with a model of individual development. *The Story of Sigurd the Volsung and the Fall of the Nibelungs* replaces individual selves with a collectivity—the language and narrative conventions of Victorian England with alien speech and storytelling. If these poems are difficult to judge by literary standards derived from the work of other poets—if they do not fit the reader's notion of what a Victorian poem is supposed to be—this should remind us that Morris, not only in politics but also in poetry, was a revolutionary.

Frederick Kirchhoff

Other major works

FICTION: *A Dream of John Ball*, 1888; *A Tale of the House of the Wolfings*, 1888; *The Roots of the Mountains*, 1890; *The Story of the Glittering Plain*, 1891; *News from Nowhere*, 1891; *The Wood Beyond the World*, 1894; *The Well at the World's End*, 1896; *The Water of the Wondrous Isles*, 1897; *The Sundering Flood*, 1897.

NONFICTION: *Hopes and Fears for Art*, 1882; *Signs of Change*, 1888; *William Morris: Artist, Writer, Socialist*, 1936 (May Morris, editor); *The Letters of William Morris to His Family and Friends*, 1950 (Philip Henderson, editor); *The Unpublished Lectures of William Morris*, 1969 (Eugene D. LeMire, editor); *The Collected Letters of William Morris*, 1984 (Norman Kelvin, editor; volume 1).

MISCELLANEOUS: *The Collected Works of William Morris*, 1910-1915 (May Morris, editor).

Bibliography

Faulkner, Peter. *Against the Age: An Introduction to William Morris*. London: Allen & Unwin, 1980. This readable introduction to Morris, with frequent quotations from his writings and contemporary criticism of his work, stresses the continuing relevance of Morris' ideas for modern readers. The six chapters are arranged according to the stages of his life, each one introduced by an excerpt from a letter Morris wrote summarizing his own life. A selected list of primary and secondary sources and an index are included.

Kirchhoff, Frederick. *William Morris*. Boston: Twayne, 1979. This book provides an overview of Morris' literary achievements, viewing them as "his central mode of self-discovery and expression." Kirchhoff stresses the interdependence of theory, experience, and emotion, and of folk art and sophisticated literary traditions in Morris' work. Includes a chronology, a select bibliography, and an index.

Lindsay, Jack. *William Morris: His Life and Work*. New York: Taplinger, 1979. In this important full-scale biography, Lindsay builds on the work of earlier biographers, with emphasis on the changes throughout Morris' life, along with the enduring influences of his childhood experience. A bibliography and an index are included.

Oberg, Charlotte H. *A Pagan Prophet: William Morris*. Charlottesville: University Press of Virginia, 1978. Oberg explores the paradoxes throughout the works of this "enigmatic Victorian" and then examines the unity in his poetry and prose fiction, which, she asserts, must be read as a living whole. Includes an index and illustrations.

Silver, Carole. *The Romance of William Morris*. Athens: Ohio University Press, 1982. Silver focuses on Morris' use of romance in this book-length study because "interwoven in the poems and romances Morris wrote throughout his life are the strands of all his other thought." Seven chapters trace the patterns in Morris' romances through his career. Illustrations, a bibliography, and an index are included.

Tompkins, J. M. S. *William Morris: An Approach to the Poetry.* London: Cecil Woolf, 1988. Tompkins fills in the gaps in previous criticism of Morris' writings by discussing the narrative poems in detail, paying attention to the sources of the tales and the links with Morris' daily life. Includes an index.

Victorian Studies 13 (Fall/Winter, 1975). This special double issue includes a reassessment of Morris in William E. Fredeman's introduction, and D. G. Rossetti's playlet on the death of William "Topsy" Morris. Six of the thirteen articles focus on Morris' poetry, including Hartley S. Spatt's essay on Morris' general theme of the transcendence of social history through an individual perspective on the past. Three articles discuss unpublished works. Color as well as black-and-white plates are included.

HOWARD MOSS

Born: New York, New York; January 22, 1922
Died: New York, New York; September 16, 1987

Principal poetry

The Wound and the Weather, 1946; *The Toy Fair,* 1954; *A Swimmer in the Air,* 1957; *A Winter Come, A Summer Gone: Poems 1946-1960,* 1960; *Finding Them Lost and Other Poems,* 1965; *Second Nature,* 1968; *Selected Poems,* 1971; *Chekhov,* 1972; *Travel: A Window,* 1973; *Buried City,* 1975; *A Swim Off the Rocks,* 1976; *Tigers and Other Lilies,* 1977; *Notes from the Castle,* 1979; *Rules of Sleep,* 1984; *New Selected Poetry,* 1985.

Other literary forms

Like many other contemporary poets, Howard Moss experimented with drama. His play *The Folding Green* was first performed in 1954 by the Poets' Theatre in Cambridge, Massachusetts, and again, in 1965, in a workshop production by the Playwrights' Unit of Theater 1965. *The Oedipus Mah-Jongg Scandal* was performed in 1968 by the Cooperative Theatre Club, Inc., in New York. A third play, *The Palace at 4 A.M.,* has been given a staged reading by the Playwrights' Unit in New York. Both *The Palace at 4 A.M.* and *The Folding Green* were published in 1980. In addition to drama, Moss published a critical study, *The Magic Lantern of Marcel Proust* (1962), and three collections of criticism: *Writing Against Time: Critical Essays and Reviews* (1969), *Whatever Is Moving* (1981), and *Minor Monuments: Selected Essays* (1986); the last discusses the work of writers ranging from Gustave Flaubert to Anton Chekhov to Katherine Anne Porter. In 1974, he published *Instant Lives,* satirical biographies illustrated by Edward Gorey. Moss was also editor of the following: *Keats* (1959); *The Nonsense Books of Edward Lear* (1964); *The Poet's Story* (1973); and *New York: Poems* (1980).

Achievements

Although widely respected for his poetry, Moss is perhaps better known for having been the poetry editor of *The New Yorker.* Since 1950, when he assumed that post, his careful editorial judgment and clearheaded vision helped to construct the environment of taste, wit, and sensibility in which many of the well-known poets writing in the English language today developed and matured. Moss opened the pages of *The New Yorker* to a rich and diverse flow of poetic talent: John Updike and David Ray; Elizabeth Bishop and Mark Strand; David Wagoner and Donald Justice; W. H. Merwin and Dave Smith; Philip Levine and Charles Simic. The list is long and impressive and could be extended almost indefinitely. Moss is one of a handful of influential editors and craftsmen who have helped give shape and direction to the flow of poetry in the twentieth century.

Moss's poetry is characterized by a lucid, often ironic voice; by evocative images; and by sure, sensitive, rhythmical language. His major concerns remained almost unchanged since they were first voiced in *The Wound and the Weather*: the passage of time, the paradox of change and permanence, the acceptance of loss and gain (of friends, of beauty, of love, of life). His own influences seem clearly marked: Wallace Stevens (visible in Moss's wordplay and in his sometimes extravagant language) and W. H. Auden (noted chiefly in Moss's carefully controlled music and in his ironic wit).

As a critic, Moss varied in his approach—from detailed New Critical textual analysis to purely subjective response. "I distrust," he said, "all theses and theories about writing, and dislike the idea of 'schools' of writing, both in the traditional and in the educational sense."

Moss received *Poetry's* Janet Sewall David Award in 1944, the Brandeis Creative Award in 1962, an Avery Hopwood award in 1963, and a grant from the National Institute of Arts and Letters in 1968. He was awarded the Lenore Marshall Poetry Prize in 1986. In 1957 and 1964, he was a judge for the National Book Awards. His *Selected Poems* was cowinner of the National Book Award in poetry in 1972.

Biography

Howard Moss was the son of David and Sonya (Schrag) Moss. When he was still a young child, his grandfather and grandmother were brought over from "the old country"—Lithuania. As a consequence, Moss writes, "I grew up in a middle-class community but was really under the care of my two grandparents, who were of another flavor unmistakably." In spite of this background, Moss was one of an increasing number of contemporary poets identified with the city and with urban life. Much of his poetry concerns itself with the metropolis—with New York City—both its moments of beauty and its moments of bleakness.

After attending public school and high school in Belle Harbor, New York, Moss studied at the University of Michigan from 1939 to 1940, then transferred to the University of Wisconsin where he received his B.A. degree in 1944. Other formal education included a summer at Harvard University in 1942 and postgraduate work at Columbia University in 1946.

After college, Moss worked for one year (1944) for *Time* magazine as a copyboy and, later, as a book reviewer. Following a short period with the Office of War Information, he was an English instructor at Vassar College for two years, served one year as fiction editor of *Junior Bazaar*, and, finally, joined the editorial staff of *The New Yorker* in 1948. He was poetry editor for the magazine until his death in 1987 at the age of sixty-five.

Analysis

One of the definitions of a poem, Howard Moss wrote, is that it "keeps the welter of life, the threat of disorientation, just under control. . . ." This sense of uneasy balance—of order poised at the edge of choas—informs Moss's editorial, critical, and poetic judgment.

As an editor, Moss established himself as one of the influential figures in American letters during the second half of the twentieth century. His strength as an editor derived primarily from his single vision of art: a dependence upon wit and intellect rather than upon spontaneity and emotion. He once said, "Though I respect and sometimes envy spontaneity in writing, I revise my work a great deal." The poems that have appeared in *The New Yorker* since the time that Moss became poetry editor reveal how clearly Moss transmitted his own vision of poetry to other poets.

As a critic, Moss's interests were far-ranging—from Proust, to John Keats, to William Shakespeare, to Jean Stafford. In his major work of criticism, *The Magic Lantern of Marcel Proust*, Moss organized the structure and content of *Remembrance of Things Past* (1913-1927) around four metaphysical concepts: gardens, windows, parties, and steeples. Although the book received mixed reviews, Moss was praised for his vivid and lucid writing. The pieces collected in *Whatever Is Moving* continued to illustrate Moss's wide range of critical interests: Walt Whitman, Robert Frost, Anton Chekhov, Elizabeth Bishop. In "The First Line," Moss presents a perceptive and original investigation into the different ways poets have used first lines to launch a poem.

As a poet, Moss's reputation grew slowly but steadily over a long and productive period, beginning in 1944, when he received the Janet Sewall David Award from *Poetry*. One criticism of his first collection, *The Wound and the Weather*, was that the poems relied heavily upon abstraction. He was recognized, however, for his skill with language, his consistency of metaphor, and his adherence to formal and traditional structures and values. *The Wound and the Weather* adumbrated many of Moss's continuing concerns: the urban setting, the preoccupation with loss, the awareness of time. The next two collections, *The Toy Fair* and *A Swimmer in the Air*, showed Moss's progress as a poet in both technique and subject matter. Howard Nemerov called *The Toy Fair* "one of the most accomplished collections of lyric poetry since the war" (*Atlantic Monthly*, September, 1954).

In his fourth book, *A Winter Come, A Summer Gone*, Moss presented, in addition to fourteen new poems, a selection of the best work from his three previous volumes—poems embodying those characteristics which have come to be associated with his poetry. The two title poems, "A Winter Come" and "A Summer Gone," are excellent examples. Both poems have the same formal structure: ten stanzas of eight lines each, shaped by an iambic pentameter rhythm, with a basically regular rhyme scheme. In each, the voice is that of the first person singular; it is a predominantly lyric voice but muted with what Moss has called, in another context, a "delicious undertone" of regret, "the way nostalgia can be redeeming or the sadness of fall pleasurable." In

"A Winter Come," the first eight stanzas sketch brief, telling vignettes of the winter season: the wind-blown leaves, the stiffened boughs, the landscape blurred with snow, the insubstantial clouds of breath on winter air, footprints of birds on "a scroll of white," frozen waterfalls, snow-covered statues. The next-to-last stanza, with its metaphor of fire as "the end of words," turns the poem on the axis of ambiguity: "By ambiguity/ We make of flame a word that flame can burn,/ And of love a stillness." The last stanza returns the poem to its now reshaped locus of winter and the bittersweet truth that "icy wind makes young blood sweet/ In joining joy, which age can never have./ And that is what all old men know of love."

In "A Summer Gone," the first two stanzas create a vivid image of the late summer seaside: "stilts/ Of slipshod timber," spiral shells, "now empty of their hosts." The next three stanzas directly address the listener, asserting, finally, "Those beautiful outsides, those thin-skinned maps/ Are part of love. Or all of it, perhaps." Stanzas VI, VII, and VIII offer metaphors of loss— loss of sight, of sound, of touch. The two final stanzas turn back to the loss of summer and look ahead to "Sad fall," colored by a thousand dyings. As in "A Winter Come," the last image is that of love: "The view/ To take is but another wintry one,/ To wait for the new nestings of the sun."

In the 1960's, Moss both widened his range of poetic techniques and probed deeper into his constant theme of loss and deprivation. *Finding Them Lost and Other Poems* received widespread critical acceptance. Moss said in an interview for *The New York Quarterly* that he was trying in this collection to change from his "usual methods." Particularly successful examples of this change were a group of poems called "Lifelines"—"attempts to get certain people I knew down on paper." In *Second Nature*, Moss essayed, in poems such as "Sands" and "Front Street," a more conversational line, approaching free verse. The sure choice of language and the ever-increasing concreteness of image, however, remained characteristic strengths of his poetry. The *Selected Poems* pulled together the strongest of his earlier verse, complemented by seven previously uncollected poems. The collection, a National Book Award winner, illustrated Moss's increasing understanding of his craft and validated his own definition of poetry as that form which "focuses, compresses, intensifies."

Buried City reinforced Moss's stature as a poet and revealed again the depth and range of his major concerns. The images here are those of the city: in the title poem, an archaeologist from some future time examines the ruins of New York City. Two subsequent volumes, *A Swim Off the Rocks* and *Tigers and Other Lilies*, turn in different directions. The former is a volume of light verse, ranging from the surreal to satiric wordplay. *Tigers and Other Lilies* is a book of poems for children—poems about plants with animals in their names.

Moss's 1979 collection, *Notes from the Castle*, reaffirmed the lucid voice, the sensitive music, and the evocative images that distinguish his poetry.

Moss's one constant was his commitment to the intellect to make sense of the world. In these poems, it is the mind that speaks—wisely and memorably—elegiac words: of gravel, of stars, of ideas. In "Gravel," there is the yearning to be "made separate/ Or to be part/ Of some great thing . . . / To be made solid." In "Stars," there is the haunting image of the speaker reaching up "to pluck the stars like words to make/ A line, a phrase, a stanza, a whole poem." In "Elegy for My Sister," one image encapsulates all the others: "What are ideas but architecture/ Taking nature to heart and sustaining/ Inviolable forms." Although the tendency to abstraction remains, Moss moves more and more toward the concrete image. Even when the abstract occurs, the poet frequently redeems it through the use of startling language and unusual contexts.

Rules of Sleep, Moss's last collection of new poetry, continues his concern with time and loss as well as his uncommon use of commonplace settings or subjects. The speaker of a meditation on Albert Einstein, for example, is Einstein's old bathrobe. Moss's penchant for urban surroundings (and his use of contemporary speech) is exemplified by a poem set in Miami Beach in which a street is "strung out on lights." There is anxiety in the poems' reflections on mortality—"the chill of what is about to happen"—but there is also a wit and calmness that keeps the fear at bay: "Everything permanent," Moss writes, "is due for a surprise."

Widely respected both as a critic and as a craftsman, Moss provided his contemporaries with a level of accomplishment that will be difficult to surpass. Perhaps his dominant strength was his single vision: his dependence upon intellect rather than emotion. That vision of art enabled him to keep the welter of life "just under control."

Robert C. Jones

Other major works

PLAYS: *The Folding Green,* 1954; *The Oedipus Mah-Jongg Scandal,* 1968; *The Palace at 4 A.M.,* 1972.

NONFICTION: *The Magic Lantern of Marcel Proust,* 1962; *Writing Against Time: Critical Essays and Reviews,* 1969; *Instant Lives,* 1974; *Whatever Is Moving,* 1981; *Minor Monuments: Selected Essays,* 1986.

MISCELLANEOUS: *Keats,* 1959 (edited); *The Nonsense Books of Edward Lear,* 1964 (edited); *The Poet's Story,* 1973 (edited); *New York: Poems,* 1980 (edited).

Bibliography

Gioia, Dana. "The Difficult Case of Howard Moss." *The Antioch Review* 45 (Winter, 1987): 98-109. Although this is primarily a review of Moss's "New Selected Poetry," it also surveys the poet's life, poetry, and career as poetry editor for *The New Yorker.* Gioia acknowledges that Moss's career at

The New Yorker has had a largely negative impact on his poetry by rob-
bing it of serious and sustained critical evaluations, and she admirably
corrects this oversight with this important evaluation of his work.

Howard, Richard. *Alone with America.* New York: Atheneum, 1980. The chapter on Moss reviews his work and illustrates the qualities that set him
apart from "the many others who are merely suave or serviceable." Among
these qualities are his rhythms, his use of conceits and puns, and his contrasts of human and universal order. Howard writes in a lean style and includes passages from major Moss works to illustrate his key points.

Leiter, Robert. "Howard Moss: An Interview." *The American Poetry Review*
13 (September/October, 1984): 27-31. Leiter's important interview provides
essential information about and by Moss, including his experience as a professor at Vassar College and as a poetry editor at *The New Yorker.* Moss
discusses the mechanics of poetry editing, composition, and structure, and
in the process reveals the criteria he uses in writing and editing his own
work.

Malkoff, Karl. *Crowell's Handbook of Contemporary American Poetry.* New
York: Thomas Y. Crowell, 1973. A succinct and informative overview of
Moss and his poetic technique, which includes a description of Moss's
stylistic evolution illustrated with a contrast between "Elegy for My Father" and "Arsenic." Malkoff suggests the poet's work is best reviewed
using the methods of New Criticism and provides the reader with a select
bibliography.

St. John, David. "Scripts and Water, Rules and Riches." *The Antioch Review*
43 (Summer, 1985): 309-319. St. John asserts that Moss has "written some
of the most powerful and moving poems of the last ten years." He argues
his case by citing a variety of Moss's works, including *Rules of Sleep,*
Buried City, and *Notes from the Castle.* The beauty, emotion, and musical
quality of Moss's works are illustrated with extensive passages from these
and other poems.

PAUL MULDOON

Born: County Armagh, Northern Ireland; June 20, 1951

Principal poetry

New Weather, 1973; *Mules*, 1977; *Why Brownlee Left*, 1980; *Quoof*, 1983; *Selected Poems, 1968-1986*, 1987; *Meeting the British*, 1987; *Madoc: A Mystery*, 1991.

Other literary forms

Unlike many other contemporary Irish poets, Paul Muldoon is, generally speaking, content to let his verse speak for him exclusively. He is less firmly attached to academia than is the norm for poets since World War II. Hence his production of articles and reviews is small and not very helpful in coming to terms with his poetry. His most notable contribution to Irish literary culture has been his idiosyncratic, and in some quarters controversial, editing of *The Faber Book of Contemporary Irish Verse* (1986). Muldoon has also published translations of a small number of poems by the important contemporary Irish-language poet Nuala Ni Dhomhnaill. The distinctive character of Muldoon's own verse invites the conclusion that translating is much closer to his imaginative inclinations than editing is. He has also edited *The Scrake of Dawn: Poems by Young People from Northern Ireland* (1979) and *The Essential Byron* (1989).

Achievements

Paul Muldoon is arguably too young for a definitive assessment of his achievement to be made. Despite the regular appearance of book-length collections, and his increasingly well-known presence internationally, particularly in the United States, his status remains somewhat overshadowed by that of older, more celebrated poets from Northern Ireland. In addition, Muldoon's fluency and inventiveness have been constants since the publication of his first precocious volume, *New Weather*, in 1973. As a result, it has been easier to take pleasure in his method than to chart the development of his aesthetic and thematic concerns. It is possible that the poet himself has experienced some of this sense of occlusion, and that this has accounted, at least in part, for his increasing tendency to write unfashionably long poems. The publication of the book-length poem *Madoc* in 1991—a work that in many senses is a typically quirky yet not wholly unexpected product of the longer poems in *Why Brownlee Left, Quoof,* and *Meeting the British*—provides a pretext for an interim report on the attainments, challenges, and difficulties of the most original Irish poet to emerge since the 1930's.

Thus, while the critical jury may still be out as to the overall significance of Muldoon's work, there is no doubt that it already signifies an impressive departure not only from that of his immediate predecessors among Northern Irish poets such as Seamus Heaney, John Montague, and Michael Longley but also from the conception of Irish poet as cultural watchdog and keeper of the national conscience promoted and embodied by the founding father of modern Irish poetry, William Butler Yeats.

Biography

Paul Muldoon was born on June 20, 1951, in the remote rural community of The Fews, County Armagh, Northern Ireland. Shortly afterward, his family moved to the no less remote area of The Moy, County Tyrone. The poet, therefore, comes from a background that is similar is many external respects to that of the poets of Northern Ireland, such as Seamus Heaney and John Montague, who have done much to put that part of the world on the literary map. This point is relevant in view of how different Muldoon's response to his background has been from that of his illustrious near-contemporaries.

After secondary education at St. Patrick's College, Armagh, Muldoon read English at Queens University, Belfast, and was graduated with a B.A. in 1971. Like many writers from Northern Ireland, particularly those of an older generation, he worked as a talks producer for the Northern Ireland regional service of the British Broadcasting Corporation in Belfast. He resigned this position in 1986 and since then has worked as a visiting professor in a number of American universities. Muldoon is married and divides his time between Ireland and the United States. Among the numerous official recognitions of his merit as a poet are his reception of two prestigious English awards, the Eric Gregory Prize in 1972 and the Geoffrey Faber Memorial Prize in 1982.

Analysis

Among the numerous phenomena for which the civil strife in Northern Ireland has been responsible since its inception in 1969 is a deluge of print— artistic, documentary, scholarly, and governmental. Of this outpouring, the material to gain the most widespread and sustained attention has been the artistic. Plays by such dramatists as Brian Friel and Stewart Parker and novels by, among others, David Martin and Benedict Kiely have touched a public nerve in those authors' native province, as well as in the Republic of Ireland and in audiences throughout the world. It is the poetry of Northern Ireland, however, that has claimed most popular and critical attention. Poets such as Seamus Heaney and John Montague have read their works to audiences of thousands on both sides of the Atlantic and beyond, while collections of their verse as well as that of others continues to be issued in large, best-selling editions. The sociology and cultural anthropology of this phenomenon remain to be written. Meanwhile, the phenomenon has seen the minority interest of poetry, dealing with obscure and unbeautiful issues in a remote part of the world, brought not merely to an educated public's awareness but also to the laudatory attention of esteemed and powerful academics. The novelty of Paul Muldoon's verse gains additional emphasis from being seen in such a context.

It will also be seen in sharper focus if the social and political context is appreciated. From the outset, Muldoon's poetry has been tight-lipped, fragmentary, seemingly at odds with a sense of wholeness, and diffident as to the existence of a singular authorizing consciousness. As a result, its predominant features are indeterminacy, randomness, and a sense of the disparate and the inconclusive, all contained within an unexceptional metric, form, and language that give each poem its deceptive readability.

Although direct environmental influences on the growth of the imagination are impossible to prove, it does seem relevant to point out that Muldoon's coming to consciousness coincided with the disintegrative threats to the social fabric of his native province. These threats of violence to civilians and forces of law and order alike, to property and the general communal infrastructure of Northern Ireland, date from 1969, when Muldoon was a freshman at Queen's University, Belfast. The threats have been both carried out and resisted. Disintegration of families, neighborhoods, and institutions has occurred, yet those entities continue to survive. Codes of self-protective speech have arisen, and things are no longer necessarily what they seem on the surface. It would be fanciful to argue that such characteristics of the poet's outer world are precisely what Muldoon's poetry reproduces, since, to begin with, such an argument overlooks the inevitable significance of form in his work. At the same time, however, there is such a degree of unpredictability, play, and opacity in his poetry that it is tempting to consider it an attractive, exuberant, puzzling, and blessedly harmless parallel universe to that of bombers and demagogues.

This does not mean that Muldoon has not addressed poems to the trials and tribulations of the Northern Ireland of his adult life. Poems such as "Anseo" in *Why Brownlee Left* (*anseo* is the Irish word for "here," meaning "present" in the poem), "The Sightseers" in *Quoof*, and the arresting and unnerving title poem of *Meeting the British*—to name well-known instances— confront in ways that are not particularly euphemistic the euphemistically named Troubles. Yet it is equally, if not more, revealing of Muldoon that he would name a collection of poems for "our family word/ for the hot water bottle" (*Quoof*), particularly since the reader has only the poet's word for it that this is what *quoof* actually means. More than any other Irish poet of his generation, perhaps, Muldoon demands to be taken first and foremost, and if possible exclusively, at his word.

Muldoon's slightly surreal, slightly whimsical, very subjective, and very oblique view of his material—his almost perverse conception of what constitutes "material" itself—sits at a seemingly crazy but refreshing angle to the modern Irish poetic tradition. Concerned more with the making of verses than with the making of statements, his work is airy, reckless, private, and provocative. Many of his poems are as much teases as they are texts in the predictable sense. Yet they can also be seen as indebted to a more intriguing tradition of Irish poetry than that inaugurated by Yeats. Muldoon's implicit rejection of the public, vatic role of the poet, his frequent absorption in the minutiae of the natural world, his deployment of fragmented narrative, his use of pastiche, his finding himself equally at ease with foreign or domestic themes, his playfulness, and the challenge of his cunning superficiality have—among numerous other devices and resources—provided a valuable counterpoint to the more solemn, preoccupied, and fundamentally historicist poetry of his Northern Irish elders. The title of his first volume, *New Weather*, has become over time a helpful phrase to describe the surprising novelty of Muldoon's poetry and its place in the canon of modern Irish verse.

The poem in which the phrase "new weather" occurs, "Wind and Tree," is in one sense not a particularly representative Muldoon work, with its talk of love and its unironic, somewhat sheepishly attention-claiming "I." The poem's elaborate metaphorical conceit of lovers being injured as trees are by wind heralds one of the most conspicuous elements in Muldoon's distinctive art, his generally shape-changing propensity, of which metaphor is a primary feature. "Wind and Tree" also provides the revealing lines, "Most of the world is centred/ About ourselves," often availed of by readers struggling for a foothold in some of the poet's less hospitable works. Much more instructive of things to come in Muldoon's work is the poem "Hedgehog," in *New Weather*, for the economy and distinctively contemporary quality of its imagery ("The snail moves like a/ Hovercraft, held up by a/ Rubber cushion of itself"), the outrageousness of its conceits (the hedgehog is referred to as "the god/ Under this crown of thorns"), and the possibility that the poem overall is a metaphor for communal and interpersonal division and defensiveness both in Northern Ireland and beyond. As the line in "Our Lady of Ardboe," from *Mules*, has it, "Who's to know what's knowable?"

By the time of the publication of *Mules* the question of knowability in Muldoon's work was not strictly rhetorical—or, to be Muldoonish about it, was strictly rhetorical, meaning that it was built into the nature of the poem, rather than occurring every so often as a detachable line from a given poem. The mysterious "Lunch with Pancho Villa," and the very novelty of an Irish poet's having something to write under such a title, is not merely a witty imaginative adventure, expressive of the poet's range and restlessness. In addition, the poem interrogates in a tone that is all the more incisive for lacking solemnity the consequences of violence and questions whether the poet's duty is to respond to what the world contains or to the contents of his own imagination.

One answer to this question—a question that may be used as a means of investigating Muldoon's increasingly complex mapping of his subjectivity—may be found in "Cuba," from *Why Brownlee Left*. Here a remembrance of family life and common usages, both domestic (a father's predictable anger) and communal (an erring daughter goes to Confession), is located in the context of the Cuban missile crisis, revealing the quirky, intimate, and reassuringly unresolved and unmechanical manner in which personal and public history overlap. This poem, ostensibly a simple narrative elaborating a vignette of memory, is a delicate essay in remoteness and intimacy, last things and initial experiences, innocence and eschatology. The poem's open rhythm (often captured by Muldoon through direct speech) leaves the reader in no doubt that the poet stands for the tender insignificances of the human realm rather than a melodramatic characterization of the machinations of history.

A comparable sense of openness, of life as new beginnings and deliberately unfinished business, is provided by the title poem of *Why Brownlee Left*, in which the material achieves significance by—as the title implies—being neither a question nor an answer. Who Brownlee is seems irrelevant. The emphasis is on what has remained "a mystery even now." The point is the leaving, the possibility of pastures new, lyrically recapitulated by the absconder's horses at the end of the poem, "gazing into the future."

Perhaps Brownlee wanted to be able to say, like the narrator in "Immrama," from the same collection, "I, too, have trailed my father's spirit"—even if the trail leads to an inconclusive and implausible end for both father and son. Conclusion is less important than continuity. Analogously, Muldoon's work suggests that a poem's happening—the multifarious activities of the words contained by and excited within a prosodic framework (itself various and informal, though necessarily final)—is of more consequence than the poem's meaning. At an elementary level, which the reader dare not overlook, perhaps the happening is more lifelike, by virtue of its free play and variety, its sometimes outrageous rhymes and syncopated rhythms, than the meaning. Though quest as a motif has been present in Muldoon's work from the outset—"Identities" in *New Weather* begins: "When I reached the sea/ I fell in with another who had just come/ From the interior"—it becomes more pronounced in the collections after *Why Brownlee Left*. The unusual title "Immrama" draws attention to this fact, as presumably it is meant to. It is the plural form of *immram*, the name in Irish for the genre of medieval Irish romances (including tales of travel to the other world) and a word that in the singular provides the title of Muldoon's first important long poem, which also appears in *Why Brownlee Left*.

In "Immram," Muldoon releases the possibilities latent or implied in not only the quirky lyrics of *Why Brownlee Left* but in his overall body of work. Using narrative in order to subvert it—a strategy familiar from, for example, "Good Friday, 1971, Driving Westward" in *New Weather*—Muldoon brings the reader through a somewhat phantasmagorical, surreal adventure that pantomimes the style of hard-boiled detective fiction. Set in Los Angeles, the story itself is too erratic and effervescent to summarize. As the title of the poem is intended to suggest, however, the material maps out a territory that is rich and strange, which may be the landscape of dream or of vision or the objective manifestation of the psychic character of quest. Lest the reader be merely exhausted by the extent of the poem's literary high-jinks—"I shimmied about the cavernous lobby./ Mr. and Mrs. Alfred Tennyson/ Were ahead of me through the revolving door./ She tipped the bell-hop five dollars"— there are important themes, such as identity, fabulation, and rootlessness, and an alert meditation on the hybrid nature of writing as an imaginative process, of which "Immrama" is a helpful rehearsal.

Much more allusive, spectacular, and demanding is Muldoon's next adventure in the long poem "The More a Man Has the More a Man Wants," from *Quoof.* Here, an increasingly prominent interest on the poet's part in the lore and legends of Native American traditional literature comes influentially into play. In particular, the various legends of jokers and shape-changers, particularly those of Winnebago literature, are availed of, not in the sense of overt borrowings or new translations but with a respect for and fascination with their spirit. Muldoon is not the first poet to pay homage to these mythical figures. The English poet laureate Ted Hughes employed them in one of his most celebrated works, *Crow* (1970, rev. 1972). The results are so different, however, that it is tempting to think of "The More a Man Has the More a Man Wants" as Muldoon's response to the senior poet.

The subject of "The More a Man Has the More a Man Wants" is change. As in the case of "Immram," scenes shift with confusing rapidity, and the inherent transience and adaptability of the persona is once again a central, enabling concern. The thematic mixture is far richer, however, in "The More a Man Has the More a Man Wants." In particular, the nature of change is not confined to Muldoon's familiar deployments, such as travel, quest, and dream. Violence as an agent of change is also explored and its consequences confronted. Here again, a certain amount of frustration will be experienced by the reader, largely because the poem, though promising to be a narrative, becomes a variety of open-minded narrative options, while the integration of the material takes place by virtue of the reader's ability to explore the possibilities of congruence within the widely diversified settings and perspectives. Sheer verve, inventiveness, unpredictability, and impenitent originality make "The More a Man Has the More a Man Wants" the poem that most fully illustrates the scope of Muldoon's ambitious aesthetic energies, through which all that is solid—including, perhaps particularly, the legacy of history—is transformed into airy, insubstantial, but memorable surfaces.

Any claim for the centrality of "The More a Man Has the More a Man Wants" must be made in the awareness of Muldoon's book-length poem *Madoc.* This poem is in effect prefaced by a handful of lyrics recognizably in the mode of, say, those in *Quoof,* among which is the superb elegy "Cauliflowers" (the incongruousness of the title is a typical Muldoon maneuver). "Madoc" itself, however, consists of a sequence of rather impenetrable lyrics, all of which are headed by the name of a philosopher. Subtitled *A Mystery,* it is certainly a baffling poem. Once again, the assertion and denial of narrative are fundamental to the poet's procedures. The source of the poem is a work of the same name written by the English Romantic poet Robert Southey, drawing in a manner vaguely reminiscent of Sir Walter Scott on the heroic legends of one of Great Britain's marginal peoples, in this case the Welsh. Muldoon, without adapting Southey's theme or prosody, seems to have adapted, in a satirical vein, Southey's method. His *Madoc* looks back to an adventure in which Southey was involved—namely, the establishment of a pantisocratic community on the banks of the Susquehanna River in Pennsylvania. The inspiration for this ill-fated scheme was the major English Romantic poet Samuel Taylor Coleridge. Casting his own mind back over the historic, not to mention romantic, dream of community, Muldoon reproduces his own puzzlement with such a project, articulating not the self-deceiving confidence of Coleridge's thought (and, by invoking the names of philosophers, of thought generally) but the fact that so little that is clear remains of what such thought asserted. In turn, or rather concurrently, a disquisition on the knowability of the world, a surreal satire on the inevitable insubstantiality of ideals, and a narrative poem whose most submerged feature is its storytelling, *Madoc* is clearly Muldoon's most sustained and substantial work, though most readers will find it easier to admire than it is to enjoy or decipher.

With *Madoc,* Muldoon takes innumerable artistic and cultural risks, among them that of seeming to be original for originality's sake. Whatever the work's merits or demerits, however, it has succeeded in drawing attention by the most provocative means possible to this poet's restless ambition, his readiness to follow no train of thought or poetic fashion other than his own. A broad critical perspective would perhaps see his work as being related to that of John Ashbery, though Muldoon's is much less solemn than Ashbery's. All that can be said with reasonable certainty about the poetry of Paul Muldoon, however, is that its liberating practices and equable temperament have succeeded in utterly changing the theory and practice of Irish poetry.

George O'Brien

Other major works

ANTHOLOGIES: *The Scrake of Dawn: Poems by Young People from Northern Ireland,* 1979; *The Faber Book of Contemporary Irish Verse,* 1986; *The Essential Byron,* 1989.

Bibliography
Birkets, Sven. "Paul Muldoon." In *The Electric Life: Essays on Modern Poetry*. New York: Morrow, 1989. An assessment of the poet's relationship to his contemporaries on the international scene. Muldoon's originality is identified and appreciated. The provision of a wider context for his work reveals its scope and interest. In particular, Muldoon's distinctive verbal deftness receives alert attention.

Goodby, John. " 'Armageddon, Armagh-geddon': Language and Crisis in the Poetry of Paul Muldoon." In *Anglo-Irish and Irish Literature: Aspects of Language and Culture*, edited by Birgit Bramsback and Martin Croghan. Uppsala, Sweden: Uppsala University Press, 1988. The title comes from Muldoon's poetic sequence "Armageddon." In using the name to pun on the poet's birthplace, the author draws attention to Muldoon's verbal dexterity. His dismantling and reassembling of language is reviewed. These practices are also related to Muldoon's background.

Johnston, Dillon. *Irish Poetry After Joyce*. Notre Dame, Ind.: University of Notre Dame Press, 1985. Chapter 6 locates Muldoon in two related ways. His connection to his immediate contemporaries is characterized. In addition, his individual voice is appraised in the overall context of modern Irish poetry. A valuable critique.

Muldoon, Paul. "Q & A: Paul Muldoon." Interview by Kevin Barry. *Irish Literary Supplement* 6, no. 2 (1987): 36-37. A rare interview. Though brief, it brings into focus Muldoon's background and its relation to his poetry. The poet's place in contemporary Irish poetry is also addressed. Useful contextual material.

Wilson, William A. "Paul Muldoon and the Poetics of Sexual Difference." *Contemporary Literature* 28 (Fall, 1987): 317-331. A theoretical approach to Muldoon. The essay addresses conceptions of sexual difference, as well as other broad pluralistic issues. The poet's formal and metrical diversity is discussed. A wide-ranging approach.

LES A. MURRAY

Born: Nabiac, Australia; October 17, 1938

Principal poetry

The Ilex Tree, 1965 (with Geoffrey Lehmann); *The Weatherboard Cathedral*, 1969; *Poems Against Economics*, 1972; *Lunch and Counter Lunch*, 1974; *Selected Poems: The Vernacular Republic*, 1976; *Ethnic Radio*, 1978; *The Boys Who Stole the Funeral*, 1979; *The Vernacular Republic: Poems 1961-1981*, 1982; *Equanimities*, 1982; *The People's Otherworld*, 1983; *The Vernacular Republic: Poems 1961-1983*, 1988; *The Daylight Moon*, 1988; *The Idyll Wheel*, 1989; *Dog Fox Field*, 1990; *The Rabbiter's Bounty*, 1991.

Other literary forms

Les A. Murray has collected several volumes of prose pieces (primarily reviews and articles): *The Peasant Mandarin: Prose Pieces* (1978), *Persistence in Folly* (1984), and *Blocks and Tackles* (1990). Of particular interest in the second book is the essay "The Human Hair-Thread," in which Murray discusses his own work and thought and the influence aboriginal culture has had on it.

Achievements

Increasingly, Murray is considered not only a major Australian poet but also one of the finest poets of his generation writing in English. His books appear in Great Britain and the United States, and his following is an international one. Moreover, the uniqueness and power of his poetic voice have caught the ear of many of his fellow poets throughout the world, for he has been hailed by Joseph Brodsky, Peter Porter, Mark Strand, and others. He is a prolific and ambitious writer, always willing to try new and unusual techniques but equally at home in the traditional forms of verse, of which he seems to have an easy and lively mastery. Murray is largely admired in Australia, where even his detractors acknowledge his accomplishments. He has received numerous awards and prizes, including the Australian Literature Society Gold Medal (1984) and the New South Wales Premier's Prize for the best book of verse in 1983-1984. He is also a frequent recipient of grants from the Literature Board of the Australia Council.

Biography

Leslie Allan Murray was born at Nabiac, on the rural north coast of New South Wales, and brought up on a dairy farm in nearby Bunyah, a locale that often figures as the subject or backdrop for his poems. He attended school in the town of Taree and then, in 1957, went to the University of Sydney, where he stayed until 1960. Between 1959 and 1960, he served in the Royal Australian Naval Reserve. He and Valerie Morelli were married in 1962 (they would have several children), and Murray worked as a translator at the Australian National University in Canberra from 1963 to 1967. After a year in Europe, he returned to Sydney, was graduated from the University of Sydney in 1969, and worked at a number of transient jobs before going to Canberra again, where he took a position in the Prime Minister's Department in the Economic Development Branch. Moving back to Sydney and refusing to work any longer in, for him, meaningless employment, Murray, in his own words, "Came Out as a flagrant full-time poet in 1971." He thereafter supported himself solely on the basis of his literary work. In addition to the books he published and those he edited, Murray wrote book reviews, contributed to newspapers and magazines, advised Angus and Robertson publishers, and gave poetry readings throughout Australia and abroad. Between 1973 and 1979, he served as editor of *Poetry Australia.*

Murray published his first book, *The Ilex Tree,* jointly with another young poet, Geoffrey Lehmann, in 1965, and quickly became known as a poet of real promise. His many subsequent volumes confirmed his status as a major voice in Australian literature.

Analysis

Readers of Les A. Murray's poetry are often attracted by the coherence of the thematic concerns that reappear consistently in his work and which are presented lucidly and imaginatively. Moreover, the stylistic features of his verse, though varied, have themselves cohered into an identifiable style uniquely his own and flexible enough to allow for the wide range of his poetic interests. Broadly, these interests may be grouped under categories of the religious and spiritual, the societal and cultural, the historical and familial, the linguistic and poetic. Murray has strong opinions about many issues facing contemporary society, and his poetry often bespeaks them. In their most reductive form, these issues would require consideration of such propositions as: Western man must rediscover a core of religious values and recover certain traditional modes of being; society should embrace a more democratic egalitarianism, avoiding the twin perils of elitism and false ideology; aboriginal attitudes regarding nature and the environment need to be better understood by white Australians and to some extent adopted; Australia itself represents an island of hope in the world, as a place where many of the divisive features undermining modern society might be finally reconciled. While such statements are virtually caricatures or distortions and far too coarse to do justice to the subtlety and rigor of Murray's poetry, they do indicate some of the general areas of his thinking. His is very often a poetry of statement, for he does not shy away from taking clear positions on matters he considers crucial, and he has none of the horror of didacticism that seems to restrain much contemporary writing. It is not, however, for his opinions or ideas that Murray is chiefly valued; rather, it is the fineness of his poetry that speaks most clearly to his readers.

In an early poem, "Driving Through Sawmill Towns," Murray renders the remoteness and tedium of life in the rural towns, those "bare hamlets built of boards," where "nothing happens" and "the houses watch each other." The evocative detail, the careful diction, the sense of quiet control convey both an appreciation of this as a way of life and an acknowledgement that it is a lonely and even desperate existence. A woman gazes at a mountain "in wonderment,/ looking for a city," and men sit by the stove after tea, "rolling a dead match/ between their fingers/ thinking of the future." It is a place one only drives through, not a place in which one wishes to live. In that sense, this poem contrasts with others in which the country life appears more salubrious, as in "Noonday Axeman" or "Spring Hail," where isolation is not necessarily loneliness.

Murray's most famous poem of rural Australia is also the one most indebted to aboriginal sources, "The Buladelah-Taree Holiday Song Cycle." It is a long poem, in thirteen sections, based in part on a translation by R. M. Berndt of "The Moon-Bone Song," a ritual poem of Arnhem Land aborigines which Murray claims "may well be the greatest poem ever composed in Australia." His poem is an attempt to use an aboriginal mode and structure to "celebrate my own spirit country," a stretch of land on the north coast between the two towns of Buladelah and Taree, where he grew up and lives as an adult and where many holiday vacationers go in the summer to enjoy the beaches and the countryside. In the same way that the aborigines celebrate their unity as a people and their harmony with the land, so Murray sees the returning vacationers, many of whom have family ties to the area, as a cyclic affirmation of ancestral values and a joyous communing with nature. In his vision, each new generation rediscovers the spiritual significance of commonplace things, as people come to possess the land imaginatively. Each section of the poem presents an aspect of this summer ritual, from the preparations made by the local inhabitants to the journey from Sydney along the Pacific Highway (represented as a glowing snake) to all the adventures, experiences, and tensions that go with a summer holiday. The poem ends with a linking of the region with the heavens above, as the Southern Cross constellation looks down upon "the Holiday." The poem is unique in its successful wedding of an aboriginal poetic structure with the matter of white Australian culture; in particular, Murray's use of place names and capitalization seems to give mythic status to the events and locations of the poem, analogous to the aborigine's sense of a "spirit of place."

In 1979, Murray published *The Boys Who Stole the Funeral*, a verse novel consisting of 140 sonnets of considerable variety. This unusual poem picked up many of the concerns and opinions prevalent in the earlier work and fashioned them into a narrative, both effective as poetry and affective as a story. In this novel sequence, two young Sydney men, Kevin Forbutt and Cameron Reeby, steal from a funeral parlor the body of Kevin's great-uncle, Clarrie Dunn (a "digger," or World War I veteran), in order to take him back home to the country where the old man had asked to be buried. Clarrie's relations having refused to pay for or honor this request, the boys have taken it upon themselves. In doing this, they set out on a journey of self-discovery as well. Such familiar Murray themes as the value of community and respect for the ordinary man are underscored repeatedly in the poem, as when the two boys get to Dark's Plain, Clarrie's old home, and are assisted by people there with the burial and with evading the police who have come to arrest them. The novel later culminates with the shooting of Cameron by a policeman. The shocked and distraught Kevin flees into the bush, falls ill, drops into a coma, and has a vision of two figures from aboriginal legend, Njimbin and Birroogun. In this vision, the central event of the novel, Kevin is put through an initiation where his soul is healed by the symbolic "crystal of Crystals," and where he is instructed by Njimbin and Birroogun (whose name modulates to Berrigan, connoting a blend of white and black Australians) in the mysteries of the spirit. Kevin is offered the Common Dish from which to eat, the vessel of common human joys and sufferings by which most people in the world are nourished. As an act of solidarity with common humanity, Kevin takes it and eats and then wakes from his comatose vision. Having been in effect reborn, he returns to live at Dark's Plain, to "keep faith" with the rural "battlers" who are the spiritual inheritors of the land. The poem as a whole is a virtuoso performance, displaying Murray's ability to handle the complex interplay of form, narrative, and character. He holds the reader's attention and, once again, interweaves aboriginal material in a convincing way.

One of Murray's preoccupations is with the notion of the vernacular; indeed, when he calls his selected poems *The Vernacular Republic*, he is reflecting upon the colloquial nature of his language and simultaneously reflecting a passionate concern which the world of his poems addresses: the need for Australia to fuse its three cultures, urban, rural, and aboriginal. Murray's vision for Australia is for a culture of convergence, where the sophisticated city dwellers, the more traditional rural folk, and the indigenous blacks can all come together to forge a society in harmony with the continent. In this, he is close to the position of the Jindyworobaks, a literary movement of the 1930's and 1940's which emphasized the uniqueness of the Australian environment and sought to align itself with aboriginal culture. Although not as narrowly nationalistic as that earlier group, Murray does see a need to avoid repeating the mistakes of Europe and America and to develop in accordance with the character and values of Australia itself, not in submission to alien and imported fashions or ideologies. For him, Australia has the possibility of becoming truly egalitarian, a place of justice and virtue for the common man, a place where what is traditional is recognizably Australian. This, for Murray, includes a certain dry sense of humor and an appreciation of an unhurried mode of living, which may be primarily a rural manner but nevertheless seems a national characteristic. His poem "The Quality of Sprawl" is a good example.

"Sprawl," in this poem, is defined through the course of eight stanzas as a way of being, at once nonchalant ("the rococo of being your own still centre"), laid-back ("Sprawl leans on things"), generous ("driving a hitchhiker that extra hundred miles home"), unpretentious ("the quality/ of the man who cut down his Rolls-Royce/ into a farm utility truck"), classless (someone "asleep in his neighbours' best bed in spurs and oilskins"), unflappable ("Reprimanded and dismissed/ it listens with a grin and one boot up on the rail/ of possibility"), and so on. It is also defined by what it is not: "It is never lighting cigars with ten-dollar notes"; "Sprawl almost never says Why Not? with palms comically raised"; "nor can it be dressed for." Murray presents it as a very attractive quality indeed, but, characteristically, he is aware of the negative element, the price one sometimes has to pay for independence of mind. "It may have to leave the Earth," he says, but then he gently undercuts his own hyperbole: "Being roughly Christian, it scratches the other cheek/ and thinks it unlikely." While not exactly turning the other cheek in Christian fashion, he does conclude with the mild warning, "Though people have been shot for sprawl." Sprawl, then, is the opposite of the uptight, aggressive, overly sophisticated self-consciousness that Murray sees around him and that he considers foreign and inappropriate for Australia—a place, perhaps, where Mark Twain's Huck Finn might have been at home. While "sprawl" may appear a public attitude and manner, it rests upon a more essential inward feature, which Murray terms "equanimity," in a poem of that title.

"Equanimity" is a poem that draws together several strands of Murray's work: His populist, bardic stance mingles with a more purely prophetic strain. Here, his democratic vistas are underwritten by a transcendental authority, based upon a personal and even sacramental experience. That experience, which he calls "equanimity," is like an influx of quiet power, an exaltation of the spirit grounded in love. "There is only love," he says; "human order has at heart/ an equanimity. Quite different from inertia," a place "where all are, in short, off the high comparative horse/ of their identity." This is the place at which people join together in a "people's otherworld," a vernacular republic of the spirit that allows for a "continuous recovering moment." It is an effortless effort, reminiscent of a Buddhist or Kantian disinterestedness: "Through the peace beneath effort/ (even within effort: quiet air between the bars of our attention)/ comes unpurchased lifelong plenishment."

Yet, foremost for Murray, this is a Christian quality; it is at the very heart of Christ's teachings and is the place from which he taught: "Christ spoke to people most often on this level/ especially when they chattered about king-ship and the Romans;/ all holiness speaks from it." To experience such equanimity would be tantamount to experiencing holiness itself, and that is precisely the sort of graceful redemption Murray seeks to convey. There can be nothing programmatic about such an attitude, but no program of reform, be it social, political, or cultural, can possibly succeed without it. That, for Murray, is the basis upon which all else proceeds, including his own poetry. For Murray, writing is like playing upon an instrument, finding out just what it can do and learning how to do it. His poems have an energy and inventiveness that reveal a delight in the resources of language and a conviction that what needs to be said can be communicated through the adequacies of poetry.

Murray's faith in the redemptive possibilities of poetry was sorely tested during the 1980's, when it became increasingly clear to him that the production of literature in Australia was tied to a commercial system fundamentally at odds with the spirit of poetry, and that the academic and critical establishment that controlled the terms under which literature was to be studied and understood was itself run by a "cabal" of "elites," notable for their "moral cowardice." In response there was a discernible retrenchment in Murray's poetry and prose, a willingness to accept his embattled position in the cultural field as a necessary corollary to his role as a virtual poet-prophet to his people. In the essays collected in *Blocks and Tackles*, Murray became more assertive about the sacramental and mysterious qualities of poetry. As he writes in "Poems and Poesies":

> Poetry models the fullness of life, and also gives its objects presence. Like prayer, it pulls all the motions of our life and being into a concentrated true attentiveness to which God might speak. "Here am I, Lord," as Samuel says in his book of the Bible. It is the plane or mirror of intuitions.

In the poems published in *Dog Fox Field*, however, the poet attends more often to his function as social critic, particularly in his denunciations of "relegation," the denial of the full humanity of others. In a poem entitled "To the Soviet Americans," a working-class man (here the abstract object of much false Marxist piety) ironically declares:

> *Watch out for the ones in jeans*
> *who'll stop you smoking and stop you working:*
> *I call them the Soviet Americans.*

The tone of these poems is often stern and unyielding, written in an age where one finds "self pity and hard drugs everywhere." Yet, this hardened voice does continue to yield up poems of sympathetic feeling, as if, once protected from the incursions of a hostile world, there is ample room for the common enjoyments of a shared living:

> Never despise those
> who fear an order vaster than reason, more charming than prose:
> surely are those who unknowingly chime with the noblest
> and love and are loved by whom they rhyme with best.
> So let your river be current and torrent and klong
> as far and intricate as your love is long. . . .

As Murray continues to write—and he is a prolific poet—the full elaboration of his vision of poetry, and of the humanity it addresses, begins to take shape. It is at once capacious, intimate, difficult, and joyful. Like Whitman, the poet he may most resemble, Les Murray is "large" and "contains multitudes."

Paul Kane

Other major works

NONFICTION: *The Peasant Mandarin: Prose Pieces*, 1978; *Persistence in Folly*, 1984; *The Australian Year*, 1985 (photographs by Peter Solness); *Blocks and Tackles: Articles and Essays*, 1990.

Bibliography

Birkerts, Sven. "The Rococo of His Own Still Center." *Parnassus* 15, no. 2 (1989): 31-48. A serious and sympathetic appreciation of Murray's poetry by a prominent critic. Birkerts highlights those poems most appropriate for inclusion in the Murray "canon," showing a keen sense of what Murray's poetic project entails. Among the first thorough treatments of Murray's poetry in the United States, this is an accessible and useful introduction.

Kane, Paul. "Sydney and the Bush: The Poetry of Les A. Murray." In *From Outback to City: Changing Preoccupations in Australian Literature of the Twentieth Century*, edited by Alexandra Cromwell. New York: American Association of Australian Literary Studies, 1988. This brief article considers what appears to be a dialectical relationship between the rural and urban elements in Murray's poetry. Out of the opposition between what he refers to as "Sydney" and "the Bush," a synthesis, at the level of style, can be discerned.

Oles, Carole. "An Interview with Les Murray." *The American Poetry Review* 15 (March/April, 1986): 28-36. This interview, which is lively, wide-ranging and informative, focuses on many of Murray's central concerns. A good introduction to the way in which Murray himself sees his own poetic project, it contains some useful background information on Australian literary politics and movements.

Taylor, Andrew. "The Past Imperfect of Les A. Murray." In *Reading Australian Poetry*. St. Lucia: University of Queensland Press, 1987. Taylor, an

Australian poet and critic himself, examines Murray's sense of time and suggests that the absence of the female in the poetry is a result of the early death of Murray's mother. This essay is part of a "deconstructive" reading of Australian poetry.

Vendler, Helen. "Four Prized Poets." *The New York Review of Books* 17 (August, 1989): 26-30. This review of Murray's work is chiefly interesting for its perplexed misinterpretation of Murray's strengths as a poet. Vendler unintentionally demonstrates how the originality and inventiveness of Murray challenge conventional notions of how contemporary poetry should be written.

Walcott, Derek. "Crocodile Dandy." *The New Republic* 6 (February, 1989): 25-28. This is a generous review by one important poet of another. Walcott makes a case for the international stature of Murray, looking at his extraordinary verbal facility and mastery of form. The sacramental quality of Murray's poetry is noted, and comparisons are made to such authors as Walt Whitman, Dylan Thomas, and Rudyard Kipling.

THOMAS NASHE

Born: Lowestoft, Surrey, England; November, 1567
Died: Yarmouth(?), England; 1601

Principal poetry

Pierce Penilesse His Supplication to the Divell, 1592 (prose and poetry); *Strange Newes, of the Intercepting of Certaine Letters*, 1592 (prose and poetry); *Summers Last Will and Testament*, 1592 (play and poetry); *The Unfortunate Traveller: Or, The Life of Jacke Wilton*, 1594 (prose and poetry); *The Choise of Valentines*, 1899.

Other literary forms

Almost all that Thomas Nashe wrote was published in pamphlet form. With the exception of a long poem (*The Choise of Valentines*), several sonnets and songs, and at least two dramas (*Summers Last Will and Testament* and *The Isle of Dogs*, 1597), all of his work was prose. His prose works include *The Anatomie of Absurditie* (1589); *An Almond for a Parrat* (1590); a preface to Sir Philip Sidney's *Astrophel and Stella* (1591); *Pierce Penilesse His Supplication to the Divell*; *Strange Newes, of the Intercepting of Certaine Letters*; *Christs Teares over Jerusalem* (1593); *The Terrors of the Night* (1594); *The Unfortunate Traveller: Or, The Life of Jacke Wilton*; *Have with You to Saffron-Walden* (1596); and *Nashes Lenten Stuffe* (1599).

Achievements

Nashe was more a journalist than an artist, if the definition of artist is one who follows the Aristotelian principles of using life as a source from which one creates a story with a beginning, middle, and end. Nashe informed and entertained his sixteenth century audience in the same way that a journalist pleases the public today. He was known in his time not as a poet or a dramatist, although he wrote both poetry and plays. He was known as the worthy opponent of the scholar Gabriel Harvey, as one who with lively rhetoric, biting invective, and soaring wit destroyed every argument the pompous Harvey could muster. He was also known to Elizabethans as the chief defender of the Anglican Church against the attack of the Puritans in the Martin Marprelate controversy. The magnificent invective found in the speeches of William Shakespeare's Falstaff, Prince Hal, and (more especially) Kent was almost certainly derived from the vituperation Nashe hurled at his adversaries.

Among modern students of literature, Nashe is remembered for his most unusual work, the picaresque novel of adventure, *The Unfortunate Traveller: Or, The Life of Jacke Wilton*. It is the story of a young page who, after serving in the army of Henry VIII, travels to Europe to find means of earning a living. The underworld realism that Nashe presents in his descriptions of Jacke

Wilton's escapades has earned him a reputation for being something other than a hurler of invective. The book is not a unified work of art; its characters, other than Jacke himself, are not particularly memorable. Its descriptions of the harshest elements of human life, such as disease, hunger, torture, rape, and murder, place it in stark contrast to the sweet absurdities of romance; it thus shows the way to the modern novel.

Biography

Thomas Nashe was born in November, 1567, the son of William Nashe, a minister in Lowestoft, Suffolk. Since no record exists of William's being a university graduate, it can be assumed that he was probably a stipendiary curate in Lowestoft, not a vicar. Although the title pages of *Pierce Penilesse* and of *Strange Newes, of the Intercepting of Certaine Letters* refer to "Thomas Nashe, Gentleman," Nashe himself denied that he was of gentle birth. From his earliest years, indeed, he disliked the propensity he found in middle-class Englishmen to pretend to be something other than what they were.

In 1573, Nashe's father was granted the living in West Harling, Norfolk, where young Thomas probably spent his early years. Nothing is known of Nashe's basic education except that it was sufficient to allow him to enter St. John's College, Cambridge, in October, 1582. In March, 1586, he received his Bachelor of Arts degree and enrolled immediately to work toward the Master of Arts degree. In 1588, however, he left Cambridge without the degree. Perhaps financial difficulties forced him to leave the university, for his father had died the year before, in 1587. Without financial support from home, Nashe likely would not have been able to continue his education; probably his college, dominated as it was by Puritans, would not look with favor in the form of financial assistance upon the satirical young Nashe, who supported the pursuit of humanistic studies over the more narrow Puritan theology then in vogue at Cambridge.

Whatever his reasons for leaving Cambridge, Nashe certainly had not the economic means to remain idle long. He followed the lead of two other Cambridge graduates who, armed with no wealth but their wits, turned to literature as a means of earning a livelihood. Both Robert Greene and Christopher Marlowe had gone to London to write and both had found moderate success. Nashe may have been acquainted with both men at Cambridge, but he certainly knew them both in London. Like Nashe, both loved poetry and detested Puritans. In the same year that he left Cambridge, he published *The Anatomie of Absurditie*, a work of inexperience and brashness.

A young writer of pamphlets in London had few opportunities to earn a living by his work. He was generally paid a flat amount for his manuscript, usually two pounds. If a pamphlet were well-received by the public, the patron to whom it was dedicated might be so flattered that he or she might feel disposed to grant the author a stipend to continue his work. Nashe's *The*

Anatomie of Absurditie, dedicated to Sir Charles Blount, was, however, of so little literary merit that Nashe probably received no more than his original author's fee.

Nashe dedicated no more works to Sir Charles; but because he did need patrons, he dedicated later works to a variety of people in a position to offer him assistance. Finally, after the dedication of *The Unfortunate Traveller* to Henry Wriothesley, the Earl of Southampton, Nashe decided that patrons were more trouble than they were worth. Hating hypocrisy in others and finding himself forced into hypocrisy in order to be paid for his work, Nashe turned to writing only for his readers and depending upon them to reward his efforts.

Perhaps what gave Nashe his biggest literary boost was the famous Martin Marprelate controversy. Nashe's part in the verbal battle was limited to the pamphlet *An Almond for a Parrat*, but the style and the vigorous prose of Martin could not help influencing Nashe. Although he was hostile to Martin's Puritanical ideas, Nashe must nevertheless have learned much from the formidable prose of his Puritan adversary, for he attacks Martin with the same devices and force of language that the Puritan propagandist used.

Nashe's entry into the Martin Marprelate controversy brought with it rewards beyond what he might have hoped. Gabriel Harvey wrote disparagingly of Nashe's part in the controversy, thus starting a new fight: the Nashe-Harvey controversy. It was in this battle of wits that Nashe found his place as a writer. Here the verbal street-fighter had the great good fortune to be attacked by a man of reputation who was inferior in wit and writing ability to Nashe. Harvey's reputation never recovered from Nashe's fierce invective. Beginning with a slap at Harvey in his Preface to Greene's *A Quip for an Upstart Courtier* (1592) and ending with *Have with You to Saffron-Walden*, Nashe earned a good reputation and a fair living from his anti-Harvey prose.

All of his previous writings were practice for *The Unfortunate Traveller*, published in 1594. A kind of pamphlet itself, but longer and more complex, the work was not particularly popular during his lifetime, but today it is his best-known work.

Nashe was hounded from London in 1597 when the authorities decided that *The Isle of Dogs*, a play he had begun, and which Ben Jonson had finished, was "seditious." Jonson was jailed and Nashe sought, but the famous pamphleteer had fled to Yarmouth, in Norfolk. By 1598, he was back in London, where *Nashes Lenten Stuffe* was entered in the Stationers' Register.

After *Nashes Lenten Stuffe*, Nashe wrote no more, and in 1601 history records a reference to his death.

Analysis

Thomas Nashe the satirical pamphleteer, who was wont to use language as a cudgel in a broad prose style, seldom disciplined himself to the more delicate work of writing poetry. Both his temperament and his pocketbook directed him to the freer and more profitable form of pamphlet prose. It is this prose that made his reputation, but Nashe did write poems, mostly lyrical in the manner of his time. No originator in poetic style, Nashe followed the lead of such worthy predecessors as Geoffrey Chaucer, the Earl of Surrey, Edmund Spenser, and Christopher Marlowe.

Nashe's interest in poetry was not slight. In typical Renaissance fashion, he believed poetry to be the highest form of moral philosophy. Following Sidney, he insisted that the best poetry is based upon scholarship and devotion to detail. Not only does poetry, in his perception, encourage virtue and discourage vice, but also it "cleanses" the language of barbarisms and makes the "vulgar sort" in London adopt a more pleasing manner of speech. Because he loved good poetry and saw the moral and aesthetic value of it, Nashe condemned the "balladmongers," who abused the ears and sensitivities of the gentlefolk of England. To him, the ballad writers were "common pamfletters" whose lack of learning and lust for money were responsible for littering the streets with the garbage of their ballads—a strange reaction for a man who was himself a notable writer of pamphlets. For the learned poetry of Western culture, Nashe had the highest appreciation.

Nashe's own poetic efforts are often placed in the context of his prose works, as if he were setting jewels among the coarser material, as did George Gascoigne, Thomas Lodge, Robert Greene, Thomas Deloney, and others. *Pierce Penilesse*, "The Four Letters Confuted," and *The Unfortunate Traveller* all have poems sprinkled here and there. The play *Summers Last Will and Testament*, itself written in quite acceptable blank verse, has several lyrics of some interest scattered throughout. Nashe's shorter poetic efforts are almost equally divided between sonnets and lyrical poems. The longer *The Choise of Valentines* is a narrative in the erotic style of Ovid.

Nashe's sonnets are six in number, two of which may be said to be parodies of the form. Each is placed within a longer work, where its individual purpose is relevant to the themes of that work. Most of the sonnets are in the English form, containing three quatrains and a concluding couplet. Following the lead of the Earl of Surrey (who is, indeed, the putative author of the two sonnets to Geraldine in *The Unfortunate Traveller*), Nashe uses a concluding couplet in each of his sonnets, including "To the Right Honorable the lord S.," which in other respects (as in the division into octave and sestet rhyming abbaabba, cdcdee) is closer to the Italian form.

In his first sonnet, "Perusing yesternight, with idle eyes," Nashe pauses at the end of *Pierce Penilesse* to praise the lord Amyntas, whom Edmund Spenser had neglected in *The Faerie Queene* (1590-1596). In "Perusing yesternight, with idle eyes," the famous poem by Spenser, Nashe had turned to the end of the poem to find sonnets addressed to "sundry Nobles." Nashe uses the three quatrains to rehearse the problem: he read the poem, found the sonnets addressed to the nobles, and wondered why Spenser had left out "thy memory." In an excellent use of the concluding couplet in this form, he decides that Spenser must have omitted praise of Amyntas because "few words could not cōprise thy fame."

If "Perusing yesternight, with idle eyes" is in the tradition of using the sonnet to praise, Nashe's second sonnet, "Were there no warres," is not. Concluding his prose attack on Gabriel Harvey in "The Four Letters Confuted," this sonnet looks forward to John Milton rather than backward to Petrarch. Here Nashe promises Harvey constant warfare. Harvey had suggested that he would like to call off the battle, but in so doing he had delivered a few verbal blows to Nashe. To the request for a truce, Nashe responds with a poetic "no!" Again using the three quatrains to deliver his message, the poet calls for "Vncessant warres with waspes and droanes," announces that revenge is an endless Muse, and says that he will gain his reputation by attacking "this duns." His couplet effectively concludes by promising that his next work will be of an extraordinary type.

The next two sonnets may be thought of as parodies of the Petrarchan style and of the medieval romance generally. Nashe, like his creation Jack Wilton, had little use for the unrealistic in love, war, or any aspect of life. The exaggerated praise of women in the Petrarchan tradition sounded as false to him as it did to Shakespeare and to the later writers of anti-Petrarchan verse. Both "If I must die" and "Faire roome, the presence of sweet beauty's pride," found in *The Unfortunate Traveller*, are supposedly written by the lovesick Surrey to his absent love, Geraldine. Both poems are close enough to the real Surrey's own sonnets to ring true, but just ridiculous enough to be seen clearly as parodies.

The first is addressed to the woman Diamante, whom Surrey mistakes for Geraldine. The dying Surrey requests that his mistress suck out his breath, stab him with her tongue, crush him with her embrace, burn him with her eyes, and strangle him with her hair. In "Faire roome, the presence of sweet beauty's pride," Surrey, having visited Geraldine's room in Florence, addresses the room. He will worship the room, with which neither the chambers of heaven nor lightning can compare. No one, he concludes, can see heaven unless he meditates on the room.

Such romantic nonsense held no attraction for Jack or for Nashe. Jack makes fun of "suchlike rhymes" which lovers use to "assault" women: "A holy requiem to their souls that think to woo women with riddles." Jack, a much more realistic man, wins the favor of Diamonte with a plain table.

The final two sonnets are also anti-Petrarchan in content. Addressed to a would-be patron to whom he dedicated *The Choise of Valentines*, both "To the Right Honorable the lord S." and "Thus hath my penne presum'd to please" ask pardon for presuming to address an overtly pornographic poem to a "sweete flower of matchless poetrie." In the octave of the former, Nashe excuses himself by declaring that he merely writes about what men really do. In the sestet, he proudly asserts that everyone can write Petrarchan love poems, full of "complaints and praises." No one, however, has written successfully of "loves pleasures" in his time—except, the implication is, him.

Nashe's earliest two lyrics, although they are very different in content, are each in four stanzas of six lines of iambic pentameter. The rhyme in each case is ababcc. The later songs, those in *Summers Last Will and Testament*, are in couplets and (in one case) tercets. Except for "Song: Spring, the sweete spring," all the lyrics are laments.

The most personal of the lyrics is "Why ist damnation," printed on the first page of Nashe's famous pamphlet *Pierce Penilesse*. Trying to gain prosperity and failing, Nashe "resolved in verse to paint forth my passion." In a logical progression, the poet first considers suicide ("Why ist damnation to dispaire and die") but decides against it for his soul's safety. He then determines that in England wit and scholarship are useless. He asks God's forgiveness for his low mood, but despairs because he has no friends. Finally, he bids adieu to England as "unkinde, where skill is nothing woorth."

"All Soul, no earthly flesh," Nashe's second lyric, is more like the anti-Petrarchan sonnets that Nashe has the Earl of Surrey write in *The Unfortunate Traveller* than it is like the other lyrics. Full of exaggerated comparisons (Geraldine is "pure soul," "pure gold"), comic images (his spirit will perch upon "hir silver breasts"), and conventional conceits (stars, sun, and dew take their worth from her), the poem is as far from Nashe as John Lyly's *Euphues, the Anatomy of Wit* (1579) is.

In *Summers Last Will and Testament*, Nashe includes four major lyrics and several minor ones. Some of the lyrics are cheery "Song: Spring, the sweete spring," "Song: Trip and goe," and "Song: Merry, merry, merry," for example. The general mood of the poems is sad, however, as the subject of the whole work would dictate: the death of summer. In watching summer die, readers, like Gerard Manley Hopkins' Margaret, see themselves. "Song: Fayre Summer droops" is a conventional lament on the passing of summer. Written in heroic couplets, the poem uses alliteration successfully in the last stanza to bring the song to a solid conclusion. "Song: Autumn Hath all the Summer's Fruitfull Treasure," also in heroic couplets, continues the theme of lament with lines using effective repetition ("Short dayes, sharpe dayes, long nights come on a pace"). Here, Nashe turns more directly to what was perhaps his central theme in the longer work: man's weakness in face of natural elements. The refrain, repeated at the end of each of the two stanzas, is "From winter, plague, & pestilence, good Lord, deliver us."

It was surely fear of the plague and of man's frailty in general that led Nashe to write the best of his lyrics, "Song: Adieu, farewell earths blisse," sung to the dying Summer by Will Summer. Nashe recognizes in the refrain which follows each of the six stanzas that he is sick, he must die, and he prays:

"Lord, have mercy on us."

In a logical development, Nashe first introduces the theme of *Everyman*: "Fond are lifes lustful ioyes." In succeeding stanzas he develops each of the "lustfull ioyes" in turn. "Rich men" are warned not to trust in their wealth, "Beauty" is revealed as transitory, "Strength" is pictured surrendering to the grave, and "Wit" is useless to dissuade Hell's executioner. In a very specific, orderly manner and in spare iambic trimeter lines, Nashe presents man's death-lament and prayer for mercy. One stanza will show the strength of the whole poem:

> Beauty is but a flowre,
> Which wrinckles will deuoure,
> Brightnesse falls from the ayre,
> Queenes have died yong and faire,
> Dust hath closed Helens eye.
> I am sick, I must dye:
> Lord, have mercy on vs.

Nashe's last poem is by far his longest. *The Choise of Valentines* is an erotic narrative poem in heroic couplets running to more than three hundred lines. With the kind of specificity that one would expect from the author of *The Unfortunate Traveller*, Nashe tells of the visit of the young man Tomalin to a brothel in search of his valentine, "gentle mistris Francis." Tomalin's detailed exploration of the woman's anatomical charms, his unexpected loss of sexual potency, and her announced preference for a dildo all combine to present an Ovidian erotic-mythological poem of the type popular in Elizabethan England. Nashe's poem must, however, be set off from Shakespeare's *Venus and Adonis* (1593) and Marlowe's *Hero and Leander* (1598), which emphasize the mythological more than the erotic. Nashe clearly emphasizes the erotic, almost to the exclusion of the mythological. Why not? he seems to say in the dedicatory sonnet accompanying the poem: Ovid was his guide, and "Ouids wanton Muse did not offend."

Nowhere, with the exception of the excellent "Song: Adieu, farewell earths blisse," does Nashe rise to the heights of his greatest contemporaries, Spenser, Sidney, Marlowe, and Shakespeare. In that poem, in the sonnet "Were there no warres," and in perhaps one or two other poems his Muse is sufficiently shaken into consciousness by the poet's interest in the subject. The remainder of Nashe's poetry is the work of an excellent craftsman who is playing with form and language.

Eugene P. Wright

Other major works

LONG FICTION: *The Unfortunate Traveller: Or, The Life of Jacke Wilton*, 1594 (prose and poetry).

PLAYS: *The Tragedie of Dido Queene of Carthage*, c. 1586-1587 (with Christopher Marlowe); *Summers Last Will and Testament*, 1592; *The Isle of Dogs*, 1597 (with Ben Jonson).

NONFICTION: Preface to Robert Greene's *Menaphon*, 1589; *The Anatomie of Absurditie*, 1589; *An Almond for a Parrat*, 1590; Preface to Sir Philip Sidney's *Astrophel and Stella*, 1591; *Pierce Penilesse His Supplication to the Divell*, 1592 (prose and poetry); *Strange Newes of the Intercepting of Certaine Letters*, 1592 (prose and poetry); *Christs Teares over Jerusalem*, 1593; *The Terrors of the Night*, 1594; *Have with You to Saffron-Walden*, 1596; *Nashes Lenten Stuffe*, 1599.

Bibliography

Helgerson, Richard. *The Elizabethan Prodigals.* Berkeley: University of California Press, 1977. Nashe and his colleagues Christopher Marlowe, Thomas Kyd, George Peele, Robert Greene, and Thomas Lodge, all with university training, formed a group of literary bohemians in London. Helgerson catalogs their escapades and relates them to their lives, which were adventurous, barbarous, and impoverished in turn. The index cross-references topics well.

Hibbard, G. R. *Thomas Nashe: A Critical Introduction.* Cambridge, Mass.: Harvard University Press, 1962. Hibbard basically tells the story of Nashe's life, giving passing attention to his poems and writings and to his theories about literature and life. Contains an index and an appendix.

Hilliard, Stephen S. *The Singularity of Thomas Nashe.* Lincoln: University of Nebraska Press, 1986. Hilliard takes a fresh look at Nashe's life and writing, discovering the distinctive qualities of his wit and style and showing how they transformed both poetry and prose. A good index ties topics together, and the bibliography provides a good source for further research.

Muir, Kenneth. *Introduction to Elizabethan Literature.* New York: Random House, 1967. This excellent single-volume guide to the period has good standard comments on Nashe and his place in Elizabethan poetry. Muir is a sound scholar with profound insights into the period. The bibliography is dated, but the full notes provide good supplementary material.

Nicholl, Charles. *A Cup of News: The Life of Thomas Nashe.* London: Routledge & Kegan Paul, 1984. This scholarly biography sets a high standard. In addition to substantial discussions of Nashe's life and writings, Nicholl includes illustrations of portraits and scenes, as well as reproductions of relevant documents. He is particularly illuminating about the poetry. The notes, bibliography, and index are all excellent.

Ostriker, Alicia, and Leslie Dunn. "The Lyric." In *English Poetry and Prose, 1540-1674*, edited by Christopher Ricks. New York: Peter Bedrick Books, 1986. This compound essay, with sections on poetry and on song lyrics, is in accordance with a practical division first initiated in the Elizabethan period. Nashe's connections with both are covered, although he is considered an incidental figure. The select bibliography lists most of the major sources.

Rhodes, Neil. *Elizabethan Grotesque.* London: Routledge & Kegan Paul, 1980. Collects a fascinating set of amusing and bizarre stories from a notably roguish period. Nashe and his fellow wits come into sight regularly. This entertaining book of literary gossip re-creates Nashe's life-style effectively. The notes make browsing easy.

HOWARD NEMEROV

Born: New York, New York; March 1, 1920
Died: Universal City, Missouri; July 5, 1991

Principal poetry

The Image and the Law, 1947; *Guide to the Ruins*, 1950; *The Salt Garden*, 1955; *Mirrors and Windows*, 1958; *The Next Room of the Dream: Poems and Two Plays*, 1962; *The Blue Swallows*, 1967; *Gnomes and Occasions*, 1973; *The Western Approaches: Poems 1973-75*, 1975; *The Collected Poems of Howard Nemerov*, 1977; *Sentences*, 1980; *Inside the Onion*, 1984; *War Stories: Poems About Long Ago and Now*, 1987.

Other literary forms

Though known primarily for his poetry, Howard Nemerov wrote novels—*The Melodramatists* (1949), *Federigo: Or, The Power of Love* (1954), and *The Homecoming Game* (1957)—and short stories, collected in *A Commodity of Dreams and Other Stories* (1959) and *Stories, Fables, and Other Diversions* (1971). Two verse dramas, *Endor* and *Cain*, are included with his collection *The Next Room of the Dream*. His criticism and reflections on the making of poetry are to be found in various volumes: *Poetry and Fiction: Essays* (1963), *Reflexions on Poetry and Poetics* (1972), *Figures of Thought: Speculations on the Meaning of Poetry and Other Essays* (1978), *New and Selected Essays* (1985), and *The Oak in the Acorn: On "Remembrance of Things Past" and on Teaching Proust, Who Will Never Learn* (1987). *Journal of the Fictive Life* is a series of candid autobiographical meditations.

Achievements

As a poet, novelist, critic, and teacher, Nemerov was a man of letters in the eighteenth century tradition. He was identified with no particular school of poetry. In the pamphlet *Howard Nemerov* (1968), Peter Meinke says that Nemerov's work explores the dilemma of "the existential, science-oriented (or science-displaced) liberal mind of the twentieth century."

Almost every available award came to Nemerov; his honors included the Bowdoin Prize from Harvard University (1940), a *Kenyon Review* fellowship in fiction (1955), a National Institute of Arts and Letters Grant (1961), a Guggenheim Fellowship (1968-1969), an Academy of American Poets fellowship (1970), the Pulitzer Prize and National Book Award (1978), the Bollingen Prize from Yale University (1981), the Aiken Taylor Award for Modern Poetry (1987), and the presidential National Medal of Art (1987). He served as a poetry consultant to the Library of Congress and as the United States Poet Laureate from 1988 to 1990. The National Institute of Arts and

Letters, the American Academy of Arts and Sciences, and Alpha of Massachusetts all claimed him as a member.

Nemerov was the poet of the modern person. His deep division of temperament and his interest in science illustrated the fragmentation and scientific bent of the twentieth century. His sense of the tragic nature of the human condition and his spiritual questing with no subsequent answers reflected the twentieth century search for meaning. Although his poetry has a decidedly religious quality, Nemerov appeared to resolve his spiritual questions by honoring life's mystery rather than by adopting specific beliefs.

Biography

Howard Nemerov was born in New York City on March 1, 1920, to David and Gertrude (Russek) Nemerov. His wealthy parents were also cultivated and saw to it that their son was well educated. They sent him first to the exclusive private Fieldston Preparatory School, where he distinguished himself as both scholar and athlete. Nemerov then entered Harvard University, where he began to write poetry, essays, and fiction. In his junior year, he won the Bowdoin Prize for an essay on Thomas Mann. Nemerov was graduated in 1937 and immediately entered the Royal Air Force Coast Command as an aviator, based in England. Subsequently, he joined the Eighth United States Army Air Force, which was based in Lincolnshire. On January 26, 1944, Nemerov was married to Margaret (Peggy) Russell (a union that produced three sons, David, Alexander, and Jeremy Seth). In 1945, when he was discharged as a first lieutenant from the Air Force, the Nemerovs moved to New York City to settle into civilian life.

During this time, Nemerov chose, against his father's will, to become a poet. This was an anguished decision, for tradition decreed that, as the only son, he should carry on the family business. As a "Jewish Puritan of the middle class," Nemerov felt keenly the separation from custom. In his *Journal of the Fictive Life* (1965), he credits his emphasis on work to a "guilty acknowledgment that I became a writer very much against the will of my father."

Since poetry customarily brings more pleasure than money, Nemerov left New York after a year to join the faculty at Hamilton College in Clinton, New York. In 1948, he became a member of the English department of Bennington College and taught there until, in 1966, he went to Brandeis University in Massachusetts. During his stay at Brandeis, Nemerov also held interim teaching appointments. He left Brandeis in 1969 to become the Hurst Professor of Literature at Washington University in St. Louis. He became Washington University's Edward Mallinckrodt Distinguished University Professor of English in 1976. He completed a writer-in-residency at the University of Missouri at Kansas City in April, 1991, shortly before his death from cancer in July.

Analysis

Howard Nemerov's poetry revolves about the theme of the absurd place of humankind within the large drama of time. It also illustrates his divided temperament, about which he wrote in _Journal of the Fictive Life_, "I must attempt to bring together the opposed elements of my character represented by poetry and fiction."

Nemerov's first three poetry collections, _The Image and the Law_, _Guide to the Ruins_, and _The Salt Garden_, demonstrate his growth from a somewhat derivative writer to a mature poet with a distinctive voice. _The Image and the Law_ is based on his dual vision, what he called "poetry of the eye" (the image) and "poetry of the mind" (the law). He tries to illustrate the "ever-present dispute between the two ways of looking at the world." _The Image and the Law_, as a first book, was competent, but was criticized for lack of unity and for being derivative. Critics found too many echoes of T. S. Eliot, W. H. Auden, William Butler Yeats, and Wallace Stevens—admittedly Nemerov's models.

Nemerov's second book, _Guide to the Ruins_, drew the same complaint, as did _The Salt Garden_. The latter collection, however, was recognized as exhibiting the beginning of his "most characteristic voice, a quiet intelligent voice brooding lyrically on the strange beauty and tragic loneliness of life," as Peter Meinke has described it.

In _The Image and the Law_ and _Guide to the Ruins_, not only is Nemerov practicing what he has learned from Yeats, Eliot, and others, but he also starts to purge himself of war-won realizations. Although _The Image and the Law_ deals mainly with the city, war, and death, it also contains religious imagery and wit. His poems wail, like an Old Testament lament—"I have become a gate/ To the ruined city, dry" ("Lot's Wife"). The poems in _The Image and the Law_ exhibit ironic detachment as well as seriousness, for to Nemerov "the serious and the funny are one." The dualism in the poems is suggested in the title.

Guide to the Ruins has a broader scope than his first collection and reveals artistic growth. The "ruins" are those created in World War II, although the war is not actually over. Again, there is duality in the poems; the poet feels trapped between art-faith and science-reality, but sides with neither wholeheartedly. His tension between the two produces a Dostoevskian religious agony that visits Christianity, but consistently returns to Judaism. Several poems in _Guide to the Ruins_ unite war and religion into a pessimism that will become more evident in later works. Paradoxically, and typical of his dualistic vision, he celebrates life not only in spite of war but also because of it.

The Salt Garden, while still exhibiting some derivation, exhibits not only the poet's own voice but also a "center," that center being Nemerov's interest in nature. True to his double vision, he contrasts "brutal" nature with "decent" humankind. The link between the two is found in liquids such as ocean and blood, which combine into humankind's "salt dream," the call of the subconscious toward wildness. The poems in *The Salt Garden* range from a decent, rational man's reflection on his garden to the nightmarish, Freudian dream "The Scales of the Eyes." A brilliant combination of the "civilized" and the "wild" is found in "I Only Am Escaped Alone to Tell Thee." By degrees, this poem shows the submerged anguish of a prosperous nineteenth century woman. The whalebone stays of her corset are a central image, leading to other images of sea, mirrors, and light, until "the black flukes of agony/ Beat at the air till the light blows out." *The Salt Garden* treats not only humanity, "brutal" nature, and the link between the two, but death as a part of "time's ruining stream." Water, sea, and blood are beyond moral categories; they are the substance of life. In this respect, according to Julia Bartholomay in *The Shield of Perseus: The Vision and Imagination of Howard Nemerov* (1972), Nemerov's perspective is biblical. Water is creative and purifying; it "sanctifies that which it permeates and recreates, for all objects are but fleeting forms on the changing surface of eternity."

Nemerov's interest in nature, which is first evident in *The Salt Garden*, continues in *The Next Room of the Dream, Mirrors and Windows*, and *The Blue Swallows*. Nature, in these poems, has objective reality; it is never merely a projection of human concerns. Like Robert Frost, Nemerov not only describes nature as something "other" than himself but also brings philosophical issues into his nature poems. In *Mirrors and Windows*, Nemerov indicates that poetry helps make life bearable by stopping it in a frame (poem). It sheds no light upon the meaning of life or death; it only reveals life's beauty or terror.

The Blue Swallows, published twenty years after his first collection, indicates further growth in Nemerov's technique and development of his philosophy of "minimal affirmation." In this book, Nemerov's paradoxical view of humanity as both helpless and indomitable is expressed in images of gulls and swallows that circle around this world, only to find it illusory and strange. His duality is expressed in symbols of physics and theology, again underlining the division between science-reality and art-faith. According to his philosophy of minimal affirmation, human beings may be crushed, but they rise "again and again," as in the end of "Beyond the Pleasure Principle." The final emphasis of the poem is simultaneously on the absurdity of life and death and the inexplicable resilience of humankind. "Beyond the Pleasure Principle" expresses the central theme of *The Blue Swallows*, a theme that was to remain constant in Nemerov's works until his later years.

Critics have commented profusely on Nemerov's witty pessimism and urbane helplessness. Though Bartholomay acknowledges Nemerov's dualistic nature, she finds other meanings in his poems besides wit and hopelessness. She sees Nemerov as a witty sophisticate who responds to life bitterly, yet she also points out his capacity to be "philosophical, subjective, lyrical, or even mystical." To support this contention she calls attention to "Runes," considered by many to be Nemerov's finest poem. Mutability is the theme of "Runes," but with a recognition of the mystery of life. The poem expresses pessimism but avoids nihilism, attacking the emptiness of modern life while affirming "the stillness in moving things." "Runes" is religious in that it is concerned with the mystery of creation and finds resolution in total submission to life's riddle.

The major artistic triumph of "Runes" is the integration of external and internal through which its paradox is resolved. This unity is achieved through the brilliant treatment of three reflexive images: two objective images—water and seed—and a subjective image—thought itself. "Runes" is perhaps the most complete expression of Nemerov's philosophy of minimal affirmation. In it Nemerov returns to the mystery of creation, in which he finds the beginnings of art. Imagination is reality's agent, revealing "the divine shadow of nature's signature on all things."

The Next Room of the Dream, a collection of poems and two verse plays, illustrates Nemerov's decision to stay close to what he calls in *Journal of the Fictive Life* the "great primary human drama." His plays *Cain* and *Endor*, based on biblical themes, illustrate his humanitarianism as well as his quest for ultimate truth. This quest is ironically expressed in "Santa Claus," which begins, "Somewhere on his travels the strange Child/ Picked up with this overstuffed confidence man," and ends, "At Easter, he's anonymous again,/ Just one of the crowd lunching on Calvary."

Nemerov's plays, however, provide no spiritual resolution to man's questions. Stanley Knock in *The Christian Century* comments, "Nemerov succeeds only in revealing the devastating emptiness of contemporary beliefs." The poem "Nothing Will Yield" sums up Nemerov's perception of human helplessness in the face of reality; even art is no solution, although poets will continue to speak "holy language" in the face of despair. In *The Next Room of the Dream*, the poems become simpler, with more precise natural descriptions and more obvious compassion for humankind.

Nemerov's dark vision mellows in his later work. In two later collections of poetry, *Gnomes and Occasions* and *Sentences*, the emphasis is spiritual, the tone elegiac. In *The Western Approaches*: *Poems, 1973-75*, the topics range from speculation about fate ("The Western Approaches") to the sterility of space travel ("The Backward Look").

Gnomes and Occasions consists of epigrams, riddles, meditations, and reflections, all poems that stress origins and ends. They have the epigrammatic style of wisdom literature—pithy, sage, and provocative. The language is rife with references to the Bible, priests, grace, and God, as well as nature. There are also the characteristic wit, irony, and doubt, as expressed in "Creation Myth on a Moebius Band":

This world's just mad enough to have been made
By the Being his beings into Being prayed.

Nemerov's interest in nature is also apparent in this book, in poems such
as "Late Butterflies" and "The Rent in the Screen," a lyric dedicated to science writer Loren Eiseley. Nemerov's sharp observations of nature are here
transformed into melancholy, sometimes irony. "The Rent in the Screen"
ends by commenting on the lives of moths and men, "How brief a dream."
Compassion for the fate of butterflies in winter ends with the dry "We take
our pity/ Back in the house,/ The warm indoors."

The publication of Nemerov's *The Collected Poems* in 1977 led to a critical revaluation of Nemerov's work. This collection (which includes all of
his poetry written through 1977) exhibits "a gradual intensifying of a unified
perspective," according to critic Phoebe Pettingell. The effect of *The Collected Poems* is to delineate the depth and breadth of Nemerov's insights.
Throughout the volume certain questions recur—questions having to do with
the nature of reality and the role of poetry in revealing the world's appearances and sometimes, perhaps, what lies beyond appearances.

Despite the increasingly religious quality of his language, Nemerov, as
usual, does not make specific religious statements. It is poetry, if anything,
that comes closest to being an intercessor between God and man, and this
link is the theme of *Sentences*. Here Nemerov applies his belief that "in the
highest range the theory of poetry would be the theory of the Incarnation,
which seeks to explain how the Word became Flesh." In a letter to Robert D.
Harvey, he wrote,

> Poetry is a kind of spiritual exercise,
> a (generally doomed but stoical) attempt
> to pray one's humanity back into the universe;
> and conversely an attempt to read, to derive anew,
> one's humanity from nature . . . In the darkness
> of this search, patience and good humour are
> useful qualities. Also: the serious and the funny
> are one. The purpose of poetry is to persuade,
> fool or compel God into speaking.

Indeed, the main theme of *Sentences* is the coherence art gives to life's
randomness. In accordance with his theory of connecting through the power
of art, the book is divided into sections entitled "Beneath," "Above," and
"Beyond;" these sections correspond to sex and power (beneath), metaphysics
and poetry (above), and human destiny (beyond). The first section is ironic,
the middle is speculative, and the last is moving. Critics generally disliked
the first part of *Sentences*, but applauded the other two sections.

After *Sentences*, Nemerov published another stunning poetry collection,
Inside the Onion. The title wryly implies his subjective-objective, romantic-

realist nature. In this book Nemerov blends the homely and the humorous into poems that avoid the dramatic and highlight the commonplace, making it arresting.

War Stories contains forty-six poems grouped into three parts: "The War in the Streets," "The War in the Air," and "The War in the Heavens." This volume is Nemerov at his metaphysical best, grounding his spiritual musings in everyday experience. His interest in science and modern events is linked to literature—for example, the advent of Halley's Comet is hailed in the language of the speech in the Anglo-Saxon epic *Beowulf* that compares man's life to a swallow's brief flight through a mead hall. These poems range from an elegy for a student to explorations of subtle psychological insights to profound spiritual observations: "Though God be dead, he lived so far away/ His sourceless light continues to fall on us" ("The Celestial Emperor").

A Howard Nemerov Reader contains selections from all Nemerov's work except his drama: poems, short stories, novels, and essays. It includes some previously unpublished poems, such as "Trying Conclusions," a meditative poem written after serious surgery. *A Howard Nemerov Reader* is a boon for those who want an overview of this writer's canon.

Nemerov's brilliant poetry and prose illustrate the opposites in his temperament: the romantic-realist, the skeptic-believer, the scientist-poet. These conflicts reflect the fragmentation and angst of modern existence. He did not employ scientific terms in a sentimental manner in his poetry but included nebulae, particles, and light-years as true poetic subjects, not simply metaphors for human concerns. Nemerov was a Renaissance man in his breadth and an eighteenth century man of letters in his satire, wit, and respect for form. His spiritual questions and his refusal of any orthodoxy, whether religious or artistic, made him a twentieth century existentialist.

Like any great figure, however, Nemerov defied categorization. He lived his life in and for literature in an age that values, as he wrote in his *Journal of the Fictive Life*, "patient, minute analysis"; he gave himself to "the wholeness of things," "the great primary human drama" in a time when some consider that loving the human story is "unsophisticated, parochial, maybe even sinful."

Many writers reach a plateau; Howard Nemerov kept growing. In his evolution, he became less bitter and more loving. As he became more complex, his language grew simpler, elegantly expressing his subtle mind and his ultimate sadness at the tragic position of humanity in the universe. Nemerov's divided nature shows in his poetry's empiricism and acceptance of objective reality and his subjective, poetic self that searched, perhaps futilely, for a definite Word of God.

Mary Barnes Bruce

Other major works

LONG FICTION: *The Melodramatists,* 1949; *Federigo: Or, The Power of Love,* 1954; *The Homecoming Game,* 1957.

SHORT FICTION: *A Commodity of Dreams and Other Stories,* 1959; *Stories, Fables, and Other Diversions,* 1971.

NONFICTION: *Poetry and Fiction: Essays,* 1963; *Journal of the Fictive Life,* 1965; *Reflexions on Poetry and Poetics,* 1972; *Figures of Thought: Speculations on the Meaning of Poetry and Other Essays,* 1978; *New and Selected Essays,* 1985; *The Oak in the Acorn: On "Remembrance of Things Past" and on Teaching Proust, Who Will Never Learn,* 1987.

EDITED TEXT: *Poets on Poetry,* 1965.

MISCELLANEOUS: *A Howard Nemerov Reader,* 1991.

Bibliography

Bartholomay, Julia A. *The Shield of Perseus: The Vision and Imagination of Howard Nemerov.* Gainesville: University of Florida Press, 1972. This book discusses Nemerov's use of "multivalent" images and other poetic techniques, and his poetry's recurrent themes. There is detailed information about the poet drawn from his letters and conversations. For the reader seeking a hypothesis about Nemerov's "religious" outlook and a careful examination of his artistic techniques, this book is an excellent source.

Knock, Stanley F., Jr. "Renewal of Illusion." *The Christian Century,* January 16, 1962, pp. 85-86. In this review of Nemerov's verse drama *Endor,* Knock shows how Nemerov transports an Old Testament story into the context of existentialism and the Cold War. Rather than "see ourselves as others see us," as Robert Burns advised, Nemerov finds hope not in the stripping of illusion, but in its renewal.

Meinke, Peter. *Howard Nemerov.* Minneapolis: University of Minnesota Press, 1968. One of the most comprehensive books on Nemerov insofar as general knowledge is concerned. It covers not only biographical data but also the effect some life incidents had on his work. There are brief comments on Nemerov's major works; naturally, however, the book is limited by its date. These volumes also trace Nemerov's rise to literary prominence, for the reviews indicate Nemerov's artistic growth and public acceptance.

Ross, Jean W. "Howard Nemerov." In *Contemporary Authors,* New Revision Series, vol. 27, edited by Hal May and James J. Lesniak. Detroit: Gale, 1989. This reference piece contains comprehensive material on Nemerov, particularly what critics have said about his work. It is particularly useful for its lists of Nemerov's works and honors. Included is the transcript of a telephone interview in which Nemerov discusses his opinion of modern poetry.

MARGARET CAVENDISH, DUCHESS OF NEWCASTLE

Born: St. Johns, England; 1624(?)
Died: London, England; January 7, 1674

Principal poetry

Poems and Fancies, 1653; *Philosophicall Fancies*, 1653 (prose and verse); *Natures Pictures*, 1656 (prose and verse); *Plays Never Before Printed*, 1668.

Other literary forms

Margaret Cavendish, Duchess of Newcastle, left many folio volumes in various prose genres. *Natures Pictures* contains a group of stories told around a winter fire; they are romantic and moralistic (disguises, abductions, wanderings, battles, reunions). The second part, a miscellaneous group of tales, has no framing device. *Grounds of Natural Philosophy* (1668) reworks her views regarding physics and medicine developed in *Philosophicall Fancies*. *Philosophical Letters* (1664) analyzes Thomas Hobbes, René Descartes, and Thomas More. Several romantic comedies, published in *Plays* (1662), have plot elements similar to the tales. The Duchess herself appears in such figures as "Lady Contemplation" and "Lady Sanspariel." The Duchess' most effective prose, and one of the century's finest biographical works, is *The Life of William Cavendish, Duke of Newcastle* (1667). Equally lively and clearly written is "A True Relation of the Birth, Breeding and Life of Margaret Cavendish, Duchess of Newcastle, Written by Herself," included in *Natures Pictures*. *The Worlds Olio* (1655) contains epistles on the branches of learning and the pleasures of reading, on the passions, fame, and education. With *CCXI Sociable Letters* (1664), it contains many interesting observations on manners and literary taste.

Achievements

As one of the first women who not only composed but also published their verses, the Duchess anticipated the disdain that she would receive and so attempted to create a persona, as did other Cavalier poets, that would help readers understand what she was doing. She developed the concept of "fancy," and the "harmless mirth" it produced, arguing that it was a woman's as much as a man's pursuit. Her poems envision the world as guided by a benevolent goddess, Natura. They movingly express humanitarian sentiments and focus on responses by women to loss of love, misfortune, and death. She utilized many genres and themes of earlier seventeenth century poetry: the pastoral, the verse-treatise, the elegy, and the verse-narrative. She is at her best when she is guided by the traditional emblems and images of lyric and narrative verse.

Biography

Margaret (Lucas) Cavendish, Duchess of Newcastle, was one of eight children afforded a privileged upbringing by her mother. Her favorite pastime
was writing, for which she neglected her reading, her languages, and her
spelling. She also enjoyed designing clothes and was known for her extravagance in dress as well as in her scientific opinions and her poetry. At nineteen,
despite her great shyness, she became a maid of honor to Queen Henrietta
Maria. In this capacity, she met William Cavendish, then Marquis of Newcastle. They married in 1645; he was thirty-three years her senior. The Duke
was a learned man, a patron of poets, and a virtuoso, a friend of Descartes
and Hobbes.

The Duke and his Lady lived happily at Welbeck Abbey after the Restoration, but during the Civil Wars and the Commonwealth the Duke was in
financial peril. He had left England after the battle of Marston Moor and
spent most of the interregnum at Antwerp. The Duchess, who met her husband at Paris, returned to London in 1652 to attempt the compounding of his
estates. It was at that time that she resumed writing poetry. She continued
in Holland, where the Duke entertained many notable visitors in politics and
the arts. The frontispiece of Lady Newcastle's *Natures Pictures* shows her
and her husband, crowned with laurel, sitting at a table with the Duke's sons
and daughters. It provides a fair picture of the congenial literary readings
and conversations that they shared.

In 1676, a commemorative volume of *Letters and Poems* in praise of Margaret Newcastle was published, with pieces by Thomas Shadwell, Henry More,
George Etherege, and Jasper Mayne.

Analysis

Seventeenth century volumes of poetry as diverse as George Herbert's *Temple*, Mildmay Fane's *Otia Sacra*, and Robert Herrick's *Hesperides* have general but significant organizing principles. This is quite clearly the case with
Poems and Fancies, despite its being very poorly printed by a craftsman who
was puzzled by the state of the manuscript and was pressed to get the book
out before the writer left England to rejoin her exiled husband. Margaret
(writers so designate her not in a spirit of condescension but to distinguish
her from her husband, Sir William) intersperses, throughout the book, transition pieces called "claspes" intended to join one section to the next. As for
"Poems," these are verse-treatises on the atomistic structure of matter which
establish the writer as a female virtuoso (one conversant in a disinterested,
amateur way with the sciences and fine arts), followed by moral discourses
including complaints about man's misuse of the world that God has placed
under his stewardship; and descriptive pieces on, for example, dispositions
to mirth and melancholy. Halfway through the work the heading "Fancies"
ushers in verses on fairies and elegiac pieces. The "claspes" do more than

divide the volume into sections. Their main function is to allow the Duchess to explain her poetic temperament or cast of mind, her reasons for writing, her disdain for niceties of poetic style, and the primacy of the intellectual content of her own verses.

In her solitary apartment, where few were brave enough, in 1652, to visit the wife of a royalist general, she wrote quickly as the thoughts were generated in her original, thoroughly idiosyncratic, and nimble intellect. Some of her explanations are attempts to justify a woman's audacity in writing poetry. Lady Newcastle is primarily concerned, however, not with what others think of her but with contemporary notions of poetry, particularly philosophical verse, narratives, and lyrics. One must focus not only on her "claspes" but also on the prefatory matter to *Poems and Fancies* in order to understand the diverse body of poetry that she produced.

Commendatory poems by her husband and his brother Charles Cavendish (Margaret's companion in London in 1652) are on the surface fulsome praises but really "harmless mirth": lighthearted punning and sprightly humor. The Cavalier and his Lady do not take themselves so seriously as to pose as national heroes or great poets. For a fit audience of like-minded readers, affable modesty and whimsical self-deprecation mark the prefatory verses. In what other spirit could one take the Duke's assertion that his wife's writings will set the ghosts of Edmund Spenser, William Shakespeare, and Ben Jonson into fits of jealous weeping? The Duchess does indeed lay claim to fame, which she frankly desires for the variety of her fancies, her manifold curiosities about the workings of nature, and the scope of her subject matter. As a female writer, she is very much aware of her uniqueness. She notes that ordering fancies is a similar kind of economy to that which women need to run households, and that verse, being fiction, is recreative to the spirit, wholesomely entertaining, and ingenuous. One part of a poetess' contribution to her readers is in defeating male sterotypes regarding female propensities to idleness, gossip, and slander.

"Fancies" is an important word to the Duchess; her usage of the word can be understood in relation to the Baconian contrast between imagination and reason. The former produced pleasant delusions, sprightly ingenuity, and alacrity of imaginings. Francis Bacon gave poetry faint praise, and the notion that fancy must be disciplined by judgment was a strong one. Lady Newcastle's own version of this dictum, stated in the "claspes," may be her emphasis on matter as opposed to niceties of style. In general, however, she is content with her fancies as a kind of self-improving, "harmless mirth," a magnanimous way for a studious and shy woman to pass the time. The Duchess had a reputation (see Samuel Pepys and Dorothy Osbourne) for eccentricity and arrogance. The prefatory materials in *Poems and Fancies*, however, suggest a writer who makes no great claims for her own poetic abilities. As with the Cavalier poets whose conventions she borrows and with whom she shares political and social as well as aesthetic values, a mind-muse analogy develops. The poetry provides recreation and reflects the amiable, benevolent disposition of the writer. In this spirit the Duchess follows Robert Herrick and Mildmay Fane with a whimsical allusion to her book as her child. As an introduction, the conceit is in her case as apt as it is conventional.

The Duchess' treatment of atoms is somewhat indebted to Bacon's new rationalism and to the encyclopedic categorizing of the phenomenal world by Guillaume du Bartas and William Davenant. The latter's metaphors from applied and theoretical sciences are similar to some of Margaret's "similizing." Her diction and iambic pentameter rhymed couplets provide a sensible framework for discursive exposition, but she does not indulge in much analysis. Atomism is merely the trapping for fanciful description, which in itself is similar to du Bartas' quaint and fantastic compilations. For example, she avers that plants are made up of branched atoms, with hooks that pull the tendrils upward from the roots. Healthy atoms are in tune with one another, like people dancing to harmonious music. Aged atoms slow down and finally move no more; this is the state of death. Sharp, arrowlike atoms make up fire; they can soar upward, while the atoms that cohere to form earth are flat and square, heavy and phlegmatic. Thus the Duchess mixes an ancient notion (the four elements) with the modern, empirical one of Thomas Hobbes (a personal friend of the Newcastles with whom Sir William held lengthy discussions).

Lady Newcastle lives in the "divided and distinguished worlds" of which Sir Thomas Browne wrote. John Donne and John Milton lived there too, but while their inconsistencies involved seeing God's signatures in the real world (however empirically, up to a point, they were willing to observe it), the Duchess' inconsistencies concern not nature and spirit, but nature and fancy. She ingenuously tells the reader that she has not read much Hobbes, Descartes, or Bacon, that her poems were written hastily and not revised to conform with what she read or recalled from her reading. She was fascinated with atomism, however, and was concerned with it throughout *Poems and Fancies*. In one place, she uses a "claspe" to explain that various atoms acting at cross-purposes within the human body are the work of mischievous fairies. The body's animal spirits can be similar tiny creatures working in nerves, muscles, and organs as the various races of mankind do in different parts of the earth, trafficking with one another through veins and arteries. This leads to the Duchess' version of the "metaphysical" metaphor of the body as a map and to other speculations bred of Renaissance skepticism. Her imagination is especially taken with microscopic convolutions of nature and with the perfections attainable within the smallest parameters of nature and art. Jonson and Herrick had similar interests. Although the Duchess cannot match their perfections in imagery or verse rhythms, she shares their imaginative empathy. "A World in an Eare-Ring" supposes a universe suspended invisibly from a lady's ear. The poem envisions a grand panorama of mortal existence: great storms and their chaos, mountains, gardens and cities, and an entire cycle of life forms, all revolving around the center or hole in the ring.

Lady Newcastle's atomism was undergoing revision as she was writing *Poems and Fancies*. In 1653, she published these revisions, alluded to on the last page of her first book, in a duodecimo volume entitled *Philosophicall Fancies*, revised two years later as *Philosophical and Physical Opinions*. Here, in a mixture of prose and verse, she is concerned with matter and motion, the former being infinite while the latter is the agent which changes the form of matter. She also deals with causes of sunlight, diseases, tides, and God as first cause. Extravagant fancies regarding sublunary worlds different from earth and beyond human control predominate. She speculates that rational spirits might so change the laws of physics as to animate trees into deer and make mermaids of water lilies.

Lady Newcastle's moral discourses are dialogues between, for example, nature and man, wit and beauty, peace and war, and discourses on love, poverty, and humility. Some of her best poetry occurs here, concerned with faculty psychology, man's stewardship of God's creation, and the humanitarian and compassionate principles which underlie nobility. For the more discursive of these verses, her predecessors would be Samuel Daniel (*Musophilus*, 1599), Fulke Greville's treatises on fame, honor, and war, and George Chapman (*Euthymiae Raptus*, 1609). For the dramatic and narrative efforts, Edmund Spenser's didactic fables, Milton's *Il Penseroso* (1645), and perhaps George Wither's and Michael Drayton's works are analogues (not, it should be noted, sources). If indeed the Duchess knew the work of these poets, it probably would have been by hearing them read rather than by close study. She was a sporadic reader, and even in childhood, she liked writing not only more than traditional feminine accomplishments such as deportment and snippets of foreign languages but also more than reading. Her widowed mother lovingly indulged these preferences.

Three of the moral discourses have considerable merit. "A Dialogue of Birds" has an effective dramatic framework: various species talk of their experiences with mankind. They speak plainly and pathetically of their sufferings brought about by man's artful cruelties, not by nature's regime, however harsh. In fact, this poem, the one on the hare, and the fairy verses suggest the folk art which John Broadbent (in *Poets of the Seventeenth Century*, 1980) attributes to her and her husband. The poem is well organized, beginning with the lark's song and ending, after a horrific recital of suffering, with the birds settling their families in their nests, and finally singing a communal hymn, the birdsong softly fading as they fall asleep. The theme of the poem is Art's perversion of Nature, which is herself benevolent and informed by love. The birds pose the question of the root of man's viciousness; they have no answer, but portray—by citing their own mistreatment—human aggression hidden under universally accepted behavior which passes for custom and sport. With that, they turn from what they cannot prevent to practical concerns such as nest-building. The rhetorical device at work here, *prosopopoeia*, was brought to perfection by Spenser, and Lady Newcastle uses it well.

"The Hunting of the Hare" is successful in the same way. It is even more accurate in its detail of the animal's furtive movements and instinctual strategies for self-preservation. The poet's personification of the animal's innocence and despair as the hounds surround him incites pathos. The theme, once again, is man's willful ignorance of the suffering he causes and his prideful desecration of nature. Margaret's humanitarianism in these and other narratives is as revealing a part of her sensibility as are her introductory verses.

"A Dialogue Between Mirth and Melancholy" was noticed favorably in the eighteenth century (in a witty sketch in *The Connoisseur*, 1774), and in the nineteenth century by Benjamin Disraeli and Leigh Hunt. They appreciated the pastoral descriptions reminiscent of *L'Allegro* (1645) and *Il Penseroso*, but the most pervasive feature is the care with which the two states of mind are balanced against each other. Notably, the Duchess, who loved retirement, lets Melancholy have the last word. It is a "white" melancholy, like that which Herrick sometimes delineates, agreeable and clean. The pleasures of retirement allow sadness to be refined away by the Duchess' guiding principle of the good life, fancy. In these verses she avoids the extravagances which mar so much of her work, including "The Hunting of the Stag," another humanitarian work, which is no sooner under way than a lengthy catalog of trees intrudes.

The Duchess' fairy poetry constitutes a microcosm of all of her concerns. In a prose introduction she justifies the existence of fairies on the basis of recent scientific discoveries about invisible but potent natural forces. As usual, these speculations resolve themselves into fanciful explanations: if air moves ineluctably through walls, fairies can invisibly go where they will. In "The Fairy Queen" Margaret spends nearly the entire poem describing the habitat of fairies, which she places in the center of the earth. She brings in the elements, the movements of the earth, and the circulation of the waters. Her humanitarianism is also evident. In the microcosm of the fairies' world, the god of love is not Cupid but the goddess Natura, a female generative principle which gives Queen Mab control over the spirit world and extends motherly beneficence to all creatures. The Duchess' interest in folklore and custom can best be seen in "The Pastime of the Queen of Fairies." This rings the changes on Hobgoblin's pranks and is very close to the speeches of William Shakespeare's Puck. Throughout all these verses one senses a preoccupation with miniature gem-like beauties, which only those with refined perceptions and respect for fancy can appreciate. The order of the universe can be seen in the order of minutest nature. The fairy verses in which some anthologists find the most attractive images (because of the succinctness with which they are stated) are in a collection of fragments, *Plays Never Before Printed* (1668).

The sources for all these poems are—in addition to Shakespeare—Michael Drayton and Herrick, writers who use this kind of pastoral without any didactic intentions, but for the ingenious play of the imagination. Newcastle's mushroom table with its dish of ant's eggs is from Herrick, as are the glowworm's eyes, used as lanterns, and snakeskin used as decoration. Mab's chariot made from a nutshell recalls Mercutio's speech in *Romeo and Juliet* (1594-1596). The differences between the Duchess' verses and those of her great predecessors lie in their verbal music and their more striking juxtapositions of the familiarity of our world with the mysteriousness of the fairies' world.

In Margaret's elegiac and lyric verses, subjects are female: their beauty, their love, their griefs, their deaths. Some of these are given the general heading of "A Register of Mournful Verses." The two most ambitious deal with a "melting beauty" whose body turns to ice and melts into the funeral urn of her loved one, and with another "mourning beauty" from whose tears flowers with bowed heads grow, and for whom the stars become fellow mourners lighting her way to the gravesite. The gods transform her into a comet. The imagery in the second of these elegies is effectively emblematic, although strained with macrocosm-microcosm analogies. The poem is well unified in its symbolic representation of universal gestures and attitudes of grief, and of grief's fateful consequences. In both poems one senses woman's isolation, and the psychological effects of the single emotion of black melancholy on the human mind. For this, Seneca is an exemplar, as Ovid is for the mysterious transformations of the women, which suggests in Margaret's work the principles of natural benevolence set forth in some of the dialogues. These and the Duchess' other elegies, especially those for a bereaved mother and for her deceased daughter, would be well complemented by emblems. Her final elegy, on her brother, is in a similar vein, attempting emotional heightening with metaphoric emblems: her heart is a sacrifice, her sighs are incense, her thoughts mourners. A mythic universality is attempted, or, more accurately, strained after. The opening and closing lines, however, are in an affecting plain style; their commonplaces about honor and fame do not spoil them.

According to the Renaissance definition, an elegy need not be limited to verses on death; it could be any serious meditative poem. A large number of the Duchess' poems might be so designated. In her short lyrical pieces, she can focus more exclusively on her "similitudes." The effects are often bizarre; her formlessness and extravagance are all too evident. A sad lover's heart becomes meat for nature's dinner. If Dame Nature has any appetite left, Margaret presents her with a "bisque" made from a young female's broad forehead, rosy cheeks, white breasts, and swan-like neck. Another conceit involves "Similizing the Heart to a Harp, the Head to an Organ, the Tongue to a Lute, to make a consort of Musique." Another compares the world of the sea to an Arcadia in which the ocean is a country green, the mast a maypole, and the sailors shepherds.

The Duchess' conceits often defy classification into Petrarchan, metaphysical, or plain (or eloquent) style. One wishes she were a bit more discreet, less spontaneously prolific, and perhaps a greater reader, like some lettered contemporaries: Lady Bedford; Lady Mary Wroth; Margaret Countess of Cumberland; Lady Falkland or her daughter-in-law, Letice Morison; or even Dorothy Osbourne, who thought her mad for attempting to write, and especially to publish, poetry. Had she been only a patroness of writers, or a letter-writer, however, she would not have been the self-possessed and courageous innovator that she was.

Jay A. Gertzman

Other major works

FICTION: *Natures Pictures*, 1656 (prose and verse).

PLAYS: *Plays*, 1662; *Plays Never Before Printed*, 1668.

NONFICTION: *The Worlds Olio*, 1655; *Philosophical Letters*, 1664; *CCXI Sociable Letters*, 1664; *The Life of William Cavendish, Duke of Newcastle*, 1667; *Grounds of Natural Philosophy*, 1668.

Bibliography

Blaydes, Sophia B. "Nature Is a Woman: The Duchess of Newcastle and Seventeenth Century Philosophy." In *Man, God, and Nature in the Enlightenment*, edited by Donald C. Mell, Theodore E. D. Braun, and Lucia M. Palmer. East Lansing, Mich.: Colleagues Press, 1988. Blaydes demonstrates how Cavendish went against the grain of male Enlightenment philosophy and established her own view of nature as a female. The book contains a useful index and a bibliography. Suitable for all students.

Grant, Douglas. *Margaret the First: A Biography of Margaret Cavendish, Duchess of Newcastle, 1623-1673*. London: Hart-Davis, 1957. The best biography of Margaret Cavendish. Grant includes illustrations and a bibliography of the Duchess' literary works. Appropriate for all students.

Mendelson, Sarah Heller. *The Mental World of Stuart Women: Three Studies*. Amherst: University of Massachusetts Press, 1987. Mendelson discusses how seventeenth century society and customs in England affected the lives of three women: Aphra Behn, Mary Rich, Countess of Warwick, and Margaret Cavendish, Duchess of Newcastle. Contains an index and a bibliography, and is suitable for all levels of students.

Paloma, Dolores. "Margaret Cavendish: Defining the Female Self." *Women's Studies* 7 (1980): 55-66. Paloma describes how Cavendish was one of the first women to write poetry, philosophy, and plays as freely as men did. Yet, in order to avoid serious censure, she had to work under the conceit that she was not a serious writer.

Perry, Henry Ten Eyck. *The First Duchess of Newcastle and Her Husband as Figures in Literary History.* Boston: Ginn, 1918. Perry's early study was reprinted in the late 1960's. It is a useful work that shows how, although the Duchess and her husband pretended to be amateurs writing inconsequential verses, they deserve a place in the canon of important British poets. Appropriate for most students.

LORINE NIEDECKER

Born: Near Fort Atkinson, Wisconsin; May 12, 1903
Died: Near Fort Atkinson, Wisconsin; December 31, 1970

Principal poetry

New Goose, 1946; *My Friend Tree*, 1962; *North Central*, 1968; *T&G: The Collected Poems, 1936-1966*, 1968; *My Life by Water: Collected Poems, 1936-1968*, 1970; *Blue Chicory*, 1976; *The Granite Pail: The Selected Poems of Lorine Niedecker*, 1985; *From This Condensery: The Complete Writing of Lorine Niedecker*, 1985.

Other literary forms

Although known primarily for her poetry, Lorine Niedecker also wrote radio plays, creative prose, and reviews. "As I Lay Dying" condenses and adapts William Faulkner's novel of the same title, and "Taste and Tenderness" centers on William, Henry, and Alice James. "Uncle," "Untitled," and "Switchboard Girl," local-color sketches, provide insight into Niedecker's family background, work experiences, and philosophy, and her reviews of the poetry of Louis Zukofsky and Cid Corman reveal Niedecker's poetics. Of her letters, which Zukofsky early praised as her best writing, her ten-year correspondence with Corman has been published, and her thirty-year correspondence with Zukofsky rests at the Humanities Research Center at the University of Texas, Austin.

Achievements

Niedecker has proved that a twentieth century American writer does not have to travel far or have exotic experiences to be able to present her culture objectively and honestly. Although in her poetry, spring floods buckle her floors and breed water bugs under her hooked rugs, the waters also reminded her of life's constant flux and helped her avoid becoming static and rootbound. Relying primarily on the past, nature, and long-distance support from a few fellow poets, she overcame the fragmentation and materialism of which so many twentieth century artists complain and to which they often succumb. Sincerity, hard work, and isolation from fame have helped earn for her a reputation as the twentieth century's Emily Dickinson. In 1978, her home state recognized her achievements by awarding her the Notable Wisconsin Writers Award.

Biography

Born on May 12, 1903, on Blackhawk Island, near the Rock River and Lake Koshkonong, three miles from Fort Atkinson, Wisconsin, Lorine Niedecker, the only child of commercial fisherman Henry E. Niedecker and his swamp-bound housewife Theresa Daisy Kunz Niedecker, never grew far from her roots. Niedecker was educated in Fort Atkinson and Beloit, where she went to Beloit College to study literature from 1922 until 1924. Returning home because her mother was becoming increasingly deaf, Niedecker married Frank Hartwig in 1928, but the couple separated in 1930 when Hartwig defaulted on a loan and lost their house. Niedecker assisted in the Dwight Foster Public Library during this period. From 1928 until 1942, she worked in Madison for the Works Progress Administration's state guide as a writer and research editor, exploring the early history of her region. She began writing radio plays during the 1930's, her interest leading her in 1942 to a brief job as scriptwriter at station WHA in Madison. She returned that year to Blackhawk Island and in 1944 began work as a stenographer and proofreader at Hoard's Dairyman, publishers of a national journal, remaining there until 1950. Her mother, completely deaf, died in 1951, and her father, in 1954. Niedecker inherited two houses on Blackhawk Island and spent some time overseeing her property while living in a small cabin nearby, which she had built in 1947; then she scrubbed floors and cleaned the kitchen at the Fort Atkinson Memorial Hospital from 1957 until 1962. In mid-1960, she started keeping company with Harold Hein, a widowed dentist and amateur artist who spent his Christmas holidays in Florida and did not want to remarry. The couple spent most of their weekends together, driving north to Manitowish Waters in June, 1961, and reading together the Thomas Jefferson-John Adams correspondence. One of Niedecker's most valued gifts from Hein was a birdfeeder, which attracted so many birds that the poet said she would have to hire a birdsitter to keep it full of seeds while she was at work. During the fall of 1962, Hein visited Niedecker less often, and in spring, 1963, she met Albert Millen, a housepainter from Milwaukee, to whom she was married on May 24, 1963, and with whom she moved to a run-down part of that city. When her husband retired, they built a two-and-a-half-room cabin on Blackhawk Island and spent most of their time there, although they traveled briefly to South Dakota and around Lake Superior. Niedecker died, on December 31, 1970, where she was born.

Niedecker began writing early but published little until late in life. She mentions an ode to Lake Koshkonong written in high school, and her first published poem appeared in her high school annual, *The Tchogeerah*, in 1922. Her poems were printed in literary journals in 1928, and in 1933 several appeared in *Poetry*. In the early 1930's, she initiated correspondence with Louis Zukofsky, who would become one of her mentors and friends. She exchanged visits and gifts with the Zukofsky family and from Louis she learned about condensation, reliance on folk dialogue, rejection slips, and publication procedures. Her first book eventually appeared in 1946. In 1960, she began to correspond with Cid Corman, who published many of her poems in his influential magazine *Origin* and who recorded her only known poetry reading a few weeks before she died. In the late 1950's and into the 1960's, she wrote many poems to Zukofsky's violinist son, Paul, and finally, in the late 1960's, when she published three volumes of poetry, she began to be recognized by a wide audience. She left three finished manuscripts, which were included in her complete writings in 1985. All of her poems, most brief and many untitled, have been arranged chronologically in *From This Condensery* and divided into seven major sections: "Early Poems," "For Paul and Other Poems," "The Years Go By," "In Exchange for Haiku," "Home/World," "North Central," and "Harpsichord and Salt Fish."

Analysis

In her review of the poetry of Louis Zukofsky, Lorine Niedecker quotes William Carlos Williams: "You cannot express anything unless you invent how to express it. A poem is not a freudian 'escape' (what childishness) but an adult release to knowledge, in the most practical, engineering manner." Niedecker used her poetry to invent herself, to discover her own wholeness. This quest for wholeness has been a persistent theme in the writing of American women since the time of Margaret Fuller. A glass cutter of words, Niedecker discards traditional poetic modes of expression *en masse*, yet selects those devices which best help her construct small stained-glass pieces, later combining some of these reflective objects into longer poems. She trims her glasslike achievements often, arranges them variously, and finally creates two outstanding large pieces: "Wintergreen Ridge" and "Paean to Place." Niedecker appropriates glass of many colors from several sources: the men and women whom she knew and read about, American society during her lifetime, nature, and art.

Of the men and women whom she knew, her father and mother engaged her most fully. In her early poems, she depicts her father building and losing houses, rocking in his chair, seining to finance his daughter's education, and wondering about the meaning of life. In "For Paul," she recalls her father's description of a warm Thanksgiving Day when he helped seine twenty thousand pounds of buffalo fish by moonlight. Other times, his "hands glazed/ to the nets." In "The Years Go By," she recalls "mild Henry" as "absent" and describes him as a catalpa tree, serene, refusing "to see/ that the other woman, the hummer he shaded/ hotly cared/ for his purse petals falling—/ his mind in the air." Niedecker also pictures her father planting trees and burying "carp/ beneath the rose" after he lost his wife. She continues that "he opened his wine tank" to "bankers on high land," wanted "his only daughter/ to work in the bank" but had left her a "source/ to sustain her—/ a weedy speech." In "North Central," she again writes of the trees her father planted, "evenly following/ the road." She walks beside them on New Year's Day and each one speaks to her: "Peace." Niedecker's father learned the "coiled celery," "duckweed," and "pickerelweeds" of the swamp but "could not/ —like water bugs—/ stride surface tension/ He netted/ loneliness." He sat rocking at

night "beside his shoes," "Roped not 'looped/ in the loop/ of her hair."
Hard work, serenity, unhappiness in marriage, planting, swamp, rocking: These
scattered details kaleidoscope into Niedecker's benediction for her father:
Peace.

Niedecker has more trouble coming to terms with her mother. The annual
spring floods soak the floors, pump, washing machine, and lilacs of "the
woman moored to this low shore by deafness," who has wasted her life in
water. Niedecker's deaf mother contradicts herself, wishing she could hear,
then complaining about "too much talk in the world." With "big blind ears"
under "high" hair, a husband with "leaky boats," a writer daughter who
"sits and floats," Niedecker's mother dies with "a thimble in her purse," her
last words urging her daughter, "Wash the floors, Lorine!/ Wash clothes!
Weed!" Daisy Niedecker parks uncharacteristically in "her burnished brown
motorless automobile," "She who wheeled dirt for flowers" waiting to be
buried in ground in which "She could have grown a good rutabaga." Daisy
grew up in marsh land, Niedecker later explains, "married mild Henry/ and
then her life was sand." Daisy, tall and thin, "took cold on her nerves," built
the fires with the wood she chopped, helped rebuild a burned house, gave
"boat" instead of birth to her daughter in the flooding spring, and philos-
ophized: "Hatch, patch and scratch,/ that's all a woman's for/ but I didn't
sink, I sewed and saved/ and now I'm on second floor."

Snow on branches later reminds Niedecker of the cotton that her mother
"wore in her aching ears," her hard work, and her protectiveness. She calls
her mother a "distrait wife," a "thorn apple bush,/ armed against life's raw
push." Niedecker tells Kenneth Cox, however, that her mother had a "rhyming, happy" father and spoke "whole chunks of down-to-earth (o very earthy)
magic." In "Wintergreen Ridge," which she considers her best poem, Niedecker remembers how her mother loved "closed gentians/ she herself/ so
closed" and identifies with her in "Paean to Place," saying they both were
born "in swale and swamp and sworn/ to water." A wealth of autobiographical material follows. Her father "sculled down" and saw her mother, who
was playing the organ but who later stopped, turned "deaf/ and away." Daisy
"knew boats/ and ropes," helped Henry "string out nets/ for tarring," and
"could shoot." Niedecker mourns the fact that her mother could not hear
canvasbacks take off and sora rails sing, and she wonders if she giggled
when she was a girl. Her question underscores the somber light in which she
sees her mother, the assonating *o*'s in "the woman moored to this low shore,"
and the following poem sustaining this sober mood:

> Hear
> where her snow-grave is
> the *You* ˎ
> 　　*ah you*
> of mourning doves

Her father, from upcountry, contemplating the stars, drawing fish from water, plants from land, rocking, lonely, wants his daughter to move to high ground. Her mother, from the swamp, enduring floods, protecting her family, closing gradually into total silence, ridicules her husband's "bright new car," declaring, "A hummingbird/ can't haul." Niedecker alternates between swamp and upland, but resides primarily in the former.

From this fragmented relationship, Niedecker must wrest her wholeness, which she does partly by observing other men and women from the present and the past. Her early poems depict her male contemporaries as J. Alfred Prufrock-like: posturing, ineffectual, directionless, out of touch with reality. Some play cards instead of chopping wood; one "strolls pale among zinnias." She later describes a prospective employer as "Keen and lovely," graceful, cultured, kind, but he does not hire her. She mentions the men who carefully build weapons to irradiate others; businessmen smoking cigarettes, leaving droppings/ larger, whiter than owls'," wearing time on their wrists, wool on their bodies, making money unscrupulously and demanding to be "jazzed" for which they pay in "nylons." She dislikes a "clean man," prefers one who falls while fishing in muddy water, "dries his last pay-check/ in the sun, smooths it out/ in *Leaves of Grass*." Niedecker mentions few modern examples of complete men.

In the past she finds many men whom she admires: John James Audubon, Michel-Guillaume-Jean de Crèvecoeur, Thomas Jefferson, John Adams, Michelangelo, William Morris, Charles Darwin, Carolus Linnaeus, Vincent van Gogh. Men who value the earth, the arts, solitude, exploration, plants, creation, equality, and humanity appeal to her. Poems on great men are sprinkled through her writing, ranging from an early short poem written from van Gogh's point of view to a long, late poem on Darwin. She compares Aeneas and Frédéric Chopin, observing that Aeneas "closed his piano/ to dig a well thru hard clay," whereas "Chopin left notes like drops of water." She ends this brief poem with Aeneas' words to Chopin: "O Frederic, think of me digging below/ the surface—we are of one pitch and flow." The high/low dichotomy which separated her parents is erased by these great men, who cooperate to bring harmony to the world. The examples supplied by great men also help Niedecker choose a partner from among her contemporaries, a man she chooses for "warmth."

Lacking models of great women from both present and past, Niedecker must create herself from within. She first deals with the female models which surround her. In her early poetry, she ridicules a lady wearing a leopard coat for being directionless and scorns women who demand only money from men and become slaves to fashion. She describes a woman who "hooks men like rugs," "covets the gold in her husband's teeth," and would "sell your eyes fried in deep grief." She rhymingly itemizes the "needs" of women: "washers and dryers, . . . bodice uplift, . . . deep-well cookers, . . . power shift." She describes an office girl who "carries her nylon hard-pointed/ breast uplift/ like parachutes/ half-pulled" which "collapse" at night among all of her material possessions.

In contrast, she mentions in later poems famous women of the past. "Who was Mary Shelley?" she asks, who eloped, wrote her novel after Lord Byron and Percy Bysshe Shelley "talked the candle down," read Greek, Italian, and bore two children who died. Margaret Fuller "carried books/ and chrysanthemums/ to Boston/ into a cold storm." Abigail Smith, who according to her suitor John Adams had faults, such as hanging her head, reading, writing, thinking, and crossing her "Leggs/ while sitting," proved to be a faithful wife. Niedecker later writes that Abigail was an architect and artist, made cheese and raised chickens, talked as an equal with Jefferson, and wrote letters that both Adams and Jefferson appreciated.

In her early poems, Niedecker writes of refusing to admit excitement or pain, the former inconvenient and the latter too great. Writing to Zukofsky's son Paul, she tells how her feelings for the boy enable her to love more fully, and in "The Years Go By," she discusses, in a manner similar to Emily Dickinson's, the ebb and flow of sorrow. The central change in a woman's life, menopause, she describes as "hot fears" in "middle life" but says in "cool years . . . who'll remember/ flash to black?/ I gleamed?" Then she begins to look back at herself, examining a photograph and remembering her "young aloofness," her wish to stay "cool," the fact that she "couldn't bake." She also begins to express her discontent with her "black office," looking forward to her "three/ days of light: Saturday, Sunday,/ memory." In "Home/World," she says her life is "a wave-blurred/ portrait" and depicts herself as a "swamp/ as against a large pine-spread—." She becomes self-conscious: Out of ten thousand women dancing on skates, she is the only one who wears boots, she remarks. Much earlier she had praised the energy of women who could work, keep a house and children, go to church, and bowl, wondering what they would think if they knew how much energy she spent on her poetry. At the time of her marriage, she visits her family cemetery, recognizing and accepting that her family line ends with her: "but sonless/ see no/ hop/ clover boy to stop/ before me." The assonating *o*'s, which she reserves for special occasions, underscore the momentous solemnity of her recognition, the rhyming *e*'s focusing attention on her as an individual. Now she can speak of the peace her father's trees bring her and compare love to a leaf, all parts relating. In "Paean to Place," about which she expressed excitement to Kenneth Cox in 1969 and stated that his questions about her background inspired the poem, she traces her life: a "solitary plover," a seven-year-old with only two dresses, a visitor to the grave of her grandfather who delighted her with folk and nursery rhymes. She recalls her love for the boy who played the violin and says,

> O my floating life
> Do not save love
>   for things
>   Throw *things*
> to the flood

She ends "Paean to Place" by describing the "sloughs and sluices" of her mind "with the persons/ on the edge."

She also felt herself to be part of American society. She expressed her concern for the social ills of her day repeatedly, discussing such topics as poverty, hunger, religion, electricity, consumerism, traffic speeding, commercialism, hunting, plumbing, private property, war, and the `atom bomb. She opposed most modern conveniences and luxuries, pleased most with her "New-saved/ clean-smelling house/ sweet cedar pink/ flesh tint" with a "Popcorn-can cover" over a hole in her wall "so the cold/ can't mouse in." She often describes *things* in terms of people and animals, maybe trying to lessen their otherness, and enjoyed such creative activities as hooking rugs, quilting, sewing, and cooking. She stresses that becoming involved with the material world leads one to wake up at night and say to oneself,

> I'm pillowed and padded, pale and puffing
> lifting household stuffing—
> carpets, dishes
> benches, fishes
> I've spent my life in nothing.

Rejecting materialism and those elements of society which thrive on it, Niedecker is especially appalled at people's desecration of nature. The "ten dead ducks' feathers/ on beer-can litter" will be covered by snow, but when man exterminated the carrier pigeon without cause, he destroyed "cobalt/ and carnelian." One of her most vehement protests involves the quiet muskrat who swims "as if already/ a woman's neck-piece." A second stanza juxtaposes the image of "Nazi wildmen/ wearing women."

Most of her nature poetry, however, exudes harmony and peace. She writes of wild swans, sandhill cranes, pheasants, pink flamingos, curlews, canvasbacks, mergansers, and warblers. Willows and poplars, cherry trees and maples, pines and catalpas dot her work. Flowers from the wild sunflower to the blue chicory to water lilies blossom, and she notes that "men are plants whose goodness grows/ out of the soil." She is especially attuned to the seasons. In winter, she watches chunks of ice swim swanlike down the river and in March notices her

> Bird feeder's
>   snow-cap
>   sliding
>   off

April brings "little/ yellows" and frogs rattling in contrast to freight trains, whereas June is hot and sticky, "a lush/ Marshmushing, frog bickering/ moon pooling, green gripping." Waxwings stain berry branches red in July, while autumn nights force her to pull her curtains because the leaves have fallen, reminding Niedecker of tree toads and her starlight talks with a boy. October she considers to be the head of spring, which is in turn the body of the year. She notices small creatures: mites in rabbits' ears, dragonflies, gophers, crickets, and frogs which stop sounding because they have turned out their lights. Only occasionally does nature frighten her, as when she hears a muskrat eat frogs and mice outside her door and when she describes a late fall weed stalk as a rapist. Generally, Niedecker presents nature as a cherished friend and often uses nature images to describe people. She also talks of multi-stratified rocks, lichens which can pulverize granite, and mosses and horse-tails which outlived dinosaurs. People are composed of and interrelated with nature. The water lily exemplifies perfect order. In her longest poem, "Wintergreen Ridge," she calls wintergreen by its Indian name, pipsissewa, which literally means "breaks it into fragments." In no other part of life does Niedecker see the absence of fragments as in nature. Parts combine to make a whole, and her immersion in nature, evident throughout her poetry but especially in "Wintergreen Ridge" and "Paean to Place," helps her to recognize and to remember her own wholeness. As she wrote to Corman in 1969, "the lines of natural growth, of life, [were] unconsciously absorbed from foliage and flowers while growing up."

Niedecker drew on the life which surrounded her for her poetry, transforming life into art by filling her subconscious, leaving herself alone, then pulling out material for her poetry. The "lava" flowed only while she wrote; then came the discipline of forming and polishing her words. Her first collected poems show her awareness of the way her contemporaries have debased language, have deified slang and narrowed their vocabularies. She early recognizes her affinity for imagism and philosophy, describes her poetic inspiration rising like feathers and gas, and realizes that wealth for her is staying in one place and writing. She mentions several poets who have influenced her, showing what type of bird she would be if depicted by H. D., William Carlos Williams, Marianne Moore, Wallace Stevens, Louis Zukofsky, E. E. Cummings, and Charles Reznikoff. Bashō and Gerard Manley Hopkins also helped form her poetry. Intellectual influences include Plato, Marcus Aurelius, Gottfried Wilhelm Leibnitz, Emanuel Swedenborg, Ralph Waldo Emerson, and Henry David Thoreau. From these thinkers, she distilled mental rigor and a belief in the soul.

Niedecker, who created her poems from familiar people and surroundings, commented that she did not want her neighbors to know she wrote because she would lose some of her finest sources of language. She used both traditional and contemporary poetic devices to shape her work: rhyme of all types, varying rhythms, alliteration, assonance, consonance, juxtaposition. She experimented with both line and stanza length, revising, arranging, and rearranging her poems into different sequences. She took seriously her mother's final words to wash, scrub, and weed, and did just that to her poems, polishing them until they gleamed with meaning and clarity, compressing them until they yielded their intrinsic forms. Her work is alive because she grounded it thoroughly in life and because she encouraged it to grow and change as she did. Filled with fragments and whole poems, the work of Lorine Niedecker reminds one that wholeness is possible even amid a chaotic world.

Shelley Thrasher

Other major works

NONFICTION: *Between Your House and Mine: The Letters of Lorine Niedecker to Cid Corman, 1960-1970,* 1986.

Bibliography

Bertholf, Robert. "Lorine Niedecker: A Portrait of a Poet." *Parnassus: Poetry in Review* 12/13 (Winter/Spring, 1985): 227-235. Probably the best complete biographical sketch of Niedecker. Bertholf clearly places her in the context of the Objectivist poetry movement. Suitable for undergraduates as well as graduate students.

Heller, Michael. *Conviction's Net of Branches: Essays on the Objectivist Poets and Poetry.* Carbondale: Southern Illinois University Press, 1985. Niedecker is considered an Objectivist poet. These essays shed light on the nature and convictions of the Objectivists. Suitable for advanced undergraduate and graduate poetry students.

Pater Faranda, Lisa. "'Between Your House and Mine': The Letters of Lorine Niedecker to Cid Corman, 1960-1970." *Dissertation Abstracts International* 44 (February, 1984): 2474A. Pater Faranda annotates the correspondence between Niedecker and fellow poet Cid Corman, who was Niedecker's editor during the last years of her life. Their correspondence has a dramatic shape to it, because it begins before her marriage and ends just before her death. This study is for students who seek detailed knowledge of Niedecker's biography.

Penberthy, Jenny Lynn. "Lorine Niedecker and Louis Zukofsky: Her Poems and Letters." *Dissertation Abstracts International* 47 (October, 1986): 1326A. Objectivist poet Louis Zukofsky corresponded with Niedecker for forty years, and his ideas substantially influenced her work. She even wrote some collage poems incorporating quotations from his letters to her. An interesting study for advanced students.

Perloff, Marjorie. "Recharging the Canon: Some Reflections on Feminist Poetics and the Avant-Garde." *American Poetry Review* 15 (July/August, 1986):

12-20. Perloff discusses how Niedecker and other women poets, such as Susan Howe, operate in the male dominated world of poetry. She points out that Niedecker was the only woman in the Objectivist movement. As a result, she is rejected by the male poetry "establishment," yet, she is dismissed by the feminists as "a male-identified woman poet."

JOHN FREDERICK NIMS

Born: Muskegon, Michigan; November 20, 1913

Principal poetry

Five Young American Poets: Third Series, 1944 (with others); *The Iron Pastoral,* 1947; *A Fountain in Kentucky and Other Poems,* 1950; *The Poems of St. John of the Cross,* 1959, 1968, 1979 (translation); *Knowledge of the Evening: Poems, 1950-1960,* 1960; *Of Flesh and Bone,* 1967; *Sappho to Valéry: Poems in Translation,* 1971, 1979, 1990 (translation); *Selected Poems,* 1982; *The Kiss: A Jambalaya,* 1982; *The Six-Cornered Snowflake and Other Poems,* 1990; *Zany in Denim,* 1990.

Other literary forms

A distinguished translator, John Frederick Nims has been most acclaimed for *The Poems of St. John of the Cross* (1959; revised, 1968, 1979). He has, as well, translated Euripides' *Andromache* for a volume in *The Complete Greek Tragedies* published by the University of Chicago Press (1959) and has published a book of his translations from various languages, *Sappho to Valéry: Poems in Translation* (1971; revised, 1979, 1990). Nims has also edited a number of books, including *The Poem Itself* (with Stanley Burnshaw and others, 1960), *Ovid's Metamorphoses: The Arthur Golding Translation 1567* (1965), and *James Shirley's "Love's Cruelty"* (1980). In 1974, he put his experience as poet, translator, and teacher to work in *Western Wind: An Introduction to Poetry.* Many of Nims's essays on poetry and translation have been collected in *A Local Habitation: Essays on Poetry* (1985).

Achievements

Nims has made an important contribution to American letters through his multiple vocations as translator, critic, editor, and teacher, as well as poet. He deserves special praise for his translations, which are consistently remarkable for their sensitivity to the sound, form, and feeling of the originals. There is no way, of course, to measure his achievements as editor, scholar, and teacher, but it is safe to say that he brings the same care and hard work to these tasks as he does to his poems. He has received a number of awards for his work, including the Harriet Monroe Memorial Prize, 1942; the Guarantors' Prize, 1943; and the Levinson Prize, 1944, all from *Poetry: A Magazine of Verse*; and the Brandeis University Creative Arts Award, 1974. In 1978, he was chosen Phi Beta Kappa Poet at Harvard. Nims has also been the recipient of grants from the Fulbright Foundation, 1952-1953, and from the National Foundation for the Arts and Humanities, 1967. In 1991 he received the $10,000 Aiken Taylor Award for Modern American Poetry, awarded by the editors of *The Sewanee Review.*

His honors and awards aside, Nims is probably undervalued as a poet. If that is true, however, he is undervalued for the right reasons. For many years he has labored against the grain of contemporary American poetry. His classic lyricism has, no doubt, failed to move a good number of readers whose expectations of poetry have been shaped largely by poets seeking to break with the traditions Nims cherishes. His stature as a poet, then, must be measured more within the context and conventions of his own poems than by comparison with other poets, or in terms of the size of his audience. "It would be comfortable," Nims has said, "to have a large audience, honestly won. But it would be shameful for the writer to say anything less well than he knows how simply to gain more readers. Any [established poet] . . . could write something that would bring him a hundred readers for every one he has now. This would be a failure."

Nims may not have received the degree of recognition given to some of his contemporaries, but one thing is clear: his place in American poetry has been "honestly won," and no poet can claim more for himself than that.

Biography

Born in Muskegon, Michigan, John Frederick Nims attended a private high school in Chicago and spent two years at De Paul University before transferring to Notre Dame to take his B.A. degree, with a double major in English and Latin, in 1937. After taking his M.A. from Notre Dame in 1939, he taught there until 1958, with periodic excursions abroad to teach at the University of Toronto, 1945-1946, at Bocconi University in Milan, 1952-1953, and at the University of Florence, 1953-1954. While at Notre Dame, he did further graduate work at the University of Chicago, and in 1945 completed his Ph.D. in Comparative Literature, with an emphasis on the history and theory of Greek, Latin, French, and English tragedy; his special interest was the English stage of the sixteenth and seventeenth centuries. After leaving Notre Dame, he taught at the University of Madrid, 1958-1960; at Harvard, 1964, 1968-1969, and the summer of 1974; at the University of Illinois at Urbana, 1961-1965; at the University of Florida at Gainesville, 1973-1977; at Williams College, 1975; and at the College of Charleston, 1981. He taught, as well, at the Bread Loaf Writers' Conference, 1958-1971, and at the Bread Loaf School of English, 1965-1969. In 1945 he began a long association with the distinguished magazine *Poetry,* serving for some years as the magazine's principal editor. From 1965 until his retirement, between wanderings, he taught English at the University of Illinois at Chicago Circle.

Such formidable academic credentials might suggest a poet literary to the point of pedantry, but literary expertise and scholarship are only a part of the equipment that Nims brings to his poetry. In a review of Nims's second collection, *A Fountain in Kentucky,* Richard Wilbur described the "I" in

Nims's poetry as "no disembodied spirit" and surely no celebrant of the erudite and esoteric. On the contrary, says Wilbur, his

adventures are not extraordinary, and he lays claim to no out-of-the-way emotions. . . . He is a family man, and owns a cat and a dog. . . . Few poets so frankly exploit their day-by-day experiences. Few poets so cheerfully present us with a world so thoroughly mundane.

Wilbur's sketch is a good likeness of Nims the poet, husband, scholar, and father. Nims's poems make it plain that Bonnie Larkin, his wife of thirty-five years, and their six children have been as much a source of inspiration as any of the considerable number of great authors in whose work he is so well-versed. When, in "Love Poem," he pays playful tribute to "My clumsiest dear, whose hands shipwreck vases,/ At whose quick touch all glasses chip and ring," he addresses no Helen, but a flesh-and-blood wife. When, in "The Masque of Blackness," Nims deals with the untimely death of a child, the death of his own son George is a haunting presence between the lines. In joy or sorrow, the sensitive father, the grateful husband, the wry and unpretentious teacher in Nims's poetry is, more often than not, Nims himself, trying to give words to that life—sweet, bitter, and salty—that he shares with his family, his students, and his readers.

Analysis

"A poem," says John Frederick Nims (with help from Dylan Thomas), "should sing in its chains like the sea!" In an age that has witnessed a broadly based rejection of the apparent restrictions of traditional poetic forms and conventions, Nims has made a career of "singing in his chains," of asserting that a poet can be both traditional and contemporary and that modern experience can find expression within the conventions of the past.

In a preface to his first published collection of poems in the 1944 anthology *Five Young American Poets*, Nims laid down some rules for himself. The poem, he insists, is "no mere meringue of sentiment. The emotion it holds is like blood in a man's body, hot and throbbing throughout, but fastened in tight channels, never seen." Imagery should be "sudden, true, and daring," diction "simple and intense," making use of whatever word best serves the poem, be it "from cathedral service or tavern riot." As to structure, the poem requires something "Mozartean . . . something stronger and shapelier than the Debussy tinkle and Wagnerian yowl to which the freer forms of poetry incline." Overseeing the whole delightful, demanding procedure is "a prodding 'Why?' . . . the poet's angel."

A survey of Nims's long career reveals these rules consistently at work; and in all that time, that same angel of wonder has never left his side. His first book-length collection proclaimed something of his intentions in its very title, *The Iron Pastoral*—a dull gleam of a word, suggestive of hardness and of subways, beside a graceful, comfortable word, evocative of ordered wilderness, of forest and field a bit greener than life. The book provides ample introduction to Nims's skill at ordering contemporary experience within traditional forms. In "Movie," the neon marquees of movie theaters blink on in iambic pentameter:

> Making a stately crossword of the night
> New stars are rising, *Gem* and *Regent*. Soon
> Great *Tivoli* takes the heaven, rose and white,
> Blanching Orion and the dappled moon.

In "Elevated," commuter trains run "Among the badland brick, the domes of tar,/ The mica prairie wheeling in the sun," gondolas in a town that "three stories up . . . is Venice," where "Flowers of the wash in highland vineyards shine." There is something at first a bit unsettling in hearing heroic quatrains and alexandrines singing in this context, something a little startling in the final image of "Colt Automatic": "at the belt a rare and terrible angel." Once one realizes, however, that William Shakespeare and John Milton would, no doubt, have gotten around to "crossword" and "quarterback," "fluoroscope" and "Florida," had they lived on a few centuries more, one can delight in Nims's rare devices.

It is no surprise that the sonnet has not escaped Nims's attention in *The Iron Pastoral*. In fact, he includes a brief sonnet sequence entitled "Foto-Sonnets." Once again, Nims's title earns its keep: "Sonnet"—the verbal "snapshot" of another age, wed to a coy misspelling typical in a city of "ALL-NITE" diners and "WILE-U-WAIT" oil changes. In a skillful blend of Shakespeare, Petrarch, and Nims, these sonnets, like pictures in an album, preserve moments from a summer vacation in New England, mementos of Provincetown, of Cape Cod, and finally, of the return to the city, the tired travelers "wrapped in tatters of salt memory." There is a density to the poems of *The Iron Pastoral*, a weight of words that, at times, overburdens the line, squeezing out articles in the bargain. More often than not, though, rereading reveals a richness that, at first reading, the eye might have taken for overindulgence and a careful flexing of the meter that first struck the ear as strain.

In his next book, *A Fountain in Kentucky*, Nims works further with the sonnet sequence. The result, "The Masque of Blackness," is one of his finest and most admired poems. Taking as its controlling metaphor the Shakespearean adage that "all the world's a stage," this narrative sequence of ten sonnets deals with the birth, brief life, and death of a child, as experienced by his parents. As the story unfolds, "in very dead of winter:/ A rumor of new breathing by late spring" places the parents in a world suddenly unreal, "since not yet real to the child," a world in which "Whether they shifted vases, turned a page/ All seemed last-minute touches on a stage." The child is born to the exultant cry, "Up with the drowsy curtain"; but the exultation is short-lived. This play, for all its glad beginnings, unfolds as tragedy. "One day they learned that sorrow wore old tweed,/ That lounging disaster spoke a soft hello." The doctors are all polite pessimism; it is their role. The mother must play hers as well, "her tight fingers round a rubber lamb/ She brought to show them all: See he can play." Perhaps the most poignant sonnet in the sequence is the eighth:

> Because someone was gone, they bought a dog,
> A collie pup, black, orange, flashy white.
> He gnawed on table legs, troubled the rug;
> His growls and pokings varied the empty night.

The sadness here is not so much in the new pet's inadequacy to the task of filling the void left in the bereaved couple's life, as in their awareness of that inadequacy. What could this creature do "in that house, with that shadow there?/ Oh nothing. They knew that." By the end of the elegy, they have learned hard lessons about this play, this life, and learned "from many-roped backstage." They have been no mere observers, however much they may wish they had been no more than that.

Throughout, "The Masque of Blackness" is marked by intensity, quantitative keenness of rhythm, and an effective use of momentum and pause within and between the lines. Like many of Nims's poems, it is preceded by an epigraph. Nims is accused by some critics of being too scholarly, too literary, in his poems, and this particular epigraph, an unidentified quotation from the opening stage directions of one of Ben Jonson's masques, may seem to support such an accusation. There is, upon further reflection, another way to look at the matter. "The Masque of Blackness" works extremely well for what it sets out to be—an elegy. There is, at times, a surreal, at times a mundane rightness to the imagery, and a psychological truth to the narrative, that are accessible to the average reader. The poem is moving in itself, although that is not to say that additional information might not make its effect still sharper. The epigraph is from Jonson's *Oberon, the Fairy Prince* (1611) an entertainment written to commemorate the installation as Prince of Wales of young Prince Henry, son of James I and Queen Anne. The Prince himself appeared in the masque as a silent, unsmiling figure, "Oberon, the Faery Prince." The other masquers, in dance, poetry, and song, celebrate the virtues of this king-to-be. Less than two years later, the Prince was dead of typhoid. A child is thus the central character in a play in which he has no lines; suddenly it is plain why Nims chose this particular epigraph. What may have seemed a mere literary ornament actually contributes to the emotional impact of the poem.

Further, Prince Henry, an intelligent lad, was a special favorite of Jonson, and the poet took some responsibility for the boy's literary education. Could this relationship have failed to remind Jonson of the death a few years earlier of his own eldest son? Taken in retrospect, the words from Jonson's elegy on his son, "Farewell, thou child of my right hand, and joy;/ My sinne was too much hope of thee, lov'd boy," are a haunting presence in the masque of *Oberon*, and, by extension, in Nims's "Masque of Blackness." If the reader learns that Nims wrote his sonnet sequence soon after the death of his own infant son, the poem's effect is only further heightened. To be able to place his own experience into a sort of constellation of reference with the death of a prince and a seventeenth century father's grief over his lost son, and to do it with skill and tact, redeems Nims from any charges of pedantry or inaccessibility.

In Nims's *Knowledge of the Evening*, there are poems of Europe and the Old World, steeped in history: "Florence," "Reflections in Venice," "Catullus," "A Frieze of Cupids." Nims, however, is less concerned with writing a poetic travelogue than he is with making the point, so aptly put by John Ciardi, that "Pompeii is everybody's home town, sooner or later." One lives with the past, whether or not one wants to, whether or not one knows it. Those who built the rooms in Nims's "Etruscan Tomb" knew it, back "when tombs were salons for living!/ Nothing had ended, that was sure." The bright paintings on the tomb walls, the rich furnishings, the "chuckle of jugs" and "crooning copper," are celebrated in the poem's refrain: *"Oh alive and alive."* The presence of the past is a theme that runs through much of Nims's work; it receives special emphasis in *Knowledge of the Evening*.

Of Flesh and Bone presents Nims at work with a fine, witty chisel, at the neglected art of the epigram. These poems, over sixty in all, are a tribute to his sense of classic brevity and concision, but, perhaps more important, they are also a tribute to his wry sense of humor. In a poem that must have given him considerable satisfaction, he answers the more iconoclastic members of the "Avant-Garde":

> 'A dead tradition! Hollow shell!
> Outworn, outmoded—time it fell.
> Let's make it new. Rebel! Rebel!'
> Said cancer-cell to cancer-cell.

The "Philosopher," lost in hypothesis, comes in for some jibes: "He scowled at the barometer: 'Will it rain?'/ None heard, with all that pattering on the pane." That august figure, the "Visiting Poet," also receives a barb: " 'The famous bard, he comes! The vision nears!'/ Now heaven protect your booze. Your wife. Your ears." These are playful poems and largely beyond comment, except to say that in each of them lies a hard kernel of homely truth.

The Kiss offers proof that Nims has paid as careful attention to the movements and conventions within his own work as to the larger tradition he gratefully accepts. The book is subtitled *A Jambalaya*, the name of a spicy French Creole stew. The imagery is not wasted, for Nims has put together a well-seasoned mixture of traditional forms and new twists, of myth and science, of the ordinary and the fantastic, with, for good measure, a sprinkling of excellent translations. In short, the book is, indeed, a jambalaya of all that Nims has learned of the art of poetry. Further, the poems have one element in common—each is a variation on "the kiss," with its many implications, from the erotic to the metaphysical.

In "The Observatory Ode," Nims indulges in wordplay and metric fireworks to commemorate Percival Lowell (brother of Amy), poet and astronomer, and discoverer of the planet Pluto, who:

> walked high ground, each long cold Arizona night,
> Grandeurs he'd jot: put folk on Mars, but guessed a planet right,
> Scribbling dark sums and ciphers at white heat
> For his Pluto, lost. Till—there it swam!
> Swank, with his own P L for monogram.

The poem is an occasional piece, the Harvard Phi Betta Kappa poem for 1978. (Percival Lowell, Nims's note informs the reader, was Phi Beta Kappa Poet in 1889.) It ranges, however, far beyond that occasion to reflect upon the miracle of life here on this earth:

> Suppose we try
> —Now only suppose—to catch in a jar
> That palmful of dust, on bunsens burn till it flash,
> Could we, from that gas aglow, Construct the eventful world we know,
> Or a toy of it, in the palm? Yet our world came so: we are . . . dust of a dying star.

Despite protests, from Edgar Allan Poe and others, that scientific inquiry saps the magic from life, Nims proclaims that the more that is known about the Cosmos the more wonderful a poem it becomes. The crystal spheres have nothing on the Universe as man is coming to know it, "Heaven's gaudy trash," this Universe, "*such stuff as dreams are made on* . . . / Yet stuff to thump, to call a spade a spade on." "No heat like this," says Nims, "No heat like science and poetry when they kiss."

Not all the "kisses" in the collection are so all-encompassing, nor so suited to public occasions. There is a translation from Plato: "That was my very soul that stole to the lips in our kissing./ Thinking to pass—poor thing!— over from me into you." There is the charming "Daughter, Age 4":

> Came traipsing to my bed today:
> No other gave so much
> Rough-and-tumble tenderness,
> Was such a flower to touch.

Nims's sense of humor is as wry as ever and transforms a linguistic discussion of "kiss" into an exercise in delight, as he pauses to

think about *kiss.*
Ugly word in the mouth, with its—ouch!—little dental-
pick *k*;
Its vowel with no music at all, and that snake-hiss of *s*'s.
. . . Not a word the lips linger on lovingly,
Although meant to mean: lingering lips.

Through more than forty poems, however, Nims lingers more than lovingly over that very word, over its various echoes. His wordplay is as brilliant as ever, but he balances his more exuberant effects with a lovely mellowness of tone and expression that is simple, muted, and intimate. In "A Summer Love," he is on potentially dangerous ground—an ice-cream cone at the end of a love affair, a sure-enough invitation to utter sentimentality. Yet the poem is so tactful, so calmly measured, that the result is anything but sentimental:

So we part,
no gift but this . . .
Our melting present in a melting world . . .
A thing not meant to last. Nor get us far.
Call it a sort of rhyme for what we are.

Such simple, straightforward elegance puts to best use Nims's years of discipline and practice. This is lyricism, ripe, sure, "honestly won," anchored firmly in the present by the weight of the past, the "lively past" that, in Wilbur's words, the poet needs "as a means of viewing the present without provinciality and of saying much in little." Nims has made very good use of that "lively past." In an era that has witnessed a great deal of irreverence, if not open contempt, toward the traditions of English poetry, he and others like him—Wilbur, for example, and Howard Nemerov—have persevered to make poetry not a "barbaric yawp" nor a "realistic" laundry list of human experience, but an ordered index of possibilities, a wondering "sort of rhyme for what we are."

Richard A. Eichwald

Other major works

PLAY: *Andromache* in *The Complete Greek Tragedies*, 1959 (translation).

NONFICTION: *Western Wind: An Introduction to Poetry*, 1974, 1983; *A Local Habitation: Essays on Poetry*, 1985.

MISCELLANEOUS: *The Poem Itself*, 1960 (edited with Stanley Burnshaw and others); *Ovid's Metamorphoses: The Arthur Golding Translation 1567*, 1965 (edited); *James Shirley's "Love's Cruelty,"* 1980 (edited).

Bibliography

Ciardi, John. *Mid-Century American Poets.* New York: Twayne, 1950. Ciardi sets his article on Nims among fourteen others describing the lives and work of Ciardi's contemporaries in the middle of the twentieth century. This volume is one of the only biographical sketches available on Nims, and so is extremely valuable to anyone studying him.

Nims, John Frederick. "John Ciardi: The Many Lives of Poetry." In *John Ciardi: The Measure of the Man*, edited by Vince Clemente. Fayetteville: University of Arkansas Press, 1987. Nims reveals his poetic bias in his praise of Ciardi. He especially admires the fact that Ciardi was a man of the world who gave up his career to write. Ciardi's experience informed his poetry, which was rich and varied.

_____. *A Local Habitation: Essays on Poetry*. Ann Arbor: University of Michigan Press, 1985. Nims builds a clear picture of his philosophy of poetry in this collection of sixteen essays. He addresses both ancient and modern poets, from Ovid to Robert Frost. This book would be very helpful to any student of Nims's work.

_____. "The Poetry of Sylvia Plath: A Technical Analysis." In *Ariel Ascending: Writings About Sylvia Plath*, edited by Paul Alexander. New York: Harper & Row, 1985. Nims examines the technical expertise found in Plath's poetry, especially *Ariel*, and so reveals his own thoughts on poetic technique. He points out that Plath worked for years to master rhythm and sound in her poetry and to sharpen her skills in metaphor and simile.

Ray, David. "John Frederick Nims." In *Contemporary Poets*, edited by James Vinson and D. L. Kirkpatrick. 4th ed. New York: St. Martin's Press, 1985. Ray provides a concise sketch of Nims and his work. He points out that Nims is an urban poet influenced by a mystical Catholicism. The article contains an easy-to-read primary bibliography and a list of Nims's achievements. A good, quick overview.

JOYCE CAROL OATES

Born: Lockport, New York; June 16, 1938

Principal poetry

Anonymous Sins and Other Poems, 1969; *Love and Its Derangements,* 1970; *Angel Fire,* 1973; *The Fabulous Beasts,* 1975; *Women Whose Lives Are Food, Men Whose Lives Are Money,* 1978; *Invisible Woman: New and Selected Poems, 1970-1982,* 1982; *The Time Traveler: Poems, 1983-1989,* 1989.

Other literary forms

Joyce Carol Oates is best known as the author of many novels, including *them* (1969), which won her the 1970 National Book Award. She is also a respected short-story writer, a playwright, and the author of several hundred critical articles.

Achievements

Many of Oates's short stories have been honored by inclusion in *The Best American Short Stories* and the *O. Henry Awards Anthology;* she won a National Book Award for the 1969 novel *them.* In addition, Oates is a member of the American Academy of Arts and Letters and has received both a Guggenheim Fellowship and a National Endowment for the Humanities grant.

Biography

Joyce Carol Oates was born into a rural working-class family in Lockport, a town in upper New York State along the Erie Canal. She is the oldest of three children, with a brother five years younger and a sister, thirteen years younger, who has been institutionalized with autism since early adolescence. Oates' early memories are of the maternal family farm, with chickens, pigs, and fruit trees. The economic depression of the 1930's kept her father, Frederic Oates, from schooling, but his talents in art and music and his capacity for joy and hard work had a profound influence on his daughter. He introduced her to the sport of boxing and the thrills of flying; as a child she saw the world of male violence from the ringside and felt the thrill of flight in an open-cockpit plane. The landscapes and people of her childhood and her parents' childhood are re-created in her literary work.

Oates was graduated Phi Beta Kappa and class valedictorian from Syracuse University in 1960 with majors in English and philosophy. She earned a master's degree in English literature at the University of Wisconsin at Madison, where, in 1961, she met and married Raymond Smith. After a period of graduate study in Texas, she moved to Detroit, where she taught at the University of Detroit. The inclusion of one of her stories in a prizewinning collection, Martha Foley's *Best American Short Stories,* prompted Oates to make the decision to become a professional writer. She continued to teach and write, moving from Detroit across the Detroit River to Windsor, Ontario, where she taught at the University of Windsor until 1978. Throughout this period, she read steadily and deeply, especially the works of William Faulkner, Franz Kafka, Friedrich Nietzsche, Thomas Mann, Henry David Thoreau, and Fyodor Dostoevski, and a favorite writer, D. H. Lawrence. She was profoundly influenced as a child by Lewis Carroll's *Alice's Adventures in Wonderland* (1865) and *Through the Looking-Glass and What Alice Found There* (1871) and the trust in instinctive, intuitive knowledge those books inspired.

In 1978, Oates and her husband settled in Princeton, New Jersey, where she began to teach at Princeton University. Her typical daily schedule would include morning writing from eight o'clock until early afternoon followed by relaxation, music (like her father, she plays the piano well), and, on some days, teaching. Her evenings are given to reading unless she is absorbed by her writing. With her husband, she edits *The Ontario Review*, a journal of new writing. She is a popular speaker at colleges throughout the United States, and at poetry readings, her enthusiasm and energy delight her audiences. She has become, like Honoré de Balzac in nineteenth century France, a "secretary to the nation," observing and re-creating her vision of post-World War II America in an astonishing outpouring of brilliant literary work.

Analysis

Living in Detroit in the 1960's, Joyce Carol Oates saw the heart of American life in the automobile manufacturer's boast, "What is good for General Motors is good for America." The city, though, erupted into hellfires of riot, exposing its underside of poverty and rage. Perhaps these events triggered Oates's interest in the Great Depression of the 1930's, her parents' struggles, and photographs of poor people in the grip of economic forces they neither understood nor controlled. Attuned to the plight of helpless people, she observed rootlessness and frustration leading to family and civil violence. The smile of consumer society that gleams in advertising and movies covers a dark and dirty reality she cannot avoid. Her vision of America reveals a nation full of tragedy heading toward ever greater violence in public and private lives. With no religious message, but rather the stance of a witness, she reveals the difficulties of Americans trying to find love and peace in a culture that leads them toward death and destruction.

The second half of the twentieth century seems a magic time to her. With a sense of wonder, she observes the panorama of American lives: family patterns that veer from contentment to fear, hatred, and worse. Questions arise: How can one know what influence one has on another person? How can one know if the encounter means love? Why is love like a fall into an abyss? Also, love has a public and private nature. The constant movement in which Americans engage effaces the private nature of love. They see and feel others in motel rooms, airports, and gas stations as they travel and become veneer people, all smooth surface from which traces of their lives are wiped away easily. What happens to love between people under these conditions? How much of a relationship is need, and what does one have to offer? How do women and men survive? Oates's work addresses these questions and others like them.

Many thinkers have compared love, sexual love as well as mystical love, to death. Oates's second great theme, related to the theme of loving, concerns the feelings of the living about dying. People can raise their hands against themselves in suicide, or diminish their lives by inhuman, mute behavior or by attacks on the human and material world around them; the death of human community happens in unlivable inner cities. As individuals, people experience the death of the ego or separate self-consciousness and entrance to a transcendental state. Transcendence can come to the artist and the mystic, and perhaps also in sex and violence. Like the poet D. H. Lawrence, whom she admires deeply, Oates questions the truth of being and nonbeing in her exploration of the boundaries and limitations in human life. The unconscious mind has much to do with the experience of life and fear of death. Dreams mediate the worlds human beings inhabit.

A third feature of Oates's poetry is found in her eye for landscape and setting. Few poets can rival her ability to paint a memorable scene. The details glitter: highways, newspaper pages staining fingers with ink, a ripe pear, a rumpled bed, and a decaying city square become visions in the reader's mind. Ultimately, Oates's poetry displays a great love for the land and people to which she belongs—a gratitude for the "multitudinous stars" and forms around her. Behind the poetry lies a mind poised, certain, unafraid, and capable of communicating honestly the contours and colors of her time.

Like Rainer Maria Rilke, Lawrence, and other modernists, Oates sees love and sexuality as the center of being; the source of both physical and spiritual energy. This recognition does not make her a sentimental or romantic poet of love. Quite to the contrary, she expresses the difficulties, limitations, and ironies that love presents. Although love is the great transforming force that accompanies growth, it most often wears a tragic face. Her source for this bitter truth is the dark side of American family life: the frequency of divorce, the incidence of rape and murder, the homeless women and children. The modern poets she reveres—W. B. Yeats, Rilke, and Lawrence—share her view; their poetry celebrates the joy of sexuality but never omits the pain, despair, or sorrow of this fundamental experience. Rilke's mature poems "Love and Other Difficulties," for example, render the dark melancholy of love beautifully.

Love experiences certainly include joy, and Oates has written enchanting poems of intimacy. In the collection *Love and Its Derangements*, the poem "Loving" describes lovers cocooned in a balloon of gauze, breathed out and invisible, a warm sac that shelters the couple from the ordinary life of people in the street. An erotic poem, "In Hot May," tells of an influx of seeds blowing onto a brick floor. They "threaten/ to turn into voices or trees or human men" as they seek the surface of female skin. The poem "Sleeping Together" evokes the blurred calm rhythm of two bodies in harmony, "hips rocked by waves of sleep," all distinctions lost in an infinite light. Wave motions are symbolized by the stanza lines' indented pattern, which suggest regular and peaceful breathing.

Yet intimacy can jar the nerves. "What I Fear . . . " tells of sleeplessness when the lovers are alert, feeling separate, dull, and "newly derailed . . . In the silence after love." The fear of drowning in a merged identity assails the speaker in "Women in Love" from *Anonymous Sins and Other Poems*. "My arms pump/ high to keep/ from drowning." Love makes its way into a person's life, flowing like water, and, like water, can refresh and nourish or flood and destroy. The rhythm of moving from oneness to separation is depicted in the poem "Where the Shadow Is Darkest" from *Angel Fire*. The poem's lovers swing in and out of their unity, but where the shadow is darkest, they are merged.

Coming-of-age experiences of young women are an important part of Oates's vision; one of her finest novels, *Marya: A Life* (1986), captures the tumults, often violent, of this period of life. Falling in love provides the topic for a humorous poem "The Small Still Voice Behind the Great Romances." The young speaker is dominated by a need for drama, a sense that death must happen for life and growth to be possible. She wants to upset time, speed it up, "to see the reel run wild, the film/ torn off its track!—I needed to die/ so I fell in love." Death occurs in sexuality, and the poem concludes in wisdom: "I died only in moods/ and ascended again/ humanly." The speaker of "A Girl at the Center of Her Life" from *Anonymous Sins and Other Poems* experiences sex without love. In a field outside town, with a young man waiting for her in a car, she feels hate yet has no skill in confronting him. She fears the reaction of other people to her change. She is "A young girl, in terror not young,/ no colt now but a sore-jointed cow/ whose pores stutter for help, help."

Similar imagery of the small but furious voice of a woman standing in the center of a moment, wind or water at the speaker's feet, informs poetry in the voice of young married women. In "A Midwestern Song" a woman has recently left her family home for life with her husband. She is bored with love and "its anatomy" and cries out *"Why do they offer me nothing more? Is there/ nothing more?"* Her imagination is alive, but her voice is mute. "A Young Wife" from *Angel Fire* displays the emotions of a woman who circles "The two-and-a-half rooms of our marriage" like a fish in her scummy fish bowl, "barely living" and fearful of her childhood nightmares. She bumps her thighs against the new bedstead, and the bruised thighs appear as an image in "Domestic Miracles." In her new and unfamiliar surroundings, the speaker feels eternal, like clay artifacts discovered by an archaeologist. Her body knows that *"something miraculous must happen."*

Marriage, family life, and children are the outward signs of the great transformations love brings. Like many women poets, Oates has written a poem titled "Marriage." Not obscure and intimidating with learned references in the manner of Marianne Moore's famous poem or propositional and narrative in the style of Denise Levertov's, Oates's poem on marriage gives the voice of a woman who needs a partial escape as she grips her skull "to stay put." She feels the heaviness of bodies. Yet the woman and her husband radiate light; they know how to love. The poem concludes with the beautifully rhythmic lines, "we touch and wander/ and draw together puzzled in the dark."

Many poets adopt an implausible voice—of a cat, a cow, or the spirit of a dead person. Oates imagines the voice of a human fetus three months before birth in "Foetal Song." As the poem begins, mother and child are in a car. The unborn infant guesses in his cave about the noises he hears: high heels pounding the floor, horns and drills in the street, jokes and arguments. The fetus likes to swim and feel comfortable. He knows the parents, months ago, agreed to let his life continue: "I am grateful,/ I am waiting for my turn." Other poems talk about the beginnings of life that did not succeed. In "Unborn Child," the speaker meditates on an aborted fetus lost early in the life process—it has "no marks of identification." This unborn child can be forgotten as it returns to the flux of life and the cycles begin again. A more urgent tone sounds in "A Woman's Song." The insistent word "pounding" dominates the poem. As the pulse of life goes on—construction of bridges, firemen shooting water from hoses, truck wheels on the roadways—in the midst of all this vitality, "children fall in clots in water/ blood flushed safe to the river," and the river continues pounding under a highway overpass. In its uncompromising picture of water and the flushing of the unborn, this poem recalls "Dark Stream," a poem by the South African poet Ingrid Jonker. The fluidity of life matches in strength the pounding vitality of human action.

Oates satirizes lives that are empty of passion in "Women Whose Lives Are Food, Men Whose Lives Are Money," the title poem of her 1978 volume. The housewives live through days bounded by regular schedules: the garbage day, the shopping mall evening. The workmen husbands eat lunches from bags that they fold and put away over the weekend. Evenings they watch handsome strangers on television, fidget through the emotions they witness, yawn, and go to bed. Their children come home and see that nothing has changed. The poem summarizes such stasis in its conclusion: "the relief of emptiness rains/ simple, terrible, routine/ at peace."

In the same volume, "Wealthy Lady" and "He Traveled by Jet First Class to Tangier" reveal in stream-of-consciousness style the fantasies and anxieties of a woman and man who have money to indulge themselves. The lady (as she sits making out checks at her eighteenth century writing desk) imagines herself smiling upon the many people who receive her charity. For a change of pace, she reviews her stock portfolio. Taking a pistol from the drawer, she imagines scenes: a lunch date, a visit to an art museum, perhaps also to a cemetery, and an adventure in the dangerous part of town; she will defend herself from attack by drawing the pistol. Finally returning to reality, she decides to cross off her list a church committee whose chairman eats indelicately. The traveling man's life is narrated in a catalog of airports, destinations, Kodak film stops, hotel room bookings (always the luxury suite), festivals, and competitive conversations. His litany of "I am only human, I am normal" reveals his obsession with self and his deep anxiety. These people have not learned to lose their egos for the contentments of love.

The poem "Making an End" from *Angel Fire* talks of male "hunger for blows that silence words." This insistence on a violent final solution (the "fifth act" of a tragedy) is "the deadliest of incantations/ the unsaying of love, love's urgency/ pronounced backward into silence. . . . " The reader feels a fear of apocalypse caused by masculine violence in place of words. The failure of politics is thus a moral failure in the exchange of blows for speech. Similarly, in "Lies Lovingly Told" from *The Fabulous Beasts*, Oates treats the male-female configuration in political power terms. The poem revises the saying "Every woman loves a fascist" to "Every man adores/ the woman who adores/ the Fascist." The femme fatale, evil destroyer of a man's wife and children, is a creation of adolescent fantasy and must not be revised. In this fantasy, the man has no responsibility but has only to feel the woman's charms. Oates's moral assessment of love in her poetry traces an arc from delight to boredom to emptiness and, finally, to oppression and violence.

As well as the polarities of love and hate, the polarities of life and death occupy a large place in Oates's poetry. Poems about accidents, near-death experiences, drownings, and suicides invite the reader to meditate with Oates on the nature of being and nonbeing. This interest in a major philosophical topic is unsurprising; Oates studied philosophy intently as a student. She earned a Phi Beta Kappa award in part by reading ancient Greek texts, and the ideas of Plato, Thales of Miletus, and Heraclitus of Ephesus, among others, contribute to her poems about the boundaries of existence.

Physical death is considered in the poem "Not-being" from *Women Whose Lives Are Food, Men Whose Lives Are Money*. Based on Plato's difficult work *Sophist*, the poem's message (spoken in the voice of a person who almost died but returned) is that Not-being is a kind of qualified Being. As the critic Thomas Chance explains, "In their mutually exclusive sense, Being and Non-being are unknowable to us. They are objective *termini*, 'located' at the outermost limits of our experience, and, like points on a compass, serve to reorient and direct our love and aspirations. Thus, only someone who 'almost' died can inform us about an undifferentiated, perfect 'consciousness' that recognizes no distinction between itself and its visible form on a mirror." If one is upset or fearful about the change that will come to each, one needs to remember, as Plato said, that one can identify with the Being in one as the fixed point for one's soul's longing. Indeed, many of Oates's poems of death show physical death itself as a local and ordinary event, even a good event. The poems "Forgiveness of Sins," "Metamorphoses," "In Case of Accidental Death," "Seizure," and "The Survivor" all disavow the common fear and terror of death. Instead, Oates says, death is not the most difficult experience.

Where Being and Non-being are extreme limits of one consciousness, suicide is an impossibility. Yet however enigmatic it may be, suicide seems real. "On the Violence of Self-Death" asks if the suicide is blameless or guilty; this is a death willed by an unhappy adult that takes time to be prepared and is not like death by accident. It presents questions—perhaps a person fights as bravely for death as others do for life. "The Suicide" asks questions in a stark, breathless style, "Was he grateful? . . . Did he marvel? . . . Was that human?" The reader senses a life-loving mind trying to address the mystery of a suicide's mental state.

More complicated than physical death is the question of the life and death of the ego. "I die because I do not die" cries Saint Teresa of Avila. So long as she holds onto the individual ego, she will not be able to live fully. When one blocks the process of maturing into one's spiritual self, one's life remains stunted, ego-centered. Life events may bring one to the threshold of transcendence—beyond the ego—and one either pulls back or takes courage and accepts change. Oates sees the ego as a shadow of death between the universe and the individual.

The death or destruction of a personality—a death in the midst of life—takes the form for Oates of an arrested growth. Many years as a college teacher have made her familiar with both the usual patterns of growth in young lives and the blockage of normal growth. A chilling poem from *Anonymous Sins*, "And So I Grew Up to Be Nineteen and to Murder," mentions nothing about murder in the poem itself. A boy with wealthy parents recounts the stages of his life. He is aware of class and race distinctions in his society, but he says he was "a good kid" eating his Cheerios for breakfast. At an expensive private school, he and a friend begin to steal things, and he worries about his height and his personality. A sense of emptiness invades him—even the telephone book cannot distinguish him; his name appears "fourteen separate times." The poet leaves the rest of his story to imagination; the reader must contemplate the poem's conclusion from the evidence of the title.

Stories of diminished lives range from the voice of a ten-year-old child in

"Three Dances of Death" (about a child who is fat, lonely, and full of wonder at the adults dancing gaily in their home bomb shelter, which is decorated to resemble a night club) to the famous writer W. Somerset Maugham,
whose words of bitterness or self-loathing are heard in the poem " 'I can
stand there in the corner. . . . ' " He says, "I am a small man. I can stand
there/ in the corner, and maybe Death will not see me." The way one looks
at death, as confused children, young adults, or aged and famous people, reveals much about one's sense of identity and self-esteem.

A further dimension of being or nonbeing comes in the consideration of
spiritual health in society at large. Each individual's tendency toward personal integration and maturity or blocked growth depends in part on the social environment. Like D. H. Lawrence and other modernists, Oates understands the materialistic, consumer-oriented society to be a huge obstacle to
human spiritual growth. In its relentless pursuit of pleasure, American society
is necessarily death-oriented, becoming saturated with desires and choking
on overabundance. In the closing lines of "American Merchandise," Oates
implies the threat of death from material bloat. After a catalog of the "goods"
everyone enjoys, she says "Even now the great/ diesels are headed in your
direction." The ninety-car, six-diesel-engine railroad caravans and eighteen-
wheel, diesel-powered trucks can run over consumers in bringing them so
much more than they need.

Like William Carlos Williams, who displayed a consuming interest in the
silk-manufacturing town of Paterson, New Jersey, Oates returns frequently in
her poems to the area of upstate New York near Lockport, where she spent
her childhood. Yet, unlike Williams, she is also a rover who takes the whole
United States and its people as her subject. Her frequent travels by car provide the settings for her thoughts on the highways, people, and places she
encounters. Some European and Pacific Ocean places figure in poems in *The
Time Traveler*, but she writes principally of the deserts, seacoasts, and inland
habitations of the United States. Her "town" might be called Detroit, the
place where she lived and taught during the riots of the late 1960's and the
automobile city crucial to America's direction in the twentieth century.

Two of Oates's poems are addressed specifically to Lockport: "City of
Locks" from *Angel Fire* and "Locking Through" from *The Time Traveler*.
Her frequent use of the idea of life "passing through us" may have been inspired by the very graphic passing through Lockport of the Erie Barge Canal, a once-vital Eastern commercial waterway. "Locking Through" describes
the experience of dropping sixty feet on the artificial waterfall of the locks.
"City of Locks" paints the city and its locks as a place of crude street names,
sullen, foamy water, workmen repairing water damage, and cars full of shop-
pers. The city of Detroit becomes the quintessential urban scene. "In the
Night" tells of sirens rising during the riots in the heart of the city. The
speaker hears them from a distance and muses, fearfully, about the shudder-

ing city. The poem recalls Denise Levertov's "Listening to Distant Guns," about the experience of hearing the guns of World War II from across the English Channel. Both poets felt the eerie contrast of battle noises and muted cries of unseen individuals.

Poems of "on the road" experiences are often dramatic and narrative. "Whispering Glades" from *The Time Traveler* gives a stream of talk from an elderly woman, a displaced Northerner retired to a Florida mobile home. She complains to her vacationing grandchildren about the flies and fleas, the worms that eat her marigolds, and her unhappy memories. "Playlet for Voices" speaks in a cacophony of small talk at a wake. The anxious hostess wants to please the guests, who arrive and depart in a flow of exclamations and questions answered hastily. "Young Love, America" is a jazzy scene near a Pepsi vending machine. A young man and woman are flirting, playing at love; this scene could be drawn by Norman Rockwell in his characteristic realism-with-nostalgia style. Similarly, "An American Tradition" evokes the rush to return gifts to the stores on the day after Christmas. In three stanzas, the poem describes a crowd waiting outside a K-Mart and entering in a rush as the doors open. The third stanza presents the mini-drama of a wife trying to return her husband's gift; he protests, she cries, and they leave. The poem combines the ingredients typical of Oates's "travelogue" poems: realistic, recognizable details and a familiar moral point. American experiences teem through this poetry: rescues, near drownings, one's house being robbed, music at a roller rink, a stuffed refrigerator in a kitchen, and always the noises of cars, trucks, jackhammers, trains, and airplanes. Oates looks into a landscape of heroism, crime, and ordinary human motivations. As she has stated, her purpose as a writer is to chronicle American life in all its breadth and depth and height.

Oates's chronicle is so rich that no single study can do it justice. The poetry, for example, has humor, water imagery, and rhythmic effects, none of which could be discussed within the present thematic emphasis. The poetry, however, forms a body of work on its own merits and does not need to be interpreted only as an adjunct to the novels and short stories, as critics have said. It pictures America and Americans in the second half of a violent and fascinating century while at the center of world power. Confused, energetic, speeding and groping their way to understanding survival conditions, Americans see themselves mirrored in these poems. Their dramas, very often melodramas, seem outrageous until the reader examines a newspaper with stories more like fiction than fact.

A future assessment of the place of poetry in the Oates canon may well increase its importance; such a reevaluation has happened with other major writers whose poetry was overlooked as the early readership more quickly perceived the message in prose. Poetry's compressed language releases its power more gradually, but intelligence and verbal brilliance combined with the "talk style" rhythm that is not yet much understood should bring a wider audience to these poems.

Doris Earnshaw

Other major works

LONG FICTION: *With Shuddering Fall*, 1964; *A Garden of Earthly Delights*, 1967; *Expensive People*, 1968; *them*, 1969; *Wonderland*, 1971; *Do With Me What You Will*, 1973; *The Assassins: A Book of Hours*, 1975; *Childwold*, 1976; *The Triumph of the Spider Monkey*, 1976; *Son of the Morning*, 1978; *Unholy Loves*, 1979; *Bellefleur*, 1980; *Angel of Light*, 1981; *A Bloodsmoor Romance*, 1982; *Mysteries of Winterthurn*, 1984; *Solstice*, 1985; *Marya: A Life*, 1986; *Lives of the Twins*, 1987 (as Rosamond Smith); *You Must Remember This*, 1987; *American Appetites*, 1989; *Soul/Mate*, 1989 (as Rosamond Smith); *Because It Is Bitter, and Because It Is My Heart*, 1990; *I Lock My Door Upon Myself*, 1990; *The Rise of Life on Earth*, 1991.

SHORT FICTION: *By the North Gate*, 1963; *Upon the Sweeping Flood*, 1966; *The Wheel of Love*, 1970; *Marriages and Infidelities*, 1972; *The Goddess and Other Women*, 1974; *The Hungry Ghosts*, 1974; *Where Are You Going, Where Have You Been?*, 1974; *The Poisoned Kiss*, 1975; *The Seduction*, 1975; *Crossing the Border*, 1976; *Night-Side*, 1977; *All the Good People I've Left Behind*, 1978; *A Sentimental Education*, 1980; *Last Days*, 1984; *Raven's Wing*, 1986; *The Assignation*, 1988.

PLAYS: *Miracle Play*, 1974; *Three Plays*, 1980.

NONFICTION: *The Edge of Impossibility: Tragic Forms in Literature*, 1972; *The Hostile Sun: The Poetry of D. H. Lawrence*, 1973; *New Heaven, New Earth: The Visionary Experience in Literature*, 1974; *Contraries: Essays*, 1981; *The Profane Art: Essays and Reviews*, 1983; *On Boxing*, 1987; *(Woman) Writer: Occasions and Opportunities*, 1988.

ANTHOLOGIES: *Scenes from American Life: Contemporary Short Fiction*, 1972; *The Best American Short Stories of 1979*, 1979 (with Shannon Ravenel); *Night Walks: A Bedside Companion*, 1982; *First Person Singular: Writers on Their Craft*, 1983.

Bibliography

Bender, Eileen Teper. *Joyce Carol Oates: Artist in Residence.* Bloomington: Indiana University Press, 1987. Bender studies Oates as both artist and critic, the recorder of American mores and moral analyst. Her double consciousness applies to her position in the academic world and the world of feminist thought. The opening chapter and lengthy conclusion will help students of the poetry to understand Oates's "revisionist" art.

Grant, Mary Kathryn. *The Tragic Vision of Joyce Carol Oates.* Durham, N.C.: Duke University Press, 1978. Grant includes poetry in her excellent study of the Oatesian tragic vision of America. Topics that illuminate the poetry are violence (in Detroit, in cities, on the road), settings, personal power and powerlessness, and literary influence. Chapter 5, "The Tragic Vision," is particularly instructive about the sense of purpose in Oates's work—to awaken Americans to their common situation.

Lercangée, Francine. *Joyce Carol Oates: An Annotated Bibliography*. New York: Garland, 1986. An ambitious and essential work that lists 423 poems by original publication and subsequent collection. A full table of contents is included for each collection of poems. Critical essays by Oates as well as criticism of her work by others receive careful and detailed annotation. The introduction by Bruce F. Michelson emphasizes her experiments in form. Several indices complete this useful reference work.

Pearlman, Mickey, and Katherine Usher Henderson. *Inter/View: Talks with America's Writing Women*. Lexington: University Press of Kentucky, 1990. Numerous interviews with Oates have been published, but this one, conducted by Mickey Pearlman, reveals topics germane to the poetry: class relations, gender relations, and the vital role of memory in her creativity. Oates talks about the biographers (whom Oates labels "pathographers") who ascribe sickness and deviance to women writers, conflating personal and professional lives in a very damaging way.

Stevens, Peter. "The Poetry of Joyce Carol Oates." In *Critical Essays on Joyce Carol Oates*, edited by Linda W. Wagner. Boston: G. K. Hall, 1979. A lengthy, detailed study of the first five collections of poems, from *Anonymous Sins* to *Women Whose Lives Are Food, Men Whose Lives Are Money*. Stevens relates themes and styles to the modernist aesthetic of D. H. Lawrence, Kafka, and Dickey and the psychic spirituality of Flannery O'Connor. He identifies major themes of modern meaninglessness, dualities of love, transcendence and limitation, and the shadow side of human existence. He finds a progression from early questioning in the poems to a declarative stance. An essential work.

Waller, G. F. *Dreaming America: Obsession and Transcendence in the Fiction of Joyce Carol Oates*. Baton Rouge: Louisiana State University Press, 1979. Although concerned mainly with the novels, this study will be useful to students of the poetry in its opening chapter, "The Obsessive Vision," and the second chapter, "The Phantasmagoria of American Personality." Both chapters are general and include mentions of poems from *Anonymous Sins*, Angel Fire, and *Love and Its Derangements*. The conclusion relies too heavily on the influence of D. H. Lawrence, but at the time the book was written such a view was natural. No index, but a very interesting bibliography of related sources, with names such as Victor Frankl, Paul Ricoeur, Paul Tillich, and Raymond Williams.

FRANK O'HARA

Born: Baltimore, Maryland; June 27, 1926
Died: Fire Island, New York; July 25, 1966

Principal poetry

A City Winter, and Other Poems, 1952; *Oranges*, 1953; *Meditations in an Emergency*, 1957; *Odes*, 1960; *Lunch Poems*, 1964; *Love Poems (Tentative Title)*, 1965; *In Memory of My Feelings: A Selection of Poems*, 1967 (Bill Berkson, editor); *The Collected Poems of Frank O'Hara*, 1971 (Donald Allen, editor); *Selected Poems*, 1974; *Early Poems 1946-1951*, 1976; *Poems Retrieved 1951-1966*, 1977.

Other literary forms

Frank O'Hara was always a poet, no matter what he wrote. His plays (published in *Selected Plays*, 1978), only a few of which are actually capable of being produced with any degree of dramatic effectiveness, are more often plays with words and visual effects than exploration of character or idea through dramatic conflict. Some juxtapose a vast variety of characters (from O'Hara's own friends to Benjamin Franklin, Marlene Dietrich, William Blake, and Generalissimo Franco), most with only a single short speech, with connections nonexistent outside of O'Hara's fertile imagination. Others of these short plays offer sustained characters speaking in non sequiturs or in monologues unheard by other characters. In one play, *Try! Try!* (written in 1950, first performed in 1951, rewritten in 1953), the monologues work in an interesting way, since there is a plot with a recognizable triangle of characters and actual dialogue, besides some poetic and psychologically suggestive monologues. Another produced play, *The General Returns from One Place to Another* (1964), uses verbal, visual, and dramatic means to satirize the American military abroad, particularly in the person of Douglas MacArthur.

O'Hara's prose has been collected in *Standing Still and Walking in New York* (1975, Donald Allen, editor). The volume consists chiefly of miscellaneous pieces on modern art and contains a small quantity of literary criticism as well.

Besides writing for *Art News*, O'Hara worked on the catalogs for various exhibits at the Museum of Modern Art, including those on contemporary American painters Jackson Pollock and Robert Motherwell. His art criticism tends to be impressionistic rather than technical, but it effectively conveys the essence of contemporary painting.

Achievements

Other than the advent of the Beat movement at roughly the same time, probably the most exciting thing to happen to American poetry is the mid-twentieth century ascendance of vital and natural voices, with all the immediacy of actual human talk, through the work of the so-called "New York Poets." Heading them were O'Hara, John Ashbery, and Kenneth Koch, with O'Hara's voice being the dominant one. Drawing elements from Walt Whitman, William Carlos Williams, Gertrude Stein, French Surrealists such as Guillaume Apollinaire and Pierre Reverdy, and the Russian poets Vladimir Mayakovsky and Boris Pasternak, O'Hara shattered the prevailing poetic standards regarding language, form, and content and forged his own verse with tremendous vigor and fire. He did not want to produce the sort of pristine, shapely work that could be found in scores of other volumes, admired by the literary establishment of New Critics for their traditional forms, metaphoric complexities, and mythic overtones. O'Hara rejected all of these familiar ingredients, writing in unfettered free verse, shifting images and metaphors wildly throughout a poem, and dealing with earthy subject matter or very personal experiences without any effort to make them seem universally significant.

Most of O'Hara's poems flow, without any attempt to structure them formally, through the free association of his surrealistic poems, where one image or word leads to another, however logically unrelated, or through the simple recording of his actual activities, thoughts, and feelings on special occasion (or not-so-special ones). Because he was so keenly in tune with his feelings, such poems work splendidly in conveying the moods that generated them, especially through the marvelously vivid vocabulary which dances across his pages.

Not least among his achievements is his lively sense of humor, sometimes just a light tone that flavors much of his work as he playfully recounts his activities or observations, sometimes satiric views of various cultural and political icons (including the movies), sometimes raucous comedy full of delightful surprises, such as the sun appearing to chat with the poet abed or a vision of bugs walking through the apartment "carrying a little banner/ which says 'in search of lanolin.'"

Delight in words and experience, surprise at the variety of existence: these are the keynotes of O'Hara's poetry, which retains its freshness and appeal far beyond the attempts of so many others to imitate it.

Biography

Although born in Baltimore and reared in rural Massachusetts, Francis O'Hara discovered a more appropriate milieu first among fellow poets and aficionados of the other arts at Harvard (where he received his B.A. degree in English literature in 1950) and subsequently in New York City. In the meantime he had spent two years in the Navy in the South Pacific and a year at the University of Michigan, where he received his M.A. in 1951 and the Avery Hopwood Major Award in Poetry for a manuscript collection of poetry (his Master's thesis). Once in New York, he rejoined fellow Harvard graduates John Ashbery and Kenneth Koch and involved himself in various arts in assorted capacities, while remaining, with the others, quite apart from the literary establishment of the day. He worked for the Museum of Modern Art, advancing from a staff position working on circulating exhibitions to an associate curatorship, selecting numerous exhibitions of contemporary American and Spanish artists and being responsible for the catalogs published in conjunction with the exhibits. He also wrote occasional articles and reviews for *Art News*, and had several plays performed. He adopted a very casual attitude toward his poetry, sending poems off to friends without keeping a copy, stuffing them in drawers, gathering material only under pressure from eager editors such as John Bernard Myers. He was intensely involved (whether as friend or lover) with many different and interesting women and men throughout these New York years until his death in a freak accident on Fire Island.

Analysis

To enter the world of Frank O'Hara is to abandon all familiar roadmaps, to give up hope for a straight and clear way through, for easily recognizable landmarks that indicate where one is going, where one has been. With "no revolver pointing the roadmarks," the reader is free to travel without preconceptions and without insistent points made by the poet. O'Hara's world is closer to Lewis Carroll's than to Robert Frost's, being constantly full of surprises, twists in the road, byways, sharp turns, cul-de-sacs, a grotesquerie of roadside attractions, and few places to stop or rest, so that one ends up nowhere near one's anticipated goal, perhaps not even at an ending at all but simply at a halt, like running out of gas. For that is how many O'Hara poems conclude—with neither a bang nor a whimper, but only a sudden cessation of the impetuous, rapid drive of words and images and feelings that has made up the poem. His poetry is exciting, startling, dizzying, frightening, overwhelming, demanding, involving, crude, elaborate, stark, disorderly, sexy, and sometimes very funny. As a poet crafting his art, O'Hara had as much gleeful fun—even when dealing with feelings considerably less than euphoric—as the liveliest child or the most daredevil racer.

O'Hara was the epitome of the New York poet: fast, frenzied, jazzy, upbeat, smart-aleck, shrewd, unzipped, down-to-earth, open, and full of action. Like his fellow New York poets (friends, some contemporaries, some followers or students from a workshop he offered), he thrived on the bustle of the city and participated in its multitude of activities. Far from being a poetic hermit in an ivory tower, he actively involved himself with people and with the other arts—notably with painters, but also with dancers and musicians. The kind of painting he favored was action painting, a style indigenous to New York and led by Jackson Pollock. Its random quality, abstractness, and emphasis

on the process of painting rather than the static permanence demonstrated·
in a still life or a portrait all have their correspondences in O'Hara's poetry.

This poetry pulses with action of all sorts—sexual, mental, emotional,
physical, natural, industrial, transportational—all the types of action, in fact,
which make up America. Action itself is the subject of some of his poems,
such as his self-styled "I do this I do that" poems. The action of the poem
may be expressed in vocabulary (colorful concrete nouns and vivid active
verbs expressing dynamic movement); in syntax (whether conventional—
using such devices as piled-up participial phrases, short sentences, and parataxis, though quite grammatically—or unconventional—omitting parts of a
sentence or letting a single word or phrase serve two different but simultaneous functions in two adjacent syntactical units); in interjections ("Hey!,"
"Yeah!"); or in rapid shifts of subject, place, or time—from stanza to stanza,
sentence to sentence, line to line, and even from one word or phrase to the
next.

"My Heat" provides evidence of all of these. The opening stanza is filled
with verbs denoting vigorous action: four finite verbs ("committed," "fell off
the balcony," "I'd force the port!/ Violate the piers"), one infinitive ("to
refountain myself"), and two present participles ("jetting," "turning in air").
Unconventional syntax and punctuation give a sensation of dizziness fitting
this turning and falling: the "if" clause seems to have two main verbs
unseparated by a conjunction or comma, both with "I" as subject; then
O'Hara does not set off what is presumably his main clause by a comma after
the subordinate clause, so that the infinitive could be regarded as part of
either the subordinate or the main clause. The verb's unfamiliarity ("refountain") also sharpens the reader's attention, as does the unclearness of its
connection with the rest of the sentence. This main clause seems to end with
the exclamation point after "port," yet the next word is another verb, presumably another main verb for the subject "I"—unless it is an imperative for
the two vocatives ending the stanza ("you bores! you asses!"). Keeping readers
alert, the very next word, "geology," at the beginning of the next stanza, not
only has nothing to do with "the balcony," "the port," or "the piers," but
also is punctuated by a question mark.

The punctuation is certainly not completely unorthodox, though it is surprising. What would give the traditional poetry reader more trouble are the
rapid shifts in imagery, but this is part of O'Hara's point: the pleasure he
takes in "jetting" from one image to whatever it suggests, the pleasure he
takes in "jetting" such words and phrases from his typewriter—all as opposed
to the "you" in this poem, who always seems a few steps behind poet "Frank,"
who proclaims, with another surprising but apt and active verb choice, "I've
kayoed your popular cant/ I'd rather jet!"

A New Critic such as John Crowe Ransom would probably throw up his
hands at the untidiness of O'Hara's metaphorical maneuverings. There is no

clear one-to-one correspondence between tenors and vehicles here; there is certainly no single picture provided out of which the meaning derives, no identifiable incident which gives rise to the poetic expression. The meaning rather resides in the exuberant movement of the poem and its words, images which—in themselves and in their transformations throughout the poem—suggest the force of creativity as well as that of sexuality.

This poem is, in fact, only one of the most compressed treatments of sexuality among O'Hara's work, from the ejaculatory "jetting" of its opening line on to the final line: "'That's no furnace, that's my heart!'" The heat of passion is inflated thus to the power of a furnace. The diffuse jetting rampant throughout the poem amply reflects the exuberant sexuality—not a sexual desire directed at a single person and thus capable of being satisfied, but rather directed at no one in particular, an all-pervasive urge, reveling in the fact of sexuality and the pleasure of the sexual feeling itself. O'Hara's images are used not as specific metaphors—he mixes them too outrageously for that—but rather as evocations of the many flavors and feelings of sexuality (or, in other poems, whatever has motivated that poetic outburst): its sweetness and beauty in roses, its violence (in violating the piers), its power (as a volcano "to melt everyone into syrup"), its self-containment, its richness, even its humor ("laughing like an old bedspring," a simile that makes a believable aural comparison as well as fitting the sexual subject matter).

O'Hara's eroticism is far from *fin de siècle* decadence, which hints at more than it tells; nor does it explicitly depict sexual acts, as in pornography. Rather, it revels in a joyous sexuality that fellow homosexual poet Walt Whitman would certainly recognize and appreciate. Only rarely does O'Hara depict an actual sexual act, as in "Twin spheres full of fur and noise/ rolling softly up my belly" for an act of fellatio. A lively choice of images ("my mouth is full of suns") and abstractions ("that softness seems so anterior to that hardness"), with a climactic hint of Apollo's chariot of the sun, raises the experience to a mythic level, but not for long. O'Hara's poetry must constantly move, never rest, and of course the moment of sexual ecstasy dissolves, even as it is achieved: "It must be discovered soon and disappear."

Sex is not, however much it may appear so from these examples, O'Hara's only concern; like Whitman, he felt intense pleasure simply in living, and since sex represents the most intense form of physical pleasure, he naturally perceived a sexual quality in his relationship with living—in all its aspects—and hence with the rest of the world. He could penetrate the world—make an impact on it, enter its multifarious experiences—just as he could penetrate a lover; he could also be penetrated by experience, by the myriad sensory impressions all around him—just as a lover might penetrate him. This openness to both roles parallels his sexual orientation; his homosexuality, indicating openness to nonstandard sexual practice, may have a share in O'Hara's Imagistic fertility, as he presents (in "Easter," for example) nonhuman and inanimate nature surging with sexuality ("it's the night like a love it all cruisy and nelly"; "the world booms its seven cunts/ like a river plunged upon and perishing"). Such images, which cannot be deciphered into metaphorical cor- respondences of tenor and vehicle with an "underlying" subject behind the metaphorical development, serve to suggest sexuality in O'Hara's more public poems (as contrasted with private poems such as "Twin spheres," written for his lover Vincent Warren) without having to be gender-specific.

In most of his poems the images shift constantly; the reader is meant to flow with the stream of O'Hara's free associations, which is often remarkably easy to do because of his vivid and emotionally evocative choice of nouns, verbs, and adjectives, even when the precise meaning of a passage remains indecipherable. "Savoy" shifts ground even more rapidly than "My Heat," yet it conveys a rich sequence of moods.

"Savoy" opens with a feeling of terror, although its cause is unclear. Like other O'Hara poems, it begins with an image which he proceeds to join to a simile—a logical enough poetic device—but the simile proceeds to take over as the poem's main concern. Yet O'Hara writes elsewhere, "How I hate subject matter!," and the reader realizes that actually neither simile nor its tenor is the subject of the poem. Looking at the extended so-called simile ("like a bespectacled carapaceous witch doctor of Rimini/ beautifying an adolescent tubbed in entrails of blue cement . . .") reveals that it is hardly to be apprehended in the manner of a Metaphysical conceit. What is a witch doctor doing in Rimini, on the Italian seacoast? How can anyone be beautified in a bath of "blue cement"? A few lines down, who is the "you" suddenly addressed? The rapid changes mirror those of a dream or nightmare, in which identities shift inexplicably. This is the method of surrealist poetry, which O'Hara brought into American poetry with a new force after it had flour- ished in Europe several decades earlier. O'Hara clearly indicates a romance with the word and whatever lively images it evokes rather than with its spe- cific literal denotation. Even in describing terrors and dangers in "Savoy," O'Hara is having fun; the pleasure is in the movement of the poem, not in discerning its "meaning."

His less surrealistic poems, however, which record his actions, are not hard to "understand" at all. Simple in form and structure, the "I do this I do that" poems, as he calls them in "Getting Up Ahead of Someone (Sun)," are, at their best, more than a mere transcription of the day's activities; they convey the quality of the poet's conscious mind and the shifting moods stirred by his activities. The most famous—and most moving—example of this sort of poem is "The Day Lady Died," which pays tribute to singer Billie Holiday upon her death but is hardly a standard elegy with explicit presentation of grief and concentration on praise for the deceased. Instead, O'Hara begins the poem—and carries on for the bulk of it—with an account of his movements, fairly random, around New York on a Friday afternoon. Suddenly he is caught short by "a NEW YORK POST with her face on it," and he is reminded of hearing Holiday ("Lady Day") sing "in the 5 SPOT," when "everyone and I stopped breathing." This last action (or rather lack of it) stunningly conveys the whole impact not only of Holiday's art but also of her death and is especially effective in stopping movement and thought after such a bustling buildup. The rest of the poem does not prepare the reader for such a conclusion at all.

Most of his "I do this I do that" poems are much less serious, and often poke fun at himself or take a delightfully lighthearted approach to the addressee, a friend or a lover, and the particular relationship they share. In fact, O'Hara's humor is one of his most characteristic traits; however, his work is quite different from light verse because it rarely satirizes and certainly does not use rhyme and rhythm. Rather, it is based on surprise, giving his readers the unexpected, as his surrealist pieces do. Yet those are rarely comic because they so constantly shift ground that the reader has no solid base to stand on, a necessity if comic surprise is to hit with true effectiveness.

A true comic gem is "Poem (Lana Turner has collapsed!)," a delightful little poem that O'Hara wrote on the spur of the moment on a ferry to a poetry reading. Written in the conversational tone at which he was so adept, it enters the world of comedy with the very first line, with its hysterical exclamation point like a sensationalistic headline (as the poem later reveals it in fact to be). The reader knows not to take this as seriously as Lady Day's death, first because of the exclamation point, then because this announcement appears at the beginning of the poem rather than at its climax, and, finally, because Lana Turner—even two decades after the poem was written—is still very much alive, having apparently suffered no serious consequences from this "collapse." The second line continues the humorous tone with O'Hara's verb choice—"I was trotting along." The speaker is obviously not a horse, nor does this verb have the intensity of suggestion of those in "My Heat"; it merely gives the reader a funny sense of the light, frolicsome quality of the poet's movements. The humor continues—and builds—stylistically with the paratactic structure of short clauses joined by coordinating conjunctions, then in content with the poet's slight disagreement with his friend about the weather (whether it was raining and snowing or hailing), and further, with the surprising apparent shift in position of the "you," who at first appears to be with the speaker and then is seen as the goal he is walking toward. The poet notes the traffic "acting exactly like the sky," using the humorous idiom of very mild outrage ("isn't that exactly like so-and-so?"). Then comes the appearance of the headline—to complete what now appears to be a flashback after the poem's opening line. The poet proceeds to assure the motion-picture star that she has no reason to collapse, there being no snow or rain in Hollywood; moreover, he refers to his own behavior at parties, where he himself has never collapsed. He concludes with an actual address to the actress—comically unpunctuated, although it encompasses an interjection, a vocative, and two short clauses unjoined by conjunctions: "oh Lana Turner we love you get up." This last line suggests that all the motion-picture star needs here is reassurance of her fans' love and an affectionately authoritative encouragement. O'Hara is implying that he cannot take this inflated problem seriously, nor should anyone else; he is gently mocking the superhuman status accorded celebrities. Of course this is a poem simply to be enjoyed, hardly to be pondered seriously. Although O'Hara certainly took poetry seriously, he also believed in enjoying it, as he did life.

Living in a throbbing city, he had countless experiences to enjoy, from attending films and ballet to walking the streets (as in the poems just discussed) to meeting with a wide range of acquaintances, for a Coke, a trip to a museum, a party, or even sex. All these experiences are celebrated in his vital poetry, through which he has vividly conveyed not only a sense of the excitement of life but also a rich sense of himself as a living person: as with Walt Whitman, it is not a mere book one encounters when reading O'Hara: "Who touches this touches a man."

Scott Giantvalley

Other major works

PLAY: *Selected Plays*, 1978.

NONFICTION: *Jackson Pollock*, 1959; *Robert Motherwell, with Selections from the Artist's Writings*, 1965; *Standing Still and Walking in New York*, 1975.

Bibliography

Breslin, James E. B. "Frank O'Hara." In *From Modern to Contemporary: American Poetry, 1945-1965*. Chicago: University of Chicago Press, 1984. O'Hara's "lunch hour poems" demythologize city poetry, contrasting him with T. S. Eliot and Allen Ginsberg. A close analysis of "On Seeing Larry Rivers' *Washington Crossing the Delaware* at the Museum of Modern Art" is made with reference to the painting, which is included as an illustration. Complemented by footnotes and an index.

Feldman, Alan. *Frank O'Hara*. Boston: Twayne, 1979. This book introduces O'Hara as a New York poet. His language, style, and degrees of coherence are analyzed. Themes of "the self," varieties of feelings, and humor are examined in succeeding chapters. The conclusion is an assessment of O'Hara's influence. Supplemented by a chronology, a select bibliography, and an index.

Holahan, Susan. "Frank O'Hara's Poetry." In *American Poetry Since 1960: Some Critical Perspectives*, edited by Robert B. Shaw. Cheadle, England: Carcanet Press, 1973. O'Hara's poems are ceremonies of naming persons, places, and things in New York; they are gestures of art in a poetic rather than a physical universe. His style is illustrated for its remarkable syntax, separating one perception from another. *In Memory of My Feelings* is analyzed as an echo of William Wordsworth.

Molesworth, Charles. " 'The Clear Architecture of the Nerves:' The Poetry of Frank O'Hara." In *The Fierce Embrace: A Study of Contemporary American Poetry.* Columbia: University of Missouri Press, 1979. O'Hara's work startles. His poems are among the most autobiographical poems in American literature, composed in several lengths and in a variety of modes. Some are surrealistic, others sentimental. Placed in a context of plastic arts, O'Hara's poetry gains more than by comparing it with other poetry. Contains notes and an index.

Perloff, Marjorie. *Frank O'Hara: Poet Among Painters.* New York: George Braziller, 1977. Perloff analyzes O'Hara's "aesthetic of attention" and surveys the early poems. Her central chapter looks at his "poem-paintings," and then his "great period" is presented. The conclusion covers the 1960's and the relationship of his poetry to John Ashbery and Allen Ginsberg. Augmented by illustrations, notes, a bibliographical note, and an index.

Vendler, Helen. "Frank O'Hara: The Virtue of the Alterable." In *Part of Nature, Part of Us: Modern American Poets.* Cambridge, Mass.: Harvard University Press, 1980. This essay reviews O'Hara's work as a genre of overproduced conversation with an incapacity to be abstract and a discomfort with form. His poetry contrasted the appeal of film with the great reality of sex. O'Hara, however, proved in his late poetry that he could capture the rhythms of America better than most of his contemporaries.

JOHN OLDHAM

Born: Shipton Moyne, England; August 9, 1653
Died: Holm Pierrepont, near Nottingham, England; December 9, 1683

Principal poetry

A Satyr Against Vertue, 1679; *Satyrs upon the Jesuits*, 1681; *Some New Pieces Never Before Publisht*, 1681; *Poems and Translations*, 1683; *Selected Poems*, 1980 (Ken Robinson, editor); *The Poems of John Oldham*, 1986 (Raman Seldon and Harold F. Brooks, editors).

Other literary forms

John Oldham's literary output was restricted to verse and verse imitation. Nevertheless, his influence in these forms produced a shaping force in English literature.

Achievements

As a notably influential although minor literary figure, Oldham is probably less recognized for any single achievement of his own than for the way he helped to shape the development of seventeenth and eighteenth century verse satire. The two major phases of his brief literary career reflect two very different satiric styles: the harshness of Juvenalian invective and the more tempered voice of Horatian conversation. Although his *Satyrs upon the Jesuits*, the harshest of the Juvenalian satires, contains Oldham's most well-known and frequently anthologized pieces, his later satires reflect a comparatively moderate tone and are now recognized as his best poems. Among these, his "imitations" of such figures as Horace, Juvenal, and Nicholas Boileau were formative in establishing a loose form of verse translation in which the original appeared in a contemporary social and literary context.

Oldham's severity in his early satires looks back to the extreme style of sixteenth century satirists; his somewhat more tempered voice in the later verses looks forward to the moderation of John Dryden and Alexander Pope. When Oldham died at the age of thirty, he had already won a firm position for himself in the development of English literature. He failed, however, to produce a satire to rival those of the great satirists who followed him and who were indebted to his limited though influential literary achievement.

Although no complete edition of Oldham's poetry exists, several partial editions are available, notably the Centaur edition of 1960 and Ken Robinson's facsimile edition of 1980. *The Poems of John Oldham* (1986; Raman Seldon and Harold F. Brooks, editors), corrects errors found in the previous editions.

Biography

John Oldham was born in the English countryside on August 9, 1653, the son of a dissenting minister. He received a solid education both at home and in grammar school, entered St. Edmund's Hall, Oxford, when he was seventeen and took his bachelor's degree in May, 1674. Sometime during this period, Oldham wrote his first poem, a long Pindaric ode "To the Memory of My Dear Friend, Mr. Charles Morwent." By this time he had confirmed, at least to himself, a lifelong commitment to the writing of poetry.

Because it was impossible to make a living from one's pen without the aid of a literary patron, Oldham assumed the position of "usher" (assistant master) in Whitgift's school, Croyden, where he remained in employment from 1674 to 1677. Although the aspiring poet had written several poems since his first ode, it was during these years that he wrote his first verse satire, *A Satyr Against Vertue* (1679). It was also during the years at Croyden that Oldham was recognized by the more prominent Restoration wits, notably the Earls of Rochester and Dorset, and Sir Charles Sedley.

As his poetic reputation grew, so did Oldham's dissatisfaction with his position at Whitgift's. Considering his tutoring duties to be little more than menial labor, in 1678 he accepted a position as a private tutor, which he kept until 1680 when he decided to move to London and become part of the literati of Restoration society. A year before the move to London, his *Satyrs upon the Jesuits* had been piratically printed, and Oldham's reputation as a promising young verse satirist was already established.

Not much is known of the time Oldham spent in London. He studied medicine for about a year, but then devoted himself wholly to poetry. He admitted to adopting the life-style of the Restoration town gentleman, engaging in drinking and debauchery, although he was quick to feel the pangs of conscience when reflecting on his excesses. During these three final years of his life, his health declined, and finally he retired to Nottinghamshire, residence of the young Earl of Kingston, who offered the poet a comfortable home where he might pursue his literary career.

It was here that, free from the social and literary demands which London society placed on him, Oldham produced some of his finest satires and imitations. In 1683, however, only three years after he had moved to London in pursuit of literary fame, Oldham contracted smallpox. He died on December 9 of that year.

Analysis

John Oldham's calling was not to the polite muse. Instead, he saw himself as inheriting the role of the poet who rails against the faults and vices of the age. His harsh Juvenalian satires and lively verse imitations were quick to attack what was wrong with society. Oldham's tone was rugged yet sharp; his poetic attitude was one of indignation. He mastered the art of the cankered muse, and left behind him some of the finest examples of vituperative verse satire.

The subjects, themes, and satirical approaches that Oldham adopted account for much of the bite in his work. Early in his career, when he wrote his most severe satires, Oldham typically addressed himself to issues which were either personally or socially repulsive to him. In *A Satyr Against Vertue*, for example, he rails against affected notions of virtue which "plague our happy state;" in the "Satire Addressed to a Friend" he complains about his own personal circumstances; and in his *Satyrs upon the Jesuits* he vents his indignation about a subject which aroused some of the most heated political and religious controversy of the age. Unlike many of his more witty contemporaries who were content to treat their subjects with humor and objectivity, Oldham focused directly on the victims of his satire—cursing them for their actions, condemning the society in which they thrived, and depicting them in the most offensive ways. While John Dryden or even the Earl of Rochester might dexterously mix censure with praise, there is no mistaking the focus of Oldham's direct accusations.

Both personal and social circumstances might account for the severity of Oldham's satiric tone. His strong sense of individualism made him an unsuitable candidate for the system of patronage, and what he perceived as the declining position of literature in Restoration England only served to confirm his individualism. It is not surprising that Oldham wrote some of his best verses after he had left London and retired to the English countryside, detached from the environment of "hack" writers and commercial values. Yet it was that very society which gave him the subjects for his satires. Political disputes between Tories and Whigs, religious controversy between Catholics and Protestants, and what many perceived as the general decadent atmosphere of London society supplied him with his best materials.

Oldham's *Satyrs upon the Jesuits*, probably written shortly before his move to London, typifies the kind of invective and raillery for which he has become so famous. In the "Prologue," Oldham describes satire as his weapon and indignation as his muse; in each of the four satires, he adopts the perspective of a different speaker who functions as the vehicle of his satiric lashes. This satiric approach made it possible for him to focus directly on his victims and at the same time vary his tone so that the satire might remain consistent in its attack and yet flexible in its point of view. The ghost of Henry Garnet, a provincial of the Jesuits who was executed in 1606 for his role in the Gunpowder Plot, speaks in the first satire, urging the Jesuits to kill and plunder, to create another "inquisition." When Oldham speaks in his own voice in the second satire, he then vents his own rage against the Jesuits with the same vigor that "Garnet's Ghost" used to plot against king and nation. Perspective shifts again in the third satire, "Loyola's Will," where Oldham speaks through the voice of Ignatius Loyola himself, founder of the Jesuit order. Here St. Ignatius, pictured on his deathbed, passes on to his followers the "hidden rules" and "secrets" of villainy. In the final satire, the perspective is even more removed as the wooden image of St. Ignatius assumes the satiric voice, exposing its own worthlessness and the emptiness of Catholic ritual.

The Juvenalian rant of the *Satyrs upon the Jesuits* has its source not only in the different perspectives that Oldham adopted in each satire, constantly allowing him to shift the focus of his invective, but also in the details of each speaker's remarks. One of the most savage passages of "Garnet's Ghost," for example, is filled with specific instructions on how to murder priests, mothers, unborn children, infants, young virgins, the aged, and the crippled. In "Loyola's Will," readers are given a gruesome picture of the dying Jesuit leader as he "heaves" and "pants" on his deathbed. The picture becomes even more gruesome in the final satire where spiders and rats find "refuge" and "religious sanctuary" in the decaying body of St. Ignatius. In depicting such scenes, Oldham was extending himself far beyond the lines of general religious satire: the Jesuits are not merely criticized; they are portrayed and condemned in vicious terms.

Satyrs upon the Jesuits was Oldham's masterpiece in his harsh Juvenalian mode. His verse translations and imitations, however, which began to consume his poetic energies, were more temperate and moderate. Several critics believe that the very act of imitation helped to tame Oldham's sharp satiric voice. Even the last of the *Satyrs upon the Jesuits*, spoken from the perspective of a dead, wooden image, was modeled in part on one of Horace's satires and is more distant and mocking in its manner.

With the verse imitations, Oldham entered the most influential phase of his brief literary career. The refined Horatian style of the translations looked forward to the moderation of Dryden and Alexander Pope. Equally influential was the theory of imitation which Oldham practiced: instead of translating the original in its own historical context, he rendered it in a contemporary English setting—at once making the classics more alive and immediate, and making his own contemporary verse more intellectually respectable. Again, both Dryden and Pope in their own imitations were to follow Oldham's practice.

Among Oldham's early imitations were "Bion's Lamentation for Adonis," which was his elegy on Rochester, and the renditions of two odes of Horace. His outstanding satiric imitations, of Horace, Juvenal, and Nicholas Boileau, were to follow in 1681 and 1682. The art of translation and imitation dominated this final phase of Oldham's career; even poems which were not strict imitations nevertheless drew on classical sources. "Spenser's Ghost" and "Satire Addressed to a Friend," two of his outstanding satires of this period, both draw on Juvenal's seventh satire. The three imitations generally considered to be Oldham's masterpieces are his renditions of Horace's ninth satire, first book (1681), Juvenal's third satire (1682), and Boileau's eighth satire (1682).

The conversational tone and comic subject of the Horatian imitation immediately distinguishes it from Oldham's earlier satiric invective. Instead of writing about plots and murder and villainy, Oldham's subject here is the poet's encounter with a bore whom he cannot manage to escape. The story is humorous, not vengeful; the "tedious chat" of the bore clearly contrasts with the bitter pleas of "Garnet's Ghost" and the deathbed speech of St. Ignatius. Contemporary social issues are satirized, but only mildly, at times almost with understatement. The Popish Plot, for example, which fired much of Oldham's invective in his *Satyrs upon the Jesuits*, becomes in the imitation a bothersome issue which the poet would just as soon dismiss. In his translation of Horace, Oldham was not only imitating the Horatian style, but adopting and perfecting a very different kind of satiric voice for himself.

The imitations of Juvenal and Boileau exemplify Oldham's mastery of this new satiric voice. Although the subject of each of these imitations is more serious than that of the Horatian piece, Oldham continues to treat his subject with a notably lighter tone. The criticism of London in his translation of Juvenal, for instance, describes the "nauseous town" as totally lacking any value or worth, but the details of the satire are often comic, especially in the portraits of the city's hairdressers, plotters, and courtiers. When Oldham describes England as the "common sewer" for France, his portraits of fops and their fashions are more often the object of humor than of indignation. The situation is much the same in his rendition of Boileau's eighth satire, which often exaggerates comedy to the point of absurdity. In this dispute between doctor and poet, man's position in the animal kingdom becomes a playful issue which Oldham easily exploits for his satiric purposes. Urbane conversation and pointed ridicule allow Oldham to treat the satire with humor: while the doctor defends, for example, man's serious position as "Lord of the Universe," the poet luxuriates in descriptions of tigers creating plots and factions, or "Whig and Tory lions" engaging in political disputes. The poet's final sustained comparison of man with an "ass" may not convince the doctor, but it makes Oldham's satire all the more engaging for its fine sense of wit.

Despite this change in tone, Oldham never lost his ability to write fiercely vigorous invective. This ability was, after all, his distinguishing achievement as a satirist and is almost always apparent in the details of his verse. One passage in the Juvenal imitation, for example, portrays London society as enslaved to money. Oldham describes everything, from court favors to the consent of lovers, as the object of purchase. London becomes more than merely an "expensive town"; it is depicted as a society which thrives on a system of social prostitution. Another passage, in the Boileau imitation, relies on the intrusion of a notably harsh subject in the midst of comparatively light satire. As the poet proceeds to ridicule man by contrasting him with animals, he pauses to make an accusation that recalls the subject matter of *Satyrs upon the Jesuits*: the "trade of cutting throats" and the "arts" of warfare and murder. Although in his best imitations Oldham had learned to moderate his depiction of the gruesome details of these arts, passages of this kind are reminders that he never entirely abandoned the cankered muse.

John Oldham will be remembered for the invective of his *Satyrs upon the Jesuits* and his contributions to the art of verse imitation. He will probably be better remembered, however, as the subject of one of Dryden's finest poems, "To the Memory of Mr. Oldham." It is an appropriate memorial, for Dryden knew only too well both Oldham's shortcomings and his achievements. The harshness of Oldham's satire, Dryden says, was a "noble error," one which could not conceal what Dryden saw as Oldham's distinguishing qualities, the "wit" and "quickness" of his best verse. "To the Memory of Mr. Oldham" both praises the poet and laments his early death, reflecting the double poetic legacy which John Oldham left behind: the accomplishments of an outstanding satirist, and the promise of literary distinction which an untimely death prevented.

Ruth Salvaggio

Bibliography
Brooks, Harold F. "The Poetry of John Oldham." In *Restoration Literature: Critical Approaches*, edited by Harold Love. London: Methuen, 1972. Brooks discusses Oldham's poetry in terms of his life and his contemporaries, sources, and genres; no Oldham poem receives extended explication. The essay is, however, valuable in terms of providing information about Abraham Cowley's influence on Oldham and the evaluation of Oldham as a better satirist than Metaphysical poet.
Hammond, Paul. *John Oldham and the Renewal of Classical Culture.* Cambridge, England: Cambridge University Press, 1983. In his revaluation of Oldham, Hammond uses the Rawlinson manuscripts to show how Oldham composed his best poems. Focuses on his subject's early indebtedness to Abraham Cowley and on the translations from Horace, Juvenal, and Nicolas Boileau. For Hammond, Oldham prepared the way for the work of Samuel Johnson, John Dryden, and Alexander Pope. The book contains a biographical chapter, a chronology, and a bibliography.
Malekin, Peter. *Liberty and Love: English Literature and Society, 1640-88.* New York: St. Martin's Press, 1981. In a chapter on the satirical aftermath of the Popish Plot, Malekin analyzes Oldham's religious satire, particularly his four satires directed at the Jesuits. For Malekin, Oldham's abusive and bitter satires, written in the Juvenalian manner, created emotional prejudice, but the lack of humor and subtlety dates and thereby weakens the poems.
Selden, Raman. "Oldham, Pope, and Restoration Satire." In *English Satire and the Satiric Tradition*, edited by Claude Rawson. Oxford, England: Basil Blackwell, 1984. Selden discusses Oldham's wide range of poetry (Roch-

esterian, Metaphysical, Ovidian, pastoral, and irony) and demonstrates, through parallel passages, Alexander Pope's extensive knowledge of Oldham's poetry. It is Oldham's rough wit that constitutes the Restoration strain in Pope's eighteenth century poetry.

_____. "Oldham's Versions of the Classics." In *Poetry and Drama, 1570-1700: Essays in Honour of Harold F. Brooks*, edited by Antony Chapman and Antony Hammond. London: Methuen, 1981. Selden describes Oldham as the most "adventurous of Augustan classicists" in his imitations of Roman satiric verse and love poetry. There are many comparisons not only between Oldham's poems and their sources but also between Oldham's versions and those of his contemporaries.

SHARON OLDS

Born: San Francisco, California; November 19, 1942

Principal poetry
Satan Says, 1980; *The Dead and the Living*, 1984; *The Gold Cell*, 1987.

Other literary forms
Sharon Olds has published several articles, including "A Student's Memoir of Muriel Rukeyser" in *Poetry East* 16/17 (1985), and "A Small Memoir on Form" in *Poetry East* 20/21 (1986).

Achievements
Sharon Olds has earned national honors for her poetry. In 1981 she won the San Francisco Poetry Center Award for *Satan Says*. Her second book, *The Dead and the Living*, won both the Lamont Poetry Selection (awarded by the Academy of American Poets) in 1984 and the National Book Critics Circle Award in 1985. She has been the recipient of a Guggenheim Foundation Fellowship, and selections of her poems have been translated into French, Italian, Chinese, Russian, and Estonian. Selections have also been reprinted in *The Norton Introduction to Poetry* and *The Norton Introduction to Literature*, among other anthologies.

Biography
Born in San Francisco in 1942, Sharon Olds lived in her native city until the age of fifteen, when she was sent to a Massachusetts boarding school. Many of her poems focus on her difficult childhood, but in one interview she describes an outwardly placid youth: "I lived near a school for the blind and sang in an Episcopal church choir with girls from that school. In the summer I went to Girl Scout camp. On special campfire nights, I would stand behind a Ponderosa pine and recite, in a loud quavery voice, home-made verses that began, 'I am the spirit of the tree'" Upon moving to Massachusetts, she became entranced with the seasons of New England.

Olds was graduated with distinction from Stanford University in 1964 and earned a Ph.D. in literature from Columbia University in 1972; her dissertation was on the prosody of Ralph Waldo Emerson's poems. She has taught poetry and poetry-writing at many institutions, including Sarah Lawrence College, New York University, Columbia University, and Brandeis University. For three years she was director of New York University's creative writing program; in August, 1991, she was appointed associate professor of English there. In 1985 she founded the Golden Writers' Workshop at Goldwater Hospital for the severely handicapped in New York. In addition to her job at

New York University, she continues to teach at the hospital and give poetry readings across the country.

Analysis

Sharon Olds's signature poems are autobiographical lyrics, many of them charged with eroticism, violence, or both. She writes frequently about her sadistic father, her victimized mother, her unhappy sister and brother, her loving, lusty husband, and her son and daughter. The best of these poems are fluid, startling in their immediacy, and filled with remarks on the genitals of her family members; she is perhaps the only poet to address "the pope's penis." Her sometimes perversely comic poems about her beastly father conjure up a contemporary version of Sylvia Plath's famous "Daddy." Yet Olds's obsessive poems about her father—who, according to one poem, tied her to a chair and denied her food—are more blatantly autobiographical than Plath's. In the course of her several collections, Olds's family members evolve into flesh-and-blood characters whose significance lies in their particularity rather than universality.

In *Satan Says*, Olds sets forth the themes that also dominate her later work. The book is divided into four sections: "Daughter," "Woman," "Mother," and "Journey." All four sections assume a self-consciously female perspective. In the first section, the poet explores her own identity as defined by relationships with her parents and sister. In the second section, she writes mostly about her sexual coming of age and her relationship with her husband. The third section contains poems about her children and about the literally creative act of giving birth; there are also four related, third-person poems about "young mothers." The final section, "Journey," contains poems about all the different relationships explored in the book's first three parts.

The title poem beginning the collection announces the poet's aim in writing so explicitly about her family: "I'm trying to say what happened to us/ in the lost past." The poems in all of her books dwell at length on "what happened to us"—the poet and the people most important to her. Olds's poetry is about one woman's connections—physical, sexual, emotional—with family members and lovers of the past and present.

Sometimes Olds celebrates her connections, as a woman, with the whole world. Among the most high-spirited poems in the book, for example, is "The Language of the Brag." In this zesty feminist manifesto about childbirth, the poet proudly elbows aside Walt Whitman and Allen Ginsberg and proclaims that the most important accomplishment is "this giving birth, this glistening verb,/ and I am putting my proud American boast/ right here with the others." The last poem, "Prayer," celebrates womanhood in a more personal way. It identifies sex and childbirth as "the central meanings" in the poet's life. After an alternating consideration of these two acts, the poet entreats herself: "let me not forget:/ each action, each word/ taking its beginning from these." For Olds, determining her own identity always involves the recognition of the body and the powerful bonds characterizing intimate relationships of all kinds.

The poet's bond with her father is especially significant in *Satan Says* and in her later volumes. In "Love Fossil," for example, the father is a dinosaur—"massive, meaty, made of raw steak,/ he nibbled and guzzled, his jaw dripping weeds and bourbon,/ super sleazy extinct beast my heart dug for." In "That Year," he is the brute whom the poet's mother divorces so "there were no more/ tyings by the wrist to the chair,/ no more denial of food/ or the forcing of foods." The father in these poems is a riveting presence, a source of terror whom the poet's imagination has transformed into an object of sexual desire.

This transformation is seen clearly in one of the "Woman" poems, "The Sisters of Sexual Treasure," where the speaker describes her sister's and her own insatiable lust after they left home: "The men's bodies/ were like our father's body! The massive/ hocks, flanks, thighs, elegant/ knees, long tapered calves—." Such incestuous eroticism is simultaneously reverent and irreverent. The poet is both bad daughter and passionate woman, a self defined by the men who remind her of her father. Yet in recognizing this, in writing out the immoral fantasies of the "lost past," she assumes a surprising amount of power. She, not her lovers or her father, is in control. This is female lust, not patriarchal oppression, on a rampage.

Throughout her first three books, Olds conveys feelings of love through forthright descriptions of sex. She relishes men, their bodies, their ability to satisfy women sexually. Her depiction of sex as a means of healing and triumphing is one way she combats the memories of an unhappy childhood. In "First Night," she describes losing her virginity in terms of a biblical migration: "The inhabitants of my body began to/ get up in the dark, pack, and move." The poem reveals the extreme importance Olds places on sexual revelation: "By dawn the migrations were completed. The last/ edge of the blood bond dried,/ and like a newborn animal about to be imprinted/ I opened my eyes and saw your face."

In *The Dead and the Living*, Olds continues to explore female sexuality, motherhood, and relationships with family members. Like her first book, this one is divided into thematic sections. The twenty poems in "Part One: Poems for the Dead" are divided into nine that are "public" and eleven that are "private." In "Part Two: Poems for the Living," the first fifteen poems are grouped as "The Family," the next eight as "Men," and the last nineteen as "The Children." The large number of poems about children shows Olds's growing interest in chronicling her children's young lives as well as her own life as a mother.

The "public" poems at the book's beginning deal with social issues and people outside the poet's immediate family. Among them are several poems based on photographs of strangers suffering, as well as a poem entitled "The Death of Marilyn Monroe." These works signal an expanded focus for Olds, but they lack the cohesion and force of the "private" poems that return to the drama of her personal history. Although the latter poems deal with the same relationships that were central to *Satan Says*, they are more gracefully executed than those in the earlier volume. In "Miscarriage," for example, Olds recollects the realization, with her husband, "that we could/ botch something, you and I. All wrapped in/ purple it floated away, like a messenger/ put to death for bearing bad news." The poem not only brings together Olds's recurring themes of love, sex, and motherhood but also contains an element of mature reflection, tempered sadness. This maturity, seen in glimpses in *Satan Says*, flowers more fully in *The Dead and the Living*.

In this book Olds continues to write memorable poems about her father. In "Fate," she declares, "Finally I just gave up and became my father,/ his greased, defeated face shining toward/ anyone I looked at." She pictures herself taking on all of his characteristics—even "his sad/ sex dangling on his thigh, his stomach/ swollen and empty." The poem, which is surprisingly triumphant, shows how much the speaker has internalized her father and how much she believes his life has shaped her own: "I saw the whole world shining/ with the ecstasy of his grief, and I/ myself, he, I, shined." Another poem, "My Father's Breasts," evokes in eleven lines the speaker's enduring love for her father. Appropriating the feminine image of breasts on her father's behalf, she remembers his chest "as if I had spent/ hours, years, in that smell of black pepper and/ turned earth." The love and nostalgia in this poem are a stark counterpoint to the anger in "The Ideal Father," which portrays a father "who passed out, the one who would not/ speak for a week, slapped the glasses off a/ small girl's face." The multiple portraits of the father reveal an aggressive yet vulnerable man—and an equally aggressive, vulnerable daughter struggling to resolve, and perhaps exorcise, her passion for the man at the center of her life.

In the poems concluding *The Dead and the Living*, Olds turns her sometimes alarmingly steady gaze on her young son and daughter. In "Six-Year-Old Boy," she writes of her son as he sleeps on the back seat of the car, "his wiry limbs limp and supple/ except where his hard-on lifts his pajamas like the/ earth above the shoot of a bulb." In "Pajamas," she describes the little girl's pajamas on the floor: "You can almost see the hard/ halves of her young buttocks, the precise/ stem-mark of her sex." The speaker's evident fascination with her children's emerging sexuality—and her willingness to transform the subject into verse—may seem exploitative to some. Many readers, however, have been impressed by her willingness to explore a maternal eroticism not often articulated in verse.

After a series of alternating poems about her son and her daughter, the book ends with "The Couple," which portrays the children asleep in the back seat of a car. Though "enemies,/ rulers of separate countries," the two now look like a child bride and groom in the Middle Ages, who find unity only in sleep, "in the solitary/ power of the dream—the dream of ruling the world." Even this poem, which is not overtly sexual in its portrayal of the children, forces the reader to acknowledge the sexuality lurking in their young, sleeping bodies.

In her third collection, *The Gold Cell*, Olds continues to write confessional, sometimes erotic poems about her family. Like the first two books, this one is divided into sections. The first part, similar to the beginning of *The Dead and the Living*, contains poems about public scenes and atrocities, including rape in "The Girl" and a baby found in a litter basket in "The Abandoned Newborn." The second part contains poems about the poet's childhood in San Francisco and about her father and mother. The third section consists of poems about sexuality, including "This," which describes the centrality of the speaker's body to her identity, and the witty "Topography," which describes lovemaking in terms of two maps pressed to each other. The last section returns to the subjects of childbirth and the poet's children.

In addition to its serious, "public" poems, the first section contains several audacious works—"The Pope's Penis," "Outside the Operating Room of the Sex-Change Doctor," and "The Solution." The first two of these poems hover between shock effect and subversive humor. Olds seems to delight in freely discussing penises; they are the totems of her verse. In "The Solution," a four-paragraph prose poem, she creates a darkly comic vision of sexuality gone wild. Single people go to huge "Sex Centers" in search of the ideal mate. Things get out of control; the whole country lines up for sexual gratification "in a huge wide belt like the Milky Way, and since they had to name it they named it, they called it the American Way." Olds's punning punchline neatly distills a wry social commentary. She mocks momentarily the overwhelming urge for sex that she celebrates so earnestly in other poems.

The family poems in the second section are among Olds's most graphic work. She metaphorically describes her father's cruel treatment of her brother in "Saturn," recollects her mother's incestuous behavior in "What if God," describes finding her father smeared with blood when she was thirteen in "History: 13," and remembers terrifying childhood drives with her father in "San Francisco." The section's last three poems, however, are loving tributes to her parents; in these, Olds moves beyond rage, fear, and eroticism toward reconciliation and acceptance.

The third section's poems about female love and sexuality begin with a young girl's perspective, move through remembrances of a young lover who died in a car crash, and end with several poems about mature love and sex. These poems are also graphic, sometimes amusing, sometimes poignant, but always written with force and conviction. Olds is at her most confident and sympathetic when writing about lovemaking. As in the concluding poem in *Satan Says*, sex remains one of the "central meanings" in her life and writing.

The poems concluding *The Gold Cell* are full of love and heightened awareness of the little things making up the poet's shared life with her son and daughter. In "When My Son Is Sick," "Gerbil Funeral," and "Liddy's Orange," Olds celebrates the homely, often unsung moments of a happy family's days together. The helpless love expressed in many of these poems contrasts with detailed imagery and sweetness of mood. Olds at least temporarily leaves eroticism behind and portrays her children as vessels of purity and goodness that she wishes fiercely to protect. Given her own traumatic childhood, the possessive love Olds expresses for her children carries a special poignance, lending a strain of dark beauty to her powerful verse.

Hilary Holladay

Bibliography

Libby, Anthony. "Fathers and Daughters and Mothers and Poets." *The New York Times Book Review*, March 22, 1987, p. 23. This brief review is an example of the ambivalent reaction Olds's poetry sometimes elicits. Libby finds Olds's frequent references to genitalia excessive and suggests that many of her poems are overdone, lacking control.

Matson, Susan. "Talking to Our Father: The Political and Mythical Appropriations of Adrienne Rich and Sharon Olds." *American Poetry Review* 18 (November/December, 1989): 35-41. Matson examines the rhetorical strategies Rich and Olds use in poems addressed to their fathers and argues that, in different ways, both poets triumph over the limitations women face in male-dominated families and cultures. The section on Olds focuses on several poems in *The Gold Cell*.

Mueller, Lisel. "Three Poets." *Poetry* 138, no. 3 (1981): 170-174. This review of *Satan Says* considers the book a significant debut but criticizes Olds's vehemence and her occasionally "uneasy metaphor."

Ostriker, Alicia. "American Poetry, Now Shaped by Women." *The New York Times Book Review*, March 9, 1986, p. 1. Placing Olds at the vanguard of contemporary poetry, Ostriker suggests that a younger generation of women poets is following in the pioneering tradition of Sylvia Plath, Anne Sexton, and Adrienne Rich.

Wright, Carolyne. Review of *The Dead and the Living*. *The Iowa Review* 15, no. 1 (1985): 151-161. This review compares Olds's second volume to a successful book of short fiction. Although Wright believes that Olds sometimes overwrites or overexplains, she praises the book's focus on family and its "concern for the larger family of humanity."

CHARLES OLSON

Born: Worcester, Massachusetts; December 27, 1910
Died: New York, New York; January 10, 1970

Principal poetry
Y & X, 1948; *Letter for Melville 1951*, 1951; *This*, 1952; *In Cold Hell, in Thicket*, 1953; *The Maximus Poems 1-10*, 1953; *The Maximus Poems 11-22*, 1956; *O'Ryan 2 4 6 8 10*, 1958 (expanded edition, *O'Ryan 12345678910*, 1965); *The Maximus Poems*, 1960; *The Distances*, 1960; *Charles Olson: Reading at Berkeley*, 1966 (transcription); *The Maximus Poems, IV, V, VI*, 1968; *Archaeologist of Morning: The Collected Poems Outside the Maximus Series*, 1970; *The Maximus Poems, Volume 3*, 1975; *The Horses of the Sea*, 1976; *The Maximus Poems*, 1983; *The Collected Poems of Charles Olson*, 1987.

Other literary forms
Charles Olson was a prolific essayist, espousing the essay form in order to advance his poetic concerns to a wider audience. His prose style can present as many difficulties as his poetry, however, difficulties to a large extent deliberately sought by Olson, who was concerned that his literary production not be consumed too easily in an era of speed-reading. With *Call Me Ishmael*, a book-length study of Herman Melville, published in 1947, Olson announced his intention to define America for his day, even as Melville had, Olson believed, for *his* time, in *Moby-Dick* (1851). Key essays published within four years of *Call Me Ishmael* include "The Human Universe" and the celebrated "Projective Verse," which, together with many others, may be found in one of several collections, namely *Selected Writings of Charles Olson* (1966), *Human Universe and Other Essays* (1965), *Pleistocene Man* (1968), *Causal Mythology* (1969), *The Special View of History* (1970), *Poetry and Truth: The Beloit Lectures and Poems* (1971), and *Additional Prose: A Bibliography on America, Proprioception, and Other Notes and Essays* (1974).

Olson's letters have also proved of much interest, and many are collected in *Mayan Letters* (1953), *Letters for "Origin," 1950-1956* (1969), and the series of volumes issuing from Black Sparrow Press of his correspondence with the poet Robert Creeley.

Achievements
With his first poems and essays, Olson caught the attention of readers ready, like himself, for a profound renaming of a present grown extremely ambiguous with the destruction of traditional values during World War II. This audience continued to grow and, with the publication in 1960 of Don Allen's anthology *The New American Poetry, 1945-1960*, a year that also saw the publication in one book of the first volume of *The Maximus Poems* and

another book of poems, *The Distances*, he was widely hailed as a leader of a revolution in poetry. Olson's section in the Allen anthology came first and was the largest; the poetry conference held at the University of British Columbia in 1963, and another, held at the University of California at Berkeley in 1965, were dominated by his presence. He remained "center-stage" until his death in 1970, and since then, his contribution has received steadily increasing attention from the scholarly community, while his influence on younger poets has continued to spread.

Olson spoke through his art to a historical moment that had come unhinged, and the cogency with which he advocated "screwing the hinges back on the door of civilization" inspired a fervor of response. Poets, editors, teachers, and lay readers formed a kind of "Olson underground," a network that disseminated the kinds of information which Olson's project favored, and these were various indeed: the founding and the decline of early civilizations (Sumer, Egypt, Greece, the Maya), the pre-Socratics, the Tarot, psychedelic drugs, non-Euclidean geometry, the philosophy of Alfred North Whitehead, and documents of the European settlement of New England—a far from exhaustive list. For the most part, Olson shunned publicity and was therefore less known to the counterculture of the 1960's than was his fellow poet Allen Ginsberg, but there can be no doubt that Olson, both in his own person and through this network, helped instigate and name the cultural revolution then attempted.

Olson's poetry instructs, deliberately, as do his essays. In this respect, it is noteworthy that his career as a teacher spanned four decades, starting at Clark University in the 1930's and resuming (after an interim during which he worked first for the American Civil Liberties Union and then in the Office of War Information) at Black Mountain College in the late 1940's. Olson continued to teach at Black Mountain until the college closed in 1956; he moved on to the State University of New York at Buffalo in 1963, where he worked for three years, and concluded his teaching career at the University of Connecticut. A partial list of his distinguished students includes John Wieners, Edward Dorn, Michael Rumaker, Fielding Dawson, Joel Oppenheimer, and Jonathan Williams. While serving as rector of Black Mountain College, from 1951 to 1956, Olson turned it into a center of the literary arts and was responsible for the publication of the *Black Mountain Review* (edited by Creeley), which gave its name to the group of writers most often published therein.

Olson was the recipient of two Guggenheim grants, in 1939 to continue his work on his dissertation on Herman Melville and in 1948 to write about the interaction of racial groups during the settling of the American West; in 1952, he received a grant from the Wenner-Gren Foundation to study Mayan hieroglyphics in the Yucatan. (It is characteristic of Olson that he completed none of these projects within the guidelines proposed but instead transmuted them into poetic essays and poetry.) In 1965, he was awarded the Oscar Blumenthal-Charles Leviton Prize by *Poetry* magazine, possibly the most prestigious award he received for his poetry. His poetry was too radical, and his life too short, for further such acknowledgment to come his way during his lifetime.

Biography

Charles John Olson was born on December 27, 1910, in the central Massachusetts town of Worcester. His mother, Mary Hines, was of Irish immigrant stock; his father, also named Charles, was of Swedish origin. Olson's giant proportions (fully grown, he was to stand six feet, nine inches) obviously came from his father's side, the elder Olson having stood well over six feet tall himself, whereas the poet's mother was barely above five feet tall. Olson's father worked as a letter carrier, a career the poet was to take up at one point in his life. From 1915 until he left home, Olson spent part of each summer with his family in Gloucester, a small seaport of Massachusetts north of Boston; he would later live there and anchor his Maximus poems in this, to him, "root city." In 1928, he entered Wesleyan University, being graduated in 1932 and receiving his M.A. there the following year; his thesis, "The Growth of Herman Melville, Prose Writer and Poetic Thinker," led him to discover hitherto unknown portions of Melville's library, and this, in turn, led to his paper "Lear and Moby-Dick," written in the course of his doctoral studies at Harvard and published in *Twice-a-Year* in 1938. Between 1932 and 1939, Olson supported himself either by grants or by teaching: at Clark University from 1934 to 1936 and at Harvard from 1936 to 1939.

In 1939, awarded a Guggenheim Fellowship, Olson lived with his widowed mother in Gloucester, laying the groundwork for what was to become *Call Me Ishmael.* In 1940, he moved to New York City, working first as publicity director for the American Civil Liberties Union and then as chief of the Foreign Language Information Service of the Common Council for American Unity. During this period, Olson met and married Constance Wilcock. From 1942 to 1944, Olson served as associate chief of the Foreign Language Division of the Office of War Information, in Washington, D.C., and during Franklin D. Roosevelt's campaign for a fourth term in 1944, he served on the Democratic National Committee. The following year, he was offered high office in the new Democratic administration but chose instead to devote himself to writing, and, with the help of Ezra Pound, whom Olson often visited at St. Elizabeth's Hospital, he published *Call Me Ishmael* in 1947.

For the next ten years, Olson's life was to be closely associated with Black Mountain College, an experiment in education being carried on near Asheville, North Carolina, where he worked first as a lecturer and subsequently, starting in 1951, as rector. Olson during this period wrote his landmark essays on poetics and the poems that made up his book *The Distances.* Through

Vincent Ferrini, a Gloucester poet, Olson met Robert Creeley, and a correspondence ensued that was to prove seminal to the movement in poetry known as "Black Mountain poetry" or "projective verse" (the latter from the Olson essay so titled). In 1954, Creeley came to teach at the college and edited the *Black Mountain Review*. Another poet, Robert Duncan—association with whom was to prove vital to Olson—also taught at Black Mountain during this time. Olson, meanwhile, had ended his first marriage (which produced one child, Katherine, born in 1951) and embarked on a second, to Elizabeth Kaiser, whom he met and married in 1954; their son, Charles Peter, was born in May of the following year.

As Black Mountain College was no longer proving fiscally viable, Olson closed it in 1956, the year that saw the publication of *The Maximus Poems 11-22* (*The Maximus Poems 1-10* had been issued in 1953). In 1957, Olson journeyed to San Francisco to read at the Museum of Art and The Poetry Center and to deliver in five lectures his "special view of history." Olson then settled with his wife and son in Gloucester, working on another volume of Maximus poems. The year 1960 was his *annus mirabilis*: He was included in the anthology *The New American Poetry, 1945-1960*, his Maximus poems were reissued as a single book, and his other poems were collected into the volume *The Distances*. Thenceforth Olson's star, in the ascendant throughout the previous decade, was much more visibly so, and he met his quickly growing audience at a number of venues, among these the Vancouver Poetry Conference (1963), the Festival of the Two Worlds in Spoleto, Italy (1965), the Berkeley Poetry Conference (1965), the Literary Colloquium of the Academy of Art in Berlin (1966), the International Poetry Festival in London (1967), and Beloit College (1968), where he delivered the lectures subsequently published as *Poetry and Truth*. Several collections of his essays were issued during this decade also. From 1963 to 1965, Olson served as visiting professor of English at the State University of New York at Buffalo; in 1969, he accepted a similar post at the University of Connecticut.

These years were marked, however, by dissipation and heartbreak. His wife died in an automobile accident in 1964; Olson's health began to fail, and, in 1969, cancer of the liver was diagnosed; he died in a New York City hospital on January 10, 1970.

Analysis

Charles Olson's poetry is political in a profound, not superficial, sense; it does not spend time naming "current events," but rather, it devotes itself to defining "the dodges of discourse" which have enabled humanity (especially in the West) to withdraw from reality into increasingly abstract fictions of life. Olson came of age during the Great Depression and admired Roosevelt's New Deal, but with the death of the president in 1945 and the bombing of Hiroshima and Nagasaki, Olson lost faith in the possibilities for liberal democracy. It did not go wide enough or deep enough in the attempt to restore humanity's lost meaning. Nor did it provide enough checks and balances against the corporate takeover of the world. Olson encouraged a resistance based on knowledge from a range of sources which he endeavored, through his essays and his poems, to bring to common attention. "Resistance," in fact, is a key word here: One of his first essays bears that title, and often, Olson's stance reminds one of the Maquis and other "underground" pockets of resistance to the Fascists during World War II. His is a sort of intellectual commando operation bent on destroying, marshaling not yards or military arsenals but modes of thought (and therefore of action) that are out of kilter with current realities and "fascistic" in their ability to crush individual senses of value that would struggle toward a coherence—where the merely subjective might transcend itself and establish a vital community. However sweeping Olson's proposals, in effect his program is reactive; such a reaction against the status quo was, as he saw it, the essential first step toward building a civilization that put people before profits. "When man is reduced to so much fat for soap, superphosphate for soil, fillings and shoes for sale," Olson wrote, the news of the Nazi death camps fresh in the minds of his audience as in his own, "he has, to begin again, one answer, one point of resistance only to such fragmentation, one organized ground. . . . It is his physiology he is forced to arrive at. . . . It is his body that is his answer." This answer led Olson to ground his poetics in the physical breathing of the poet, the vital activity that registers the smallest fluctuations of thought and feeling. Language had become separated from being over the centuries of Western civilization, so that, for example, it became more important to carry out orders than to consider their often terrible consequences. In the words of Paul Christensen, "The denotational core of words must be rescued from neglect; logical classification and the principles of syntax must be suppressed and a new, unruly seizure of phenomena put in their place." Civilization, to the extent that it alienates one from one's experience of the actual earth and the life that arises therefrom, has failed, and it supplants with "slick pictures" the actual conditions of human lives.

Therefore, it has become necessary, Olson argues, to deconstruct the accepted authorities of Western thought, while seeking to preserve the thought of such persons who, throughout history, have warned against systems of ideation that debase human beings. In Olson's vision, one of the great villains is Aristotle; one of the heroes, Apollonius of Tyana. With Aristotle, "the two great means appear: logic and classification. And it is they," Olson continues in the essay "Human Universe," "that have so fastened themselves on habits of thought that action is interfered with, absolutely interfered with, I should say." Olson in this same passage points out: "The harmony of the universe, and I include man, is not logical, or better, is post-logical, as is the order of any created thing." As for classification,

What makes most acts—of living and of writing—unsatisfactory, is that the person and/or the writer satisfy themselves that they can only make a form . . . by selecting from the full content some face of it, or plane, some part. And at just this point, by just this act, they fall back on the dodges of discourse, and immediately, they lose me, I am no longer engaged, this is not what I know is the going-on. . . . It comes out a demonstration, a separating out, an act of classification, and so, a stopping.

In "Apollonius of Tyana, A Dance, with Some Words, for Two Actors," Olson addresses the reader through the medium of a contemporary of Christ, Apollonius, and the play's one other character, Tyana, the place of his origin, as well as through himself, as narrator/commentator. This last tells how Apollonius "knows . . . that *his* job, at least, is to find out how to inform all people how best they can stick to the instant, which is both temporal and intense, which is both shape and law." Apollonius makes his way through the Mediterranean world of the first century A.D., which "is already the dispersed thing the West has been since," conducting "a wide investigation into the local, the occasional, what you might even call the ceremonial, but without . . . any assurance that he knows how to make objects firm, or how firm he is."

Apollonius, readers are told, learned from his journeyings

that two ills were coming on man: (1) unity was crowding out diversity (man was getting too multiplied to stay clear by way of the old vision of himself, the humanist one, was getting too distracted to abide in his own knowing with any of his old confidence); and (2) unity as a goal (making Rome an empire, say) had, as its intellectual pole an equally mischievous concept, that of the universal—of the 'universals' as Socrates and Christ equally had laid them down. Form . . . was suddenly swollen, was being taken as a thing larger a thing outside a thing above any particular, even any given man.

These descriptions of the confusions which beset Apollonius clearly apply to those Olson himself was encountering, and therefore readers look to find, in Apollonius' solutions, those of Olson. This part of the work, however, rings less convincingly: Olson makes some rhetorical flourishes, but in the end the reader is simply told that Apollonius has learned that he must "commit himself"; he has also learned that Tyana (surely a figure for Olson's Gloucester) is intimately connected with his endeavor.

Olson's brilliance when specifying the major ills, and his vagueness when speaking to their cure, his inability to resolve the inherent contradictions between the latter and the former (how shall the individual make himself responsible for many of the elements in a society in whose false unity and swollen forms he himself is caught and of which he is a part?), all so clearly to be seen in this piece, persist throughout his canon. It is the problem he recognizes in Melville, who finds splendid embodiment for his society's evils in Ahab but who can never create a convincing hero. Large answers, the sweeping solution, evade Olson by the very nature of his method, which is to focus on particulars, even on "the blessing/ that difficulties are once more."

These difficulties include the obvious truth that Olson is trammeled at the outset by the very tricks of discourse he would overthrow: Witness, for example, his sweeping generalization, near the beginning of his essay "Human Universe": "We have lived long in a generalizing time, at least since 450 B.C." Again, and on the other hand, given that he is urgent about reeducating his contemporaries to eradicate society's evils before it is too late, his refusal to write in received forms was bound to delay dissemination of his message. Moreover, while he was embodying the difficulties and the particularities in highly difficult and particular forms, and thereby rendering these virtually inaccessible except by the slow "trickle-down" process which accompanies aesthetically responsible art, he was given, in both poem and essay, to assertion without supporting evidence—such is the nature of the intuitive perception he espoused, as against a stupefied insistence on proof—and thereby to alienating many more conventionally trained readers.

That Olson could not accomplish his project was a result of its inherent impossibility; this failure, however, in no way erases the spellbinding body of his poetry. His magnificent embodiment and evocation of the dilemma in which he found himself remains as both consolation and exhortation. He gave a rationale for free (or, to use his own term, Open) verse, of which his own work is the most telling demonstration; he gave a scale and a scope to poetry which inspired and continue to inspire other poets and which make his own among the most compelling of all time. If his more general prescriptions regarding society—true as they still ring, particularly in their diagnostics—have been largely ineffectual against the momentum of social change (surely, from Olson's point of view, for the worse), his speculations, conjecture, and assertions concerning the practice of poetry stay valid, viable, and vital. Moreover, his insistence that the poet (as Percy Bysshe Shelley thought, a century and more before) be lawgiver to those of his day must be a salutary thorn in the side of any practitioner of the art.

The power of Olson's finest poems stems from a double movement: The poet strives to fill his poem with the greatest variety of subject matter that he can; the poet strives to empty his poem of everything he has brought into it. The plethora of subject matter (information, often conflicting) is there to say that the world is absolutely fascinating—its details are fit matter for anyone's attention; the act of emptying these out is to say nothing is as important, as worthy of attention, as the moment about to come into being. A quick topic sentence ("What does not change/ is the will to change"; "As the dead prey upon us,/ they are the dead in ourselves"), broad enough in application, allows Olson to bring in all manner of materials by logical or intuitive association that somehow fit under its rubric: Meditation upon change (in his early poem "The Kingfishers") leads, first, to a recalled cocktail party conversation that touched upon the passing of the fashion for kingfishers' feathers; this soon leads Olson to recall Mao Tse-tung's speech upon the success of his revolution; and, a dialectic having now been set up between West (tyrannized by its markets—"fashion"—and associated with a dying civilization) and East (Mao's revolution, source of the rising sun), the poem proceeds to "dance" (a favorite term of Olson's for the poetic act), its details representing East/novelty/uprising in among those representing West/ stagnation/descent, in a vocabulary variously encyclopedic, colloquial, hortatory, cybernetic, lyrical, prosaic. It is a collage, then, but one filled with movement, bearing out Olson's dictum "ONE PERCEPTION MUST IMMEDIATELY AND DIRECTLY LEAD TO A FURTHER PERCEPTION." Yet the poem ends: "shall you uncover honey/ where maggots are?// I hunt among stones," and while to one reader this may suggest that the poet's weight is thrown on the side of those details which belong to the "East/novelty/ uprising" sequence, to a reader who bears in mind that *all* these details now are of the past, it suggests that the poet opts for the present/future, which, being as yet all potential, is blank—as a stony landscape.

Ends, however, are only tiny portions of their poems and cannot cancel the keen pleasure a reader may take in tracing meaning among such enigmatically juxtaposed blocks of constantly altering language, while being carried along at such various velocities. There are many striking formulations— often evidently stumbled on in the compositional process, which appears to unfold before the reader's very eyes (and ears); these often appear as good counsel ("In the midst of plenty, walk/ as close to/ bare// In the face of sweetness,/ piss"; "The nets of being/ are only eternal if you sleep as your hands/ ought to be busy"). Syntax—at times so filled with baffles and circumlocutions as to be more properly parataxis—brilliantly evokes the difficulties Olson would name, even court; nouns carry much of the freight, whereas adjectives are scarce (description Olson thought not projective, not able to break the circle of representation); verbs tend to be those of concealment and discovery and of social acts—talking, urging, hearing, permitting, obtaining, and the like. Because his notation favors the phrase over the sentence, in Olson's poetry words can appear to leap from the page, freed significantly of their usual subjections. Although on occasion Olson (an accomplished orator) segues into a Roman kind of rhetoric, for the most part he stays true to his aim, namely, to attack a universe of discourse with a poetry not only of particulars but also particulate in its construction. As indicated earlier, each of these elements helps constitute an intense dialectic whose synthesis occurs only as the abolition of its components: "It is undone business/ I speak of, this morning,/ with the sea/ stretching out/ from my feet."

While Olson's poetry appeared as a number of volumes during his lifetime, these are now contained in two texts: *Maximus Poems* and *Archaeologist of Morning* (containing all of his non-Maximus poems). "Maximus" is the poetic figure Olson created to "speak" poems (sometimes called letters) to the people of Gloucester and, by extension, to any who would be people of "a coherence not even yet new"—persons of that vivid and imminent future which is the Grail to Olson's search and labor. Maximus knows the history of the geography of this seaport and, by extension, of both pre- and post-settlement New England; of the migratory movements of Europe and the ancient world; of other civilizations which, at some (usually early) stage, discovered the will to cohere, which Olson praised. He is to some degree based upon Maximus of Tyre, a maverick sage akin to Apollonius of Tyana from the second century A.D., although Olson appears not to have investigated this historical personage with much thoroughness, preferring, no doubt, not to disturb the introjected Maximus he was finding so fruitful. The significance of the city of Gloucester in these poems is complex but has to do with a place loved so well that it repays its lover with a battery of guarantees and tokens, enabling him to withstand the greased slide of present culture, the suck of absentee ownership and built-in obsolescence. It is for Olson the place where, in William Wordsworth's terms, he first received those "intimations of immortality" that even in the beleaguered present can solace and hearten. In his attachment to its particulars, his heat for its physical reality, the reader is invited to discover feelings for some actual place or entity akin to that of the poet, thereby to be led to the commitment essential to an awakened sense of life and a practice of person equal "to the real itself."

David Bromige

Other major works
SHORT FICTION: *Stocking Cap: A Story*, 1966.
PLAYS: *The Fiery Hunt and Other Plays*, 1977.
NONFICTION: *Call Me Ishmael: A Study of Melville*, 1947; *Mayan Letters*, 1953; "Projective Verse," 1959; *Human Universe and Other Essays*, 1965; *Proprioception*, 1965; *Selected Writings of Charles Olson*, 1966; *Pleistocene Man*, 1968; *Causal Mythology*, 1969; *Letters for "Origin," 1950-1956*, 1969; *The Special View of History*, 1970; *On Black Mountain*, 1971; *Additional Prose: A Bibliography on America, Proprioception, and Other Notes and Essays*, 1974; *Charles Olson and Ezra Pound: An Encounter at St. Elizabeth's*, 1975; *The Post Office*, 1975; *Muthologos: Collected Lectures and Interviews*, 1978-1979 (2 volumes); *Charles Olson and Robert Creeley: The Complete Correspondence*, 1980 (8 volumes; George F. Butterick, editor).
MISCELLANEOUS: *Selected Writings of Charles Olson*, 1966; *Poetry and Truth: The Beloit Lectures and Poems*, 1971.

Bibliography
Cech, John. *Charles Olson and Edward Dahlberg: A Portrait of a Friendship*. Victoria, Canada: English Literary Studies, University of Victoria, 1982. Cech describes the relationship between these two longtime friends

and writers. Provides interesting background for students interested in literary movements of the time. Includes a bibliography.

Evans, George. "A Selection from the Correspondence: Charles Olson and Cid Corman, 1950." *Origin*, 5th ser. 1 (1983): 78-106. Evans presents the first fourteen of 175 letters between Olson and Corman. In 1950, Corman was attempting to launch a new poetry magazine. He writes to Olson to persuade him to take on the position of contributing editor. Interesting to all students of the Objectivist movement.

Heller, Michael. *Conviction's Net of Branches: Essays on the Objectivist Poets and Poetry.* Carbondale: Southern Illinois University Press, 1985. Corman was a major figure in the Objectivist poetry movement. These essays shed light on the nature and convictions of the Objectivists. This study is suitable for advanced undergraduate and graduate poetry students.

Olson, Charles. *Charles Olson and Cid Corman: Complete Correspondence, 1950-1964.* Edited by George Evans. 2 vols. Orono: National Poetry Foundation, University of Maine, 1987. Evans presents the 175 extant letters between the founder of *Origin* magazine and its contributing editor. They reveal that Olson was initially skeptical of Corman's aims, fearing that Corman was starting a magazine with too broad a scope to serve the needs of the Objectivist poets.

_____. *Letters for Origin, 1950-1956.* Edited by Albert Glover. New York: Paragon House, 1989. Cid Corman founded *Origin* magazine as a forum for Objectivist poets, and he hired Charles Olson to be its contributing editor. Their letters discuss the struggles of the fledgling periodical and of the Objectivist poetic movement. For serious Corman students.

GEORGE OPPEN

Born: New Rochelle, New York; April 24, 1908
Died: Sunnyvale, California; July 7, 1984

Principal poetry
Discrete Series, 1934; *The Materials*, 1962; *This in Which*, 1965; *Of Being Numerous*, 1968; *Alpine*, 1969; *Seascape: Needle's Eye*, 1972; *Collected Poems*, 1975; *Primitive*, 1978.

Other literary forms
In addition to his poetry, George Oppen published several reviews and essays. Of these, two are central to an understanding of his work: "The Mind's Own Place," published in *Kulchur*, and "A Letter," published in *Agenda*, in 1973. Oppen's many published interviews and his extensive correspondence with both American and British writers provide an in-depth look into Oppen's poetics and his sense of poetry's place in the contemporary world; *The Selected Letters of George Oppen* was published in 1990.

Achievements
In a long and distinguished career, Oppen never wavered from that which Ezra Pound in 1934 noted of his work: its commitment to sustained seriousness, craftsmanship, and individual sensibility. Out of this commitment, Oppen created one of the most moving and complex bodies of poetry of the twentieth century.

Oppen was one of the original Objectivist poets; his work can be associated with that of William Carlos Williams, Pound, and the Imagists. Yet more than any other poet associated with that group, he was to develop a radical poetics of contingency, a poetics as wary of formalist assumptions about art as it is about naïve realism in poetry. His unique combining of imagery and rhetoric, the breadth of his subject matter, and its nearly populist strain have made his work extremely important to younger poets.

In recent years, with the receipt of the Pulitzer Prize for Poetry in 1969 and an award for his distinguished contribution to poetry from the National Endowment for the Arts and with increasing critical attention (much of it contained in *George Oppen: Man and Poet*, published in 1981), Oppen's place in twentieth century poetry is beginning to be recognized as one of major significance.

Biography
George Oppen was born on April 24, 1908, in New Rochelle, New York, into a middle-class family. Within a short time, he had moved with his family, who were in the theater business, to San Francisco, a city which has been

both an inspiration and a resource for much of his poetry. In 1926, at a small college in Oregon, he met Mary Colby, and they were later married. Of their relationship, Mary wrote that it was not simply love but the discovery that "we were in search of an esthetic within which to live." For both, it meant distancing themselves from their pasts and striking out into new territory, both geographical and psychic. This departure was not so much a break with the past as a desire to obtain distance from and insight into it, for in this, as in all of their subsequent travels, the Oppens sought to live close to, and understand, ordinary working people.

Together, the Oppens hitchhiked to New York City, completing the last leg of the journey on a barge through the Erie Canal. In New York they met Louis Zukofsky and Charles Reznikoff, whose friendship and influence were to shape Oppen's poetry significantly over the years. These poets, with the encouragement of William Carlos Williams and Ezra Pound, formed themselves into the Objectivists, one of the most significant groupings in the field of twentieth century poetry, and began publishing one another's work.

In 1930, the Oppens traveled to France and Italy, meeting Pound and Constantin Brancusi; returning to the United States, the couple became involved in labor organizing and other left-wing political movements, an involvement which for Oppen ultimately led to a twenty-five-year hiatus from writing poetry. This political commitment led the Oppens to flee to Mexico during the McCarthy period, where Oppen began to write poetry again. This work, collected in *The Materials*, and touching on the themes of Oppen's past, his travels, and his sense of contemporary urban life, brought Oppen immediate recognition as a unique and powerful voice in contemporary poetry.

In 1960, the Oppens returned to the United States, living alternately in New York, San Francisco (where they eventually settled), and Maine, places which play a prominent role in Oppen's poetry. Oppen died in Sunnyvale, California, southeast of San Francisco, in 1984.

Analysis

In one of George Oppen's poems, the poet is being driven around an island off the coast of Maine by a poor fisherman and his wife. The landscape, the lobster pots and fishing gear, the harbor, and the post office are noted, and the poet is, unaccountably, moved by a nearly metaphysical sense of passage. The experience is at once intimate and remote, and the poet is moved to exclaim to himself: "Difficult to know what one means/ —to be serious and to know what one means—." Such lines could be emblems for Oppen's entire career, for, of contemporary poets, none has more searchingly investigated through poetry the attempt to mean, to examine how language is used, and so to account for the very vocabulary of modernity.

For Oppen, inquiry is synonymous with expression. In a world of mass communication and of a debased language riddled with preconceptions about the nature of reality, the poet, according to Oppen, must begin in a completely new way; he must begin, as he says in one poem, "impoverished of tone of pose that common/ wealth of parlance." In Oppen, this is not so much a search for a language of innocence or novelty as it is a resolve against making use of certain historical or elegiac associations in language, a desire on the part of the poet not to be bewitched (as the philosopher Ludwig Wittgenstein warned) by conventional ways of speaking and of making poetry.

Oppen's entire body of work can be seen as a modern test of the poet's capacity to articulate. The terms of his poetry are the common meanings of words as they attempt to render the brute givens of the world of appearance. For this reason, Oppen has called his work "realist"; it is realist in the sense that it is "concerned with a fact (the world) which it did not create." In a way, the subject of all Oppen's poetry is the nature of this encounter, whether with the world or with others. The task for the poet is neither to beautify sentimentally nor to categorize such encounters but to render their living quality, to make the poet's relatedness to the facts into something felt. As Oppen acknowledges in one of his poems, "Perhaps one is himself/ Beyond the heart, the center of the thing/ and cannot praise it/ As he would want to."

In all Oppen's work, there is an attempt to render the visual datum accurately and precisely; this is in keeping with the Imagist and Objectivist techniques at the root of Oppen's poetics. The aim of the technique, however, is more philosophical than literary; it is to establish the material otherness of the visual event. In the poems, objects and landscapes obtrude and reveal their existence as though seen for the first time. *Discrete Series*, Oppen's first book, is nearly procedural in its epistemological insistence on what is seen. The short lyrics which compose its contents are less like poems than they are the recording of eye movements across surfaces juxtaposed with snatches of statement and remembered lines from older poetry and fiction. The white space of the page surrounding these elements becomes a field of hesitations, advances, and reconsiderations, and the burden of meaning in the poem resides in the reader's recomposition of the fragmented elements. It is as though a crystal or prism had been interposed between poet and subject.

By the time Oppen had resumed writing poetry in the late 1950's, he had greatly modified his reliance on visual sense as a source of knowledge. One of the chief distinctions of his poetry remains its persuasive powers of registration, as in a poem written in the 1960's where "the north/ Looks out from its rock/ bulging into the fields," or from a poem of the 1970's where the sun moves "beyond the blunt/ towns of the coast . . . fishermen's/ tumbled tumbling headlands the needle silver/ water. . . ." Such imagery evokes the solidity and palpability of the world, and, at the same time, suggests its ungainliness and its obdurate self-referential quality which contrasts sharply with the usual visual clichés.

This sense of the visual, however, is for Oppen only one element in a dialectical occasion in which poetic truth resides neither in the object nor in the poet but in the interaction between the two. If, as Oppen would insist, the poet's ultimate aim is truth, then what is seen has the possibility of being a kind of measure: seeing precedes its verbalization and therefore offers an opportunity for an open response to the world. This opportunity is hedged about with all one's conditioned reflexes, the material which the poet must work through to arrive at a sense of the real. It is through this struggle that Oppen's poetics, though they are concerned with ambiguity and paradox, strive for a clarity that is both immediate and complex. Oppen has described this as an attempt to write poetry which "cannot not be understood."

This process can be seen at work in *The Materials*, the first of Oppen's major collections to be written and published after his twenty-year hiatus from the world of poetry. The book's underlying theme, carried through its forty poems, is clearly signaled in its epigraph from the philosopher Jacques Maritain, "We awake in the same moment to ourselves and to things." Oppen's "subjects" are these awakenings, which are capable of transcending the usual notions of self and society. In one of the book's major poems, "The Return," amidst "the dim sound of the living" the impingement of the natural world becomes a moment in which "We cannot reconcile ourselves./ No one is reconciled, tho we spring/ From the ground together—." Nor is this estrangement eased by a sense of history or community; these are fictions in their way, and to look closely at them is to feel "The sense of that passage, is desertion, betrayal, that we are not innocent of loneliness." The poem ends with an image of the poet's old neighborhood "razed, whole blocks of a city gone . . ." in which "the very ceremony of innocence" has been drowned.

In Oppen, such loss of innocence is not to be mourned; rather, it is the very beginning of a purer association between individuals and between the individual and the world, based on a language shorn of old, inauthentic mythologies. "Leviathan," the last poem in *The Materials*, insists that "Truth also is the pursuit of it," that "We must talk now. Fear/ is fear. But we abandon one another."

Oppen's next book, *This in Which*, is an exploration of the nature of such "talk." Here the poet's search is for a "substantial language of clarity, and of respect," based on a willingness to look fully, without illusion, at the human condition. It is "possible to use words," the poet says, "provided one treat them as enemies./ Not enemies—Ghosts which have run mad." Comparing modern consciousness to that of the primitive Mayans and their mythic view of life, "the poor savages of ghost and glitter," Oppen reminds the reader that it is necessary to examine squarely the "terror/ the unsightly/ silting sand of events." The critic Hugh Kenner, in discussing Oppen's method of stripping language of its historical associations, suggests that an apt motto for his work (and for that of the other Objectivist poets) might be "No myths." "Art,"

Oppen warns, "also is not good for us/ unless . . . it may rescue us/ as only the true/ might rescue us."

These themes, the need for a demythologizing poetics and a language adequate to render the fullness of reality, are brought to culmination in *Of Being Numerous*, the book-length poem which many critics consider to be Oppen's masterpiece. *Of Being Numerous* is concerned with the deepest notions of community and the basis on which community might be established: what is meant by humanity, ethics, and love. The poem is, in a sense, an interrogation of these terms, an attempt to discover whether they can truthfully be retained in the light of what humanity has become. For Oppen, the word "community" represents, in the present, an expression of the individual's psychic needs, of the effect of anxiety on contemporary life. Hence, in Oppen's view, the very notion of community is, at best, flawed and irrational. Humanity, the poem tells us, is "bewildered/ by the shipwreck/ of the singular"; thus, "we have chosen the meaning/ of being numerous." Given this situation, there is now only "a ferocious mumbling in public/ of rootless speech." Against this mumbling, Oppen seeks to set the truth-value of poetic speech. The poem attempts, not to lull one into another false sense of community, but to clear the air of bankrupt sentimentality about community and to genuinely reestablish it on a recognition of one another's essential aloneness. This is to discover, the poem continues, "Not truth, but each other." The poem's last word, "curious," overshadows the argument of the poem, for it is Oppen's intention to lead the reader to this understanding, not by rational means, but by the dynamics of aesthetic response. In such a response is to be found "our jubilation/ exalted and as old as that truthfulness/ which illumines speech."

Oppen's last work, beginning with *Seascape: Needle's Eye* and continuing through his final collection, *Primitive*, involves a radical departure from the poetry that had come before. In the earlier poems, especially in *Of Being Numerous*, Oppen created a restrained but rhetorically powerful amalgam of statement and imagery, a poetry which, like a Socratic dialogue, aimed at undermining conventional thought and attitude. In the later poems, the chaos and flux of life and the ever-partial mythologizing that language enacts are embodied in a troubled and moving voice that seems to embrace deeply the contingency and indeterminacy of life.

In these poems, syntax, punctuation, and rhythm are wrenched into a compelling new tone; words and phrases are enjambed and repeated, then modified into a poetic architecture which in its cadence expresses a new urgency, as in this excerpt from *Seascape: Needle's Eye*:

> Pride in the sandspit wind this ether this other this element all
> It is I or I believe
> We are the beaks of the ragged birds
> Tune of the ragged birds' beaks.

Such poetry seems at once immensely sophisticated and primordial; it is sophisticated inasmuch as behind its strange and powerful technique lies the history of the use and misuse of language. At the same time, it strikes the reader as a kind of first poetry, fashioned out of an unconditioned and open sense of life.

Such poems range across all the characteristic themes of poetry, love, death, politics, and being; yet the ambiguity of their claims, rather than diminishing them, adds a new, previously unheard richness to the verse. This richness is in the service not only of the present but also of history. As Oppen notes in *Primitive*, harking back to the very beginning of his career and his insistence on the visual, "the tongues of appearance/ speak in the unchosen journey . . . the words out of that whirlwind his." In Oppen, this "unchosen journey" has been transformed into a powerful poetry of both collective and individual pain and loss, into a desire to make "a music more powerful," a music meant to redeem humanity "till other voices wake us or we drown."

Michael Heller

Other major work
NONFICTION: *The Selected Letters of George Oppen*, 1990.

Bibliography
Freeman, John, ed. *Not Comforts/But Visions: Essays on the Poetry of George Oppen*. Budleigh Salterton, Devon: Interim Press, 1984. This volume, intended to introduce Oppen to British readers, contains contributions by poets and critics. Truly an appreciation for the uninitiated. The essays survey Oppen's work rather than analyze the poems.
Hatlin, Burton, ed. *George Oppen, Man and Poet*. Orono, Maine: National Poetry Foundation, 1981. This homage dedicated to Oppen and his wife is an anthology of twenty-eight articles and two separate bibliographies, all but six published for the first time. The essays are well organized, and good bibliographies appear in notes. Two essays (by John Peck and Rachel Blau DuPlessis) give political and philosophical contexts to the poetry. Contains an index and two personal memoirs by Mary Oppen.
Ironwood 5 (1975). This special issue devoted to Oppen is really a celebratory bouquet. It contains, among other things, an "Introductory Note on Poetry" by Charles Tomlinson, seven poems by the poet, and an interview, photographs, and memoirs by Charles Reznikoff and Mary Oppen ("France 1930-33"), and a critical essay by Rachel Blau DuPlessis ("What Do We Believe to Live With?"). Supplemented by a bibliography.
Ironwood 13 (Fall, 1985). This second special issue on the poet contains a number of excellent essays, memoirs, and appreciations. This volume contains more critical work than the first volume and a different selection of

critics, poets, and scholars are presented. An excellent publication.

Paideuma 10 (Spring, 1981). This journal, normally dedicated to Ezra Pound studies, is a memorial to George Oppen. It contains a collection of more than thirty appreciations, poems, explications, biographical sketches, and memorials, and it begins with Pound's preface to Oppen's *Discrete Series*. This, like the first *Ironwood* special issue, is really a commemorative collection of material on the poet's life and work.

Tomlinson, Charles. *Some Americans: A Personal Record*. Berkeley: University of California Press, 1981. The British poet, Tomlinson, tells of his encounters with many major artists during the mid-twentieth century. Includes a character sketch of George and Mary Oppen.

JOEL OPPENHEIMER

Born: Yonkers, New York; February 18, 1930
Died: Henniker, New Hampshire; October 11, 1988

Principal poetry

The Dutiful Son, 1956; *The Love Bit and Other Poems*, 1962; *In Time: Poems, 1962-1968*, 1969; *On Occasion*, 1973; *The Woman Poems*, 1975; *Just Friends/Friends and Lovers*, 1980; *At Fifty*, 1982; *Poetry: The Ecology of the Soul*, 1983; *New Spaces: Poems, 1975-1983*, 1985.

Other literary forms

In addition to writing book reviews and critiques, introductions and jacket blurbs, Joel Oppenheimer worked on the primary level as a printer and typographer. He was also a regular columnist for *The Village Voice* from 1969 to 1984.

Oppenheimer wrote several plays which have been performed off-off-Broadway: *The Great American Desert* (1961), *Miss Right* (1962), and *Like a Hill* (1963). Oppenheimer's collection of short stories, *Pan's Eyes*, was published in 1974. Through the aficionado's eyes, he has viewed popular American culture in *The Wrong Season* (1973) and *Marilyn Lives!* (1981). *The Wrong Season* re-creates the year 1972 from the point of view of a disappointed New York Mets baseball fan. With interviews, photographs, personal narrative, and poems, *Marilyn Lives!* looks at the life of Marilyn Monroe.

Achievements

For the first fifteen years of his writing career, Oppenheimer worked, in the tradition of William Carlos Williams or Wallace Stevens, outside the university to support himself and his writing, mostly as a production manager for printing firms. Beginning in 1969, he became an active presence at various universities, teaching and giving poetry readings. His work was recognized by his appointments as director of the St. Mark's Poetry Project and the New York City Teachers and Writers Collaborative, as well as by such awards as the Creative Artists Public Service Fellowship (1971) and the National Endowment for the Humanities (1980). In addition, he held the poet-in-residence positions at the City College of New York and at New England College and visiting professorships at St. Andrews Presbyterian College in North Carolina and the Black Mountain II College at the State University of New York at Buffalo. In his own words, his achievement was that he "made poems and children much of his adult life, and also a living."

Biography

Joel Lester Oppenheimer was born in Yonkers, New York, a son of a leather goods retailer; he was the youngest of three boys. He went to Cornell University (1947 to 1948), wanting to become an architect, but—compromising with his mother—he enrolled in civil engineering. He left Cornell for the University of Chicago, where he stayed only briefly.

For the next three years (1950 to 1953), Oppenheimer attended Black Mountain College, enrolled as a painter/writer. Here he met and was influenced by such men as Robert Creeley, Charles Olson, Robert Duncan, and Jonathan Williams. Remembering his grandfather, who had founded a printing union, Oppenheimer tried to start his own press. He shortly abandoned it, however, after completing only one or two jobs.

Leaving Black Mountain, Oppenheimer worked in various print shops for the next fifteen years, mostly as a production person, mediating between advertisers' demands and the printer's experience. He worked first in Washington, D.C. (living in Olson's apartment); and later in Rochester, New Hampshire; Provincetown, Massachusetts; and New York City.

For two years beginning in 1966, Oppenheimer directed the Poetry Project at St. Mark's in the Bowery, followed by one year directing the New York City Teachers and Writers Collaborative. In 1969, he began writing for *The Village Voice*, and after teaching part-time at the City College of the City University of New York, in 1970 he was offered a part-time but untenured position as poet-in-residence. On leave from City College, he taught, again as poet-in-residence, at New England College in New Hampshire. He also taught poetry workshops and seminars at the State University of New York at Buffalo's "Black Mountain II Summer Arts Program." In 1982, Oppenheimer became associate professor of communications and poet-in-residence at New England College. He died in New Hampshire in 1988.

Analysis

This "sports-loving Jewish intellectual/ writer" ("Dear Miss Monroe"), who "still grew up a jew in/ yonkers new york" admits at one moment that "finally i am through with it, with/ the american dream, a dream that ran through/ all my ancestors who fought here for you/ america" ("17-18 April, 1961"). Don't believe him. Joel Oppenheimer's own language and ideas give him away. His book *On Occasion* includes "Life," the poem, and "Life," a subsection of the collection. Two major sections are entitled "Liberty" and "The Pursuit of Happiness."

Not only does the triumvirate of American independence reign throughout his work, but the language of his poetry also shows that he has not abandoned America. Instead of the Christmas jingle "not a creature was stirring, not even a mouse," he writes, "inside the/ window/ not even a/ football game not even/ a haiku disturbing/ us" ("Found Art"). He defines "contra naturam" as "the pot which boils while/ watched" ("The Zoom Lens"). Beginning "The Riddle," he asks, "what/ s gray and comes in quarts"; answering, "is an elephant or my brain." His biblical allusions take the form of "it/ is very hot/ my sweat runneth over, even if/ my belly be not sheaved/ wheat" ("The Bye-Bye Happiness Swing"). He reaffirms or readjusts the platitudes "love *is* a/ many-splendored thing" ("Untitled") and "it's the world we live in/ we can't eat our cake or have it/ either" ("Four Photographs by Richard Kirstel"); and he haunts one with an echo of the now classic radio line, "who knows what shadows lurk in the hearts of old girl friends" ("Come On Baby"). As he exclaims in "Poem Written in the Light of Certain Events April 14th, 1967," "finally, i am here, goddamnit!/ i am american, goddamnit!"

Only an American would take and insist on such liberties with language. Oppenheimer insists not only that one can take liberties with language, but also that it is language that gives us our liberty and freedom. He vehemently defends that right, to "defend that truth/ that is our inheritance" ("Poem in Defense of Children"). The fight is against those that would take it away— "the first amendment was here/ before mendel rivers or lbj" ("A Dab of Cornpone")—as well as against those who would equally damage individual freedom by manipulation and lies. Echoing Williams' complaint against T. S. Eliot, he rejects language that is not part of and does not express one's own experience: "there is the problem of words, how/ to sound like language, and/ one/ s self" ("The Great American Novel").

Oppenheimer's American heritage runs from Thomas Jefferson, through Davy Crockett and Andrew Jackson— "andy/ show them all. once/ a free man ruled the free" ("The 150th Anniversary of the Battle of New Orleans"). His other ancestors include such persons (and literary banners) as Walt Whitman (I sing of myself), William Carlos Williams ("no ideas but in things"), Ezra Pound ("make it new"), and Charles Olson ("form is but an extension of content"). His immediate kin he addresses in "The Excuse":

> dear god, dear olson, dear
> creeley, dear ginsberg, my
> teachers and makers, bring
> me again to light, keep
> me from lies. . . .

These influences are political and literary. Many of Oppenheimer's poems are politically directed, created in the protesting air of the late 1950's and 1960's. Oppenheimer, however, does not separate politics from life, life from art, art from politics or life—"after all man is a/ political animal" ("The Innocent Breasts"). All directly affect how one lives, and how one says one wants to live—"we have forgotten/ we once carried a flag into battle that/ read don't/ tread on me" ("17-18 April, 1961").

Life, however, in these United States as he states in "17-18 April, 1961" has somehow found it

> . . . better to lie and hope not
> to get caught, than to behave honorably.
> well, this has been true of the world
> all along, but it was not supposed
> to be true of you, america

Oppenheimer finds that America has ignored the simple tenets of life, liberty, and the pursuit of happiness. Instead of honor and justice, his poem "Keeping It" expresses how one lives by fear and deception:

> the world we live in
> is not what we sing,
> and we are afraid we will
> fall prey to that we
> are most afraid of, the
> truth.

In the world that Oppenheimer perceives, truths about how man is created are no longer self evident: "we are all incapable/ it seems of living in that/ environment we were created/ for . . . " ("A Prayer"). In "Sirventes on a Sad Occasion" (1967), an old woman loses control of her bowels walking up the stairs to her apartment. She tries to hide the accident, feeling inadequate and inhuman for it. Oppenheimer can only ask, sadly, "this is a/ natural act, why will you/ fear me for it. . . . " Without these truths the world is unnatural, alien, often hostile.

Against such threats, one must preserve one's liberty. "The Surgeon in Spite of Himself" endures his fear because "master of my fate and captain/ of my soul, i know that i will." Liberty, built into the Declaration of Independence, is a fundamental need; Oppenheimer declares, in "A Treatise": "all that matters is/ the built-in mechanism/ of self-preservation."

Oppenheimer's poetry is filled with slogans: "to live my own life" and "to thine own self be true." These might be taken as mere egotistical or selfish desires. Oppenheimer might respond, "So what?" Liberty is necessary to make and define one's self; he insists on a voice, the personal voice and poetic voice being one and the same. Oppenheimer's ideal is the self-made man—Crockett, Jackson, Jefferson, his grandfather who began his own printing union—all men of action who looked to themselves and into themselves for freedoms: "freedoms (freedoms you might only/ have, anyhow, if you look deep inside/ yourself where all freedom is to be/ found . . . " ("17-18 April, 1961").

Oppenheimer's poems, as one title specifically indicates, provide "Some Suggested Guidelines" as to how one can live freely in this world; and they encourage individual action. His advice starts, of course, with himself. "Notes Toward Lessons to Be Learned at Thirty" advises taking care of his body; it provides advice on coffee, cigarettes, fresh fruit, and "the loveliest ass in the world." "Sirventes Against Waiting" underscores three lessons: "you do what you can . . . what you have to . . . [and] what you want to." Oppenheimer's faith in America, then, comes down to a faith in the self. His declaration of independence is "the simple/ declaration of the/ faith a man must have,/ in his own balls, in/ his own heart" ("Keeping It").

Not all of Oppenheimer's poems are political. Many are love poems—love that varies and that takes as many forms as do the women he invokes— Artemis, Persephone, Diana, Medusa, and Marilyn Monroe. *The Woman Poems* presents his fourfold synthesis of Woman—Good Mother, Death Mother, Ecstasy or Dancing Mother, and Stone or Tooth Mother—all embodied in the mythical figure of Mother Goddess. As a true democrat, he loves and lusts after them all, equally. His poems, in addition, are filled with tenderness, affection, and hope—for friends, children, and parents. There is fighting and plain sex; there are elegies, celebrations of births and weddings, and blues. A poem in *New Spaces: Poems, 1975-1983* celebrates a marriage (and in the process touches on the relationship between art and life), noting that people ask for poems as "blessing on their union"; he adds, "the wonder is/ we keep writing/ they keep getting married."

Oppenheimer's definition of happiness invokes the old-time notion of a little peace and quiet—"this much/ will a little quiet do,/ and peace, in our times" ("Modern Times")—and a little honesty and decency. Happiness is having one's own space, "asking for/ space to build our own perimeters/ in defense of such" ("Poem for Soho"). Happiness for Oppenheimer is not so much being happy as pursuing happiness. Happiness is the labors of Hercules, not their completion; or, more apt, the labors of love. It is the act of happiness, not the state, which seems more real. In fact, the last poem of *On Occasion* is "The Act":

> as i do
> it is as it is
> does as it does
> as i am it is
> is as is is as
> i do as i do
> as it does as it
> does as it is
> as is is

All active, simple verbs, "The Act" defines, blends with, but does not constrict, personal pronouns and direct objects. The act defines itself and oneself. "The Act" summarizes Oppenheimer's self and his world in language, idea, and act.

Steven P. Schultz

Other major works

SHORT FICTION: *Pan's Eyes*, 1974.

PLAYS: *The Great American Desert*, 1961; *Miss Right*, 1962; *Like a Hill*, 1963.

NONFICTION: *The Wrong Season*, 1973; *Marilyn Lives!*, 1981.

Bibliography

Beach, Christopher. "Interview with Joel Oppenheimer." *Sagetrieb* 7 (Fall, 1978): 89-130. An informative interview conducted ten years before the poet's death. Contains Oppenheimer's comments on his contemporaries and poetry in general, interspersed with personal detail. This lengthy document gives an excellent portrait of the poet. His personality surfaces as he reflects on topics and figures in American poetry.

Landrey, David W. "Simply Survival: David Budbill and Joel Oppenheimer." *Credences*, n.s.1 (Fall/Winter, 1981/1982): 150-157. This article explores the two poets' shared quest for life, knowledge, and understanding, their different approaches to their work, and their shared need for a changed sense of self through poetry. Particularly significant is the discussion of Oppenheimer working from the inside out. Several themes are pointed out and short examples given.

Oppenheimer, Joel. *Poetry, The Ecology of the Soul: Talks and Selected Poems.* Edited by David Landrey and Dennis Maloney. Buffalo, N.Y.: White Plains Press, 1987. This excellent collection is preceded by an introductory appreciation by David Landrey. The volume contains a number of poems, three informative talks, and a bibliography of Oppenheimer's work. The lectures on the Black Mountain poets and on *The Woman Poems* are of particular importance because of what they reveal about the poet's craft.

Sylvester, William. "Joel Oppenheimer Talks About His Poetry." *Credences*, n.s.3 (Fall, 1985): 69-76. This transcription of several conversations with Oppenheimer lets the poet speak for himself about his craft, his career, his early influences from theater and film, and so on. Although it is a bit rambling, it does give one a strong sense of who Oppenheimer was and what informed his thinking.

Thibodaux, David. *Joel Oppenheimer: An Introduction.* Columbia, S.C.: Camden House, 1986. This study provides an overview of Oppenheimer's work and examines closely his literary themes, including the significance of images, motifs, and symbols. Approximately half the book is devoted to poetry. The remainder discusses fiction, drama, and nonfiction prose. An excellent bibliography cites several useful journal articles on specific poems, interviews, reviews, and the like.

GREGORY ORR

Born: Albany, New York; February 3, 1947

Principal poetry
Burning the Empty Nests, 1973; *Gathering the Bones Together*, 1975; *The Red House*, 1980; *We Must Make a Kingdom of It*, 1986; *New and Selected Poems*, 1988.

Other literary forms
In addition to his poetry, Gregory Orr has published a critical study, *Stanley Kunitz: An Introduction to the Poetry* (1985).

Achievements
Although the models for Orr's writing can be found in the "deep imagery" of Robert Bly and the visionary lyrics of W. S. Merwin (as well as in the European poetry translated by these poets and others), Orr's poems have spoken with a distinctive voice from the beginning, compelled as much by inner necessity as by outside example. Several things characterize his poems: they are very brief; their diction is clipped; they are cleanly articulated; they thrive on imagery and rejoice in metaphor ("The water;/ a glass snake asleep in the pipes"); they revolve around dramatic situations; they do not explain but break off quickly, so that one is left with a silence in which echoes of the poem reverberate.

Orr's concept of the image comes largely from Surrealism: a "variant of symbol." In a statement prepared for "The Inward Society," a symposium on Surrealism held at the University of Virginia (published in *Poetry East*, Spring, 1982), Orr remarks that "Surrealism kept alive the poet's notion of the self as that which mediates between inner and outer worlds; as that which focuses and constellates perceptions of the world." This mediation between the self and the world is central to Orr's work, which began its explorations and excavations in the interior, with dreams and the anxieties of the unconscious, but which has recently begun to summon realistic scenes from his waking life.

A number of Orr's poems are parables: "The Ambassadors," the early sequence "The Adventures of the Stone," and "The Man in the Suit of Mirrors." As his work has become more realistic, this emblematic mode (close to allegory, with the same mechanical predictability) has receded. The newer poems are more celebratory and undisguised, drawing on the resources of dream life to heighten the realism, which is now in the foreground. All Orr's work seeks to transcend his private griefs, but to accomplish this, he must go deeper into the source of that pain. He must unmask what is hidden:

"I stand at the sink/ washing dinner plates/ that are as smooth as the masks/ my grief once wore" ("After the Guest"). Orr's poems, in the words of "The Bridge," continually call out: "Return to yourself."

Biography

Gregory Orr's childhood in the Hudson River Valley was disrupted by two deaths. When he was twelve, he accidentally shot and killed his brother, a scene described in his sequence of seven short poems, "Gathering the Bones Together":

> A gun goes off,
> and the youngest brother
> falls to the ground.
> A boy with a rifle
> stands beside him, screaming.

When he was fourteen, his mother died in Haiti, a time recalled and reawakened in "Black Moon" and "Haitian Suite." Orr's early work, obsessed with grief and guilt, transforms these deaths into dream imagery, which may seem like an evasion, a looking-away, but which is actually an intensification. The porcelain face of "The Doll" is disfigured by a "bullet hole/ like a black mole" on its cheek. Orr's losses do not disappear: they leave behind shells, husks, evidence of their absence, like the doll he carries "in a glass jar," like the snails, "little death-swans," and like the coat his great-grandfather made from his favorite horse, "because when the horse died/ he wouldn't let it go" ("A House in the Country"). Orr's poems occupy a world "where the dead and half/ dead live together" ("Lullaby Elegy Dream").

The poems of his first three collections represent an exorcism (but not an exclusion) of his demons, a coming to terms with what he has seen and sensed as fate: "a lugged burden/ of the invisible and unforgiving dead." In the same poem ("On the Lawn at Ira's"), Orr admits that now he is "mostly/ happy, even . . . blessed among so many friends." The working-through of grief began at the very center, in dreams, but completed itself by breaking out of the cave of darkness into the light of everyday life.

Orr received a Master of Fine Arts degree from Columbia University and now teaches at the University of Virginia, where he is director of the writing program. He lives in a farmhouse near Charlottesville, Virginia, with his wife Trisha and their two daughters.

Analysis

Since the poems of Gregory Orr represent a symbolic journey, it is not surprising that maps are of central importance in his work. The opening poem of Orr's first book ends with "A moth lands on the toe of my boot./ Picking it up, I discover a map on its wings" ("When We Are Lost"). Dream and memory both offer maps to the lost wayfarer, clues to a mystery that neither the conscious nor the unconscious mind alone can apprehend completely. More and more, Orr's work has sought to bring these two worlds—of darkness and of light, roughly speaking—into consonance. If his first three books can be said to constitute a trilogy, they resemble, in general outline, the three stages of Dante's *The Divine Comedy* (c. 1320): descent, purgation, and enlightenment. The poems attempt to become "accurate maps/ for the spirit's quest:/ always death at the center/ like Rome or some oasis/ toward which all paths tend" ("Song of the Invisible Corpse in the Field"). The poems of memory that dominate *The Red House* have not been ignited to consume the poems of dream and nightmare. Rather, the dream imagery heightens Orr's close observation of the outer world.

The titles of Orr's early poems usually furnish coordinates for the dream terrain that will follow: "When We Are Lost," "Lines Written in Dejection, Oklahoma," "Manhattan Island Poem." These down-to-earth titles, flat and explanatory, ground the poems in the electrical sense. They act as a kind of documentation, safe passage into an alien world. The simple act referred to in the title "Washing My Face" leads to an illumination of the no-man's-land between dreaming and waking. The complete poem is only three lines long: "Last night's dreams disappear./ They are like the sink draining:/ a transparent rose swallowed by its stem." The poem is nearly a haiku, both in length and content, but its dependence on connectives ("They are like") keeps it in the Western hemisphere. Each line elaborates on the line before it: statement, then simile, then metaphor. If the process should go on, it would become baroque, but Orr's inclination is always to stop while the poem is still uncluttered. The process depends upon clarity and quickness of metaphor.

The first two lines of the poem are flat declaratives. They are joined by "like" because the comparison is an obvious and easy step. Metaphor demands more of a leap, and what comes in the final line is strong enough to electrify both statements. The rose may be an overworked symbol in itself, but its transparency (and unreality) brings back the full mystical force of the flower. Whereas T. S. Eliot's rose in *Four Quartets* (1943) blends into fire, Orr's dissolves into water. The clear rose being "swallowed by its stem" resembles a film run backwards; the natural process is reversed. It is both an apt comment on forgetfulness and a snapshot of a real sink draining: a picture, yet beyond a picture; a surreality.

In "Beginning," a poem from his first book, Orr writes that "you will make each journey many times," a prediction—or prophecy, or curse—that touches upon the importance of journeying in his poems and the even greater importance of obsession, the repetition of charms, the consultation of oracles. The locus of the earlier poems is a blank arena: the bareness of snow and "the way the word sinks into the deep snow of the page." The blankness extends indoors, into "empty rooms" with "bare walls." Even when a child's drawing becomes a window, the means of escape and the journey's starting point ("The Room"), the path merely adds distance to emptiness: "Far ahead in the valley, I saw the lights/ of a village, and always at my back I felt/ the white room swallowing what was past." The last image represents one of Orr's obsessions, an image out of the brothers Grimm, in which breadcrumbs (providing a trail back to the familiar world) are eaten by birds, the same "flock of sparrows" that is "eating your footprints" in "The Wooden Dancer."

The fear of the past disappearing is countered by the persistence of memory that one finds in dreams, the tokens left behind as outward signs of an invisible presence. Orr's central poem, "Gathering the Bones Together," unites these two obsessions just as the poet confronts the greatest trauma of his life: the accidental killing of his brother.

The poem begins with an epigraph that is Orr's rethinking of an earlier poem, "The Sleeping Angel": "When all the rooms of the house/ fill with smoke, it's not enough/ to say an angel is sleeping on the chimney." Orr rejects the relatively easy myth of the sleeping angel in favor of examining the inner smoke. It is "not enough" to offer solutions that quell the greater mystery. The drama of the poem begins with the abandonment of costumes.

"A Night in the Barn" is the first section of the poem. A boy, referred to in the third person, "keeps watch/ from a pile of loose hay." He is guarding a "deer carcass (that) hangs from a rafter," a portent of what will follow. (In "Spring Floods," the dead brother is likened to a deer "high in a tree, wedged/ there by the flood.") The rustling of pigeons and the German shepherd that "snaps its jaws in its sleep" create an ominous music, a mood of anxiety and dread. Between these descriptions of the night scene, the prophetic dream is revealed: the "death that is coming." Yet the vision narrows in the aftermath of death, the gathering of bones in an empty field. It is a sentence fit for the inferno, the reparations that the boy must pay to the dead, the impossible task of reassembling a skeleton and making the dry bones sing.

The accident, the killing, is set forth with complete simplicity in part two, which is untitled. Another deer has just been killed. On the way to retrieve the body, "a gun goes off."

In the third section, the point of view switches from third person to first. Although he is hiding, the boy feels compelled to reveal himself through speech. Already the events have been transformed through terror into nightmare images: the "glass well/ of my hands," in which the brother drowns. The leaves, "shaped like mouths" (an image that recalls Jean Cocteau's movie, *Blood of the Poet*, 1932), litter the ground outside: a silent chorus of grief and accusation. As though the world had been flooded, the leaves form a "black pool" in which snails glide like "little death swans." The water, following the dryness of the barn, immerses the boy in his guilt. The world has become alien and threatening. Nothing is more disturbing than the underwater silence, so different from the laughter and chattering just before the accident.

The water imagery is replaced by smoke in the poem's middle section. This smoke from an unseen fire has made everyone weep, has turned "people into shadows." It is, of course, smoke from the pyre, the imaginary bone-fire for the dead brother, and even after the funeral it remains in the pillows, to be smelled "when we lie down to sleep."

In the fifth section of the poem, the "glass well" becomes "a house of black glass" where the boy visits and talks with his dead brother. It is another world, separate from the familiar one, close to fairy tale and close to madness; the clarity of glass is turned into the "dark night of the soul." Yet the voice is naïve: "My father says he is dead,/ but what does that mean?" The disorientation of the boy is reinforced by the reference to "a child/ sleeping on a nest of bones" that follows. It is the same brother, yet it is not. The brother he visits is the ghost of the one he knew in life. The child he carries (like the one preserved in "The Doll") is the image of the brother in death, "a red, leaf-shaped/ scar on his cheek." The wound is like a leaf, which has already been likened to a mouth. The certainty of the boy's communion with the dead is offset by his uncertainty about the destination to which he is traveling, loaded down with the weight of his guilt and remorse.

"The Journey" is described in the penultimate section: "Each night, I knelt on a marble slab/ and scrubbed at the blood." This act of devotion and expiation is fruitless: the stain is too deep, the gravestone too permanent. When his own bones "begin to burn," the boy begins his journey, still ignorant of his destination and destiny. The slab remains under his feet, "a white road only as long as your body." The whiteness contrasts with the "house of black glass." Everything disappears in the course of the journey except this movable stretch of road, which is as inescapable as a shadow.

In "The Distance," the last section of the poem, a winter scene is recalled, when "a horse/ slipped on the ice" (another accident), "breaking its leg." The boy watched the carcass burn. The speaker says that, when he killed his brother, he "felt my own bones wrench from my body." When he walks beside the river, what he gathers are both his own bones and those of his dead brother, which "have become a bridge/ that arches toward the other shore": a passageway like the white road of the marble slab, yet offering a way to reconnect with all that has been lost, a way to "gather at the river" and to atone for the taking of life. The bridge, one of Orr's key images, recurs in another poem as "this bridge/ of poems: a thousand/ paper coffins/ laid end to end" ("Before We Met"). All the elements of the poem coalesce in this final section: animals, fire, water, bones, the road. The poem ends on the aspiration to unite the two shores, to span the moving waters.

This construction project is echoed and qualified by two poems later in the same volume. In "The Project," the speaker plans "to generate light/ with no outside source." The parable about this Thomas Alva Edison of the psyche goes on to elaborate, in terms resembling Franz Kafka, how this is to be accomplished in a burrow (which must be read as both a grave and a kind of subway to the underworld). The speaker wants to capture the "faint light" given off by his body in the darkness. He supposes it comes from the bones (Orr's bridging material) but once the flesh is scraped away, "the light was gone too." The ending resembles Marco Polo's argument, in Italo Calvino's *Le città invisibili* (1972, *The Invisible Cities*), that without stones there can be no arch. Without the life of the flesh, in all its voluptuousness, there can be no life. Stripping everything down to the bare bones is not an act of renewal but of denial.

In "The Builders," however, the feat is accomplished: a windowless hut is "filled with light," but it is the light given off by love. The couple, in quarrying the field of white stone and carrying it "strapped to our backs" (like the body of the dead brother in "Gathering the Bones Together"), have reclaimed the white stone of the grave slab for their rebuilding. The surroundings are still bleak, and the elements are the same, but the scene has been transformed by the love of the living. Instead of black windows, there are none at all, but this retreat is a necessary step toward self-forgiveness and eventual benediction.

This rapprochement is achieved in the main sequence of *The Red House*, assisted by an epigraph from William Wordsworth's *The Prelude* (1850). The close attention to physical detail, to the inner life of the ordinary, is new to Orr's work. The Haiti of his "Haitian Suite" springs to life in the exuberant images of a "flamboyant tree" and a girl who squats "to fill/ her calabash at the gurgling spring/ in the gully." Part of the impression is conveyed by the sound, musically more alive than before. The title of the collection suggests both the vivacity of new color and a grounding in domestic peace, the gift to be simple—as opposed to the restless participles of *Burning the Empty Nests* and *Gathering the Bones Together*. The images that predominate belong to the light:

> In the barn's huge gloom
> light falls through cracks
> the way swordblades
> pierce a magician's box.

The ecstasy of the passage which ends "Morning Song" comes from the awareness that the swords do not represent danger, but rather the magician's power to keep things whole.

The new poems glory in the senses: "bluebottle flies . . ./ magnetized to the gleaming/ scales of a carp"; "his father's red car crossing/ the flats, dragging huge plumes of dust" (both from "The Ditch"). After the passage through "Gathering the Bones Together" the road leads clearly to this exultation. It may disappoint some of Orr's early disciples and devotees, but it is a necessary continuation of a journey that has turned out to be different from the repetitive, futile path of Sisyphus; Orr is fortunate to have come upon a new landscape, which is, in fact, the old one which had been lost through grief.

One of the side effects of the change has been a greater interest in other people. Love has cleared the way for this interest: "So many years/ before the soft key of your tongue/ unlocked my body" ("Before We Met"). Now the open door admits "Neighbors," such as Edith, with a "photo on the mantel:/ her Texas Ranger husband" and Christopher Augustinovich, who "jabbered about his youth/ in the Czar's army."

"The Drawing Lesson" introduces Mr. Knight and re-creates a realistic scene that leads, quite naturally, to something from another world:

> To loosen my wrists, he tried to teach me
> the bones: I was supposed to hold the two
> delicately-curved pieces of rosewood
> in one hand and clack them deftly together
> to music.

After so much emblematic use of "bones," it is a pleasant surprise to come upon the witty and frightening play on the word in this poem. More than anything else, this passage demonstrates the growing delicacy of Orr's poetry, which accompanies the affection he lavishes upon what he portrays.

Through this affection, and through the many songs that go into *The Red House*, Orr approaches the affirmations and discoveries of Rainer Maria Rilke, giving himself over into other beings, alive with "The 'new life' of freedom" mentioned in "Leaving the Asylum." This poem represents his coming to terms with the grief of his childhood, a litany that has released him:

> Hollow tree
> though I am, these things I cherish:
> the hum of my blood, busily safe
> in its hive of being; the delicate
> oily kiss my fingertips give
> everything they touch; and desire,
> a huge fish I drag with me
> through the wilderness:
> I love its glint among the dust and stones.

Light and music rise out of the desolation: the poems are free to become songs of celebration.

John Drury

Other major work

NONFICTION: *Stanley Kunitz: An Introduction to the Poetry*, 1985.

Bibliography

Glück, Louise. "On Gregory Orr's Poems." *The Iowa Review* 3 (Fall, 1973): 86-88. Glück examines the characteristic persona assumed in Orr's poetry, one of solitude of the narrator, inevitability of events, and ambiguity of experiences. This highly personal and compelling evaluation of Orr's poetry includes ruminations on the cinematic quality of his poems and their sense of necessity, irreversibility, and dream-logic.

Harris, Peter. "A Shelter, a Kingdom, a Half Promised Land: Three Poets in Mid-Career," *The Virginia Quarterly Review* 63 (Summer, 1987): 426-436. This enlightening essay examines Orr's distinct vision of psychic, surreal images. Harris studies the battle between abstraction and specific, familiar and metaphysical, body and soul, and hidden and known in Orr's work. *We Must Make a Kingdom of It* is the featured text, and stanzas of several poems are used to illustrate key points.

Kohl, Greg. "Transparency and Prophecy: Gregory Orr's 'Burning the Empty Nests.' " *The American Poetry Review* 14 (July/August, 1975): 40-42. Kohl has a very specific and explicit agenda in his exploration of *Burning the Empty Nests*: He seeks to determine the influences of shamanistic experiences and techniques and identify the value of shamanism in dealing with personal and social experience as found in Orr's poetry. To this end, he is successful, but limits the appeal of his work to Orr's scholars.

Lazer, Hank. Review of *The Red House* by Gregory Orr. *The Iowa Review* 11 (Winter, 1981): 148-156. Lazer asserts that this work is Orr's finest due to its sophisticated exploration of two lyric modes: an expressionistic imagery inspired by Georg Trakl and the persuasive, lyrical tone of Theodore Roethke's greenhouse poems. Orr uses his distinct lyric voice to explore his obsession with grief, precipitated by the death of his mother and brother.

Lehman, David. "Politics." *Poetry* 122 (December, 1973): 178-180. Lehman addresses the lack of political references in Orr's first book of poetry, *Burning the Empty Nests*, explores the stark landscapes evoked by the poet, and analyzes Orr's tendency to "turn nature inside out." Acknowledging the influence of W. S. Merwin and Robert Bly on Orr's work, the author asserts Orr's poetry is unique, in part, due to the tension between his spare writing style and dense imagery.

Leo, John Robert. "Finding the Imagination." *Poetry* 128 (November, 1976): 106-108. This work examines the elements Orr unites in his poetry, such as text and illustration, surface and depth, child and adult, and nature and artifice. Also explored are the themes of "home," interior landscapes, and the primitive dream world. Leo defends Orr against critics who argue the poet's work has become increasingly fragmented and reductive.

WILFRED OWEN

Born: Oswestry, England; March 18, 1893
Died: Sambre Canal, France; November 4, 1918

Principal poetry
Poems by Wilfred Owen, 1920 (Siegfreid Sassoon, editor); *The Poems of Wilfred Owen*, 1931 (Edmund Blunden, editor); *The Collected Poems of Wilfred Owen*, 1963 (C. Day Lewis, editor); *Wilfred Owen: War Poems and Others*, 1973 (Dominic Hibberd, editor).

Other literary forms
Like many of the poets and artists of his time, Wilfred Owen professed a strong interest in the theater and supposedly drafted a play while recovering from shell shock in Craiglockhart Military Hospital in 1917, although no manuscript has appeared. Owen's letters, which have been collected, deserve mention for two reasons. First, the style reflects both the poetic temper of the man and the adherence to detail reflective of an age of correspondence which will probably never return. Second, and perhaps more important, Owen's letters record the transitions typical of most British soldiers who survived on the front for a long time: from resolve to do the soldier's duty, to disgust, fear, and depression, to the solemn acceptance of fate that extended service produced. One is fascinated by Owen's attempt to depict his life on the front for his naïve family and friends, as well as his ability to do so in spite of censorship.

Achievements
Many commentators have emphasized that Owen exhibited more potential to continue and enlarge the craft of poetry than any of the soldier-poets of World War I. He was a technician, an innovator, a "poet's poet" long before he was a proud soldier, a horrified combatant, a victim. The kinds of criticisms applied to Rupert Brooke (immature, too much style and too little substance) or Siegfried Sassoon (limited, more propaganda than art) have little validity when it comes to Owen. Indeed, in spite of his early death and limited canon, several twentieth century poets (among them W. H. Auden and Stephen Spender) have publicly stated their admiration for Owen's work or have used or expanded his methods. A notable dissenting voice is that of William Butler Yeats, who shocked many writers and critics by excluding Owen's work from his *Oxford Book of Modern Verse* (1936). Yeats defended his decision in a famous venomous blast, writing to Dorothy Wellesley that Owen was "unworthy of the poet's corner of a country newspaper. He is all blood, dirt, and sucked sugar stick . . . (he calls poets, 'bards,' a girl a 'maid,' and talks about 'Titanic wars'). There is every excuse for him, but none for those who

like him."

Owen's champions, however, far outnumber his detractors. It is true that all of his work, from earliest to latest, is characterized by a kind of romantic embellishment, an intensity that borders on parody. This was more of a problem early in his career; as he matured, he assimilated the devices of John Keats, Percy Bysshe Shelley, and Lord Byron (among others), creating effective juxtapositions and dramatic tensions. This change was perhaps a result of the sophisticated and shocking material he found in his war experience.

Shocking the war poems are. Certainly among the most descriptive and horrifying of their era, they continue to penetrate minds supposedly benumbed by exposure to the twentieth century. In what became the Preface to his first published volume of poetry, Owen wrote: "Above all, I am not concerned with Poetry. My subject is War, and the pity of War. The Poetry is in the pity." Indeed it appears true; of the many horrifying experiences suffered by the artists who recorded their experience in World War I (Robert Graves, Sassoon, Isaac Rosenberg, Edward Thomas, Brooke, and others), it is Owen's cries which are the loudest and most anguished. Owen seems to have been more outraged than most by the lamentable tragedy of fine young men lost in the struggle. What is surprising, however, is that the resultant verse is never self-indulgent, self-pitying; rather, Owen was able to focus his vision outward. He concluded sadly in the Preface previously cited that "all a poet can do today is warn." Owen's disgust with the war he experienced and despised is readily apparent, but it goes beyond immediacy and is elevated to prophecy as well.

Another of Owen's goals, through all the years of fighting and suffering, was to cling to his artistic voice, to expand his abilities, to become a better poet. He sought new ways to use language, and his mastery of alliteration, onomatopoeia, assonance, and dissonance have been often cited. Perhaps his most consistently brilliant device was the use of slant rhyme (or "half rhyme" or "pararhyme" as it has been called), the subtle and effective mixture of vowel dissonance and consonant assonance most often effectively employed at the end of his lines (for example, "cold" and "killed").

The effect of Owen's expert use of form (he was a master of sonnets and elegiac mood) and his fluency (both traditional and experimental) was to suggest a poet who would have been very much at home with modernism, but who never would have forgotten his literary heritage. In fact, an observation often made concerning the poetry of Thomas Hardy, that his was the soul of the nineteenth century anticipating twentieth century innovations, applies equally well to Wilfred Owen. That Owen was able to sustain his brilliance under the stress of battle makes the reader appreciate his achievement all the more.

Biography

Wilfred Edward Salter Owen was born in Oswestry, Shropshire, England, on March 18, 1893, the first child of Tom and Susan Owen. Owen's mother was a devout and cautious woman; his father was an active, rough-hewn, hardworking sort who was nostalgically attracted to the sea and those who sailed it. The early years of their marriage, and Owen's childhood, were sometimes difficult, characterized by several moves, frequent if not severe financial difficulties, and tensions produced by his parents' conflicting characters. Their union produced four children. Owen's younger brother Harold became a successful artist and devoted much of his adult life to chronicling the life of his more famous war-poet brother.

Owen was sent to Birkenhead Institute for his first years of schooling; his father approved of the discipline for which the school was noted, but Owen probably profited most from an adoring teacher and early exposure to the pleasures of literature. He also showed a great interest in religious matters, much to the delight of his mother. In 1907, the family moved to Shrewsbury, where Owen enrolled in the technical school. There he read diligently and began to compose serious essays (some on politics, some on art theory) and put down his first attempts at verse.

Somewhat confused about his future after his matriculation examination at London University in 1911, Owen accepted an opportunity to become a lay assistant to the Vicar of Dunsden. His activities were many-faceted, from the intellectual (extensive reading and attending lectures) to the practical affairs of the parish (playing with children and assisting the poor). His poetry began to mature, not so much in its subject matter as in its increasing flexibility of language. For reasons that remain unclear, Owen became disenchanted with his commitment to the vicarage and left Dunsden. After a period of contemplation, during which he struggled with his health, he was offered, and he accepted, a post to teach English at the Berlitz School in Bordeaux. He enjoyed the experience and the climate was beneficial, even as the clouds of war gathered over Europe.

Because Owen was in France during the "exhilarating" first part of the war, a time when nationalism and enthusiasm for battle possessed young men like him in England, his wavering emotions regarding the conflict are understandable. He had left his job in late 1915 to assume a position as a private tutor to a well-to-do family in Merignac, France. His correspondence reveals a confused but honor-bound attitude toward his own responsibilities: appalled at the destruction and suffering so near by, confident and proud of his ability to serve, excited at the prospect of taking his gift for poetry into battle. He briefly investigated business opportunities, flirted with but rejected the idea of joining either the French Army or the Italian Cavalry, and in September, 1915, returned to England, where he enlisted with the Artists' Rifles.

During his training he sought not only to become a fine soldier but also to become familiar with many people active in literary circles of London. He met Harold Monro of *The Poetry Review* and lived briefly in a flat adjacent to the magazine's offices. Owen performed admirably as a soldier and claimed to enjoy his work, though he appeared uncomfortable, out of place with his peers. He was well liked, however, and in June, 1916, 2nd Lieutenant Owen was attached to the 5th Battalion of the Manchester Regiment.

After a few months of polishing, Owen was sent with thousands of his fellows to the front. The Somme offensive, begun in July, 1916, had been stalled tragically for several months, and war planners had determined to begin another push as the new year began. Immediately, Owen was struck by the difference between the grotesque reality of the war zone and the appallingly inaccurate depictions of the war at home. These sentiments, together with supportive vivid details, were relayed home regularly. Still, he took comfort in his devotion to duty and in writing, criticizing, and discussing poetry, pleasures which he never neglected.

Writing and fighting with distinction for six months, Owen showed signs of suffering from the strain and was finally sent to Craiglockhart Military Hospital, where he was diagnosed as suffering from neurasthenia, or shell shock. His stay there was to be crucial, not only for his health but for his poetic and intellectual development as well. Owen participated in many of the therapeutic activities offered by the hospital. Also at Craiglockhart was Siegfried Sassoon, the distinguished soldier, poet, and most recently a virulent antiwar spokesman. The two became friends and eventually Sassoon became audience and critic for the work which began to reveal Owen's growing artistry. Robert Graves, a friend of Sassoon and a regular visitor to the hospital, also encouraged Owen to continue his work. In December, Owen was dismissed and returned to London, where he pursued other contacts in the literary establishment. (Later, in 1920, Sassoon became responsible for collecting and publishing selections of Owen's poetry.)

In spite of his increasing disgust at the carnage of battle, amply evident in his poems of this time, Owen was compelled to return to the war, and during the summer of 1918 he was granted permission to cross to France. Participating in the heavy fighting preceding and during the armistice talks, Owen became a respected and competent soldier (he won the military cross). Invigorated artistically by his friendship with prominent writers during his recuperation, he sent poems and lively letters back to England. On November 4, 1918, one week before the armistice, Owen was killed while leading his troops across the Sambre Canal.

Analysis

Wilfred Owen's most memorable, and often cited, works reveal several characteristic traits. Romantic imagery dominates his work, regardless of whether it is war-inspired. Owen was a passionate disciple of Keats; he made pilgrimages to Keats's shrines and felt a personal affinity for the great Romantic poet. There is also brutal realism in Owen's war descriptions. Had Owen not been there himself, the reader might be tempted to believe the verse exaggerated, such is its power. The poetry is also characterized by the sensual glorification of male beauty and bravery, and the hideous waste of wartime slaughter. Such elements have prompted a plentitude of conjecture about Owen's personal relationships; but the sentiment with which he glorifies male qualities in his early years, and the depth with which he expressed his concern for his fellows in his war years are not, in his case, cause for prurient speculation by the psychological critics. The simple fact concerning Owen's poetry is that he wrote about his comrades in ways that were never offensive and always eloquent.

Innovations and experiments with the potential of language give Owen's best work a quality that is more of the modernistic than the Edwardian or Georgian temper. In spite of its strength and ferocity, however, there is an equally noticeable fragility. Owen's earliest extant attempts at poetry (according to Jon Stallworthy, it is probable that his first efforts were burned by his mother at his death, at the poet's request) reflect a somewhat awkward sentimentalism. He laboriously expresses his adoration for the muse in "To Poesy." The poem, an odd beginning for one who would later write that he was "not concerned with poetry," contains a variety of religious, erotic quest images (none very effective) designed to signify the "purer love" of his aesthetic principles. Also noticeable at this time in Owen's poetic infancy are poems and fragments which either imitate Keats or illustrate his exultant emotions after having visited locales associated with Keats's life and work. Again, the sentiments are apparent, if hardly laudable artistically, as in "SONNET, written at Teignmouth, on a Pilgrimage to Keats's House." Its sestet begins: "Eternally may sad waves wail his death,/ Choke in their grief 'mongst rocks where he has lain." Still, the young poet shows signs of searching for more sophisticated methods. A revealing fragment from an early manuscript shows that Owen had penciled in lines to attract attention to the interesting effect of half-rhymed words, "tomb, home," "thou, below," "spirit, inherit."

The effect which one experiences when turning from Owen's earlier works to his mature verse is dramatic indeed. "Bent double, like old beggars under sacks,/ Knock-kneed, coughing like hags, we cursed through sludge," begins "Dulce et Decorum Est," one of his most often cited depictions of the reality of war. An interesting juxtaposition established at the beginning is that of the simple exhaustion of the troops who "marched asleep . . . lame . . . blind . . . drunk with fatigue," and the nightmarish, almost surreal atmosphere of the battle, lighted by "haunting flares," pierced by the "hoots" of artillery fire, and pervaded by the sickening presence of gas. The soldier who has donned his gas mask looks through "misty panes" at thick green light, as if submerged in a "green sea." The nightmare is unrelieved by the passage of battle as the persona sees "in all my dreams," without relief, a comrade who was unable to survive the attack, who lurches grotesquely, "guttering, choking, drowning." After witnessing these events, the reader is drawn more intimately into the scene, as the persona uses the second person, asking directly if "you too" could imagine witnessing eyes "writhing in his face" and blood that "gargles from froth-corrupted lungs." As Owen builds the intensity and visceral detail of his description, he is preparing the reader for the ironic and bitter conclusion which utilizes a tag from Horace (*Odes*, III. 2.13), familiar to schoolboys and used to glorify the war effort: *Dulce et decorum est pro patria mori* (It is sweet and honorable and proper to die for your country). For Owen, and surely for most readers, however, the sentiments expressed in the phrase can now only be considered an "old lie" which cannot honestly be told to children anymore. Owen brilliantly half-rhymes in the last three lines the words "glory" (what children seek) and "mori" (what happens to them in war).

Another nightmare vision serves as the stimulus for a greatly admired work. "Strange Meeting" recounts a frightful reverie, an encounter between two soldiers in hell. Their confrontation, unified by dramatic dialogue, is inspired by the horrors of war, but it also serves as an occasion for Owen to comment on poetic principles and to prophesy (quite accurately and depressingly) on the nature of the new century.

Owen begins by describing his descent down "some profound dull tunnel," arriving at a shattered place where "encumbered sleepers groaned." He is surprised when one of these fellows jumps up; there is a moment of recognition not only between them but also of their mutual circumstance, standing "in Hell." Owen comforts his opposite in a dramatic understatement, suggesting that even "*here*" (italics added), dead, in hell, there "is no cause to mourn." Such was the gruesome reality above ground, alive, in battle. The stranger is in no mood to be assuaged, because he too had been a poet who ventured and strove for "the wildest beauty in the world." Thus, the poet's life is lost, but that loss is not to be lamented nearly as much as the loss of the truth he might have written, the "truth untold." The ultimate tragedy is not temporary, but lasting, as future generations will be unaware of the truth of war which the poet could have recorded. Instead of rejecting the past, those generations will embrace it, probably with devastating efficiency. Had he lived, the poet would also have battled, not with instruments of war, but with his "courage" and "wisdom." His would have been a war to dominate men's minds, fought when men wearied of bleeding and death, a soothing message of "truths that lie too deep for taint" that would have flowed from his "spirit."

Owen does not wish to end the poem at this abstract level, seeking instead to pull the reader back to the immediacy of war. Even though the setting is highly contrived, Owen provides a "surprise ending" which serves two purposes: to impress upon the reader the brutal infighting characteristic of many

World War I battles, and to ridicule the notion of nationalism and emphasize the common humanity of all the war's combatants. The early "recognition," a foreshadowing device, had not been between friends but between enemies, as the poet-narrator had evidently slain the poet-prophet with a bayonet. Rather than continuing either the hostilities or the discussion, the soldier who had been thus murdered offers a simpler, but more final and disturbing alternative: "Let us sleep now. . . ."

In other poems Owen draws attention to the waste of young men slaughtered. "Arms and the Boy" (an ironic revision of the opening of Vergil's *Aeneid*, c. 29-19 B.C., "Arms and the Man I sing. . . .") is a three-stanza portrait of youthful innocence confronting the awful mysteries of the instruments of war. He emphasizes the apparent discomfort as a boy tests a bayonet "keen with hunger for flesh" and caresses a bullet which seeks "to nuzzle in the hearts of lads." These gestures are not natural for youngsters whose "teeth seem for laughing round an apple" (the immediate thought here is of a soldier's death-grimace). Moreover, the human animal was not designed for battle; there are "no claws behind his fingers supple." His appearance is of gentle, delicate demeanor, a face framed with "curls," as opposed to the brutish nobility of animals which possess "talons" and "antlers."

Similar sentiments, now supported by religious imagery, are expressed in "Anthem for Doomed Youth," a sonnet which illustrates Owen's fusion of the traditional elegiac mood with the realities of modern warfare. The opening question serves as an example: "What passing-bells for these who die as cattle?" The answer is that the only possible form of lamentation for the war dead is the cacophonous sounds of war, "the stuttering rifle's rapid rattle." Not only are religious ceremonies out of the question, but they would also be a "mockery." Here Owen shows the extent to which his disillusionment with organized religion had gone. Instead of the glow of holy candles, the poet finds light in "their eyes." They will wear no "pall," but will be recognized and remembered through the "pallor of girl's brows." The essence of this poem is that in such times as these, Christianity seems incapable of providing its traditional comfort. The memorial of the dead soldiers will not be "flowers" but memories held by "patient minds." Their legacy, sadly and not of their making, is but darkness, at "each slow dusk drawing-down of blinds."

In a sense, Owen's poetic legacy can also inspire darkness for the reader. His work is highly educational, however, and thus valuable, especially when read in the context of World War I and in contrast to that of some of his fellow soldier-poets. The reader, ultimately grateful for the work that Owen left, is intrigued by what he might have become.

Robert Edward Graalman, Jr.

Other major works

NONFICTION: *Collected Letters*, 1967 (Harold Owen and John Bell, editors).

Bibliography

Breen, Jennifer. *Wilfred Owen: Selected Poetry and Prose*. London: Routledge, Chapman & Hall 1988. Breen does an excellent job of giving a brief analysis of Owen's major poems and supports her opinions by subjectively looking at his personal correspondence to gain insight for her analysis. This short book is organized by a chronological table of contents and contains a limited bibliography.

Hibberd, Dominic. *Owen the Poet*. Athens: University of Georgia Pres, 1986. This excellent book presents Owen as a single identity, not as a poet whose works are traditionally studied as being either before the war or after it. Hibberd examines Owen's growth to "poethood," his imagination, and his understanding of himself, and complements this approach with an exhaustive bibliography and a concise index.

Lane, Author. *An Adequate Response: The War Poetry of Wilfred Owen and Siegfried Sassoon*. Detroit: Wayne State University Press, 1972. Analyzes Owen's poetry from the aspect of the cataclysmal effect of the war on the use of poetic language. Owen's influence from John Keats is considered as he replaces traditional, figurative images with realistic scenes from the battlefield and weaves them into his verses.

Owen, Harold, and John Bell, eds. *Wilfred Owen: Collected Letters*. London: Oxford University Press, 1967. Follows the life of Owen from the time he was five until his death at the age of twenty-five, through his letters to his family and friends. While not providing critical analysis of his poetry, this fascinating collection gives the reader rare insight into the personality of this gifted poet. Supplemented by a complete index.

Simcox, Kenneth. *Wilfred Owen: Anthem for a Doomed Youth*. London: Woburn, 1987. This study of Owen begins with his interaction with his family, focusing on his influential mother. His religious background is highlighted as Simcox reviews the major issues in Owen's poetry, amply augmented with examples from his primary works. Supplemented by a comprehensive index.

Stallworthy, Jon, ed. *The Poems of Wilfred Owen*. New York: W. W. Norton, 1985. An intensive study into the chronological sequence of 103 poems and twelve fragments by Owen. Aims to offer factual footnotes to allow readers a more concise foundation to formulate their own explications.

White, Gertrude. *Wilfred Owen*. New York: Twayne, 1969. White traces Owen's maturation as a poet from dreamy, romantic imagery to the harsh realities of World War I. Discusses his standing with other war poets and stresses that genre is more important than chronology in focusing on his development. Offers a somewhat dated bibliography and index.

DOROTHY PARKER

Born: West End, New Jersey; August 22, 1893
Died: New York, New York; June 7, 1967

Principal poetry
Enough Rope, 1926; *Sunset Gun*, 1928; *Death and Taxes*, 1931; *Not So Deep as a Well*, 1936.

Other literary forms
In addition to Dorothy Parker's verse—not serious "poetry," she claimed—her principal writings, identified by Alexander Woollcott as "a potent distillation of nectar and wormwood," are several collections of well-crafted short stories: *Laments for the Living* (1930), *After Such Pleasures* (1933), and *Here Lies* (1939). These stories focus on the superficial, pointless, barren lives of middle- and upper-class Manhattanite women of the flapper and early depression times, unhappily dependent on men for their economic support and emotional sustenance. Parker also wrote witty drama reviews for *Vanity Fair* (1918-1920), *Ainslee's* (1920-1933), and *The New Yorker* (1931); and terse, tart book reviews for the *The New Yorker* (1927-1933) and *Esquire* (1959-1962). "Tonstant Weader Fwowed Up," her provoked, personal reaction to A. A. Milne's *The House at Pooh Corner* (1928), typifies her "delicate claws of . . . superb viciousness" (Woollcott). Parker's major plays are *The Coast of Illyria* (1949), about Charles and Mary Lamb's tortured lives, and *The Ladies of the Corridor* (1953), three case histories of death-in-life among elderly women.

Achievements
Parker's poems, stories, and reviews, wisecracking and wary, were the toast of New York in the 1920's and early 1930's. She presented a brittle, world-weary, cynically urban view of life appealing to pseudosophisticates—who, indeed, were the subjects of many of her writings. Her literary coterie, the verbally glib, self-promoting journalists of the Algonquin Round Table, were minor writers in relation to their major contemporaries, such as Ernest Hemingway, William Faulkner, and Eugene O'Neill, and later estimates see her work as flashy but not penetrating. Yet, although many of her characters seem superficial, her women being "self-absorbed snobs, her men philanderers, scoundrels, or subservient husbands" (Arthur F. Kinney, *Dorothy Parker*, 1978), Parker's stories have remained perennially popular. Serious critical assessment has been negligible in recent years, except for Kinney's work. Nevertheless, as the editors of the recent anthologies of Parker's works (Viking, 1973; Penguin, 1977) and the authors of occasional encyclopedia articles have noted, the repeated themes of Parker's poetry and prose are

ever contemporary; anxieties, social hypocrisy, waning or unequal love between the sexes, failures of human sympathy and communication.

A few poems and various *bons mots* continue to be anthologized ("Men seldom make passes/ At girls who wear glasses"), though since the advent of World War II, Parker's poetry, itself highly derivative, has had little or no influence on subsequent writers of verse, light or otherwise. Today, as the poetry of the contemporaries with whom she was most often compared, Elinor Wylie and Edna St. Vincent Millay, is being treated with renewed critical respect, Parker's reputation continues to languish. To call her, as Kinney does, "the most accomplished classical epigrammatist of her time" is praise of very limited scope. Some feminists perceive Parker as a kindred spirit in her concern for the chronic, debilitating, and also demeaning dependence of women upon their husbands or lovers.

Biography

Dorothy Rothschild Parker Campbell was the daughter of a prosperous Jewish clothier, Henry Rothschild (no relation to the banking family), and the Protestant Eliza Marston, who died shortly after childbirth. Her childhood loneliness was exacerbated by her mixed religious ancestry and the fact that her hated stepmother sent her for some years to the Blessed Sacrament Convent school in West End, New Jersey. She later said she wanted to write her autobiography if only for the sake of calling it *Mongrel*, an epitomization of her self-image as "a mongrel that wanted to be a thoroughbred."

After a year (1911) at the fashionable Miss Dana's School in Morristown, New Jersey, Parker gradually developed as a writer. Her first job was to write fashion blurbs and drama criticism for *Vanity Fair* (1916-1920). She later wrote short stories for *The New Yorker*, irregularly from 1926 to 1955; Hollywood film scripts at intervals, 1934 to 1954; and *Esquire* book reviews, 1959 to 1962.

Through her associates at *Vanity Fair*, Parker, whose wisecracking wit and cynical demeanor epitomized for many the insouciant flapper spirit of the 1920's became a charter member of the *bons vivants* of the Round Table at the Algonquin Hotel. Other founders include Robert Benchley, Robert Sherwood, Alexander Woollcott, Franklin P. Adams, and Harold Ross, who later established *The New Yorker*. Over daily lunches they exercised through endless wordplay the careful concern for precise and vivid (and, some would say, smart-alecky) language that characterized their writing. Parker's reputation for finesse as a punster caused more outrageous witticisms to be attributed to her than she deserved, though this quintessential response to Franklin P. Adams command to use "horticulture" in a sentence is authentic: "You can lead a horticulture but you can't make her think." At the Algonquin, Parker met many theater people and lesser literati to whom later critics attribute her downfall. Because the literary shallowness of her admirers led them to exaggerate her early reputation, and because Parker believed them, she failed to fulfill her early promise of developing into a serious writer of enduring distinction. From them she learned to value terse expression, and to engage in satiric repartee that culminated in the typical sardonic punch lines of her verse after 1920. From them, especially, she came fervently to believe in the importance of not being earnest.

Beneath the surface gaiety lay an unstable personal life reflected in Parker's continual heavy drinking. Her marriage to Edwin Pond Parker (1917 to 1928) was succeeded by two marriages to the bisexual actor-writer Alan Campbell. They were married from 1934 until 1947 and from 1950 until 1963, when Campbell died of an overdose of sleeping pills, just as Edwin Parker had done. Campbell, Lillian Hellman, and others nurtured Parker, but they could not control her drinking and her worsening writer's block that kept her from finishing many of her literary attempts during the last fifteen years. Her sad and bitter old age ("People ought to be one of two things, young or dead") was ended by a fatal heart attack in her decrepit hotel room where she was found dead on June 7, 1967. Her acerbic self-assessment echoes the contemporary judgment of Parker as "a woman who outlived her time."

Analysis

Dorothy Parker's slight reputation as a poet rests on three slender volumes of verse with funereal titles: *Enough Rope, Sunset Gun,* and *Death and Taxes*—collected in 1936 with five additional poems in *Not So Deep as a Well.* Although her poems on the whole are highly restricted in scope and depth, her poetic techniques became somewhat more sophisticated and more effectively controlled during the decade when these books were published.

The major motifs of Parker's poems are love, loneliness, and death. Loneliness and death, however, are usually variations on the theme of romantic love—exploited or exploitative, betrayed, feigned, unrequited, abandoned, lost. Parker finds the relations between men and women disagreeable and duplicitous: "Scratch a lover and find a foe." In Parker's limited poetic world, women as epitomized by the narrative persona are doomed to perpetual emotional dependence on men, whose indifference, fickleness, and callousness drives them to the despair implied in the books' macabre titles. Love relationships, so fleeting and superficial, are based on appearance ("A curly mouth . . . long, tapered limbs") and "dust-bound trivia" ("The Searched Soul") that foreordain their failure. Lovers kiss—and invariably tell ("A Certain Lady"). If they swear that their passion is "infinite, undying," one or both are bound to be lying ("Unfortunate Coincidence"). Dalliance, not marriage, is the aim of the men, and sometimes of the women, for lovers are numerous, faceless, and somewhat interchangeable: "I always get them all mixed up" ("Pictures in the Smoke").

The narrative female persona from whose perspective nearly all the poems are presented plays one of two characteristic roles. In one role the rejected lover, dominated by her own grief and a sense of unworthiness, tries to cope with her own devastation. This penitent suppliant sometimes seeks a new love, wanting to give away her heart, "the wretched thing," "now to that lad, now to this." Otherwise, she dies, literally or figuratively. On occasion she lies "cool and quiet," finding the grave a tranquil antidote to the fever of unrequited love ("Testament"). At other times she returns as a ghost to haunt her lover "In April twilight's unsung melody" ("I Shall Come Back").

The other role, however, is the image most commonly associated with Dorothy Parker, the wisecracking wit of the Algonquin Round Table. This narrative persona, worldly-wise and weary, knows that it is always "just my luck to get/ One perfect rose" instead of "one perfect limousine." She knows, too, as a lover, "my strength and my weakness, gents" is to love only until her passion is reciprocated ("Ballade at Thirty-Five"). She realizes that, as a latent romantic, she is bound to be "spectacularly bored" with a constant lover ("On Being a Woman"), and to prefer inappropriately one who is "sudden and swift and strong" to a wealthy wooer—"Somebody ought to examine my head!" To cope, she undermines her sentiment with cynical punch lines, either one-liners or couplets: "I shudder at the thought of men . . . I'm due to fall in love again" ("Symptom Recital"). She relishes the calculated insult ("I turn to little words—so you, my dear/ Can spell them out") as much as the imagined injury: if she had a "shiny gun" she could have "a world of fun" shooting her antagonists ("Frustration").

These contrasting personae alternate poems in Parker's collections and the intermittent presence of the cynic undermines the credibility of the rejected lover. Once conditioned, readers expect a witty riposte or a slangy word ("Here's my strength and my weakness, gents") to shift the poem from seriousness to satire, as indeed it often does. Though anticipated, the slang startles, as in "Coda" ("For art is a form of catharsis/ And love is a permanent flop") and provokes laughter in hitherto serious contexts. Even if the author meant some of her poems to be taken seriously, as individually they might be (see "Transition"), the cynical persona and her attendant language establish the prevailing comic tone for Parker's collected verse. Thus Parker's poetic techniques reinforce the impression that her verse is primarily an exercise in verbal ingenuity rather than a presentation of authentic emotion or experience.

Composed mostly of simple iambic quatrains or couplets, Parker's lyric poetry lacks the formal complexity, structural finesse and variations, and metaphorical ingenuity that add interest to much other poetry on the same themes, such as the love poetry of John Donne, William Shakespeare, John Keats, or Emily Dickinson. Kinney has favorably compared Parker's techniques and control of meter and line to Horace, Martial, Catullus, Heinrich Heine, and her contemporaries Elinor Wylie and Edna St. Vincent Millay. Although Parker may have read the classical authors, it seems likely that she learned their techniques from the verse of her companion of the Algonquin Round Table, Adams, whose "Conning Tower" column in the *New York World* sported such whimsies as "Give me the balmy breezes! . . . / Wind on my cheek and hair!/ And, while we're on the topic,/ Give me the air." Adams and Parker share control, compression, precise diction, and a fondness for puns—perhaps all that one can or should ask of light verse.

The difficulty is that the techniques and diction which make Parker's light verse comical and airy simply seem banal when applied to poetry that purports to be of greater seriousness. The imagery is predictable—stormy seas, softly dropping rain, withering flowers to denote an absent or lost lover; the rejected maiden "a-crying," or sleeping chastely, or mourning "whenever one drifted petal leaves the tree" for the dream that "lies dead here." Moreover, the language in some of the more serious poetry is too often self-consciously anachronistic: "what shallow boons suffice my heart" or uncomfortably poetic—"e're," "lay a-drying," "Little will I think. . . ."

One could apply to Parker's poetry the judgment that she herself applied to the performance of a famous actress, who ran "the gamut of emotions from A to B." Within that restricted compass, her comic verse succeeds where her more serious poetry fails.

Lynn Z. Bloom

Other major works

SHORT FICTION: *Laments for the Living*, 1930; *After Such Pleasures*, 1933; *Here Lies*, 1939.

PLAYS: *Close Harmony*, 1924 (with Elmer Rice); *The Coast of Illyria*, 1949; *The Ladies of the Corridor*, 1953.

Bibliography

Cooper, Wyatt. "Remembering Dorothy Parker." *Esquire* 70 (July, 1968): 56-57, 61, 110-114. This rich and reliable portrait of Dorothy Parker in her last years offers insights into her life and work and assesses her place in American literature.

Keats, John. *You Might as Well Live: The Life and Times of Dorothy Parker.* New York: Simon & Schuster, 1970. This standard, popular biography, thin in places, is based on extensive research. Some facts and interpretations have been amended or superseded. The literary judgments tend to be sparse and overwhelmingly adulatory. Contains a bibliography.

Kinney, Arthur F. *Dorothy Parker.* Boston: Twayne, 1978. In this excellent study of Parker's life and work, Kinney incorporates facts recorded for the first time and provides the first full critical assessment of her writing. The author traces the sources of Parker's writing and assesses her final achievement in order to locate what he views as her significant and unique contribution to American literature. Kinney calls Parker the best epigrammatic American poet of the century. Contains a bibliography and extensive notes and references.

Labrie, Ross. "Dorothy Parker Revisited." *Canadian Review of American Studies* 7 (Spring, 1976): 48-56. Labrie discusses Parker as a child of the 1920's, with her mixture of wit and skepticism, her uneven taste, and her concern with the American myths of glamour and success. According to Labrie, Parker is drawn in her writing toward vividness and candor but also toward an austerity of form.

MacDermott, Kathy. "Light Human and the Dark Underside of Wish Fulfillment: Conservative Anti-Realism." *Studies in Popular Culture* 10 (Spring, 1987): 37-53. In one of the few and excellent critical studies of Parker's work, MacDermott compares Parker's realism to that of Robert Charles Benchley, S. J. Perelman and P. G. Wodehouse. Delves beneath the surface of Parker's work to reveal its essentially complex nature.

LINDA PASTAN

Born: New York, New York; May 27, 1932

Principal poetry

A Perfect Circle of Sun, 1971; *Aspects of Eve*, 1975; *The Five Stages of Grief*, 1978; *Waiting for My Life*, 1981; *PM/AM: New and Selected Poems*, 1982; *A Fraction of Darkness*, 1985; *The Imperfect Paradise*, 1988; *Heroes in Disguise*, 1991.

Other literary forms

Linda Pastan has written an autobiographical essay, "Roots," that appeared in a volume edited by William Heyen entitled *American Poets in 1976* (1976).

Achievements

Since the appearance of Pastan's first book, critics have praised the lucidity of her language, the freshness of her metaphors, and the consistency of her accomplishment. She has been appreciated as an artist of what she herself calls "dailiness"—contemporary domestic life. She has won a fellowship from the National Endowment for the Arts and a Maryland Arts Council grant, as well as several literary awards: *Mademoiselle*'s Dylan Thomas Poetry Award, the Alice Fay di Castagnola Award, the Bess Hokin Prize, and the Maurice English Award. *PM/AM* was nominated for an American Book Award. In 1991, Pastan was named Poet Laureate of Maryland.

Biography

The daughter of Jacob L. and Bess Schwartz Olenik, Linda Pastan is of Jewish lineage. Her father, the son of Russian immigrants, was a surgeon, and Pastan married a molecular biologist, Ira Pastan, in 1953. She earned a B.A. from Radcliffe College in 1954, an M.L.S. from Simmons College in 1955, and an M.A. from Brandeis University in 1957. Mother of three children—Stephen, Peter, and Rachel—she and her husband reside in the Maryland countryside, near Potomac. She has been poetry editor of the literary magazine *Voyages*, has lectured at the Bread Loaf Writers' Conference in Vermont, and has taught graduate workshops in poetry at American University. From 1986 to 1989, Linda Pastan served on the governing board of Associated Writing Programs. Although Pastan received recognition for her poetry while a student, winning *Mademoiselle*'s Dylan Thomas Award (the runner-up was Sylvia Plath), she did not work regularly on her poetry for ten years and did not publish a collection until 1971. Since that time her books have appeared regularly, and she has received other prizes as well as critical praise in leading literary journals. Pastan has acknowledged the influence and support of the poet William Stafford and has been labeled a "Post-Confessional" poet, interested in sincerity as well as going beyond the personal.

Analysis

Like many American poets since Walt Whitman, Linda Pastan has made poetry from her experience, but she has been much less optimistic than the Whitman who wrote "Song of Myself" (1855), "Crossing Brooklyn Ferry" (1856), and "Passage to India" (1870). Starting with her first book, published when she was nearly forty, Linda Pastan has seen the human individual as subject to such forces as genetics, mortality, gravity, climate, fate, and God. Not that the individual is powerless: in love her characters can choose to be wise or foolish, passionate or subdued, faithful or not; and Pastan thinks highly of artistic and domestic accomplishments. Unlike Whitman, however, she never suggests that the individual can transcend mortal limits.

A survey of Pastan's favorite metaphors suggests that most of their sources are autobiographical: her Jewish heritage, her childhood in New York City, her education and interest in literature, her medical knowledge stemming from her father's and husband's scientific interests, Greek and biblical mythology, a later interest in Asian culture, flora and fauna of her adult life in the Maryland countryside, the behavior of her offspring and husband, and vacations near the ocean. Yet to concentrate only on the origins of her imagery would be to ignore Pastan's vision and craft.

Starting with her first book, she tried various means of shaping material into poems and of arranging poems into collections. The four parts of *A Perfect Circle of Sun* conform to the seasons. *Aspects of Eve* alludes to the biblical story of Eden, and in this book Pastan relies more frequently on narratives, like "Folk Tale" and "Short Story," to present material in a more comprehensive, dramatic fashion. Elisabeth Kubler-Ross's description of the process of mourning underlies *The Five Stages of Grief*, and Pastan continues the quest for Kubler-Ross's final stage, Acceptance, in *Waiting for My Life* and the new poems in *PM/AM*. The most compelling shaping principle in Pastan's poetry, however, is mythology—especially the story of Adam and Eve, with its emphasis on the Fall (see *Aspects of Eve* and *The Imperfect Paradise*), and the character of Penelope as depicted in Homer's *Odyssey* (c. 800 B.C.), legendary for her patience and domesticity. It is important to stress that the relationship between such myths and Pastan's own life is reciprocal: the myths help to frame her experience, but she also questions them, returning obsessively to meditate on their meaning and reinvent them—to tell them, that is, in her own way as a result of her experience.

It would therefore be inaccurate to suggest that Pastan has tucked her entire life into a pattern prescribed by any single myth. Instead, one should place mythological allusions into the more comprehensive "story"—the interplay of Pastan's persona and the forces affecting her. "Persona" is an important concept: Pastan has acknowledged that her poems are not strictly or merely autobiography, calling "the poetic 'I' . . . more like a fraternal than an identical twin." What one finds in her poetry, then, is the tragic story of human limitation. Since Pastan depends upon favorite metaphors, this analysis will examine their roles in the story.

She mentions many forces she cannot control. In "Last Will," she acknowledges that her children's only important inheritance is "in the genes," and in "balancing act: for N." she portrays the generations as acrobats "hooked together// by nerve/ and DNA." While hospitalized in "Accidents," she senses future accidents "waiting to happen." "On the Question of Free Will," one of her meditations on the Eden story, questions human freedom, hinting that "God's plan" may prevail.

Her most frequent metaphor for human vulnerability is the weather. As she says in "Hurricane Watch," "Some live in the storm's eye only./ I rise and fall/ with the barometer,/ holding on for my life." *A Perfect Circle of Sun* establishes the ambivalent vision of the annual cycle that applies to all of her work: Winter is both death and beginning; the energy of spring can start growth or turn chaotic; summer, she says, is only winter in a "disguise of leaves"; and autumn is more a time for dirges than for harvest. Pastan's habitual and resourceful use of the weather reflects her sense of mortality. In "Hurricane Watch," the persona inhabits "a storm cellar/ of flesh," recalls "a blizzard of cells" in a microscope, and admits that "at times/ the hairs on my arm lift,/ as if in some incalculable wind." Her pessimism is such that she says "I read my palm as though it were a weather map/ and keep a hurricane watch/ all year." While fresh, lucid metaphors are essential to the success of this poem, it is worth noting Pastan's characteristic use of short lines, here suggesting her own tentativeness. Yet in the preceding line, "Some live in the storm's eye only," she lets a sentence about others run unbroken to its end, suggesting their greater courage.

As Pastan charts the seasons, she often refers to trees. In "Each Autumn," she writes, "We put our leaves in order,/ raking, burning, acknowledging,/ the persistence of time." In "After Agatha Christie," she implies her skepticism of summer by calling a tree's leaves "its false beard." Leaves ready to fall in "Consolations" are "scrolls bearing/ the old messages." "There is an age when you are most yourself," she remembers her father saying, and in "Something Above the Trees," which is written in a Malaysian form called *pantoum*, she wonders, "Was it something about the trees that made him speak?" The nearly unpunctuated poem "Family Tree" plays on the traditional *ubi sunt* theme by asking, "How many leaves/ has death undone . . . ?" Throughout this poem, Pastan chants the names of trees, and she finally declares that she will not drink to the New Year, in which her mother will die and her grandson be born. Instead, she broods on burned leaves' telling "the long story/ of smoke." In "Donatello's Magdalene," a fifteenth century wood sculpture of Mary Magdalene inspires one of Pastan's most inventive and anguished tree metaphors. After describing the sculpture, Pastan asks how many of its branches were "stripped/ and nailed/ to make each crucifix?" In this case, by alluding to the suffering and death of Jesus, Pastan adds a religious or mythic factor to her usual symbolic equation of trees with mortality.

The metaphors already discussed—weather and trees—play the roles, respectively, of agent and victim in Pastan's story of human limitation. Yet one natural metaphor—the sea—contains both roles. References to the sea enter her work in *Aspects of Eve*. Many later poems have coastal settings, usually with beaches, allowing Pastan to pit the individual against the awesome force of the ocean and introduce the impermanence of sand to characterize human life and relationships. Moreover, she often applies the verbs "to swim" and "to drown" to the human condition.

Pastan's most sustained metaphoric use of the sea occurs in the final four poems in the section of *The Imperfect Paradise* subtitled "Balancing Act." In "A Walk Before Breakfast," she dreams of an entire life like a vacation, "with the sea/ opening its chapters/ of water and light." "The Ordinary Weather of Summer," however, concludes pessimistically, with her imagining the last summer she and her husband will both be alive, when they walk up from the surf "on wobbly legs," "shaking the water out of our blinded eyes." "Erosion," the last poem of the group, expresses both optimism and pessimism. "We are slowly/ undermined," she declares, thinking of the slippage of sand, and adds, "The waves move their long row/ of scythes over the beach." Nonetheless, the sea appears "Implacably lovely," and the couple tries to stop the erosion. She has to admit, though, that "one day the sea will simply/ take us." The final stanza contains the most rewarding metaphors. Pastan allows, "We are made of water anyway," and says she has felt it "in the yielding/ of your flesh." She also thinks of her husband as sand, "moving slowly, slowly/ from under me."

Having acknowledged that the forces facing the individual are "implacable," Pastan still places considerable emphasis upon human endeavor and accomplishment. Her people raise families, sustain professions, initiate projects and hobbies, love and hurt one another. In other words, though subject to the forces of creation, they are far from passive. Indeed, Pastan exerts herself metaphorically to depict human effectuality, even in the face of finally overpowering forces.

One reliable metaphor of human accomplishment, often implicit, is art. Many of Pastan's poems have been inspired by works of art, and she frequently mentions her own reading and working at poems. One of her tenderest love poems, "Prosody 101," uses poetry itself as a metaphor. She begins by noting that she was taught that surprise, not regularity, was essential to poetry. (By writing the poem in blank verse, an unusual choice for her, Pastan can let the metrical pattern create rhythmic surprises.) Then, after describing surprises brought on by the weather, she relates a situation in which her husband startles her. He has acted so much like "a cold front" that she expects she might leave him, but he unexpectedly laughs and picks her up, making her feel young and alive—making her realize, "So this is Poetry."

Pastan has also dedicated a significant portion of her adult years to domestic concerns. In fact, the poems in the second part of *Waiting for My Life* depict her acceptance of "dailiness" as a vocation. In "Who Is It Accuses Us?" she angrily answers that domesticity is anything but safe. "You who risk no more than your own skins/ I tell you household Gods/ are jealous Gods," she declares, thinking of how they poison one's "secret wells/ with longing." Her autobiographical essay "Roots," in which she tells of postponing her career in poetry to raise her family, acknowledges the duties of home life as an important source of metaphor. She talks specifically of her identification with Penelope, Ulysses' wife in the *Odyssey*, who told her importunate suitors that she would choose a husband to replace the long-absent Ulysses when she finished a tapestry. Each day she worked on it, and each night tore out that day's work. Appropriately, throughout Pastan's poems one finds references to various types of needlecraft—lace, knitting, sewing—and two provocative meditations on the Penelope myth—"At the Loom" and "Rereading *The Odyssey* in Middle Age"—appear in *The Imperfect Paradise*. Images of closets, hallways, televisions, and entire houses also pervade Pastan's writing. Not surprisingly, kitchens supply some of the most compelling domestic metaphors. In "Soup," an angry persona likens her life to an "icebox . . . full/ of the homelier vegetables." A mellower view develops in "Meditation by the Stove," a poem that harkens to the traditional use of kitchen fire to symbolize nurturing (as in many fairy tales, such as the Cinderella stories). Amid the baking of bread and looking after children, the persona acknowledges the disruptive presence of passion, but commits herself to domestic responsibility: "I have banked the fires of my body/ into a small domestic flame for others/ to warm their hands on for a while."

While there are references to her father's work as a surgeon, the primary male occupation in Pastan's poems is gardening—a passion of her husband's, which resonates with the story of the Garden of Eden. Pastan is alert to forsythias, locusts, lady slippers, bloodroot, milkweed, trillium, dandelions, onions, corn, and bees, as well as the work involved in tending plants. Her fine six-sonnet sequence "The Imperfect Paradise" contains the fullest portrayal of the gardener—devoted to spring, naming "everything in sight." His endeavors are such that he can seem godlike, destroying trees so that flowers flourish and carting off trapped squirrels so that birds can have the seed intended for them. Toward such activity Pastan's persona is often antagonistic. "In the Absence of Wings" portrays the gardener as her warden, holding her in his "maze of hawthorn and yew." Now that her children have grown, her father has died, and her writing of poems seems near an end, she wanders to a place where snow and flowers alternate. Still longing, she is like the mythical Daedalus before he invented the wax-and-feather wings that enabled him and his son Icarus to escape the power of King Midas: "The horizon is the thread/ I must tie to my wrist" "as I come/ to the vine-scrolled gatepost/ of the labyrinth."

A final major metaphor of human endeavor—travel—is also ambiguous. More often than not, movement implies potentiality. Pastan writes of morning being "parked/ outside my window" in "Final," and in "To a Daughter Leaving Home," a girl's first tentative bicycle rides represent her maturation. Absence of movement represents failure. In "Waiting For My Life," for instance, the persona regrets her lack of initiative. She has stood at bus stops waiting for her life "to start," and even when she makes her way onto a bus she has no sense of direction or purpose. An even more frightening aspect of this metaphor lies in the fact that travel is not necessarily a matter of intention. The journey of life, especially progress toward death, is not merely one's own doing. "They seemed to all take off/ at once," Pastan writes in "Departures," referring to the deaths of several female relatives. The second stanza of "The Accident" may be the most eloquent passage on this theme. She imagines death as "an almost perfect ending": the icy road leading to a lamppost, the post being "a hidden exit . . . where the past/ and the future collide/ in one barbarous flash/ and only the body/ is nothing,/ disappearing at last/ into certainty."

Pastan's discomfort with the fact that human efforts, regardless of their nature or immediate ends, lead finally to death makes her portrayal of the body highly distinctive. In "At the Gynecologist's," perhaps echoing Sylvia Plath's poem *Ariel* (1965), Pastan characterizes herself in the stirrups of the examining table as "galloping towards death/ with flowers of ether in my hair." The body is the focal point—even the battleground—in Pastan's story of human limitation. There is little celebrating of sensuality in her poems, in fact little visual description. Rather, she focuses on callouses, cramps, anesthesia, infection, rash, scars, bruises, bandages, migraine, root canal surgery, bypass surgery, mammograms, X rays, EKG's, sonograms, insomnia, and (not surprisingly) hypochondria. The poem "Teeth" emphasizes physical decline and collapse, characterizing teeth as "rows of crumbling/ headstones."

If Pastan's concern lay only with perpetuating her youth or physical beauty, however, her poetry would lack its tragic dimension. Her real interest is moral, her preoccupation with bodily misfortune a reflection of her worry about her own failures. Yet her views are far from absurdist: she recognizes and values accomplishment. Her persona admits to "a nature always asking/ for the worst" and laments her "sins," "all my old faults," and various missed opportunities. Yet amid threatening forces, people can live admirable, even heroic lives. The often-praised early poem "Emily Dickinson," which links health and morality, praises Dickinson not for eccentricity but for "the sheer sanity/ of vision, the serious mischief/ of language, the economy of pain."

In Pastan's tragic story of human limitation, not only does the body journey toward death, but the self, as she says in "Low Tide," is "the passionate guest/ who would inhabit this flesh," an entity—call it "soul"—eventually separate from the body. With age, medical charts become one's "only autobiography," she says in "Clinic." The human individual exists subject to forces—natural and perhaps supernatural—that surpass one's ability to control. Weather and the sea represent such forces, and trees reflect the individual's position in relation to them. The human being, however, has the freedom—or curse, if one recalls the Fall in Genesis—to exert oneself in significant ways. Thus, according to Pastan, we travel until, to quote "Clinic" again, "we stop/ being part of our bodies/ and start simply/ to inhabit them."

Jay Paul

Bibliography

Franklin, Benjamin, V. "Theme and Structure in Linda Pastan's Poetry." *Poet Lore* 75 (Winter, 1981): 234-241. This article summarizes Pastan's first four books and discusses the "fatalistic" nature of Pastan's vision, arguing that she is both "anguished" and "indomitable." She acknowledges frustration, but she is also a "realist who sees that proper understanding of one's realities is essential for living."

Gray, Richard. *American Poetry of the Twentieth Century.* London: Longman, 1990. While this book does not comment on Pastan, the chapter entitled "Formalists and Confessionalists: American Poetry Since the Second World War" surveys poetry contemporary with and relevant to Pastan's. See the section entitled "From Formalism to Freedom: A Progress of American Poetic Techniques Since the War."

Ingersoll, Earl G., et al. *The Post-Confessionals: Conversations with American Poets of the Eighties.* Rutherford, N.J.: Fairleigh Dickinson University Press, 1989. Stan Sanvel Rubin's "Introduction" provides a detailed definition of "The Post-Confessionals" (15-23) and links Pastan with her contemporaries. "'Whatever Is at Hand': A Conversation with Linda Pastan" (135-149), recorded in 1976 and updated in 1987, discusses Pastan's interest in mythology and science, the theme of death, and the influence of William Stafford, especially upon her writing habits.

Pastan, Linda. "Roots." In *American Poets in 1976*, edited by William Heyen. Indianapolis: Bobbs-Merrill, 1976. Pastan charts her development from an early longing for escape, through an obsession with reading and then writing, into a difficult time when wifely duties precluded writing. Writing about Penelope gave Pastan a way out of her dilemma. In closing, she admits that "the road to discovery . . . loops backward."

_____. "Unbreakable Codes." In *Acts of Mind: Conversations with Contemporary Poets*, edited by Richard Jackson. Tuscaloosa: University of Alabama Press, 1983. In this 1979 interview, Pastan discusses her close involvement with nature. She explains that some of her metaphors create a sense of safety. She also tells how she organized her first books and stresses that there are only a few poetic themes of significance: aging, dying, passion, and identity.

Smith, Dave. "Some Recent American Poetry: Come All Ye Fair and Tender Ladies." *American Poetry Review* 11 (January/February, 1982): 36-46. In this unusually insightful review (of *Waiting for My Life*), Smith argues that Pastan's central theme is desire—an asking both what people want and what deserves their allegiance. He also notes the profundity and "innocence" in Pastan's telling of her main story—death.

KENNETH PATCHEN

Born: Niles, Ohio; December 13, 1911
Died: Palo Alto, California; January 8, 1972

Principal poetry

Before the Brave, 1936; *First Will and Testament,* 1939; *The Dark Kingdom,* 1942; *The Teeth of the Lion,* 1942; *Cloth of the Tempest,* 1943; *An Astonished Eye Looks Out of the Air,* 1945; *Outlaw of the Lowest Planet,* 1946; *Selected Poems of Kenneth Patchen,* 1946, 1958, 1964; *Panels for the Walls of Heaven,* 1946; *Pictures of Life and Death,* 1947; *To Say If You Love Someone,* 1948; *Red Wine and Yellow Hair,* 1949; *Orchards, Thrones and Caravans,* 1952; *The Famous Boating Party,* 1954 (poetry and prose); *Poems of Humor and Protest,* 1954; *Glory Never Guesses,* 1955; *A Surprise for the Bagpipe Player,* 1956; *Hurrah for Anything,* 1957; *When We Were Here Together,* 1957; *Poemscapes,* 1958; *Because It Is,* 1960; *The Love Poems of Kenneth Patchen,* 1960; *Hallelujah Anyway,* 1966; *Doubleheader,* 1966; *But Even So,* 1968; *Collected Poems of Kenneth Patchen,* 1968; *Love and War Poems,* 1968; *There's Love All Day,* 1970; *Wonderings,* 1971.

Other literary forms

Although mainly known as a poet, Kenneth Patchen, a dedicated experimentalist, rejected normal genre distinctions, participating in radical new forms of prose, concrete poetry, poetry-and-jazz, picture poems, and surrealistic tales and fables, as well as other innovations. His first published prose work, a short story entitled "Bury Them in God," appeared in a 1939 collection by New Directions. Two years later, in 1941, he published his most celebrated prose work, a pacifist antinovel entitled *The Journal of Albion Moonlight.* After that, his prose work began to appear irregularly between the publication of his numerous books of poetry.

Achievements

An extremely prolific writer, Patchen published roughly a book a year during his thirty-six-year writing career from 1936 to his death in 1972. Besides poetry, his artistic works consisted of prose and drama, silkscreen prints, paintings and drawings, hand-painted books, and even papier-mâché animal sculptures. Holding strongly to his belief in the "total artist," Patchen experimented with a wide variety of artistic forms, influencing a generation of poets with his creative energy.

Patchen also played a role in initiating the Poetry-and-Jazz movement in San Francisco during the 1950's. With Kenneth Rexroth and Lawrence Ferlinghetti, Patchen began reading his poetry to jazz accompaniment at the Cellar, a small club in San Francisco, in 1957. Patchen's own innovations in this area began six years earlier when he read and recorded his *Fables and*

Other Little Tales (1953) to a jazz background. As early as 1945, in his novel *The Memoirs of a Shy Pornographer*, Patchen had presented a two page list of "the disks you'll have to get if you want a basic jazz library."

In addition to the Poetry-and-Jazz movement, Patchen made important contributions to at least three other areas of poetic experimentation. First, in the 1950's, Patchen began to work with surrealistic fable and verse forms in such works as *Fables and Other Little Tales*, *Hurrah for Anything*, and *Because It Is*. Second, as an early experimenter in concrete poetry in this country—see, particularly, *Cloth of the Tempest*, *Sleepers Awake* (1946), and *Panels for the Walls of Heaven*—Patchen provided American poetry with a uniquely visual poetic form in which the poet is concerned with making an object to be perceived rather than merely read. Patchen's third contribution, also involving visual expression, is his fusion of painting and writing forms. Many of Patchen's books include self-painted covers, drawings printed with poems, and picture-poem posters. Such "painted books" as *The Dark Kingdom*, *Panels for the Walls of Heaven*, *Red Wine and Yellow Hair*, and *Poemscapes*, illustrate Patchen's impressive skill as a painter. Although he usually refused to exhibit his paintings, claiming that he preferred bookstores to art galleries, in 1969, a few years before his death, he finally conducted a one-man art show at the Corcoran Gallery in Washington, D.C.

Patchen received a Guggenheim Fellowship in 1936, the Shelley Memorial Award in 1954, and a cash award of ten thousand dollars in 1967 from the National Foundation of Arts and Humanities for his lifelong contribution to American Letters. A small but moving volume entitled *Tribute to Kenneth Patchen* (1977), published after the poet's death, attests the great respect in which he was held by contemporaries, publishers, critics, and friends.

Biography

Kenneth Patchen was born into a working-class milieu in Ohio's industrial and mining area, an environment that helped to forge his reputation in the late 1930's and 1940's as a significant proletarian poet. His father, Wayne Patchen, had spent more than twenty-five years working in the steel mills, where both Patchen and his brother also worked for a time. As Larry R. Smith writes in his biography *Kenneth Patchen* (1978), "much like D. H. Lawrence's mining background in England, Patchen's roots in a hard working yet culturally wasted community of poor and semi-poor gave him an early sense of strength and violation." In his early childhood, the family moved to nearby Warren, Ohio, where Patchen received most of his schooling. The town is located a few miles from Garretsville, the birthplace of Hart Crane.

In Warren, Patchen began writing poetry. He also spent two summers working in the steel mills with his brother and father to earn tuition money for his brief attendance at the University of Wisconsin in 1929. Following this successful year at the university, Patchen wandered around the United States and Canada, working at odd jobs, writing poetry, attending Columbia University for a while, and eventually meeting Miriam Oidemus, the daughter of Finnish immigrants, whom he was to marry in June, 1934, and with whom he would spend the rest of his life.

With the exception of a brief period in Santa Fe, New Mexico, and a short stay in Hollywood in 1937, the Patchens lived in and around Greenwich Village from 1934 to 1950. Although his marriage was happy, Patchen spent a good part of his life in intense physical pain caused by a serious back disability that began in 1937 when Patchen tried to separate the locked bumpers of two cars that had collided. In 1950, a writer's committee, consisting of such notables as T. S. Eliot, W. H. Auden, E. E. Cummings, Thornton Wilder, and William Carlos Williams, gave a series of readings to earn money for Patchen to have corrective surgery.

Finding a renewed sense of mobility after the surgery, Patchen and his wife moved to San Francisco where, in 1954, he befriended Kenneth Rexroth and Lawrence Ferlinghetti, with whom he collaborated in 1957, after a second spinal fusion, to create the Poetry-and-Jazz movement. By 1956, the Patchens were living in Palo Alto, at the southern end of San Francisco bay, which was to become an important artistic center. In 1959, following a surgical mishap after prescribed exploratory surgery, further surgery was cancelled and Patchen returned to Palo Alto to a bedridden life of almost constant pain. The 1960's, despite his disability, were productive years for Patchen, resulting in such books as *Because It Is*, *Hallelujah Anyway*, *But Even So*, and his *Collected Poems*, as well as several recordings of his works and an exhibition of his art in Washington, D.C.

By the time of his death in January, 1972, Patchen had gained a sound reputation as one of America's most influential avant-garde poets and "painters of poems." His experimentation with new forms, whether poetic or painterly, as well as his insistence on living the life of the "total artist," despite excruciating pain and deteriorating health, point unmistakably toward a quality that made him the greatly respected artist he was: action even in the face of chaos and pain. "The one thing which Patchen cannot understand, will not tolerate, indeed," wrote Henry Miller, "is the refusal to act. . . . Confronted with excuses and explanations, he becomes a raging lion."

Analysis

One way to trace the development of Kenneth Patchen's vast poetic output is to posit a shift from the emphasis upon class-consciousness and protest in the poetry of the 1930's to 1940's to a later concern with a sense of wonder and with the spiritual and irrational side of existence. Another and perhaps more compelling approach is to view the entire body of Patchen's work as both spiritual and revolutionary, marked by the antiestablishment anger of the Old Testament prophets, who condemned the greed of the secular world while celebrating the coming of a just and sacred Kingdom of God.

In his first book of poetry, *Before the Brave*, Patchen combines a vision of revolution with the wonder of the spiritual world. While lashing out angrily at the "sightless old men in cathedrals of decay" ("Letter to the Old Men") and the police with "their heavy boots grinding into our faces . . ." ("A Letter to a Policeman in Kansas City"), he still confirms, in Whitmanesque terms, the ability of humanity to seize control of events:

> O be willing to wait no longer.
> Build men, not creeds, seed not soil—
> O raise the standards out of reach.
>
> new men new world new life.

In contrast to the world of the "culture-snob" and the emptiness of "civic pride," Patchen's prophetic voice calls out for a world of unity and wonder, for a "jangling eternity/ Of fellowship and spring where good and law/ Is thicker love and every day shall spawn a god."

In another of his so-called "protest" books of the 1930's, *First Will and Testament*, Patchen again combines or synthesizes the dual impulses of spiritual wonder and revolutionary zeal. In a poem called "A Revolutionary Prayer," he cries: "O great good God/ I do not know that this fistful of warm dirt/ Has any mineral that wills that the young die. . . ." Here the miner's son, Patchen, looks to the lesson of the ore that he, his father, and his brother had mined to confirm the injustice of war. Similarly, in "The Soldier and the Star," Patchen contrasts the grace, wonder, and wholeness of nature with the destruction of warfare. In the opening four lines he writes: "Rifle goes up:/ Does what a rifle does/ Star is very beautiful:/ Doing what a star does."

In all Patchen's poetry, life's energy and fruitfulness is contrasted with the mechanical, dead, and often violent world of the warmakers and the ruling elite. Throughout his work runs a triple vision that serves to direct his approach to the world. First is the painful reality of alienation and corruption, of a brutal, ruling monolith that forces people to move toward violence and control rather than growth and human fulfillment. In his earlier poetry this force often takes the form of an actual ruling class in the language of Marxist ideology, while in later works it appears as the nebulous darker side of human nature depicted by Mark Twain in his later works. Second is the need for humankind to become engaged in or committed to the fullness of life, unity, and social solidarity. Third is the sense of wonder and imaginative power that opposes the brutal side of human nature.

The corruption and alienation that Patchen sees running rampant in society is characterized largely by capitalist greed and human violence. Although the first evil is emphasized in his earlier works, the second emerges and is stressed throughout his entire poetic career. "War is the lifeblood of capitalism; it is the body and soul of fascism," wrote Patchen in his novel, *The Journal of Albion Moonlight*, and it is mainly in his poetry that Patchen vividly depicts the bloody force of war. In such poems as "I DON'T WANT TO STARTLE YOU" and "Harrowed by These Apprehensions" (*First Will and Testament*), as well as in the later, more subtle antiwar works such as "In the Courtyard of Secret Life," from his 1957 book, *When We Were Here Together*, Patchen's pacifist sentiments, which he held his entire life are powerfully expressed.

Faced with chaos, alienation, and violence, Patchen believed that the poet must not fall into apathy or bitterness but rather must adopt a worldview in which belief, love, and action are possible. In the face of nothingness, Patchen offers the richness of being; in the face of chaos, he offers unity and order; and in the face of despair and confusion, he offers belief. In the poem "No One Ever Works Alone," from *Panels for the Walls of Heaven*, Patchen further pursues his prophetic faith that a new order will soon sweep away the injustice and evil of the outmoded system. "O Speak Out!," urges Patchen, "Against the dead trash of their 'reality/ Against 'the world as we see it.'/ Against 'what it is reasonable to believe.'"

Ultimately, for Patchen, the path that leads from destruction to unity is the path of love. "There is only one power that can save the world," writes Patchen in "The Way Men Live Is a Lie" (*An Astonished Eye Looks Out of the Air*), "and that is the power of love for all men everywhere." Though it is a rather prosaic statement, this affirmation illustrates the poet's unswerving belief in the need for commitment to and engagement in the energy of life as opposed to the forces of death that always threaten to engulf humanity. Love, both sexual and spiritual, is an important weapon in that struggle.

Apart from love, another element that maintains unity in life, and one that is particularly evident in Patchen's later books, is a sense of wonder, or, one might say, childlike amazement toward life. In a 1968 interview with Gene Detro, Patchen speakes of the absolute necessity of childlike wonder. Losing this sense, for Patchen, would be equivalent to death. In "O Fiery River" (*Cloth of the Tempest*), Patchen warns that "men have destroyed the roads of wonder,/ And their cities squat like black roads/ In the orchards of life."

For Patchen, as for such Romantic poets as William Blake and William Wordsworth, the most perfect paradigm for wonder is to be found in the innocence of the child. In describing the wonder that exists between two people in sexual union, for example, Patchen speaks of how coming to his beloved Miriam's "wonder" ("For Miriam") is "Like a boy finding a star in a haymow" (*The Teeth of the Lion*). Like Blake in his *Songs of Innocence* (1789), Patchen finds a kind of salvation from injustice and pain in the world of childlike wonder. "Children don't want to know," writes Patchen in "O What a Revolution," a prose poem from *The Famous Boating Party*, "They want to increase their enjoyment of not knowing." In "This Summer Day" (*An Astonished Eye Looks Out of the Air*), the child serves as a metaphor for both life and death. "O Death," writes Patchen, "must be this little girl/ Pushing her blue cart into the water," while "All Life must be this crowd of kids/ watching a hummingbird fly around itself."

As vividly as tanks and the "rustless gun" represent, for Patchen, the horror of history and the blind destructiveness of patriotism, the image of the child and childlike wonder (depicted often in collections of tales and verse such as *Fables and Other Little Tales*, *Hurrah for Anything*, and *But Even So*) represents the innocence, energy, and potential of life's richness. The critics who accuse Patchen of being a poet of dreary negativism ignore the fact that, throughout his poetry, Patchen offers a continuous prophecy of a world of wonder and delight that will inevitably shine through the universal darkness. As a revolutionary and a prophet, Kenneth Patchen was never far removed from the vision of humanity's enormous potential.

Donald E. Winters, Jr.

Other major works

LONG FICTION: *The Journal of Albion Moonlight*, 1941; *The Memoirs of a Shy Pornographer*, 1945; *See You in the Morning*, 1948.

FICTION: *Sleepers Awake*, 1946; *They Keep Riding Down All the Time*, 1947; *The Famous Boating Party*, 1954 (poetry and prose).

SHORT FICTION: *Fables and Other Little Tales*, 1953; revised as *Aflame and Afun of Walking Faces*, 1970.

PLAYS: *The City Wears a Slouch Hat*, 1942 (radio play); *Don't Look Now*, 1959; *Patchen's Lost Plays*, 1977.

MISCELLANEOUS: *In Quest of Candlelighters*, 1972.

Bibliography

Morgan, Richard G. *Kenneth Patchen: A Collection of Essays*. New York: AMS Press, 1977. A comprehensive and diverse collection of articles and essays on Patchen, with a foreword by Miriam Patchen. From reviews and radio interviews to critical analyses, this is a must for all who are interested in this poet.

_____. *Kenneth Patchen: A Comprehensive Bibliography*. New York: Paul Appel, 1978. A comprehensive, annotated, descriptive bibliography of primary and secondary works. Essential for the Patchen scholar.

Nelson, Raymond. *Kenneth Patchen and American Mysticism*. Chapel Hill: University of North Carolina Press, 1984. A full-length and important literary criticism of Patchen that attempts to secure him a place among contemporary poets without the stigma of "cultist following." Discusses his major works and his leanings toward the mystical in his poetry. An appreciative study of Patchen that concedes, however, that his work is uneven.

Nin, Anais. *The Diary of Anais Nin, 1939-1944*. Vol. 3. New York: Harcourt

Brace Jovanovich, 1969. Contains a short biographical sketch of Patchen during his New York days. Favorably analyzes his work *The Journal of Albion Moonlight.*

Smith, Larry R. *Kenneth Patchen.* Boston: Twayne, 1978. This study attempts to correct misunderstandings about Patchen by placing him in the context of his independence. Notes that his love poetry combines "hard realism with a visionary idealism." Discusses also his "poetry-jazz" form, which was one of his highest achievements.

COVENTRY PATMORE

Born: Woodford, England; July 23, 1823
Died: Lymington, England; November 26, 1896

Principal poetry

Poems, 1844; *Tamerton Church-Tower and Other Poems*, 1853; *The Angel in the House*, 1854-1862 (2 volumes; includes *The Betrothal*, 1854; *The Espousals*, 1856; *Faithful for Ever*, 1860; and *The Victories of Love*, 1862); *Odes*, 1868; *The Unknown Eros and Other Odes*, 1877 (2 volumes); *Amelia*, 1878; *A Selection of Poems*, 1931, 1948; *Poems*, 1949.

Other literary forms

Coventry Patmore's prose works include essays, a biography, numerous letters, and aphoristic collections. His *Essay on English Metrical Law* was published in 1856 (a critical edition was published in 1961). More than twenty years later he published his first book of prose, a biography of the poet Barry Cornwall entitled *Bryan Waller Procter* (1877). He published an account of his success in managing his estate at Heron's Ghyll in *How I Managed and Improved My Estate* (1888). His major collections of prose are: *Principle in Art* (1889); *Religio Poetæ* (1893); and *Rod, Root, and Flower* (1895).

A five-volume edition of his *Works* was published in London in 1907. No edition of his letters exists, but many can be found in Basil Champneys' *Memoirs and Correspondence of Coventry Patmore* (1900) and in *Further Letters of Gerard Manley Hopkins* (1956, Claude C. Abbott, editor), the latter volume containing Patmore's correspondence with Hopkins.

Achievements

Patmore has often been referred to as a man and a poet of contradictions, and his achievements—as both—are equally contradictory. He was one of the most popular of all Victorian poets. *The Angel in the House* had gone into a sixth edition by 1885, and by the time of his death in 1896 it had sold more than 250,000 copies. He was widely read throughout the British Empire as well as in the United States and other countries. He was also, however, one the most quickly forgotten of Victorian poets. His reputation went into eclipse in the late 1860's and early 1870's, enjoyed a brief revival in the late 1870's and early 1880's, and then fell into a critical and popular decline that has never been reversed. Patmore is one of the few Victorian poets whose work is not in print even in an edition of selected poems.

The reasons for these oddly varying extremes of reputation are not hard to find. True to his contradictory nature, Patmore was a poet who could and did speak to the "common reader" in an intelligible manner, but he often spoke of mystical and esoteric subjects far beyond the grasp—or even concern—of those same readers. He gave his audience vignettes of domestic bliss—usually of the upper-middle-class variety—offering comfort in times that seemed to threaten the nuclear family and even the Empire's economic underpinnings, yet he included in these vignettes stark confrontations with emotional and spiritual absurdities intimately connected with the vicissitudes of love. Most significant, perhaps, he was able to couch profound psychological and emotional insights in apparently simple—and simplistic—aphorisms.

Patmore's poetry gained for him his great popularity, but his thought was often more adaptable to prose. It was in his poetry, however, that he was best able to reveal his artistry and his philosophy in a harmonious blend of lyrical beauty and rich perception. His poetry had for its subject one idea: love. In fact, at least ninety-five percent of his poems deal with love in one form or another. From his earliest musings to his last philosophical treatises in verse, he was preoccupied with the manifestations of divine and human love.

Patmore's early work betrayed his affinity with the Pre-Raphaelites in its overindulgence in description for description's sake, especially in the overabundant use of adjectives before nouns and in the awkward use of Nature as a substantive character. By the time Patmore wrote *The Angel in the House*, however, he had much better control of his language. His style underwent further change and refinement so that by the time of *The Unknown Eros* he had eliminated virtually all of the verbal "deadwood" from his work; even when the language fails in concision, it is usually because the thought attempted is, in itself, incommunicable. Along with control of style, Patmore gained control of emotion. His late poetry best reveals this control when he treats subjects that would easily lend themselves to the worst excesses of Victorian sentimentalism.

While not a systematic philosopher, Patmore was a profound and comprehensive thinker. He undertook to explain—as well as such a phenomenon could be explained—the very idea of Love, easily the most irrational, mysterious, and misunderstood of human emotions. He went even further and attempted to explain the love between God and human beings in terms of human love. What Patmore attempted was *explanation* and not merely the ecstatic recounting of mystical experience. In order to explain, he believed that he first had to experience and then to know his subject (ironically, a very scientific attitude for someone who despised science). He used his life as such an experiment, and his poetry is his record of the results.

Biography

Coventry Kersey Dighton Patmore's life falls roughly into four periods, the latter three of which correspond to his three marriages. The first period, up to his first marriage, was dominated by his father, Peter George Patmore.

Peter Patmore was a man devoted to the arts, intent upon social climbing, and steadfast in his devotion to friends. His life, unfortunately, was beset with problems and scandals. Peter was the man to whom William Hazlitt wrote some of the letters later published in *Liber Amoris* (1823), letters in which the married Hazlitt confessed to a degrading love affair with a young girl. When the book was published, both author and recipients were critically condemned for, at least, a serious breach of taste. Two years earlier, in 1821, Peter had been a second in a duel during which his principal was killed, there being reason to believe that Peter's ignorance of the rules of duelling led to the death. In any event, he was condemned for his role in the affair and actually left the country to avoid prosecution. On his return, Peter married Eliza Robertson, a young Scotswoman of strict religious beliefs and practices.

Peter later speculated in railway shares, lost a great deal of money, and fled to the Continent, leaving the twenty-two-year-old Coventry and his siblings without support. Finally, in 1854, Peter published *My Friends and Acquaintances*, a book of memoirs that was poorly received and that managed to rekindle the flame of controversy surrounding the duel of years earlier. Peter died in the following year.

Despite his tumultuous life, Peter was a father who encouraged Coventry's poetic gifts early in life, insisting that his son publish his first volume of poems when he was only twenty-one. Peter had always encouraged Coventry's love of literature, and the two often read and discussed various authors. Perhaps in response to his wife's stern religious beliefs, Peter offered his children no religious training, preferring to treat the Bible as merely a work in the body of literature for which he had much respect. Peter was concerned enough with Coventry's education, however, to send him to Paris in 1839 to improve his French. There Coventry fell in love with the daughter of Mrs. Gore, an English novelist who had a salon in the Place Vendôme. His love, however, was not reciprocated, and the bitterness of the affair became entangled with his bitterly anti-French sentiments, feelings that lasted most of his lifetime. While in Paris, Coventry began to explore the question of religious belief, seeking principles by which he could live and to which he could devote his work.

In 1842 Coventry visited Edinburgh and the home of his mother's family. There the religious questioning that had begun in Paris was intensified by a personal experience that brought him in contact with the Free Kirk piety and severity that surrounded him. This discomfiting episode became entangled with his anti-Scottish sentiment, also a feeling that lasted all his life.

For some time afterward, Patmore dabbled in reading, painting, and chemistry, conducting experiments in his own laboratory. He earned a meager living by translating and writing for the periodical reviews. In 1844, at the insistence of his father, he published his first volume, *Poems.* In 1846 he was given a post at the Library of the British Museum. Two years later he became engaged to Emily Augusta Andrews, the daughter of a Congregational minister. They were married in Hampstead in 1847.

The Patmores settled in Highgate, where they entertained such visitors as Robert Browning, Alfred, Lord Tennyson, Thomas Carlyle, and John Ruskin, not to mention Dante Gabriel Rossetti and others of the Pre-Raphaelite Brotherhood. They were very popular with their visitors and seemed to enjoy their "court" in this suburb of London.

Patmore continued his work at the British Museum, and Emily bore six children over the course of their marriage. From all that can be learned, this was indeed a happy marriage, one in which Emily felt the joys of love, home, and motherhood as much as Patmore reveled in being the "breadwinner," patron, and husband to such a family. One record of the marriage is, of course, *The Angel in the House*; the first two parts—those dealing with courtship and marriage—were published in 1854 and 1856. The second installment in this poem, *The Victories of Love*, was also published in two parts in 1860 and 1863. This work anticipates and reflects the event that shattered the happiness of Patmore's fifteen years of marriage: in 1862 Emily died of tuberculosis.

Patmore never recovered from the death of his first wife. In spite of his two later marriages, it was to his first wife and marriage that he always looked when he sought inspiration. The emotional and spiritual completion—as well as the physical ecstacy—that he celebrated in *The Angel in the House* and later poems was never duplicated in his other unions.

For two years after Emily's death Patmore continued to work at the British Museum and sought to provide the warmth and guidance for his children that would have been given by Emily. In February, 1864, at the insistence of his friend Aubrey de Vere, he obtained a leave of absence and journeyed to Rome. There, the leanings he had felt even during his marriage to the stringently anti-Catholic Emily became irresistible and he converted to the Catholic Church, being received by a Jesuit, Father Cardella.

While in Rome, Patmore met his second wife, Marianne Byles. In a small comedy of errors, Patmore first proposed to her and then learned of her personal vow to become a nun. Thinking the vow irrevocable, he withdrew his proposal. When he learned that she could easily obtain a dispensation to revoke the vow, he proposed again, and was accepted. Then he learned that she was not, as he had first assumed, the poor traveling companion of a wealthy woman but was the wealthy heiress herself. Again, he withdrew to protect his freedom of idea and propriety. His friends, however, urged him to reconsider, and he agreed to the marriage. He returned to England before Mary (as she was known) to prepare his children for their new mother. In July, 1864, they were married.

This second marriage produced no children, but it provided Patmore with the opportunity to purchase an estate of four hundred acres near Uckfield in

Sussex, known as Heron's Ghyll, into which his family and new wife moved in 1868; he had resigned from the British Museum in 1865. For six years, Patmore ran the estate successfully, surrounding himself with the comforts of the country and spending happy hours with his children and wife. He continued writing poetry and encouraged his wife in her literary project, a translation of St. Bernard's *On the Necessity of Loving God* (c. 1126-1141), which was later published. In 1874, Patmore sold Heron's Ghyll to the Duke of Norfolk for £27,000, realizing a profit of £8,500; he even published a pamphlet on his success as an estate manager. In 1875, the family moved to Hastings and remained there until 1891.

In 1877, Patmore published *The Unknown Eros*, a series of odes dealing primarily with the nature of human and divine love. In the same year he made a pilgrimage to Lourdes, after which he more fully devoted himself to the Blessed Virgin. In 1878, he published his final collection of poems, *Amelia*. After 1879 he wrote virtually no poetry, concentrating rather on expressing his difficult philosophy in prose.

Mary died in 1880. In 1881 Patmore married Harriet Robson, who had entered the household as a domestic during Mary's final illness. In 1882, Emily, Patmore's daughter, who had become a sister of the Society of the Holy Child Jesus, died. One year later, Henry, the youngest of the six children by Emily, died. In that same year, Harriet gave birth to a child, Francis Epiphanius, known as Piffie. Patmore, already sixty, greatly enjoyed the delights of the child—delights that helped to offset the grief he suffered at the death of so many of his loved ones.

In 1891, the Patmores moved to Lymington, where Patmore spent the remaining five years of his life in virtual seclusion. He made occasional trips to London, wrote reviews and columns for the *St. James's Gazette*, and continued writing prose, the first collection of which had been published in 1889 and the last of which would be published a year before his death in 1896.

Analysis

Coventry Patmore began his poetic career, as did many of his contemporaries, under the influence of the burgeoning interest in the Middle Ages that forced its way into many poems of the period. The poems in his first two volumes, published in 1844 and 1853, are filled with knights (both ancient and modern), long journeys on horseback through lush and wild countryside, and, of course, maidens and damsels in need of love or rescue. These early works are quite conventional and, frankly, dull. They attempt to deal with his favorite topic, love, but they stand too much in awe of the subject, afraid to assert with conviction any insight the young poet might have had. Rather, they present lovers meeting, wooing, wedding, and dying—and little else.

These poems are of interest, however, for what they reveal about Patmore's increasing poetic abilities. The earliest of them, especially, are filled with excesses of description that reflect the poet's immaturity and uncertainty. One example, from "The River," will suffice;

> The leafy summer-time is young;
> The yearling lambs are strong;
> The sunlight glances merrily;
> The trees are full of song;
> The valley-loving river flows
> Contentedly along.

It is significant to note that within six lines there are eight modifiers, words attempting to convey complete pictures in themselves but that, through their conventionality, become clichés. The diction fails to "paint" the kind of vivid word-picture the poet was aiming for. Between this early style and that of *The Angel in the House* there is a tremendous gap—and one that shows how far Patmore had progressed by the time he published his most popular poem.

Of the early poems, however, there is one that demands special attention. Entitled "A London Fête," this work of forty-seven lines of four-stress iamb rhymed variously in open quatrains and couplets is unusual for Patmore. The subject is a hanging at Newgate, attended by a mob of curious and excited people. The poem is stark and realistic in its presentation of the bloodthirsty nature of the people "enjoying" this spectacle. Mothers jostle with other mothers to give their babes a good view; young girls tear their garments to provide themselves with rags to wave; sots yell out the doomed man's fate in Hell. The execution takes place, and the crowd releases a cry of joy. As they leave, one baby strings its doll to a stick, and the mother praises this "pretty trick." Two children catch and hang a cat. A pickpocket slinks off to ply his trade elsewhere. Two friends chat amicably. Two people, who fought over the best vantage point, leave to settle their score "with murderous faces."

The poem is an early revelation of Patmore's elitist politics. Throughout his life, he feared (even hated) the idea of democracy and its resultant "mob." The people depicted in this poem are that very mob: drunks, thieves, murderers, and, worst of all, mothers who do not know what is best for their children, or do not care. Although the poem gives voice to Patmore's political prejudices, it is extremely effective nevertheless. Its style is compact and journalistic; its impact is heightened by its one figure of speech: a simile comparing the howling mob to the mob of damned souls in Hell as they rejoice over the addition of another to their fold. The condemnation conveyed is so complete as to disallow any attempt at rebuttal, poetic or otherwise. What is unusual about the poem, in addition to its not being about love, is that it is concerned with one specific event treated as such and left to stand on its own. Later in his career, Patmore seemed unable to isolate and then reincorporate specific events in his poetry. In seeking the significance of the event, he sometimes felt obliged to introduce a prologue (or several) or to elaborate upon the event immediately upon his telling it. One of the faults of *The Angel in the House* is this insistence on commentary of occasionally excessive length. That fault, however, is nowhere to be found in this early, and quite moving, poem of political and social contempt.

Patmore's popularity as a poet was achieved with the publication of *The Angel in the House*. This was to be his epic poem celebrating Love, Woman, Home, and God in six books. He finished only four of them: the two published as *The Angel in the House* in 1854 and 1856 and the two published as *The Victories of Love* in 1860 and 1862. The first two books concern a happy marriage between two true lovers; the second two books concern a marriage that begins without mutual love but ends in a state of shared happiness; the final two books, one can conjecture, would have dealt with a good marriage gone bad or a bad marriage that remained bad.

The Angel in the House is the story of the courtship and marriage of Felix and Honoria. The poem begins with a prologue set on their eighth anniversary and ends on their tenth. The two books, with their twelve cantos each, cover, respectively, the betrothal and the marriage. The poem is Felix's gift to his wife, as a celebration of the bliss they have enjoyed and as a record of the emotions both felt throughout the course of their love and courtship. Each canto consists of a number of preludes (usually two, but no more than five) followed by an ode that contains the main "episode" or occurrence of that canto. These odes are divided into smaller numbered units. The rhyme is open quatrain and the meter is four-stress line, usually iambic.

The cantos provide a roughly chronological account of the courtship and marriage; the chronologically arranged material falls within the odes, while the preludes range freely, dealing with any number of questions pertaining to Love but always applying them to the coming incident. How this schema works can be seen, for example, in Canto VI of Book I, "The Dean," in which Felix asks the Dean for his daughter's hand in marriage. The first prelude, *"Perfect Love Rare,"* is a meditation on and apostrophe to Love as well as a lament that, indeed, perfect (that is, pure) love is a "privilege high" to be enjoyed by only the few who merit such reward. The poet goes on to add that

> A day [in Love's] delicious life
> Though full of terrors, full of tears,
> Is better than of other life
> A hundred thousand million years.

Thus, the opening prelude, through its conventional hyperbole, offers "evidence" of the rarity of perfect love (but, of course, hints that such rarity will be achieved in the coming match).

The next prelude, *"Love Justified,"* is simply that, a justification of the poet's choice of a mate—as much choice, that is, as love allows. The poet concludes the prelude by claiming that his song will prove that "This little germ of nuptial love,/ . . ./ The root is . . ./ Of all our love to man and God." From the seeking of the rare in the first prelude, the poet carries his readers in the second into the realm of the earthly and attainable and offers a "logical" justification for the action.

The third prelude, "*Love Serviceable*," is an even more intense call to action. Here the poet asserts that the noble lover does not care about his own fate but only about the happiness of his beloved. His quest for her is, after all, to make her happy; failure in that quest would result in both his and her lack of fulfillment and joy. Thus, he must devote his every attention to obtaining his goal, for "He does not rightly love himself/ Who does not love another more." Another strong reason for taking action is offered in this prelude as the canto progresses to the ode containing the action.

There is, however, one final prelude, "*A Riddle Solved*," that reads:

> Kind souls, you wonder why, love you,
>   When you, you wonder why, love none.
>   We love, Fool, for the good we do,
>   Not that which unto us is done!

The riddle thus solved by the altruistic nature of true love, the canto moves to the ode, divided into four parts. Felix is visiting the Dean's family. In the first part of the ode, the ladies leave to take tea outside. In the second part, the Dean and Felix make small talk over trifling matters. In the third part, Felix makes his plea for the daughter's hand. In the fourth part, the Dean, giving him his best wishes, sends him out to woo Honoria, who is having tea. Thus, the canto focuses on the act of Felix's seeking Honoria's hand but prefaces that act with observations on the rarity of perfect love, justifications for pursuing such a rare phenomenon, and insights into the nature of true love in such pursuit. The reader is, then, quite prepared for the act and its outcome by these philosophical probings that stand at the head of each canto.

The relationship among the preludes and between the preludes and odes is well handled by Patmore and provides much of the structural integrity of this long, thoughtful poem. By including such preludes, Patmore is able to take incidents with apparent meaning and amplify or alter such meaning to suit his didactic purpose. Usually behind such manipulation is the motive of revealing something to the readers that should have been quite obvious but was hidden by the mundaneness of the everyday occurrence. Such insight is one of the strengths of the poem.

The mundaneness of the subject matter, however, contributes to the poem's major flaw, and it is a significant one. Patmore was attempting to mold the everday to the poetic and the poetic to the everyday. By further attempting to imitate the epic mode, he was forcing a gravity and significance upon his subject matter which it simply could not bear.

The poem's other principal fault—especially from a modern reader's point of view—is the philosophy upon which it is built, an extreme Victorian male chauvinism. Throughout the cantos there is constant reference to the most offensive stereotypes of women; they are foreign lands, whose customs can never be understood by men; they are frail children in need of a paternalistic husband; they are empty-headed vessels in need of man's intelligence; they are objects to be sought and possessed; they are long-suffering companions put on earth to please their men; they are parts in need of a whole. In fairness to Patmore, it must be admitted that he viewed man as equally incomplete and dependent upon woman for completion, but the poet insisted on basing his philosophy on "unequal equality," and, to echo George Orwell, man was "more equal than woman"—at least in Patmore's conservative worldview.

This male chauvinism is also apparent in *The Victories of Love*, the third and fourth books of *The Angel in the House*. The poem, written as a series of verse letters, is not as successful as its predecessor. It lacks a true emotional focus, its style is much less direct, and its structure is not as tightly controlled. The two books consist of nineteen and thirteen letters, respectively, written in four-stress couplets. The effect of such a scheme is monotony, which further undercuts the impact of the poem.

The "victories" of the title refer to the effort of the two lovers whose story is unfolded through the many letters. Frederick Graham, a cousin of Honoria, is deeply in love with her when she weds Felix (at the close of *The Angel in the House*). He embarks on a long sea voyage to try to overcome his passion, but, as his letters to his mother show, he is unable to do so. In desperation for "a change," he marries Jane, whom he does not really love, although she grows to love him. The remainder of the poem recounts their marriage, the birth and death of some of their children, and their "victories" in establishing first respect, then concern, and finally love for each other. Unfortunately, Jane dies, leaving Frederick with a still-unabated passion for Honoria, a passion he again tries to lose by going to sea. He does, however, see his remaining child married to Honoria's (the subjects, perhaps, of the unwritten fifth and sixth books of the epic).

In this poem, Patmore attempts far to much. He tries to imitate prattling, gossipy old ladies in strictly rhymed couplets; he tries to convey genuine emotions regarding love and honor and felicity in verse letters; and he tries, again, to justify his view of women by placing too much of the philosophical burden on the shoulders of poor dying Jane, whose letters to her mother, mother-in-law, and husband just prior to her death do not escape the maudlin extremes that Patmore was usually able to avoid. Jane pleads with Frederick to accept that: "Image and glory of the man,/ As he of God, is woman. Can/ This holy, sweet proportion die/ Into a dull equality?" Perhaps Patmore himself realized the significant falling-off in effectiveness in these two books of his projected six and abandoned the idea of an epic on the Household of Love.

If *The Angel in the House* proved to be Patmore's most popular work, his final major volume of poetry, *The Unknown Eros and Other Odes*, has certainly proved to be his best collection. This volume, also published in two parts, consists of two books, the first containing a proem and twenty-four odes, the second eighteen odes. In these odes Patmore, loosening the hold of traditional prosody, uses a variety of meters and rhyme schemes to treat his favorite topic—Love—and his next-favorite topic—the political and social decline of England and her empire. As a poet of analogies, Patmore saw the similarities in his love for Woman and for God and his love for his country. Likewise, he saw the decline and death of his beloved as a reflection of the decline and death of his beloved country, and *vice versa*. These analogies appear throughout the odes, both explicitly and implicity. In fact, the poet boldly announces in the proem that it may be "England's parting soul that nerves [his] tongue" and gives him the impetus to break his years of silence with these odes designed to restore to his beloved (woman and country) some of the luster lost by either death or dying.

Part of the strength of these odes lies in their variety of subject and mode. Here Patmore's prosody, more relaxed and much more colloquial, comes closer to capturing the essence of speech he so vainly sought in his earlier works; these odes seem almost effortless in their flow and offer no resistance to the reader in terms of language. They may, however, continue to resist the reader in terms of the density of their thought, the political theories expounded, or the philosophical basis of the majority of the observations. In spite of such barriers, these odes succeed as no other of Patmore's poems do in their eloquence, their emotional impact, and their profundity.

The first twelve odes in the first book form a thematic unit on love and denial of love by death; the odes are probably based on Patmore's experience with his first wife, Emily. The first few odes focus on time and its passage. Beginning with the fifth ode, there is a distinct unit on his loss at the death of his wife, on his memory of her, on his fears and hopes, and on his remarriage. These poems are some of the finest Patmore wrote, containing emotions that manage to travel more than a century between then and now with grace and meaning. "The Azalea," "Departure," and, especially, "The Toys" show Patmore at his most mature and controlled; he is able, as few of his contemporaries were, to touch a poignant note lightly enough to allow the reverberations to have their full impact on the reader. There is moralizing here, and some preaching as well, but all is blended with a sensitivity unsurpassed in his other work, including his best prose. That sensitivity is well reflected in his superbly economical style; here is one example from "Eurydice," in which he addresses his lost mate:

Thee, whom en'n more than Heaven loved I have,
And yet have not been true

> Even to thee,
> I dreaming, night by night, seek now to see,
> And, in a mortal sorrow, still pursue
> Thro' sordid streets and lanes. . . .

Here, as in his earliest work, there is an abundance of modifiers; but now each one is charged with meaning, effectively holding readers before allowing them to move on to the next complementary and expansive link in an emotional chain.

True to his extremes, Patmore balances his best with some of his worst poetry in these odes. His political odes are not nearly as successful as the personal, nor are they, in themselves, good verse. They are marred by long-windedness, awkward lines, and, too often, repugnant ideas.

The second book of odes continues the mixture of personal and political observations but contains some of his most difficult work, the odes in which he uses the classical myths to expound his ideas on human and divine love. Some of them simply do not fulfill their intention, and most of the political odes are also unsuccessful. The personal poems, however, such as "The Child's Purchase," are generally very moving.

After *The Unknown Eros and Other Odes*, Patmore wrote very few poems, and these are generally rather bland when they are not offensive. For example, *Amelia* returns to the theme of the sacrificing woman and has a young girl weep over the grave of her lover's former betrothed; that, however, is not enough: she actually takes the dead woman's ring and swears to wear it for *her* sake because "dear to maidens are their rivals dead." Here Patmore succeeds in straining—some would say rupturing—plausibility, as he does in "The Girl of All Periods," in which a "feminist" who smokes cigarettes and reads George Sand is "put in her place" by a few sly male compliments.

Patmore insisted that his poetry was not original, in meter or insight. He even abhorred the charge of "originality" when he heard it applied to himself. By this insistence on drawing from wells already much-frequented, Patmore placed himself as a poet in a very vulnerable position. Even profound insights can become monotonous if they are constantly delivered in simple aphorisms. To that temptation to be aphoristic, Patmore too often succumbed. It is unfortunate that so much of his best poetry and his best thought lie buried. Whether this arch-conservative Victorian poet's work will again be popularly read is open to question. What is certain is this: his works deserve attention.

Richard F. Giles

Other major works

NONFICTION: *Essay on English Metrical Law*, 1856; *Bryan Waller Procter*, 1877; *How I Managed and Improved My Estate*, 1888; *Principle in Art*, 1889; *Religio Poetæ*, 1893; *Rod, Root, and Flower*, 1895; *Memoirs and Correspon-*

dence of Coventry Patmore, 1900 (Basil Champneys, editor).
MISCELLANEOUS: *Works*, 1907.

Bibliography

Gosse, Edmund. *Coventry Patmore*. New York: Charles Scribner's Sons, 1905.
The earliest book-length critical study published on Patmore, designed to
complement the "official" biography of the Patmore family published by
Basil Champneys. Full of anecdotes and personal accounts, it is nevertheless an important critical work on Patmore.

Oliver, E. J. *Coventry Patmore*. New York: Sheed & Ward, 1956. A short,
accessible biography on Patmore suggested for the beginning reader. Discusses love as the focus of his life, his family life, and his mystical leanings that put him at odds with clericalism. Examines the importance of
place and background in his poems.

Patmore, Derek. *The Life and Times of Coventry Patmore*. New York: Oxford University Press, 1949. A biography of Patmore written by his great-
grandson. Although considered unreliable, it contains much of interest in
bringing to light Patmore's family, his upbringing, and the shaping of his
poetry.

Reid, John Cowie. *Mind and Art of Coventry Patmore*. London: Routledge &
Kegan Paul, 1957. A full-length study of Patmore and a valuable resource for
scholars of his work. Explores the influences on Patmore and his thought,
and his "doctrine" of love as expressed in his poems. Particularly noteworthy is the chapter on the odes, *The Unknown Eros and Other Odes*.
Includes an extensive bibliography.

Weinig, Mary Anthony. *Coventry Patmore*. Boston: Twayne, 1981. An appreciative introduction to Patmore, noting that his poems are "rooted in immediate experience of life and love and marriage." Contains strong critical
commentary on *The Angel in the House*, and on *Faithful for Ever* (1860).
Includes a separate section on his odes, which Weinig considers the best
access to Patmore for the modern reader.

THE PEARL-POET

Born: England(?); fl. in latter half of the fourteenth century

Principal poetry

Pearl, Patience, Cleanness (Purity), Sir Gawain and the Green Knight, Saint Erkenwald(?).

In addition to the four poems that constitute the unique British Library manuscript, Cotton Nero A.x. (c. 1400), *Saint Erkenwald*, an alliterative poem describing the miraculous life of a seventh century bishop of London, has been attributed to the Pearl-Poet. Since 1882, scholars have argued that *Saint Erkenwald* shares a common diction, a similar style and dialect, and a peculiar phraseology with the poems of the Pearl-Poet. They further argue that *Saint Erkenwald* may be dated 1386, when the feast days of the bishop saint were given special status in London, thus making it contemporary with the Cotton Nero poems.

One modern editor of *Saint Erkenwald* (Clifford Peterson), however, has suggested an early fifteenth century date for the poem, which is extant only in a late fifteenth century manuscript. Scholarship, furthermore, has cast doubt on the attribution by showing that the common language is not unique to these poems and by arguing that the similar stylistic elements are best understood as reflecting the formulaic character of alliterative poetry. Therefore, it is best to limit the corpus of the Pearl-Poet to the four poems of the Cotton Nero manuscript.

Other literary forms

Even though the Pearl-Poet experimented with a variety of genres, he is best remembered for his four Middle English poems.

Achievements

The work of the Pearl-Poet (also called the Gawain-Poet after his other major poem) was essentially lost until the nineteenth century. *Sir Gawain and the Green Knight* was first edited in 1839, to be followed twenty-five years later by the other three poems of the manuscript. Over the past hundred years, these poems (whose titles are modern, not found in the manuscript) have gained a secure place in Middle English poetry. Although attention has focused on *Pearl* and *Sir Gawain and the Green Knight*, considered masterpieces of their respective genres, the two verse homilies have more recently been the objects of much critical study as well.

A contemporary of Geoffrey Chaucer, the Pearl-Poet has often been compared to medieval England's most famous poet. Like Chaucer, he worked in a variety of genres and experimented with various verse forms. His poetry, like Chaucer's, shows a knowledge not only of the Bible and its commentaries, but also of the new vernacular literature of the Continent. Again like Chaucer, he analyzes moral issues in narratives that create characters who are often unaware or confused by their situations. However, the Pearl-Poet must be judged apart from Chaucer, for he worked in a distinctly different poetic tradition, that of the Alliterative Revival, not Chaucer's French courtly style.

The poetry that flourished in northern and western England in the second half of the fourteenth century probably continued and modified (rather than reinvented) the Old English accentual and alliterative line. In contrast to the verse forms employed by Chaucer, which became the usual patterns of most English poetry after his time, the alliterative long line concentrates on stresses alone and does not count syllables. The unrhymed long lines of *Cleanness* and *Patience*, for example, include four key stresses generally separated into two half lines by a caesura, the first three stresses falling on alliterating syllables. The pattern may be diagramed as follows: Á Á ns Á X́. These alliterative long lines (sometimes grouped in quatrains), skillfully developed by the Pearl-Poet, impart a surprisingly dramatic and active feeling to *Cleanness* and *Patience*. The alliterative tendency toward variation and realistic description prevents the verse homilies from disappearing into the mist of abstraction.

In *Sir Gawain and the Green Knight* the poet turns again to this traditional form, but arranges the lines in descriptive and narrative stanzas of varying length, rounded off by five shorter alliterating lines comprising a "bob and wheel," a device not unique to the poet but most skillfully employed by him. The one-stress line of the "bob" and the four three-stressed lines of the "wheel" rhyme ababa. These rhyming lines impart rhythmic variety to the poem and serve to sum up the major topic of the stanza and to emphasize key images and themes.

The mixture of alliteration and rhyme is more thorough in *Pearl*. Departing more freely from the tradition of the alliterative long line in the direction of the octosyllabic line of Chaucer's early poetry, *Pearl* is composed of 101 twelve-line stanzas, which resemble in both form and spirit the sonnet of later English poetry. Each stanza develops three rhymes in linked quatrains (aba-bababbcbc). These tightly structured stanzas are further grouped into twenty larger sections through the concluding repetition of key words and phrases forming a refrain for each stanza. The larger sections are also linked by concatenation, the device of repeating a key word from the final line of a previous stanza in the first line of a following stanza. These intricate poetic devices perfectly mirror the intricacy of the themes and arguments of the *Pearl*, a poem highly admired for its form and considered by Thorlac Turville-Petre in *The Alliterative Revival* to be "the finest of all the poems in rhyming alliterative stanzas."

Biography

As W. A. Davenport has aptly remarked, "Though the *Gawain*-poet may not have existed, it has proved necessary to invent him." Certainly, there is no external evidence to "prove" that the four poems found only in a single manuscript are by a single poet. It may be that the poems were crafted by a small school of poets working together closely at a court in the northwest Midlands during the late fourteenth century. As A. C. Spearing has argued, however, the principle of "Ockham's razor" suggests that it is more reasonable to postulate that the Pearl-Poet was a single poet of genius writing in a unique Middle English dialect (probably north Cheshire or south Lancashire, but with Scottish, French, and Scandinavian forms). The poems share to a remarkable extent imagery, diction, and stylistic features that cannot be entirely accounted for by a common alliterative tradition. More important, readers of the four poems are continually impressed by what Malcolm Andrew and Ronald Waldron, the poems' most recent editors, have called a "conviction of an individual poetic personality" and an "unbroken consistency of thought." The analysis of the four poems below will suggest, moreover, that they are thematically related.

Nevertheless, the Pearl-Poet remains unknown. The manuscript can help scholars locate him approximately in place and time, and the poems can provide clues to his interests and knowledge. Like other poets working in the Alliterative Revival, he perhaps was attached to the household of an aristocrat of the northwest Midlands. The manuscript (probably not in the poet's hand) includes twelve rough illustrations of the four poems (published in Charles Moorman's 1977 edition of the manuscript), suggesting to some that the poet may have had the support of a wealthy patron. Certainly, the poems reflect a familiar knowledge of court life, as well as an interest in contemporary religious issues, a thorough knowledge of the Vulgate Bible and its commentaries, and some awareness of French poetry and perhaps even the poetry of Dante and Boccaccio. Some scholars have argued that the descriptions, debates, and specialized diction of the poems suggest that the poet was trained as a priest or a lawyer, that he may have sailed or been, like Chaucer, on a diplomatic mission. Such arguments, however, deduced as they are from the four poems, provide little help in understanding his poetry.

Even more fruitless and really very misleading are the various attempts to identify the poet with certain historical figures of the late fourteenth century. These nominees have included the Oxford philosopher referred to by Chaucer in *Troilus and Criseyde* (1382), Ralph Strode; the poet Huchown of the Awle Ryale; and other names from the period, such as John Erghome, John Prat, and, most recently, Hugo de Mascy or John Massey or simply the "maister Massy" praised by Thomas Hoccleve. What readers would gain should such scholarly speculation finally attach a name to the Pearl-Poet is not clear, for modern interest in the poet is the result of interest in his superb poetry, and it is unlikely that the little which is known about these candidates for poetic fame will affect interpretations of the poems.

Analysis

All four poems attributed to the Pearl-Poet reflect a great concern with establishing the distinctions between the temporal and sublunary viewpoint of human beings and the eternal and unvarying positions of God. This outlook is not uncommon in the art and thought of the later Middle Ages. It is the foundation of scholastic thought. Like scholasticism, furthermore, the arts were not content to establish only the distinctions between human and divine; they sought also to merge and synthesize the sacred and the secular. As long as the hierarchy of values was kept clear, allegiance to the divine and the human need not be in contradiction; it was possible to serve, for example, both the Virgin Mary and the courtly lady. However, if human sinfulness and obstinacy reversed the hierarchy, placing the earthly garden of delights above the promise of paradise regained, then the synthesis of earthly and divine was shattered and man was left to inherit the results of his folly.

The Pearl-Poet was thus an artist of his time not only in distinguishing between the earthly and the heavenly but also in showing how the two spheres could merge and interrelate. His greatness, however, lies in his sympathetic investigation of man's situation in the face of the divine. Man as creature is subordinate to his creator, and there is no room for doubt that man's rebelliousness is disastrous, because the Lord can become "wonder wroth." Yet, as Malcolm Andrew and Ronald Waldron conclude, the poet shares "a spirit of sympathetic identification with human frailty besides a zealous dedication to ideal virtue."

The distinctions between, yet juxtaposition of, human desires and divine standards are explored by the Pearl-Poet by concentrating on three ideals. These encompass a variety of social and Christian values, best summed up by the concepts of cleanness (understood as the divine requirement of purity in both body and soul), of truthfulness to duty and to God (and thus including loyalty, obedience, and faithfulness), and, finally, courtesy (a chivalric ideal given religious significance by the poet).

In three of the four poems, the poet creates a major character with whom readers sympathize yet who must come to learn of the differing values of mankind and the divine. In these poems, the major characters undergo a three-part mysterious journey: in *Patience*, a voyage in the belly of a whale; in *Pearl*, a visionary pilgrimage glimpsing the New Jerusalem; and in *Sir Gawain and the Green Knight*, a fantastic quest to meet an enchanted opponent. The characters face a divine or supernatural demand or challenge and are left quite befuddled, surprised, or overwhelmed by what they experience. More important, in each poem, the character is moved from a narrowly human and basically self-centered outlook to an awareness of man's essentially subordinate and often ignorant position in relation to the divine. Surprisingly, none of the characters has changed drastically by the end of the poems, although readers are left to assume that the new perspectives they have gained will lead to such change.

The fourth poem, *Cleanness*, also shares this three-part movement, but it presents not a journey of a single character to a mysterious or foreign land, but the history of mankind as outlined in the Old Testament and interpreted within the context of the New Testament. By concentrating on three key moments when the divine intervened in human history, the poem highlights the results of man's unwillingness to conform to the divine.

The four poems of the Pearl-Poet are of great artistic merit. In verse of great beauty, they include passages of vigorous narrative, realistic description, and dramatic intensity. They describe extremely violent situations as well as peaceful gardens, sailors as well as an enchanted green knight, the suffering of the dying as well as the joy of the saved. Drawing from a wide range of sources yet including much that is original, the poems are carefully crafted and structured. They are compelling not only for their presentation of deeply moral and human concerns, but also for their imaginative power.

The Pearl-Poet's shortest and most simply structured poem, *Patience*, is a verse homily teaching the need for man to submit his will to God and to act faithfully and humbly. Like traditional medieval sermons, it establishes this theme in an introductory prologue and illustrates it in an *exemplum*, a narrative example intended to support the preacher's main argument. In the case of *Patience*, the narrative centers on the prophet Jonah. It is a dramatic expansion of the biblical account found in the Book of Jonah.

The poet's choice of Jonah may seem odd, since the usual Old Testament figure representing patience is Job. The poet may have felt that the best way to explore the virtue of patience (which might be viewed as rather passive and uninteresting) was through negative examples (as, again, in *Cleanness*). Certainly Jonah's sulking pride and abortive attempt to flee from the command of God serve as examples of what patience is not. It may also be that Jonah was selected because, although his human rationalizing and severely limited understanding of God's nature place him in conflict with the divine, he does ultimately accept the will of God. Finally, Jonah's figurative significance in medieval exegesis as an Old Testament type of Christ may be significant. As evident in numerous commentaries, sermons, and popular literature, Jonah's three-day entombment within the belly of the whale typifies the death of Christ and his resurrection on the third day.

The association of Old Testament story with New Testament event is not unusual in medieval poetry. Medieval theology understood the Old Testament as prefiguring the New, and often interpreted the stories of the Jewish people as signifying Christian belief. The story of Jonah is thus told by the poet to exemplify the beatitudes preached by Christ in the Sermon on the Mount. These are recited in the prologue of *Patience*, and it is the last beatitude, interpreted as Christ's promise of heaven for those who endure patiently, that provides the poet's theme. The beatitudes certainly are classic examples of

Christ's teaching that false earthly goals and aspirations are not to be confused with the true ideals of Heaven. Whereas man seeks riches, boldness, pleasure, and power, Christ praises poverty, meekness, purity, and patience. *Patience* tells how Jonah must come to recognize the distinction between human and divine in order to act truthfully and to obtain the mercy of God.

Although the four divisions of *Patience* in the manuscript accord with the four chapters of the biblical account, the poem's narrative actually moves in three parts: first, Jonah desperately attempts to avoid the command of God, rejects his role as prophet, and sets sail to escape the power of God; second, after being swallowed by the whale, he accepts his duty and faithfully obeys God and prophesies the destruction of Nineveh; finally, while sulking because Nineveh is not destroyed, he learns of God's grace, love, and mercy.

Jonah is at first the epitome of man's foolish opposition to God. The poet sympathetically imagines Jonah's motives for rejecting the prophetic mission and presents his fear as understandable; nevertheless, Jonah's flight from God, his attempt to hide, is obviously ridiculous. The God who created the world, the poet ironically comments, has no power over the sea! The power of the creator over his creation, however, becomes clear to all. Even the pagan sailors who at first pray to Diana and Neptune learn to worship the Hebrew God. At the height of the storm, Jonah, wakened from his unnatural sleep, recognizes the Creator's power and identifies himself to the sailors as a follower of the world's creator. From this point Jonah submits himself to the will of God and, in the belly of the whale, learns to act faithfully as a prophet.

He also prays for mercy, but it is not until the third part of the story, after Jonah has prophesied the destruction of Nineveh and its citizens actually repent, that the prophet of God learns the true nature of God's grace. Although now aware of the awesome power of God over his creation, Jonah remains earthbound in his attitudes. Since Nineveh is saved, he feels humiliated. Again, rather than accepting God's will (the ultimate meaning of patience for the Pearl-Poet), Jonah reacts angrily, sulks childishly, and wishes he were dead. His wish does not come true, however, and through the remainder of the narrative Jonah learns that God not only controls but also loves his creatures.

Interestingly, in condemning what he does not understand, Jonah sets forth one of the major themes developed in the works of the Pearl-Poet: the bounty of God's grace. This grace is described in chivalric terms, as God's courtesy, and is linked to God's patience. Jonah prays for mercy in the belly of the whale, but now desires—because of his pride in preaching the very prophecy that he sought to avoid—that God turn against the repentant Nineveh and destroy the city. While the Lord patiently seeks to change him, Jonah's final attitude is not made clear since the poet suddenly concludes with his epilogue urging patient acceptance of one's position and mission in life. The last lines of the narrative are the words of God, whose patience is displayed not only toward Nineveh but also toward Jonah. Thus, although the career of Jonah may be a negative example of patience, the courtesy of God reflected in his patience and grace becomes the positive representation of ideal patience.

The poet's much longer verse homily *Cleanness* (sometimes called *Purity*) also mixes negative and positive examples, although there is no doubt that the negative receives the bulk of his attention and that God's righteous wrath, rather than his patience, becomes most evident. Again, one of Christ's beatitudes provides the theme: "Blessed is he whose heart is clean for he shall look on the Lord." The promise to the blessed clean, however, is not developed as much as the threat of damnation for the unclean. In his prologue, for example, the poet concentrates on yet another New Testament passage, Christ's parable of the wedding feast. This rather harsh analogy comparing the kingdom of heaven to a king who has a guest thrown out of a wedding feast because he is improperly dressed receives a lengthy exposition, concluding with a list of the forms of uncleanness by which man hurls himself into the devil's throat.

In his conclusion, the poet notes that he has given three examples of how uncleanness drives the Lord to wrath. These three Old Testament examples are arranged in chronological order, thus establishing the poem's three-part movement through the history of salvation: from the destruction of the world by the Flood, through the annihilation of Sodom and Gomorrah by fire, and finally to the overpowering of "the bold Belshazzar." The three are linked by shorter Old Testament stories as well. The Flood is introduced by the fall of Lucifer and the angels, leading to the fall of Adam; the destruction of the two cities is preceded by the stories of Abraham and Lot and their two wives; and Belshazzar's feast is interwoven with the fall of Jerusalem under Nebuchadnezzar and his eventual conversion.

Like the story of Jonah, the Old Testament stories retold in *Cleanness* have typological significance in medieval theology. Each of the three major examples of God's wrath prefigures the Last Judgment. Combined with accounts of the fall of Lucifer and the origin of sin, this typological significance gives the poem a universal sweep from creation to doomsday, symbolically encompassing the entire Christian understanding of history. The emphasis, however, is on judgment, which is clearly the moral of the introductory parable of the wedding feast: "Many are called but few are chosen."

Judgment is particularly severe against the unclean, for the Lord of heaven "hates hell no more than them that are filthy." The concept of cleannness includes innocence, ceremonial propriety, decency and naturalness, physical cleanliness, and moral righteousness. Their opposites are encompassed by the concept of filth, which includes all manner of vices, sacrilege, sodomy, lust, and the arrogance of spirit that elevates man's earthly desires above God's requirement of truthfulness. God floods the world because sinfulness is out of control. Not only did man sin against nature, but devils copulated with human beings, engendering a breed of violent giants as well. Similarly, the Sodomites practiced unnatural vices, filling a land that was once like paradise thick with filth so that it sunk into the earth under the weight of its own sins. The Lord is equally angered by blasphemy and sacrilege, as Belshazzar learns when he defiles the vessels of the temple in "unclean vanity."

Lack of truthfulness, although not arousing the violent wrath of God to the same extent as lack of cleanness, is represented in the minor *exempla* of the poem. The stories of Lucifer and Adam exemplify the results of disobedience. Sarah's mocking the word of God when told she would bear a child reflects human lack of faith, for she prefers worldly reason to divine wisdom. Lot's wife is turned into a pillar of salt for two faults, the results of her "mistruth." She disobeyed a direct command not to look at the doomed Sodom, and she set salted food before the two angels, thus angering the Lord for her ritual uncleanness. King Zedekiah and the Jewish nation were similarly found untruthful; they proved disloyal to their duties as God's chosen people and blasphemously worshiped idols.

The minor examples suggest that the lack of truthfulness is the cause of the uncleanness that ultimately leads to mankind's doom. They also expand the concept of filth beyond sexual misconduct to include the improper relationship between the natural and the supernatural, leading to unnatural perversion and sacrilege. Thus, the sexual intercourse of fallen angels and sinful human beings is punished by the flood because it represents unnaturalness on a cosmic scale. The Sodomite attempt to attack sexually the two angels visiting Lot is the most villainous example of their sacrilege. Although Lot's attempt to shift their lust from the angels to his two virgin daughters seems horrible, it is an attempt to keep the city's perversion on a human scale. Belshazzar's profanation of the sacred vessels consecrated to God is the final example of man's blasphemous desire to overturn the proper relationship between the human and the divine.

This long series of Old Testament stories linking untruthfulness to uncleanness is, luckily, broken by a few representatives of truth and cleanness: Noah, Abraham, Lot in his hospitality, the prophet Daniel, and Nebuchadnezzar after his conversion. This right relationship between man and God evident in truth and cleanness is, furthermore, described by the poet in terms of courtesy. After the flood, for example, God promises never to send another universal deluge and establishes man once again as he was before the fall—as ruler over the earth. This new covenant between God and Noah is described by the poet as spoken in courteous words. As in *Patience*, the Pearl-Poet understands God's mercy and grace as reflecting divine courtesy. Early in the Introduction to *Cleanness*, for example, he couples the need for purity with courtesy. Similarly, when explaining how the divine became human, the poet notes that Christ came in both cleanness and courtesy, accepting and healing all who "called on that courtesy and claimed his grace." Here, then, is the key to the right relationship between the human and the divine.

Less overtly didactic than *Cleanness* and *Patience*, *Pearl* sets forth its main ideas by creating two characters: a dreamer who mourns the loss of a pearl and a beautiful young girl who speaks in a dream from the vantage of heaven. The dreamer, who narrates the poem in the first person, is earthbound in his outlook, mourning and complaining, like Jonah in *Patience*, against his fate. He rather foolishly debates theological issues with the visionary maiden, who speaks with divine wisdom. This relationship between a naïve narrator and an authority figure representing truthfulness is typical of the poem's genre: the dream vision. Such is evident in the early but highly influential *The Consolation of Philosophy* by the sixth century philosopher Boethius, as well as in the fourteenth century masterpiece of the genre, William Langland's *The Vision of William Concerning Piers the Plowman*. The human dreamer, schooled by the agent of the divine, is also a feature of the New Testament Book of Revelation, the poem's most important source. However, the rather passive role of John during his apocalyptic visions is avoided by the poet. *Pearl*, as A. C. Spearing and others have noted, presents its teachings by means of "a dramatic encounter."

Unfortunately, attention has been diverted from analysis of this dramatic encounter by the scholarly arguments attempting to identify the meaning of the lost pearl. According to some scholars, the lost pearl represents the poet's daughter (and the poem thus is an elegy in her memory), who died at a "young and tender age" before she was two. Postulating such an occurrence may help explain the dreamer's mourning at the beginning of the poem, but the problem with reading the poem as an elegy is that it identifies the foolish narrator with the poet and equates the dream's fiction with historical and biographical events about which nothing is known. Certainly it is not the case, as A. C. Cawley writes in the Introduction to his edition of the poem, that "there would be no poem" if the poet's daughter had not died—or that the poet in *Pearl* "was recording an actual vision he had experienced."

On the other hand, rejecting the naïve biographical reading of the poem as an elegy for the poet's daughter need not imply that those who argue that the poem is an allegory are closer to the truth. This reading interprets the pearl as representing some Christian concept or ideal that has been lost or misunderstood. Identifications, all with limitations, include the purified soul, virginity and innocence, the grace of God, and even the eucharist. However, *Pearl* is not a consistent allegory in the tradition of *Everyman* or John Bunyan's *The Pilgrim's Progress*. Its characters and objects are not static but dynamic, symbols that shift as the dreamer gains fuller self-knowledge and greater awareness of the divine.

The growth in the dreamer's knowledge takes place as the poem moves through three settings. The narrator at first describes a beautiful garden, luxurious in its growth. This ideal earthly garden is nevertheless time-bound. In August at the height of the season, it blooms with flowers and natural beauty, but the garden is subject to change and all will decay. It is here that the narrator has lost his pearl, here that he comes to mourn, mortally wounded by his loss, and here that he falls asleep, his spirit setting forth on a marvelous adventure while his body remains in the garden. At this point, the pearl is to be understood as a lost jewel, "pleasant for a prince," perfect, round, radiant, smooth, and without spot. The narrator's grief over the loss of this precious but earthly object, however, is to be judged as excessive. The narrator seems vaguely aware of his problem, since he refers to his "wretched will," but he must learn to put his treasure in heavenly, not earthly, things.

The second setting is introduced immediately. Now the dreamer finds himself in another garden, even more radiant and dazzling than the first. The dreamer is in a garden that is beyond change, a beautiful setting that makes him forget all grief. This is the Earthly Paradise lost by Adam for his sin and reached by Dante near the conclusion of his ascension through Purgatory in *The Divine Comedy* (a possible source for *Pearl*). Here, the dreamer comes to a river which he cannot cross and on the far bank sees a beautiful, gleaming maiden dressed in white. She is associated with the pearl by her appearance and purity and by the fact that she is adorned with pearls. Whether or not this association implies an elegiac reading of the poem, it is clear that the maiden (and thus the pearl) represents the beauty, perfection, and eternity of the soul beyond the ravages of place and time. The maiden identifies herself as the bride of Christ, a traditional symbol for the righteous soul, derived from Revelation 19:7-9. Her status as bride and her position in Heaven will become the main focus of her debate with the dreamer.

The poem's third setting, the New Jerusalem, is described by the pearl maiden and only glimpsed by the dreamer. This setting is clearly beyond the reach of the dreamer as long as he lives, at least in this world. When he foolishly attempts to cross the river separating the earthly paradise where he stands from the New Jerusalem whence the pearl maiden speaks, he is startled from his dream and awakes to find himself in the very garden where he fell asleep. However, this third setting, along with the maiden's discussion of Christ's parable of the pearl of great price, provides yet another significance of the pearl—Heaven itself. The maiden's advice to the dreamer is to forsake the mad world and purchase Heaven, the spotless and matchless pearl. He is, she scolds, too concerned with his earthly jewel.

The close associations of the pearl with smoothness and with roundness, whiteness, and brightness are extended in the poem so that the pearl comes to symbolize perfection and purity. The traditional symbolic significance of the circle and sphere as representing the soul and eternity is also developed in the poem, both in its imagery and in its symmetrical structure, with each stanza linked by concatenation from beginning to end. This linking device has been compared to a chain and to a rosary. The poem's final line, furthermore, echoes its first, the 101 stanzas implying not only the completion of a full circle but also the beginning of another. The whole suggests eternity. The centrality of the number twelve, traditionally the apocalyptic number, is also appropriate; it appears repeatedly in the Book of Revelation. Thus, the image of the pearl, the vision of Heaven, and the poem itself merge into one. As Thorlac Turville-Petre concludes, "Heaven, the pearl and the poem are all constructed with the same flawless circularity, an idea which reflects the words at the beginning and the end of the Apocalypse: 'I am Alpha and Omega, the beginning and the end, saith the Lord.'"

Thematically the poem is also concerned with Heaven and its perfect nature, order, and ideals. Much of *Pearl* develops a debate between the pearl maiden and the obtuse earthbound dreamer. As in *Cleanness*, a parable of Christ is at the center of the poem's teaching. The parable of the workers in the vineyard is particularly suitable, because it represents sharply the distinction between man's sense of worth and reward based on reason and a general sense of fairness and God's loving gifts of mercy and grace tendered equally to all. Christ tells how the owner of the vineyard pays those workers who labored for only an hour the same amount as those who labored all day. This apparent unfairness elicits protests and grumbling from the latter, and the dreamer foolishly allies himself with them by similarly complaining to the pearl maiden. The expectation of earth is simply not met in Heaven. The parable makes the point cogently: the last will be first and the first last.

From the divine perspective, no man is worthy of Heaven. Salvation is a gift of God. This gift is an example, the pearl maiden argues, of God's courtesy. Thus, although the ideals of cleanness and truthfulness remain important in *Pearl*, the poet here concentrates on the ideal of courtesy as his basis for exploring the nature of Heaven. God is portrayed as a noble and courteous chieftain, and the Virgin Mary is known not only as the Queen of Heaven—her traditional title—but also Queen of Courtesy. All the righteous become, in fact, kings and queens, members of the chivalric court of equals because they are members of Christ's body through courtesy. The poem thus expands the traditionally social virtues of the chivalric ideal into a religious concept with a wide range of applications. In addition to the usual sense of the term to signify good breeding, proper speech, kind manners, and unhesitating generosity, in *Pearl* courtesy connotes as well the freely given grace of God and the loving relationship between man and the divine lost on earth through sin but available in Heaven.

As a romance in the chivalric tradition dealing with knights of renown and beautiful courtly ladies, *Sir Gawain and the Green Knight* quite naturally also examines the ideal of courtesy. It is not discussed as a characteristic of Heaven, for the romance limits its focus to earthly heroes and events, although they may be superhuman and altogether marvelous. Courtesy is examined as a characteristic of the Arthurian court and especially of Gawain, the nephew of King Arthur, a favorite of the charming ladies of court, and the epitome of chivalry. His character does, however, merge secular ideals with religious devotion. This merger is evident in his elaborate shield, described and explained at length by the poet. Decorated with a pentangle, the "endless knot" suggesting eternal ideals, the shield reflects not only Gawain's bravery, generosity, truthfulness, cleanness, and courtesy, but also his devotion to the five wounds of Christ and the five joys of the Virgin. Yet, through the mysterious challenge of the Green Knight, Gawain and the chivalric ideas he represents are both tested severely. When the requirements of courtesy come into conflict with truthfulness and cleanness, even the perfect knight may fail.

Although the poem is generally divided into four parts, the testing of the knight takes place as the hero moves through three locales. At first Gawain is portrayed at the Arthurian court, feasting over Christmas and celebrating the New Year with King Arthur, the knights of the Round Table, and Queen Guinevere. Here he is tested in his duty as a knight when the reputation of Camelot is threatened. Acting courteously and bravely, he accepts the challenge of the Green Knight, whom he beheads—only to be told by the enchanted figure that Gawain's turn for the return blow will come in a year and a day. As J. A. Burrow notes, this test of courage in combat is the easiest for Gawain to pass, for it involves an obvious knightly virtue—truthfulness to his word—in conflict with the desire for life, and brave knights often face such challenges successfully.

The hero's second locale is the court of Bertilak at Hautdesert, where a year later Gawain rests on his journey to meet the unknown Green Knight. Here, Gawain is welcomed in a chivalric court and undergoes a much more subtle test. At this court the ideals of truthfulness and cleanness come into conflict with the demands of courtesy. Burrow sees Gawain here as "subjected to one of the most complex and elaborately contrived test situations in all medieval literature." After agreeing with Bertilak to exchange each evening whatever he gains during the day, Gawain is tempted by Bertilak's beautiful wife. She approaches him in bed for three mornings, calling on his reputation as a courtly lover. Gawain must overcome this threat to cleanness and loyalty to his host while remaining courteous to the lady. This he accomplishes through his great talent for gentle speech. Each morning the lady settles for a kiss from Gawain, which he passes on to his host each evening. The host, who has spent his days hunting, similarly gives Gawain his winnings. On the third morning, however, apparently successful in turning back the lady's sexual advances, Gawain accepts a green girdle from her. That evening he does not give it to Bertilak, ostensibly because he would be discourteous in revealing the lady's gift, but also because the green girdle's magical powers will protect him when he faces the Green Knight the following day. Thus, in one decision,

Gawain fails the test of truthfulness by breaking his word to Bertilak, and the test of bravery by carrying an enchanted girdle to the Green Chapel.

Finally, Gawain journeys to the poem's third locale, the Green Chapel. Here he meets the Green Knight, who three times swings his axe over the bowed head of Gawain. The third time, he knicks the skin, symbolizing Gawain's failure at Hautdesert in his third temptation. The Green Knight now reveals himself as Bertilak and explains that he has known all along of his wife's morning rendezvous with Gawain. The whole adventure, Gawain discovers, has been instigated by the enchantress, Morgan le Fey, as a means of testing Arthur's court. Although Bertilak praises Gawain's performance under this test, the hero himself is humiliated and angry. He has failed the test of bravery and truthfulness and now, in an antifeminist harangue, he also reveals his lack of courtesy.

Like *Pearl*, *Sir Gawain and the Green Knight*, after 101 stanzas, ends where it begins. Recalling the introduction, the poem returns to Camelot. Gawain, however, has been changed by his experience, and although the knights and ladies of the round table—along with many modern readers—believe he has acted as honorably as can be expected of any mortal, Gawain takes his failure very seriously.

The poet has shown that earthly virtues alone, even those of the greatest knight, fail. Human values and societies are by definition sinful and subject to the ravages of time and weaknesses of the flesh. Thus, the poet introduces the Arthurian court with references to the fall of Troy, war, and betrayal. Furthermore, the ideal societies of Camelot and Hautdesert represent vulnerable and artificial islands of civilization surrounded by wild nature and affected by the changing seasons. By the end of the poem the dominant symbol of Gawain's character has been changed. Instead of the pentangle, he is now associated with the green girdle, which he wears as a penitential reminder of his failure.

Gawain's marvelous adventure is narrated in the third person, but the point of view is generally limited to Gawain's perceptions of events. The result is a masterful story with suspense and awe in which the reader, surprised like the hero by the unfolding plot, sympathizes with the hero's bewilderment. As Larry Benson and other scholars have shown, the plot artistically combines several traditional romance and folklore motifs into a seamless whole. Like *Pearl*, it is symmetrically structured: it counterpositions the two courts, two feasts, two journeys of the knight, and his two symbols, and it balances the three temptations of Gawain with Bertilak's three hunting expeditions and the three blows of the axe at the Green Chapel. Also like *Pearl*, it includes descriptions of great natural beauty, and, like *Patience*, it creates a character overwhelmed by the supernatural. Like *Cleanness*, *Sir Gawain and the Green Knight* relates a narrative of strange visitors and violent deeds in vigorous and forceful verse filled with realistic details. It shares with the other poems of the Cotton Nero manuscript many stylistic and thematic features, and remains the greatest work of the Pearl-Poet.

                                                    Richard Kenneth Emmerson

Bibliography

Conley, John, ed. *The Middle English "Pearl": Critical Essays.* Notre Dame, Ind.: University of Notre Dame Press, 1970. The twenty essays in this volume, published originally since the 1940's, represent a variety of critical approaches and include general interpretations of the poem as well as more specialized studies. Middle English and foreign-language quotations are followed by modern translations.

Gardner, John, ed. *The Complete Works of the Gawain-Poet.* Chicago: University of Chicago Press, 1965. Gardner's long introduction/commentary discusses what is known about the poet in question. Describes conventions and traditions in the poems, analyzes the poems themselves, and offers notes on versification and form. Gardner's own modern verse translations of the poet's works, including *Saint Erkenwald*, compose the body of this volume.

Howard, Donald R., and Christian Zacher, eds. *Critical Studies of Sir Gawain and the Green Knight.* Notre Dame, Ind.: University of Notre Dame Press, 1968. This collection of twenty-three essays includes two essays of introduction and background followed by discussions of critical issues, style and technique, characters and setting, and interpretations. Quotations are in Middle English, with Middle English alphabet characters.

Moorman, Charles. *The Pearl-Poet.* New York: Twayne, 1968. This volume is an excellent introduction to the anonymous writer of *Pearl, Patience, Purity*, and *Sir Gawain and the Green Knight.* Biographical information is by necessity replaced by more general information about the fourteenth century. Includes a chapter that examines each poem in turn, a chronology, and an annotated bibliography.

Spearing, A. C. *The Gawain-Poet: A Critical Study.* Cambridge, England: Cambridge University Press, 1970. After a brief discussion of the Middle Ages, the alliterative tradition, and the question of authorship, this book devotes one chapter to each of the four poems attributed to the poet. The extensive quotations from the poetry have not been modernized, although only modern alphabet letters are used.

ROBERT PINSKY

Born: Long Branch, New Jersey; October 20, 1940

Principal poetry
Sadness and Happiness, 1975; *An Explanation of America*, 1979; *History of My Heart*, 1984; *The Want Bone*, 1990.

Other literary forms
Mindwheel (1987) is a kind of metanovel: an interactive electronic computer game in the form of a novel. Robert Pinsky has also written poetry criticism: *The Situation of Poetry* (1976) and *Poetry and the World* (1988).

Achievements
Pinsky has won many outstanding literary and academic awards, including Woodrow Wilson fellowships in 1962 and 1966 and a Fulbright Award in 1965, a year he also won the Stegner Fellowship in Poetry. The National Endowment for the Humanities awarded him a fellowship in 1974, and in 1979 he won the Oscar Blumenthal Prize for Poetry. In 1980 he won three significant awards: the American Academy and Institute of Arts and Letters Award, the Saxifrage Prize, and a Guggenheim Foundation Fellowship. In 1984 he garnered a National Endowment for the Arts Fellowship, and in 1985 he won the William Carlos Williams Prize, which is awarded by the Poetry Society of America. In 1988 he was a nominee for the National Book Critics Circle Award in Criticism.

Biography
Robert Pinsky was born in 1940, in the coastal town of Long Branch, New Jersey, a locale that figures prominently in many of his nostalgic and autobiographical poems. Pinsky completed his undergraduate studies at Rutgers University, then moved to the West Coast to undertake graduate studies at Stanford University, where he came under the powerful influence of the critic-poet Yvor Winters. After taking a Ph.D. in English at Stanford, Pinsky taught at Wellesley College for several years before becoming a faculty member at the University of California at Berkeley and then at Boston University.

Analysis
Like many of the creative writers in the second half of the twentieth century, Robert Pinsky is closely identified with the university and may be accurately described as a major poet-critic. As a graduate student, Pinsky was charmed and influenced profoundly by the work of Yvor Winters, one of the most important poet-critics of the twentieth century and a man who is memorialized as the "old Man" in Pinsky's long poem "Essay on Psychia-

trists," which appears in his first volume of poetry, *Sadness and Happiness*. From Winters, Pinsky learned the virtues of clarity in thought and diction as well as a rigorous attention to poetic meter and other details of craftsmanship. Even in the freest of his free verse, the reader will detect no slackness or raggedy edges in the lines of Robert Pinsky: a quiet elegance and reassuring feeling of control seem to guide all of his poetic compositions.

Under the influence of Winters, Pinsky developed a fondness for certain poets such as Fulke Greville, Robert Herrick, Thomas Hardy, Robert Bridges, and Wallace Stevens. While at Stanford, Pinsky became especially interested in the nineteenth century English Romantic poets, an enthusiasm that resulted in a dissertation on the work of Walter Savage Landor and a lifelong passion for the great odes of John Keats. Pinsky's first published work, in fact, was not a book of poetry but his dissertation on Landor, which appeared under the title *Landor's Poetry* (1968). In that work, Pinsky began to sketch out the architecture of his critical beliefs, key ideas that would be fully examined in his two other important books of criticism: *The Situation of Poetry* and *Poetry and the World*.

To some extent, all of Pinsky's critical theories trace their roots to his close reading and analysis of Landor's poetry. Pinsky develops the notion that all great poetry (classical, modern, or contemporary) possesses three unmistakable characteristics: the expression of universal sentiments (love and death, for example), the use of history, and the use of mythology, not merely as decoration but as a true archetype or universal symbol (as in the work of Carl Jung).

In *The Situation of Poetry*, Pinsky began to refine and clarify his critical thinking, a process that undoubtedly contributed to the growth of his poetic craftsmanship. Pinsky began to move toward statements that suggest the social responsibilities of poetry and the necessity of having a poetry that is humanly comprehensible, with real people and real ideas at its center. That general theory does not imply the desirability of a simplistic or merely didactic kind of poetry, but Pinsky does insist that poetry have a human center and that relationships, memory, and personal experience become the touchstones of this kind of poetry. Too much modern poetry, he believes, is unnecessarily pretentious, intent on creating a cool, noninvolved attitude. This kind of poetry is the sort that comes from creative writing programs and writing workshops at their worst, a sort of ready-made poetry that relies on superficial effects such as surrealism without making important statements. For that reason, famous poets such as Charles Simic and May Swenson fall short of the mark, in Pinsky's estimation. He admires a poetry that does not shrink from making abstract statements about life, a poetry that relies heavily on discursive statement, proportion (in thought and formal arrangement), and naturalness (appropriateness of language).

At first sight, Pinsky seems to be a reductionist, wanting to weed out any poets who do not fit his tidy definition. Actually, his program is generous and expansive, more in keeping with the spirit of two great American poets who also lived in the state of New Jersey, Walt Whitman and William Carlos Williams. What Pinsky wants, finally, is a poetry firmly based in human experience, as he explains in a chapter entitled "Conventions of Wonder": "The poem, new or old, should be able to help us, if only to help us by delivering the relief that something has been understood, or even seen, well." Poetry, then, is the ultimate form of knowledge, and for Pinsky himself that knowledge will come through poems about his father, his daughter, and his hometown. Personal poems are the key to universal poetry in this view, and for that reason Pinsky is particularly impressed by the poetry of John Keats, Wallace Stevens, T. S. Eliot, Robert Creeley, A. R. Ammons, Frank O'Hara, Louise Bogan, and, to a lesser degree, Sylvia Plath and John Ashbery. Bad poets are those who show marks of insincerity, or of self-conscious flaunting of an adopted poetic identity or persona. Their verse sounds like an echo of the English literature classroom; among them would be poets such as Robert Lowell, Theodore Roethke, and John Berryman.

These heterogeneous groupings of good and bad poets suggests that Pinsky is a complex thinker, and that his distinctions depend upon the ultimate effect of poems rather than upon their particular verse forms or metrical patterns. What the poet has to say about human experience counts more in the long run than how it is said. This complex grouping also prepares the reader for Pinsky's third book of poetry criticism, *Poetry and the World*, an especially well-written critical analysis in which a kind of wholeness or inclusiveness becomes the sought-after ideal, a goal that incorporates all the varieties of Pinsky's taste (from Keats to Creeley). Pinsky's admiration for the poet Elizabeth Bishop is based on the duality of her approach, her ability to remain in the world and yet simultaneously transcend it. Pinsky admires Robert Frost, William Carlos Williams, Jean Toomer, Philip Levine, and John Ashbery because they are also in and out of the everyday material world in their poetry. Also, they use a kind of metalanguage or "heteroglossia"—that is, a contrasting mixture of ordinary Anglo-Saxon or American speech and Latinate words or exotic diction. Their poetry results in a realistic complexity that mirrors the actual way Americans speak and think at representative points during the twentieth century.

The first poem of Pinsky's *Sadness and Happiness* serves as a kind of illustration of his desire to espouse a human-centered poetry and proves that Pinsky is the rarest of all critics: one who actually practices what he preaches. That opening poem, significantly titled "Poem About People," offers the reader a catalog of ordinary American types, such as gray-haired women in sneakers, buying their weekly supply of soda pop, beefsteaks, ice cream, melons, and soap at the local supermarket, and young male workers in green work pants and white T-shirts that cannot conceal bulging beer bel-

lies. Between all these types there is a gulf of emptiness, the realm of dark
spaces that can be filled only with love and tenderness, a recognition that in
spite of unlovable aspects each human being absolutely requires love. This
poem makes a great pronouncement on the need for compassion in all human undertakings (one of Pinsky's consistent themes), for without this compassion life would be intolerable. It is also unthinkable that human beings
could, indeed, be human without the potential for compassion and love to
fill the dark spaces that surround them. That love may be impossible to attain for some, but it is the fundamentally unifying dream of the human
spirit. It is significant that the poem unifies all the contrary states of human
life, which is why Pinsky includes Nazi and Jewish elements in the poem
and why Pinsky, himself a product of Jewish tradition, wishes "to feel
briefly like Jesus."

This theme of human compassion can be expressed on the most elemental
plane as well. The poet need not feel cosmic love for the human race but
merely a sympathetic appreciation for the tedium and occasional boredom
inherent in the ordinary passage of time, what the church fathers during the
medieval age called *taedium vitae*. In "Waiting," Pinsky composes a kind of
minimalist poem that takes the form of a list or string of images (air, a rake
handle, the stone of a peach, a dirty Band-Aid, junk in a garage) that become odd little markers of time slipping by, things unimportant in themselves but remembered simply because they create the texture of life as it is
lived. These inconsequential minutiae help to create a sense of expectancy, a
quickening desire for something better in life.

Perhaps that lack of fulfillment explains why the poet symbolizes this inescapable tedium in the act of watching trains go by, a kind of hypnotic involvement that goes on and on without any great conclusion—a fitting symbol for the everyday, the quotidian. Finally, by beginning and ending the
poem with this image of watching trains, the poet suggests a kind of circular
entrapment, as if human life can be summarized in this sad but touching
gesture. What keeps the poem above the plane of triviality on the one hand
and cynicism on the other is Pinsky's careful handling of the tone, which is
unvaryingly compassionate without ever descending to pity or sarcasm.

In the title poem of this volume, "Sadness and Happiness," Pinsky meditates on the great mood swings that define the human condition, the fundamental peaks and valleys of the human emotional condition, beginning with
another image of unfulfilled desire, this time symbolized not by watching a
train but by shopping for a new house. Pinsky opens this long poem (of thirteen parts) with the image of a short-changed American family visiting model
homes every Sunday in a futile and desperate attempt to realize their impossible dream. Then he shifts abruptly to a sexual image of *post coitum triste*
(or depression after love) to suggest sadness and happiness in a more immediate and personal way. In fact, his successes and failures as a lover and poet

become one of the major themes in the poem. He admits that his primary problem is a comic-tragic self-awareness, a kind of egotism that makes him see himself as a star of the film of his life, in which he is grotesquely transformed into medieval knight, blues singer, and jazz musician. The comic absurdity of all these roles, including the additional one of Petrarchan love poet, makes him confess his shame and pride. There is a grotesque quality, after all, about a film star, "tripping over his lance, quill, phallic/ symbol or saxophone." Later in the poem, this same line of imagery returns when he sees himself (again comically) as a kind of "Jewish-American Shakespeare"—or even Longfellow. Perhaps another role he might play is that of the worn-out old jazz musician whose outpourings consist no longer of melodious notes but of repugnant phlegm and vomit, caused by excessive consumption of cheap wine and gin. Yet as the poem draws to its conclusion, Pinsky becomes lyrical and serious, noting that somehow his eyes have learned to have visionary experiences, to see beyond the here and now, to appreciate and feel gratitude for the unmediated beauty of young women and even small triumphs such as the perfect home run he hit during a sandlot game (an image that has stayed with him ever since it occurred).

Sadness and happiness, then, are always juxtaposed in this unpredictable drama called human life, and they can take on unusual dimensions, as when "Sadness and Happiness" becomes the name of a bedtime game Pinsky, the loving father, plays with his young daughters, who must tell him one happy and one sad thing that occurred on that particular day. In so doing, they are like the poet and the artist because they are organizing life itself—the most difficult and the most rewarding of all accomplishments.

The final sections of *Sadness and Happiness*, entitled "The Street of Furthest Memory" and "Essay on Psychiatrists," constitute some of Pinsky's most important writing. In the poems that make up these subsections of the larger book, he offers some of his truest observations about his life as a poet, exploring all the roots of his being, adopting a manner that is clinically precise but tenderly nostalgic and touchingly autobiographical. In effect, these sections could be seen as touchstones of his own poetic theories, proofs of a very special kind that poetry can be abstract and personal, rational and emotional, all at the same time.

Perhaps the key to achieving this marvelous yoking of private and public sentiments is the recognition of place and hometown in American life. Within a country as mobile and shifting as the United States, a sense of roots becomes a precious tool for aesthetic and personal introspection. To be denied roots is to be denied identity, as the writer Alex Haley demonstrated in his great saga *Roots* (1976).

For Pinsky the locus of all the deep emotions summed up by the term "nostalgia" is the community of Long Branch, New Jersey, a seaside settlement with resemblances to the more famous Atlantic City (decaying neighborhoods, ethnic enclaves, and dilapidated boardwalks along the beach). In "Salt Water," a splendid nostalgic essay that Pinsky tellingly includes with the critical essays in *Poetry and the World*, he describes Long Branch as a place famous for having been visited by Abraham Lincoln and painted by Winslow Homer, and also celebrated for having produced the renowned literary critic M. H. Abrams and the controversial novelist-essayist Norman Mailer. Yet Long Branch is also the location of cheap bars and honky-tonks, burned buildings, junkyards, and various underworld hideaways, including one used by mobster Vito Genovese.

For Pinsky, it is the private, personalized history of Long Branch that matters most, a complicated narrative web made of countless strands and details, such as the details in the poem "To My Father." Pinsky's father, Milford, was an optician, and his shop is evoked by such details as glass dust, broken spectacles, and lenses in every possible dimension and shape, all in the service of showing Pinsky's filial affection. "To My Father" occurs in an earlier section of the book ("Persons"), suggesting how pervasive and obsessive these images are for the poet. "The Street of Furthest Memory," which is the title poem of the Long Branch section, fills in more of the details, offering a panorama of tarpaper shacks, cheap luncheonettes, awnings flapping in the rain—images that somehow are still filled with sweetness for the poet because they are endowed with the wonder of childhood, in much the same way as William Wordsworth endowed the Lake District of England with all his sense of childhood enthusiasm.

In "Pleasure Pier" Pinsky is transported to the arcades and carnival atmosphere of his boyhood, the fake Oriental façades, the pinball machines, the boat ride, the Fun House, and the imaginary scene in which he dies dramatically, having rescued the girl of his dreams from flames that even in retrospect feel all too real. Another imaginative reconstruction occurs in "The Destruction of Long Branch," in which the poet imagines himself burying the Long Branch of his numinous childhood under miles and miles of artificial turf rather than have it buried under the squalor and decay that seem to be its inexorable fate.

The last of the Long Branch poems, and one of the most successful, is "The Beach Women," a work that perfectly captures the mores of the 1950's with references to best-selling books by John O'Hara, Herman Wouk, and Grace Metalious and allusions to cultural icons such as oval sunglasses, *Time* magazine, sweatshirts, and floppy dungarees. The poem creates a focal point on the beach where rich women come to pick up their young lovers, while young Bob Pinsky, clerking at the drugstore, admires their tanned bodies and painted nails and is reduced to selling them

> Perfume and lipstick, aspirins, throat lozenges and Tums,
> Tampax, newspapers and paperback books—brave stays
> Against boredom, discomfort, death and old age.

Sadness and Happiness concludes with one of Pinsky's most quoted and celebrated works, a long twenty-one-part poem called "Essay on Psychiatrists," in which the word "essay" is employed in its eighteenth century sense of the discursive treatment of a subject. Pinsky offers no plodding essay in prose form to the reader but, rather, a series of twenty-one closely interlocking poems that deal with the role of therapy in the modern world, the history of madness, the role of logic and reason, and the theories of Pinsky's mentor, Yvor Winters. The poem shifts in mood from serious to whimsical and back again, always offering Pinsky's sharp insights on the human condition. In section VII, "Historical (*The Bacchae*)," Pinsky treats the idea of madness and loss of control in the context of Greek mythology. He firmly connects the myth to the realities of modern life, including a group of actors in Cambridge, Massachusetts, who perform the ancient play of Euripides in which the worshipers of Bacchus are whipped into an insane frenzy and tear limbs from living creatures. In the midst of the sea of chaos stands the figure of Pentheus, a rock of stability, whom Pinsky admires for "reason . . . good sense and reflective dignity." It is clear that Pentheus serves here as a tidy summation of Pinsky's personal and aesthetic ideals. Pinsky later dismisses many of the patients of psychiatrists in a rather whimsical way because they miss the seriousness of the whole enterprise, primarily because they view psychiatry as another consumer product, a small part of trendy lives fashioned around Ann Landers, designer glassware, and Marimekko drapes.

Later in the poem Pinsky quotes his literary idol Walter Savage Landor, who once undertook an imaginary conversation with Fulke Greville and Sir Philip Sidney, great thinkers whom Pinsky regards as his own psychiatrists because they taught him that truth never appears in a pure or undiluted form. In this recognition, the poet believes, lies his own sanity.

In section XX, "Peroration, Concerning Genius," Pinsky offers a brilliant and moving portrait of his pipe-smoking mentor, Yvor Winters, delivering a magnificent lecture on madness in English poetry. Winters expounds on his theory that around the middle of the eighteenth century, at the same time as the rise of capitalism and the scientific method, the logical underpinnings of Western intellectual life collapsed. The result was catastrophic for the practice of poetry, because poets were still on the scene, and they were filled "With emotions and experiences, and no way/ To examine them. At this time, poets and men/ Of genius began to go mad." A list of madmen follows, including such notables as the poets Thomas Gray, William Collins, Christopher Smart, William Blake, and Samuel Taylor Coleridge, and their modern counterparts, Hart Crane and Ezra Pound. This passage is one of the revealing moments in all of Pinsky's published writing because it offers the formative conditions and catalysts for his own work—his desire to escape the crudeness of capitalism and science, while insisting on logic and reason as ways of warding off the great wave of madness that tends to overwhelm any poet working in the postindustrial age. Like his mentor, Pinsky believes that only wisdom can arm the poet against attacks of madness. Temporary, faddish, or clever speech is not enough; one needs the highest forms of poetry to survive this onslaught, because poetry, finally, offers truth.

In *An Explanation of America*, Pinsky addresses his daughter, using her as a focal point for his meditations on American culture and social history in much the same way that he used his father and the town of Long Branch to anchor his thoughts about growing up and discovering one's identifying roots. *An Explanation of America*, despite its somewhat grandiose title, is in fact a collection of a dozen poems, three groups of four, each group with a proper subtitle. In part 1, "Its Many Fragments," Pinsky is at his most personal, writing persuasively and passionately about his daughter, her habits, and her idiosyncrasies. For example, she chooses the *nom de plume* Karen Owens and under this disguise reveals her innermost thoughts about childhood in an "Essay On Kids." In games she does not choose the conventionally desirable parts such as Mother or Princess but prefers instead to be cast as Bad Guy, Clown, or Dragon. Although talkative, and good at spelling, she exhibits a somewhat wobbly penmanship: "you cannot form two letters/ Alike or on a line." Besides, she still sucks her thumb. Like any doting father, however, he loves her for her gazing eyes full of "liberty and independence."

Liberty and independence are highly resonant words in the vocabulary of patriotism, but Pinsky bewails what Americans have made of those patriotic opportunities in "From the Surface," a poem that depicts the sleaziness that all too often typifies contemporary American life. The poem begins with a shocking image of a scene from an X-rated film, which is followed by a dizzying sequence of other images of day-to-day life, including cars crashing, people dressed up as Disney cartoon animals, a collie, a pipe and slippers, tennis rackets, two people kissing on Valentine's Day, a napalmed child from the Vietnam War, a hippie restaurant—all the good and bad that make up the visible surface of America, a documentary of what Americans are and what they dream as opposed to what they should be.

One of the goals Americans might desire is a nation in which everyone took voting seriously again, Pinsky explains to his daughter in "Local Politics" (although he realizes that she may not actually read this poem or any of the others in the book). A utopian America would be one, Pinsky insists, in which citizens no longer view the critical act of democracy, voting, as a necessary evil.

In "Countries and Explanations," voting becomes a way of protecting the many places that make up the United States, the ground in which the roots of identity will thrive. These places include the rutabaga farms of northern Michigan and better-known places such as Levittown, Union City, Boston, Harlem, and Pinsky's own Long Branch. These sites were all once part of a nation before the United States became a country "of different people living in different places."

This preoccupation with place continues in part 2, "Its Great Emptiness," which evokes the vastness of scale and simplicity of effect that define the American prairie. Almost like Walt Whitman or Carl Sandburg, Pinsky sees the prairie and its settlers in broad, epic terms, and he narrates a brief story of Swedish and German immigrants who harvest the grain until there is a horrible accident in which a man is chewed up by the threshing machine. Events such as this provide a starting point for a true mythology of American workers and immigrants. Instead, Pinsky notes in "Bad Dreams," Americans tend to read and interpret their experiences in terms of European or foreign models, as if they had no proper sense of identity. In "Horace, Epistulae, I, xvi," his poetic comment on Horace's first epistle, Pinsky also notes that unless Americans can break away from the shackles of their self-imposed materialism, they can never discover their own identity. A similar fate awaited the ancient Romans, he implies.

Pinsky believes that a glorious American union is possible in real political terms, because he sees the process already underway at the level of language, specifically in the unifying effects of American names, which nevertheless preserve a distinct racial and ethnic flavor. These names may be French, Spanish, Scottish, Italian, or German in origin. A "Yankee" is just a *jankel* or Dutchman, after all. Thus the Germanic Mr. Diehl could hire boys with Italian surnames to work for him. America is a patchwork quilt of names, including Eagles, Elks, Moose, and Masons. Pinsky ends this magnificent poetic meditation by echoing Robert Frost's "The Gift Outright," when he concludes that America is "so large, and strangely broken, and unforeseen." It is in that "unforeseen" that all the promise and potential lie, waiting to be tapped.

If *Sadness and Happiness* was directed toward Pinsky's father and *An Explanation of America* toward his daughter, then *History of My Heart* is addressed to his mother, whose powerful will and even stronger imagination created the matrix in which young Robert thrived. The title poem narrates his mother's imaginary memory of seeing Fats Waller and two girlfriends when she was still a girl and worked at Macy's during school vacations. This magical moment is replayed on a more pedestrian scale by young Robert at a Christmas party, dancing erotically with his girlfriend, then going out into the snow, just like Fats Waller. His mother gives him his name not only in the legal sense but in a physical one, too, since she has a printer make up a lead slug with the twelve letters of his name (ROBERT PINSKY) reversed on their surface. In the end of his adolescence, all of her claims upon him, except perhaps her claim as a catalyst for his imagination, prove powerless. Robert goes off into his own world, playing his saxophone, and, like adolescents everywhere, tries desperately to attract the notice of the world. That, he concludes, is the history of his heart, since the saxophone player-poet is still craving the attention of an audience.

In *The Want Bone*, Pinsky returns to the themes and interests expressed in *Landor's Poetry* and *Sadness and Happiness*, especially the great theme of compassion based on a deep sympathy for human needs and desires (as symbolized by the "want bone") and the use of religious symbolism and mythology (especially his use of apocryphal material loosely based on the life of Christ). This apocryphal material figures prominently in the first poem of the collection, "From the Childhood of Jesus." In this bizarre and arresting tale, Jesus is depicted as a precocious five-year-old boy who apparently violates the Sabbath by fashioning twelve clay sparrows and by damming the river to make a little pool from which the birds might drink. A self-righteous Jew immediately complains to Joseph about the boy's apparent profanation of the holy day, but Jesus claps his hands, and the clay birds miraculously flutter their wings and fly away. The son of Annas the scribe appears and destroys Jesus' dam. Jesus curses him, and the son of Annas begins to wither and die. The poem ends with the boy Jesus crying himself to sleep as the twelve birds fly continually throughout the night.

In this rewriting, retelling, or reinventing of scriptures, Pinsky is putting his theories about religious symbolism and mythology into practice. Clearly, he seeks to emphasize in this paradoxical tale that sympathy (or faith) is what Jesus will require in his mission on earth, and that his powers of creation are, indeed, godlike even if he chooses to curse the nonbeliever. Most important in the tale are the birds that have taken off and will not land— until they become the twelve chosen apostles.

"The Want Bone," the title poem of the collection, is a generous and complex work of art, enticing and subtle, a poem that manages in sixteen lines to compress the whole history of human desire—and perhaps the history of life itself—in a brilliant sequence of fresh and startling imagery. Like all of Pinsky's poetry and criticism, "The Want Bone" enshrines the great qualities of balance (the word "O" is positioned at the very center and end of the poem), clarity of language and imagery (images such as "the tongue of the waves"), precise diction ("swale," "gash," "etched," and "pickled"), and precision of thought (a movement, a kind of zoological and historical evolution from the waves of the ocean to the rapacious mouth of the shark, whose jaw provides the literal "want bone" of the title). Finally, like all of Pinsky's work, "The Want Bone" is a supremely human utterance, not merely because it is the product of a human artist but also because its meaning is fundamentally human, a celebration of human desire, an evocation of all the "wanting" that may never be fulfilled. The "O" is thus a great zero of emptiness and frustration and simultaneously a resounding "O" of exultation and unalloyed joy—a perfect symbol for the mysterious complexity that Pinsky manages to discover again in the best of his poetry. As the bleached jaw of the shark seems to sing, so, too, may the poet say to the world: "But O I love you."

Daniel L. Guillory

Other major works

MISCELLANEOUS: *Mindwheel*, 1987.

NONFICTION: *Landor's Poetry*, 1968 (dissertation); *The Situation of Poetry*, 1976; *Poetry and the World*, 1988.

Bibliography

Lehman, David, ed. *Ecstatic Occasions, Expedient Forms: Sixty-five Leading Contemporary Poets Select and Comment on Their Poems.* New York: Macmillan, 1987. Lehman's concept in this volume appears to be superficial, but the choices of poems and the quality of the authors' commentaries are unusually high throughout the volume. Pinsky explicates "The Want Bone" with candor and shares his enthusiasm for the use of the word "O." His remarks are incisive and revealing.

Molesworth, Charles. "Proving Irony by Compassion: The Poetry of Robert Pinsky." *The Hollins Critic* 21 (December, 1984): 1-18. Molesworth is a distinguished critic, and his interpretations here are well worth the time of any interested reader. He deals with three major topics, generously illustrating all three: Pinsky's use of discursive poetry, the role of irony in his work, and the all-important theme of compassion.

Parini, Jay. "Explaining America: The Poetry of Robert Pinsky." *Chicago Review* 33 (Summer, 1981): 16-26. Parini has written widely on the subject of contemporary poetry, and this short study gives an excellent account of the connection between Pinsky's critical theories and the volume *An Explanation of America.*

Pinsky, Robert. Interview by Adam J. Sorkin. *Contemporary Literature* 25 (Spring, 1984): 1-14. Although one might have wished for an even longer interview, this intelligent and wide-ranging interview, if read sensitively, can give abundant insight on the role of certain autobiographical elements in Pinsky's poetry, such as his hometown of Long Branch and the influence of Yvor Winters, his mentor.

Tangorra, Joanne. "New Software from Synapse Takes Poetic License." *Publishers Weekly* 227 (April 19, 1985): 50. Even though Tangorra's piece is relatively brief, it offers an intriguing glimpse at another side of Pinsky's creative expression—his electronic novel-game *Mindwheel*, the construction of which provides some fascinating clues about how Pinsky's mind works and about how he organizes material in more traditional formats, such as those of poetry.

SYLVIA PLATH

Born: Boston, Massachusetts; October 27, 1932
Died: London, England; February 11, 1963

Principal poetry
The Colossus and Other Poems, 1960; *Three Women*, 1962; *Ariel*, 1965; *Uncollected Poems*, 1965; *Crossing the Water*, 1971; *Winter Trees*, 1971; *Fiesta Melons*, 1971; *Crystal Gazer*, 1971; *Lyonesse*, 1971; *Pursuit*, 1973; *The Collected Poems*, 1981; *Selected Poems*, 1985.

Other literary forms
Sylvia Plath was a prolific writer of poetry and prose. Her first publication was a short story, "Sunday at the Mintons'," which appeared in *Mademoiselle* in 1952. Throughout the remainder of her life, her stories and prose sketches appeared almost yearly in various journals and magazines. Ted Hughes edited a selection of these prose works, *Johnny Panic and the Bible of Dreams* (1977, 1979). Plath's extensive diaries and journals were also edited by Hughes; they were published as *The Journals of Sylvia Plath* in 1982. Her mother has edited a collection of letters written by Plath to her between 1950 and 1963, *Letters Home* (1975). Plath's work in other forms included a poetic drama, *Three Women*, that was aired on the BBC on August 19, 1962; an autobiographical novel, *The Bell Jar*, published under the pseudonym "Victoria Lucas" (1963); and a popular children's book, *The Bed Book* (1976).

Achievements
Plath's poetry, like that of Hart Crane, will be read, studied, and known for two reasons: for its intrinsic merit, and for its bearing on her suicide. In spite of efforts to disentangle her poetry from her life and death, Plath's reputation and impact have fluctuated with public interest in her suicide. Almost immediately after her death, she was adopted by many members of the feminist movement as an emblem of the female in a male-dominated world; her death was lamented, condemned, criticized, and analyzed as a symbolic gesture as well as an inevitable consequence of her socialization. Explanations for her acute mental anguish were often subsumed in larger arguments about her archetypal sacrifice.

With the publication of *The Bell Jar* and the posthumous collections of poetry, however, her audience grew in diversity and appreciation. *The Collected Poems* (1981) was awarded the Pulitzer Prize for Poetry in 1982. While she never lost her value to the feminist movement, she gained other sympathetic readers who attempted to place her in a social and cultural context that would help to explain—although certainly not definitively—her artistic success and her decision to end her life.

It is not difficult to understand why Plath has won the respect of a wider audience. Her poems transcend ideology. Vivid, immediate re-creations of mental collapse, they are remnants of a psyche torn by severely conflicting forces. Yet Plath's poems are not merely re-creations of nightmares; were they only that, they would hardly be distinguishable from reams of psychological case histories. Plath's great achievement was her ability to transform the experience into art without losing its nightmarish immediacy.

To retain that immediacy, Plath sometimes exceeded what many readers consider "good taste" or "aesthetic appropriateness"; she has even been convicted of trivializing universal suffering to the level of individual "bitchiness." The texture of her poetry demands closer scrutiny than such judgments permit, for Plath was one of the few poets to adhere to Theodor Adorno's dictum: "To write lyric poetry after Auschwitz is barbaric." In one sense, Plath redefined *lyric* by using that mode in a unique way. Plath's Auschwitz was personal but no less terrifying to her than was the horror of the German death-camps to the millions who died there and the millions who learned of them later. For Plath, as for the inmates of Auschwitz, survival became paramount, but her Nazis were deep in her own psyche and her poetry became a kind of prayer, a ritual to remind her of her identity in a world gone mad. As a record of such experiences, Plath's poetry is unexcelled in any tradition.

Biography

Few poets demand that we know as much about their lives as Sylvia Plath does. Her intensely personal poetry was often rooted in everyday experiences, the knowledge of which can often open obscure references or cryptic images to fuller meaning for the reader.

Plath's father, Otto, was reared in the German town of Grabow and emigrated to the United States at the age of fifteen. He spoke German, Polish, and French, and later majored in classical languages at Northwestern University. In 1928 he received his Doctor of Science degree in applied biology from Harvard University. He taught at Boston University, where he met Aurelia Schober, whom he married in January, 1932. In 1934 his doctoral thesis was published by Macmillan as *Bumblebees and Their Ways*, and he became recognized as an authority on this subject. Beginning about 1935, Otto's health declined; he stubbornly refused any kind of medical treatment, assuming his illness to be lung cancer. When, in August, 1940, he stubbed his toe and suffered immediate complications, he submitted to medical examination. He was diagnosed as suffering from diabetes mellitus, a disease he could possibly have conquered had he sought treatment earlier. The condition of his toe worsened, however, and on October 12 his leg was amputated. He died on November 5 from a pulmonary embolus.

Plath's mother had also been a teacher—of English and German. At Otto's request, she gave up her career and devoted her time to housekeeping. Of Austrian ancestry, she too spoke German as a child and took great interest in Otto's scientific research and writing as well as in her own reading and in the teaching of her children.

Plath's early years were spent near the sea in her native Massachusetts, where she passed much of her time with her younger brother, Warren, exploring the beaches near their home. A very bright student, she consistently received high grades in virtually all of her subjects, and won many awards.

In September, 1950, Plath began her freshman year at Smith College in Massachusetts, the recipient of a scholarship. She continued her brilliant academic record, and at the end of her third year she was named guest managing editor of *Mademoiselle* and given a month's "working vacation" in New York. In August, 1953, after returning from New York, she suffered a nervous breakdown and attempted suicide. She was hospitalized and given shock treatments and psychotherapy. She returned to Smith for her senior year in February, 1954.

Plath won a full scholarship to study German at Harvard in the summer of 1954. She returned to Smith in September; in January, 1955, she submitted her English honors thesis, "The Magic Mirror: A Study of the Double in Two of Dostoevsky's Novels," and graduated *summa cum laude* in June. She won a Fulbright Fellowship to study at Newnham College, Cambridge University, and sailed for England in September.

After one semester of study, she briefly toured London and then went to Paris to spend the Christmas break. Back in Cambridge, she met Ted Hughes at a party on February 25, 1956. They were married on June 16 in London. That summer she and Hughes toured France and Spain. She was awarded a second year on her Fulbright; Hughes began teaching at a secondary school. She completed her year of study, and, in 1957, she submitted her manuscript of poetry, "Two Lovers and a Beachcomber," for the English tripos and M.A. degree at Newnham College. In June, 1957, she and Hughes sailed for the United States, where she would be an instructor in freshman English at Smith College. She enjoyed her teaching and was regarded as an excellent instructor, but the strain of grading essays led her to abandon the academic world after one year. She and Hughes remained in Boston for the following year, both trying to earn a living by writing and part-time work. In the spring of 1959 Hughes was given a Guggenheim fellowship; meanwhile, Plath was attending Robert Lowell's seminars on poetry at Boston University.

In December of 1959 the couple returned to England, settling in London after a brief visit to Hughes's Yorkshire home. Plath was pregnant with her first child, and it was during these months in early spring that she learned of the acceptance by William Heinemann of her first book of poems, *The Colossus*, for publication in the fall. On April 1, Plath gave birth to her daughter, Frieda. Her book was published in October, to generally favorable reviews.

In February, 1961, Plath suffered a miscarriage, and in March she underwent an appendectomy. That summer, Plath and Hughes purchased a house in Croton, Devon, and went to France for a brief vacation. In August they moved into their house in Devon, and in November Plath was given a grant to enable her to work on *The Bell Jar*.

On January 17, 1962, Plath gave birth to her second child, Nicholas. Within a period of ten days in April she composed six poems, a sign of her growing desire to fit into the village life of Croton and of her returning poetic voice.

In June, Plath's mother arrived from America and remained until August. In July, Plath learned of Hughes's affair with Assia Gutman. On September 11, Plath and Hughes journeyed to Ireland; almost immediately Hughes left Plath and went to London to live with Gutman. Plath returned alone to Devon, where, with her children, she attempted to rebuild her life. She wrote extensively: twenty-three poems in October, ten in November. She decided, however, that she could not face another winter in Devon, so she found a flat in London and moved there with her children in the middle of December.

That winter proved to be one of the worst on record, and life in the flat became intolerable. The children were ill, the weather was cold, there was little heat, the pipes had frozen, and Plath was suffering extremes of depression over her separation from Hughes. On January 14, 1963, *The Bell Jar* was published to only lukewarm reviews. Her mood worsened, and on February 11, 1963, Plath committed suicide in the kitchen of her flat.

Analysis

In many ways, Sylvia Plath as a poet defies categorization. She has been variously described as a lyricist, a confessionalist, a symbolist, an imagist, and a mere diarist, but none of these terms can adequately convey the richness of approach and content of her work. Perhaps the proper way to identify Plath is not through a process of exclusive labeling but through inclusion and synthesis. All of these terms aptly describe the various modes of discourse that work effectively in her poetry and her prose.

She was definitely a lyricist, capable of creating great verbal beauty to match feelings of peace and tranquillity. Her lyricism can range from a simple but effective evocation of a Spanish sunrise ("Southern Sunrise") in which adjectives and metaphors balance finely against the simple intent of the word-picture, to a very Hopkinsian ode for her beloved ("Ode for Ted"), in which a blending of delicacy of emotion with startling diction is achieved. Even toward the end of her tortured life, she was able to return to this mode in a few of her last poems, the finest of which is "Nick and the Candlestick," in which transcending not only the usual maudlin and mawkish treatment of maternal love but her own emotional plight as well, she is able to re-create a moment of genuine tenderness that emerges from her wholly realistic viewing of herself and her young son. This lyrical trait was not restricted to whole poems; quite often in the midst of utter frustration and despair Plath creates images or sounds of great beauty.

Plath's poetry is largely confessional, even when it is lyrical. Most of her confessional poetry, however, is not at all lyrical. Especially in her last years, she used this mode frequently, personally, and often viciously. She seldom bothered to create a persona through whom she could project feelings; rather, she simply expressed her feelings in open, exposed, even raw ways, leaving her self equally exposed. One such poem is "The Jailer," written after her separation from Hughes. The focus is the authorial "I," which occurs twelve times (together with the pronouns *my* and *me* that occur thirteen times) within the poem's forty-five lines. This thinly disguised persona imagines herself captive of her lover/husband (the jailer of the title), who has not only drugged her but also raped her; she has become, in her degradation, a "Lever of his wet dreams." She then imagines herself to be Prometheus; she has been dropped from great heights to be smashed and consumed by the "beaks of birds." She then projects herself in the role of a black woman being burned by her captor with his cigarettes. Then she sees herself as a starved prisoner, her ribs showing after her meals of only "Lies and smiles." Then she sees herself as persecuted by him because of her rather frail religious belief (her "church of burnt matchsticks"). She is killed in several ways: "Hung, starved, burned, hooked." In her impotence to wish him the harm she feels he deserves, she retreats to slanders against his sexuality, making him impotent as well. She is paralyzed: unable to attain freedom through his death (by her wishes) and unable to escape her own imagination and her own psyche's fears. She ends the poem by unconsciously revealing her worst fear: "What would the light/ Do without eyes to knife, what would he/ Do, do, do without me?" She seems reconciled to the pain and suffering that awareness brings, but, by repeating "do" three times, she shows that she cannot face her awareness that her lover has already assumed another active role, that he is performing on his new victim the same deeds he performed on her. Written only four months before her death, this poem shows Plath at both her strongest and her weakest. She is in command of the poetic form and language, but the emotions running through the words are in control of her. This same phenomenon occurs in many of Plath's other confessional poems, but especially in "Daddy," perhaps her most infamous poem. There she also seems able to control the artistic expression within the demands of the poem, but she ultimately resorts to "screaming" at her father, who is transformed into a "Panzer-man," a "Fascist," and a "bastard."

Plath used many symbols throughout her poetry, some assuming the value of motifs. While her mode was not, in the strictest literary sense of the word, symbolic, she frequently resorted to symbols as primary conveyors of meaning, especially in some of her most personal and most obscure poems. The moon held a special fascination for her, and it recurs throughout her entire poetic output. Colors—especially white—take on greater significance with each appearance. In the same manner, trees become larger and more significant in her later poems. Fetuses and corpses, although less often used, are two prominent symbols in her poetry. Animals move in and out of symbolic meaning in both her poetry and prose. The sea is second only to the moon as one of her favorite symbols. Other recurring symbols include: bees, spheres (skulls, balloons, wombs, heads), mirrors, flowers, and physical wounds. This is only a partial list, and the meaning of each of these symbols in any particular context is governed by many factors; but the mere repetition shows that Plath allowed them to assume special value in her own mind and imbued them with special meaning in her poems.

Plath was also capable of creating imagistic poems, word-pictures intended to evoke a specific emotional response. Using an economy of words and an artist's eye (Plath did sketch and draw for a brief period), she could present a picture from her travels in Spain ("Fiesta Melons"), ships tied up at a wharf in winter ("A Winter Ship"), or a beach scene in which her eye is attracted by an incongruous figure ("Man in Black").

Perhaps Plath's greatest talent lay in her ability to transform everyday experiences—the kind that would be appropriate entries in a diary—into poems. Her poetry is a journal, recording not only full-fledged experiences but also acute perceptions and a wide range of moods. One such poem based on an everyday happening is "Medallion," in which the persona tells of discovering a dead snake. In fact, if the lines of the poem were simply punctuated as prose, the piece would have very much the appearance of a diary entry. This style in no way lessens the value of the piece as poetry. It is, indeed, one of Plath's most successful works because it is elegantly easy and colloquial, exemplifying one more mode of expression in which the poet excelled.

As Plath developed as a poet, she attempted to fuse these various modes, so that, by the end of her life, she was writing poems that combined any number of symbols and images into a quasilyrical confessional poem. What remains constant throughout her life and the various modes in which she wrote, however, is the rooting of the poem in her own experience. If Plath is to be faulted, this quality is perhaps her greatest weakness: she was not able to project her personae a great distance from herself. Plath was aware of this limitation (she once wrote: "I shall perish if I can write about no one but myself"), and she attempted to turn it into an advantage. She tried to turn her personal experiences and feelings into a vision. Her vision was in no way comprehensive, nor did it ever receive any systematic expression in prose, but it did govern many of her finest creations, especially in her later poetry, and it does account for the "lapses of taste" that many readers find annoying in her.

One of her last poems will serve as an example of how this vision both limited and freed Plath's expression. "Mary's Song" is a complex of religious imagery and the language of war, combined to express feelings of persecution, betrayal, impending destruction, and, at the same time, defiant hope. The poem is very personal, even though its language works to drown the personal voice. An everyday, ordinary scene—a Sunday dinner in preparation, a lamb cooking in its own fat—suddenly provokes violent associations. It is the Sunday lamb whose fat sacrifices its opacity. The fire catches the poet's attention—fire that crystallizes window panes, that cooks the lamb, that burned the heretics, that burned the Jews in Poland. The poet re-creates the associations as they occurred to her, as it was prompted by this everyday event of cooking. Her vision of the world—bleak, realistic, pessimistic—demands that the associations follow each other and that the poem then turn on the poet herself, which it does. The victims of the fire do not die, she says, implying that the process has somehow transformed them, purified them. She, however, is left to live, to have the ashes of these victims settle on her eye and in her mouth, forcing her to do a psychic penance, during which she sees the smokestacks of the ovens in Poland as a kind of Calvary. The final stanza returns the poet to her immediate plight: her own heart is a holocaust through which she must travel; it too has been victimized by fathers, mothers, husbands, men, gods. She ends by turning to her own child—her golden child—and lamenting that he too will be "killed and eat[en]" by this same world.

This poem shows how Plath's vision worked to take a moment in her day and, rather than merely entering it mechanically in her journal, transform it into a statement on suffering. The horror of death by fire for heretics and Jews in Poland is no less horrible, she says, because her horror—a heart that is a holocaust—is as real as theirs was; nor is her horror any the less horrible because other victims' horror was so great or so real. Plath's vision works to encapsulate this statement with its corollary in virtually all of her later confessional pieces.

While Plath's vision remained, unfortunately for her, fairly consistent, the personae through which she expressed that vision often varied widely. In some poems there is no reason to assume the presence of any persona; powerful, sometimes psychotic emotions brush aside any obstacle between Plath and her reader. This shortened distance can be seen in such poems as "The Disquieting Muses," "On the Decline of Oracles," "Full Fathom Five," "Lesbos," and "Lady Lazarus," all poems written with a specific person in mind as both the subject of the poem and the object of the feeling, usually anger, expressed therein. In these works, Plath does little to create a mask behind which she could create feelings analogous to her own. Rather, she simply charges frontally and attacks whoever she feels has somehow wronged her. As a result of too much frontal assault and too little consideration for the poetic mode, some of these poems are not as successful as those in which she is at least in control of the poetic medium.

On the other hand, Plath could at times be a bit too detached from her persona, trying to force personal sentiment into a statement intended to have universal significance. One example of this kind of distancing is "Maudlin," a poem rooted in Plath's experience but one which attempts to moralize without sufficiently providing the moral, or literal, groundwork. Its cryptic images—a sleep-talking virgin, "Faggot-bearing Jack," and "Fish-tailed girls"—drive the reader to hunt for clues outside the poem, weakening the basis for the moralizing that takes place in the last two lines. The poem seems to be based on a birth that Plath witnessed during one of her visits to a hospital with a medical student. The "sleep-talking virgin" is the expectant mother (thus Plath indulged her love of dark and comic irony), rambling on in her drug-induced stupor. "Jack" is the child, reluctant to emerge from the mother (hence, "in his crackless egg"), a male bearing a "faggot" (a penis). He finally emerges with his "claret hogshead" (the placenta) to take his place with the dominant sex in the world ("he kings it"). This scene is behind the poem, but it can't be reconstructed from the poem itself: the reader must turn to *The Bell Jar* and other prose. Without an understanding of this scene— knowledge of what is literally occurring—the reader is not only unprepared for the moral at the end of the poem, but is also unwilling to accept such a pat bit of overt sermonizing, especially after pondering the cryptic clues. The poet simply warns her readers, especially women, that such pain as the mother suffers in childbirth results from the loss of the maidenhead. "Maudlin" is one of the few poems by Plath that actually needs less distance between the poet and her persona; it stands as an example of the other extreme to which Plath occasionally went, confusing her readers in an attempt to "depersonalize" her poems. A similar poem is "Among the Narcissi," about her ailing neighbor in Devon: it lacks the presence of the persona, it lacks a perspective, and it lacks a reason for its stark diction.

Such failures, however, were not typical: few of her poems suffer from excessive detachment. Rather, her recurring struggle was against uncontrolled subjectivity and self-dramatization. Two poems written in October, 1962, demonstrate the difficulties Plath faced when her poetic persona was simply herself, and her poetry less an act of communication than a private rite of exorcism. The first poem, "By Candlelight," presents a winter night's scene of a mother and her young son. The first stanza represents the exterior environment as threatening to break through the windows and overwhelm the two characters in cold and darkness. The next stanza focuses on the reality given the child by the light that fights the darkness (the candlelight of the title). The next stanza presents the awakening of the child and the poet's gazing on a brass figure supporting the candle. That figure is the focus of the final stanza, in which the little Atlas figure becomes the child's sole heirloom, his sole protection "when the sky falls." The poem is Plath's lamentation on her inadequacy, as a mother, as a human being, and as a poet, to ward off the world that threatens to break through the window. Her perception is made graphic and horrifying, as the surroundings take on an autonomy beyond human control. The tone of this poem is submissive, not even rebellious; the poet writes as therapy for her wounded self, as justification for resorting to words when all else fails.

"Nick and the Candlestick," written five days later, reveals changes in the poet's psyche that make the poem more assertive and alter its tone. Even the very beginning of the poem reflects this change of tone: "I am a miner." At least now the poet has assumed some sort of active role, she is doing something other than resorting to mere words to ward off mortality. She does, in fact, assume the role of a target, a lightning rod to attract the overwhelming forces toward her and away from the child. Even her small gestures—decorating their "cave" with rugs and roses and other Victoriana—have taken on great significance as acts to ward off the reality outside the window. The poet is able to end on a note of strengthened resignation, almost challenging the world to hurl its worst at her, for her child has been transformed by her into her own messiah, "the baby in the barn." The process by which this quasi-religious transformation and salvation has occurred accounts for the major differences in tone in these two poems; but, again, without reference to Plath's life, the reader cannot be expected to grasp this process.

The tonal fluctuation and the inconsistent and varied personae in Plath's poems are rooted in her personality, which is capable of adopting numerous, almost infinite, masks. Plath played at many roles in her life: wronged daughter, brilliant student, coy lover, settled housewife, poet of promise, and mentally disturbed woman. Her life reflects her constant attempt to integrate these masks into what she could consider her identity—an irreproachable and independent psyche that needed no justification for its existence. Her life was spent in pursuit of this identity. She attempted to reassemble her shattered selves after her first suicide attempt, to exorcise selves that seemed to her too horrible, and to invent selves that she felt she should possess. Her poetry overwhelms its readers with its thematic consistency, drafted into this battle by Plath to help her survive another day, to continue the war against a world that seemed always on the verge of undoing the little progress she had made. Her personae were created from her and by her, but they were also created *for* her, with a very specific intent: survival of the self as an integrated whole.

In her quest for survival, Plath uncannily resembled Hedda Gabler, the title character of the 1890 Henrik Ibsen play. Like Hedda, Plath viewed the feminine self as a product created and manipulated by traditions and bindings far beyond the control of the individual woman. Also like Hedda, Plath felt that by rejecting the traditional demands placed on women, she could take one step toward assertion of an independent self. Plath's reactions to these traditional demands can be seen in "All the Death Dears," "The Ghost's Leavetaking," and "Magi," but the bulk of her poetry deals not so much with rejection of demands as with the whole process of establishing and maintaining identity. Masks, roles, charades, lies, and veils all enter Plath's quest and all recur throughout her poems.

In "Channel Crossing," an early poem, Plath uses the excitement of a storm at sea to suspend temporarily the identity of the persona, who reassumes her identity when the poem ends and she picks up her luggage. Identity is depicted as a fragile, dispensable entity. The nature of identity is also a theme in "The Lady and the Earthenware Head," in which the head is a tangible mask, a physically separate self that the persona seeks unsuccessfully to destroy. Here, instead of fragility, Plath emphasizes the oppressive durability of a prefabricated self. Identity's endurance, if it violates one's personal sense of self, is a terrible burden. That quality is displayed in "The Bee Meeting." Here the persona is a naked, vulnerable self that assumes identity only when the villagers surrounding her recognize her need for clothing, give her the clothing, and respond to the new self. The poem ends with the implication that her *perceived* identity will prove to be permanent, despite any efforts she might make to alter these perceptions. Identity becomes a matter of perception, as is clearly stated in "Black Rook in Rainy Weather." In this poem the persona concedes to the artist's perception the very power to establish the artist's identity. The dynamic of power between perceived and perceiver is finely balanced in this poem. In "A Birthday Present," the balance is tipped by the duplicity of veils and what they hide in identities that are established within personal relationships.

Toward the end of her life Plath's concern with identity became defensively rebellious. In "Daddy," she openly declares her rebellion, severing the demands and ties of tradition that so strangled her earlier in her life and in her poetry. She adopts several methods to achieve her end of freedom: namecalling, new identities, scorn, humiliation, and transfer of aggression. Her freedom rings false, however; the ties are still there. "Lady Lazarus" reveals Plath's awareness of the lingering ties and stands as an encapsulation of her whole life's quest for identity—from passivity, to passive resistance, to active resistance, and finally to the violently imagined destruction of those people who first gave and then shattered her self: men. This poem contains meaning within meaning and exposes much of Plath's feelings about *where* her identity arose. She saw herself as a product of a male society, molded by males to suit their particular whims or needs. Her contact with females in this context led inevitably to conflict and competition. This duality in her self was never overcome, never expelled, or, worse, never understood. Having failed to manipulate her manipulators, she tried to find identity by destroying her creators. Set free from the basis she had always known even if she despised it, she had nowhere else to go but to the destruction of the self as well.

Plath realized this quandary. In "Words," a poem written ten days before her death, she looked back:

Years later I
Encounter them on the road—
Words dry and riderless,
The indefatigable hoof-taps.
While
From the bottom of the pool, fixed stars
Govern a life.

The words with which she had striven to create a self—a meaningful self that would integrate her various sides in a harmonious whole and not merely reflect "daddy's girl," "mommy's girl," "big sister," "sorority Sue," or "Mrs. Hughes"—these words had turned "dry and riderless." They too had failed her, just as her family, friends, husband, and her own self had failed her. She had sought identity in traditional places—parents, school, marriage, and work—but had not found enough strands to weave her various selves together. She had sought identity in unorthodox places—the mind, writing, Devon, and hope—but even these failed her.

Plath finally conceded her failure to create a self that would satisfy her and the world about her. She reviewed a life that she had tried to end earlier. Even then she had been forced to regroup, forced to continue inhaling and exhaling. The truth of the real world that had threatened to overwhelm her collection of masks throughout her life had finally yielded to her on one point. She asked ten days before her death: "Once one has seen God, what is the remedy?" The perfection of death that had haunted her throughout her life seemed the only answer. Her final act was her ultimate affirmation of self in a world that would not let her or her words assume their holistic role.

Richard F. Giles

Other major works

LONG FICTION: *The Bell Jar*, 1963.
NONFICTION: *Letters Home*, 1975; *The Journals of Sylvia Plath*, 1982.
CHILDREN'S LITERATURE: *The Bed Book*, 1976.
MISCELLANEOUS: *Johnny Panic and the Bible of Dreams*, 1977, 1979.

Bibliography

Axelrod, Steven Gould. *Sylvia Plath: The Wound and the Cure of Words*. Baltimore: The Johns Hopkins University Press, 1990. Calling his book a "biography of the imagination," Axelrod makes sophisticated use of psychoanalysis, feminist and other recent critical theory, and biographies of the poet to interpret her life and work, including not only her major poems but her letters and journals as well. Supplemented by an extensive bibliography of primary and secondary sources.
Barnard, Caroline King. *Sylvia Plath*. Boston: Twayne, 1978. Contains an open-

ing chapter on Plath's life, a second chapter on her autobiographical novel, *The Bell Jar*, and several chapters that discuss her poetry in chronological order. A concluding chapter on her life and work, informative notes, an annotated bibliography, and an index make this volume a good introduction.

Bundtzen, Lynda. *Plath's Incarnations: Woman and the Creative Process*. Ann Arbor: University of Michigan Press, 1983. The critic's approach is shaped by the "current feminist awareness of the difficulties peculiar to being a woman and an artist." Bundtzen probes the reasons for Plath's suicide and takes issue with earlier works on the poet, such as Butscher's biography. Includes extensive notes and an index.

Butscher, Edward. *Sylvia Plath: Method and Madness*. New York: Seabury Press, 1976. The first critical biography of Plath by a poet. Based on extensive interviews with Plath's friends and colleagues, although without the cooperation of Plath's family or estate, Butscher defines the poet's life and art in controversial terms, calling her the "bitch goddess," a term he takes from D. H. Lawrence to describe "fierce ambition and ruthless pursuit of success."

Newman, Charles, ed. *The Art of Sylvia Plath*. Bloomington: Indiana University Press, 1970. An early but still valuable collection of criticism, with seven major articles on Plath's poetry and fiction, a section of reminiscences, and another of short reviews. Includes Plath's pen drawings, an annotated checklist of criticism, and a bibliography of Plath's poetry.

Stevenson, Anne. *Bitter Fame: A Life of Sylvia Plath*. Boston: Houghton Mifflin, 1990. Written with the cooperation of the executor of Plath's estate, Stevenson's book presents a rather harsh view of the poet and a defense of her husband, the poet Ted Hughes. Stevenson, a fine poet, presents several provocative readings of Plath's poetry. Her book should be read in conjunction with Linda Wagner-Martin's biography.

Wagner-Martin, Linda. *Sylvia Plath: A Biography*. New York: St. Martin's Press, 1987. A more detached and sympathetic biography than Butscher's and Stevenson's accounts. Presents Plath as a feminist in "a broad sense of the term" and concentrates on the poet's "identity as a writer." Based on nearly two hundred interviews and limited cooperation from the Plath estate, Wagner-Martin presents the most balanced view of Plath.

STANLEY PLUMLY

Born: Barnesville, Ohio; May 23, 1939

Principal poetry
In the Outer Dark, 1970; *How the Plains Indians Got Horses,* 1973; *Giraffe,* 1973; *Out-of-the-Body Travel,* 1977; *Summer Celestial,* 1983; *Boy on the Step,* 1989.

Other literary forms
Throughout the 1970's, Stanley Plumly contributed critical essays and book reviews to *The American Poetry Review.* His best-known essay, "Chapter and Verse," appeared in two parts in the January and May, 1978, issues.

Achievements
In his essay "Chapter and Verse," Plumly explains his belief that the direction of contemporary American poetry is away from a strict reliance on imagery and toward a stronger emphasis on rhetoric, on the centrality of the poem's voice and the speaker's attitude. His own poems stand as strong examples of this aesthetic. For his first book, *In the Outer Dark,* Plumly received the Delmore Schwartz Memorial Award. In 1973-1974, he received a Guggenheim Fellowship.

Biography
Stanley Ross Plumly was born in 1939 in the small Quaker town of Barnesville, Ohio, and grew up in the lumber and farming regions of Ohio and Virginia. After receiving his B.A. degree from Wilmington College, Plumly attended Ohio University, where he studied writing and literature with Wayne Dodd and where he received an M.A.

Plumly has taught writing at Louisiana State University, Ohio University, the University of Iowa, Princeton, Columbia, and the University of Michigan. In 1979, he joined the faculty of the University of Houston, directing and teaching in the writing program there until 1985, when he moved to the University of Maryland at College Park.

Analysis
T. S. Eliot said that writing poems is a way of escaping personality. Stanley Plumly holds a similar view. Only when one abandons an intense internal focus, Plumly believes, can one see the outer world clearly. Such a clarity typifies Plumly's own poetry. This freeing oneself of the confines of personality allows one to absorb the outer world more fully, a world that Plumly's poems reveal to be mysterious.

For Plumly, such an escape from personality does not mean, however, a poetry that is impersonal. On the contrary, in his own poetry Plumly establishes a very intimate voice. His "out-of-the-body travel" allows him to understand nature, the outer world, more clearly, but he can also understand his own distinctive place in the natural world. He is able to stand apart from and observe himself at the same time.

The poems in *Giraffe* clearly exemplify this concern with escaping personality. In this volume, Plumly repudiates confessional poetry because it allows the poet to indulge in his or her own psychological struggles and leads nowhere. The poet, Plumly suggests, must enter the world outside himself, no matter how dark, foreign, or foreboding, and live in it. In the transcendental tradition of Ralph Waldo Emerson or Hart Crane, Plumly sees entry into the outer world as a means by which one can intuit a sense of his or her own place in the natural order of things, thereby realizing a more harmonious existence with nature.

This focus on nature is often manifested in poems whose subjects are animals, plants, or trees. Horses, for example, appear in several poems, particularly in *Giraffe*, where they represent a kind of sacred, spiritual union with nature. Plumly's examination of the natural world also points to his admiration for his fellow Ohio poet, James Wright. Like Wright, Plumly aims to see the natural world anew and, through fresh imagery, to make it live in his poems.

Another important similarity to Wright's work is Plumly's spare style, which follows Wright's ideal of a reliance on the "pure, clear word." The diction in Plumly's poems is direct but quiet, and the resonating emotive quality of the language often leans toward lyricism.

Plumly's poetry, however, is distinguished stylistically in several ways. The poems most often begin in an intense state of emotion and move toward an understanding of those feelings. Thus, a poem's forcefulness often depends on the strength of its closure, and it is this strength in particular which contributes to Plumly's individual style. The poems build toward a final moment of epiphany in which often contradictory emotions are condensed into a single clarifying image, as in "Wrong Side of the River" (*Out-of-the-Body Travel*). In this poem two people try to communicate from opposite banks of the river:

> . . . you began shouting and I didn't
> want you to think I understood.
> So I did nothing but stand still,
> thinking that's what to do on the wrong side
> of the river. After a while you did too.
> We stood like that for a long time. Then
> I raised a hand, as if to be called on,
> and you raised a hand, as if to the same question.

In this example, Plumly depends in the last two lines, as he often does, on repetition, and on the strong cadence that results from it. The chantlike effect makes the poem's emotional resonance all the more powerful.

As this passage suggests, Plumly is concerned with questions that are common to everyone. In many of the poems these are questions of loyalties to and relationships with parents, or questions about why certain childhood memories remain so strong and recur so often. In Plumly's major collections, several poems center on a father-son relationship. In the earlier volumes, *In the Outer Dark* and *Giraffe*, the son has difficulty accepting the father's death because the father-son relationship in life had been incomplete. The son resents the father's passing and cannot let go of his father because an understanding between the two had not been achieved. In *Out-of-the-Body Travel*, however, the son has become more forgiving of the father for dying before a mutual understanding between them had been reached.

Many of the poems, particularly those whose subject is the father or another relative, also focus on the steadfastness of early memories. These poems reflect Plumly's belief in the shaping importance of early experiences. In "This Poem" (*Out-of-the-Body Travel*) he writes: "The first voice I ever heard/ I still hear, like the small talk in a daydream." These lines also illustrate Plumly's notion that traveling out of oneself enables one to turn back and look more clearly *at* oneself and to understand in retrospect the experiences that contribute to forming one's individuality. It is also by so doing that one sees one's similarities to others in the world.

The poems comprising *In the Outer Dark*, as the title suggests, are about outer darkness, but they are also about inner light, the power of the imagination and the feeling mind to illuminate. The poems are rich with contrasting images of light and dark. Inextricably caught up in the imagery and ideas of light and dark are the related subjects of time and space. Plumly considers the dark in "Now the Sidewise Easing into Night" as the embodiment of space. In this poem the dark has walls; it measures distance. Light, on the other hand, connotes openness, the physical and metaphysical sense of infinite possibility. In "All the Miles of a Dream," for example, men travel across snowy fields toward light: "The light sat in the window// and was the only direction/ all the miles of a dream/ can offer three men moving across such spaces."

The title poem reflects a similar concern for coming to terms with the complexities of time and space. In this poem, people move toward one elusive center at which they never arrive. As suggested by the title of another poem, "Arriving at the Point of Departure," time propels people in such a way that their arrival points are also their points of departure. Plumly sees poetry, however, as a vehicle that can stop time and allow people to reflect on a single moment. In "Rilkean Autumn," he writes:

> Tomorrow the pump will freeze.
> But today, thought, in the held moment,
> sucked to a single drop,
> still wags at the lip of the tap.

Such held moments for Plumly often depend on the absence of ego, and it is in such moments that the imagination sees beyond the confines of personality. Furthermore, many poems, such as "Chinese Jar," suggest that only when the outer world seems darkest and most silent does one's inner spirit become most active, most fully engaged. This creates a compelling tension in the poems. The held moment, the narrated experience, appears still, while the poem's emotion, the feeling discovered from the moment, resonates with powerful intensity. These moments are most often memories: digging potatoes with his father, driving in the car with his mother, listening to the wind in Kansas. In silence and darkness, then, Plumly suggests, the spirit recharges itself by transcending the self and entering more directly into the moment. This in turn enables one to perceive finally and more fully the significance of a moment.

Understanding the significance of one's memories, a dominant concern throughout all three volumes, is especially important in *In the Outer Dark*. Several poems speak of the son's inability to accept the finality of his father's death. "My father," writes Plumly in "Arriving at the Point of Departure," "breaks down into the slightest memory at random." The title, then, also describes memory as that point of both departure and arrival. The experiences that shape people also return to them as memory throughout life, or as reminders, Plumly suggests, of who they are.

Stylistically, the poems in this volume reflect Plumly's thematic concerns of time and space. The poems narrate experiences that happen sequentially in time but also capture those experiences completely in one moment, the moment of each poem itself. Consequently, the emotions of a poem come to the reader whole and distilled with the poem's closure.

Ten poems in *Giraffe* were published earlier in 1973 in a chapbook entitled *How the Plains Indians Got Horses*. As both titles suggest, many of the poems have animals as subjects, but more important, the poems in *Giraffe* are about how man can learn from animals to become more a part of the natural world. Again, the lesson is to center on transcendence of self in order to identify one's proper place in the order of nature—to achieve harmony with the outer world. As the last few lines of "Mile of the Animal" indicate, animals achieve such harmony because they have "the distance beyond the body." Addressing an anonymous animal, Plumly writes: "Your mind throws down its perfect shadow/ at your feet. You begin to walk,/ away from yourself, not simply out of the dark." Similarly, in the title poem "Giraffe," the giraffe, a shy, gawky creature, is described lovingly as embodying that harmony in which it is unafraid to

> stand still
> in a camouflage of kind
> in a rare daylight
> for hours,
> the leaves spilling
> one break of sun
> into another,
> listening to the lions.

Horses, the subjects of several poems in this volume, also exemplify this compatibility with nature. In "How the Plains Indians Got Horses," a horse is described in majestic terms, as more than human. An Indian chief, tired and hungry, sees a horse for the first time, and at the end of the poem he

> rise[s] from [his] body
> as from the ground
> onto this other, second of itself, horse
> and rider.

In the prose passage by Franz Kafka, entitled by Plumly "The Wish to Be a Red Indian," which ends the book, a rider becomes one with his horse, leaning into the wind and giving up his spurs and reins as unnecessary. He allows the horse to carry him where it will, and he hardly notices "when the horse's neck and head would be already gone." The union with nature is accomplished. The journey through life, Plumly suggests, is a similar kind of travel, in which acceptance and appreciation of the new and unknown landscapes beyond and outside the self can make the person whole, at one with the world.

For this reason Plumly thinks the ability to move beyond the self is essential. Movement inward, as Plumly shows in the poem "Jarrell," about Randall Jarrell's continual progression toward suicide, is unhealthy. The confessional poets, Plumly implies, perhaps best represented by Jarrell, John Berryman, and Sylvia Plath, exemplify this illness. Because of their preoccupation with self, they are unable to participate in those out-of-the-self activities that Plumly believes feed and fulfill the human spirit.

The language and tone of the poems in *Giraffe* reveal the mind of an observer who has traveled beyond the self and is in awe of the natural world, as if seeing it for the first time. The images and the uniqueness of the similes, such as the giraffe who "bends like a bow/ over the water," convey Plumly's admiration for the animals. The language and tone also bring to mind the poems of James Wright's *The Branch Will Not Break* (1963), especially the well-known poem "The Blessing," in which the poem's speaker says, upon realizing the horses' harmony of power and gentleness and how much a part of their world he is, that "if [he] stepped out of [his] body [he] would break/ into blossom." The poems in *Giraffe* resonate with a similar kind of joy, a spiritual fullness that comes from the deliberate projection of the self into the natural world.

The poems in *Out-of-the-Body Travel* examine more closely the ability of the past to inform the present, to shape personality, and to determine how one perceives the world. Although the poems in this volume continue to focus on a movement out of the self, the self, through memory, receives added emphasis. The powerful relationships of father and son, the subject of several poems in this volume as well, exemplify this concern. In the title poem, for example, the narrator realizes that, although his relationship with his father has been troublesome, certain retained associations with his father have influenced his perceptions of the world. The narrator recalls his father playing the violin, slaughtering a bull, and laying his hand on his (the son's) feverish forehead. Each of these memories associated with the father represents a kind of travel from the body. The son comes to understand, through memory, how his father contributed to shaping his own concept of transcending the self.

Similarly, in the long poem "For Esther," the son comes to understand how his mother also contributed to shaping the same concept. In this poem, the speaker remembers his childhood love of watching the trains and playing along the tracks. Afraid for him, however, his mother cautioned him away from the tracks. The narrator was thus caught between his desire to participate in the world, to hop a train, perhaps, or simply to play along the tracks regardless of the danger, and his mother's "orders" to be only an observer, to watch the trains from a distance. The strong details of the poem suggest that the narrator has learned from his mother another, perhaps better, way to travel: "It's what we hear all night,/ between Troy and anywhere, what you meant// to tell me, out of the body, out of the body travel."

The ties to one's past, the poems in *Out-of-the-Body Travel* assert, are strong, and the images convey this strength. In "The Tree," for example, a family tree's roots and branches are described as "inlaid" into a man until "the man's whole back, root and stem [are] veins." Similarly, in "Iron Lung" the strength of the past entraps the poem's persona in the same way that an iron lung entraps, although, in this poem, it is largely through dreams that the past does its entrapping. As with several poems in this volume and the two earlier ones, the strength of the past shows itself in the son's feelings of being victimized by the sins of the father. "Iron Lung" ends, however, with the son's realization that dreams may end in daylight—the iron lung lifted:

> Once there was a machine for breathing.
> It would embrace the body and make a kind of love.
> And when it was finished it would rise
> like nothing at all above the earth
> to drift through the daylight silence.

The poems in *Out-of-the-Body Travel* perhaps represent Plumly's greatest strides in establishing a unique voice. His imagery in this volume is inventive, apt, and beautiful. In the poem "Rainbow," for example, he describes a standard poetic subject, a sunset, but in a striking new way: "Taking its time/ through each of the seven vertebrae of light/ the sun comes down"; at the end of the poem, "It looks as if the whole sky is going down on one wing."

The poems in *Summer Celestial* continue Plumly's explorations of memory and of the relationships that it mysteriously captures. In the poem "Virginia Beach," he writes: "Sometimes when you love someone/ you think of pain— how to forgive/ what is almost past memory." The poems describe nature and landscapes in Plumly's typically graceful way. In "Chinese Tallow," he writes of a tree quite unlike the family tree of "The Tree" in *Out-of-the-Body Travel*—he wants to see it "large with the rain inside it"; he wants to "wake in a room bright with small dark leaves." Again in this volume there is the play between the inner world and the outer world of nature, between imagination and sensory details. The tone of *Summer Celestial* is generally more hopeful than that of the previous volume; emphasis is more on characters and the events in which they are involved than on the inner life of the poet himself. In *Boy on the Step*, however, published six years later, darkness becomes more dominant. The title poem is a sonnet sequence that combines images of the clearing of a forest with references to the Holocaust; in the poem "Infidelity," a child sees his mother pushed from a car by her angry husband.

Nance Van Winckel

Other major works
NONFICTION: "Chapter and Verse," 1978.

Bibliography

Dodd, Wayne. "Stanley Plumly." *The Ohio Review* 25 (1980): 33-57. An excellent, probing, and wide-ranging interview in which the poet discusses the characteristics of American poetry, the nature of lyric poetry, the synesthetic qualities of poetry, and aspects of the narrative. Plumly also discusses his views of his own writing style, his approach to story-telling, and poets who have influenced his work.

Heyen, William. *American Poets in 1976*. Indianapolis: Bobbs-Merrill, 1976. Plumly discusses his poems, "The Iron Lung," "Now That My Father Lies Down Beside Me," *Out-of-the-Body Travel*, and "Horse in the Cage." The poet comments on the inspiration and real-life events that precipitated his works, the practical and aesthetic issues related to the poems, and the writers who have influenced his distinct poetic voice.

Stanton, Maura. "On Stanley Plumly's Poems." *The Iowa Review* 3 (Fall, 1973): 92-93. Stanton views the imagery of the body and its state of sleep and death in Plumly's work. References to these images are noted and discussed in "Dreamsong," "In Sleep," and "Light." The issues that emerge include the meaning of escape from the body, the "other" of objective reality, the memory and reality, and the literal and metaphorical death.

Stitt, Peter. "On Stanley Plumly." *The American Poetry Review* 9 (March/April, 1980); 16-17. An in-depth examination of Plumly's book, *Out-of-the-Body Travel*, and the theme that recurs in many of his poems: the death of his father. Stitt explores the various technical and stylistic methods used by Plumly to explore this subject with enduring spirituality rather than pathos and self-pity. Stitt also celebrates Plumly's verbal, lyrical, and figurative density.

Young, Vernon. "A Belated Visit." *Parnassus: Poetry in Review* 8 (Fall/Winter, 1979): 297-311. Young deals with the broad issues raised by Plumly's poetry such as diction problems, reconstruction of reality, the religious and ritualistic connotations of his language, and the purge of suffering. Young points to the shortcomings of Plumly's poems as well as his strengths to provide an uncommonly balanced assessment of the poet's work.

EDGAR ALLAN POE

Born: Boston, Massachusetts; January 19, 1809
Died: Baltimore, Maryland; October 7, 1849

Principal poetry

Tamerlane and Other Poems, 1827; *Al Aaraaf, Tamerlane, and Minor Poems*, 1829; *Poems*, 1831; *The Raven and Other Poems*, 1845; *Eureka: A Prose Poem*, 1848; *Poe: Complete Poems*, 1959; *Poems* (Volume I of *Collected Works*), 1969.

Other literary forms

Edgar Allan Poe wrote several major essays of literary criticism, in addition to numerous book reviews for magazines. Especially important are his reviews of Nathaniel Hawthorne, containing Poe's theory of short fiction, and his reviews of the works of English and American poets, which explain much of his theory of the poetic imagination. Poe's philosophical speculations are found in his book-length *Eureka: A Prose Poem* (1848) and in his "Marginalia." In the former he attempts no less than a complete theory of God and the universe. Although he was untrained in science, some of his ideas about the nature of space and time clearly anticipate significant discoveries in twentieth century theoretical physics. He was one of the founders of the short story, and today's "category fiction" owes two of its most popular and enduring types to Poe: the detective story and the story of "Gothic" horror. He also wrote a verse drama, *Politian* (1835-1836), and a novella, *The Narrative of Arthur Gordon Pym* (1838).

Achievements

Even if Poe were read less frequently than he is today, he would still have to be regarded as an important and an influential figure in American literature. He established basic principles for analyzing poetry which have subsequently been modified but never abandoned. Before Poe, American critics saw their job as protecting the public from European decadence and revolutionary ideas. Poe maintained that the critic should rather protect readers from bad poetry, and remind poets to live up to their potential. He was also among the first to introduce theoretical considerations into book reviewing. He believed that the critic must judge poetry by a definite body of standards rather than by the vague and impressionistic criteria so often resorted to by his contemporaries. He pioneered in insisting that a poem is an aesthetic object and that its existence can be justified solely on aesthetic grounds. He was also concerned to make poetry accessible to a wide public, something which often irritated his fellow reviewers.

Poe was one of the first American poets to be famous in his own lifetime, and has remained, with Robert Frost and Walt Whitman, one of America's three best-known poets. His command of the entire range of technical devices available to the poet, especially of sound effects, remains unsurpassed. While his subject matter is narrow and sometimes idiosyncratic, he has written some of the finest lyrics and descriptive poems in the language. Poe's poetry was never completely ignored in nineteenth century America, but it was in France after 1850 that he was most admired. His theory and practice had an enormous influence on French—and later on British and American—poetry, particularly on the Symbolist movement of the later nineteenth century. The Symbolists admired Poe's conception of ideal beauty, his use of atmosphere, his command of the musical qualities of language, and his notion of the poem as a rationally constructed work. Perhaps most important, he influenced the symbolists, and through them much of twentieth century poetry, with his insistence that art is an appropriate instrument for dealing with the subjective and the transcendent in human life. The list of great artists who acknowledged him as an important influence on their work would have to include the poets T. S. Eliot, William Butler Yeats, Dante Gabriel Rossetti, and Charles Baudelaire; the dramatists August Strindberg and George Bernard Shaw; and the composers Claude Debussy, Maurice Ravel, Serge Prokofiev, Alban Berg, and Igor Stravinsky.

Biography

Edgar Allan Poe was born to parents who were professional actors. Poe always believed that he inherited his talents as a reciter of verse especially from his mother, and it is not farfetched to see his lifelong concern for the effect of the poem on the reader as an outgrowth of this early exposure to the stage. One of the most important events of his early life was the death of his mother when he was not yet three, and his poetry bears the imprint of his various attempts to find an ideal woman adequate to her memory. Since his father abandoned the family about this time and probably died shortly thereafter, young Edgar was taken into the family of John Allan, a merchant from Richmond, Virginia. It was from Allan that Poe took his middle name. From 1815 to 1820 the family lived in England, where Poe acquired much of his early education as well as his first exposure to the Gothic style which figures so prominently in the atmosphere and settings of his work. Back in Richmond, Poe studied the Classics in several schools, and entered the University of Virginia, where he seems to have impressed his teachers and fellow students with his knowledge of languages. He ran up large gambling debts which Allan refused to pay, however, forcing Poe to drop out of school. Thus began an estrangement from Allan which lasted until Allan's death six years later. At eighteen Poe enlisted in the United States Army, rising within two years to the rank of sergeant-major. Already at eighteen he had managed to have a slim volume of verse published, followed by another when he was twenty. At about that time he requested (with Allan's approval) a discharge from the Army so that he could apply to West Point. He entered the Academy in 1830 and did well, but when Allan again refused him necessary financial support he felt that he had no choice but to get himself expelled in order to find a job. He left West Point with enough material for a third volume of poetry, which appeared that year (1831) when he was still only twenty-two.

Poe now set himself to making a career in the world of professional letters, which he pursued with mixed success until his death eighteen years later. His financial circumstances were often desperate as he moved from one eastern city to another looking for work as a writer or editor of literary magazines. In 1836 he married his cousin, Virginia Clemm, and in 1839 received his first job as an editor. In 1841 he became editor of *Graham's Magazine*: the first of two periodicals whose circulation he increased dramatically while in charge. Yet sometimes erratic behavior and frequent problems with alcohol cost him jobs even when his actual performance was adequate. The journalistic world of the 1830's and 1840's was characterized by fiercely polemical writing, full of vituperation and personal attacks—a style which Poe practiced with great zest and ability. Despite his attacks in print on his fellow writers, some of them aided him in times of unemployment and stress.

In 1842 Poe's young wife burst a blood vessel, and her deteriorating health over the next five years added greatly to the anxiety caused by lack of money. Poe's mother-in-law was an important source of strength to the couple during these years. Amazingly, he was able to turn out dozens of first-rate poems, reviews, and stories for the magazines even while fighting off problems of health and finances. The publication of his poem "The Raven" in 1845 made him famous, enabling him to begin earning good money as a public reciter of poetry. When Virginia finally died in 1847, Poe himself became desperately ill, and even after recovering he never regained his old resiliency. In 1848 he became engaged to one of several women whom he was seeing, Mrs. Sarah Whitman, who attempted with some success to help him conquer his problems with drinking. In what was to be the last year of his life he felt more secure with Mrs. Whitman, with a regular income from lecturing and writing, and with his popularity in Richmond society. In the early fall of 1849, on his way to Philadelphia to help a woman edit her poems, he stopped off in Baltimore and began drinking. He was found senseless in a polling place and taken to a hospital, where he died a few days later on October 7 at the age of forty.

Analysis

The poetry of Edgar Allan Poe cannot be understood adequately apart from his concepts of the role of the poet and of poetry in human life. Probably few poets have followed their own theories more completely than Poe did, and his great popularity with all sorts of readers is due in large part to his consistency in producing certain universally appealing effects. A Poe setting, atmosphere, or situation is instantly recognizable. Specific poems of his have so passed into the common literary heritage that readers with only the slightest acquaintance with his work can quote lines and phrases from such poems as "Annabel Lee" and "The Raven." Yet the very ease with which bits of Poe can be absorbed tends to obscure the fact that all of his poetry is based on carefully thought-out principles of artistic creativity. Poe contended that the poet must be concerned above all with the effects to be produced on the reader. Further, only certain effects are proper to poetry. Poetry must take beauty as its sole province, leaving logic and truth to prose. The poet must do everything in his power to create an intense impression of beauty, marshaling verse form, imagery, rhythm, rhyme, and subject matter in this effort. By "beauty" Poe meant something quite specific: the pleasurable excitement of the soul as it reaches for a perfection beyond this earth. This yearning for an unattainable, supernal beauty means that the subject matter of poetry will almost inevitably be melancholy. Logic and reason as we ordinarily think of them cannot be the poet's concern because ultimate beauty can be grasped, if at all, only aesthetically, not rationally. The universe itself is essentially a work of art, not a logical construct to be analyzed.

The task of poetry, then, is to induce a state of mind in the reader corresponding to the exaltation felt by the soul as it explores the limits of perception in search of ideal beauty. Further, since the intense excitement thus produced cannot be sustained over long periods, a poem by definition must be rather brief: one of Poe's best-known principles is that a long poem is a contradiction in terms. As the poet seeks appropriate images for ideal beauty, he should avoid the concrete, ordinary objects of everyday life, since these are corporeal, not spiritual, and therefore impede the mind's progress toward perfection. The realms of dream, fantasy, the subconscious, and glimpses of life after death are what the poet will find most congenial. These realms cannot be represented directly in language, since they cannot be grasped directly by human beings. Nevertheless, poetry can approach them more nearly than can other kinds of writing because it depends on powers of suggestion, of intuitive imagining, of rhythmical effects which bring the soul some sense of what ideal beauty must be. The poet becomes a careful calculator of effects. Nothing must be allowed into the poem which violates the unity of impression which the poet desires to create in the reader. Brevity will aid here, also, since a very long poem would, according to Poe, dilute and finally destroy the unity of impression for which the poet strives.

In his poetry Poe returns again and again to a few basic themes, and to explore the subtle variations he weaves on his themes is one of the principal pleasures of reading his verse. Poe's first important treatment of the poet's relation to the world is found in his "Sonnet—To Science," published when he was twenty. It is an important question for Poe because according to his theory the poet will find much in the world that is a barrier to the attainment of ideal beauty. This poem begins by seeming to hail science, but its purpose is actually the reverse, as quickly becomes apparent. Like time itself, the speaker says, science alters everything without regard for human feeling. It peers into every corner of our lives, preying especially upon the poet's heart. In a series of effective rhetorical questions, the speaker demands to know how the poet can love science when it deprives the imagination of inspiration, destroys the power of myth, and prevents him from soaring into worlds of ideal beauty. For Poe, "science" was synonymous with "logic" and "truth"— all representing an approach to reality by means of consecutive reasoning, attention to material objects, and mathematical calculation. The poet should shun such ways of thinking, for the very nature of his activity emphasizes the indefinite, the ideal, the symbolic. Even by protesting, as he does in this poem, the dominance of science in the world, Poe seems to wish not to alter the situation so much as to declare that the poetic and scientific ways of viewing reality are irreconcilable.

Another very important poem, "Romance," provides a version of this position in more personal terms and makes its point through imagery more than through argument. In "Romance" (entitled "Preface" in some collections) the contrast is not between poetry and science but between the ideal world of the imagination and the painful world of everyday reality. In the first of two richly suggestive stanzas, he shows us Romance as a "painted paroquet." The speaker sees only the reflection of this beautiful bird in the water of "some shadowy lake." Yet it had been a familiar sight to him because it had taught him his alphabet when he was a child in "the wild wood." Through the bird's being visible only by reflection, Poe may be saying that poetry cannot communicate truth directly, but only as truth is comprehended in the beautiful. The second stanza contrasts dramatically with the first. If the childhood years of immersion in Romance may be imaged as a colorful paroquet, the adult period of almost unceasing "tumult" and "unquiet" are figured as "eternal Condor years." Now as an adult the speaker has no time for the idle concerns of everyday—he must always be watching for the return of the Condor. He concludes this contrast of images by saying that even when an hour of calm is allowed him and he returns briefly to the beauties of Romance, his conscience would reproach him did not his heart "tremble with the strings." The poem "Romance" represents Poe's version of a familiar Romantic myth: the years of childhood with their heightened imaginative vision are in many ways preferable to the adult's dependence on fact and reason. For Poe specifically, these early years were more attractive because he identified them with a type of poetry which most nearly approached ideal beauty. "Romance" is almost unmatched in the Poe canon for the way the subtle variations in the rhyme scheme (aabbcdcdee and deedeffgfgf) and the regular iambic tetrameter rhythm unobtrusively reinforce the emotional impact of the poem.

Poe may be better known for his poems of longing for a lost love than for those on any other subject. He works various modulations on the theme. The woman may personify the pure Classical beauty of ancient Greece and Rome ("To Helen"); or she may represent some version of the popular nineteenth century theme of the Sleeping Beauty who may never awaken ("The Sleeper"). The speaker in the poem may be a surviving husband or lover ("Annabel Lee"); or he may himself be dead or recovering from a brush with death ("For Annie"). The poem may be totally taken up with longing for the lost love ("To One in Paradise"); or her loss may provide an excuse to treat another subject (such as the relationship of body and soul, in "Ulalume"). Finally, the poem may be an intensely personal monologue, like several already named; or it may take the form of a dialogue or brief drama where two speakers debate how the dead should be mourned ("Lenore"). Whatever the mode of treatment, Poe's poetry (as well as his stories) makes clear that the death of a beautiful woman was for him the supremely interesting subject, since, if ideal beauty is ultimately unattainable, it follows that the most appropriate tone of a poem is melancholy, and certainly there can be no subject more melancholy than the loss of beauty through death.

The autobiographical element in this mixture must be noticed, whatever cautions have to be added in interpreting its appearance in an art form. Poe lost his mother as a young child, and was not close to his stepmother. At fifteen, an older woman whom he loved as a combination of mother and romantic lover died (she was the mother of a friend), and his age undoubtedly made the loss all the more traumatic for him. He watched his wife die a horrible death from tuberculosis, and during the last two years of his life he was declaring his love to several women almost simultaneously. One of these women was widowed from a man whom she had married years before instead of Poe himself. It will not do, of course, to assume that the sole or even chief explanation of these poems' meaning is the frequency with which Poe himself experienced such loss. The importance of any theme in a writer's work is not how it reflects the events of his life, but what meaning it has for him in the work itself. In Poe's case the meaning centers on the ways in which the loss can be made to embody the effects of yearning for supernal beauty: thus the frequency in these particular poems of memories, dreams, prophetic visions of the future, and of other expressions of the need to transcend earthly concerns and achieve illumination (however partial) in an imagined land of perfect beauty and truth. Very often the lost woman inhabits a kind of twilight zone, and the speaker in the poem, acting as mourner, guards her memory here on earth while re-creating the effects of the realm of spiritualized beauty which the beloved now presumably inhabits.

The poem which most fully reveals Poe's typical treatment of this theme is "Ulalume," written near the end of his life. Readers new to Poe often do not notice that he wrote "Ulalume" to be recited aloud (as he did "Annabel

Lee" and "The Bells"). This device undoubtedly explains the somewhat obvious repetition of certain words, especially rhyme words, and the great emphasis on regularity of rhythm found in the poem. Readers keeping the circumstances of the composition of this poem in mind will be less likely to regard its versification as overdone; or, alternatively, they will not be as likely to ignore the narrative thread for the musical effects.

It is autumn of a particularly important year, the speaker's "most immemorial" year. He wanders with his Soul through a semireal, semi-imaginary landscape characterized by gloominess, but also by images of titanic struggle. As he so often does, Poe here provides a vivid *sense* of spiritual extremity without identifying its cause. He is more interested, especially at the beginning, in emotional effect than in analysis, since his initial need is to transport the reader to another level of consciousness. Neither the speaker nor his Soul note the time of year, however, because they concentrate so intensely on their inward gloom. The strange landscape through which they travel affects them like the music of Auber or the magic colors in the paintings of Robert Weir. Poe knew that his contemporaries would recognize the artists to whom he referred; thus he could call in his aid his readers' awareness of certain musical and "painterly" effects to complement the aural effects of the recited words.

As the night advances, two brilliant lights appear in the sky: one is Diana, the Moon, and the other is Venus. (In Poe's poetry, the Moon is always "colder" and "more distant" than Venus, probably because the haziness of Venus in the sky could more easily symbolize the vague outlines of ideal beauty). Here, Venus observes sympathetically that the speaker yet mourns the loss of someone, so the goddess of love has risen in the sky to lead the mourner to a "Lethean peace of the skies." The Soul mistrusts Venus, but the speaker urges them to go on, guided by "this tremulous light." This seems to be a variation on Poe's favorite idea that the realm of ideal beauty will somehow be a better guide, a surer inspiration for human beings, than will the transient beauties of this world. The speaker therefore pacifies his Soul with soothing words, and they proceed on "to the end of the vista" (a line emphasizing Poe's concern that his readers see this landscape as one in a painting), where they find a tomb. On the door is written the name of his lost love: Ulalume. The speaker now remembers that it was on this very night of the previous fall that he journeyed here—not with his Soul but with the body of his beloved. "What demon has tempted me" to come here again? he wonders. He can offer only a tentative answer: that the spirits guarding this place have some greater secret than this to hide. They have therefore created this "spectre of a planet" (Venus) to mislead earthly beings.

If this secret is the nature of the Soul's existence in the realm of ideal beauty, as seems likely, then "Ulalume" offers one of Poe's last comments on the difficulty of reaching that realm. Thus the poem ends not with an answer but with a question. The ultimate human tragedy would be to have to give up hope of ever finding ideal beauty. Even the Soul as companion on the quest is not sufficient guarantee of finding it, for the Soul fears confronting the truth. Poe's poems on the loss of a beautiful woman are important, then, not only for their articulation of the theme of ideal beauty, but also for the theme of the imaginary landscape which embodies and controls the means of the search.

Poe always maintained that objects do not lend themselves readily to the metamorphosis that the artist wishes to impose on them. Therefore he should not represent the objects themselves in his work, but the ideas and feelings they inspire. Poe further believed that words can evoke mental states without referring directly to phenomena. Thus an imaginary landscape is superior to an actual one because the artist can create a total, unified effect without being hindered by unmalleable objects. It is in the imaginary landscapes of Poe's poetry that readers will recognize the closest connections to his fiction. Several poems featuring such landscapes, in fact, such as "The Haunted Palace" and "The Conqueror Worm," were originally parts of short stories. These poems tend to be of two kinds: those that look backward in time to a shadowy memory of primal innocence, and those that look forward to an apocalypse which will substitute for this sad earthly existence a higher, purer one.

One of Poe's most successful poems on the latter theme is his "The City in the Sea" because of its concise descriptive power and marriage of sound and meaning. At the opening of the poem, Death occupies a throne in a strange city lying somewhere "within the dim West." Here the souls of the dead abide. The city resembles "nothing that is ours," and it is surrounded by "melancholy waters." The sun does not shine on this city: its light comes from out of the sea. It is a lurid light, revealing buildings suspended in air, with Death surveying all from his "proud tower." The sea around the city, like a "wilderness of glass," is "hideously serene." And yet the city is not completely removed from time and motion, for the speaker detects faint movement, a redder glow to the water, a "breathing" of time. He foresees that when this motion increases sufficiently, the city will sink into the waters, and even Hell itself shall bow to it. Poe seems to mean that Death shall at last itself be conquered. In an earlier version of this poem, Poe shows Death as being forced to find other worlds whose inhabitants he can hope to control— perhaps representing Poe's wish that we will somehow be able to break down the barriers that separate us from the eternal. A paraphrase cannot do justice to the compact energy and power of this poem. There are, in fact, less successful poems by Poe which make his argument on this point more explicit. In "Dreamland," for instance, the speaker is able to pass through the strange landscape of postmortal existence, although he can behold it "but through darkened glasses." It is a place where those who have suffered most in this life may find surcease.

The other theme in the imaginary landscape poems is one of looking not forward to the apocalypse but backward to the primordial innocence first treated by Poe in a different way in "Romance." This group of poems is very important in Poe's total output for its working out of one of his key ideas: that the outline of the poet's life may serve as a model to explain the meaning of all our earthly existence. Poe's most concise and successful poem on this theme is "The Haunted Palace." There was once, in "the greenest of our valleys," a beautiful palace, guarded by good angels. The valley was perpetually fair, under the dominion of "Thought." At that time, travelers could see in the windows of this palace spirits "moving musically" to the laws of harmony. The ruler of this realm was surrounded by beings who carried out his will in "voices of surpassing beauty." Evil, however, invaded the palace and the valley, destroying their perfection; their ideal beauty is now but a "dim-remembered story." Travelers through this valley now see in the windows of the palace forms that move to discordant sounds, while, "like a ghastly rapid river," a hideous throng continually rushes out.

"The Haunted Palace" is one of Poe's most explicitly allegorical poems. The images on which the poem depends form a system of symbols which add up to something like the following: As an infant, the poet enjoyed psychic integrity, unified consciousness, and harmony with nature. Time, however, betrayed him; rational language and philosophy estranged him from his visionary self. As an adult, a captive of the everyday world, he longs continually for his former condition when he had unbroken communion with ideal beauty and universal truth. So different is his fallen state from his former one that he can only touch his visionary self through reverie and dream. The only escape from the now hideous palace and its discord is death, and the dying are only too eager to rush out of the palace as quickly as they can. Ultimately, then, Poe's poems on the imaginary landscape are part of the same fabric as those on the poet in the world and those on the loss of a beautiful woman. Ideal beauty can be conveniently represented as a beautiful woman, whose death signifies loss of the original psychic integrity and innocence; as the beautiful bird whose reflection brings us all we know of truth but is replaced by the terrifying condor; and as the palace haunted by pure mind and perfect harmony and the valley forever green, until they are invaded by discord and mere logic.

To read the poetry of Edgar Allan Poe is to enter a world at times so bizarre that some have dismissed it as juvenile fantasy, absurd posturing, or sound without sense. Admirers of Poe are wisest if they acknowledge in his poetry a little of each of these elements. His accomplishments in lyric and descriptive poetry, however, are very impressive. His command of vivid images and subtle rhythms and sound effects (particularly alliteration and assonance) raises his subjects to a level of keen interest for a very wide range of readers. The very regularity of his lines and stanzas makes them easier to remember than those of many other poets. His psychological insight, especially into the abnormal subconscious, is unmatched, at least in nineteenth century poetry. Although his essay "The Philosophy of Composition" makes demonstrably untrue claims concerning his composition of "The Raven," its importance (as the French were the first to recognize) is that it taught poets the importance of unity, coherence, structure, and economy; of knowing how something will affect a reader; of the dullness and insipidity of didactic verse. Poets as well as readers of poetry will always read Poe to benefit from these not inconsiderable accomplishments.

Mark Minor

Other major works

LONG FICTION: *The Narrative of Arthur Gordon Pym*, 1838.

SHORT FICTION: *Tales of the Grotesque and Arabesque*, 1840; *The Prose Romances of Edgar Allan Poe*, 1843; *Tales*, 1845.

PLAY: *Politian*, 1835-1836.

NONFICTION: *The Letters of Edgar Allan Poe*, 1948; *Literary Criticism of Edgar Allan Poe*, 1965; *Essays and Reviews*, 1984.

MISCELLANEOUS: *The complete Works of Edgar Allan Poe*, 1902 (17 volumes); *Collected Works of Edgar Allan Poe*, 1969, 1978 (3 volumes).

Bibliography

Buranelli, Vincent. *Edgar Allan Poe*. 2d ed. Boston: Twayne, 1977. A thematic approach that deals with Poe's poetry and prose, the history of his reputation, recent critical attitudes, and the permanence of Poe's best work, which Buranelli analyzes as a "retreat" from and "return to reality." The notes and select annotated bibliography provide a good introduction to Poe's scholarship and criticism.

Carlson, Eric W., ed. *Critical Essays on Edgar Allan Poe*. Boston: G. K. Hall, 1987. An extensive, heavily documented introduction surveys the essays in this volume, which is divided into sections on "Poe's contemporaries," "Creative Writers on Poe," and "Modern Criticism." All three sections contain important commentary on the poems, which are easily located in the detailed index.

Hoffman, Daniel. *Poe Poe Poe Poe Poe Poe Poe*. Garden City, N.Y.: Doubleday, 1972. A perceptive, if sometimes overly ingenious, study of Poe's personality and work. As the title suggests, Hoffman finds many Poes, a man and artist of many masks. He traces the coherence of the poet's work through the unity of his images.

Quinn, Arthur Hobson. *Edgar Allan Poe: A Critical Biography*. New York: Appleton-Century-Crofts, 1941. The first comprehensive biography to correct errors in earlier treatments of Poe's life and work, this informative but dry biography is still indispensable for a thorough, reliable account of the poet's development.

Regan, Robert, ed. *Poe: A Collection of Critical Essays.* Englewood Cliffs, N.J.: Prentice-Hall, 1967. The introduction focuses on Poe's reputation. Poe's poetry is slighted, but the general essays on his art, especially by Floyd Stovall and Richard Wilbur, are essential reading. The select bibliography is inadequate.

Symons, Julian. *The Tell-Tale Heart: The Life and World of Edgar Allan Poe.* New York: Harper & Row, 1978. A short biography of Poe. Although Symons concedes that his biography is not a work of "original scholarship," he provides the best short life of Poe with a chapter on his poetry, a succinct, annotated bibliography, and an index.

Walker, I. M., ed. *Edgar Allan Poe: The Critical Heritage.* London: Routledge & Kegan Paul, 1986. The introduction is an in-depth description and analysis of the critical reception of each of Poe's books from 1827 to 1848. Walker includes the important reviews of *Poems*, The Raven and Other Poems, general estimates, obituary notices, reviews of his collected works, and "views from abroad."